ABODE
UNDER THE
DOME

STATE GUESTS AT RAISINA HILL: 1947-67
and their subsequent visits

Dr. Thomas Mathew

PUBLICATIONS DIVISION
Ministry of Information and Broadcasting
Government of India

Contents

PHOTOGRAPHS:

Introduction: DR. THOMAS MATHEW

State Guests: PHOTO CELL (PC)
                     Rashtrapati Bhawan

                     PHOTO DIVISION (PD)
                     Ministry of Information and Broadcasting

                     US EMBASSY

An elevated view of Rashtrapati Bhavan

सत्यमेव जयते

PRESIDENT
REPUBLIC OF INDIA

Foreword

I am indeed happy that a publication, 'Abode under the Dome' would be soon released. It is a part of the initiative aimed at documenting the history of Rashtrapati Bhavan and how it was the chosen place of residence of several eminent world leaders who visited India in the first two decades of India's independence. They had come to meet the leaders of the newly independent nation and understand for themselves what this diverse nation stood for. Among those who visited India during this period were Kings, Princes, Heads of State, Heads of Government and Marshalls.

It is interesting that almost all of the leaders who visited India during this period stayed at the Rashtrapati Bhavan (or the Government House as it was earlier known), making it a treasure trove of information regarding these visits. Many of the important meetings that the Indian leaders had with the visiting dignitaries were also held here.

The task of documentation was, however, not easy. Most files relating to the visits were either destroyed or untraceable. In several cases, even when the files were traced, the information in them was scarce. A reconstruction of these visits had to be painstakingly undertaken sourcing information from diverse sources. Dr. Thomas Mathew, Additional Secretary in the President's Secretariat, was entrusted with this task. In about nine months, he has produced this book which covers 52 visits of 32 leaders from 1947-67. It also includes their subsequent visits to India.

This work is a product of extensive research and is a narrative on how the Government House or Rashtrapati Bhavan spared no effort in caring for its guests, adhering to traditional Indian culture, as exemplified in the philosophy of *atithi-devo-bhava* literally meaning 'the Guest is God'. The book also very thoughtfully details the part played by the staff members of Rashtrapati Bhavan's Guest Wing in making each and every honoured guest feel valued and at home. It captures fascinating information on these visits; how the world leaders were welcomed in India, their impressions about our nation and how their visits to India changed the way they and, consequently, the world looked at our country.

I am confident that this well researched book will be a valuable addition to the existing literature on how our great leaders welcomed their counterparts around the world, the context of each visit and the impressions of these visiting Heads of State about India in the first two decades since India's independence. It is a virtual journey down an important and defining period of Indian history.

I wish the Volume well.

Pranab Mukherjee
July 20, 2015

A view of Rashtrapati Bhavan from the Forecourt on Republic Day

Preface

President Pranab Mukherjee would soon be completing three years in office. During the last three years he has taken several important initiatives which include the opening of the Rashtrapati Bhavan to the general public and increasing their access to the various heritage structures in the Presidential complex. Besides these, he has also taken the initiative to record for posterity the wealth of information that Rashtrapati Bhavan holds. As a part of this effort, he had desired that a book be brought out on how Rashtrapati Bhavan has been a witness to history, an important part of which was the hosting of scores of Heads of States/Heads of Governments and world leaders, in the Rashtrapati Bhavan.

Especially in the first two decades of India's independence, the Government House/Rashtrapati Bhavan had the honour of becoming a temporary abode for the visiting dignitaries. It was, therefore, important to record for posterity, these visits, the context in which they were undertaken and the impressions these visiting world leaders carried about India.

As many of the records regarding the visits were unavailable and many incomplete, information had to be pieced together from various books, particularly biographies, newspapers, interviews and online resources. This was indeed a difficult task that was undertaken by Dr Thomas Mathew, Additional Secretary in Rashtrapati Bhavan. It is also remarkable that the book has been brought out within a short span of around nine months has covered 52 visits of 32 leaders during the period 1947–67 and their subsequent visits.

The research has been able to contextualise the visits, how the leaders were received by the people of India, the impressions they carried with them about our nation and its leaders when they returned to their homes. During the research, he has also been able to unearth some very interesting information.

I have no doubt that this dimension of history, dealing with the visits of Heads of States/Heads of Governments, may have remained buried in the various offices of Rashtrapati Bhavan and lost with time if it were not for this book.

I wish the Volume well.

Omita Paul
Secretary to the President
July 20, 2015

Rashtrapati Bhavan dressed up for Republic Day

Introduction

*The view of Vijay Chowk, North and South Blocks from the
Dome of Rashtrapati Bhavan on Republic Day*

Sitting majestically at the apogee of the slope of Raisina Hill is Rashtrapati Bhavan, the domineering element of Lutyens' New Delhi. The city itself was built to symbolise the might of Britannia and its central cynosure was Government House. The edifice was conceived and constructed combining the disparate icons of Western and Eastern architecture, which it does magnificently, moulding the two styles into the rhythmic harmony of a 100-string philharmonic orchestra.

The building was emblematic of the Imperial power of the British Empire, with India as the brightest jewel in its crown.

Today, it stands as an enduring icon of Indian democracy – the ultimate triumph of the people to which it truly belongs and as a symbol of the freedom they wrenched from the mighty British.

Since India's independence in 1947, the building has been home to the 'protector' of the Indian Constitution, the President or the *Rashtrapati*. The only interregnum was during the transition phase, before India became a Republic, when an Englishman, ironically, the last Viceroy, became the caretaker Governor–General and was later succeeded by India's own, C Rajagopalachari.

India's "tryst with destiny" began when the clock struck 12 on the midnight of August 14, 1947. The birth generated great interest around the world in the new nation whose large geographical size could qualify it to be a continent and a population that was the second largest in the world.

The evincing of sudden interest was understandable. Until independence, India was a colony, whose material and human resources could be harnessed at short notice and at will, by orders from London. All this changed and an independent India could now voice its own opinion, support or oppose issues, positions or nations. This freedom exercisable on international issues was a new dimension that other powers had to factor in their strategic calculus. Equally important was the sustainment of the pluralistic political system in India, more so for the unpredictable consequences its failure could spawn.

India also had some of the tallest democratic leaders in the world. Comprehending their philosophy and the destiny they were charting for the nation was important to the large powers in a globe divided into antagonistic blocs of the Cold War.

India's support, if not at least its neutrality, was something the major powers could ill-afford to ignore. Therefore, engaging with India became a priority. With much at stake, many Heads of State/Government were keen to visit and meet its leaders.

For centuries, India was also a mystery to many – from the common man around the world to the leaders of the most powerful nations. As President Eisenhower confessed during his visit to India in 1959, his desire to visit the country was partly because he was intrigued by it. The reality was that India was a nation that foreign leaders desired to see for themselves, understand what its culture embodied and the enigma it presented to them.

In the two decades after India's independence, the world's 'who's who,' therefore, came calling. Indeed, the rush to India

Rashtrapati Bhavan through the magnificient Entrance Grill

was such that, one foreign newspaper wrote in January 1958, "In the last two years, New Delhi has become a favourite stopping-off point for political leaders of many nations."[1]

The Building

Government House, now Rashtrapati Bhavan,[2] was built on Raisina Hill, which was under the fiefdom of the Jodhpur rulers. It was constructed after the capital of British India was shifted to Delhi, after its announcement at the Delhi Durbar held on December 12, 1911. It was not the first time that Delhi was chosen as the capital. It incidentally was also the choice of several rulers including Yudhisthira of the Pandava Kingdom as described in the *Mahabharata* and in the 17th century, of Shah Jahan, the 5th Mughal Emperor who built Shahjahanabad.

The foundation for the Viceroy's House was laid in 1914 but work came to a virtual standstill until April 1920 because of the First World War. It was only in April 1921, that the work resumed in right earnest and by December 1929, the building was more or less complete in all respects.[3]

The building by any standards is mammoth. It occupies an area of five acres; spread over four floors, the lower basement, upper basement, main and first floors. With 340 rooms, 37 fountains and 227 towering columns, the building is a marvel described as embodying "architecture in excelsis."[4] It covers an area of 2.1 million square feet inclusive of the internal courts, making it larger than the Palace of Versailles, which is not used as a residence today. It is slightly smaller than the Palace of Westminster, which has also ceased to be a royal residence. In any case, these buildings do not brook comparison with an existing office and residence of the President.

The construction itself was a gigantic task. As the area was rocky, large quantities of stone had to be blasted before it could be removed. Around 23,000 labourers and 3,000 stonecutters worked feverishly to complete the building. The materials used for the construction itself were of unimaginable proportions and their transportation, shifting etc., was a logistical nightmare that led to the construction of a railway line around the building to move material.

Perhaps, the quantity of the material used can be imagined better if one visualises the area required to spread three-quarters of a billion bricks in a single layer – they would cover 34,600 football fields. Other materials used in the construction included one-and-a-quarter million cubic feet of stone and 100,000 cubic feet of white marble from the famed quarries of Makrana and Alwar, the former famous for having supplied marble for the Taj Mahal. Green marble was obtained from Marwar, yellow from Jaisalmer, pink from Alwar, Makrana and Haripas and deep chocolate marble from Italy, used for a small portion of the Durbar Hall. When completed, Government House cost Rs 15.41 million,

Stone piers with elephants and urn on the side of the Main Gate

inclusive of electrical installations, furnishing, upholstery and carpets but excluding sanitary fittings and "drainage".[5]

The Architectural Style

The architectural style to be adopted for the building was a very contentious issue. Sir Edwin Lutyens, who designed the building, initially conceived it in Western style. As a devoted classicist and a protagonist of the Renaissance style, Lutyens opposed the blending of Indian architecture in the construction of Government House. His hostility emanated from his "dislike of all things Indian."[6] So dogmatic was he in his views that he held that any merging of the two styles would be disastrous.

Lord Hardinge, who was Governor-General and Viceroy from 1910-1916, during the crucial phase of the planning of Imperial Delhi and the construction of Government House, opposed Lutyens with equal fervour. He was determined not to allow Lutyens' writ to run. To counter him, Hardinge canvassed support at various quarters of the British decision-making body, arguing that Eastern and Western styles should be merged for the building in the Imperial capital. He even took the fight to an almost personal level contending that the future would hold him responsible for a Government House that was badly designed. Three architects, Herbert Baker (knighted later in 1926), Sir Swinton Jacob and John A Brodie also lent Hardinge a helping hand in convincing Lutyens. Finally, running out of friends and options, Edwin Lutyens combined Renaissance and Indian architectural styles, fusing them into a seamless new style for Government House. It resulted in "one of the great masterpieces of 20th-century architecture and the culmination of an architectural quest to find a unique Anglo-Indian Imperial style."[7]

King George V rechristened Government House as Viceroy House in 1929. Churchill, however, preferred to call it Viceregal Palace, symbolising perhaps the continuing desire of the British Empire to retain control over India, despite unmistakable evidence that the 'Brightest Jewel in the Crown of the Empire' was slowly shifting from its authority.

In the end, however, Government House which was conceived to symbolise the Imperial power of the British Empire, did not serve that purpose for its creator for long. In just 18 years after it was completed with all the splendour, pomp and pageantry associated with the British Empire, the majestic building passed into the hands of the 'natives', something which its creator never imagined would happen when the birth of the capital was announced, 36 years before India's independence.

The Stately Drive

A Head of State/Government arriving at Rashtrapati Bhavan leaves behind India Gate, which stands majestically on Rajpath. As his motorcade climbs the slope separating the two Secretariat buildings, the dome and its drum - the only visible part of Rashtrapati Bhavan from Vijay Chowk - become expansive as if a huge new building has surreally risen from the confines of the ground.

As the motorcade arrives at the main gate, it is met by The President's Bodyguard (PBG), the senior-most regiment of the Indian Army, raised in 1773 by Lord Warren Hastings when he was the Governor of Bengal. The men who stand not less than six feet tall, numbering 48, dressed in their winter or summer ceremonial uniforms with swords or lances in hand, are seated on their handsome steeds. Presenting a national salute, 35 of them transport the arriving dignitary into an ephemeral world of Imperial splendour. The motorcade is then escorted in a grand rectangular formation to Rashtrapati Bhavan through the intricate wrought-iron gates, whose design was considered so important that the Viceroy himself approved it.[8] Today, these gates are opened only for the President and visiting Heads of State.

Entrance Grill

At the top end of the two main gates, rising majestically to a measured height of 26 feet from the ground, are lantern-like shapes, each having a Star of India at their terminal. On both sides of the main gate are two replicas of Galloper Guns that the Viceroy's Bodyguard used in 1890 and two porticos which together take the shape of a saddle.

On either side of the gates are similar shaped smaller gates. Adjacent to these are stone piers on which a pair of white stone elephants, "carried" a stone lantern each. These stone lanterns have now been replaced by lanterns made of gun metal. Each of these lanterns also held aloft a British known. In the centre is the pier that supports an "enriched circular urn."[9] Each urn had a similar crown perched higher than even the main gate demonstrating, perhaps, to any viewer, the superior authority it commanded over everyone, including the representative to whose house the gates provide access.

The Imperial crowns were removed after independence, yet their apex point today has a measured height of 30.67 feet. The gate opens to the red gravelled stately path, or the Viceroy's Court as it was called, leading to the main building. Flanking the Viceroy's Court are four long stretches of water channels carved out of red stone, with fountains. Two large fountains are situated on both sides, at the beginning and end of the Viceroy's Court, before it becomes the Forecourt.

The Jaipur Column

Passing through the Viceroy's Court, at a further distance of 556 feet from the main gate, the motorcade reaches the Jaipur Column. The Column, which derives its name from the Kingdom of Jaipur, was built by Maharaja Madho Singh, as a mark of his kingdom's loyalty to the British with the approval of Lord Hardinge. It stands at an awe-inspiring height of 145 feet or 45 metres.

The Viceroy's Court

Map of Lutyens's 'New City' engraved at the base of Jaipur Column

w seat of a car, the apex point of the Column eludes
y conveying a picture of the endless domination of a
sted with the responsibility of protecting the building,
distance of 523 feet from it. The Column stands at
two lateral roads from the south and north, which
the left and right there are rows of short, thin, pink
illars mounted with lions on their haunches.

is built in sandstone and has a shaft carved in the
British oak leaves. Above it is a large sandstone egg.
terminates with a five-ton copper lotus that could
to six inches in a strong breeze. Above it is a six-
of India, made of glass which was erected in 1930.

tern side of the base of the Column is a plan of
envisaged then which is engraved similar to the
picted on the obelisk of the Place de la Concorde
map also contains the engraved position of major
On the west of the base is an inscription which

w your thought with faith
leed with courage
ife is a sacrifice
men may know
reatness of India"

when dignitaries were ceremonially welcomed at the
motorcade usually bypassed the Jaipur Column and
ght to the Forecourt or the South or North Courts.
special circumstances was any form of Guard of
esented to a visiting Head of State in the Forecourt.
tion was extended to dignitaries with hereditary
if they were not on State Visits but were calling on
f State of the country. One such instance was the
haraja Padma of Nepal (see pages 102 to 103).

ceremonial welcome is held in the Forecourt of
Bhavan for which a set of different procedures
stablished. As the motorcade arrives at the Jaipur
scorted by the PBG, the Ceremonial Guard
t gives the dignitary a general salute, accompanied
n salute. Each round is fired every 2.5 seconds.

is synchronised to end by the time the dignitary
in any case, before he reaches the Saluting Dais.
owed by another salute at the dais and thereafter, the
thems of both countries are played. The dignitary
d with an Inter-Services Guard of Honour and then
to a designated area. In this designated area, the
tees to the ceremony are introduced to the visiting
ereafter, the Head of State/Government meets the
ntire programme at the Forecourt is concluded in
-minutes. According to tradition, the Head of State

then goes to Rajghat to pay respects to the memory of the
'Father of the Nation'.

The Forecourt

Passing the Jaipur Column, the visiting dignitary arrives at the
Forecourt of the building. From this vantage position, the view
of the 12 Tuscan columns at its centre may evoke in the visitor,
an imagery of the Pantheon and Roman architecture at its peak.

These columns rest on the *veranda* which is accessed from
the Forecourt by 32 stately steps. Climbing them may evoke
yet another imagery; this time one of the diminution of the
climber as the columns get more proximate and appear bigger
with the building rising majestically over them.

The main flight of 32 stately stairs ends with the *Ashoka
[Rampurva]* Bull that occupies the centre point on the
veranda. It was retained out of the several artefacts displayed
in the Durbar Hall after they were exhibited in the Indian
Art Exhibition in London in 1947-48. It was done at the
instance of Prime Minister Jawaharlal Nehru who wanted
the bull placed in Rashtrapati Bhavan.[10] The two wings of the
building on the south and north also add to the perception
of gigantism of the construction.

Columns of smaller size stand above the three archways on
each side of the Tuscan pillars. The archways lead to the North
and South Courts. Similar sized columns also rise above the
solitary entry on each of the two wings the building has on
its north and south. Five fountains on the top of the building,
visible from Forecourt, two each on either side of the 12 Tuscan
columns, two others at the beginning of the wings and one on
the south above the guest wing, add to the building's allure.

Visible also from the Forecourt are the Indian elements that
testify to the transformation of Lutyens from a die-hard
opponent of Indian architectural style to a fusionist of Western
and Eastern forms. These are the capitals of the columns that
have carved bells on them. Square *chhatris* (Hindi for umbrella)
on the top of the building are another similar feature.

The Dome & The Durbar Hall

The most prominent Indian element visible from the
Forecourt is the copper dome. It sits almost like the crown
of the building with its bamboo-weave-like grill running
around. Both these elements were copied from the 1st century
BC *Stupa* at Sanchi.

The dome occupies the highest point of the building and is
at a height of 180 feet, eight inches from ground level. The
compulsive desire to make the dome the highest peak in the
vicinity resulted in its rather pointed shape. Lord Hardinge
was determined to ensure that no other structure in the area
was taller than the dome. He floated a balloon to assess how
tall the dome would look after the Secretariat had been built.

The Star of India

The lit Star of India

President's Bodyguard in ceremonial formation on the steps to Durbar Hall

Perhaps, an irony that the dome symbolised went largely unnoticed. It was that the dome, which occupies the highest point of the magnificent building, had even at the acme of foreign rule, symbolised the dominance of an Indian style over a British creation. It was therefore, only natural for this symbol to augur well for the ruled and portentous for the British.

The President's own flag with its four quadrants used to fly on the dome until 1971. In its upper left quadrant, the state seal represented authority and an elephant in the upper right quadrant symbolised justice and equality. In the lower left, the scale was the symbol of equality and fraternity; while lotus-bearing flowers and buds in the lower right quadrant represented peace and plenty. After 1971, the national flag flies on the Rashtrapati Bhavan dome.

Crossing the *veranda* on which the 12 columns rest and climbing another 14 steps above, the visitor arrives at the Durbar Hall, which has been witness to history like no other hall or room at Rashtrapati Bhavan. It is here that the transition of power took place as the band played '*God Save the King*' for the last time on June 21, 1948 when C Rajagopalachari was sworn-in as the first and last Indian Governor-General. A 31-gun salute then announced the transition of power from the British Empire to India. '*Jana Gana Mana,*' the national anthem of the country was played for the first time to mark the swearing-in of the Indian Head of State.

The Accommodation

The accommodation in the building is divided into five blocks. The South West Wing was built as the Viceroy's Wing. It has 31 rooms spread across three floors, including 10 bedrooms. The South East Wing was reserved for the *aides-de-camp* (AsDC) to the Viceroy and bachelor guests. It housed the office of the Military Secretary to the Viceroy (MSV) and had 25 different rooms.

The North West Wing was designated for guests and it had 29 rooms out of which 20 were guest bedrooms. The North East Wing housed the clerical and technical staff of the Private Secretary to the Viceroy. It also housed the Superintendent, Viceregal Estates and had a total of 36 rooms.

The residential wing of the Viceroy or the Head of State continued to be in the South West of the building with suites named after former British Viceroys even after India gained independence. It did not, however, remain that way for long. The first Indian occupant, Governor-General C Rajagopalachari, chose to move into a more modest set of rooms in the North West Wing and the more luxurious South West Wing, became the Guest Wing.

The Dwarka Suite

The Dwarka Suite Sitting Room

The Dwarka Suite Loggia

President's Bodyguard in the Guest Wing Corridor

President's Bodyguard in the State Corridor

The Guest Wing has three floors. The ground floor during the period covered by this book (1947–67), originally had two bedrooms. One of these was partitioned to make another room taking the total number available to three. These bedrooms and appurtenant areas together cover a total area of 6,120 square feet. The first floor, with its two suites and an equal number of bedrooms and similar areas has an area of 17,094 square feet. The second floor, with its seven bedrooms and associated areas covers an area of 15,408 square feet, taking the total number of bedrooms in the Guest Wing to 14 and the total area to 38,622 square feet.

The first floor is normally reserved for the Heads of State/ Government, their spouses and other senior members of delegations and it has the regal magnificence designed to transport a visiting dignitary to Viceregal splendour. Many dignitaries who stayed here have echoed their wonderment. The words of President Eisenhower, who stayed in the Guest Wing in 1959, perhaps, describe it best. He wrote, "Although I have, through many years, become largely insensitive to the appointments of the quarters where I lay my head, I must confess I experienced a feeling of amazement in the Rashtrapati Bhavan."[11]

At the heart of the Guest Wing are the Dwarka and Nalanda Suites. They were earlier named the Irwin and Reading Suites and were occupied by the Viceroy and Vicereine respectively. This was, however, not how it was planned during the construction of Government House.

A less known fact is that the larger of the suites, the Dwarka Suite, was not originally planned as the bedroom of the Viceroy, but of his spouse. In the original completion drawings of 1931, this was designated as "Her Excellency's Bed Room." Similarly, the Reading Suite was designated for the Viceroy in the original drawing as "His Excellency's Bed Room." No records were, however, traceable that revealed how the Viceroy later got the better of the deal.

The cynosure of the first floor is the Dwarka Suite and is usually earmarked for the Head of State or the principal visitor. It has the largest of the bedrooms in the Guest Wing with a dimension of 40 feet, 10-and-a-half inches by 19 feet, 11 inches. It is regally appointed and showcases some antique furniture pieces designed by Lutyens. The Suite has two rooms attached to it–one sitting room and a private dining room and it also has a bathroom fitted with a rarely-seen antique shower that has some features of the most modern jacuzzis.

The second most prestigious suite is the Nalanda Suite, which is normally allotted to the spouse of the visiting Head of State/ Government. It is 24 feet, 10 inches by 20 feet, four-and-a-half inches. Both these suites are served by a large common Loggia measuring 55 feet by 16 feet, which has a breathtaking view of the Mughal Gardens that again seldom fails to draw on of world leaders. President Eisenhower was one ator. Referring to the beauty of the Gardens he eyond the Loggia "lay the beautiful Mogul Gardens, e palace much of its dignity and grandeur."[12]

wo decades covered in this book, all the Heads of rnment, stayed with their main delegation in this However, the number of those choosing to stay here cline after the 1980s. The last prominent occupant o stay here before the turn of the millennium was peth II, in 1997.

ent Pranab Mukherjee became the 13th Head of a, the Guest Wing was restored and refurbished. ion work was completed using some antique rnishings and decorative pieces, which had been the storerooms of Rashtrapati Bhavan. The rooms d with minimal changes to their original layout and tation. Priceless items including the jacuzzi with were restored and made fully functional in the

first floor of the main Guest Wing. The entire 14-room Guest Wing was also modernised to include a Business Centre.

In January 2014, the restoration was completed. Heads of State/Governments have once again begun staying in the Guest Wing. President Pranab Mukherjee was delighted to host the King of Bhutan, Jigme Khesar Namgyel Wangchuk, from January 6-10, 2014; the President of the People's Republic of Bangladesh Abdul Hameed and his wife Rashida Khanam from December 18-20, 2014 and the President of the People's Republic of Afghanistan Mohammad Ashraf Ghani from April 27-29, 2015.

The Ashok Hall

Though the Durbar Hall is more majestic in terms of its height and shape, it is less regal than the ornate Ashok Hall, which served as the State Ballroom before India's independence. Magnificently appointed, it rests on a sprung wooden floor, and has a central dance floor and three vestibules. It was

*Painting gifted by Shah of Iran, Fateh Ali Shah, in
the Rectangular Panel on the Ceiling of Ashok Hall*

*Painting of Persian Lady on
the North Centre of Ashok Hall*

The Ashok Hall

Painting of Persian poet Nizami on the South Centre of Ashok Hall

The Grand Open Staircase

designed to facilitate refreshing breeze to bl
dancers through a wide tunnel between the Ba
its own loggia to the north.

The Hall has a Persian style carpet (105 feet by 6
inches) woven in India. Six multi-tiered chandel
ceiling and another six can be found around the l
candelabras on its walls and crystal sconces fixe
the lighting is grand and delectable. Large Fren
opening to the garden, and the mirrored walls g
view of the dancers in motion.

The most striking feature of the Hall, howeve
ceiling breathtaking frescos that flow down t
arches end. These frescos were, however, not pla
the construction of Government House. The ini
was to paint on the ceiling, a design that resembl
Subsequently, a painting on a large oval mou
central rectangular shape, which was gifted by Fa
the Shah of Iran to King George IV, became the
the ceiling.

The painting portrays the Emperor and his 22 s
on horses. The Emperor is depicted thrusting h
a lion while others are shown engaging in the le
activity of hunting antelopes. Painted Persian ins
the ceiling enhance its beauty.

Vicereine Lady Willingdon, however, was not c
the lonely painting standing in splendid isolation
ceiling. She, therefore, requisitioned the services
artist, Tomasso Colonnello, who extended the hu
with the help of 12 Indian artists who painted di
surface. The paintings on the sides were in comp
on hung canvas pieces of 75 feet by 16 feet. The
portray royal processions with elephants and hors
in beautiful harnesses followed by royalty, dignitari
amongst others. They also contain floral designs
animals of prey like lions and leopards leaping o
Adding to the majestic look of the Hall are tw
central arches on the southern and northern sides
southern arch is a recessed alcove that has a pai
Persian poet, Nizami. On the north, there is a p
Persian Lady which is similarly placed.

After India's independence, the Ashok Hall has
variously. Important official functions were and a
If the occasion demands, the loft, an area desig

The Banquet Hall

orchestra, serves as the location from where the band plays the national anthem. It was also a preferred venue for swearing-in ceremonies, though it is now seldom used for this purpose. It, however, continues to be used for the introduction of dignitaries who are invited to the banquets held in honour of visiting Heads of State. During the period covered, it was usual for the President of India to accompany a visiting leader from the Dwarka Suite to the Ashok Hall. Escorted by AsDC, they walked through the Guest Wing Corridor and crossed the Grand Open Staircase to reach Ashok Hall. The entire path taken by the leaders was usually decorated with flowers and flower pots. The *sowars* of the PBG, standing with lances in hand, lent an Imperial ambience. The Grand Open Staircase particularly transformed into a grand spectacle, adding to the majestic setting of banquets. The introductions take place under the southern arch after the Indian President arrives with the visiting dignitary.

During the period that has been covered in this book, this Hall also doubled up as an auditorium for cultural shows during the visits of several world leaders. The cultural shows for the President of the Soviet Union, Kliment Efremovich Voroshilov (1960) and the President of the UAR, Gamal Abdel Nasser (1966) for instance,

were held here. It has also served as the venue for the signing of agreements as in 1980 during the visit of the Soviet President, Leonid Brezhnev.

The Banquet Hall

To the south of the Ashok Hall is the Banquet Hall or the State Dining Room. It is here that the Prime Ministers and Presidents hosted banquets for visiting Heads of Government and Heads of State during the period covered by the book. The practice of the Prime Minister hosting banquets for the Heads of Government at Rashtrapati Bhavan has, however, been discontinued. They are held at Hyderabad House after its renovation in the 1980s.

The 104 feet long, 34 feet wide and 35 feet high Banquet Hall with Burmese teak panelling is strikingly elegant and will seldom fail to impress anyone privileged to be invited to dine here. The 28 fluted pilasters rising to a height of 13 feet, one-and-a-half inches from the ground, made from single piece Burmese teak logs, add to the Imperial décor of the Hall. Each of the pilasters ends with two gorgeous bells, carved from wood, on their capitals. Huge glass windows with French louvres overlook the grand Mughal Gardens imparting a sense of space and elegance to the Hall.

A cornice made of wooden elephant motifs, another Lutyens' innovation, runs all along the top of the pilasters. The same motifs were copied and inverted to form the legs of the dining room consoles. A full-sized portrait of the 'Father of the Nation' greets visiting Heads of State/Government and guests from the southern end of the Hall. Portraits of the former Presidents of India on the wooden panes give the Hall a sense of history.

If the Hall imparts an unmistakable Imperial décor, banquets held here are no less impressive. Every banquet in Rashtrapati Bhavan is an elaborate and special affair where every invitee is treated like a royalty. Unbeknown to the guests, is the elaborate planning and the clockwork precision with which every banquet is conducted.

Every detail – from the subtle method of identifying every vegetarian to the butlers through an indigenous method of placing a small red rose in a vase in front of them, to the offering of *paan*, the Indian chew consisting of betel leaves, areca nut with other combinations as the guests depart is a well-choreographed affair. One butler is assigned to two guests, a ratio that was decided on the basis of the two separate plates that a bearer could carry in both hands. This ensures that all guests are served simultaneously.

As soon as guests arrive, they are ushered to their designated seats according to the table plan prepared on the basis of seniority of the guests. The more important dignitaries are seated closest to the Heads of State who face each other at the centre of the table.

At the head of the table on the southern side stands the Head Butler who controls a discreet set of three lights: blue, green and red. Guests take their seats only after the Heads of State arrive and are seated. At this point the blue light is switched on by the Head Butler. This is an indication for hot towels to be offered to the guests. As soon as the guests wipe their hands, the Butlers remove the used towels, beginning from the centre and moving outwards.

The green light is now switched on and the first course is served. When the red light is switched on, the table is cleared and this system is adhered to for all courses. The Head Butler switches on this light as soon as the Heads of States finish their course. After all the courses, follows the finger-bowl service, after which tea/coffee is served. During the duration of the dinner, live music is played from the band gallery on the southern side of the Hall. They are on a mezzanine floor with high walls and therefore can be heard and not seen. As the guests leave, the Indian tradition of eating *paan* after a meal is maintained, and two assistants offer *paans* to the guests.

In the past, during the two decades that this book covers, Presidents of India have hosted banquets and lunches not only for visiting Heads of Government at Rashtrapati Bhavan but also for Heads of States. For instance President Dr Rajendra Prasad hosted a State Banquet for Prime Minister of Pakistan, Liaquat Ali Khan in 1950 and he also hosted a lunch for the Canadian Prime Minister John Diefenbaker in 1958. Rashtrapati Bhavan too was not used only by the President of India to host visiting leaders.

Prized collection of the "Star of India" crockery used mainly for banquets.

It was also not unusual for the Vice President of India to host a visiting dignitary at Rashtrapati Bhavan. For instance, Vice President Dr Sarvepalli Radhakrishnan hosted the US Vice President Lyndon Johnson in 1961. It was particularly commonplace for the Indian Prime Minister to host foreign Heads of Government at Rashtrapati Bhavan. For instance Prime Minister Jawaharlal Nehru hosted a banquet for the Polish Prime Minister Józef Cyrankiewicz in 1957. Even in the absence of the Prime Minister, banquets were hosted by the Government of India for a visiting Head of Government as was done during the visit of the Afghan Prime Minister, Shah Mahmoud Khan Ghazi in 1951.

During the first two decades after independence, the sequence of the banquet speeches and the toasts that followed them, according to accessed material, had a different pattern and sequence. The speeches were made at the end of dinner and before coffee/tea was served. The procedure was for the butlers and all other supporting staff to leave the room after the main courses were served. It was the signal for the host to make the speech, concluding it normally with a toast to the visiting dignitary or to the Head of State of that country. This was followed by the playing of two bars of the national anthem of the Head of State/Government to whom the toast was raised. Similarly, when the visiting dignitary delivered

Crockery used for small parties and in the Guest Wing

Silverware used in banquets

The Morning Room

a speech and concluded it with a toast, two bars of the national anthem of India were played. Today the practice has changed and no bars of the national anthem are played after the toasts. The banquet speeches too are made before the dinner begins.

During the period 1947–1967, the cutlery and crockery used both for banquets and for service in primarily the Dwarka and Nalanda Suites during the stay of the Heads of State/Government and other dignitaries, were exquisite, exclusive and relics of the British Raj. The two most used brands were the prized collection of the 'Star of India' and the more exclusive 'Bleu De Roi' sets.

The former was mainly used for banquets. The sets of this crockery were made by T. Goode & Co., South Audley St., London. W; Cauldon Ltd., England and Pellatt & Wood, 25 Baker St., London. W. The latter, the first set of which was reportedly created and presented to King George V and Queen Mary, when they visited the factory in 1913 was fewer in number. They were primarily made of white china and had a royal blue border and a gold rim or gold filigree pattern. Rashtrapati Bhavan had a 15-set dinnerware and smaller sets of this brand. These sets were, however, reserved mainly for service in the first floor suites. The Bleu De Roi crockery bear the marking Alfred Meakin, England.

The Committee Room

Besides the above two brands, crockery from T. Goode & Co., London, was also used for service in the suites particularly on the first floor. Crockery made by Johnson Bros, England; George Jones & Sons, England and J&G Meakin, England were usually reserved for service in the suites and for small parties. All the above sets of crockery are no more in use and whatever remains of them have been shifted to the Rashtrapati Bhavan Museum.

The information relating to the use of the cutlery and crockery was gleaned from interviews that the author had with Ram Chander who worked as Chief Butler in Rashtrapati Bhavan and Abdul Majid who worked as Head Butler.[13] They also shared an interesting tale that they said was passed on by their fathers who had served as Butlers before 1947 during the time of the British. They showed the author a beautiful plate, which they said, would change colour in case any poisoned food was placed on it. The author did not, however, test the veracity of the claim. Perhaps, it must have been a clever stratagem of someone to dissuade any local employee from pursuing any insidious design.

The Informal Rooms

The informal rooms are on the ground floor on the western side of the state corridor that runs north to south and forms

The Yellow Drawing Room

The Thinkers Loggia

The Grey Dining Room

the main passage to the Study (another name for the office of the President). They are the Morning Room, the Committee Room, Western Garden Loggia, the Yellow Drawing Room and the Grey Dining Room. In actuality, however, it would be a misnomer to term them informal rooms. These rooms were also used for formal meetings, during the visits of State Guests in the first two decades after India's independence.

The Morning Room was originally known as the Vicereine's Card Room. It is connected to the Study and has subtle frescoes on the ceiling with gold leaf work, a large fireplace and paintings on the walls. The paintings depict the 6th century frescoes on the famous Ajanta Caves. It has a sublime ambience, with the décor melding with the ceiling to give it the soft touch of the hues of the morning sun. The room was mainly used by Presidents to meet visiting Heads of State. Out of the 52 visits covered, no less than10 Heads of State called on the Indian President in this room. They included Prime Minister Liaquat Ali Khan (April 1950), Premier Chou En-lai (June 1954) and the President of the USSR Leonid Brezhnev and Madame Brezhneva (December 1961).

The Committee Room is panelled with teak from the floor to the ceiling, in a bid to give it a more serious, official air. In the 52 visits covered, the room was used no less than four times for formal meetings. They included the meeting of Prime Minister Jawaharlal Nehru and Members of the Planning Commission with Marshal Voroshilov, Chairman of the Presidium of the Supreme Soviet Republic (January, 1960); the tripartite

The South Drawing Room

The North Drawing Room

talks between Indira Gandhi, President Nasser and President Tito (October 1966) and the meeting of Prime Minister Indira Gandhi with President Nixon and his delegation (July 1969).

The Yellow Drawing Room gets its name from its golden-yellow motif on the floor and the Jaisalmer stone pillars of its fireplace. Out of the 52 visits covered, this was used the most and on no less than 20 occasions. These included the introduction of the entourage of Crown Prince Akihito and Princess Michiko to the President of India, Dr Rajendra Prasad and the introduction of the staff of the Indian President to the Prince and Princess (November 1960). It was used for the same purpose during the visit of President Dwight Eisenhower (December 1959) and for a farewell tete-a-tete with, Queen Elizabeth II of England and the President of India, KR Narayanan (October 1997).

The Grey Dining Room is a large rectangular room with a white and green marble floor. Two lion-headed fountains each on the north and south give it an air of elegance. It has a coffered ceiling and beautifully embellished plaster mouldings with square motifs. The room also has paintings of the Himalayas. It was one of the favourite rooms for holding luncheons and dinners for smaller groups.

During the 52 visits covered, it was used on not less than eight occasions. It was also the venue of the longest press conference held at Rashtrapati Bhavan (by Premier Chou En-lai in April 1960). Luncheons were also hosted by President Dr S Radhakrishnan for the Crown Prince of Kuwait (November 1964) and by the Prime Minister of India, Lal Bahadur Shastri, for King Mahendra of Nepal (November 1965).

The West Loggia has large pillars and is today called the Thinker's Lounge and was not used as frequently as the other informal rooms.

Formal Rooms

In Lutyens' blueprint, there were two formal rooms, the North Drawing Room and the South Drawing Room that are on both sides of the Durbar Hall. The North Drawing Room is perhaps the most well appointed of all the rooms, with the possible exception of the Study in Rashtrapati Bhavan. It has grand Burmese teak panelling and has two prized paintings of the swearing-in of India's first Governor-General, C Rajagopalachari and India's first Prime Minister, Jawaharlal Nehru. It is in this room that the President meets the visiting Heads of State/Government for talks and *tete-a-tetes.*

The South Drawing Room is another elegantly appointed room with beautiful fluted pilasters that rise from the floor to the ceiling with broader capitals on top. Its ceiling is embellished

The Victoria Regia Lily fountain in the Mughal Gardens

जाफरी
JAFFERI
(Marigold)

with plaster moulding, and its walls are hung with oil portraits of royalty and Company School paintings. It was also used as a Reception Room. Out of the 52 visits covered, it served as a reception area for the press and photographers during the visit of Queen Elizabeth II in 1983. It was also used by the Vice President of India, Krishan Kant and his wife Suman Kant to call on Queen Elizabeth II in October 1997.

Mughal Gardens

This is a beautiful 15-acre garden that combines several Persian and British features. Two canals, 18 feet wide, cross the garden from north to south and two others with the same width intersect to form a 200 foot square island in the centre spanned by four low bridges.

Fountains were designed in the model of the Victoria Regia Lily. Four of these stand at the crossings of the canals and have 16 red stone petals, the lowest tier of which rests almost on the flowing water below and touches the four corners of the junction. In a marvel of architecture, slotted margins of the leaves direct the flow of water step-to-step, in alternating falls.

A pair of almost similar fountains rises from the centre of the two pools on the west. These stand out higher than the others

The Circular Garden in the Mughal Gardens

and are adorned with 18 petals. The garden's square central lawn that has an area of 6,645 square feet serves as the main area for holding 'At Home' receptions by the President of India on Republic and Independence Days and in honour of visiting dignitaries (for Pakistan Prime Minister Mohammed Ali Bogra

The Mughal Gardens and the Central Lawn

in 1955 and Queen Elizabeth II in 1961 for instance). It has also been used by Presidents for hosting lunches and tea parties for visiting leaders.

The Indian Welcome

When world leaders came to India on State Visits, their first choice of residence was invariably Government House, now Rashtrapati Bhavan. Foreign leaders reluctantly chose to stay elsewhere only when accommodation was not available 'under the dome'. Rashtrapati Bhavan was the most preferable 'home away from home' with all its symbolism when other options would have made it look less regal.

The Governor-Generals and the Presidents have extended to all dignitaries who were their guests the traditional and famed Indian welcome. According to Indian culture, guests are to be treated as Gods, with the respect and care that no other culture demands. This social practice has its mooring in the Sanskrit words, *"Atithi Devo Bhava"* meaning "the Guest is God" contained in the *Taittiriya Upanishad* which equates guests at par with the mother, father and teacher.

The treatise also lists the five steps to be followed while receiving guests. These include the use of fragrance or incense to uplift the mood of the guests; an earthen lamp for visibility; offering of eatables including fruits, milk, sweets and other refreshments; applying *tilak* to convey warm wishes and the well-being of guests, and fresh flowers for good memories of the visit. These traditions were followed with appropriate modifications by the staff inculcated with the spirit of *"Atithi Devo Bhava"* when guests were welcomed to the abode of the Indian President.

Several distinguished visitors to Rashtrapati Bhavan have remarked on the special welcome and reception they received over and above the grandeur and pageantry to which almost all Heads of State/Government are accustomed to and receive here too, maybe with a splendour unmatched in several respects. The welcome left a deep imprint on the minds of several visitors who stayed at Rashtrapati Bhavan. It led to many guests expressing their appreciation of their unique experience at Rashtrapati Bhavan even in disregard to the strict protocol they were accustomed to usually follow.

Olive Diefenbaker, the wife of the Prime Minister of Canada, for instance, sent a hand-written letter after their stay in 1958, to President Dr Rajendra Prasad in which she thanked him for what she said was, "privilege of staying" at Rashtrapati Bhavan and for the "wonderful and kindly care" that she received 'under the dome'. She described it as an "unforgettable" experience (please see letter at page 278).

The US Vice President, Lyndon Johnson too reacted with similar emotions after his stay at Rashtrapati Bhavan in 1961. He wrote to President Dr Prasad and said, that he and Lady Bird would "always cherish" the "wonderful hospitality at

Rashtrapati Bhavan." He even disregarded the levels of protocol after the visit and wrote to the Military Secretary to the President and thanked him for the "courtesies" shown by the "fine staff" of Rashtrapati Bhavan to him and Lady Bird which "proved Indian hospitality to be legendary" (please see letter at page 316). Queen Elizabeth II of England, famous for her adherence to formality, sent a hand-written letter to President Giani Zail Singh in 1983 thanking him and said, "We shall always have the happiest memories of our stay in Delhi and in Hyderabad"(please see letter at page 244).

From the response of the dignitaries who stayed under the dome, the discernible conclusion that could be reached is that they left with a feeling no different from what they experienced when they left their own homes. The reason was the 'Indian Welcome.' Right from the warm reception at the airport to the ceremonial welcome that they received on arrival at the South Court till their departure, nothing was spared to make their visit special and memorable. The tradition of *"Atithi Devo Bhava"* followed by the staff at Rashtrapati Bhavan ensured that the stay of the distinguished guests under the dome was memorable.

Covering the Visits

Deciding on the visits to be covered posed a serious dilemma. More than a hundred Heads of State/Government and other very important personalities had visited India during the first two decades of India's independence. The aim was to cover all such visits as possible where the principals stayed in Government House/Rashtrapati Bhavan.

With this objective in mind, it was decided to cover the visits decade-wise to make the volumes manageable. To our disappointment, however, there were very few files of the visits that we could find. Many of them were lost, destroyed or untraceable. An earnest effort to locate or recover the files from even the old records that had escaped the shredders and incinerators met with little success.

The absence of any record whatsoever on the stay of several leaders at Government House/Rashtrapati Bhavan, most disappointingly constrained us to exclude many important visits.

Consequently, we could cover only 52 visits of 32 Heads of State/ Government/leaders during the period 1947–67 who had stayed 'under the dome'. The only exception where a leader whose visit was covered though he did not stay in Government House/ Rashtrapati Bhavan, was that of Maharaja Padma Shumshere Jung Bahadur Rana of Nepal who visited Government House in 1949. This departure was made as it was the only visit during the transition period, when Lord Mountbatten was the Governor-General of India and for which records are available.

As many files were not traceable, we have not been able to cover all visits of several leaders. Only the visits where there was some evidence of the leaders having stayed at Rashtrapati Bhavan have been included in this book. Many of the files that survived did not also contain adequate information. Some of them had only single sheets of paper. Nevertheless, such visits were included when it was possible to recreate them using information from diverse sources.

Within the above serious constraints, an attempt has been made to contextualise every visit covered, detail the programmes of leaders, their reception by the people of India, her leaders, and their impression of India's democracy and of the country as they left the nation. The book, therefore, suffers from the drawback that the visits of some leaders and some visits of many have not found treatment in this work.

Nevertheless, I must confess that the research for this book was both exacting and tedious, especially as it had to be completed within a short span of nine months. The most challenging part was the reconstruction of the visits from various bits and pieces of information dispersed in various documents, including thousands of newspaper reports, the majority of them dating back over half a century. To fill gaps in information, some of the staff,

who had served in Rashtrapati Bhavan during the relevant period, were reached at some of the remotest locations of the country, biographies of leaders combed and history books searched.

The satisfying part of it, however, was that the end product makes it appear as if all the demands on time and the effort expended was worth it. Before concluding, it must be said that this volume would not have seen the light of day if it were not for the constant reminder of the Secretary to the President that I had no other option, but to complete the task and the equally regular encouragement of the President, an historian himself. They leavened my spirit.

I hope that this book gives you a peek into life 'under the dome' and takes you through some of the less known pages of history.

Happy reading!

Notes

[1] "Leaders Visit India: The Arrival of Czech Premier Inaugurates Round of Tours," *The New York Times*, January 4, 1958, p. 3.

[2] The date on which the Government House was renamed as Rashtrapati Bhavan has been variously indicated in many works. The Government House was, however, renamed as Rashtrapati Bhavan on August 15, 1951. The Secretary to the President, BK Gokhale, communicated the order of the President in this regard, to Col. B. Chatterjee, MSP. Records, President's Secretariat, Rashtrapati Bhavan, File No. 109-Est/51, 1951.

[3] Records, President's Secretariat, Rashtrapati Bhavan, File No. B-III/17/15-B, 1947.

[4] Philip Davies, *Splendours of the Raj: British Architecture in India, 1660–1947* (London: John Murray (Publishers) Ltd, 1978), p. 228.

[5] Records, President's Secretariat, File No. B-III/17/15-B, 1947.

[6] William Dalrymple, *City of Djinns: A Year in Delhi* (Gurgaon: Penguin Books India, 2004), p. 84.

[7] Davies, *Splendours of the Raj*, p. 227.

[8] Records, President's Secretariat, Rashtrapati Bhavan, File No. B-VI/327, 1927.

[9] Arthur S.G. Butler, *The Architecture of Sir Edwin Lutyens: Volume II* (London: Country Life Limited, 1950), p. 42.

[10] Records, President's Secretariat, Rashtrapati Bhavan, File No. 518, 1949.

[11] Dwight D. Eisenhower, *The White House Years: Waging Peace, 1956–1961* (London: William Heinemann Ltd., 1956), p. 500.

[12] Ibid., p. 501.

[13] Ram Chander and Abdul Majid (2015), personal interview by Thomas Mathew, New Delhi, April 5, 2015. Ram Chander had joined Rashtrapati Bhavan on May 11, 1971 and retired as Chief Butler on June 31, 2012. Abdul Majid joined Rashtrapati Bhavan on June 18, 1957 and retired as Head Butler on May 31, 1993.

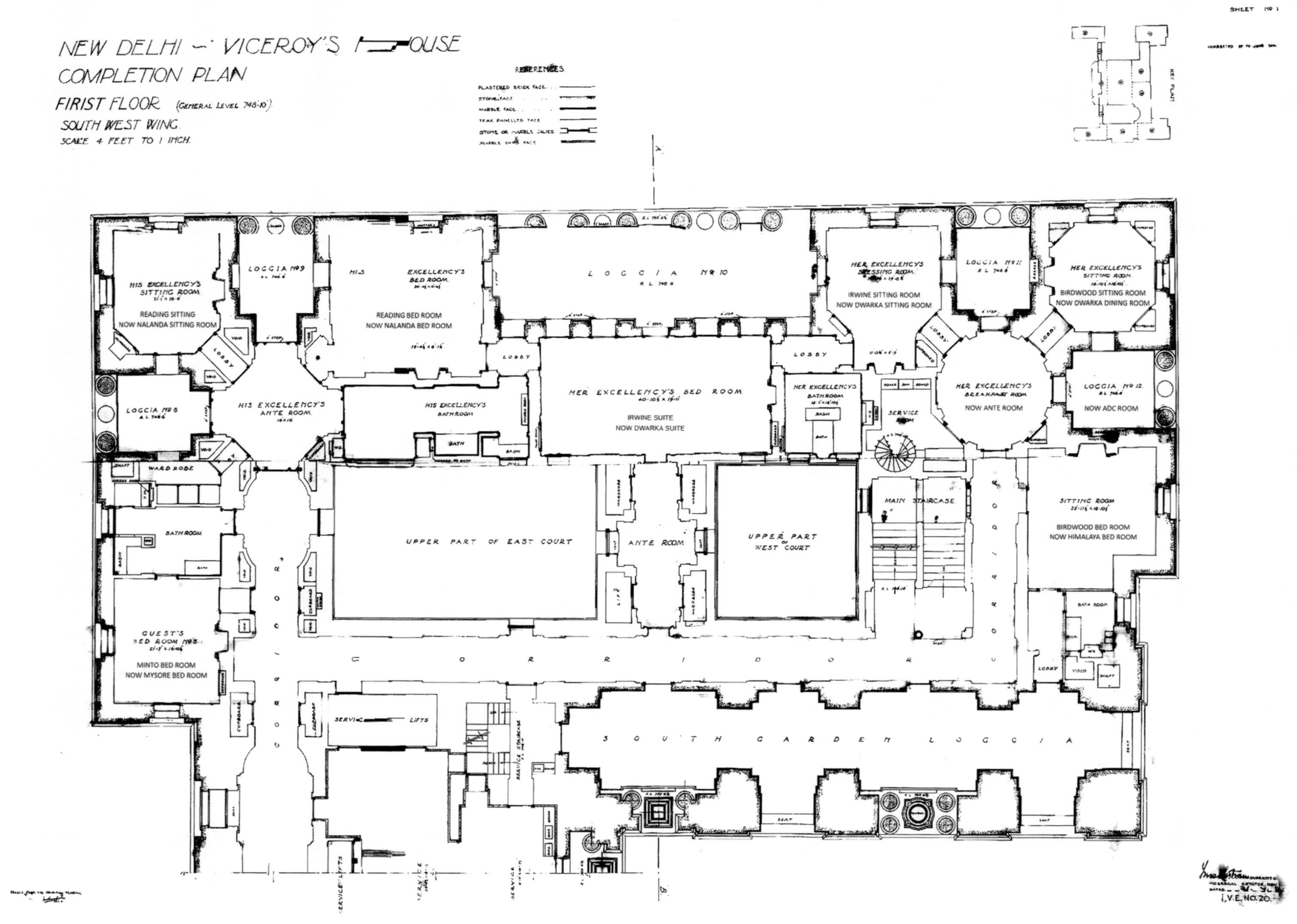

The original drawing of the Viceroy's living quarters (now Guest Wing). The new names of the suites have been inserted in blue on the original drawing.

STATE GUESTS

AT

RAISINA HILL: 1947–67

AND THEIR SUBSEQUENT VISITS

A view of the North Court at dusk.

The visits have been arranged in alphabetical order according to continents. Within continents, too, they have been arranged alphabetically according to countries, as they were called, at the time of the visits. Within the countries, the visits have been arranged chronologically. In the case of multiple visits by one dignitary, the chronology is based on the first visit. When a dignitary has visited multiple times, all subsequent visits have been included irrespective of the years they may have taken place in, provided the first visit fell within the two decades of 1947–67.

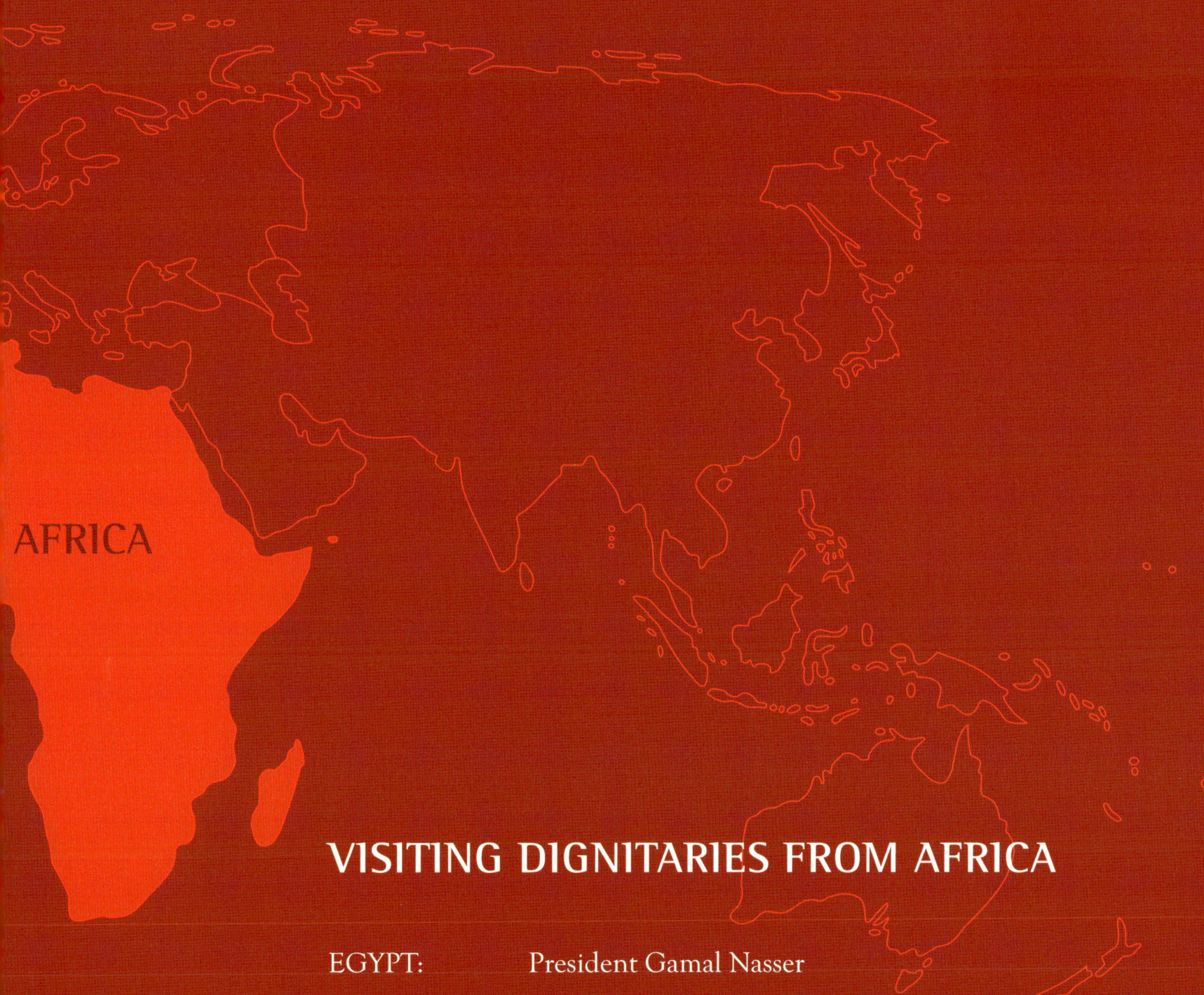

AFRICA

VISITING DIGNITARIES FROM AFRICA

EGYPT: President Gamal Nasser

GHANA: Prime Minister Kwame Nkrumah

The President of the United Arab Republic, Gamal Abdel Nasser, arrived on a State Visit to India from October 20-27, 1966, to attend the third Non-aligned trilateral meeting Summit. Although this was not his first visit to India,[1] it was the first time that President Nasser would not be received by his friend, the late Indian Prime Minister Jawaharlal Nehru, on his arrival.

Gamal Abdel Nasser was born on January 15, 1918, to a poor family in the village of Beni Murr near Alexandria in Egypt. When he was only eight, Nasser was sent to Cairo to stay with his uncle Khalil Hussein, who was earlier arrested for his involvement in anti-British demonstrations.[2] The stories that Gamal Nasser heard from his uncle had a great influence on the young man and he too began participating in anti-British activities. During one such demonstration in which he participated, Gamal Nasser received a blow to the forehead that left a lifelong scar. After six months of studying law at the Faculty of Law, Cairo University, Gamal Nasser joined the Royal Military Academy from which he graduated in 1938 and subsequently joined the Egyptian Army.

Visit of

H.E. Mr Gamal Nasser

President of the United Arab Republic

October 20-27, 1966

While serving in the army in Sudan he met three fellow officers, one of whom was Anwar el-Sadat, who would succeed Gamal Nasser as President of the UAR one day. The four formed a secret revolutionary organisation, the Free Officers, with the aim of overthrowing the British as well as the Egyptian royal family who were believed to be supporting foreign dominance over Egypt.

The revolutionary organisation captured power on July 23, 1952, in an almost bloodless *coup d'état*. King Farouk was ousted and the Revolutionary Command Council of officers assumed authority under Nasser's leadership. Not long thereafter, in 1956, President Nasser consolidated his power by promulgating a new constitution making Egypt a socialist Arab State and ushering in a one-party rule with Islam as the State religion. By this time, he also earned the name as a crusader in the Arab struggle against foreign domination. Largely due to President Nasser's spirited role in the 1956 war of Egypt against the French, British and Israeli forces, his name had become a household word in the Arab world.

President Nasser had also gained international stature by this time. It was primarily his association with Prime Minister Nehru, President Sukharno and President Tito, and their founding of the Non-Aligned Movement that catapulted him on to the world stage. The 1955 Bandung Conference, held in Jakarta, Indonesia, where a declaration on the promotion of world peace and cooperation was made, was a defining moment and a milestone in President Nasser's transformation into a global figure.

The leaders of India, Yugoslavia and the UAR/Egypt spearheaded the Non-aligned Movement steering many nations away from Cold War military blocs. They met at

Facing page:
President Dr Radhakrishnan (left) with
President Nasser at Rashtrapati Bhavan in
October 1966. Credit: PC

short intervals to reinvigorate the organisation and counter the continuing challenges spawned by superpower rivalry. It was for one such Summit in 1966 that President Nasser arrived in Delhi on a four-day trilateral meet of the leaders of India, Yugoslavia and UAR. This was the third such conference after those held in Brioni in 1956 and Cairo in 1961.[3]

President Nasser's arrival plans, the composition of his delegation and his programmes in India received considerable attention in the Ministry of External Affairs (MEA). Though President Nasser's participation in the Summit was decided well in advance, the details of his plans came only shortly before his arrival. It was on October 12, with less than 10 days before his arrival, that a telegram was received about the Arab leader's programme.[4] The telegram was, however, notable for its unusual openness. President Nasser, said the telegram, had informed that he would prefer to reach Delhi on the evening of October 20, at 5.45, but "before sunset,"[5] because he wanted to "relax in the friendly atmosphere of India in New Delhi itself."[6]

The Secretary to the UAR President, Abdel Maguid Farid, also conveyed that President Nasser was specifically desirous of utilising his stay in India as a vacation to recuperate from his ill-health. The communication further added that the UAR President would not be inclined to travel out of New Delhi but would prefer to see places of archaeological importance in the city "in the company of the Prime Minister in a relaxed atmosphere."[7]

The composition of President Nasser's delegation was also not finalised until the last moment and it led to some anxiety in the MEA. In a telegram dated September 24, 1966, to the Chief of Protocol (COP), APA Pant, of the MEA, Indian Embassy officials at Cairo lamented that they still did not have, despite "repeated requests,"[8] any information regarding the possible composition of President Nasser's entourage. "Obviously President Nasser has not yet made up his mind," said the telegram apologetically, "especially as there has been a great Governmental shake-up and new Ministers have come into prominence."[9]

Whether President Nasser would be accompanied by his wife or not also became the subject of a discreet enquiry by the Indian Government. A telegram was sent from the Foreign Office to the Indian Embassy in Cairo informing them that while the President of India would be sending a formal invitation to the President of the United Arab Republic (UAR) shortly, they "might enquire and mention incidentally that Madame Tito is coming."[10] The Indian Embassy duly did so, and discovered that Madame Nasser could not come to India, because the Nassers were expecting a grandchild.

The Indian Embassy also sent a list of suggested places that the President might like to visit during his stay in New Delhi. Their proposal included seeing village industries and industrial estates, a trip to Ranchi and Bangalore. The Foreign Office in

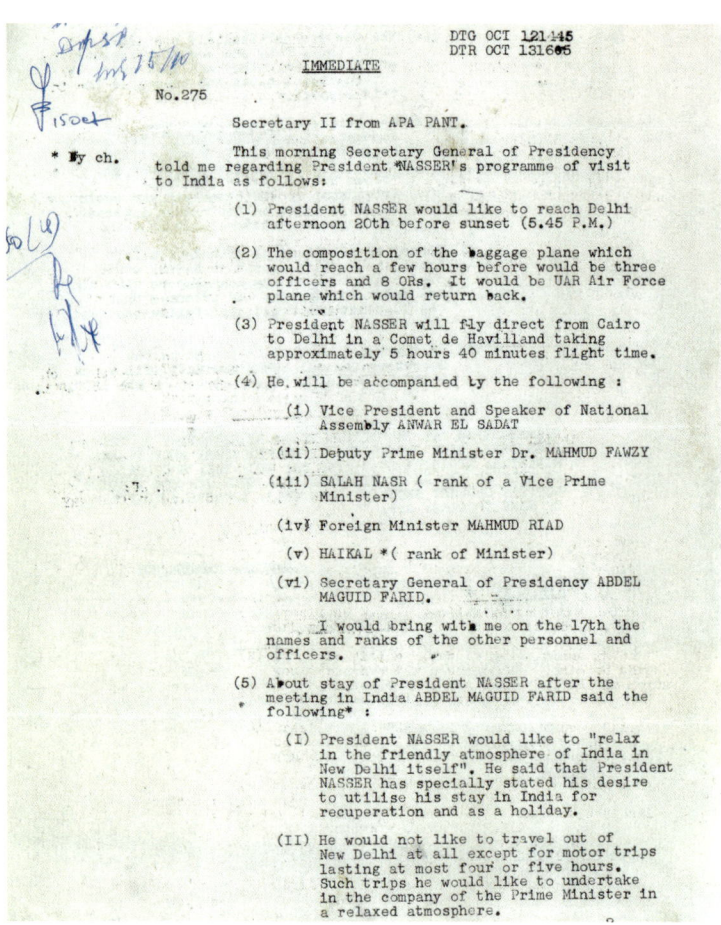

Communication intimating President Nasser's desire to "relax in the friendly atmosphere of India in New Delhi."

New Delhi, however, quickly dismissed these suggestions. In a terse reply, to the India Embassy in Cairo, MEA said, "We have considered your suggestions but do not find them practicable in short time available."[11]

As President Nasser's aircraft touched down, a 21-gun salute boomed in welcome. Impeccably dressed in a grey suit, a smiling UAR President alighted from the plane to a ceremonial welcome. He was received by President Dr Radhakrishnan and Prime Minister Indira Gandhi.[16] The 5000[17] strong crowd that had gathered at the airport also joined the celebrations with cries of "Long Live Nasser."[18]

The Mayor of New Delhi, Nuruddin Ahmed, greeted the UAR President, garlanding him with marigold flowers. Thereafter, President Nasser was presented an Inter-Services Guard of Honour by three detachments of 50 men each from the Indian Army, Navy and Air Force.[19]

After the Guard of Honour and introductions at the special enclosure, President Dr Radhakrishnan delivered the traditional welcome address and referred to President Nasser as a "tested and trusted friend of India,"[20] "a great friend of our country"[21] and a "great servant of the Arab people."[22] He recalled the historical and friendly relations that the two nations had shared since ancient times and complimented President Nasser on his growing stature describing him as the force behind Arab unity and nationalism.[23]

President Nasser reciprocated declaring that his visit would help consolidate a relationship between "brothers" who had made numerous contributions to the service of the contemporary world and in solving its problems. Real peace, said the UAR President, was still a distant dream, but he was glad to work with Prime Minister Indira Gandhi and President Tito to reaffirm the principles adopted at Bandung.[24] Before concluding his speech, President Nasser paid an emotional tribute to the memory of his friend, the late Indian Prime Minister, Jawaharlal Nehru. Referring to him, President Nasser said, "my dear friend – indeed the friend of humanity as a whole."[25] His references to Prime Minister Nehru brought into focus the close bonds that the two leaders had forged on the foundations of their common worldviews and their desire to lead their countries out of the chains of poverty and colonialism. It particularly reflected the influence Prime Minister Nehru had

on President Nasser. As journalist and biographer, Jean Lacouture had opined, the influence that the Indian leader had on President Nasser was significant. Commenting on the meeting between the two leaders on the Nile, and the impact it had on President Nasser, he wrote, "Nehru's influence was less keen, but the five hours the two men spent on the Nile on February 13, 1955, were to plant in Nasser a spirit which would inspire him in the course of the following years – the spirit of Bandung."[26]

After the welcome ceremony, President Nasser drove to Rashtrapati Bhavan in the Indian President's Mercedes Benz. The 10–mile drive afforded President Nasser a view of the enthusiastic crowds that had lined the streets. They waved paper flags and cheered as the motorcade drove past, adding to the joyous mood of the city that was in the grip of excited anticipation of the two important festivals of *Dussehra* and *Durga Pooja* that were fast approaching. Buntings and streamers welcoming President Nasser added more colour to an already festooned city and even Parliament Street which is not normally decorated had a paper arch of flowers.[27]

(R-L): President Dr Radhakrishnan, President Nasser, Prime Minister Indira Gandhi and Vice President Dr Zakir Husain at Palam Airport, Delhi, in October 1966. Credit: PC

From Vijay Chowk, the motorcade was escorted to the Forecourt of Rashtrapati Bhavan by the impressive President's Bodyguard (PBG). The arrival of the UAR leader was something that even the staff of the President's Secretariat and their families were loath to miss. So they had lined up along the grassy lawns of the Forecourt to get a glimpse of the leader.

When President Nasser arrived at the Forecourt, he was received by Major General GS Gill, Military Secretary to the President (MSP). The PBG had also lined up in the corridors leading to the Guest Wing and the Himalaya Suite[28] that was reserved for President Nasser. Thereafter, President Nasser was greeted by President Dr Radhakrishnan who presented his Personal Staff to the Arab leader after which the UAR delegation was conducted to the Yellow Drawing Room for tea and refreshments.

The accommodation for President Nasser and his delegation had given protocol officials at Rashtrapati Bhavan some anxious moments. Invariably visiting Heads of State stay in the regal Dwarka Suite. This may also however have been the first time, that not one, but two Heads of State would be staying 'under the dome' at the same time. The question as to who would stay in the Dwarka Suite had no easy answer. After long deliberations, the matter was resolved on the basis of the *inter se* seniority of the leaders and the Himalaya Suite was allotted to President Nasser. Marshal Tito stayed at the Dwarka suite as he was the senior of the two leaders having become President nearly three-and-a-half years before President Nasser and had also arrived in Delhi earlier than the Arab leader.

President Nasser had also arrived with a large entourage of 80 members. All of them could not be accommodated in Rashtrapati Bhavan as Marshal Tito and his delegation were occupying five suites/rooms. Consequently, only select members were accommodated in Rashtrapati Bhavan. Zakaria Mohieddin, Vice President of the UAR, stayed in the Bombay Bedroom and Anwar el-Sadat, Speaker of the National Assembly, stayed in the Pepsu Bedroom. The rest of the delegation was allotted rooms according to their seniority in the remaining rooms/ suites. Those who could not stay at Rashtrapati Bhavan were accommodated in the Ashoka Hotel.

On the evening of their arrival, Marshal Tito and President Nasser had dinner at Prime Minister Indira Gandhi's residence, which was elegantly decorated for the occasion. The portico was rearranged in traditional Indian style with flowers surrounding the bronze statue of a Goddess, while earthen lamps placed nearby lent the ambience a warm glow.[29] When the guests arrived they were personally received at the portico by Prime Minister Gandhi.

The traditional theme was also extended to the dinner menu. The fare included *Tandoori Chicken, Seekh Kebab, Potato Balls, Naan and Tandoori Roti* along with Cauliflower Polonaise and Water Chestnuts. *Phirni* and *Apsara* made up the dessert.[30] The dinner also gave the leaders an opportunity to have informal[31] discussions with other guests – that included the UAR Vice President, Zakaria Mohieddin; the Yugoslav Foreign Minister, Marco Nikezic; the Indian Home Minister, GL Nanda and the

(Facing L-R): President Tito, President Dr Radhakrishnan (delivering banquet speech), President Nasser and Madame Broz Tito at Rashtrapati Bhavan in October 1966. Credit: PC

ALLOTMENT OF ROOMS

Name of Guests	Rooms	Phone. 35321/Ext. Nos.
H.E. Mr. Gamal Abdel Nasser, President of the United Arab Republic.	Himalaya Suite— Bed Room Sitting Room	89 66
H.E. Mr. Zakaria Mohieddin, Vice-President of the United Arab Republic.	Bombay Bed Room	114
Mr. Anwar El Sadat, Speaker of the National Assembly, UAR.	Pepsu Bed Room	109
Mr. Salah Mohamed Nasr, Deputy Prime Minister, UAR.	Godavari Bed Room	104
Mr. Mohamed Ahmed, Secy. to the President of the United Arab Republic.	Neelam Bed Room	202
Dr. Ahmed Abdel-Rahman Sarwat, Private Physician to the President of the United Arab Republic. Dr. Salah-Eddine Gabr, Director General of the Medical Supplies of the President.	Gautam Bed Room	42
Mr. Chorif Mahmoud Sami, Private Secretary Mr. Galal-Eddine Mohamed Farag, Private Secretary.	Dufferin Bed Room	185
Attendants	Marble Hall No. I Marble Hall No. II Service Room attached to Himalaya Suite.	

Room Allocation Plan.

Indian Foreign Minister, Swaran Singh – on the agenda of the tripartite meeting scheduled to begin the following day.[32]

October 21 for President Nasser began with a visit to *Rajghat* at 9.05 am, where he paid homage to Mahatma Gandhi and placed a wreath on the *samadhi*. President Nasser also paid his respects at the *samadhis* of late Prime Ministers, Jawaharlal Nehru and Lal Bahadur Shastri.[33] He was accompanied by the UAR delegation and escorted by the Indian Union Minister for Irrigation and Power, Fakhruddin Ali Ahmed.

Among the wreaths President Nasser had laid, the one he had placed on the *Samadhi* of the Father of the Nation was notable for its stunning beauty and design. It was specially flown from the UAR and was made of white lotus buds and ferns. It was placed on the *samadhi* that was "decorated in geometrical patterns with petals of jasmines, marigold and red roses."[34] In all likelihood, this must have been the solitary instance of a wreath being imported from the country of a visiting Head of State to India.

After the visit to the *samadhis*, President Nasser returned to Rashtrapati Bhavan, and called on the President for tea in the Rajaji Room[35] at 10.30 am. The meeting lasted for a little over 20-minutes, after which the Indian Prime Minister called on President Nasser.

At 11.30 am, the leaders and their delegations assembled in Rashtrapati Bhavan's grand Ashok Hall, taking their places around the circular teak table. Microphones had been set up around the table for the meeting. The meeting, however, began with an embarrassment of sorts as a glitch in the sound system led to some uncomfortable moments. The microphone that Prime Minister Gandhi was to use failed. The Indian Prime Minister waited, while flustered officials desperately worked to make it functional. Failing in their task, they tried to hand her the microphone of President Nasser's interpreter, but found that they could not, as it had become inextricably tangled in wires. Eventually Prime Minister Indira Gandhi had to make do with Nasser's microphone that was a good yard away from her. Her voice did not carry, and as a consequence, her remarks, briefly explaining her Government's approach to the problems of colonialism, racialism and disarmament,[36] unfortunately, could not be heard in the Press Gallery.[37]

Speaking on the occasion, President Tito asserted that in the last two or three years, the policy of non–alignment had gained more followers, since it had dawned on nations that catastrophe could be averted only by adhering to the "principles of co–existence and peaceful international cooperation."[38]

At 8.30 that evening, President Dr Radhakrishnan hosted a dinner at the Banquet Hall in Rashtrapati Bhavan, in honour of President Nasser of the UAR and President Tito of Yugoslavia and Madame Tito. It was a rare instance of one banquet being organised in honour of two Heads of State.

The House Party, consisting of President Tito, President Nasser and Madame Tito met the President of India in the Rajaji Room, before walking to the magnificent Ashok Hall, along corridors where the PBG had lined up in their splendid uniforms with their lances in hand. As was done during banquets, the Ashok Hall, its precincts and the Banquet Hall were adorned with beautiful flower arrangements. Lights came on in the Mughal Gardens and fountains began to play presenting a mystical view for the guests in the Ashok Hall.

Guests, who arrived via the South Sunken Road and the South Court, alighted at the South Entrance of the West Subway and were then escorted to the Ashok Hall by the President's Personal Staff. Here they assembled in a horse-shoe pattern under the central arch, with wives standing to the right of their husbands. As the President of India and the Guests of Honour entered, the band played the national anthems of the Yugoslavia, UAR and India in succession. The guests were then introduced to the two Heads of State and Madame Tito.

With introductions over, the guests were escorted to the Banquet Hall for the elaborate dinner. The specially selected menu included *Asparagus Soup*, *Grilled Fish* and *Vegetable Cutlets* as appetisers. The main course included traditional Indian fare such as *Chicken Mosallam* and *Khoya Mattar Curry*, with sides of *Stuffed Capsicum* and *Dahi Bara–Chutney*.

After the main courses were over, the *khidmatgars* (butlers) cleared the tables and left the Hall as instructed, as was the practice before toasts were raised. President Dr Radhakrishnan was the first to speak. He began welcoming the two Heads of State as "friends of this country."[39] He elaborated on the relevance and goals of non-alignment and drew commonalities in the policies of all the three countries that were aimed at steering clear of Cold War alliances. He ended saying, "I am very glad that we have the pleasure of meeting our old friends here and telling them how much we appreciate their endeavours for peace."[40] He concluded his speech by raising a toast to President Tito, Madam Tito and President Nasser. This was followed by the band playing the two bars of the national anthems of Yugoslavia and UAR.

President Nasser began his reply addressing guests at the banquet as, "Dear friend, Brethren."[41] He complimented President Dr Radhakrishnan for his achievements, especially his "ability to blend past heritage with future aspirations."[42] He reiterated the importance of the bonds that the three countries shared and lauded the similarities in their policy priorities. Then President Tito, too, replied to President Dr Radhakrishnan's toast.

The banquet ended with fruits and coffee. Thereafter, the guests were escorted to the Ashok Hall for a Cultural Programme of classical Indian dances that showcased the very best of India's cultural heritage.

The next few days were devoted to discussions on strategies to further strengthen the Non-Aligned Movement. The tripartite meeting ended with a joint statement. This was followed by a press conference, in which the three leaders answered questions that were put to them by the large gathering of the press corps.

On the evening of October 24, Prime Minister Indira Gandhi hosted an "At Home" at 6.00 in the Mughal Gardens. As the 200-odd guests arrived, President Nasser, President Tito and Madame Tito were conducted to the Yellow Drawing Room from where they were escorted to the Central Lawns of the Mughal Gardens. A band, positioned near the West Fountain in the Central Lawns, entertained guests with carefully selected music. As the sun began to set, casting an amber glow over the Gardens, the lights were switched on and fountains began to play, adding a sublime touch to the already beautiful surroundings.

President Tito left India on October 25, but President Nasser stayed behind for another two days until October 27. President Nasser's first programme on the morning of October 25 was a visit to the Nehru Memorial Museum on Teen Murti Marg. He walked quietly around the grounds of the museum with perceptible melancholy and spent a large part of the morning in the massive library that houses many of Prime Minister Nehru's original manuscripts. The visit was evidently emotional for the Arab leader. Its manifestation was unmistakable, when he paused in front a life-sized portrait of the late Indian Prime Minister hanging in the lobby and kept looking up at the face, for a good five minutes.[43]

President Nasser was admittedly pleased with the manner in which the museum was organised. He opined that it was a fitting tribute to the memory of the departed leader. He added that Prime Minister Nehru's documents were, "well-collected and well-preserved."[44] After the visit, by 12.30 pm, he returned to his suite in Rashtrapati Bhavan, to prepare for the Prime Minister's luncheon which was to be held in the stately Grey Dining Room.

The Household Staff at Rashtrapati Bhavan were given, as they usually are, a detailed list of instructions to be followed to ensure that the luncheon was meticulously organised and was a memorable one. Plants in pots and vases with beautiful flowers were tastefully arranged in the halls through which the guests would pass, as also in the Yellow Drawing and the Grey Dining Rooms. Personal Staff were dressed in special uniforms - white patrol jackets, blue overalls, aiguillettes and miniature

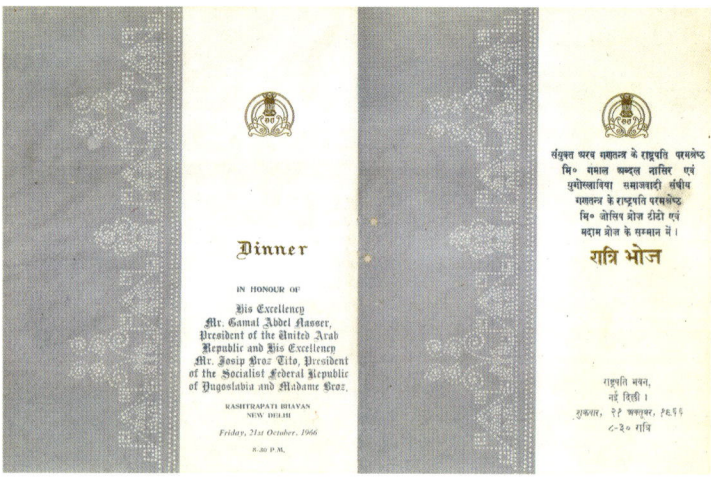
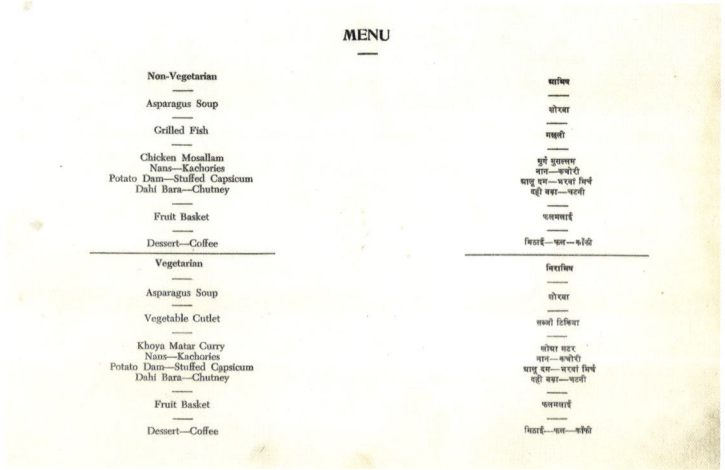

Menu of the banquet held in honour of President Nasser, President Tito and Madame Jovanka Broz Tito in 1966.

(L-R): President Nasser, President Dr Radhakrishnan, Madame Tito, President Tito and Prime Minister Indira Gandhi at Rashtrapati Bhavan in October 1966. Credit: PC

medals. The *khidmatgars* on duty wore white/cream *achkans* with matching *churidar* pyjamas.

The movement of the invitees was arranged with clock-wise precision. The first trickle of guests arrived at 1.00 pm. They had driven up the South Sunken Road to the South Court, where they alighted at the South Entrance of the West Subway. They were received by the smartly dressed Personal Staff of Rashtrapati Bhavan and were conducted to the Yellow Drawing Room. Prime Minister Indira Gandhi joined the visitors at five minutes past 1.00 pm and President Nasser arrived in the Yellow Drawing Room ten minutes thereafter, escorted by the Deputy Military Secretary to the President (DMSP) and an *aide-de-camp* (ADC). As the guests sat down to their meal, the band of the "3 Grenadiers" Regiment positioned outside the Grey Dining Room played selected music for the duration of the luncheon.

The luncheon was not a long affair. It ended at 2.30 pm, after which President Nasser, the Guest of Honour, took leave of the Prime Minister and was escorted by the DMSP and the ADC to his suite. Thereafter, *aides-de-camp* (AsDC) escorted the rest of the UAR delegation to their suites. The Personal Staff of the President of India bid the remaining guests good-bye, after Prime Minister Indira Gandhi took her leave and departed for her residence.

In the evening, Prime Minister Indira Gandhi held talks with President Nasser in the Himalaya Suite. The discussions which lasted about an hour were chiefly on Indo-UAR bilateral relations.[45] After the discussions, the Foreign Ministers of India and the UAR continued the talks.[46]

Following the meeting with Prime Minister Indira Gandhi, President Nasser travelled to the Ashoka Hotel, to attend a reception held in his honour by the Heads of the Arab and African Missions in Delhi. Vice President, Dr Zakir Hussain; Prime Minister, Indira Gandhi; the Minister for External Affairs, Swaran Singh; Cabinet Ministers and the diplomatic corps were amongst those who attended the reception.[47]

On October 26, the penultimate day of the visit, President Nasser hosted a banquet in honour of President Dr Radhakrishnan at the Ashoka Hotel, where he expressed his gratitude and that of his delegation for the warmth shown to them by the people of India and especially President Dr Radhakrishnan. Referring to Prime Minister Indira Gandhi as "an excellent daughter to an excellent father,"[48] he stated that in these tripartite and bilateral talks he had the opportunity to see her as "a great disciple of an illustrious professor."[49] Speaking of the deep bonds uniting India and the UAR, he affirmed that the relationship was one which "constituted a genuine and healthy example of relations between developing countries, sharing the same past, the same struggle and the same aspirations."[50]

At the reception, President Nasser also raised a toast to his "dear friend President Radhakrishnan, for the distinguished and valiant Lady Indira Gandhi, for an ever-strong and revived Arab-Indian Friendship."[51] Responding to President Nasser, Indian President Dr Radhakrishnan affirmed that Indo-Arab friendship would be further strengthened.

President Nasser's visit had generated much public interest. Apart from the presents from the Indian Government, there was also a surprise gift that awaited his acceptance from an unexpected source. It came in a mysteriously wrapped paper parcel that was addressed to the President of UAR. It aroused suspicion and none at Rashtrapati Bhavan displayed the courage to unwrap the parcel until a Sikh sentry bravely undid the parcel to check its contents. To everyone's astonishment, it contained a neat little silver penknife, sent by a student in Delhi as a token of respect and love for President Nasser. The gift was handed over to the UAR President who gladly received it.[52] The plane that President Nasser would use for his return flight was an issue that became a subject of discussion between the Indian Embassy at Cairo and the MEA. The Indian Embassy had suggested that India should make President Nasser and his party an offer to fly them from Cairo to New Delhi and back in a special chartered Air India plane. "The expense of this charter," said the memo "should be borne by us. This would have very good emotional and political impact. It would also have great commercial advantage for Air India."[53] The plan however, did not materialise.

President Nasser had arrived in New Delhi in a Comet, de Havilland, and the same aircraft finally flew him back to Cairo on October 27. That morning, two Cadillacs and a Rolls Royce formed the Presidential motorcade which drove through the streets of New Delhi to the airport. The Indian President escorted President Nasser to the airport, where the visiting dignitary was received by the Vice President, the Prime Minister, the Minister of External Affairs and the COP. He witnessed the farewell ceremony seated under a special *shamiana*, erected to protect assembled dignitaries from the sun. Thereafter, President Nasser was escorted to the Saluting Base. Dignitaries stood solemnly to attention while the national anthems of the UAR and of India were played by the Inter-Services Band.

After inspecting the Guard of Honour, the Arab leader was presented to the invitees to the departure ceremony. After the good-byes, President Nasser walked to the foot of his aircraft, where he was garlanded by the Mayor of New Delhi. A 21-gun salute boomed forth as President Nasser ascended the steps of the aircraft that would take him back to Cairo after what would be his last visit to India.

President Nasser died on September 28, 1970. The Arab world was grieved and as the Lebanese newspaper, *Le Jour*, wrote on his death, "One hundred million human beings – the Arabs" became "orphans."[54] He was 52.

Notes

1 From the various public sources, it is understood that Nasser had visited India in 1955, 1960 and 1966. Only the 1966 visit has been covered as the records relating to the other visits were not traceable.

2 Sam Witte, *Gamal Abdel Nasser* (New York: Rosen Publishing Group, 2004), pp. 9-12.

3 "Tripartite Meet Will Discuss Big Power Pressures," *The Hindu* (New Delhi), October 20, 1966, p. 1.

4 Records, President's Secretariat, Rashtrapati Bhavan, File No. 30/CER/210.

5 Ibid.

6 Ibid.

7 Ibid.

8 Ibid.

9 Ibid.

10 Ibid.

11 Ibid.

12 "Special PO Cachet for Summit," *The Hindustan Times* (New Delhi), October 21, 1966, p. 3.

13 Records, President's Secretariat, File No. 30/CER/210.

14 Ibid.

15 "Tito, Nasser Given Warm Welcome," *The Hindustan Times* (New Delhi), October 21, 1966, p. 3.

16 Ibid.

17 J. Anthony Lukas, "Tito and Nasser in India for Talks," *The New York Times*, October 21, 1966, p. 3.

18 "Tito, Nasser Given Warm Welcome," p. 3.

19 Ibid.

20 Ibid.

21 "Warm Welcome to Tito and Nasser in Delhi: Talks With P.M. To-day," *The Hindu* (New Delhi), October 21, 1966, p. 1.

22 Ibid.

23 "Tried and Tested Friends," *The Hindustan Times* (New Delhi), October 21, 1966, p. 6.

24 Ibid.

25 Ibid.

26 Jean Lacouture, *Nasser: A Biography* (London: Secker & Warburg, 1973), p. 155.

27 "Tito, Nasser Given Warm Welcome," p. 1.

28 Records, President's Secretariat, File No. 30/CER/210.

29 "P.M.'s Dinner to Tito & Nasser," *The Hindu* (New Delhi), October 21, 1966, p. 1.

30 Ibid.

31 Ibid.

32 "Leaders Discuss Agenda," *The Hindustan Times* (New Delhi), October 21, 1966, p .1.

33 "Presidents Lay Wreaths," *The Times of India* (New Delhi), October 22, 1966, p. 9.

34 Ibid.

35 This room is in the Family Wing in the northern side of the building.

36 K. Rangaswami, "Non-alignment More Valid Now Than Ever," *The Hindu* (New Delhi), October 22, 1966, p. 1.

37 K. Rangaswami, "Frank Exchange of Views at First Informal Meet," *The Hindu* (New Delhi), October 22, 1966, p. 1.

38 Rangaswami, "Non-alignment More Valid Now Than Ever," p. 1.

39 Ministry of External Affairs (1995), Government of India, MEA Library, Foreign Affairs Records 1966, Volume XII, accessed May 23, 2015, http://mealib.nic.in/?pdf2554?000.

40 Ibid.

41 Ibid.

42 Ibid.

43 "Visit to Nehru Museum," *The Times of India* (New Delhi), October 26, 1966, p. 1.

44 Ibid.

45 "Nasser-PM Talks on Bilateral Ties," *The Hindustan Times* (New Delhi), October 26, 1966, p. 1.

46 Ibid.

47 "Indira-Nasser Talks on World Situation," *The Times of India* (New Delhi), October 26, 1966, p. 1.

48 "Nasser Hopes Ties with India will Grow," *The Times of India* (New Delhi), October 27, 1966, p. 9.

49 Ibid.

50 Ibid.

51 Ibid.

52 "It was Merely a Pen friend," *The Times of India* (New Delhi), October 24, 1966, p. 1.

53 Records, President's Secretariat, File No. 30/CER/210.

54 "Nasser's Legacy: Hope and Instability," *Time*, October 12, 1970, accessed May 24, 2015, http://content.time.com/time/subscriber/article/0,33009,942325,00.html.

D r Kwame Nkrumah, Prime Minister of the first independent African nation, Ghana, came on an 18-day State Visit to India from December 22, 1958 to January 8, 1959.

Born on September 21, 1909, in Nkroful on the Gold Coast, to a family of goldsmiths, Kwame Nkrumah came from a humble background. He received his education in Mission schools and took up teaching, after he completed his degree studies from Achimota College in Accra, in 1930. The desire to pursue further education took Kwame Nkrumah to the US, where he studied at the Lincoln University in Pennsylvania.

During his student days in the US, he was drawn to politics and led the African Student's Organisation of the United States and Canada, as its President. Kwame Nkrumah left for London in 1945, where he organised the Fifth Pan-African Congress in Manchester. In 1947, when the United Gold Coast Convention (UGCC) was formed, Kwame Nkrumah was invited to become its General Secretary.[1]

Visit of
H.E. Dr Kwame Nkrumah
Prime Minister of Ghana

Working for the independence of the Gold Coast, Kwame Nkrumah gradually expanded his mass base and became a prominent face in the liberation movement. He led the younger revolutionary group of the Convention and advocated that the organisation pursue a new direction with the aim of liberating the nation from the colonial yoke. This resulted in a split in the UGCC and in June 1949, Kwame Nkrumah launched the Convention People's Party (CPP) with the aim of achieving 'self-governance now'. On January 21, 1950, Nkrumah was arrested but this did nothing to dampen his spirit and his rising popularity could not be doused. In 1951, his party contested elections and stormed to power winning 34 out of the 38 electoral seats in the Legislative Assembly.[2] Kwame Nkrumah himself won a stunning victory, securing 22,780 votes out of a possible 23,122 from the Accra Central seat.[3] He was released from prison and became the leader of Government Business and, in 1952, the Prime Minister of the Gold Coast.[4]

After six years in office as Prime Minister, Nkrumah finally succeeded in his mission of liberating his country. On March 6, 1957, he "presided over the Gold Coast's independence as Ghana."[5] As the leader of a nascent independent nation, Prime Minister Nkrumah took up the mammoth task of building his country from scratch. In a bid to attract foreign investment, he built and fostered friendly ties with several countries around the globe. He commanded mass popularity and adulation, prompting his admirers to refer to him as *Osagyefo* (meaning the Redeemer).

As a leader who fought for the independence of his nation from colonial domination, he found common cause with India's Prime Minister who had waged a similar battle and campaigned for the liberation of colonies. The Nehru-Nkrumah friendship was in

Facing page:
President Dr Prasad (left)
greeting Prime Minister Dr Nkrumah at
Rashtrapati Bhavan
in December 1958. Credit: PD

fact older than India–Ghana relations. Prime Minister Nkrumah had met Prime Minister Nehru on the side lines of the Bandung Conference held in 1955 and both leaders had developed close bonds. Their friendship grew and it gained in strength during Nkrumah's tenure as Prime Minister.

In 1958, Prime Minister Nehru extended a formal invitation to Prime Minister Nkrumah to visit India, which the Ghanaian Prime Minister gladly accepted. The "goodwill" visit was planned during the festive season of Christmas and New Year.

Prime Minister Nkrumah was keen to visit India to learn from its deft handling of issues since it gained independence. He was particularly impressed with India's handling of her post-colonial domestic imperatives. He in fact "wanted to see at first-hand how India had tackled economic and political problems during the 11 years of her independence."[6] Another objective of the visit was to promote his idea of the "liberation and unification" of the African continent.[7]

On the eve of his departure to India, an incident almost derailed his visit. The Army and Police discovered a plot hatched by two Members of the Parliament of the opposition party. The plot was to assassinate the Prime Minister at Accra Airport as he boarded the flight to India. They tried to bribe a non-commissioned officer to carry out the assassination. The unearthing of the plot did not, however, unhinge the plans of the Ghanaian leader. A stoic Prime Minister Nkrumah went ahead with his State Visit and arrived in India on an Air India International aircraft, called the "Rani of Chittor."[8]

The Ghanaian Prime Minister began his visit in Bombay, instead of Delhi where Heads of State/ Government normally arrive. Prime Minister Nkrumah's flight landed at Santa Cruz Airport on December 22, 1958, at 5 pm. He was warmly received by the Finance Minister of Bombay, Jivraj Mehta, who then introduced the Ghanaian Prime Minister to the Mayor of Bombay, SS Mirajkar and the Sheriff, BD Garware.

The absence of Bombay's Chief Minister, YB Chavan, did not dampen the enthusiastic welcome. The airport had been beautifully decorated and the flags of both countries flew prominently from different locations. After the initial introductions, the Indian Navy presented the Prime Minister of Ghana a Guard of Honour, after which Jivraj Mehta introduced members of the Bombay Cabinet and members of the diplomatic corps to the visiting Prime Minister. Speaking to media correspondents at the airport, Prime Minister Nkrumah said that this was the longest flight he had ever been on.

The Ghanian leader had arrived with a 12-member entourage that included the Minister of Works, Emmanuel Kobla Bensah; Member of Parliament, Atta Nantogmah and Development Commissioner, Robert Jackson. The "Rani of Chittor" had also flown a four-year-old passenger, Philomena Erzuah, the

Allotment of Rooms for Guests in Rashtrapati Bhavan
(24th December 1958 to 3rd January, 1959).

Name of Guests.	Rooms.	Phone 43401/Ex. No.
1. The Hon'ble Dr. Kwame Nkrumah, Prime Minister of Ghana.	Dwarka Suite	63 & 46
2. The Hon'ble Emmanuel Kobla Bensah, Minister of Works.	Tagore Suite	1 & 47
3. The Hon'ble Atta Nantogmah, Member of Parliament.	Himalaya Suite	89 & 66
4. Sir Robert Jackson, Development Commissioner.	Dakshin Bedroom	152
5. Mr. A. L. Adu, O. B. E., Permanent Secy., Ministry of External Affairs.	Bombay Bedroom	114
6. Mr. E. K. Okoh, Secretary to the Cabinet.	Pepsu Bedroom	109
7. Mr. R. J. Moxon, O. B. E., Secretary, Ministry of Information & Broadcasting.	Godavari Room	104
8. Miss Erica Powell, Private Secretary to the Prime Minister.	Mysore Room	83
9. Mr. Sam Morris, Press Officer to the Prime Minister.	Neelam Bedroom	202
10. Mr. Nyamekeh, Personal Attendent ...	Gautam Bedroom	42
11. Mr. Yankey, Personal Attendant ...		

Room Allocation Plan

daughter of the High Commissioner of Ghana to India, who was travelling with the Prime Minister's delegation to meet her parents in Delhi.

After the airport reception, Prime Minister Nkrumah left for Raj Bhavan accompanied by Jivraj Mehta. Huge crowds had gathered on the roads at several junctions on the way, and they waved and cheered the visiting Prime Minister.[9] The next day, December 23, Prime Minister Nkrumah visited several places of interest in Bombay that included the Atomic Energy Establishment in Trombay, the Radio-Chemistry Laboratory, the thorium plant, India's first nuclear reactor – *Apsara* and the Aarey Milk Colony. Later, the visiting Prime Minister was accorded a Civic Reception at the Kamala Nehru Park.

Mayor Mirajkar welcomed the Ghanaian Prime Minister who had arrived for the reception donning his traditional attire. The Mayor conveyed the good wishes of the people of India to the people of Ghana. Speaking at the reception, Prime Minister Nkrumah declared that his ambition was to liberate all of Africa from colonial exploitation. Ghana "will be the spring-board for the liberation of every part of the African continent from colonial exploitation," he said.[10] On his return to Raj Bhavan, Prime Minister Nkrumah met a group of 50 African students who were studying in various universities in India and acquainted them of "the political developments in Africa."[11]

On Christmas Eve, Prime Minister Nkrumah boarded Indian Air Force Viscount, "*Pushpak*," to Delhi. The plane landed at Palam Airport at 2.45 pm. Prime Minister Nkrumah, dressed in a dark suit, came down the steps and was warmly received by his "old friend" Prime Minister Nehru. A crowd of around 1,000 people too had gathered at the airport to welcome the African leader. Conspicuous among them was a group of colourfully dressed Ghanaian students who sang and danced in traditional Ghanaian style celebrating the arrival of their Prime Minister.[12]

The Ghanaian Prime Minister was accorded a Guard of Honour by an Inter-Services contingent drawn from the Army, the Navy and the Air Force. After he had inspected the Guard of Honour, he met the other dignitaries present at the airport. The visiting Prime Minister was then escorted to a specially erected rostrum from where he and Prime Minister Nehru addressed the gathering at the airport. Welcoming his Ghanaian counterpart, Prime Minister Nehru hailed him as "the symbol not merely of the newly won independence of Ghana but of the wider question of African freedom."[13] Prime Minister Nehru also referred to India's solidarity with Prime Minister Nkrumah's freedom struggle and hoped that the visiting Prime Minister would see the similarity in the policies of the two countries.[14]

Replying to the welcome address, Prime Minister Nkrumah acknowledged the cheering crowd that had gathered at the airport and said that he hoped his visit to India would strengthen the friendly relations between the two countries. He added: "Although I have never visited this country, India in a real sense has always been known to me. I have been influenced in much that I have been able to carry out by the ideas of that great man, Mahatma Gandhi, and your [Nehru's] own superb and human example."[15]

After the welcome ceremony, the two Prime Ministers drove to Rashtrapati Bhavan in an open Cadillac, which was followed by other cars from the President's Garage. They drove via Willingdon Crescent, Talkatora Road, Parliament Street, Vijay Chowk and Rajpath. The ceremonial route was colourfully decorated and flags of the two countries fluttered from poles erected on either side of the roads.

The route taken by the motorcade was also lined by cheering crowds. They were particularly thick near Parliament House and Rashtrapati Bhavan.[16] Deeply moved by the outpouring of goodwill, the visiting Prime Minister did not fail to wave at the cheering crowds.

On his arrival at Rashtrapati Bhavan, Prime Minister Nkrumah and members of his entourage were received by the Comptroller, President's Household (CPH). The guests were then conducted to

Prime Minister Dr Nkrumah (left) with Vice President Dr Radhakrishnan at Rashtrapati Bhavan in December 1958. Credit: PD

their respective suites. The Ghanaian Prime Minister stayed in the Dwarka Suite. The Ghanaian Minister of Works, Bensah stayed in the Tagore Suite and Robert Jackson in the Dakshin Bedroom. Other members of the entourage were also accommodated in Rashtrapati Bhavan.

Prime Minister Nkrumah began his engagements in Delhi by paying a visit to *Rajghat* at five that evening. On reaching the *samadhi* of the Father of the Nation, Prime Minister Nkrumah paid homage to a leader whom he greatly admired and whose teachings had helped Ghana achieve independence. He also signed the Visitor's Book at *Rajghat*. The Ghanaian Prime Minister then met the Indian Prime Minister in the External Affairs Ministry and discussed subjects of mutual interests. These included the recent developments in Ghana, Guinea, and Africa, and the just concluded Accra Conference in which several African countries participated. India's Defence Minister, VK Krishna Menon; Commonwealth Secretary, JM Desai; Bensah and Ghana's High Commissioner to India, JB Erzuah also attended the talks which lasted about an hour. That night, Prime Minister Nkrumah attended a banquet hosted in his honour by the Prime Minister of India. The State Banquet was held in the grand Banquet Hall and it began at 8.15 pm. Prime Minister Nehru and Prime Minister Nkrumah received the guests at the entrance of the Ashok Hall. Thereafter, the guests proceeded to the Banquet Hall for the grand dinner. The services of Gorkha Regimental Centre

Band were also requisitioned for the event. They played a medley of songs during the course of the dinner.

After the main course, as the host, Prime Minister Nehru delivered his speech with his usual eloquence. He said that in India, the Ghanaian leader was "doubly welcomed both for the sake of Ghana and for the sake of Africa and the new movements and urges that are moving there, moving the minds and hearts of millions and millions of people...I trust that your brief visit to India will enable you to realise to some extent what our own aims, objectives and ideals are."[17]

At the end of his speech, Prime Minister proposed a toast to the Queen of England, Elizabeth II. The toast was raised to the Queen as, unlike India, independent Ghana which had joined the Commonwealth of Nations upon gaining independence in 1957, had not opted to become a Republic. The Queen of England was therefore the Head of State of Ghana. After the toast, the Gorkha Band played two bars of Ghana's national anthem.

In reply to Prime Minister Nehru's address, Prime Minister Nkrumah thanked his host for his kind words, and spoke about the influence that the Indian leader had on him. He said, "Some time ago when I was a student in the United States, I read a book, the Glimpses of World History, and the part that interested me most was the Chapter dealing with Africa. I said to myself. 'Why

Prime Minister Nehru delivering banquet speech at Rashtrapati Bhavan. Seated opposite Prime Minister Nehru is Prime Minister Dr Nkrumah. (December 1958). Credit: PD

can't that man be in Africa?' I am only saying this to show that if I am here today, the purpose is to see if I can advance the inspiration which I personally have found trying to read some of your [Nehru] books and also about Mahatma Gandhi."[18] Speaking about African independence, Prime Minister Nkrumah said that the entire continent of Africa needed to be freed from the chains of colonial bondage. Towards the end of the speech, he struck an enthusiastic note and said that he hoped to renew the friendship between the two countries. He also thanked Prime Minister Nehru for the warm reception that he had been accorded from the day of his arrival. He concluded by proposing a toast to the Indian Head of State, President Dr Rajendra Prasad, and the Gorkha Band played two bars of the Indian national anthem.

The banquet was followed by a dance and music recital that had been specially organised by All India Radio at Rashtrapati Bhavan's behest. It included *Pung Cholom*, a Kashmiri Folk Song, *Bharatnatyam*, a *Sarod* Recital, a Group Dance, and *Kathak*. The 30-minute programme, which started at 9.30 pm, was held in Rashtrapati Bhavan's Cinema Hall and was attended by almost 100 guests.

The next morning, on December 25, Prime Minister Nkrumah called on the Vice President of India Dr Sarvepalli Radhakrishnan at the latter's residence. After an hour's meeting with the Vice President, Prime Minister Nkrumah had a meeting with the Defence Minister of India, Krishna Menon. The Prime Minister returned to the residence of the Vice President at 1 pm and had lunch with him. Later, he toured the "India 1958" exhibition. This exhibition organised at Mathura road, New Delhi, showcased India's modernisation and development since independence. After the exhibition, Prime Minister Nkrumah attended a reception held in his honour by the Delhi Branch of the African Student's Association at the Sports Club of India at 4.30 pm.

Welcoming the visiting dignitary, the Chairman of the Association, John Kakonge, said that the "world has come to regard him [Prime Minister Nkrumah] as one of the chief spokesmen for the rights of the African people."[19] In his reply, the visiting Prime Minister reminded the gathering that Africa was still under the dominance of six colonial powers and that this had to change. He also told the students that it was their "duty to clear all the artificial barriers and work for the greater unification of the people of the African continents."[20] At the reception, Prime Minister Nkrumah freely mixed and exchanged views with the African students. The British High Commissioner and the Ethiopian Ambassador also attended the reception.

It was Christmas Day and the High Commissioner of Ghana hosted a dinner for his Prime Minister at 8.30 pm at 2, Golf Link Area. The Prime Minister of India and several dignitaries attended it.

The next day, December 26, began with a visit to the University of Delhi, where Prime Minister Nkrumah was awarded the Honorary Degree of Doctor of Letters at a special investiture ceremony.

Handing over the degree in his capacity as the Chancellor of the University, Vice President Dr Radhakrishnan said: "I wish to assure you that you have our full support and sympathy in your attempts to build up a new Africa."[21] Prime Minister Nkrumah, in his short acceptance speech, replied: "May I take this opportunity, within the walls of this University, to pay a tribute to two men of India, whose writings among others contributed for me the sum total of my political thinking, Mahatma Gandhi and Jawaharlal Nehru?".[22]

Later that day, at 11.45 am, Prime Minister Nkrumah called on President Dr Prasad, at Rashtrapati Bhavan, and had lunch with him. After the call, Prime Minister Nkrumah was free for the day and chose not to leave Rashtrapati Bhavan. He ate a quiet "dinner at residence," and thereafter, watched a cultural programme organised for him at the Rashtrapati Bhavan.[23]

On December 27, Prime Minister Nkrumah visited Air Force Station, Palam, where he enjoyed a carefully planned programme. Escorted to the Station by Air Vice Marshal Arjan Singh, Prime Minister Nkrumah drove "along a park of different types of fighters, fighter–bombers, intruders, trainers and rescue planes."[24] On his arrival, he was presented a Guard of Honour. He was also given a short ride in an Indian Air Force Bell helicopter.

The Air Station staged a 50-minute "air display" for the visiting Prime Minister.[25] India's Defence Minister, Krishna Menon, and the Ghanaian Minister of Works, Bensah were also present on the occasion. At the end of the show, the Ghanaian Prime Minister presented a "beautiful ivory piece, carved into a drummer playing on two 'talking' drums, by a Ghanaian craftsman" to the Chief of the Air Staff, Air Marshall S Mukerjee.[26]

At 11.30 am, the Prime Minister visited the National Physical Laboratory and the Indian Agricultural Research Institute in the city. After the visit, the Prime Minister returned to Rashtrapati Bhavan for lunch.

At 5.00 that evening, the Municipal Corporation of Delhi hosted a Civic Reception in honour of Prime Minister Nkrumah. It was held at the Red Fort, the usual venue where visiting Heads of State/ Governments were felicitated. In spite of the dipping mercury of Delhi's December month, a large crowd had gathered at the venue. *The Hindu* reported that the icy cold weather did not prevent the congregation of a large gathering at the event.[27]

Upon his arrival at the Red Fort, Delhi's Mayor, Aruna Asaf Ali welcomed Prime Minister Nkrumah describing him as the "standard-bearer of the freedom of the African continent."[28] She drew parallels between the trials, tribulations and sufferings that the Indian leaders and Prime Minister Nkrumah had to endure in their determined quest to wrest freedom from imperial domination. She also followed the practice of presenting the welcome address to visiting dignitaries who are accorded Civic Reception by the Municipality, and presented Prime Minister Nkrumah the speech framed in brocade.

GHANA

PRIME MINISTER

4th January, 1959.

My dear President,

    I would like to thank you very sincerely for your most generous hospitality to me and to my party during our stay in New Delhi. I would be grateful if my appreciation could be conveyed to all members of your staff at Rashtrapati Bhavan for the kindness and consideration which were shown to us.

    It was a very great pleasure to me to be able to meet you and I value the opportunity that was afforded me to have a short discussion with you.

    My visit to India has been a most memorable occasion for me. I have been greatly interested in the various projects and establishments which I have seen and I have been touched by the goodwill and the warmth of my reception wherever I have been here. My one hope is that I shall be able to return some day and see more of your great country.

With warm personal regards.

Yours very sincerely,

Kwame Nkrumah

His Excellency Dr. Rajendra Prasad,
    President of India,

Letter of thanks from Prime Minister Dr Nkrumah to President Dr Prasad.

In his reply, Prime Minister Nkrumah said that India and Ghana would foster closer relations with the "passage of time."[29] He added that his visit to India was "the fulfilment of a long-cherished desire." Referring to the success that India had achieved in securing its people the freedom of democratic choice, he said, "we, in Ghana have watched your attempt to consolidate political freedom."[30] Prime Minister Nehru also spoke on the occasion. His address revolved around the continuing exploitation of the nations of the African continent by colonial powers. He said that the exploitation and repression that plagues Africa would be put to an end by the rise of nationalism sweeping that continent. Prime Minister Nehru declared that India "stood for the freedom of all people and racial equality" and would support such national liberation movements.[31]

Prime Minister Nkrumah met with the Indian Prime Minister later that evening at the latter's residence. The meeting lasted for over an hour and was also attended by the Commonwealth Secretary, MJ Desai and the Indian High Commissioner to Ghana, BK Kapur. As the day's events came to an end, Prime Minister Nkrumah had dinner in his suite at Rashtrapati Bhavan.

The morning of December 28 started with a visit to the Community Project in Alipore. Prime Minister Nkrumah also met Prime Minister Nehru that morning, and in the afternoon, he had lunch at Prime Minister Nehru's residence at Teen Murti Bhavan. A polo match was next on the agenda and the Ghanaian Prime Minister reached the Jaipur Polo Ground at 3.30 pm to witness a match and a mounted display. Later that evening he attended a reception held in his honour at Hyderabad House by the High Commissioner of Ghana.

The next morning, Prime Minister Nkrumah addressed a press conference at Vigyan Bhavan. Speaking to media correspondents and responding to an array of questions, Prime Minister Nkrumah outlined his percept of an African Union whose foundation lie "in a popular urge and was not merely an intellectual idea being promoted by top African leadership."[32] He further added that Ghana and Guinea had decided to set up a joint constitution commission to obviate the possibility of the Balkanisation of the continent once all the countries became free. Recounting his experience in India, Prime Minister Nkrumah said that he was quite impressed with what he had seen so far. What particularly caught his fancy was the use of "motor-cycle rickshaws as a form of simple and cheap transport"[33] in India. The Ghanaian Prime Minister observed that he was "trying to learn from Mr Nehru and India's experience as Ghana was confronted with many similar problems."[34]

After the press conference, Prime Minister Nkrumah met the Members of the Planning Commission at Udyog Bhavan. Later on, the Ghanaian Prime Minister met Prime Minister Nehru over lunch at the latter's residence. He also addressed a gathering at the Indian Council of World Affairs, and was the Guest of Honour at a reception hosted by the Indian Foreign Affairs Association.

That night at 11.00, Nkrumah left for Nangal to visit the multipurpose Bhakra Nangal dam. He left by a special train from the ceremonial platform at New Delhi Railway Station. After the visit, Prime Minister had lunch at *Sutlej Sadan* in Nangal. Thereafter, he and his entourage left by road to the city of Chandigarh which impressed him immensely. Prime Minister Nkrumah termed it "fascinating" and commented that it was "well-planned," with a "fine blending of old and new trends in architecture."[35] From here, the delegates took a train to Jhansi, a city famous for its forts. The Ghanaian Prime Minister was accorded a Guard of Honour on his arrival in Jhansi at 9.00 am on December 31. Thereafter, he witnessed some military exercises at Babina, home to a large military establishment, and had lunch there.

It was New Year's Eve and as the city celebrated, so did the visiting Prime Minister. That night at 8.00 the visitors dined at the Black Elephant Institute in Jhansi. At 2.00 am on New Year's Day, a special train took Prime Minister Nkrumah to Agra. He arrived at 9.00 am and visited the most famous monument in India, the Taj Mahal, the Agra Fort and *Itmad–ud–Daula's* Tomb. After a trip to Fatehpur Sikri in the afternoon, Prime Minister Nkrumah left for Delhi by train at midnight.

With only one day remaining for his visit to Delhi to end, on January 2, 1959, the Ghanaian Prime Minister recorded a message, which was broadcast on All India Radio. This was followed by a reception hosted by the Indo-Ghana Association at the Imperial Hotel. At the reception, the Goldsmith's Union of Delhi presented Prime Minister Nkrumah with a golden medal "as an 'expression of fraternal affection of the men of the same profession.'"[36] Nkrumah acknowledged this gift amidst loud cheers and wittily stated, "Yes, it is true. My father was a goldsmith."[37] At 8.30 pm, the Ghanaian Prime Minister hosted a banquet at the Ashoka Hotel for his Indian hosts.

Speaking at the banquet, Prime Minister Nkrumah profusely thanked the Indian people for the warm welcome that had been accorded to him throughout the country. He said that Ghana had "in many ways followed in the footsteps of India, except in one thing – that of declaring the country a Republic within the Commonwealth," which he hoped would soon be accomplished.[38] He hoped that his visit would further strengthen the friendly ties between the two countries.

Prime Minister Nehru, in his reply, said that the country had welcomed the Ghanaian Prime Minister for a variety of reasons the most important of which was that, Prime Minister Nkrumah symbolised the African people "emerging into freedom."[39] Indira Gandhi, Krishna Menon, and members of the diplomatic corps also attended the reception.

At 9.00 am of January 3, Prime Minister Kwame Nkrumah left for Bangalore in a special Viscount aircraft. An official press release was issued at the end of his visit to Delhi. It encapsulated the content of the several rounds of informal talks that were held between the two Prime Ministers. It also covered the issues that the two leaders had agreed upon, including the "lessening of international tensions, the removal of colonial domination and the promotion of understanding between nations."[40]

Prime Minister Nkrumah landed at the Hindustan Aerodrome in Bangalore and was warmly received by the Minister of Law and Labour, T Subramanya; Cabinet Ministers and other Government officials. On January 4, Prime Minister Nkrumah sent a note addressed to the Indian President thanking him for the "generous hospitality" that was extended to him. In the letter, he also said that he wished to convey his thanks to all the staff at Rashtrapati Bhavan. After his visit to Bangalore, the Ghanaian Prime Minister arrived in Mysore on the same day and spent two days in the city before returning to Bangalore.

In Mysore, Prime Minister Nkrumah visited the Bandipur Game Sanctuary on the same day of his arrival in the city. Accompanied by the Maharaja of Mysore, the Ghanaian Prime Minister had gone to the sanctuary on an adventurous drive that could have led to disastrous consequences. As they were driving, a wild elephant attacked the vehicle "in which they were standing."[41] It only fled after an alert Maharaja of Mysore fired a shot at it staving off a crisis. After his trip to Mysore, Prime Minister Nkrumah returned to Bangalore for a day's stay. He flew back to Ghana on January 8, 1959, after making brief halts in Poona and Bombay. The visiting Prime Minister was given a "hearty send–off" at the Bombay airport and he boarded an Air India International flight at 6.30 pm.[42]

Prime Minister Nkrumah's visit to the country further strengthened relations between India and Ghana. In 1960, after Ghana became a Republic, Kwame Nkrumah became its President. Six years later, he was overthrown in a military coup, while on his way to Peking on a peace mission. He was granted asylum in Guinea where he spent his days in exile. He died on April 27, 1972 in Bucharest where he had gone for medical treatment.[43] He was 62.

Notes

1 "Kwame Nkrumah," Encyclopaedia Britannica, accessed May 28, 2015,

http://www.britannica.com/biography/Kwame-Nkrumah.

2 Daurius Figueira, *Tubal Uriah Butler of Trinidad and Tobago Kwame Nkrumah of Ghana: The Road to Independence* (Lincoln: iUniverse, 2007), p. 1948.

3 Robert Addo-Fening, "Gandhi and Nkrumah: A Study of Non-Violence and Non-Co-operation Campaigns in India and Ghana as an Anti-Colonial Strategy," *Transactions of the Historical Society of Ghana*, vol.13, no.1, June 1972, p. 82.

4 Ibid., p. 83.

5 Harris M. Lentz, *Heads of States and Governments: A Worldwide Encyclopaedia of Over 2,300 Leaders, 1945 through 1992* (London: Fitzroy Dearborn Publishers, 1995), p.316.

6 *Panaf Great Lives*, Kwame Nkrumah (London: Panaf Books, 1974),p.154.

7 Ibid.

8 "Enlarging Union of Ghana & Guinea," *The Times of India* (New Delhi), December 23, 1958, p.1.

9 Ibid.

10 "Ghana will be Base for Freedom Fight in Africa," *The Times of India* (New Delhi), December 24, 1958, p.1.

11 Ibid.

12 "Delhi's Cordial Welcome to Ghana Premier," *The Times of India* (New Delhi), December 25, 1958, p. 1.

13 "Warm Welcome on Arrival at Palam," *The Hindustan Times* (New Delhi), December 25, 1958, p. 1.

14 Ibid.

15 Ibid.

16 Ibid.

17 Ministry of External Affairs (1995), Government of India, MEA Library, Foreign Affairs Records 1958, Volume IV, accessed May 10, 2015,18 http://mealib.nic.in/?pdf2546?000.

18 Ibid.

19 "Liberation of Africa," *The Times of India* (New Delhi), December 26, 1958, p.7.

20 Ibid.

21 "Honorary Degree Conferred," *The Hindu* (New Delhi), December 27, 1958, p. 3.

22 Ibid.

23 Records, President's Secretariat, File No. 30/CER/75.

24 "Visit to Palam Air Force Station," *The Hindu* (New Delhi), December 28, 1958, p.4.

25 Ibid.

26 Ibid.

27 "India–Ghana Friendship," *The Hindu* (New Delhi), December 28, 1958, p.4.

28 "Dr. Nkrumah Hailed as Symbol of African Awakening," *The Times of India* (New Delhi), December 28, 1958, p. 9.

29 Ibid.

30 Ibid.

31 Ibid.

32 "Concept of African Union Outlined," *The Times of India* (New Delhi), December 30, 1958, p. 1

33 Ibid., p. 7.

34 Ibid.

35 "Praise for Chandigarh," *The Times of India* (New Delhi), January 1, 1958, p.8.

36 "Dr. Nkrumah is One of Us," *The Times of India* (New Delhi), January 3, 1959, p.7.

37 Ibid.

38 "India–Ghana Friendship is Strengthened," *The Times of India* (New Delhi), January 3, 1959, p. 1.

39 Ibid.

40 "Large Measures of Accord Between Premiers," *The Time of India* (New Delhi), January 4, 1959, p. 9.

41 "Dr. Nkrumah's Escape from Elephant," *The Times* (London), January 6, 1959, p.8.

42 "Hearty Send-Off to Dr. Nkrumah," *The Times of India* (New Delhi), January 9, 1959, p. 5.

43 "Africa: Death of a Deity," *Time*, May 18, 1972, accessed on May 27, 2015, http://content.time.com/time/subscriber/article/0,33009,943444,00.html.

VISITING DIGNITARIES FROM ASIA

AFGHANISTAN: Prime Minister Shah Mahmoud Khan Ghazi

BURMA: Chairman of the Revolutionary Council
of the Union of Burma, Ne Win

CAMBODIA: Prince Norodom Sihanouk

CEYLON: Prime Minister SWRD Bandarnaike

CHINA: Premier Chou En–lai

IRAQ: President Abdul Salam Mohammad Arif

JAPAN: Prince/Emperor Akihito

JORDAN: King Hussein–bin–Talal

KUWAIT: Prime Minister Sheikh Sabah Al–Salim Al–Sabah

NEPAL: Maharaja Padma Shamshere Jung Bahadur Rana
Maharaja Mahendra Bir Bikram Shah Dev

PAKISTAN: Prime Minister Liaquat Ali Khan
Prime Minister Mohammed Ali Bogra
Governor-General Malik Ghulam Mohammed

VIETNAM: President Ngo Dinh Diem

ASIA

One of the first Heads of Government to visit India after the country gained independence, was the Prime Minister of Afghanistan and Commander-in-Chief of the Afghan Armed Forces, Marshal Shah Mahmoud Khan Ghazi. He came on a four-day visit from January 15-19, 1951.

Unlike many of the visiting Heads of State/Government, Prime Minister Khan was no stranger to India. The youngest son of Sardar Mahmoud Yusuf Khan, he was born in the year 1888[1] in the city of Dehradun, now in the Indian State of Uttarakhand. His affection for India largely grew from the natural bond he developed for the country, on whose soil he took his first steps as a toddler. This bond was further strengthened, when he made the country of his birth his chosen haven, during his exile from Afghanistan.

Mahmoud Khan had always displayed a strong desire to pursue a career in the Armed Forces, which he eventually did. He rose to become a Marshal in the Afghan Army. He earned encomiums for his leadership as a military commander in the third Anglo-Afghan War of 1919 and was later recognised for his decisive role in the quelling of the 1928 civil wars in Afghanistan.

Visits of

H.R.H. Marshal Shah Mahmoud Khan Ghazi

Prime Minister of Afghanistan

Mahmoud Khan served as Minister of War under his brother King Mohammed Nadir Shah, who ruled Afghanistan from 1929 until his assassination in 1933. He was appointed Prime Minister nearly 13 years later, on May 19, 1946[2] under the rule of his nephew, Mohammed Zahir Shah, son of Nadir Shah. Holding several important positions in the Afghan hierarchy, he worked towards closer ties with India, his personal bonds playing an influencing role.

Afghanistan as a nation was always linked to India through historical, commercial and cultural ties. The immense popularity of *Kabuliwala*, a highly acclaimed and touching short story by Rabindranath Tagore, about the fatherly relationship between a vendor of dry fruits from Afghanistan and a little Indian girl in Calcutta, is just one of the examples of the cultural affinity the two societies shared. The departure of the British in 1947 changed the geo-political landscape of South Asia and impelled the leaders of both nations to craft policies as separate Nation States while simultaneously focusing on maintaining close bilateral ties. It was in this context that the visit of the Afghan Prime Minister assumed importance.

The January 1951 Visit

Marshal Shah Mahmoud Khan Ghazi first visited India as the Prime Minister of his nation, when he was *en route* to the United States for medical treatment. The US was at this time working towards bettering its relations with Afghanistan and had

Facing page:
(L-R): Prime Minister Shah Mahmoud Khan Ghazi with Minister of Education, Maulana Azad and Home Minister, C Rajagopalachari at Willingdon Airport (now Safdarjung Airport), Delhi, in January 1951. Credit: PD

(L-R): President Dr Prasad, Home Minister C. Rajagopalachari, Prime Minister Shah Mahmoud Khan and Afghan Ambassador to India, Najibullah Khan, at Rashtrapati Bhavan in January 1951. Credit: PC

made special arrangements influenced by the stature of Prime Minister Khan and the determinant role he could play in the formulation of his country's policies.

A special US Air Force Dakota carrying the Prime Minister and his entourage from Kabul landed at Willingdon Airport (now known as the Safdarjung Airport) in the evening of January 15, 1951. The entourage comprised of Prime Minister Ghazi's two daughters, Her Royal Highness Princess Nazifa, aged 22 and Her Royal Highness Princess Najia, aged 17. Besides them, the Prime Minister's Chief of Protocol (COP), Mohammad Ali Khan and his personal physician, Dr Faqir Khan formed his delegation.

As the Prime Minister, dressed in "grey trousers, a camel brown greatcoat and a round Afghan cap,"[3] alighted from his aircraft, he was warmly received on his arrival by independent India's first and last Indian Governor-General, C Rajagopalachari, who had, by then, been inducted into the Nehru Cabinet as Home Minister. He represented the Government of India in the absence of Prime Minister Jawaharlal Nehru, who was away in London, attending a conference on the Korean crisis. Also present were

Maulana Abul Kalam Azad, the Union Education Minister; Colonel B Chatterjee, Military Secretary to the President (MSP), who represented the President of India; some Cabinet Ministers, Service Chiefs and other dignitaries.[4]

Speaking in Persian, the Afghan Ambassador to India, Sardar Najibullah Khan, introduced the visiting Prime Minister to the various Cabinet Members, Ambassadors, High Commissioners and members of the diplomatic corps who had come to the airport. Escorted by the Indian COP, IS Chopra, the Prime Minister then inspected a Guard of Honour presented by an Inter-Services contingent.

After the welcome, Prime Minister Ghazi addressed the media, stressing the importance his country attached to maintaining close relations with India. It was, therefore, no surprise that he told the media that he was happy to meet the "leaders of a sister nation,"[5] and that he prayed for India's prosperity. He went on to add that he hoped that the place he was born in and the place that was his home now would be forever united in friendship and trust.

After addressing the press, the Prime Minister and his entourage left for Government House (now Rashtrapati Bhavan) in the luxury cars sent for them from the President's Garage. The Indian Home Minister, C Rajagopalachari, accompanied Prime Minister Ghazi in a Humber, a British manufactured car that was flying the Afghan flag. The MSP accompanied the two Princesses in a Pontiac, a luxury car manufactured in the US. The COP and the physician to the Prime Minister drove in another well-known American luxury car, a Buick.

If the welcome at the airport was warm, the one at Government House was no less. On arrival, the Prime Minister and his retinue were escorted to the well-appointed Guest Wing on the southern side of Government House. Arrangements for the Prime Minister's stay and that of his entourage's were meticulously drawn up and nothing was left to chance.

In keeping with tradition, Prime Minister Ghazi stayed in the Irwin Suite. The two Princesses stayed in the Reading Suite, Mohammed Ali Khan in the Birdwood Suite and Dr Faqir Khan, in the Minto Bedroom.

Security was particularly tight for the visit. During their four-day stay, the Guest Wing was cordoned off and guests and visitors were screened before they were allowed access into the building. Only those who were cleared in advance were permitted to meet the Prime Minister. Even the *khidmatgars* (butlers), *khalassis* (door attendants), sweepers and liftmen assigned to the Guest Wing were subject to rigorous security checks.

At 6.30 pm, the visiting Prime Minister called on the veteran Congress leader, freedom fighter, close associate of Mahatma Gandhi and India's first President, Dr Rajendra Prasad. The two leaders met in the President's stately Study.

The following day, on January 16, Prime Minister Ghazi visited *Rajghat* and paid his respects at Gandhi's *samadhi*. The visiting Prime Minister then met with C Rajagopalachari at 1, York Place (now Motilal Nehru Marg), after which he had lunch at the Afghan Embassy. The evening was reserved for a State Banquet that was hosted by the "Government of India"[6] in Prime Minister Ghazi's honour. The President's Secretariat spared no effort to make the banquet memorable. Despite all the meticulous planning, in the

(L-R): Home Minister C Rajagopalachari, President Dr Prasad, Prime Minister Shah Mahmoud Khan and Afghan Ambassador to India, Najibullah Khan, at Rashtrapati Bhavan in January 1951. Credit: PC

hustle and bustle of activities, the Afghan National Flag and the musical score for the national anthem of Afghanistan could not be located. Much to the relief of the Deputy Military Secretary to the President (DMSP), the Royal Afghan Embassy came to the rescue and Abdul Kayoum, First Secretary at the Embassy, ensured that both the flag and the score reached the venue immediately, thus, saving the day for the President's Secretariat.

The President of India arrived at the Ballroom, precisely at 8.15 pm, upon which the national anthem of India was played. Thereafter, the President of India received the Afghan Prime Minister. *Aides-de-camp* (AsDC) then presented guests to the President and the visiting Prime Minister. Thereafter, the guests were escorted to the State Dining Room. The famous band of the Bombay Engineers Group, also known as the Bombay Sappers, a regiment in the Indian Army's Engineering Corps, which was specially requisitioned for the evening, played a medley of select songs during the banquet. The 60 distinguished invitees who attended included Cabinet Ministers, heads of diplomatic missions of countries in the Middle and near East. The High Commissioner of Pakistan to India, the Ambassadors of Russia and the People's Republic of China and other diplomatic officials also attended the banquet.

After the main courses were served, the band stopped playing. The practice that was obtaining in the initial decades after India gained independence, the representative of the host country, usually the President or the Prime Minister of India as the case may be, delivered the banquet speech before coffee were served. This was followed by the speech of the guest of honour. As the President of India was present at the banquet, he addressed the guests and proposed a toast to the health of the King of Afghanistan. Thereafter, according to tradition, two bars of the Afghan National Anthem were played. This was followed by the address of C Rajagopalachari. The Indian Home Minister explained to the guests the reason for the absence of Prime Minister Jawaharlal Nehru at the banquet. He said, "Our Prime Minister is absent abroad [sic], engaged in waging the sacred battle of peace."[7] He added that he had confidence in Nehru's diplomatic capabilities, and said, "I have no news, but I instinctively feel he will win the difficult battle."[8] At the end of his address he raised a toast to "drink to the health of His Royal Highness the Prime Minister of Afghanistan, in water – the divine element that holds in its secret store all the power that sustains life."[9]

His Royal Highness Shah Mahmoud Khan Ghazi, thereafter addressed the guests and proposed a toast to the President of India, following which two bars of the Indian national anthem were played. Prime Minister Shah Mahmoud Khan Ghazi, then raised a toast to C Rajagopalachari and said, "for the health of the beloved follower of Mahatma Gandhi, Shri Rajagopalachari, and the prosperity of the Indian nation."[10] He expressed his deep gratitude to the President and the members of the Indian Government for the hospitality and warm reception accorded to him. He stated that the Afghans had always cherished the hope of a free India, and that

it gave them immense happiness to see India not only free but also fighting ceaselessly "for the peace and happiness of Asia and the world."[11] His Royal Highness expressed his deep condolence on the demise of one of India's great freedom fighter and a brilliant administrator, Sardar Vallabhbhai Patel, whose memory", he said, "will remain alive always."[12]

After the banquet, some "talkies" (movies) were screened for the visiting dignitary in the Cinema Hall from 10.00 pm to 11.00 pm. Thereafter, the dignitaries retired for the night.

The rationale of raising toasts during banquets, however, became an issue of some deliberations after this rather western tradition was once again followed during the visit of the Afghan Prime Minister. President Dr Rajendra Prasad, raised this issue with Union Minister, Shriprakash in a personal letter dated January 17, 1951. In it, the President expressed his reservations on continuing with the practice of raising toasts during banquets. He wrote, "though we neither drink wine nor offer it to our guests and I feel it quite ridiculous imitating it by filling the wine glass with water or cold drinks. When I was there I felt it to be quite a meaningless exercise." Opining thus, he requested Shriprakash to suggest an alternative method by which good wishes could be conveyed during a State Banquet, "without imitating this tradition"[13] of raising a toast. No alternative could, however, be found and the practice continues. Even today, toasts are raised with anything but an alcoholic drink. Evidently, the query of the Indian President did not get enough traction to engender a change in the form of a toast being used as a medium to convey good wishes.

Prime Minister Shah Mahmoud Khan (Left) with President Dr Prasad at Rashtrapati Bhavan in January 1951. Credit: PC

The next day, on January 17, Prime Minister Ghazi met several members of the Indian Cabinet, including Defence Minister Baldev Singh and Finance Minister CD Deshmukh in the Yellow Drawing Room at Government House. The meetings were only interrupted for lunch which was served at 1.00 pm at the residence of India's Education Minister, Maulana Abul Kalam Azad at King Edward Road (now Maulana Azad Road).

In the evening, Prime Minister Ghazi attended a dinner at the Imperial Hotel on Queensway (now Janpath) which was hosted by the Afghan Ambassador Dr Najibullah in his honour. At 6.00 am on January 19, 1951, Prime Minister Ghazi and his entourage left for the United States on board a Pan American World Airways flight from Palam Airport. The MSP, Colonel Chatterjee, accompanied Prime Minister Ghazi to the airport. The Home Minister, C Rajagopalachari, was unable to bid the Afghan Prime Minister farewell and the MSP conveyed the Minister's best wishes to the Prime Minister.

As his flight was airborne, Prime Minister Ghazi sent a telegram to President Rajendra Prasad, conveying his sentiments on the hospitality that was extended to him and his delegation during their stay in India. In the telegram he said, "Before crossing the Indian border I address my deep gratitude and sincere thanks to your Excellency for the warm reception and generous hospitality

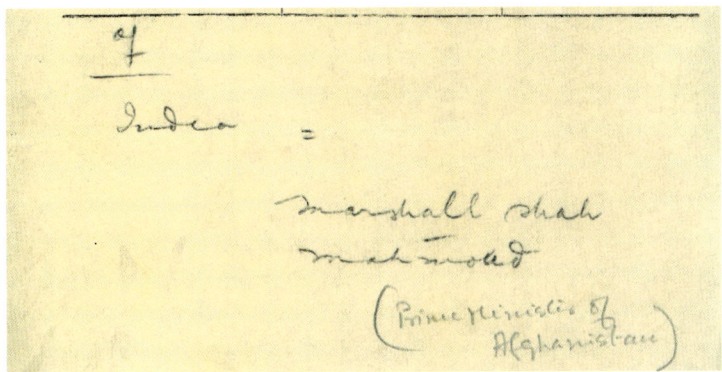

Telegram of thanks from Prime Minister Shah Mahmoud Khan to President Dr Prasad.

that your Excellency extended to me...my best wishes for your Excellency's health and the prosperity of India."[14]

The visit of the Afghan Prime Minister was a success. *The Times of India* reported that the Indo–Afghan "amity, which is being steadfastly fostered...received a new stimulus this month as a result of the visit of the Prime Minister of Afghanistan, Marshal Shah Mahmoud Khan."[15]

The September 1951 Visit

A few months later, Prime Minister Shah Mahmoud Khan Ghazi visited India again on his return journey to Afghanistan from the United States. He arrived in Bombay on the morning of September 1, 1951, from London, by the RMS Strathnaver. Prime Minister Ghazi was accompanied by his two daughters and the COP, Sardar Mohammad Ali. The visiting dignitaries were received by the Chief Minister of Bombay, BG Kher; the Afghan Ambassador Dr Najibullah and other Indian dignitaries.[16]

The Afghan Prime Minister spent three days as the Guest of the Governor of Bombay and left for Delhi on September 3 by Frontier Mail. Before boarding the train, Prime Minister Ghazi inspected a Guard of Honour presented by "the city police at the Bombay Central station."[17] The Governor of Bombay, Raja Maharaj Singh; Chief Secretary to the Bombay Government, MD Bhat and the Saudi Arabian Consul-General, amongst others, saw him off at the station.

Prime Minister Ghazi arrived in Delhi on September 4 and was warmly received at the Railway Station by the Indian Prime Minister Jawaharlal Nehru and his Cabinet Ministers. A lot had changed on Raisina Hill since the Afghan Prime Minister's last visit. "Government House" had now been renamed "Rashtrapati Bhavan."[18] Various suites and rooms also got new names dropping British names in preference of Indian ones. During this visit, the Afghan Prime Minister stayed in the Dwarka Suite, the erstwhile Irwin Suite.

The next day, September 5, the visiting Prime Minister informally addressed the Members of Parliament. In his speech to them in the Central Hall of Parliament House, he emphasised the ancient ties that existed between India and Afghanistan, and expressed that hope that the "'reciprocal desire of sincerity and cordiality' would draw the two countries closer together."[19] He added that the foreign polices of Afghanistan and India were similar in many respects and that they stood "for their rights and the 'rights of their brothers'."[20] Responding to the address, Prime Minister Nehru remarked that the "relations between the two countries were not governed by geographical proximity, but by common ideals and interests."[21]

Later that evening, Prime Minister Jawaharlal Nehru hosted a State Banquet in honour of his Afghan counterpart. At the banquet, Prime Minister Nehru, while proposing the toast, described the visit of the Afghan leader and termed it as a "great event", and requested the visiting Prime Minister to convey the message of friendship to the people of Afghanistan.[22] Speaking at the banquet, the Afghan Prime Minister highlighted the similarities in the foreign policies of both countries, and stated that they aimed at fostering "most friendly relations with all."[23] Several notable dignitaries, including the heads of foreign missions in Delhi, Ministers of the Government of India and high officials, attended the banquet.

During his stay in Delhi, the Afghan Prime Minister visited the Indian Air Force Station at Palam and some other military establishments in Delhi.[24] Besides, he visited the University of Delhi, where he and Dr Najibullah interacted with students and professors. He was also scheduled to visit the National Military Academy in Dehradun, his birthplace, on September 7.

On September 8, Prime Minister Shah Mahmoud Khan Ghazi left Delhi for Kabul via Amritsar. Prime Minister Nehru, heads of different diplomatic missions, Dr Najibullah and other dignitaries were at the Delhi Railway Station to bid him farewell.

Prime Minister Ghazi's visit to India not only strengthened relations between the two countries but also brought into focus the need to check what they perceived as Pakistan's destabilising policies. As the Indian Home Minister said, "Indian foreign policy held that friendly relations were essential between India and Afghanistan – geographically separated by Pakistan. When we two are sound in friendship, we will squeeze anyone in between in the same embrace of affection – a pincer movement for peace, so to speak."[25]

Shah Mahmoud Khan Ghazi continued as Prime Minister of Afghanistan until 1953, when there was a backlash against his liberal policies. He was overthrown that year by Lieutenant General Mohammed Daud Khan, brother-in-law and first cousin of the King[26] with the backing of the conservatives in Government and religious leaders. Shah Mahmoud Khan Ghazi died on December 27, 1959. He was 71.

Notes

[1] Harris M. Lentz, Heads of States and Government: A Worldwide Encyclopaedia of Over 2300 Leaders, 1945 through 1992 (London: Fitzroy Dearborn Publishers, 1995), p. 18.

[2] The exact date of the appointment has been a matter of some uncertainty. While most of the sources record that he was appointed in May 1946, there is no such consensus on the date. May 19, 1946 has been indicated as the date along with May 14, 1946 in the book Heads of States and Government: A Worldwide Encyclopaedia of Over 2300 Leaders, 1945 through 1992 (London: Fitzroy Dearborn Publishers, 1995) by Harris M. Lentz.

[3] "Afghan Premier Arrives in New Delhi," The Statesman (New Delhi), January 16, 1951, p. 1.

[4] Ibid.

[5] "Afghan Premier Arrives in New Delhi," p. 1.

[6] "Mr. Nehru's Efforts for Korean Peace," The Times (London), January 17, 1951, p. 5.

[7] Ibid.

[8] Ibid.

[9] "Indo-Afghan Friendship," The Times of India (New Delhi), January 17, 1951, p. 1.

[10] Ibid.

[11] Ibid.

[12] Ibid.

[13] Records, President's Secretariat, Rashtrapati Bhavan, File No. 2/51.

[14] Ibid.

[15] "Delhi Diary," The Times of India (New Delhi), January 21, 1951, p. 4.

[16] Ibid.

[17] "Afghanistan's Premier," The Times of India (New Delhi), September 4, 1951, p. 7.

[18] No direct or primary evidence on the date or year when the Government House was renamed as Rashtrapati Bhavan could be found. There are some records in Rashtrapati Bhavan that indicate that the name was changed in the month of August or September of 1951. Some newspaper reports also indicate the same. There are certain Government and other writings that, however, indicate that the name was changed on January 26, 1950 when India became a Republic. However, in this book, reliance has been placed more on contemporaneous Government records available in the archives Rashtrapati Bhavan and contemporaneous newspaper reports to conclude that in all likelihood, the name was changed in 1951.

[19] "Baseless Interpretations of Indo-Afghan Ties," The Times of India (New Delhi), September 6, 1951, p. 1.

[20] Ibid.

[21] Ibid.

[22] Ibid.

[23] "Afghanistan for Amity," The New York Times, September 6, 1951, p. 13.

[24] "Pakhtoonistan's Claim to Freedom," The Times of India (New Delhi), September 9, 1951, p. 1.

[25] "Indian Expectation of Success," Cairns Post, January 18, 1951, accessed April 9, 2015, http://trove.nla.gov.au/ndp/del/article/42694890

[26] "Shah Mahmud Khan: Prime Minister of Afghanistan," Encyclopaedia Britannica, accessed April 9, 2015, http://www.britannica.com/EBchecked/topic/537698/Shah-Mahmud

General Ne Win, Chairman of the Revolutionary Council of Burma, came to India as the Head of State of his country for the first time in February 1964, two years after coming to power. It was, however, a private visit[1] though it was seldom that a Head of State undertakes a private visit to a foreign country. It was more so, as it was to personally enquire about the health of the Head of Government of a neighbouring country, in this case, India's Prime Minister, Jawaharlal Nehru, who had suffered a stroke about a month earlier.

The visit began to take shape after a telegram was received by the Indian Foreign Secretary from the Indian Embassy in Rangoon on February 6, 1964. The telegram stated that General Ne Win wished to "pay a private visit to Delhi for about two days to enquire into Prime Minister's health, over which he is much concerned."[2]

Ne Win was born on May 24, 1911, in Paungdale, Burma (now Myanmar) to a Sino-Burmese[3] district revenue surveyor.[4] He was named Shu Maung ("the apple of one's eye")[5] at birth by his parents, a name that he later changed to Ne Win ("brilliant as the sun").[6]

Visits of

H.E. General Ne Win

Chairman of the Revolutionary Council of Burma

Ne Win joined the military when he was young. Later, he closely associated himself with the Burmese resistance movement against foreign powers drawing inspiration from India's independence movement, and the philosophies of Nehru and Bose.[7] It first fought the British, and then the occupying Japanese forces during the Second World War.

Ne Win rose rapidly through the military hierarchy, to become the Commander-in-Chief of the Burmese Army. When Burma faced ethnic and secessionist unrest and Prime Minister U Nu was not able to restore order, Ne Win seized power in a *coup d'état* ousting him in 1962.

The coup that brought Ne Win to power adversely affected Indo-Burma relations. His request to visit the ailing Indian leader Jawaharlal Nehru was a part of his efforts at repairing relations with India. Since the arrival was not planned after diplomatic discussions that normally precede the visit of Heads of State, there was little advance notice to make arrangements. Further, General Ne Win had desired to return to Burma before February 11 to meet Chinese Premier Chou En-lai, who was scheduled to visit Rangoon three days later. This meant that the visit had to be arranged barely 48 hours after the Indian Embassy had communicated that General Ne Win was desirous of visiting Delhi. This meant that the only window that was available for the visit was from February 8 –10.[8]

In the telegram of February 6, 1964, there was another aspect that needed attention. Burmese officials had unambiguously indicated that General Ne Win desired that

Facing page (L-R): General Ne Win (second), President VV Giri & Madame Ne Win at Rashtrapati Bhavan in January 1970. Credit: PC

(L-R): President VV Giri, Madame Ne Win and General Ne Win at Rashtrapati Bhavan in January 1970. Credit PC

the visit should be "very informal and without [ceremony] and also without putting unnecessary strain on the Prime Minister."[9] Another communication conveyed that there should be no Guard of Honour, no special reception ceremony or any outside guests invited for dinners or social functions.[10] Nevertheless, it was the visit of a Head of State and both the Ministry of External Affairs (MEA) and the President's Secretariat swung into action to welcome General Ne Win. He arrived by a Union of Burma Airways (UBA) Viscount aircraft that landed in New Delhi's Palam Airport from Rangoon at 1.30 pm, on February 8, 1964. General New Win was accompanied by his wife Madame Ne Win and an entourage of eight.

They were welcomed on their arrival by the Vice President of India, Dr Zakir Husain; Indira Gandhi; Finance Minister of India, TT Krishnamachari; Deputy Minister of External Affairs, Dinesh Singh and others. At the airport, General Ne Win declined to speak to the hundred-strong members of the press gathered outside the airport, except to say that his visit was a private one.[11]

Since there was no ceremonial welcome, General Ne Win directly drove to Rashtrapati Bhavan. Though it was a private visit, the Burmese delegation was accommodated in the various suites of the Guest Wing.[12] After lunch, General Ne Win, with his Cabinet

and Foreign Secretaries, called on Vice president Dr Zakir Husain later in the day.[13]

On the afternoon of February 8, the Prime Minister of India and the Chairman of the Revolutionary Council of Burma began their meeting at the former's house at Teen Murti Bhavan. Prime Minister Nehru's daughter, Indira Gandhi received General Ne Win, Madame Ne Win and the Burmese Ambassador, Madame Aung San on the porch and conducted General Ne Win to her father's study upstairs.[14] General Ne Win and Prime Minister Nehru conferred for an hour, without any aides or interpreters.[15] Meanwhile, Madame Ne Win and Madame Aung San had tea with Indira Gandhi.

That evening, Vice President Dr Zakir Husain hosted a dinner in honour of General Ne Win at Rashtrapati Bhavan. This was a quiet affair, unlike the banquets hosted for visiting Heads of State. As advised by the Burmese authorities, the invitations were limited to its Ambassador, its staff of the Embassy and Cabinet Ministers.

For the President's Secretariat, however, it was business as usual. The Ashok and the Banquet Halls looked stately, with fresh flowers imparting a flash of colour to the decor. The tiered chandeliers in both Halls sparkled, casting subtle silhouettes on the painted ceilings and walls. The only difference was that there were fewer guests to enjoy the imperial splendour that night. An hour-long cultural programme in the theatre at Rashtrapati Bhavan followed the dinner.[16]

On the morning of February 9, 1964, Dinesh Singh; Foreign Secretary, YD Gundevia and the Chief of Army Staff, General Chaudhri, called on General Ne Win in the Rashtrapati Bhavan and held general discussions on matters concerning both countries.[17] General Ne Win later called on the Prime Minister once again before departing for Rangoon. He was seen off by Vice President Dr Zakir Husain, Lal Bahadur Shastri, Indira Gandhi, Minister of Scientific and Cultural Affairs Humayun Kabir, and the Burmese Ambassador to India.[18] A sizeable crowd of both Indian and Burmese citizens was also present at the airport to see off the visitors.

The 1970 (January) Visit

In January 1970, General Ne Win arrived in India for a weeklong visit from January 15 to 22. It was once again an "informal" visit.[19]

At 1.00 pm on January 15, 1970, a UBA Boeing 737, bearing the call sign of UNIONAIR 489, touched down at New Delhi's Palam Airport.[20] General Ne Win, his wife and a delegation of 17 were warmly welcomed by the President of India, VV Giri and his wife; Prime Minister, Indira Gandhi; Minister of Defence, Jagjivan Ram and select members of the diplomatic corps.[21]

There were neither speeches nor introductions. The Guard of Honour was dispensed with, as the visit was informal. At the request of the Chairman of the Revolutionary Council, communicated in a telegram to the Indian Ministry of External Affairs from the Embassy of India in Rangoon, on January 14, 1970, the airport was kept off limits for the press. There was just one photographer from the Press Information Bureau (PIB) to cover the visit for official records.

General Ne Win's staff had also informed the Indian establishment that he would not be holding any press conference. If they had any queries, his Secretary General, Ko Ko, who was in charge of handling press coverage, was to be contacted. The officials at the Indian Embassy in Rangoon, however, had informed the Burmese authorities that they could not provide any guarantees as India had a free press.[22]

After the informal reception at the airport, the Burmese delegation was driven to Rashtrapati Bhavan, where accommodation for the entire delegation was arranged. General Ne Win and his wife stayed in the Dwarka Suite.[23]

President VV Giri (seen in side profile and fourth from right) proposing a toast to General Ne Win (facing, second from right) at Banquet at Rashtrapati Bhavan. Prime Minister Gandhi is on his right. (January 1970). Credit: PC

(L-R): Prime Minister Indira Gandhi, General Ne Win, President VV Giri and Madame Ne Win at Rashtrapati Bhavan in January 1970. Credit: PC

That same afternoon, General Ne Win called on the President of India. The meeting lasted half-an-hour. After the meeting, the Indian Prime Minister called on the General and discussed Indo-Burmese relations, and regional and global issues. In accordance with a request from the Burmese side, the discussions were kept strictly confidential.[24]

At 8.30 pm, on January 15, President VV Giri hosted a dinner in honour of General Ne Win. The setting was grand and the Banquet Hall was readied as if it were a State Banquet but there were to be neither any outside invitees nor any formal addresses. The President nevertheless, proposed a toast to "Ne Win Chairman of the Revolutionary Council of Burma, and his charming wife Madame Ne Win" conveying the "warmest sentiments of friendship and goodwill for the people and Government of Burma and their continued peace and prosperity." He also expressed his hope that the "age-old ties" between the two countries "will be broadened and strengthened day by day." A cultural programme in the Rashtrapati Bhavan's private theatre followed the dinner.[25]

Early on the morning of January 16, General Ne Win travelled to *Rajghat* and to *Shantivana*, where he laid wreaths on the memorials of Mahatma Gandhi and Jawaharlal Nehru, respectively. After paying his respects to the departed Indian leaders, he returned to Rashtrapati Bhavan, where he ate a quiet lunch en suite.[26]

The afternoon was spent in discussions with the Indian Prime Minister, as well as the Minister for External Affairs, Dinesh Singh and officials from both countries. They dealt with the issue of the people of Indian-origin living in Burma.[27] General Ne Win's nationalistic policies had adversely affected the sizeable

Indian population residing in Burma since the late 1800s. In 1960, they numbered around 500,000 and played important commercial roles. Within two years of General Ne Win coming to power, the people of Indian origin had fled Burma *en masse*, leaving behind their valuables and possessions.[28] Decisions concerning these people were taken during the discussions. After the meeting, General Ne Win had the evening to himself. He spent the time enjoying a game of golf at the Delhi Golf Club,[29] after which he returned to Rashtrapati Bhavan for dinner and retired for the night.

General Ne Win spent the next morning visiting the Indian Agricultural Research Institute. There he was shown, how rice could be fitted into a multiple-cropping system throughout the year. He spent an hour discussing agricultural techniques with the scientists and expressed fervent hope that Indian and Burmese scientists should have the chance to work together in future.[30] He then had a scheduled meeting with the Minister of Foreign Trade, BR Bhagat. At the end of the 45-minute-long meeting, there was increased hope of boosting Indo-Burmese bilateral trade.[31] Later that morning, there was another meeting with the Minister of Industrial Development, Internal Trade and Company Affairs, Fakhruddin Ali Ahmed, as the Chairman of the Revolutionary Council had shown an interest in establishing heavy industries in his country with Indian collaboration.[32]

At 1.15 pm, General Ne Win and Madame Ne Win, attended a lunch hosted by the Indian Prime Minister, Indira Gandhi, at her residence at 1, Safdarjung Road, in honour of the Chairman of the Revolutionary Council. The lunch was followed by a short programme of folk dances.[33]

The next morning, on January 18, the General visited *Gandhi Darshan* (now *Gandhi Smriti* and *Darshan Samiti*). In the evening, at 8.30, General Ne Win hosted a dinner at the residence of the Burmese Ambassador to India, on Shantipath in Chanakyapuri, which was attended by the President of India and others.[34]

After spending four days in the capital, on 19 January, General Ne Win and his entourage left Rashtrapati Bhavan at 9.30 am and arrived at Palam Airport 15 minutes later. There was no ceremonial send-off. A special UBA Boeing 737 was waiting at the airstrip to take the delegation to Agra. In Agra, the Burmese leader, his wife and the delegation visited the Taj Mahal, the Agra Fort and Fatehpur Sikri during the day, only to return to the Taj Mahal to see it by moonlight.[35]

The next day, the delegation travelled to Gaya from Agra at 12 noon. The General visited the Mahabodhi Temple that very evening. In a three-hour ceremony, General and Madame Ne Win gilded the image of the Buddha with gold plates — the most sacred Buddhist ritual. It was the first time this service had been performed at the temple since 1953.[36]

On the morning of January 21, the Burmese delegation departed Gaya for Rajgir, another sacred site of pilgrimage for Buddhists. Later that day, they reached Nalanda and visited the ancient excavations and the museum there. After halting for the night at the Gaya Circuit House,[37] on January 22, 1970, at 9.00 am, General Ne Win and his entourage returned to Rangoon. Though there was no formal ceremony, officials of the Government of Bihar bade him goodbye at the airport.[38]

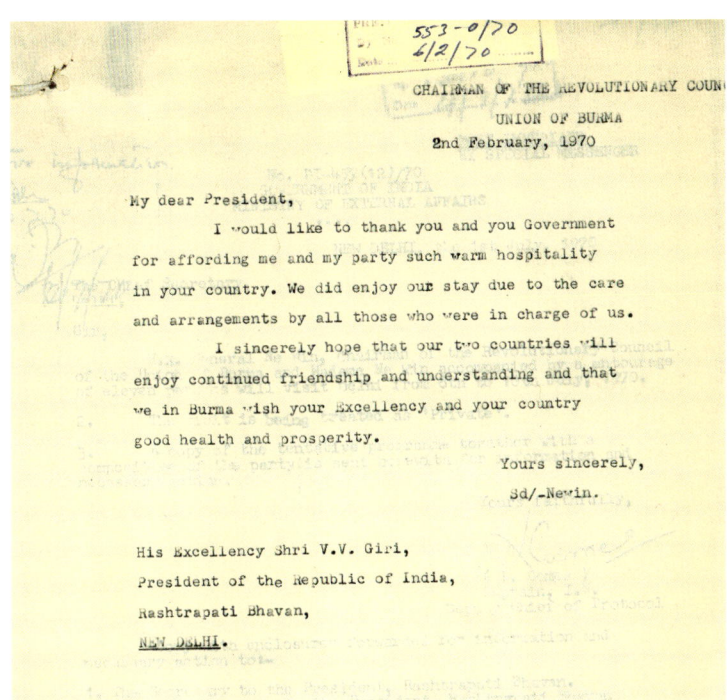

Letter of thanks from General Ne Win to President VV Giri.

From his special aircraft, on the flight to Rangoon, General Ne Win sent a note thanking President Giri for the "warm welcome and hospitality" accorded to the delegation during their stay in India.[39] He sent another letter on February 2, after reaching Rangoon, expressing warmer sentiments.[40] He addressed President VV Giri as "My dear President," and he thanked him and the Government of India for the "warm hospitality." He added that they enjoyed their stay. It was, he wrote, "due to the care and arrangements by all those who were in charge of us."[41]

On February 2, contrary to all expectations, a joint statement was released in New Delhi. It said that the Premier of Burma and the Prime Minister of India had discussed matters of interest to both countries. Cooperation, especially in trade and industry was expected to get a boost, it added.[42]

The 1970 (July) Visit

General Ne Win made a brief, two-day stop in India while returning to Rangoon from England on July 8, 1970, where Madame Ne Win had undergone a surgery. The main purpose of this halt was to hold discussions with Prime Minister Indira Gandhi.

In the wee hours of the morning of July 8, at 4.15, General Ne Win accompanied by his wife and a delegation of 13, landed at New Delhi's Palam Airport on a special UBA flight. As the President of India, VV Giri, was away at the time, the Vice President of India, Gopal Swarup Pathak, received the guests at the airport along with Prime Minister Gandhi, some Ministers and senior officials. As in the case of the previous two arrivals, there was no ceremonial reception as this too was treated as a "private" visit. Therefore, the General, his wife and the entourage were driven straight to Rashtrapati Bhavan.

Despite it being a private visit, the President's Bodyguard (PBG) did not let the occasion pass without imparting a touch of colour to General Ne Win and his entourage's arrival at Rashtrapati Bhavan. In their attractive white ceremonial summer uniform and their knee-high boots, the PBG had, by 4.30 am, lined the route from the alighting point in the South Court to the Dwarka Suite. It added a ceremonial and warm touch to an occasion otherwise devoid of the pomp and grandeur that accompanies the reception of the Heads of State at Rashtrapati Bhavan. The Burmese flag was also flown from the roof of Rashtrapati Bhavan above the Guest Wing.

On their arrival, the Military Secretary to the President (MSP) escorted General Ne Win and Madame Ne Win, Vice President GS Pathak and Prime Minister Indira Gandhi to the Dwarka Suite. Here they were served light refreshments by the liveried butlers of Rashtrapati Bhavan. The rest of the delegation was conducted to the Guest Loggia by the President's *aides-de-camp* (AsDC). They were served light refreshments here and thereafter escorted to their respective suites/rooms.

As the Indian President was out of station, Vice President Pathak hosted a lunch at 1.15 pm in honour of the visiting dignitary. The Vice President and his wife arrived via the South Sunken Road and were escorted to the Dwarka Sitting Room where the Vice President called on the Chairman of the Revolutionary Council.

At 1.12 pm, the Vice President, his wife, General and Madam Ne Win, escorted by the MSP and an ADC of the President, left the Dwarka Sitting Room and reached the Yellow Drawing Room, which has a spectacular view of the grand Mughal Gardens and the famed Victoria Regia lily-shaped fountains. Soft drinks were served, after which the guests stood in line with their "wives on their right" and were introduced to General and Madam Ne Win. Thereafter, they were conducted to the elegant rectangular Grey Dining Room where they were seated according to a carefully decided seating plan. The guests enjoyed the lunch as the 2-Rajput band, whose services were requisitioned, played a selection of light music.[43]

During the course of his brief visit, the Chairman of the Revolutionary Council met Prime Minister Indira Gandhi twice. The talks were confidential. Other than these engagements, General Ne Win's schedule was rather light.

General Ne Win's third visit to India came to an end on the morning of July 10, 1970. The Burmese guests left Rashtrapati Bhavan at 4.50 am and reached Palam Airport at 5.05 am. The Burmese President was seen off by the Vice President and other dignitaries.

General Ne Win and Madam Ne Win were evidently pleased with their stay at Rashtrapati Bhavan. This was manifest in the letter dated July 24, 1970 that General Ne Win wrote to the President of India. He thanked President Giri for the hospitality he had received at Rashtrapati Bhavan. He also politely inquired after the health of President Giri's daughter, who had also, incidentally, like Madam Ne Win, undergone surgery in England.

President Giri replied saying, "It is very kind of you to write to me and make enquiries about the health of my daughter. She is all right now and here with me at Delhi." The President added his apologies for not being able to meet the General, and wrote, "I am sorry I missed the opportunity of meeting you and Madame Ne Win on your way back home. I am glad that you found your stay here comfortable. I trust Madam Ne Win has fully recouped her health by now."[44]

In 1988, General Ne Win was deposed by a popular uprising. He was placed under house arrest, though he remained an influential figure in the Burmese armed forces. He died in 2002. He was 91.

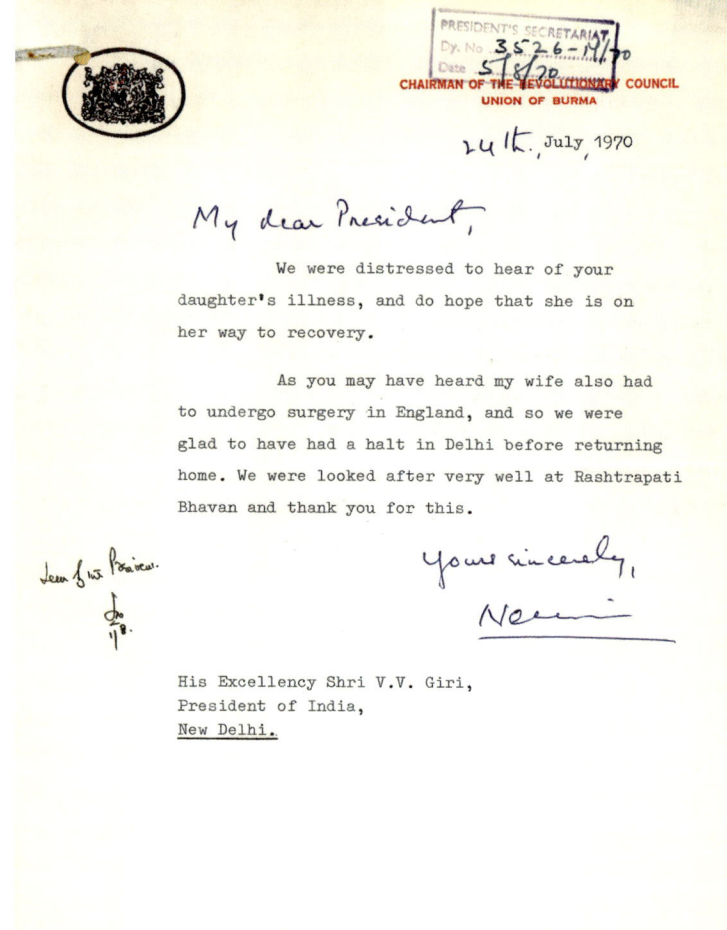

General Ne Win's letter to President VV Giri enquiring about his daughter's health.

Notes

[1] From the various public sources, it is understood that Ne Win had visited India in 1959, 1964, 1965, 1966, 1968, 1970, 1974 & 1980. Only the 1964 and 1970 visits have been covered as the documents relating to other visits were not traceable.

[2] Records, President's Secretariat, Rashtrapati Bhavan, File No. 15(3)/64.

[3] Martin Smith, "General Ne Win," *The Guardian*, December 6, 2002, accessed June 10, 2015, http://www.theguardian.com/news/2002/dec/06/guardianobituaries

[4] "General Ne Win," *The Telegraph*, December 6, 2002,

accessed June 11, 2015, http://www.telegraph.co.uk/news/obituaries/1415295/General-Ne-Win.html

[5] Eric Pace, "Ne Win, Ex-Burmese Military Strongman, Dies at 81," *The New York Times*, December 6, 2002, accessed June 10, 2015, http://www.nytimes.com/2002/12/06/world/ne-win-ex-burmese-military-strongman-dies-at-81.html

[6] "General Ne Win," *The Telegraph*.

[7] *Maung Maung, Burma and General Ne Win* (Bombay: Asia Publishing House, 1969), p. 39.

[8] Records, President's Secretariat, File No. 15(3)/64.

[9] Ibid.

[10] Ibid.

[11] "Burma Desires Direct Sino-Indian Discussions," *The Times of India* (New Delhi), February 9, 1964, p. 1.

[12] "Nehru, Ne Win Review Asian problems," *The Hindustan Times Weekly* (New Delhi), February 9, 1964, p. 1.

[13] Ibid.

[14] "Ne Win Confers with Nehru," *The Hindu* (New Delhi), February 9, 1964, p. 1.

[15] "Burma Desires Direct Sino-Indian Discussions," p. 1.

[16] Records, President's Secretariat, File No. 15(3)/64.

[17] Ibid.

[18] "India's Appraisal of Chinese Menace Conveyed to Ne Win," *The Hindustan Times* (New Delhi), February 10, 1964, p. 1.

[19] Records, President's Secretariat, File No. 15(3)/64.

[20] Ibid.

[21] G.K. Reddy, "Ne Win in Delhi to Forge Closer Ties in Face of Chinese Hostility," *The Hindu* (New Delhi), January 16, 1970, p. 1

[22] Records, President's Secretariat, File No. 15(3)/64.

[23] Ibid.

[24] "Informality Marks Ne Win Visit," *The Hindustan Times* (New Delhi), January 16, 1970, p. 1.

[25] Ibid.

[26] Ibid.

[27] "Talks on Future of People of Indian Origin in Burma," *The Times of India* (New Delhi), January 17, 1970, p. 1.

[28] C.P. Cook, "Burma: The Era of Ne Win," *The World Today*, vol.26, no.6, June 1, 1970, p. 261.

[29] Records, President's Secretariat, File No. 15(3)/64.

[30] "Team to Burma for Talks on Trade Expansion," *The Hindu* (New Delhi), January 18, 1970, p. 1.

[31] "STC Office Likely in Rangoon," *The Times of India* (New Delhi), January 18, 1970, p. 1.

[32] "PM and Ne Win Agree on Indian Settlers Issue," *The Hindustan Times* (New Delhi), January 17, 1970, p. 1.

[33] Records, President's Secretariat, File No. 15(3)/64.

[34] Ibid.

[35] Ibid.

[36] "Ne Win Performs Gilting Ceremony in Bodh Gaya," *The Hindu* (New Delhi), January 21, 1970, p. 1.

[37] Records, President's Secretariat, File No. 15(3)/64.

[38] "Close Identity of Views Stressed," *The Times of India* (New Delhi), January 23, 1970, p. 10.

[39] Records, President's Secretariat, File No. 15(3)/64.

[40] Ibid.

[41] Ibid.

[42] Records, MEA Library, Foreign Relations, 1970, accessed June 14, 2015, http://mealib.nic.in/?pdf2558?000

[43] Records, President's Secretariat, File No. 15(3)/64

[44] Ibid.

The Prince of Cambodia, Norodom Sihanouk, paid a short two–day visit to India from November 19-20, 1956. The visit was at the invitation of Prime Minister Nehru, to attend the grand celebrations that marked the 2,500th *Buddha Purnima*. This was, however, not the Prince's first visit.[1] He had spent three hours in India on his way to Europe on a goodwill visit in May of the same year.

Born on October 31, 1922, Prince Sihanouk was educated in the best primary school in Phnom Penh and later in Saigon and France. He was coronated in 1941, when he was just 19-years-old. Cambodia was then a part of French Indochina. In 1955, two years after Cambodia won independence; Sihanouk abdicated the throne, in favour of his father, to contest the elections. In the Parliamentary elections held that year, Sihanouk received an overwhelming mandate, and he became Prime Minister of Cambodia.

Prince Sihanouk was a man of varied interests. He was a "film–maker, journalist, editor and impresario."[2] Of his royal life, he wrote, "Being a prisoner of protocol, fawned on by all sorts of time-servers awaiting my favours, was something I detested...I saw only impeccably dressed citizens amidst banners and welcoming arches, and a wall of officialdom was raised as a barrier against social reality. I hated this but, as a God–King, I had to submit to it."[3]

Visit of

H.R.H. Prince Norodom Sihanouk

of Cambodia

Relations between India and Cambodia date back to historic times: nurtured by their shared religious and cultural commonalities. In addition, the close friendship between the two leaders helped further strengthen the bilateral ties. Prime Minister Jawaharlal Nehru had long regarded the Prince as a younger brother; and Prince Sihanouk unmistakably admired the Indian leader for his intellect and independent vision. This close bond did, however, cause certain diplomats some anxious moments on how to deal with situations rooted in the closeness.

One instance of such a proximity-induced predicament was recounted by the Former Indian Ambassador to the Kingdom of Cambodia, Dinesh K Patnaik. He recalls an incident, where the Cambodian King made a somewhat familial demand of Prime Minister Nehru in 1954. This was at a time when arrangements were being made for the Prime Minister to visit Vietnam. India had requested the Cambodian Government for over-flight clearance. This was denied as Prince Sihanouk was insistent that the Indian Prime Minister visit Cambodia as well, during the Vietnam trip. Prime Minister Nehru instantly agreed and clearance was granted.[4]

The close bonds between the two leaders even spilled over into areas of international diplomacy. Prime Minister Nehru used his familiarity with Premier Chou En-Lai to introduce Prince Sihanouk to the Chinese leader in Bandung. The relationship

Facing page:
Prince Norodom Sihanouk (left) with
President Dr Prasad at Rashtrapati Bhavan in
November 1956. Credit: PD

Prime Minister Nehru (left) with Prince Sihanouk at Rashtrapati Bhavan in November 1956. Credit: PD

between the Cambodian leader and the Premier would mushroom into a long and fruitful friendship.

The admiration that Prince Sihanouk had for Prime Minister Nehru was evident during the Prince's various visits to India. When he first visited for three hours in May 1956 on his way to Europe, he attributed the reason for his stop-over, to meet, "my greatest friend Mr Nehru whom I admire very much."[5] Prime Minister Nehru had met Prince Sihanouk at the airport and had also seen him off. The personal bond that existed between the two leaders was apparent even during this brief halt. During the stop-over, the Cambodian Prime Minister was accompanied by his five-year old daughter. It was a happy Indira Gandhi who took care of her and presented her with two gifts - some Indian dolls and an affectionate kiss on the Princess's cheek.[6]

The Prince's admiration for Prime Minister Nehru never waned. During a banquet given in honour of the Prince at Rashtrapati Bhavan in 1963, when he said that, "Cambodia is deeply indebted to India; and I will add that I, for my part, am much indebted personally to India's great leader, Shri Jawaharlal Nehru."[7]

Prince Sihanouk adopted Prime Minister Nehru's non-alignment philosophy for Cambodia and stated that he followed only one principle in politics, "the defence of the independence, the territorial integrity and the dignity of my country and my people."[8]

When Prime Minister Nehru passed away in 1964, the Prince dedicated a boulevard to his memory. Dedicating the Jawaharlal Nehru Boulevard in Phnom Penh in 1965 the Prince said, "The first navigators, Indian merchants and *Brahmins* brought to our ancestors their Gods, their techniques, their organisation. Briefly, India was for us what Greece was to the Latin Occident."[9]

Prince Sihanouk arrived at New Delhi's Palam Airport with a small entourage of five members at 50 minutes past midnight on November 19, 1956. The delegation included his Technical Advisor, Son Sann; Private Secretary, Colonel You-Heng; *aide-de-camp* (ADC), Colonel Meas-Houl[10] and two highly respected personalities from the *Buddhist Sangha* - the Venerable IV-Tuot and the Venerable Ket-To, who had also been invited to India to witness the *Buddha Purnima* celebrations by the Indian Prime Minister.

President Dr Prasad (Left) with Prince Sihanouk at Rashtrapati Bhavan in November 1956. Credit: PD

As a practising Buddhist, the Prince encouraged the ideology of 'Buddhist Socialism' in his country integrating *Theravada* Buddhist principles with modern ideas like democracy.

India had elaborate plans for the *Buddha Purnima* celebrations. Being the birth place of Buddhism and home to the most holy places of Buddhist pilgrimage, India was at the centre of all the religious festivities. Bodh Gaya in Bihar, the small town where Buddha attained *nirvana*, was the venue for the global celebrations. A number of events including conferences and symposiums were scheduled in different cities across India; the first of which was inaugurated by Nehru in Calcutta. Buddhist pilgrims had flocked to the country congregating to worship at holy Buddhist sites like Sanchi, Kushinagar, Sravasti and Sarnath.

A high-powered committee to oversee the arrangements was appointed with Indian Vice President, Dr S Radhakrishnan as Chairman and Chief Ministers of several states as its members. Almost 80 delegates from 23 countries gathered in New Delhi for a four-day symposium starting November 26, 1956.

The subject of the conference, being held in collaboration with UNESCO, was on the contribution of Buddhism to the arts, letters and philosophy. Eminent Buddhists from the United States, Germany, Ceylon and Japan were expected to participate as well. Prince Sihanouk had let it be known that Ray Buc, the Chairman of the Buddhist Association of Cambodia; Sam Sary, Member of the Royal High Council and M Eng Meas, Member of the Cambodian Parliament would also join the festivities.[11]

The guest list included the former Prime Minister of Burma, U Nu; His Holiness the Dalai Lama and the Panchen Lama of Tibet; His Highness Prince Dhani-Nivet Kromamun Bridiyalkh Briddhiyakom of Thailand and Bhutan's Rani Chuni Dorji.[12]

Public meetings, exhibitions of Buddhist art, visits by foreign Buddhist scholars, a shadow play by Uday Shankar, a publication of 40 volumes of Buddhist scripture, the screening of documentary films, a publication of *Tripitaka* in Pali and Sanskrit, commemorative *Buddha Jayanti* postage stamps and the building of a monument in New Delhi, were just some highlights of the celebrations.[13] A week-long tour of the Buddhist shrines in India, starting December 3, was also arranged for the delegates.

The Prince was intent on ensuring that his visit was productive and included as many meetings with Nehru as possible. He even insisted that he be met by Prime Minister Nehru on his arrival.[14] Prince Sihanouk had on his agenda, discussions related to the problems being faced by Cambodia, as well as issues concerning world peace, in particular, the invasion of Egypt by Israel, the situation of Britain and France,[15] and the subsequent withdrawal of forces on US, Soviet and UN pressure.[16]

Speaking at the airport, Prince Sihanouk said that Cambodia welcomed the UN's call for a ceasefire between Israel and Egypt but added that great nations should have the courage to settle the heart of the problem, lest the crisis erupt again. He said, "My country believes that only objectivity, logic, realism and conciliation can be the guides in our attempt to find a genuine solution to the problems facing the UN. On their solution will depend world peace and consequently, the future of humanity."[17]

Prince Norodom Sihanouk was a Guest of the State and stayed in the Dwarka Suite of Rashtrapati Bhavan. The Venerable Ket-To and the Venerable IV Tuot stayed in the Nalanda and Tagore suites respectively. Commander Meas-Houl was accommodated in the Mysore Room, Colonel You-Heng in the Bombay Bedroom and Son Sann, in the Pepsu Bedroom.[18]

Prince Sihanouk's first day began on November 19, on the hour at 10 in the morning when he called on Prime Minister Nehru. Later, at noon he called on the Indian President, Dr Rajendra Prasad at Rashtrapati Bhavan. That evening, the Prince visited the *Buddha Jayanti* Pavilion,[19] before returning to attend a dinner hosted by Prime Minister Nehru in his honour.

The Prince could not however extend his stay. He had to be back in Cambodia to welcome the Chinese Premier, Chou En-Lai. The Prince, therefore, scheduled his return trip on the morning of November 20.

Accordingly, Prince Sihanouk departed for Calcutta aboard Indian Airways Corporation Flight 401 accompanied by three officials: Son-Sann, You-Heng and Meas-Houl.[20] In view of the departure of the Prince, a representative of the *Buddha Jayanti* Celebration Committee called at Rashtrapati Bhavan that morning and escorted the two monks who had accompanied the Prince, out of Rashtrapati Bhavan and into the Ashoka Hotel.

Major General Yadunath Singh, Military Secretary to the President (MSP), represented the President and bade the Prince farewell. As a mark of the happiness at the hospitality he had received in India, the Prince left presents for Indira Gandhi, the MSP and his wife, the Comptroller, President's Household (CPH), the President's *aides-de-camp* (AsDC), Security Officer Khub Chand and some others.[21]

Prince Sihanouk spent a long and eventful life in his strife-torn country, during which time Cambodia was ravaged by war and genocide under the Khmer Rouge. He fled Cambodia in 1979, before Vietnam invaded his country and returned only in 1991. He was crowned King once more in 1993, but by this time he was past 70 and his health was rapidly failing. King Sihanouk retained his throne until he abdicated it once again, in 2004. He was 81.

He was diagnosed with cancer and spent his last years in North Korea and China. He passed away in Beijing on October 15, 2012. He was just 16 days short of his 90th birthday.

Notes

[1] From the various public sources, it is understood that Sihanouk had visited India in 1956, 1958, 1959 and 1963. Only the 1956 visit has been covered as the documents relating to other visits are not traceable.

[2] Martin Woollacott, "King Norodom Sihanouk obituary," *The Guardian*, October 15, 2012, accessed May 5, 2015, http://www.theguardian.com/world/2012/oct/15/king-norodom-sihanouk.

[3] Norodom Sihanouk and Wilfred Burchett, *My war with the CIA: The memoirs of Prince Norodom Sihanouk as related to Wilfred Burchett* (Harmondsworth: Penguin Books, 1974), p. 162.

[4] Dinesh K Patnaik, "Sihanouk's India connection," *The Phnom Penh Post*, October 30, 2012, accessed May 5, 2015, http://www.phnompenhpost.com/national/sihanouk%E2%80%99s-indian-connection.

[5] "Prince Norodom has 3 Hour talks with Mr. Nehru", *The Times of India* (New Delhi), May 22, 1956, p. 1.

[6] Ibid.

[7] Ministry of External Affairs (1995), Government of India, MEA Library, Foreign Affairs Records 1963, Volume IX, accessed May 5, 2015, mealib.nic.in/?pdf2551?000.

[8] Elizabeth Becker and Seth Mydans, "Norodom Sihanouk, Cambodian Leader Through Shifting Allegiances, Dies at 89," *The New York Times*, October 14, 2012, accessed May 14, 2015, http://nyti.ms/RJLhU5 .

[9] Patnaik, "Sihanouk's India connection."

[10] Records, President's Secretariat, Rashtrapati Bhavan, File No. 255.

[11] "Prince Norodom in Delhi," *The Hindustan Times* (New Delhi), November 20, 1956, p. 1.

[12] "23 countries to be represented," *The Times of India* (New Delhi), November 20, 1956, p. 6.

[13] Senaka Weeraratna, "1956- A year of National and Religious Awakening," Asian Tribune, accessed May 5, 2015, http://www.asiantribune.com/news/2011/05/16/1956-%E2%80%93-year-national-and-religious-awakening.

[14] "Prince Norodom in Delhi," p. 1.

[15] Ibid.

[16] Ibid.

[17] Ibid.

[18] Records, President's Secretariat, File No. 255.

[19] "Prince Norodom," *The Times of India* (New Delhi), November 20, 1956, p. 7.

[20] Records, President's Secretariat, File No. 255.

[21] Ibid.

The Prime Minister of Ceylon, Solomon Bandaranaike, visited India and stayed at the Rashtrapati Bhavan from December 1–6, 1957, while attending the Commonwealth Parliamentary Conference. The Conference, which was held between December 1–10, 1957, was co-hosted by India, Pakistan and Ceylon. This was also the first time that this Conference was being held in India.

Hailing from an elite Ceylonese Christian family, Solomon West Ridgeway Dias Bandaranaike was born in Colombo on January 8, 1899. His father Sir Solomon Dias Bandaranaike was an advisor and Chief Native Interpreter to the Governor of Ceylon, Sir Joseph West Ridgeway, who was one of the most powerful personalities in British Colonial Ceylon. Sir Ridgeway was not only young Solomon's godfather, but also the reason for Bandaranaike's rather long name.

Visit of

November 30 to December 7, 1957

H.E. Mr S W R D Bandaranaike

Prime Minister of Ceylon

Bandaranaike had his initial degree education in Ceylon, before he enrolled at Oxford University in 1919. The years he spent there stood him in very good stead in the legislature of Ceylon.[1] He was called to the Bar in 1925 and soon acquired a reputation of being an erudite lawyer. A votary of the federal political structure and systems of local governance, Bandaranaike was an active advocate of Sinhalese interests within the country. His rise through the political hierarchy in Ceylon, as a ministerial member of the United National Party (UNP) and a founder member of the Sri Lanka Freedom Party (SLFP), saw him become Prime Minister in 1956, when he won a landslide victory and headed a four-party coalition.

The Ceylonese Prime Minister was a staunch advocate and supporter of non-alignment, as was the Indian Prime Minister Jawaharlal Nehru. The Prime Ministers shared a close relationship and Prime Minister Bandaranaike went on record to say that there was a general agreement between him and the Prime Minister of India on almost all important international problems.[2] The proximity of the leaders also helped in forging closer national ties between the two countries.

With the Commonwealth Parliamentary Conference scheduled to begin on Monday, December 2, 1957, Prime Minister Bandaranaike arrived in India via Air Ceylon Flight No. 102, at 5.00 on the evening of Saturday, November 30. He landed at Santa Cruz Airport in Bombay and was driven straight to Raj Bhavan. He stayed there until the morning of December 1. Later that day, he emplaned for New Delhi with Prime Minister Jawaharlal Nehru. Prime Minister Nehru was flying to New Delhi from Poona via Bombay. Based on their overlapping travel arrangements, Indian Government officials had decided that the two Prime Ministers could fly together to New Delhi.

Facing page:
Prime Minister Solomon Bandaranaike (left)
with President Dr Prasad at Rashtrapati Bhavan
in December 1957. Credit: PD

(Front row, R-L): Prime Minister Nehru, Prime Minister Bandaranaike and Speaker of Lok Sabha, Ayyangar at Palam Airport, Delhi, in December 1957. Credit: PD

Prime Minister Nehru arrived in Bombay by a special Ilyushin aircraft, "*Meghdoot*" and landed at Santa Cruz Airport at 10.30 am on December 1. He went straight to the VIP lounge, where he was received by his sister, Krishna Hutheesing, and the two spent a considerable time chatting. The Ceylonese Prime Minister was already at the airport, having arrived there a few minutes earlier. The "*Meghdoot*" was refuelled and with both Prime Ministers aboard, it took-off for Delhi with the flags of both nations fluttering alongside one another.

They arrived at Palam Airport's VIP bay just before 3.00 pm. The large group of dignitaries receiving them included several Indian Cabinet Ministers; Sir Richard Aluwihare, the Ceylonese High Commissioner in India; MA Ayyangar, Speaker of the Lok Sabha; Sardar Hukam Singh, the Deputy Speaker of Lok Sabha; Krishnamurthy Rao, Chairman of the Rajya Sabha; MRA Baig, the Chief of Protocol; members of the diplomatic corps and many other senior Government of India officials. The Deputy Military Secretary to the President (DMSP), Lieutenant Colonel M Ghufran received the Ceylonese Prime Minister on behalf of the President of India.[3] The press had also gathered in large numbers expecting to elicit some comments from the Ceylonese Prime Minister.

Prime Minister Bandaranaike was the first to step off the aircraft, followed closely by Prime Minister Nehru. As a visiting Head of State, Prime Minister Bandaranaike was presented with a Guard of Honour, which he inspected while the Services Band played the national anthems of both Ceylon and India.

The large press corps that was keen to get the Ceylonese Prime Minister to speak, however, met with little success, as the eloquent leader gave very little away. On being queried about his talks with Prime Minister Nehru, he replied in jest, "I had the pleasure of having a little talk with your Prime Minister, my good friend."[4] His reply to a supplementary question on the topic of their discussion was handled with even more aplomb. Prime Minister Bandaranaike smiled, and quoted a line from *Alice in Wonderland*, "We talked of cabbages and kings."[5] After having charmed the journalists, he added, on a serious note, that he hoped to have informal talks with the Indian Prime Minister on issues that concerned both countries during his stay in New Delhi. He nevertheless said that these talks would not, by any means, be a "full-dress discussion."[6]

Prime Minister Bandaranaike was accompanied by G de Souza, Permanent Secretary and his Private Secretary, DW de Alwis.[7] Maitripala Senanayake, Minister for Transport and Works of Ceylon, dropped out of the State Visit at the very last minute, despite earlier indications that he would be accompanying the Prime Minister. Rashtrapati Bhavan had received word that Senanayake would not be accompanying the Ceylonese Prime Minister, as late as November 30.

The motorcade that left Palam Airport for Rashtrapati Bhavan moved with regal elegance. Leading the cavalcade was a DeSoto,

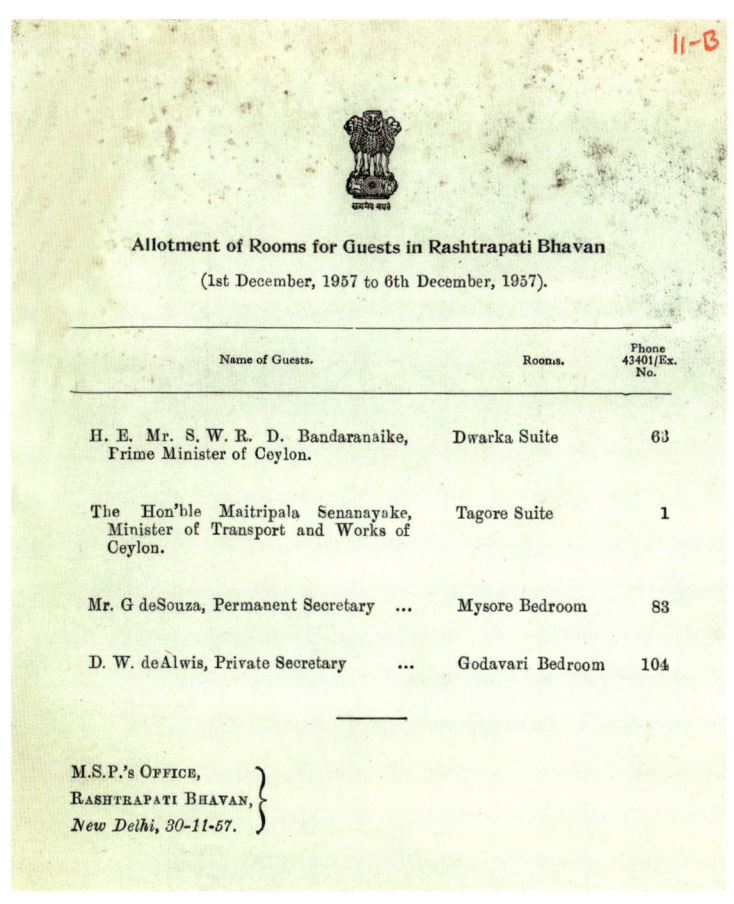

11-B

Allotment of Rooms for Guests in Rashtrapati Bhavan

(1st December, 1957 to 6th December, 1957).

Name of Guests.	Rooms.	Phone 43401/Ex. No.
H. E. Mr. S. W. R. D. Bandaranaike, Prime Minister of Ceylon.	Dwarka Suite	63
The Hon'ble Maitripala Senanayake, Minister of Transport and Works of Ceylon.	Tagore Suite	1
Mr. G deSouza, Permanent Secretary ...	Mysore Bedroom	83
D. W. deAlwis, Private Secretary ...	Godavari Bedroom	104

M.S.P.'s Office,
Rashtrapati Bhavan,
New Delhi, 30-11-57.

Room Allocation Plan.

bearing the two Prime Ministers. A Plymouth, other guest cars and a Fargo Lorry constituted the rear, bearing other members of the entourage and their luggage.

The Prime Minister of Ceylon occupied the Dwarka Suite; G de Souza stayed in the Mysore Bedroom and DW de Alwis was given the Godavari Bedroom.[8] The Tagore Bedroom, which had been reserved for Senanayake, remained unoccupied.

As is normally done, Rashtrapati Bhavan made elaborate security arrangements for its guests. A communication sent by the Military Secretary to the President (MSP) to BL Chhiber, Deputy Superintendent of Police at Rashtrapati Bhavan, listed in detail, the need to have sentries posted at strategic points in the building. One sentry was posted at the South Court from 6.00 am to 9.00 pm every day and kept it clear in case any of the Ceylonese entourage, or indeed the Prime Minister, chose to use this way.

A special sentry was appointed to keep watch over the cars in the parking lot, from 7.00 am until such time as the cars were garaged for the night. Policemen were detailed on duty in the grand Durbar Hall to ensure that no "unauthorised person" went down the marble staircase. "Men posted at the roof," and particularly above the Dwarka Suite were instructed to be extra vigilant.[9]

After a quiet lunch en suite on December 1, Prime Minister Bandaranaike called on President Dr Rajendra Prasad for tea in the latter's Study at 5.00 pm. Thereafter, the two leaders attended

Prime Minister Bandaranaike (left) with President Dr Prasad at Rashtrapati Bhavan in December 1957. Credit: PC

a dance and music recital at the All India Fine Arts and Crafts Theatre. Prime Minister Bandaranaike retired for the day after a quiet dinner in his suite.

The Commonwealth Parliamentary Conference opened on December 2. It was a ceremonial event held in the circular Central Hall of the Parliament House. The Central Hall had been witness to many important assemblies since its inauguration nearly 30 years ago. The sound of trumpets echoed through the halls of Parliament House, announcing the arrival of President Dr Rajendra Prasad, Vice President Dr Radhakrishnan, Prime Minister Nehru, Prime Minister Bandaranaike, the Chief Pakistani Delegate[10] and 13 leaders of other delegations.

Welcoming the delegates, President Dr Prasad said, "It would be a bad day for us and for others, too, if anything were to happen which would, in any way, weaken this bond."[11] As joint host, Prime Minister Bandaranaike emphasised in his welcome address, that even if the Commonwealth was "not bound together by the crimson thread of a common blood...[it was] bound together by the golden thread of a common tradition."[12] He added that this tradition was that of democracy, and although its forms might change in the future, the essentials – including free elections, sovereignty of Parliament and independence of the judiciary – would go down in history, as Britain's greatest contribution to human welfare.[13] The message from the Prime Minister of Pakistan was read out by Law Minister Abdus Sattar. It praised the democratic values of the Commonwealth but recommended the need for remedies to strengthen the "structural weakness" of the body and the development of a mechanism for the amicable settlement of disputes among member countries.[14]

The first day of the Conference ended with a speech by Vice President Dr Radhakrishnan, who appealed to all nations to promote and encourage humility, charity and understanding in the international arena.[15] From Parliament House, Prime Minister Bandaranaike returned to Rashtrapati Bhavan and attended the 'At Home' reception which was hosted by the President of India in the beautiful Mughal Gardens at 5.15 pm.

After the function, at 7.00 pm, he attended a reception at 3, Hardinge Avenue (now Tilak Marg), hosted by the High Commissioner for Ceylon. Prime Minister Bandaranaike then returned to the Dwarka Suite and after a quiet dinner, he travelled to the All India Fine Arts and Crafts Theatre to attend a *Bharatanatyam* performance by renowned *danseuse*, Kamala Laxman.

The morning of December 3 was packed with seminars and discussions with delegates attending the Conference. The day also happened to be President Dr Rajendra Prasad's 73rd birthday. Starting his day with his usual *puja* (prayer), President Dr Prasad received a steady stream of visitors. Prime Minister Bandaranaike joined in the celebration and garlanded President Dr Prasad.

Later in the day, the visiting Prime Minister had lunch with the Indian Prime Minister at his residence, Teen Murti Bhavan. Thereafter, he went to Parliament House and remained there till about 4.00 pm. The Ceylonese Prime Minister left the meeting early, to attend a reception organised in his honour by the Maha Bodhi Society at Birla Mandir on Mandir Marg. Shortly before 6.00 pm, another 'At Home' was held by the President and the members of the Indian branch of the Commonwealth Parliamentary Association. To round off what had been a busy day, Prime Minister Bandaranaike had a quiet dinner in his suite at Rashtrapati Bhavan.

After attending the Conference on the morning of December 4, Prime Minister Bandaranaike returned to Rashtrapati Bhavan for a quick lunch-break. He later attended an 'At Home', hosted in his honour by the Indian Prime Minister at 5.00 pm at Teen Murti Bhavan. After the 'At Home', Prime Minister Bandaranaike addressed the Indian Council of World Affairs.

Speaking at the Council's Headquarters in Sapru House, Prime Minister Bandaranaike delved into the topic: "The Problem of Democracy in Asian Countries."[16] He elaborated on the various concepts and types of democracies, categorising India and Ceylon as "democratic socialists"[17] and China as "semi-communist."[18] Prime Minister Bandaranaike further elucidated on his idea of democracy and described it as a "combination or the agglomeration of a number of individual liberties and collective liberties."[19]

He also delved on other problems confronting the Asian countries, the most challenging of which, he said, was steering free of power-bloc politics.[20] Emphasising the need to stay non-aligned in an atmosphere that compelled countries to choose sides, the Ceylonese Prime Minister emphatically said, "We are not going to lump ourselves into this power bloc or the other power bloc. We want to be free. To look about us. To take what is useful and beneficial to us — may be from the East or West...may be from anything else — in building up our new society as suits us best. That is the philosophy behind the theory of neutralism and co-existence which your country follows and my own is following now."[21] The word "now" was uttered in a deliberate undertone, causing the crowded hall to break into delighted laughter. Amidst more laughter, the Ceylonese Prime Minister added that those who were following this policy were being accused of sitting on the fence.[22] "The democratic idea is a very pious idea," he said gravely, "I think it is an idea that must all try to achieve and preserve."[23] His main theme revolved around the importance of democracy, its development in Asia, and the use of the occasional referendum with which Governments might safeguard their sovereignty.[24]

Prime Minister Bandaranaike attended the Conference for just one more day on December 5, 1957. This day had much the same programme, with conference sessions and interactions with delegations consuming most of his time. He had lunch with Prime Minister Nehru once again at Teen Murti Bhavan at 1.15

pm, and spent the evening attending an exhibition polo match, before driving to a dinner hosted by the Indian Vice President, Dr Radhakrishnan, at the Ashoka Hotel.

After an early night, Prime Minister Bandaranaike was up bright and early on the morning of December 6. Breakfast was served to him *en suite* after which he left Rashtrapati Bhavan at 7.30 am, reaching Palam Airport in 15 minutes. He was accompanied by the DMSP, who represented the President of India.

Prime Minister Bandaranaike and his entourage left for Bombay at 8.00 am, by an Indian Airlines Corporation's British manufactured Viscount Aircraft and arrived at Santa Cruz Airport at 11.15 am.[25] In Bombay, he halted for one day. During his stay in the city, he visited the Bhabha Atomic Research Centre and evinced keen interest in the Canada–India nuclear reactor that was then under construction. He was shown around the facility by Dr Homi J.Bhabha, Chairman of the Atomic Energy Commission and Secretary of the Atomic Energy Department of the Government of India.[26]

He left for Colombo on December 7. Before his departure, Prime Minister Bandaranaike addressed the press and made a brief statement. He said that he had held talks with the Indian Prime Minister on the sensitive issue of Indian settlers in Ceylon. At 9.30 am, he boarded an American TWA flight, for Colombo.[27]

On September 25, 1959, Prime Minister Bandaranaike was shot in full public view by a Buddhist monk on the veranda of Tintagel, his home in Rosmead Place, Colombo. He succumbed to his injuries on September 26, 1959. He was 60.

Notes

[1] Yasmine Gooneratne, *Relative Merits: A Personal Memoir of the Bandaranaike Family of Sri Lanka* (London: C. Hurst & Company, 1986), p. 84.

[2] Ministry of External Affairs (1956–1957), Government of India, Ministry of External Affairs, Report 1956–1957, Government of India, Ministry of External Affairs – A : States in Special Treaty Relations with India, accessed April 28. 2015, http://mealib.nic.in/?pdf2483?000

[3] Ibid.

[4] Ibid.

[5] Ibid.

[6] Ibid.

[7] Records, President's Secretariat, Rashtrapati Bhavan, File No. 30/CER/9

[8] Ibid.

[9] Ibid.

[10] As Pakistani Prime Minister II Chundrigar could not attend the Conference, the Pakistani delegation was represented by Law Minister Abdus Sattar.

[11] "Commonwealth Link Needs to be Developed," *The Hindustan Times* (New Delhi), December 3, 1957, p. 1.

[12] S.W.R.D. Bandaranaike, *Speeches and Writings* (Colombo: Information Division of the Department of Broadcasting and Information, 1963), p. 402.

[13] "Asian Members Reaffirm Faith in the Commonwealth," *The Times* (London), December 3, 1957, p. 9.

[14] "Commonwealth Link Needs to be Developed," p. 1.

[15] "Strengthening of Bonds of Commonwealth," *The Times of India* (New Delhi), December 3, 1957, p. 1.

[16] Bandaranaike, *Speeches and Writings*, p. 405.

[17] "Conflict between Right and Left," *The Hindustan Times* (New Delhi), December 5, 1957, p. 3.

[18] Ibid.

[19] Bandaranaike, *Speeches and Writings*, p. 407.

[20] Ibid., pp. 411–412.

[21] Ibid.

[22] "Conflict between Right and Left," p. 3.

[23] Bandaranaike, *Speeches and Writings*, p. 411.

[24] "Two Party System," *The Times* (London), December 6, 1957, p. 9.

[25] Records, President's Secretariat, File No. 30/CER/9

[26] "Mr. Bandaranaike," *The Times of India* (New Delhi), December 7, 1957, p. 11.

[27] "Mr. Bandaranaike," *The Times of India* (New Delhi), December 8, 1957, p. 7.

On June 25, 1954, Chou En-lai, the first Foreign Minister and Premier of a barely four-year-old People's Republic of China, arrived in India on a three-day visit. He came at the invitation of the Indian Prime Minister, Pandit Jawaharlal Nehru, who was keen to develop close relations with the new country. The Prime Minister had already made known his intention, when India recognised China on December 30, 1949, barely two months after Mao's revolutionary forces ousted Chiang Kai-Shek from the mainland. It had also made India one of the first non-socialist countries to recognise the new Government.

Chou En-lai was born on March 5, 1898, in Huai'an, in Jiangsu province. His family was originally from Shaoxing, in the Zhejiang province, where generations worked as Government "clerks" during the late Qing dynasty. He grew up in a China that was rapidly changing, and his travels to Europe as a young man sharpened his views of the world and China's position in it.

Chou En-lai made his mark playing a significant role in establishing the Communist Party, which was struggling for political control in China. He also played an active role in consolidating China's resistance against the Japanese invasion in 1938.

June 25–28, 1954
November 28 to December 10, 1956
December 30, 1956 to January 1, 1957
April 19–26, 1960

Visits of

H.E. Mr Chou En-lai

Premier of the People's Republic of China

In the 1950s, Chou En-lai was elevated to the post of Foreign Minister and Premier, and became Chairman Mao's trusted man. He rose to an eminence and stature that prompted Henry Kissinger to comment of Premier Chou En-lai as "the most impressive" foreign statesman he "had ever met" and had ranked him "equally with de Gaulle."[1]

The 1954 Visit

The invitation to visit India was extended to Premier Chou En-lai by Prime Minister Nehru through the Defence Minister, Krishna Menon at the Geneva Conference of 1954 that was held to bring an end to the Korean War.[2] The invitation was readily accepted and Premier Chou En-lai rerouted his travel plans to spend four days in India before returning to Peking (modern Beijing).

Premier Chou En-lai's visit and its details were, however, kept under tight wraps at the request of the Chinese Government. They had desired that the visit be kept a secret until the Chinese leader landed in Delhi. Speculation was, however, rife in Delhi that something unusual was afoot. The newspaper *Times of India*, for instance, reported that Pandit Nehru had postponed his customary 10-day trip to Simla that was planned for the summer, after the Geneva Conference.

In a rather unusual gesture, India sent a special aircraft to bring the Chinese Premier and his 15-member entourage to New Delhi from Geneva. The aircraft, a four-engine

Facing page:
(L-R): Prime Minister Nehru,
Vice President Dr S Radhakrishnan,
Premier Chou En-lai and
President Dr Prasad, at
Rashtrapti Bhavan
in June 1954. Credit: PC

Air India International Constellation, the "*Maratha Princess*"[3] left Bombay early on the morning of June 22, 1954. The Chinese Premier could not, however, depart for Delhi as planned as his talks with the French Premier, M Pierre Mendes-France, got extended by a day. Consequently, he arrived in the capital a day later than originally scheduled.[4]

It was a sunny day, as days in the month of June are in the north of India, when the plane carrying Premier Chou En-lai touched down at New Delhi's Palam Airport on Friday, June 25, at 7.10 am. On board, the Chinese Premier had enjoyed a sumptuous Indian meal elaborately served to him by the Indian crew. As his subsequent conduct evidenced, he was delighted that the Indian Government had sent him a special plane in which he could travel in comfort.

As the plane taxied to a halt, a beaming Premier Chou En-lai shook hands with all the crew members and handed each of them a packet of "high-class" Chinese cigarettes.[5] As a token of his appreciation for flying him and his delegation to Delhi, the Chinese Premier presented AC Gazdar, Commander of the Constellation, a copy of Pictorial China, and a personally autographed edition of *New China*[6], along with a handwritten note thanking him. He wrote: "I enjoyed the wonderful flight. I am thankful to the Government of India for sending this beautiful plane to bring me from Geneva. I have also to thank the members of the crew for their efficiency."[7] As an afterthought, Premier Chou En-lai added a postscript to the note which read, "The efficiency of these Indian pilots is very high," and this "should be emulated by the pilots of the Chinese Airlines."[8]

Nattily dressed in a "dark blue Chinese tunic and a velvet beret,"[9] the Chinese Premier stepped out of the Constellation aircraft into the Delhi summer sunlight with his entourage behind him. He was garlanded with ropes of myriad-hued flowers, a traditional Indian gesture of welcome, before shaking hands with a visibly delighted Prime Minister Jawaharlal Nehru.

Premier Chou En-lai later inspected a ceremonial Guard of Honour drawn from the Indian Army and Air Force and held up his right arm in salute. He was then introduced to the Cabinet Ministers, the Chiefs of the Army, Navy and Air Force and the representatives of those countries that had recognised Mao's Government and were, therefore, invited to the welcome ceremony.[10] In view of the restrictions, the United States, France, Canada and several Latin American countries were not represented at the airport.

The welcome at the airport was more than ceremonial. Besides the official congregation that usually received foreign leaders on state visits, there was a large throng of people who had arrived at the airport to welcome the Chinese leader. Wire enclosures were

Premier Chou En-lai (left) and President Dr Prasad (both with hand raised in salute) being escorted to the Reception in Mughal Gardens at Rashtrapati Bhavan by AsDC in June 1954. Credit: PC

erected at the airport, from where they could greet the visiting dignitary. The Government had also stepped in to make special arrangements for transporting people who had desired to come to the airport to greet the Chinese Premier. Additional buses were, for instance, pressed into service for the purpose. The crowds reacted excitedly when their eyes fell on the Chinese Premier. Despite being at considerable distance from where the aircraft had come to a halt , the crowds erupted in cheers on seeing Premier Chou En-lai and their frenzied shouts of, "Long live the friendship between India and China!" and "Long live Mao Tse-tung and Chou En-lai"[11] could be heard on the tarmac.

The visit had also generated considerable interest in the press corps and almost 100 journalists were at the airport to cover the ceremony. Premier Chou En-lai did not disappoint them. Before he left the airport, he addressed the journalists and said that he was "honoured and pleased"[12] to visit India. He added that the 960 million peoples of the two countries were an important constituent of world peace and expressed his desire for closer India–China relations. The interest of the media in the visit was so intense that the entire reception and press address was filmed and the recording was taken to China, the United Kingdom and the United States where it was telecast.[13]

After the reception at the airport, Premier Chou En-Lai and his delegation[14] were driven to Rashtrapati Bhavan where they stayed in the recently refurbished rooms and suites of South Wing. The refurbishing was done in Indian style in the beginning of 1954 using decorative fabric and handmade village products.[15]

Shortly after his arrival at Rashtrapati Bhavan at 9.00 am, Premier Chou En-lai visited *Rajghat* with the Chinese Ambassador and the Indian Chief of Protocol (COP) and laid a wreath at Mahatma Gandhi's memorial. He then met Pandit Nehru at the Ministry of External Affairs (MEA) and later Vice President Dr S Radhakrishnan at the latter's residence on 2, King Edward Road (now Maulana Azad Road).

After the two engagements, Premier Chou En-lai called on President Dr Rajendra Prasad at 11.00 am. They met in the cheerfully decorated Morning Room, which was cooled by a gentle breeze, wafting in from the Mughal Gardens through the open windows. The two leaders exchanged pleasantries with the help of interpreters over cups of tea served in white bone-china.

During the meeting, the Chinese Premier had requested that his schedule for the first day be kept flexible to include a private meeting with Prime Minister Nehru. This was immediately agreed to. Subsequent to the meeting with the President, Premier Chou En-lai had a quiet lunch with his advisers *en-suite* after which he met Prime Minister Nehru for top-secret discussions. The meeting started at 3.30 pm and continued until 6.15 pm with only a single interpreter present. The talks reportedly covered a

President Dr Prasad (left) with Premier Chou En-lai (seated opposite) at Rashtrapati Bhavan in June 1954. Credit: PC

whole host of topics that ranged from politics and international relations to issues of mutual concern.

Later Premier Chou En-lai changed into more formal attire and departed for the Chinese Ambassador's reception that was held in his honour at Jind House early that evening. From there, a Presidential car brought the Chinese leader back to Rashtrapati Bhavan, where he was the Guest of Honour at an 'At Home' reception, hosted by the President of India on the sprawling lawns of Rashtrapati Bhavan's Mughal Gardens.

The evening was clear and the weather as fine as can be on a summer evening in Delhi. In this pleasant setting, the two leaders, engrossed in intense conversation, walked down the paved pathways of the beautifully landscaped Mughal Gardens escorted by *aides-de-camps* (AsDC) in spotless white uniforms. The reception began at 7.00 pm, just as dusk set in, casting an amber glow over the trees, plants and the carefully manicured lawns of the Gardens. Nearly 400 guests, including Ministers, diplomats, officials and prominent citizens, had been invited to meet the Chinese Premier.[16] Amongst those who attended the reception was the Indian Vice President.

The reception lasted for an hour, after which Prime Minister Nehru and Premier Chou En-lai travelled together to Teen Murti Bhavan, where the Indian Prime Minister hosted a dinner in honour of his counterpart. This dinner at Prime Minister Nehru's residence was Premier Chou En-lai's last engagement for the day.

Saturday began with a sightseeing trip that began in the early hours of the morning. With China's red five-starred 'Kuochi' flag fluttering on the flag mast of the black Presidential limousine, Premier Chou En-lai covered 40-miles traversing the new and old cities of Delhi. He was accompanied by the Chinese Ambassador and various dignitaries of the Delhi Government.[17]

Their first stop was the famous Qutub Minar, where Premier Chou En-lai climbed up the winding steps for a panoramic view of Delhi. He explored Chirag Dilli and the tiny, vibrant temple town of Kalkaji and thereafter stopped by at Jamia Millia Islamia University. He also visited the displaced people's colonies in Nizamuddin, Jangpura and Lajpat Nagar. The reception accorded to the visiting Premier at *Kasturba Niketan* in Lajpat Nagar, the home of displaced women and children, was particularly an emotional and moving interlude for the Chinese leader. There he was greeted by an elderly refugee woman in the traditional Indian manner by applying a saffron mark on his forehead. She also "smothered him with the weight of garlands."[18] Premier Chou En-lai, was demonstrably touched and "his eyes [were] wet with tears."[19]

After his tour of the city, at quarter to nine in the evening, Prime Minister Nehru hosted a State Banquet in honour of his counterpart at Rashtrapati Bhavan.[20] The banquet was held in an exquisite setting. The sheer magnificence of the wood-panelled Banquet Hall came to life under the mellow lights of the intricately tiered chandeliers. Delicate crystal stemware and shining silver cutlery were set out on the long tablecloth of pure white damask, with the Star of India crockery that had been brought to India by Lady Willingdon during her time as Vicereine, taking the pride of place. Flowers in myriad colours were delicately arranged at intervals along the table.

The banquet too was an elaborate affair and considerable thought and gone into the kind of fare to be served to the Chinese Premier. After detailed discussion, a conscious decision was taken to serve only Indian cuisines. Accordingly, different cuisines from various States in the country were on offer.[21] After the main courses were served, Prime Minister Nehru delivered his banquet speech. Speaking in Hindi, he welcomed Chinese Premier Chou En-lai and said that despite their individual backgrounds, India and China had sustained a 2000 year-long friendship. He concluded with a toast to Chairman Mao Tse-tung. Replying to the Indian Prime Minister, Premier Chou En-lai, speaking in Mandarin, declared that the Chinese Government and people attached great importance to their friendship with India. He acknowledged India's role in bringing about a successful armistice to the Korean War and raised a toast to the President of India, Dr Rajendra Prasad.[22]

At 6.00 am on Sunday, the next day, Premier Chou En-lai left for Agra. He returned to the capital at noon, in time to attend a Civic Reception at the historic Red Fort. The Chinese Premier drove to the venue from Rashtrapati Bhavan with the Indian Prime Minister in an open limousine. All along the three-mile route, the crowd was dense. The people who had lined the roads cheered the two leaders as their motorcade passed by. Thousands had also gathered on the spacious lawns of the *Diwan-i-Khas* of the Red fort. When the limousine finally came to a halt at the venue, Premier Chou En-lai was greeted by the people who were excited to see him. Premier Chou En-lai acknowledged the vast cheering crowd by folding his hands.

Sham Nath, President of the Delhi Municipal Committee, welcomed the Chinese Premier. Responding to the welcome address, Premier Chou En-lai, speaking in Mandarin, said that he had brought to India the "friendship of the Chinese people," and would take the "profound friendship of the Indian people for the Chinese people." He ended his reply with the cry, "Long live friendship between the people of China and India. Long live peace in Asia. Long live world peace."[23] After the speeches, Premier Chou En-lai was presented with an ivory screen, a replica of one of the famed marble screens at the Taj Mahal and Pandit Nehru's address in Hindi that had been printed on an elegant silken scroll.[24]

After the reception, the Chinese Premier returned to Rashtrapati Bhavan and resumed talks with the Indian Prime Minister. After the talks, both the leaders had dinner at the Chinese Embassy. The final meeting between Prime Minister Nehru and Premier Chou En-lai took place on the afternoon of June 27, 1954. Later that evening, both the leaders held a joint press conference in the Grey Dining Room at Rashtrapati Bhavan. This was, however, not an ordinary press conference. It was a carefully regulated affair. Questions had to be submitted 24 hours in advance.[25] A total of 62 questions were received.

The Chinese leader was not particularly forthcoming at the conference and chose not to be expansive, and merely answered that his talks with Pandit Nehru had been helpful in furthering Asian and global peace. To most other questions, he chose only to say that their answers would be contained in the joint communiqué that was to be issued the same day. By the end of the conference, Chou-En-lai had only answered five questions.[26]

On the night of June 27, the Chinese Premier called on Dr Rajendra Prasad and bid him farewell. To commemorate the visit, the President presented Premier Chou En-lai a silver-framed autographed photograph of himself. The return gifts would, however, come later.

As the Chinese motorcade left Rashtrapati Bhavan, the President, Vice President and Prime Minister found personal gifts awaiting them. The parcels contained fragrant Chinese teas, exquisitely drawn Chinese scrolls and books on New China. The Military

Secretary to the President (MSP), Major General Chatterjee, and his staff, received some beautiful Chinese paper paintings.[27]

On the morning of June 28, Premier Chou En-lai left for Rangoon at the invitation of the Prime Minister of Burma, by the Air India International plane, the "Bengal Princess."[28] On board, a pleasant surprise awaited the Chinese Premier. Special baskets of delicious *Dussehri* mangoes had been secretly loaded onto the plane on Prime Minister Nehru's instructions. As soon as the aircraft was aloft, these mangoes were served to the Premier and his entourage. The Chinese delegation savoured the mangoes so much that they reportedly described them as fruits of "paradise."[29]

Pandit Nehru was visibly pleased with the visit and it had demonstrably lifted his spirits. It was apparent by his unusually cheerful mood. Journalists, who caught up with him before he left the capital for his usual 10-day vacation to Simla, were rather astonished by his buoyant demeanour. Replying to a question from one of them who queried if he were pleased with the talks of the past three days, he laughed and said, "Well, I am always pleased – except that rarely I am not."[30]

Premier Chou En-lai (second from left) in conversation with President Dr Prasad at Rashtrapati Bhavan in November 1956. Credit: PC

Premier Chou En-lai (left) with Prime Minister Nehru in November 1956. Credit: PD

The 1956 Visit

After the previous visit of Premier Chou En-lai, India–China relations improved considerably. Later that year, Prime Minister Nehru visited Peking at the invitation of the Chinese Premier. The two countries cooperated on a number of issues relating to Taiwan, Tibet and the People's Republic of China's membership to the United Nations amongst others.

The Chinese Premier's second visit, unlike the previous one, was not shrouded in secrecy. It was a part of his six-nation tour of Pakistan, Afghanistan, Nepal, Burma and Laos besides India. This time too, the Chinese Premier came in an Indian Airlines Skymaster jetliner that was sent to him to Cambodia from where he flew to Delhi. The aircraft made a brief stop at Agra, from where Indian Air Force Vampire jet fighters escorted the Premier's plane to the capital.[31]

The Skymaster touched down at Palam Airport's VIP Bay, at 10 minutes past four on the cool evening of November 28, as the crowds that had gathered there shouted, "Long live Indian–Chinese friendship"[32] and their excited greetings rendered the air. Upon alighting the stairs, the Vice President of India, Dr S Radhakrishnan and the Indian Prime Minister, Jawaharlal Nehru received the Chinese Premier. The Chinese leader was also welcomed by two of Tibet's most holy men – the Dalai Lama and the Panchen Lama, who were in India in connection with 2,500th anniversary of the death of Lord Buddha.[33] Thereafter, Premier Chou En-lai was presented a Guard of Honour and both he and his Vice Premier, Marshal Ho Lung, who was a part of the delegation, took the salute as the Air Force band played Arise, China's national anthem.[34] After the Guard of Honour, Premier Chou En-lai delivered the customary address that a visiting Head of State/Government does on arrival. He highlighted the growing friendship between the two countries, and promised to return to India during Christmas.

The reception that the Chinese leader received was enthusiastic and he was garlanded with multiple ropes of marigold flowers. As he passed the excited crowds of children, union members, communists, common folk and clerks from some Government offices who were given special leave to witness the reception, he was showered with rose petals. Yet there was something lacking in the welcome. It was not rapturous and spontaneous. As one newspaper chose to report, he was greeted with "disciplined enthusiasm."[35]

From the airport, the Chinese Premier and his delegation drove straight to Rashtrapati Bhavan. On arrival at its South Court, they were received by the Comptroller, President's Household (CPH) and the Personal Staff of the President. They were then escorted to the Yellow Drawing Room for refreshments by the AsDC following which the visiting dignitaries were conducted to their respective suites/rooms.

During this visit, the MEA had sent a rather long advisory to Rashtrapati Bhavan on the arrangements that the President's Secretariat may make for the Chinese delegation. It included the food, lodging, furnishings and entertainment preferences of the Chinese Premier. It also came with a note on the "types of presents that would be appreciated" by the visiting delegation.[36]

The advisory on the food was particularly as interesting as it was elaborate. It is not known if the serving of the primarily Indian fare during the previous visit of the Chinese Premier prompted the advisory. The lists of his preferences, however, lend credence to the conclusion that this may have been the case.

Among the food preferences listed were the Premier's liking for all kinds of seafood such as "Crabs, Lobsters, Oysters, Prawns, Sea-slugs etc."[37] The advisory also contained information that the Chinese, as a rule, do not eat mutton and the "meats" that should be served to them should preferably be "Spring-chicken,

> FOOD.
>
> His Excellency Mr. Chou-en-Lai likes all kinds of Seafood such as Crabs, Lobsters, Oysters, Prawns, Sea-slugs etc.
>
> 2. The Chinese, as a rule, do not eat mutton. The meats to be served should, therefore, preferably be Spring-chicken, Duck, Turkey and game such as Partridges, Quails, etc. Ham and Pork, when served should be minced. Mutton dishes such as Kabab or meat balls in Indian style may be served. All meats are eaten very tender by the Chinese. Curd and Cheese are not liked. With breakfast a glass of hot milk should invariably be served. The Menu for breakfast should include eggs.
>
> 3. Fruit and fruit juices are liked. Indian coffee is very much appreciated. Indian tea, however, is not much liked. Chinese 'LU CHA' green tea should invariably be served.
>
> 4. Heavily spiced or very hot food is not desirable but a variety of Indian dishes from different regions, such as Bengali fish, Tandoori Chicken, Tikka Kabab, Dosa and Upana would be welcomed.

Advisory on food preferences of Premier Chou En-lai.

Duck, Turkey and game such as Partridges, Quails, etc. Ham and Pork, when served should be minced."[38] The above advisory flew in the face of the subsequent one which said that "mutton dishes such as Kabab and meat balls in Indian style may be served". The befuddled President's Household, however, catered for both as an abundant precaution.

The Premier's preference for special Indian coffee was specifically noted, as was the bar on serving the "not much liked" Indian tea. The direction that "Chinese 'Lu cha' green tea" should "invariably be served",[39] persuaded the President's Secretariat to stock it in adequate quantities. The advisory also ironically contained under the item "Food," the need to compulsorily offer "'India' cigarettes" on all occasions. Special orders were consequently placed on The Imperial Tobacco Company for despatching consignments to their agents at various places where the Premier was expected to visit.[40] With regard to the "Lodging & Furnishings", the Premier's particular liking for "roses and tube-roses" was indicated which were specially ordered by the President's Secretariat.[41]

In the "Entertainment" preference section, it was stated that "Chou-En-Lai has indicated that he would very much like to see modern and classical Indian dancing ballet and drama and meet Indian artistes both of the stage and screen."[42] Arrangements were also made to stage a cultural show for him. It was communicated that as "Presents" they would like "Indian made Equipment and Toys for Nurseries such as 'Kay Bee' Education Art Equipment."[43]

The detailed advisory sent the President's Secretariat scurrying for procuring the various items required to prepare the Premier's preferred dishes and hone their skills at cooking them. Since it was in the winter month of November that he arrived, the availability of seafood being more than in the summer, the kitchen staff did not have to spend much time surveying the various markets to buy what the Premier preferred to eat. Shri Abdul Majid, who joined as Junior Butler on June 18, 1957 and retired as Head Butler on May 31, 1993 recalled that the cooks in the Kitchen of Rashtrapati Bhavan were specifically informed of the preferences and several of them had refined their culinary skills before the Premier came to live in the 'Abode under the Dome'.[44]

Premier Chou En-lai's schedule during this visit was more hectic than his previous one. On November 29, the President of India hosted a lunch for the Chinese Premier in the Mughal Gardens at 1.15 in the afternoon under the pleasant November sun. He later visited both Houses of Parliament before attending a reception of the India-China Friendship Association. That evening, the Chinese Premier was the Guest of Honour at a banquet hosted at the Ashoka Hotel by the Indian Prime Minister.

During this visit too, a Civic Reception was organised for the Premier. The venue, this time, was New Delhi's more spacious Ramlila Grounds, in the heart of the capital. At the reception, more than 100,000 people congregated to hear him. The entire area was lit for the event and decorated with more than 40,000 multi-coloured light bulbs. Nearly 5,000 Indian and Chinese flags fluttered overhead in the evening breeze imparting a festive look to the venue.

At the reception, both the leaders spoke about the importance of strengthening bilateral relations and with other Afro-Asian countries. The gaiety of the evening was, however, slightly marred by a low-intensity bomb that went off on the ground. The Indian Prime Minister, who was standing near the microphone when the bomb exploded, appealed for calm and diffused the situation, which could have otherwise resulted in a stampede. As the incident unfolded, Premier Chou En-lai sat stoically behind his Indian counterpart.

From December 1, 1956, the Chinese Premier travelled to various cities in the country in the Indian President's aircraft, "Raja Humsa".[45] He visited Poona, Bombay, Madras and West Bengal. At every stop, the Premier was met by cheering crowds. On December 10, the Chinese Premier, dressed in a black tunic, boarded an Indian Airlines Skymaster from Dum Dum Airport in Calcutta, for Burma. The Chief Minister of Bengal and other dignitaries bade him farewell. After climbing the stairs of the plane, at the doorway, Premier Chou En-lai turned back and looked out over the crowd of politicians and pressmen who were assembled on the tarmac and said "Namaste" several times, to the cheers and applause of the people.[46]

The 1956 / 1957 Visit

By Christmas Eve, arrangements were already underway for Premier Chou En-lai's second visit of 1956. Intimation had arrived on December 24, through a letter addressed Lieutenant Colonel M Ghufran, the Deputy Military Secretary to the President (DMSP) from the MEA requesting accommodation for the Premier and his 30-member entourage for two days, beginning December 30, 1956.

At 12.40 pm, on December 30, the Chinese Premier's plane landed at Palam Airport. Following a ceremonial welcome, the Premier was driven to Rashtrapati Bhavan in a black Cadillac, while his entourage travelled behind in a Packard, a Plymouth and other cars sent by the President's Secretariat.

Premier Chou En-lai stayed in the Dwarka Suite when he was in Delhi. Members of his rather large entourage were accommodated in various suites of Rashtrapati Bhavan's Guest Wing. Marshal Ho Lung, the Vice Premier, stayed in the Nalanda Suite. Chang Yen, Deputy Director of the Premier's Office of the State Council and Pu Shou-chang, Secretary of the Premier's Office of the State Council stayed in the Tagore Suite. Since accommodation was limited, 14 members of the entourage shared seven rooms in Rashtrapati Bhavan, while eight members of the press were accommodated at the Ashoka Hotel.

The President's Secretariat had also made several special arrangements for the visit. As it was informed that Premier Chou

(Seated, L-R): Premier Chou En-lai, President Dr Prasad and Foreign Minister of China, Chen Yi, at Rashtrapati Bhavan in April 1960. Credit: PC

En-lai would be working late during his stay, a special request was made by the DMSP, Lieutenant Colonel M Ghufran, to the Director General of Post and Telegraphs to ensure that the Rashtrapati Bhavan Post Office remained open from 12 noon to 10.00 pm on December 30, 1956 and from 7.00 am to 1.30 pm on January 1, 1957. The Director General was requested to facilitate prompt receipt, dispatch and delivery of letters, parcels, telegrams etc. Memos were issued, barring staff from peeping out of office windows as dignitaries came or went, and to maintain silence until the guests left. Restrictions were also imposed on the entry of visitors to Rashtrapati Bhavan during the stay of the Chinese delegation. This led to the closing of the Rashtrapati Bhavan museum to the public from December 30–31.

Additional vehicles were also arranged for the use of the Chinese delegation. Eight special taxis were hired from Pearey Lal Transport Private Ltd. in Janpath and placed at their disposal. They were positioned on standby in the President's Garage for the duration of the Premier's stay. Equal attention was paid to the attire of the drivers. When some drivers had been found wanting in maintaining the required standard of the uniform they wore, a stern memo was issued to the Manager of the company. The visit of the Chinese

Premier Chou En-lai (left) with His Holiness the Dalai Lama (extreme right), in January 1957. Credit: PD
(Photo Division's documents indicate that the photo was taken on January 1, 1957. No other source could, however, be located confirming such a meeting.)

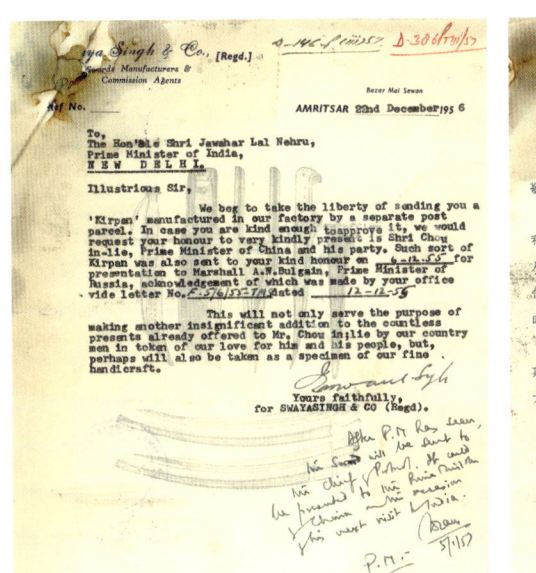
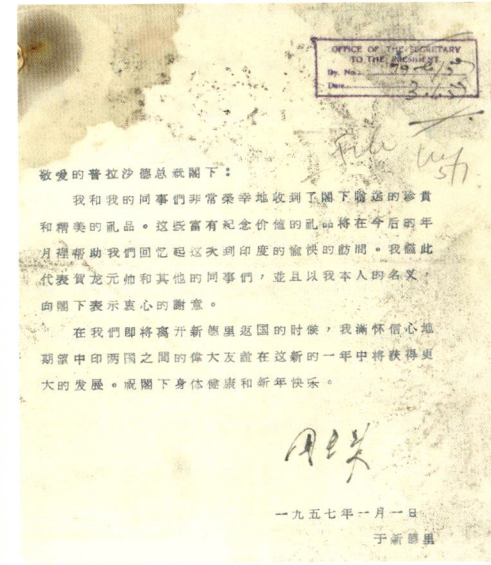
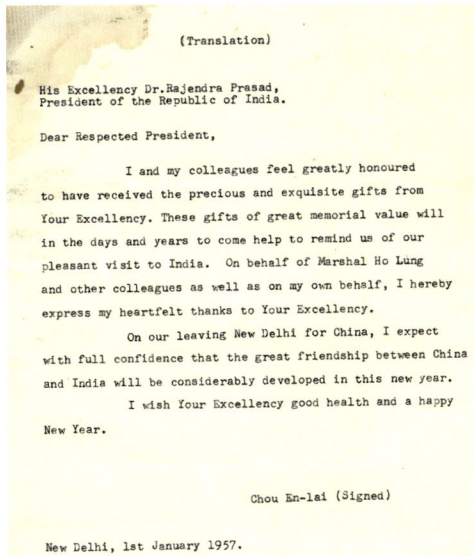

Special request to present a 'Kirpan' to Premier Chou En-lai.

Letter of thanks in Mandarin from Premier Chou En-lai to President Prasad and its translation.

Premier had also generated much interest among the public in the country. It emboldened an admirer of the Chinese Premier to send him a special gift. It came with a rather interesting letter dated December 22, 1956, addressed to the Prime Minister. The sender was from a sword manufacturing company called Swaya Singh & Co. in Amritsar. In the letter, he stated that they were taking the "liberty of sending a *kirpan*"[47] manufactured by the company to be presented to "Shri Chouin-lie[48] [sic], Prime Minister of China and his party." The letter also added that a similar *kirpan* was sent to the Prime Minister for presentation to "Marshall AN Bulgain [sic], Prime Minister of Russia."[49]

The *kirpan*, Swaya Singh said, would be "another insignificant [sic] addition to the countless presents already offered" to the Chinese Premier as a "token of our love for him and his people" and would also be evidence of the "specimen of our fine handicraft."[50] NK Seshan, Private Secretary to the Prime Minister, recorded on a small slip and sent the letter to the COP. On the slip, it was noted that the Prime Minister had seen and that he had desired that it be sent to the COP. The *kirpan* was thereafter presented to the Prime Minister of China and it was duly recorded by the DMSP on January 25, 1957.

On the night of December 30, 1957, the Chinese delegation left Rashtrapati Bhavan for Nangal. Two three-ton Lorries, one Fargo Lorry and one Fargo van were deployed at the South Court to transport the luggage of the Chinese delegation. AsDC personally ensured that transport vehicles arrived on time. The Transport Superintendent supervised the loading of the Chinese Premier's luggage into the Lorries. Guests got into the waiting open Cadillac, Packard and Plymouth from the President's Garage which drove them to New Delhi Railway Station.

As they usually do when delegations leave Rashtrapati Bhavan, select Personal Staff of the President had lined up in their frock coats, replete with sashes and aiguillettes with gleaming swords hanging at their sides. They were also there to receive Premier Chou En-lai and his entourage when they returned from Nangal. The Chinese delegation left for Patna by air, at 1.30 that afternoon.

The Chinese Premier was evidently pleased with the presents he received from the President that he wrote a letter on January 1, 1957, and sent it along with an English translation. In it, he expressed his "heartfelt" thanks for the gifts and also wished the President good health and a Happy New Year.

The 1960 Visit

Premier Chou En-lai returned to India three years later on another invitation from Prime Minister Nehru. It was sent through the Indian Ambassador to China, Gopalapuram Parthasarathy. The Chinese Premier accepted the invitation but cautioned that he would be travelling to Nepal from India and would also have a large party with him and that this would mean that they would have an equally large amount of luggage. Nevertheless, the Premier wrote that he would be happy to stay in India for seven days.[51]

The visit, however, came during troubled times. The public opinion had become unfavourable towards China. Just days before the Chinese Premier arrived in India, a crowd of nearly 5,000 marched to the gates of Prime Minister Nehru's home, protesting against the visit.

As during the previous visits, Premier Chou En-lai and his delegation arrived in Delhi in an Indian aircraft. He came by an Indian Air Force Viscount on April 19, 1960 at 5.00 pm. The aircraft was escorted by eight Vampire jets of the Indian Air Force. Rashtrapati

Bhavan had, by 4.30 pm, dispatched a motorcade comprising of an open Cadillac, a green Cadillac, a DeSoto and four station wagons, a Fargo Lorry and a van, for the visiting delegation.

The plane carrying Premier Chou En-lai touched down at Palam Airport at 5.00 pm, with the golden rays of the evening sun glimmering on the metal body of the plane. An anxious Prime Minister and select members of the Indian Cabinet were present to welcome the Premier and his delegation. The Premier stepped out of the aircraft wearing a light grey tunic and matching trousers, smiling thinly at those present to receive him. Shaking hands with the Prime Minister, he stated: "Both of us need peace. Both of us need friends."[52] President, Dr Rajendra Prasad had also sent a bouquet of flowers welcoming Premier Chou En-lai.

At the airport, both the leaders made their customary speeches. Prime Minister Nehru spoke in Hindi and Premier Chou En-lai in Mandarin. Though an open Cadillac was sent for the use of the Chinese Premier, Prime Minister Nehru and Premier Chou En-lai, chose to travel in a closed Cadillac instead for security reasons. In view of the tense atmosphere and the prevailing anti-Chinese

sentiment in the capital, the motorcade was also rerouted avoiding crowds, busy roads and junctions.

When the Premier arrived at Rashtrapati Bhavan, he was received by the MSP, who introduced the Premier to the Personal Staff assigned to him and his entourage for the duration of their stay. The guests were then escorted to their suites. Premier Chou En-lai's entourage, this time comprised 37 members including Ministers, officials and members of the Chinese State Press. Interestingly, no military advisor was part of the Chinese delegation. Following the usual practise, as the head of the delegation, the Premier stayed in the Dwarka Suite. A total of 18 guests stayed at Rashtrapati Bhavan and the suites/rooms were earmarked for them according to their seniority.

The following day, Premier Chou En-lai called on the President in his Study at 10.00 am. After the call, he held talks with the Indian Prime Minister, but the tone and tenor of the discussions between the two leaders were different this time. While the Chinese Premier Chou En-lai tried to downplay the differences between the two nations as a temporary difference in opinion,[53] Prime Minister Nehru believed that the differences were serious and a misfortune for the entire world.[54]

The writing on the wall was, however, unmistakable. The signs were ominous. All evidence pointed to the widening rift between

Letter from Premier Chou En-lai to Prime Minister Nehru confirming his visit to India in 1960.

Communication of Premier Chou En-lai's travel plans of 1960.

the two nations. The atmosphere was charged. In view of this, the security officials carefully restricted the movement of the Chinese Premier within the city and a closed black car was earmarked for his travel. The security for the Premier was strengthened to a formidable level to create a buffer between him and the public. A lot had obviously changed since his first visit in 1954. The Indian establishment nevertheless adhered to protocol in the way it dealt with the Chinese delegation.

On the evening of April 20, 1960, a grand State Banquet was held at 8.30 in honour of the Chinese Premier in Rashtrapati Bhavan's Banquet Hall. It was hosted by Pandit Nehru and attended by 110 guests, who included select Cabinet Ministers, high officials from both India and China and diplomats from countries that recognised Peking (Beijing). For the first time, All India Radio was permitted to install microphones in the Banquet Hall and the addresses of the two leaders were broadcast live to the nation.

There were, however, hints in the banquet speeches that India-China relations were under strain. In his toast to Premier Chou En-lai, Prime Minister Nehru said as much: "We are meeting here today to do honour to the Prime Minister of China who is our respected guest not only in his individual capacity, but also as the representative of a great nation.... We meet here at a difficult and crucial moment in the world's history and in our own relations."[55] However, he assured his Chinese counterpart and said, "We shall endeavour to do our utmost so that our efforts may lead to success and to the maintenance of peace with dignity and self-respect of both our great nations."[56]

Premier Chou En-lai replied in a similar tone. After thanking the Indian establishment for its efforts, he said, "this should not, nor can it, shake the foundation of the long standing friendship between our two peoples... I am deeply convinced that the profound friendship between our two peoples is unshakable."[57]

On the next day, the President hosted a lunch at Rashtrapati Bhavan, in honour of the Chinese Premier. The arrangements for the President's lunch were, as usual, grand. Flowers spilt out of pots and vases along the Grand Open Staircase in the Ashok Hall and the Banquet Hall. Fountains spouted streams of water in the Forecourt of Rashtrapati Bhavan, as the guests drove up through the South Sunken Road and South Court. The Band of the 3rd Guards, in position in the Band Gallery of the Banquet Hall was, however, instructed to only play light music.[58] On the following day of April 22, Vice President Dr Radhakrishnan hosted another lunch in honour of the Chinese Premier at his residence, 2 Maulana Azad Road. A third lunch was hosted by Jawaharlal Nehru at his residence, Teen Murti Bhavan, on the next day.

Premier Chou En-lai's schedule during this visit was, however, relatively light. There was only one special event; a dance recital organised by All India Radio, that was held in the Ashok Hall of Rashtrapati Bhavan. This time the 'At Home', was hosted by the Minister of Home Affairs in Rashtrapati Bhavan's Mughal Gardens on April 25.

Over the next few days, the leaders of both countries engaged in intense talks that lasted for many hours. They did not, however, prove to be constructive and it was reported that most of them ended in deadlocks.[59] Eventually, a joint communiqué was issued by both the Prime Ministers declaring that the talks had been inconclusive. The Chinese Premier was scheduled to leave on the next day.

On the eve of his departure, Premier Chou En-lai held a press conference that began at 10.45 pm on April 26, in the Grey Dining Room of Rashtrapati Bhavan. It was to be a conference that would hold the record of being among the longest, if not the longest ever held in Rashtrapati Bhavan. The conference concluded only at 1.00 am on the next day.

The press conference was attended by more than 150 correspondents from various countries. Before answering questions, the Chinese Premier announced that he would read out a statement and said, "I would be willing to listen to any questions raised by any of you and I would like to answer all that I could answer. And if you are not very tired, it does not matter if our Conference lasts rather a long time."[60]

He went on to add that they have prepared "their note papers" so that the questions and answers of the conference will not only appear in Indian papers and said, "will also be issued by our New China News Agency and all the answers today will be published in our papers."[61] He also offered to send an English magazine in China called the *Peking Review* which he said would have a full text of the interview.

Further, he invited the press correspondents to leave their addresses with the Chinese team, if they so wished to receive a copy of the *Peking Review*. He went on to claim that the Chinese too have freedom of press and said, "So let us have this gentleman's agreement to show our freedom of press."[62] After this announcement, he read out a written statement which described the relationship between the two countries in positive terms.

The statement, however, sought to communicate the impression that the disputes between the two countries could be settled amicably. Towards the end of his statement, the Chinese Premier strived to convey that even the boundary question and the other contentious disputes would not endanger peace and good-relations between the two countries. He said, "The Chinese Government holds that Sino-Indian friendship is of extremely great significance between the 1,000 million people of the two countries and to the Asian and world peace. This friendship should not be, nor can it be, jeopardised because of the temporary lack of settlement of Sino-Indian boundary question."[63]

In the last paragraph of his statement, he said that the Chinese Government "has unshakable confidence in a settlement of the Sino-Indian boundary question and the strengthening of the friendship between the two countries, and that it will exert unremitting the efforts for this end."[64] He went on to add that he has "invited Prime Minister Nehru to visit China at a time convenient to him."[65]

Towards the end of the conference, the Premier's replies reflected certain optimism. When a press correspondent asked, "Did the Prime Ministers consider what would follow if the officials did not agree on the outstanding issues any more than did the Prime Ministers,"[66] Premier Chou En-lai replied that he did not like to take a "pessimistic attitude because he has confidence in the friendship between China and India...if necessary, he himself or his colleagues may come again for the sake of enhancing friendship between the two great nations."[67] As subsequent events would testify, his professions of optimism bore an inverse correlation with the unfolding reality.

The visiting dignitary departed India for Kathmandu at 10 minutes past 8 on the morning of April 26, 1960. Unlike in the past, it was two Chinese Ilyushin aircraft that ferried the Premier and his entourage to Nepal. The aircraft had in fact been conducting trial flights in Indian airspace since the beginning of April.

After the Chinese Premier had departed, when Pandit Nehru was asked about the former's press conference of the previous night, he avoided making any comments, stating that he had not yet read the whole proceedings of the press conference. *The Times of India* stated that in the press conference, the Chinese Premier was "oozing optimism and seemed to think that though no agreement has been reached in the present talks, in the future India would and should show a spirit of accommodation on the western (Ladakh) sector in return for the Chinese spirit of accommodation on the eastern (McMahon line) sector."[68] When Pandit Nehru was asked to share his opinion on this, he blatantly said, "There is no question of barter in these matters."[69]

Addressing the Lok Sabha on the same day, Pandit Nehru said, "There was no meeting ground at all."[70] He also said that there was little probability of him visiting China in response to the invitation that had been announced by the Chinese Premier. On a question raised in the Parliament about the possibility of using force, Pandit Nehru retorted, "You either have war or something called talks or steps. You cannot have both."[71]

Despite the Chinese declarations of friendship, war broke out between the two countries, a little over two years after the visit of Premier Chou En-Lai.

Chou En-lai served as his country's Premier for 27 years from October 1949 until he died of cancer on January 8, 1976. He was 77.

Notes

[1] Richard Nixon, Leaders: *Profiles and Reminiscences of Men Who Have Shaped the Modern World* (New York: Warner Books Edition, 1982), p. 229.

[2] "Chinese Indian Relations," *The Times* (London), June 26, 1954, p. 6.

[3] "Memorable Scenes at Palam Airport," *The Hindustan Times* (New Delhi), June 26, 1954, p. 9.

[4] "Mr Chou's Visit Delayed: Arriving Tomorrow," *The Times of India* (New Delhi), June 24, 1954, p. 1.

[5] "Chou's Present to Gazdar," *The Hindustan Times* (New Delhi), June 26, 1954, p. 9.

[6] New China is a 1950 Soviet documentary film directed by Sergei Gerasimov. It entered the 1951 Cannes Film Festival.

[7] "India's Air Pilots," p. 6.

[8] Ibid.

[9] "Mr. Chou En-Lai in Delhi," *The Hindu* (New Delhi), June 26, 1954, p. 6.

[10] Ibid.

[11] "Nehru and Chou Open Secret Talk," *The New York Times*, June 26, 1954, p. 1.

[12] "Mr. Chou En-lai in Delhi," *The Hindu* (New Delhi), June 26, 1954, p. 6.

[13] Ibid.

[14] As all records of the visit were not traceable, the exact size of the delegation could not be ascertained. The suites/rooms in which the dignitaries stayed also could not be ascertained for this reason.

[15] "Mr. Chou En-Lai in Delhi", *The Hindu* (New Delhi), June 26, 1954, p. 6.

[16] "President's Reception," *The Hindu* (New Delhi), June 26, 1954, p. 6.

[17] "Villagers' offerings to Chou En-Lai," *The Hindustan Times Weekly* (New Delhi), June 27, 1954, p. 1.

[18] Ibid., p. 7.

[19] Ibid.

[20] "Rousing reception to Mr. Chou planned," *The Times of India* (New Delhi), June 25, 1954, p. 7.

[21] "Mr. Chou En-lai in Delhi," *The Hindu* (New Delhi), June 26, 1954, p. 8.

[22] "Mr. Chou thanks India for armistice in Korea," *The Times of India* (New Delhi), June 28, 1954, p. 5.

23 "China's ties with India," *The Hindu* (New Delhi), June 28, 1954, p. 1.

24 "Delhi's Reception to Mr Chou," *The Times of India* (New Delhi), June 28, 1954, p. 7.

25 "Cooperation in Asia", *The Times* (London), June 28, 1954, p. 8.

26 "Chou En-lai on talks with Nehru," *The Hindu* (New Delhi), June 28, 1954, p. 1.

27 "Exchange of Souvenirs," *The Hindustan Times* (New Delhi), June 29, 1954, p. 1.

28 "Consolidation of Peace," *The Hindu* (New Delhi), June 29, 1954, p. 4.

29 "Exchange of Souvenirs," p. 1

30 "Prime Minister to Take Rest," *The Times of India* (New Delhi), June 29, 1954, p. 7.

31 "Chou and Nehru open India talks," *The New York Times*, November 29, 1956, p. 1.

32 Ibid.

33 Ibid., p. 24.

34 Ibid.

35 "Mr. Chou En-Lai in Delhi," *The Times* (London), November 29, 1956, p. 10.

36 Records, President's Secretariat, Rashtrapati Bhavan, File no. 266.

37 Ibid.

38 Ibid.

39 Ibid.

40 Ibid.

41 Ibid.

42 Ibid.

43 Ibid.

44 Abdul Majid (2015), personal interview by Thomas Mathew, New Delhi, June 15, 2015.

45 "Closer Sino-Indian Ties Called For," *The Times of India* (New Delhi), December 2, 1956, p. 1.

46 "Mr. Chou En-lai's Parting Message to People," *The Times of India* (New Delhi), December 11, 1956, p. 1.

47 A *Kirpan* is a small sword or dagger which is carried by Sikh Men as part of their religious faith.

48 The name of the Chinese Premier has been quoted exactly as it is in the letter. Evidently, the sender of the letter had again used another word "insignificant" perhaps wanting to use the word "significant".

49 Records, President's Secretariat, Rashtrapati Bhavan, File No. 268-A.

50 Ibid.

51 Records, President's Secretariat, File No. 15(4)/60.

52 "Delhi's subdued welcome to Chou," *The Statesman* (New Delhi), April 20, 1960, p. 1.

53 "Reciprocal acceptance of 'Present Actualities,'" *The Times of India*, (New Delhi), April 26, 1960, p. 1.

54 "Speeches at State Banquet to Chou," *The Statesman* (New Delhi), April 21, 1960, p. 10.

55 Ibid.

56 Ibid.

57 Ibid.

58 Records, President's Secretariat, File No. 15(4)/60.

59 "Tension likely to be reduced," *The Times of India* (New Delhi), April 27, 1960, p. 9.

60 Record, President's Secretariat, File No. 15 (4)/60.

61 Ibid.

62 Ibid.

63 Ibid.

64 Ibid.

65 Ibid.

66 Ibid.

67 Ibid.

68 Tension likely to be reduced," p. 9.

69 Ibid.

70 Paul Grimes, "Chou 'Hard Rock' Nehru declares," *The New York Times*, April 27, 1960, p. 5.

71 Ibid.

As the spring of 1964 waned, the President of Iraq, Abdul Salam Mohammad Arif landed in Delhi on a one-week State Visit from March 26 to April 1. This was President Arif's first visit to India and he was to stay in Rashtrapati Bhavan for the three days he was spending in Delhi.

Born on March 21, 1921, Abdul Salam Mohammad Arif came from a family of merchants. After graduating from military college, he joined the Iraqi Army, and later served as a "Commander in the Arab–Israeli war of 1948."[1]

Arif rose to political prominence when King Faisal II was ousted from power in 1958. Arif had played a crucial role, along with Abdul Karim Kassem in deposing the Hashemite King. Soon, a new Government was formed under Kassem and Arif was appointed Deputy Prime Minister in the new dispensation. He was also given the post of Minister of Interior and Commander-in-Chief of the military, but was relieved of these posts after he fell out with Kassem. Now as his country's Ambassador to West Germany, a discontented Arif engineered a coup against Kassem. The plan was unsuccessful[2] and Arif was sentenced to death. Destiny, however, stepped in and in 1961, Kassem pardoned Arif. Two years later, in 1963, Arif staged yet another coup, this time with the support of the Ba'ath Party. This attempt was successful and Arif emerged as the President of Iraq.

Visit of

H.E. Field Marshal Abdul Salam Mohammad Arif

President of Iraq

A fervent supporter of the Palestinian cause, President Arif's policy was in alignment with India's. Not only did India maintain close relations with the Arab countries but India and Iraq also shared close economic and cultural ties that dated back many centuries. President Arif's visit to India in 1964, therefore, was seen as another step towards strengthening India–Iraq bilateral relations.

President Arif's visit to India was not a result of the extensive consultations that usually precede the foreign visit of a Head of State. The Iraqi President was only scheduled to visit Pakistan in March 1964 and a visit to India was not on the cards. Delhi extended an invitation only after President Arif conveyed on December 12, 1963, that he hoped his proposed visit to Pakistan would not pave the way for any misunderstanding with "friendly India."[3]

The invitation was accepted by President Arif. Soon, another issue emerged relating to the duration of the stay of the Iraqi President in both countries. There was frenetic communication between the Indian Embassy in Baghdad and the Foreign Office in New Delhi. The Ministry of External Affairs (MEA) worked "to ensure that his visit to India is not of lesser duration."[4]

President Arif laid the issue to rest by deciding to spend equal number of days in both countries. Later, yet another matter relating to the aircraft that the Iraqi President would use to arrive in India from Pakistan became a bone of contention. The Pakistani

Facing page:
President Mohammad Arif (left) with
President Dr Radhakrishnan
at Rashtrapati Bhavan in
March 1964. Credit: PC

President, Ayub Khan, had offered to fly President Arif to Delhi in his private Viscount aircraft.

The use of a Pakistani aircraft did not find favour with the MEA and an offer was made to send an Indian Air Force Constellation BG 575 to fly President Arif to India. The Foreign Office quoted the precedent of Pakistan following such a practice. It said that Pakistan had "followed the practice of sending their own plane to bring dignitaries from India, for example in taking Mrs Kennedy from New Delhi to Lahore."[5]

This issue was, however, settled after the Iraqi Ambassador communicated that President Arif had already accepted President Ayub Khan's offer and that it would be embarrassing for him to turn it down at this stage.[6] India acquiesced and also agreed to permit Pakistani flight PK109 to ferry the Iraqi entourage to Delhi.

The Iraqi President landed at Palam Airport on March 26, at 12.00 noon to a 21-gun salute. He had flown to India aboard a Pakistani aircraft, Viscount J751. His 22 member entourage comprising of Iraqi Foreign Minister, SA Hamid; two other Ministers, the Army Commander, senior officials, press crew and personal staff came in another Pakistani aircraft.[7]

Dressed in a black suit, President Arif alighted from the aircraft to a full ceremonial welcome. The President of India, Dr Sarvepalli Radhakrishnan; Union Minister without portfolio, Lal Bahadur Shastri; Minister of State of the MEA, Lakshmi Menon and the Mayor of Delhi, Nuruddin Ahmed were at the airport to receive the visiting Head of State.[8]

President Arif was then presented an Inter-Services Guard of Honour. This was followed by the customary address of both the Presidents. President Dr Radhakrishnan welcomed his Iraqi counterpart referring to the age-old ties between the two countries, and expressed the hope that the two would "become closer in the years to come."[9] He complimented the Iraqi President on his role during the Arab League Summit, especially for his declaration at the Summit that "Iraq would not resort to military force in settling problems."[10]

Replying to the Indian President, President Arif thanked him for the warm reception. In what would seem like an acknowledgement of President Dr Radhakrishnan's speech on the old ties the nations' shared, he added that Baghdad "was a 'haven of learned men of all countries' during the Abbasside Caliphate and Indian physicians were quite prominent then."[11] The Iraqi President also expressed his optimism on the future of Indo-Iraq relations and said that the relationship between the two nations would become stronger.[12]

After the reception at the airport, the visiting dignitaries drove to Rashtrapati Bhavan in a motorcade of cars mainly drawn from the President's Garage. A huge crowd had gathered all along the ceremonial route to catch a glimpse of the visiting leader. It was especially thick near Rajpath. As the motorcade approached Vijay

(Seated, L-R): President Arif with President Dr Radhakrishnan at Rashtrapati Bhavan in March 1964. Credit: PC

President Arif delivering banquet speech at Rashtrapati Bhavan. Seated opposite is President Dr Radhakrishnan (in white turban). (March 1964). Credit: PC

Chowk, the President's Bodyguard (PBG) escorted it through the majestic gates of Rashtrapati Bhavan. They arrived at the South Court and were welcomed by the officers of the President's Secretariat and escorted to their accommodation. In keeping with protocol, the Iraqi President stayed in the regal Dwarka Suite.

After having rested for a while, President Arif called on the Indian President at 4.30 pm in his Study at Rashtrapati Bhavan. He then visited Mahatma Gandhi's *samadhi* at *Rajghat* where he paid his respects.

Later in the evening, at 8.30, President Dr Radhakrishnan hosted a State Banquet at Rashtrapati Bhavan in honour of the Iraqi President. Special arrangements were made as usual for the event. The Ashok Hall, the Grand Open Staircase and the Guest Wing corridors were specially decorated for the banquet.

At the appointed time, the President of India and the President of Iraq arrived at the Ashok Hall and stood at attention under the arch on the southern side. The band played the national anthem of both the nations, after which the guests were introduced to the two Presidents. A lavish banquet followed.

After the last course of the dinner was served, President Dr Radhakrishnan proposed a toast to the visiting President. In his speech, the President referred to the common cultural and spiritual ties that bound the two nations. He complimented President Arif on his efforts towards effectuating peace and democracy in his country, and said, "The way in which you have dealt with the problems of the Kurds gives us hope that

you will be able to consolidate your country soon."[13] He further complimented the visiting President and remarked: "It is a matter of great gratification to us that you Mr President are doing everything in your power to work for this kind of peace in the world, friendship among nations and you have exhorted all your friends to avoid resort [sic] to violence."[14] Concluding his speech, the President proposed a toast to the "health of the President of Iraq, Field Marshal Arif."[15]

In his short reply, President Arif acknowledged the common ties that both the countries shared and opined that the bonds extended beyond commercial practices and involved "traffic in ideas."[16] He thanked the "Government and the people of India for the warm welcome accorded to him."[17] The elaborate dinner was followed by a dance and music programme, which showcased India's ancient dance forms reflecting the culture and ethos of the nation.

On the morning of the next day, March 27, 1964, President Arif visited the National Physical Laboratory and the Indian Agricultural Research Institute. Later in the afternoon, he attended the *dhuhr*[18] prayers at the Jama Masjid, the largest Mosque in India built in the 17th century by the Mughal Emperor Shah Jahan, where more than 5,000 devotees had congregated for prayers. Thereafter, he returned to Rashtrapati Bhavan and had lunch in his suite.

After a few hours of rest, at 3.45 pm, President Arif visited the *dargah*[19] at Hazrat Nizamuddin, which is one of the world's most renowned shrines. The head priest, Khwaja Pir Zamin Nizami, welcomed the Iraqi President and presented him a replica of the holy shrine. Speaking in Arabic, the head priest in his welcome address recalled Hazrat Nizamuddin's ancestral links with Iraq and the spiritual bonds that the two countries shared.[20] Responding to the cordial welcome, President Arif acknowledged that the "Nizamuddin Aulia was as much respected in his country as in India."[21]

Later that evening at 6.00, a grand Civic Reception was held at the *Diwan-i-Khas*, Red Fort in honour of the Iraqi President. Lal Bahadur Shastri, many Parliamentarians and members of the diplomatic corps amongst others attended the reception. The event commenced with the Mayor of Delhi Nuruddin Ahmed welcoming the visiting President and urging him to convey the "warm greetings and good wishes of the Indian people to the people of Iraq."[22]

Speaking at the reception, the Iraqi President thanked the gathering for the warm reception that had been accorded to him. He spoke about the common cultural ties that bind both countries, and hoped that his visit would "achieve a broader cooperation" for the benefit of the international society.[23] Concluding his address he said, "Our two governments have a common policy based on peaceful co-existence and active contribution towards non-alignment and world peace."[24] The visiting President was presented an "ivory element bridge"[25] on the occasion. He concluded the day's events after attending a reception hosted for him at 7.30 pm by the Iraqi Ambassador.

The next day, March 28, President Arif visited the Okhla Industrial Estate and the National Museum in the morning. In the afternoon, at 12.30, he had a 30-minute meeting with Prime Minister Jawaharlal Nehru at his residence, Teen Murti Bhavan. The discussions mostly centred on the Kashmir issue. Pandit Nehru explained India's stand on the subject to dispel any misperception that the Iraqi leader may have formed during his visit to Pakistan. After the meeting President Arif attended a lunch hosted by Prime Minister Nehru at his residence in honour of the visiting dignitary. Lal Bahadur Shastri, other Cabinet Ministers including MC Chagla, Education Minister and the leader of the Indian delegation in United Nations Security Council on Kashmir, were amongst those who attended the lunch.

Later that evening, at 8.30, the Iraqi President hosted a dinner in honour of his Indian counterpart. The next morning at 9.00 after a ceremonial farewell at Palam Airport, he and his entourage emplaned for Agra on an Indian Air Force Super Constellation. Before reaching the airport, however, a message from the Iraqi President to the President of India was dictated to the wireless tower at Safdarjung Airport. In the message, he thanked President Dr Radhakrishnan for the "generosity and warm welcome" shown to them and said that "the tradition [al] and historic ties" between the two countries had created a "surer foundation" that would bring, he said, "progress and prosperity to our people and the promotion of peace among all nations."[26]

At Agra, the Iraqi President visited the Taj Mahal and Agra Fort and later left for Hyderabad in the afternoon. In Hyderabad, the Iraqi President visited several places including the Charminar, Salarjung Museum and the Mecca Masjid. The Osmania University at Hyderabad also conferred the Iraqi President an Honorary Degree.

The details of the conferment programme were finalised with the University by the Indian Embassy in Baghdad in advance. In a communication dated March 14, 1964, the Indian Embassy had informed the Foreign Office in New Delhi the measurements required to stitch the robe that the President would have to wear during the award ceremony.

MEA had proposed the conferment of an Honorary Doctorate on the Iraqi President and the University of Osmania was not the first choice. Since the visit of the Iraqi President had suddenly materialised, MEA was hard pressed for time to approach various universities and then decide on one to confer the honorary degree.

It had initially approached the Aligarh Muslim University, but the attempt failed. An anxious MEA immediately approached Osmania University, though it feared that it may not be "feasible" for them to organise it at such short notice. Rajasthan University was also approached as an alternative, to confer the degree on the Iraqi President."[27] However, before Rajasthan University could take a final decision, Osmania University relented and President Arif was conferred with the Honorary Doctorate.

The following day, March 30, President Arif travelled to Bangalore where he visited the Hindustan Aircraft and Hindustan Machine Tools, the Indian Telephone Industries and the Arts and Crafts

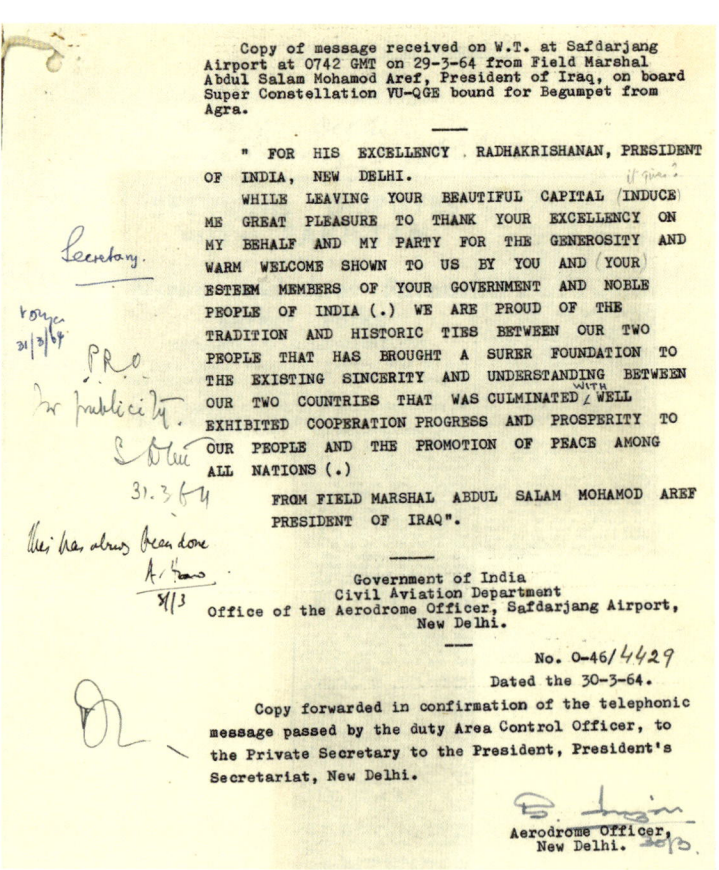

Message of thanks from President Arif to President Dr Radhakrishnan.

Emporium. The Bangalore leg of the journey had been specially scheduled to highlight the country's technical advancement and the visit to these renowned establishments served that goal.

After a night's halt in Bangalore, President Arif travelled to Poona the next morning on March 31, where he visited the National Defence Academy and had lunch with the cadets. At ten minutes to four in the late afternoon, the Iraqi President emplaned for Bombay, the final stopover in his weeklong visit to India. After arriving in Bombay, in the late hours of the evening, President Arif attended a reception hosted by the Indo-Arab Society in his honour. At the reception, Executive Vice President of the society, Dr Rafiq Zakaria, presented the Iraqi President with an exquisite silver salver.[28]

The next day the Iraqi President visited the Atomic Energy Establishment, his last engagement in India. After this visit, President Arif left Indian shores for home, on the afternoon of April 1 from Santa Cruz Airport, Bombay. The Vice President of India, Dr Zakir Hussain, Vijayalakshmi Pandit, sister of Prime Minister Nehru and former Governor of Maharashtra, and the Chief Minister of Bombay, VP Naik, amongst others, were present at the airport to bid farewell to the Iraqi leader. On behalf of the Government, Vijayalakshmi Pandit gifted a Kashmiri carpet to President Arif. He was also presented an "album of photographs" containing photos taken during his stay in Bombay.[29] The Ministers who accompanied him were presented with gifts in silver.

Before boarding the flight, President Arif sent a note to President Dr Radhakrishnan thanking him for having invited him to India. It read: "We feel that our visit has achieved benefits for the mutual interest between our countries the result of which may I proudly say shall be for the betterment of our people and all people of the world whom we wish all progress and prosperity."[30]

On the day of his departure, a joint communiqué was also released in New Delhi, signed by both Prime Minister Nehru and President Arif, which revealed "a wide area of agreement between India and Iraq on various subjects of mutual interest."[31] Hailed as a significant outcome of this visit, the communiqué covered commonality of views on a range of subjects pertaining to foreign policy issues, nuclear disarmament and non-alignment.[32] Importantly, it also stressed the need for direct bilateral discussions for resolving Indo-Pakistan disputes.[33]

The joint communiqué was remarkable for the expression of the Iraqi President's "gratification at the fact that India was the homeland of 50 million Muslims and millions of persons belonging to other faiths, who enjoyed the fullest freedom of religious faith and worship on a basis of complete equality."[34]

This visit of President Arif further deepened India-Iraq relations. After his return, Arif continued to be President for another two years until his death on April 13, 1966, in a helicopter crash. He was 45.

Notes

[1] Harris M. Lentz, *Heads of States and Governments: A Worldwide Encyclopaedia of Over 2,300 Leaders, 1945 through 1992* (London: Fitzroy Dearborn Publishers, 1995), p. 409.

[2] Ibid.

[3] Records, President's Secretariat, Rashtrapati Bhavan, File No. 15(11)/63.

[4] Ibid.

[5] Ibid.

[6] Ibid.

[7] "Arif Hopes for Closer Indo-Iraq Relations," *The Hindustan Times* (New Delhi), March 27, 1964, p. 4.

[8] "Welcome to Arif at Airport," *The Hindustan Times* (New Delhi), March 27, 1964, p. 1.

[9] "Arif Hopes for Closer Indo-Iraq Relations," p. 4.

[10] Ibid.

[11] "Welcome to Arif at Airport," p. 1.

[12] Ibid.

[13] Ministry of External Affairs (1995), Government of India, MEA Library, Foreign Affairs Records 1964, Volume X, accessed March 19, 2015 http://mealib.nic.in/?pdf2552?000

[14] Ibid.

[15] Ibid.

[16] Ibid.

[17] Ibid.

[18] The *dhuhr* or the "noon prayer" is the prayer offered after mid-day by Muslims.

[19] A *dargah* is an Islamic shrine built over the grave of a revered saint, often a Sufi.

[20] "Aref Assures India of 'Broader Co-operation,' " *The Times of India* (New Delhi), March 28, 1964, p. 8.

[21] Ibid.

[22] Ibid.

[23] Ministry of External Affairs (1995), Foreign Affairs Records 1964, Volume X.

[24] Ibid.

[25] "Aref Assures India of 'Broader Co-operation,' " p. 8.

[26] Records, President's Secretariat, File No. 15(11)/63.

[27] Ibid.

[28] "Aref Promises To Do His Bit," *The Times of India* (New Delhi), April 1, 1964, p. 1.

[29] "Kashmir Carpet Presented," *The Times of India* (New Delhi), April 2, 1964, p. 3.

[30] Records, President's Secretariat, File No. 15(11)/63.

[31] "Settling Disputes with Pakistan," *The Statesman* (New Delhi), April 2, 1964, p. 1.

[32] Records, President's Secretariat, File No. 15(11)/63.

[33] Ibid.

[34] Ibid.

On November 27, 1960, the newly wed royal couple, Prince Akihito and Princess Michiko of Japan arrived on their first State Visit to India. They stayed in India until December 6.

The visit was influenced by the close historic bonds shared by the two nations. These bonds predate India's independence and the threads of commonalties of the two nations were evident in many facets of their relations. For instance, the Japanese name for India – 'Tenjiku' – translates to 'Heavenly Abode,' signifying the embodiment of a special place for the nation in their culture that is inseparably linked to Buddhism.

Many instances bear evidence to the continuing and cordial relationship the two nations enjoy. The late 1940s and the 1950s provided some interesting evidence of it. Perhaps the best instance of it came when the children of Tokyo sent a request for a baby elephant and Prime Minister Nehru did not disappoint them. He dispatched one named 'Indira' in 1949 to them. Again, when Prime Minister Nehru visited Japan in 1957, he recalled to mind the love Japanese children have for pachyderms and he presented them two more baby elephants.

Economic cooperation between the two countries was also strong. Japan was amongst the first countries to make sizeable investments in India. It was in the context of such strong relations that the visit of the Crown Prince and Princess of Japan took place and assumed great importance as it exemplified the burgeoning relationship between the

Visits of
Crown Prince/H.M. Emperor Akihito
of Japan

two countries.

On his last trip to Japan in 1958, the President of India, Dr Rajendra Prasad, expressed the hope that the Japanese Emperor would someday entertain the idea of visiting India. Two years later, on April 12, 1960, President Dr Prasad sent the Emperor a formal letter extending a "most cordial invitation" to the Crown Prince and Princess to come to India on a State visit. In his reply dated September 14, 1960, Emperor Hirohito accepted the invitation. He informed the Indian President that his son Prince Akihito would travel to India representing him and that Princess Michiko would be accompanying the Prince.[1]

Born on December 23, 1933, Akihito, the 125th descendent of Emperor Jimmu, was the eldest son and fifth child of His Majesty Emperor Hirohito and Empress Nagako of Japan. As royal tradition demanded, Prince Akihito was separated from his parents and raised by tutors from the tender age of three.[2] He soon excelled in many fields. He was fond of music, became an expert cellist and an authority "on fish." A former tutor, Elizabeth Gray Vining in her 1952 book *Windows for the Crown Prince* opined that, "He has a better than average mind, clear, analytical, independent, with a turn for original thought. He is aware of his destiny; he accepts it soberly."[3] At 25, he became the first royal in his family to break the 2600-year-old Imperial Japanese tradition by

Facing page:
(L-R): Prince Akihito and
Princess Michiko with
President Dr Prasad at Rashtrapati Bhavan in
November 1960. Credit: PC

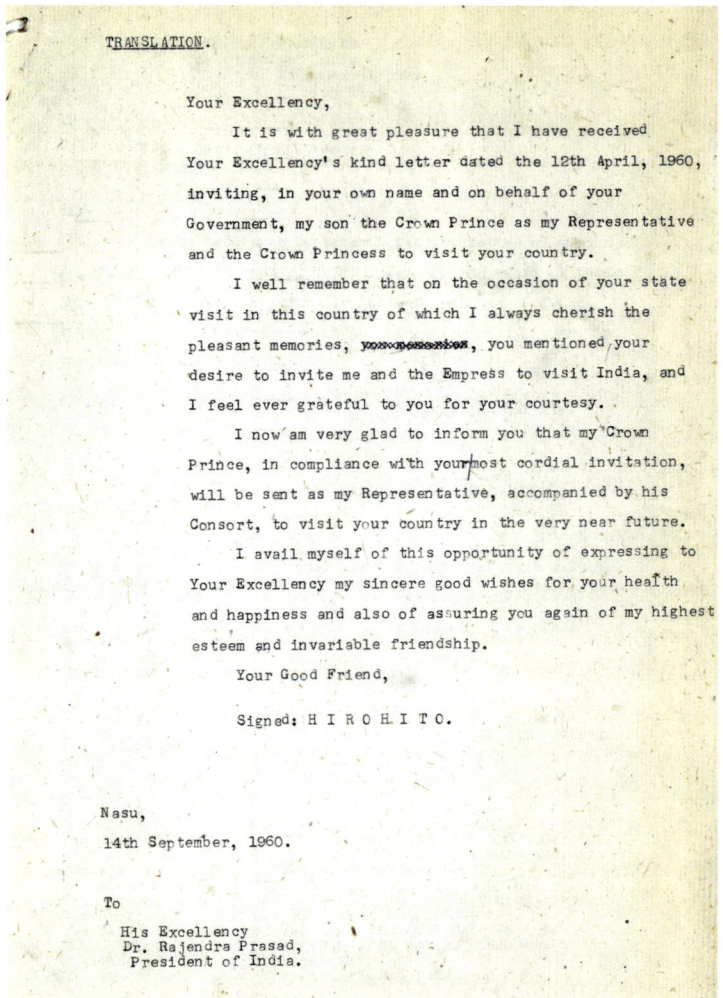

Your Excellency,

It is with great pleasure that I have received Your Excellency's kind letter dated the 12th April, 1960, inviting, in your own name and on behalf of your Government, my son the Crown Prince as my Representative and the Crown Princess to visit your country.

I well remember that on the occasion of your state visit in this country of which I always cherish the pleasant memories, xxxxxxxxxx, you mentioned your desire to invite me and the Empress to visit India, and I feel ever grateful to you for your courtesy.

I now am very glad to inform you that my Crown Prince, in compliance with your most cordial invitation, will be sent as my Representative, accompanied by his Consort, to visit your country in the very near future.

I avail myself of this opportunity of expressing to Your Excellency my sincere good wishes for your health and happiness and also of assuring you again of my highest esteem and invariable friendship.

Your Good Friend,

Signed: H I R O H I T O.

Nasu,
14th September, 1960.

To

His Excellency
Dr. Rajendra Prasad,
President of India.

Translation of letter from Emperor Hirohito to President Dr Prasad accepting his invitation.

marrying a commoner, Michiko Shoda, something that divided the opinion of the country between the traditionalists and the change-loving modernists.[4]

At 10.30 pm on November 27, 1960, a special Japan Airlines turbo-jetliner called "City of Osaka," flew in from Addis Ababa and touched down at Bombay's Santa Cruz Airport. It carried the Crown Prince, the Princess and an 11-member delegation.[5] The entourage included the Counsellor of Foreign Affairs, Yukihisa Tamura and the Princess's Chief Lady-in-Waiting, Sumiko Makino. The Crown Prince and Princess had been touring several countries since their wedding in April 1959 and their visit to India was part of this trip.

A large gathering of senior officials of the State Government received the Crown Prince and Princess at the airport. They included the Chief Secretary to the Government of Maharashtra, NT Mone; the Japanese Ambassador to India, N Nasu and his wife; the Japanese Consul-General in Bombay, T Yoshioka; the President of the Japanese Association, R Miyoke and the Vice President of the

Indo-Japanese Association, Murarji Vaidya.[6] Despite the lateness of the hour, there was a large gathering of onlookers that had gathered at the airport to catch a glimpse of the royal couple.

Prince Akihito and Princess Michiko emerged from the aircraft to a warm welcome. Prince Akihito looked dashing in his white summer suit and a straw hat, while his wife's stylish European dress complemented his elegant attire. After the reception ceremony at the airport, the royal couple were driven to Raj Bhavan where they stayed for the night.

The couple spent a quiet morning at Raj Bhavan the next day. Thereafter, they had lunch at the Japanese Consul-General's residence. Later, they visited the Aarey Milk Colony, where they were briefed on the working of milk plants and the "economics of dairy farming."[7] Prince Akihito, who was carrying two cameras, took "photographs of the buffaloes in the stables and of the scenery around the Colony."[8] The couple also planted an *Ashoka* sapling in the garden of the Aarey Guest House, which was located within the Colony's premises.[9] At 6.15 pm, the couple met with Japanese residents in Bombay at Kashmir House, the residence of the Japanese Consul-General.

The next day, the Prince and Princess visited Taraporewala Aquarium after which they emplaned for Delhi on the hour at 12 noon. From Alwar onwards, the "City of Osaka" was escorted by a flight formation of eight Indian Air Force jet fighters.[10] After a three-hour flight they landed at New Delhi's Palam Airport to the sound of a 21-gun salute. The President of India Dr Prasad, warmly received the Crown Prince and Princess on their arrival. They were also greeted at the airport by Vice President Dr S Radhakrishnan, Prime Minister Nehru, Cabinet Ministers, the Mayor of Delhi Sham Nath and several other important dignitaries. The Mayor of Delhi extended a traditional welcome by garlanding the royal couple and Japanese and Indian children presented bouquets to a smiling Princess.[11]

The Chief of Protocol (COP), MRA Baig then escorted the Crown Prince to the Saluting Base, where he was presented a Guard of Honour. After inspecting it, Prince Akihito was escorted to the special enclosure where select invitees were introduced to him by COP Baig.

In his address at the airport, President Dr Prasad welcomed the royal couple to India, and recalled the commonalities shared by both countries. He hailed Japan as an example of growth and development for India, and lauded its assistance to India in its development. He added that the visit was the "most auspicious and significant event in the history of Indo-Japanese relations."[12] In his reply, Prince Akihito, praised India as a place, "where one of the great civilizations of mankind originated," and expressed his immense pleasure to be in the country.[13]

After the reception, the royal couple drove to Rashtrapati Bhavan. The President of India and the Crown Prince sat in an open

(Seated, L-R): Prime Minister Nehru, Prince Akihito, Princess Michiko and President Dr Prasad at Rashtrapati Bhavan in November 1960. Credit: PC

Allotment of Rooms for Guests in Rashtrapati Bhavan
(29th November to 3rd December, 1960).

Name of Guests.	Rooms.	Phone 35321/Ex. Nos.
His Imperial Highness the Crown Prince of Japan.	Dwarka Suite	63 & 46
Her Imperial Highness the Crown Princess of Japan.	Nalanda Suite	54
Mr. Yukihisa Tamura, Counsellor of the Ministry of Foreign Affairs.	Bombay Bedroom	114
Mrs. Sumiko Makino, Chief Lady-in-waiting to HIH the Crown Princess.	Himalaya Suite	89 & 66
Mrs. Ken Harada, Specially attached to HIH the Crown Princess.	Dakshin Bedroom	152
Dr. Mitsumasa Hoshikawa, Physician of the Crown Prince's Household.	Pepsu Bedroom	109
Mr. Saneaki Ijuin, Chamberlain to HIH the Crown Prince.	Godavari Bedroom	104
Mr. Minoru Hamao, Chamberlain to HIH the Crown Prince.	Neelam Bedroom	202
Mrs. Eiko Nawa, Lady-in-waiting to HIH the Crown Prince.	Mysore Room	83
Mr. Kumesaku Inaba, Secretary of the Crown Prince's Household.	Tagore Suite	1 & 47
Miss Matsuyo Ishii, Assistant Secretary of the Crown Prince's Household		

Room Allocation Plan.

Cadillac, and, while the Princess and the Indian Prime Minister travelled in a separate car of the same make.[14] The royal couple's luggage was transported by a Fargo van while a Jeep and another Fargo Lorry carried the baggage of the entourage.

The streets were adorned with banners and colourful buntings and hundreds of people had gathered along the route to Rashtrapati Bhavan, cheering and welcoming the royal couple as the motorcade drove past. *The Hindustan Times* reported that several "villagers [had] come from long distances in bullock and camel carts" to cheer the Japanese couple and that the crowds were at their thickest in "Connaught Place."[15]

When the motorcade reached Vijay Chowk, it was received by the President's Bodyguard (PBG) and escorted to the Rashtrapati Bhavan in a grand ceremonial formation. On their arrival, they were received by the Military Secretary to the President (MSP) and the Personal Staff on duty was introduced to them. The royal couple was then escorted to the Guest Loggia where refreshments were served. Prince Akihito stayed in the regal Dwarka Suite, while Princess Michiko, in the exquisite Nalanda Suite. Members of the entourage were accommodated in other suites/ rooms, which included the Bombay Bedroom, the Himalaya Suite, the Dakshin Bedroom, the Pepsu Bedroom, the Godavari Bedroom, the Neelam Bedroom, the Mysore Room, the Tagore Suite and the Pratap Bedroom.

Elaborate arrangements had been made at Rashtrapati Bhavan for the royal couple's stay. Special dress regulations were issued for the visit. For the duration that the couple was in residence, the President's Personal Staff were dressed in impressive formal attire – frock coats, aiguillettes and sashes. Civilian staff members wore short, black buttoned-up coats with white or black trousers and black shoes.

On the hour at 6.00 in the evening, Prince Akihito accompanied by Princess Michiko, called on President Dr Prasad in his Study at Rashtrapati Bhavan. During this time, the members of his delegation gathered in the Yellow Drawing Room, awaiting the arrival of the President and the royal couple. After the call on, the President and the royal couple were escorted to the Yellow Drawing Room. Here the members of the visiting entourage were introduced to President Dr Prasad. Thereafter, the Personal Staff of the President was introduced to the Prince and Princess.

Half an hour later, Prime Minister Nehru called on the Crown Prince in the Dwarka Sitting Room. President Dr Prasad also called on Prince Akihito a while later. This was, however, not the last engagement of the day. In the evening, on the hour at eight, the President of India hosted a glittering banquet in honour of the Crown Prince and Princess of Japan.

The Ashok Hall and the adjoining rooms and passages were exquisitely adorned for the banquet. Masses of flowers in a whole host of different shades were delicately arranged in the Ashok Hall, the Grand Open Staircase, the Guest Loggia, the Banquet Hall and the Yellow Drawing Room.

Guests arrived at the South Entrance via the South Sunken Road and were received and escorted to the Ashok Hall by the Personal Staff of the President, where they awaited the President and the royal couple. After the President and the royal guests arrived at the Hall, national anthems of both the countries were played in succession and the guests were introduced to the principals. Thereafter, the Guests of Honour and the other invitees were conducted to the Banquet Hall where an elaborate dinner was served by Rashtrapati Bhavan's *khidmatgars* (butlers).

It was no ordinary evening. The Maratha Regimental Centre Band, whose services were specifically requisitioned for the evening, played a medley of soft music while the different courses were served. The soft music, the subtle splash of colours of the varied hues of flowers and the exquisitely tiered chandeliers added to the grandeur of the Banquet Hall.

After the main courses were served, President Dr Prasad addressed the distinguished invitees. He recalled his visit to Japan, some two years ago and said he had returned to "India with the lasting

Prince Akihito delivering banquet speech at Rashtrapati Bhavan in November 1960. Credit: PC

(L-R): President Dr Prasad, Prince Akihito and Princess Michiko with artists of cultural programme at Rashtrapati Bhavan in November 1960. Credit: PC

impression that the bonds that link us will grow stronger as time passes, for our ideals are the same and spring from the same ancient traditions." Referring to the tour of the Crown Prince and Princess, he said that their visit "will reinforce these ties of understanding and mutual regard and strengthen our efforts for the establishment of lasting peace in the world."[16] The Indian President also thanked Japan for its cooperation and extending assistance to India.

He referred to the transition taking place in Japan and said that "Japan is a striking example of a rapidly changing society in which traditional patterns are gracefully adapting themselves to modern requirements."[17] He concluded his address with a request to the Crown Prince to take back with him, "a message of affection, friendship and goodwill from the people of India to his Imperial Majesty and the people of Japan."[18] Thereafter, President Dr Prasad raised a toast to the health of "His Imperial Majesty the Emperor of Japan," the Crown Prince, Princess and to the happiness and prosperity of Japan.

In his reply, the Crown Prince recalled the deep impression that the Indian leaders had left in the minds of the people of Japan during their several visits to his country. He added that he appreciated India's devotion and commitment to peace. Towards the end of his speech, he made some touching observations on his visit. Striking a personal note, he said his visit to India had been one of the

"happiest" and most "unforgettable" experiences of his life. He then raised a toast "to the health of His Excellency The President and the prosperity of the Republic of India."[19] Dessert and coffee followed by an exquisite ballet in the Ashok Hall brought the curtains down on the Japanese royal couple's first day in New Delhi.

The next morning, on the hour at ten, Prince Akihito and Princess Michiko drove to *Rajghat*, where they paid their respects at the memorial of Mahatma Gandhi. Thirty minutes later, they arrived at India Gate to attend an event organised by the National Discipline Scheme in the Children's Park. On their arrival, some 4000 schoolchildren welcomed the royal couple.

Later, the Prince and Princess attended a lunch hosted by Prime Minister Jawaharlal Nehru in their honour at Teen Murti Bhavan. Indian Vice President, Dr S Radhakrishnan; the Maharajkumar of Sikkim and some Cabinet Ministers[20] were amongst the select few who attended the lunch. The royal couple then returned to Rashtrapati Bhavan.

The Crown Prince laid the foundation stone of the India International Centre (on Max Mueller Marg) at quarter to four in the afternoon. Speaking on the occasion, the President of the Centre, CD Deshmukh stated that the Centre's principal aim was to promote "understanding and amity among the different communities of the world by 'undertaking or promoting the study of their past and present cultures, by disseminating or exchanging knowledge thereof and by providing such other facilities as would lead to their universal appreciation.' "[21] The Prince, in his address, said that India had become "one of the most important crossroads of Eastern and Western cultures as evidenced by successive visits of so many distinguished scholars and artists of world renown in recent years."[22] He spent almost an hour at the venue and thereafter returned to Rashtrapati Bhavan.

The evening was reserved for the Civic Reception hosted by the Delhi Municipal Corporation in honour of the Royal Couple at the Red Fort. Prime Minister Nehru arrived at Rashtrapati Bhavan at half past five to accompany the royal couple to the historical site. Mayor Sham Nath welcomed the Prince and Princess on their arrival at the venue.

In his reply to the welcome address, Prince Akihito spoke of the deep kinship that the people of Japan had always felt for the people of India. He said, "The Japanese people believe that in the near future India will achieve immense success in her endeavours and hope that this great nation will co-operate in establishing peace and prosperity in Asia and through it world peace."[23]

Prime Minister Nehru also spoke at the reception and referred particularly to the warm welcome that the Japanese royal couple had received in India. He said that the "welcome given to them since they arrived here, was not a formal one. There was something deeper and heart-warming in it."[24] At the reception, the Mayor presented a beautifully carved sandalwood box to Prince Akihito and a *Banarasi stole* to Princess Michiko.[25]

Later that evening, around 7.00, the royal couple attended a reception at the Japanese Ambassador's residence on Ashok Road, New Delhi. Here they met some of the Japanese residents in the city. After the dinner with the Ambassador, the royal couple returned to Rashtrapati Bhavan and retired for the night.

The next morning, December 1, 1960, the royal couple started the day with a visit to the village of Nistoli, in the Community Development Block in Loni, Ghaziabad, a city on the outskirts of Delhi. This was the first time that the couple had a "glimpse of rural India."[26] Residents of the village cheered the royals as they walked around, visiting first the community centre and later the local youth club. They also stopped by the children's school to watch a physical training display by the students. Prince Akihito took photographs of the paintings on the earthen wall of a local resident's house with his personal camera, while Princess Michiko watched the wife make *chapattis* (local bread made of wheat flour) with great interest.

The Prince and Princess returned to Rashtrapati Bhavan and half an hour later, travelled to Chelmsford Club to meet the members of the Indo-Japan Friendship Association. At half past one that afternoon, Prince Akihito hosted a lunch at the Japanese Embassy.

Later that afternoon, Prince Akihito and Princess Michiko witnessed a spectacular 90-minute display of horsemanship staged by the PBG for the royal couple and select members of the Delhi Polo Club at the Jaipur Polo Ground. The show finished around 5.00 pm. There were no other scheduled engagements for the day and the royal couple spent the evening in their suites at Rashtrapati Bhavan.

Prince Akihito's second last day in New Delhi, December 2, was spent travelling around the city visiting places of scientific interest. He went to the National Physical Laboratory and the Indian Agricultural Research Institute. Prince Akihito was particularly impressed by the equipment and techniques that were being employed by Indian scientists. In particular, he was "pleased to note that Indo-Japanese collaboration had resulted in remarkable progress in scientific research."[27] While the Prince was visiting institutions, the Princess spent the morning at the After-care Home for Women.

The royal couple had lunch with the Japanese Ambassador, before they returned to Rashtrapati Bhavan to attend the President's 'At Home' that was hosted in their honour. The reception began at half past four in the evening in the misty expanse of the Mughal Gardens. Elaborate arrangements had been made. All the fountains in the Jaipur Column area, North and South Courts, Durbar Hall and Mughal Gardens were switched on by 3.30 pm. 300 chairs had been arranged in small groups in the garden and buffet tables were placed at several places in the Central Lawns. The President and his guests of honour were escorted from the Morning Room to the Central Lawns in a ceremonial procession. Trumpeters sounded fanfare that was timed to end as the procession reached the edge

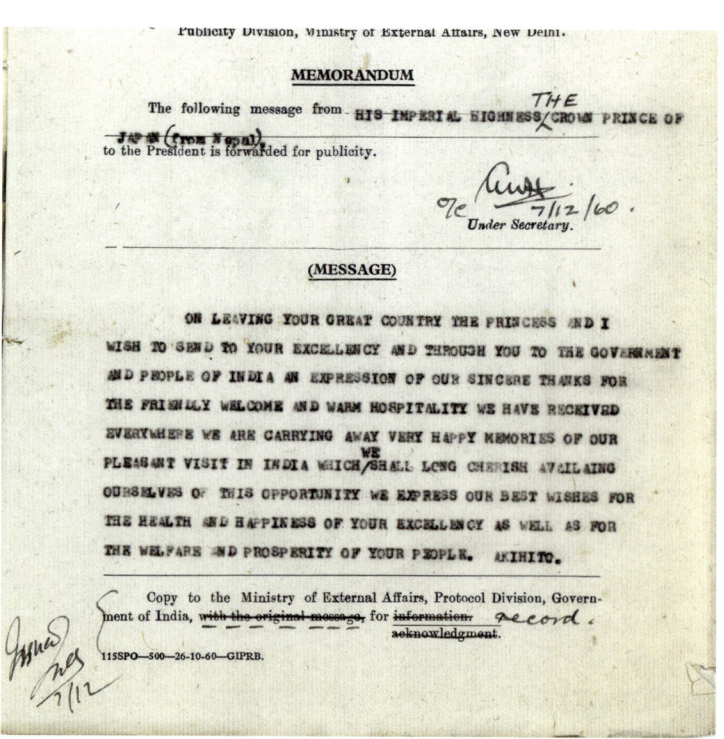

Message of thanks from Prince Akihito to President Dr Prasad.

(Front row, L-R): Sharmistha Mukherjee, Empress Michiko, Emperor Akihito, President Pranab Mukherjee, Prime Minister Dr Manmohan Singh and his wife Gursharan Kaur in the Forecourt at Rashtrapati Bhavan in December 2013. Credit: PC

of the lawn. It was an elaborate reception and the invitees were treated to a high tea. Vice President Dr Radhakrishnan, Prime Minister Nehru, Cabinet Ministers, Parliamentarians, Supreme Court Judges, diplomats, officials were amongst the dignitaries who attended the reception.[28]

Later, at 8.30 pm, Prince Akihito hosted a banquet at the Ashoka Hotel in honour of President Dr Prasad. A total of 200 guests including Prime Minister Nehru, Vice President Dr Radhakrishnan and several other dignitaries attended the reception. Speaking on the occasion, the Crown Prince thanked the people and the Government of India for the warm welcome and the thoughtful arrangements made for them. He appreciated the "strenuous efforts being made by the leaders and the people of 'this great Republic for their interest and for the common good of mankind.' "[29] At the end of his address, Prince Akihito proposed a toast to the good health of the Indian President, and to the prosperity of the Indian nation.[30] In reply to the Crown Prince's toast, President Dr Prasad commented on the growing co-operation between the two countries. He also referred to the endearing nature of the royal couple and said, "You have won our hearts with your great charm and courtesy and the keen interest you have so kindly evinced in our country."[31]

At five past eight on the morning of December 3, the royal couple departed the stately premises of Rashtrapati Bhavan for the airport. The President of India and Prime Minister escorted them to the airport. The royal couple emplaned for Agra on board the "City of Osaka" after a 15-minute ceremony at the airport, where the President and the Prime Minister bade them goodbye. The Prince and Princess were in India for a few more days and visited Gaya and Patna They departed for Kathmandu on December 6.

After arriving in Nepal, Prince Akihito wrote a warm letter to President Dr Prasad expressing his sincere thanks for the friendly welcome and warm hospitality that they received in India. He wrote, "We are carrying away very happy memories of our pleasant visit in India which we shall long cherish."[32]

When his son returned home, the Emperor of Japan, His Imperial Majesty Hirohito, sent a telegram on December 9, 1960, addressed to President Dr Prasad, expressing the same sentiments as his son had done two days ago. The telegram read: "On the home–coming of my son Crown Prince Akihito who visited your country as my representative together with his consort I hasten to express my sincerest thanks to Your Excellency for the most cordial reception and hospitality accorded them by Your Excellency and for the warm welcome extended to them by your Government and people during their memorable visit in your country."[33]

The 2013 Visit

After the death of Emperor Hirohito on January 7, 1989, Crown Prince Akihito succeeded his father to become the 125th Emperor of Japan, though he formally ascended the *Chrysanthemum Throne*

Emperor Akihito inspecting a Guard of Honor in Forecourt at Rashtrapati Bhavan in December 2013. Credit: PC

almost two years later, on November 12, 1990. Under Emperor Akihito, bilateral ties between India and Japan strengthened significantly. It was further evidenced when Japan became one of the few countries that had "bailed India out of the balance of payment crisis."[34]

It was a testimony to the higher trajectory that Indo-Japanese relations were traversing. Emperor Akihito with his wife Empress Michiko returned to India in 2013, 53 years after they had first come to India on their honeymoon. The six-day visit from November

30 to December 5, 2013, was widely hailed as a significant event symbolising the attainment of a "peak level in bilateral relations."[35] It was special also for the reason that the Japanese Emperor who seldom travelled abroad, was setting foot on Indian soil for the first time in that capacity.

The Emperor and Empress arrived in Delhi in a special plane at ten past five in the evening on November 30. In another testimony to the close ties both nations shared, in a departure from the revised protocol, Prime Minister Dr Manmohan Singh received and welcomed the

(Front row, L-R): President Pranab Mukherjee, Sharmistha Mukherjee, Empress Michiko and Emperor Akihito at Rashtrapati Bhavan in December 2013. Credit: PC

President Pranab Mukherjee presenting a gift to Emperor Akihito at Rashtrapati Bhavan. Empress Michiko looks on. (December 2013). Credit: PC

Empress Michiko and President Mukherjee exchanging toast at the banquet at Rashtrapati Bhavan in December 2013. Credit: PC

Japanese Emperor at the airport. The couple was thereafter warmly received by Foreign Minister Salman Khurshid and other dignitaries present at the airport. After the reception, the Japanese Emperor left for Hotel Taj Palace where he stayed in the Capital.

The Japanese Emperor had a heavy schedule the following day, December 1, 2013. Among the scheduled events, was a lunch hosted by the Prime Minister of India at his residence. He also met with representatives of the Japanese expatriates and concluded the day's events with a dinner at the residence of the Japanese Ambassador.

On the next morning, December 2, the Japanese Emperor and Empress were accorded a grand ceremonial reception at Rashtrapati

Bhavan. Emperor Akihito's motorcade was escorted to Rashtrapati Bhavan by nine Inter-Services outriders from Hotel Taj Palace. As the motorcade entered the main gate of Rashtrapati Bhavan at 9.45 am, the outriders branched off. The PBG, who were positioned here, presented a National Salute and escorted the Emperor's motorcade in a grand ceremonial formation. As the motorcade reached the Jaipur Column, a 21-gun salute was fired in honour of the Emperor. The motorcade was escorted to where the gravelled path or the Viceroy's Court ends and the Forecourt begins.

President Pranab Mukherjee and Prime Minister Dr Manmohan Singh warmly received the visiting dignitaries as soon as they

President Pranab Mukherjee (left) and Emperor Akihito (right) in the North Drawing Room at Rashtrapati Bhavan in December 2013. Credit: PC

(Facing): Emperor Akihito delivering banquet speech at Rashtrapati Bhavan. Seated to his right is Vice President Hamid Ansari and on the Emperor's left is Prime Minister Dr Manmohan Singh. Seated opposite the Emperor is President Mukherjee and on his right is Empress Michiko. (December 2013). Credit: PC

alighted from the car. Emperor Akihito was then conducted to the Saluting Dais where a Guard of Honour 'presented arms' to him. This was followed by the national anthems of Japan and India. After inspecting the Guard of Honour, the Japanese Emperor was escorted to the enclosure where the specially invited dignitaries were introduced to him and the Empress.

After the grand ceremonial reception, the visiting dignitaries left for *Rajghat*, where they placed a wreath on the *samadhi* of Mahatma Gandhi. The evening was reserved for the State Banquet that the Indian President hosted in honour of the royal couple.

Emperor Akihito and Empress Michiko arrived at Rashtrapati Bhavan at 7.30 that evening and called on President Mukherjee in the North Drawing Room. After a brief exchange of views, the royal couple and President Mukherjee accompanied by his daughter, Sharmistha Mukherjee, were escorted to the Ashok Hall at 8.10 pm by the MSP, the Deputy Military Secretary to the President (DMSP) and the *aides–de–camp* (AsDC).

After the two leaders arrived under the central arch of the Ashok Hall, the band played the national anthems of Japan and India. A host of dignitaries including the Vice President, Indian Prime Minister, the Chief Justice and the Speaker of Lok Sabha, amongst others, had arrived at the Ashok Hall where they waited to be introduced to the royal couple. After the national anthems, the guests were introduced to the dignitaries, in the order of their seniority. The introductions were followed by some brief moments of interaction, during which soft drinks and dry fruits were served. The guests thereafter proceeded to the Banquet Hall and stood behind their respective chairs according to the table plan. Soon afterwards, the royal visitors, the President, his daughter, the Vice President and other senior government leaders were escorted by the AsDC to

the Banquet Hall and sat at the middle of the table, opposite each other. President Pranab Mukherjee was seated opposite Emperor Akihito. Empress Michiko was seated to the right of the President and to the left of his daughter. The Vice President, Hamid Ansari was seated to the Emperor's right and India's Prime Minister Dr Manmohan Singh to the Emperor's left.

Banquet protocols had undergone a change since Emperor Akihito's last visit over five decades ago. This time the banquet began with speeches, unlike in the past, when they were delivered after the main courses were served. President Mukherjee in his speech welcomed the Japanese Emperor and Empress and

Emperor Akihito (left) with President Pranab Mukherjee (right) at Rashtrapati Bhavan in December 2013. Credit: PC

remarked that India was delighted to receive the royal guests after a gap of 53 years. Speaking on the commonalities between the two nations, President Mukherjee said that the, "India-Japan partnership is based on the bedrock of shared values of democracy, the rule of law and individual rights."[36] He added that, "the presence of the Emperor and Empress of Japan in India was a historic milestone in bilateral relations, heralding a further deepening of the time-tested friendship, solidarity and co-operation that have always characterised relations between India and Japan."[37]

Replying to the President's address, Emperor Akihito expressed his pleasure on re-visiting India and referred to further strengthening of the bonds between the two countries. Emperor Akihito also thanked "the Parliament of India on behalf of the people of Japan for paying tribute to Japan's atomic bomb victims in August every year."[38]

After the banquet, the Emperor and Empress spent 15 minutes in the same Dwarka Suite where the former had spent four nights during their last visit to India, providing them an occasion to revisit old memories. Thereafter, the Emperor, Empress, the Indian President and his daughter met in the North Drawing Room for a farewell *tete-a-tete*, with select aides from both sides. The meeting lasted for about 10-minutes. After the brief exchange of views, the distinguished guests left for their hotel. The following day, December 3, the couple visited several places in Delhi including the India International Centre and the Japanese School in Vasant Kunj.

The Emperor and Empress left Delhi in the late morning hours of the next day in a special aircraft. They emplaned for Chennai, and after spending an eventful day there, left India for Tokyo on December 5, 2013.

Emperor Akihito continues as the monarch of Japan. He is 81. Empress Michiko is 80.

Notes

[1] Records, President's Secretariat, Rashtrapati Bhavan, File No. 15(3)/60.

[2] Steven R. Weisman, "Japan's Imperial Present," *The New York Times*, August 26, 1990, accessed June 1, 2015, http://www.nytimes.com/1990/08/26/magazine/japan-s-imperial-present.html.

[3] Michael Walsh, "Akihito: The Son Also Rises," *Time*, January 16, 1989, accessed June 1, 2015, http://content.time.com/time/magazine/article/0,9171,956717,00.html.

[4] "Japan: The Girl from Outside," *Time*, March 23, 1959, accessed June 1, 2015, http://content.time.com/time/magazine/article/0,9171,892335,00.html.

[5] "Japanese Crown Prince Arrives," *The Times of India* (New Delhi), November 28, 1960, p. 1.

[6] Ibid.

[7] "Japanese Prince Visits Aarey," *The Times of India* (New Delhi), November 29, 1960, p. 3.

[8] Ibid.

[9] Ibid.

[10] "Thousands Cheer Prince Akihito," *The Hindustan Times* (New Delhi), November 30, 1960, p. 1.

[11] "Japanese Royal Visitors in Delhi," *The Times of India* (New Delhi), November 30, 1960, p. 1.

[12] "Thousands Cheer Prince Akihito," p. 1.

[13] Ibid.

[14] Ibid.

[15] Ibid.

[16] Records, President's Secretariat, File No. 15(3)/60.

[17] Ministry of External Affairs (1995), Government of India, Foreign Affairs Records 1960, Volume VI, accessed March 10, 2015, http://mealib.nic.in/?pdf2548?000.

[18] Ibid.

[19] Ibid.

[20] "Japanese Prince Opens International Centre," *The Times of India* (New Delhi), December 1, 1960, p.1.

[21] Ibid.

[22] Ibid.

[23] Ibid.

[24] Ibid.

[25] "Common Bond with Japan," *The Times of India* (New Delhi), December 1, 1960, p. 1.

[26] "Prince Akihito," *The Times of India* (New Delhi), December 2, 1960, p. 7.

[27] "Co-operation Between Japan & India," *The Times of India* (New Delhi), December 3, 1960, p. 7.

[28] Ibid.

[29] Ibid.

[30] Records, President's Secretariat, File No. 15(3)/60.

[31] "Co-operation Between Japan & India," p. 7.

[32] Records, President's Secretariat, File No. 15(3)/60.

[33] Ibid.

[34] Ministry of External Affairs (July 2014), Government of India, "India-Japan Relations," accessed May 18, 2015, http://www.mea.gov.in/Portal/ForeignRelation/Japan_-_July_2014_.pdf.

[35] H.S. Prabhakar, "A Sign of Strong Ties with Japan," *The New Indian Express*, December 7, 2013, accessed May 17, 2015, http://www.newindianexpress.com/columns/A-Sign-of-Strong-Ties-with-Japan/2013/12/07/article1931914.ece.

[36] "India, Japan Share Vision of a New Asia: President Pranab Mukherjee," *The Economic Times*, December 3, 2013, accessed 17 May 2015, http://articles.economictimes.indiatimes.com/2013-12-03/news/44710491_1_president-pranab-mukherjee-new-asia-india-and-japan.

[37] Ibid.

[38] Press Information Bureau (December 2013), Government of India, "Emperor and Empress of Japan Call On the President," December 3, 2013, accessed May 17, 2015, http://pib.nic.in/newsite/PrintRelease.aspx?relid=100984.

It was in the brumal season of 1963 that the King of Jordan, Hussein-bin-Talal came to India on his maiden visit. The 13-day trip, from December 3-16, was undertaken at the invitation of the Indian President, Dr Sarvepalli Radhakrishnan.

India's ties with Jordan date back to historical times with commerce and trade dominating the relations. The spices from India often travelled to Petra (situated in Jordan) on their way to other markets. Politically, too, at the fundamental level, both nations were in agreement on several important international issues. On the Palestinian problem, for instance, India's policies differed little from those of Jordan. The support of Jordan during the India-China war of 1962 was another instance of the similar vectors in the foreign policy of both nations.

King Hussein was barely 28 when he received President Dr Radhakrishnan's invitation. Though he was comparatively too young to adorn the mantle of a ruler, and termed by some as a "Boy King", his age belied his capabilities. People soon found him to be a man of sagacity and stratagem. Even at a young age, he was known for his deft handling of complex foreign policy issues. In the words of the noted historian Avi Shlaim, King Hussein was a "man of slight build who possessed a powerful personality and immense political stature."[1]

Visit of
H.M. King Hussein-bin-Talal
of Jordan

Born to the Hashemite ruling family on November 14, 1935, Hussein-bin-Talal was the eldest of four siblings. He completed his basic education in Jordan and Egypt and later studied at some of the best institutions in England, including Harrow and the Royal Military Academy, Sandhurst. At the age of 16, he survived a close brush with death when his grandfather, King Abdullah, was shot and killed while offering prayers at a mosque in Jerusalem. Hussein, himself, had a miraculous escape after a "bullet aimed at him struck a medal on his uniform."[2]

After the death of his grandfather, Hussein's father, Talal bin Abdullah, was coronated King but his rule was short-lived. In just about a year, he had to abdicate due to a serious medical condition and his son, Hussein-bin-Talal, became King of Jordan. Hussein was just 17 then and had to wait for another year before he could officially ascend the throne in 1953. Once he assumed power, he led his nation from a British mandate to an independent nation-state.

King Hussein was an inveterate hunter, a skilled horseman, scuba diver and loved fishing in deep seas. He was a competent pilot and a skilled driver.[3] He evinced great interest in foreign policy matters, particularly on finding a solution to the Arab-Israeli conflict. So determined was his pursuit of this goal, that even his own Arab brethren had expressed reservations about his intentions. His position on many international issues and those

Facing page:
President Dr Radhakrishnan (left) with
King Hussein-bin-Talal
at Rashtrapati Bhavan in
December 1963. Credit: PC

of India had a striking vectoral similarity. His visit to India was, therefore, seen as a logical progression in the strengthening of Indo-Jordanian relations.

The King of Jordan landed at Palam Airport in Delhi at the stroke of noon on December 3, 1963, in a special Swissair Boeing DC-8. He was accompanied by an entourage of eight members, including the Chief of the Royal Court, Bahjat Al-Talhouni; Minister to the Royal Court, Hazim Nusseibeh and the First Secretary to His Majesty, Prince Raad Ibn Zeid.

Dressed in an olive green tunic and traditional Arab headgear, a "youthful" King Hussein stepped out of the aircraft to a ceremonial welcome and a 21-gun salute. He was warmly welcomed by President of India, Dr Radhakrishnan; the Vice President, Dr Zakir Husain; Prime Minister, Jawaharlal Nehru and Delhi's Mayor, Nuruddin Ahmed, amongst others.

An Inter-Services Guard of Honour was presented to him after which, the Jordanian King was escorted to the special enclosure where he met the other dignitaries present. Delivering his welcome address, President Dr Radhakrishnan greeted the visiting King by describing him as "one of the youngest rulers in the world," and expressed the hope that he would have a "profitable and interesting

time" in India.[4] King Hussein responded to the President's welcome speech and thanked him for "his kind words," adding "that India and Jordan stood for the same principles and ideas."[5]

After the airport reception, the Jordanian King, accompanied by the Indian President, drove to Rashtrapati Bhavan in a Mercedes Benz with President Dr Radhakrishnan seated on the left. Two Cadillacs and five "guest cars" from the President's Garage formed part of the ceremonial motorcade. As the cars approached Vijay Chowk, the President's Bodyguard (PBG) escorted the motorcade to Rashtrapati Bhavan.

The Military Secretary to the President (MSP), Major General DGR Rajwade, received the guests at the alighting point in the Forecourt. To welcome the visiting King, the Personal Staff of the President had lined up inside the corridor leading to the Guest Wing. They were introduced to King Hussein by President Dr Radhakrishnan. The Jordanian dignitaries were then conducted to the Guest Loggia where refreshments were served before being escorted to their respective suites / rooms.

The elegantly appointed Dwarka Suite became the temporary home of King Hussein-bin-Talal. Prince Raad Ibn Zeid stayed in the Nalanda Suite. Bahjat Al-Talhouni stayed in the Himalaya

Seated: King Hussein (left) with President Dr Radhakrishnan at Rashtrapati Bhavan in December 1963. Credit: PC

Suite, while Hazim Nusseibeh was accommodated in the Dakshin Bedroom. The rest of the entourage was hosted in the Bombay Bedroom, Pepsu Bedroom, Mysore Bedroom, Tagore Bedroom and Neelam Bedroom.

At half past four that evening, King Hussein called on President Dr Radhakrishnan in the Morning Room. Thereafter, the two leaders proceeded to the Yellow Drawing Room, where King Hussein presented his accompanying delegation to the Indian President. Thereafter, President Dr Radhakrishnan introduced his Personal Staff to the King.[6]

That evening, Prime Minister Nehru called on King Hussein at Rashtrapati Bhavan and had a half-an-hour discussion, primarily on world issues. Also present at the meeting were the Deputy Minister for External Affairs, Dinesh Singh; the Special Secretary in the Ministry of External Affairs, Rajeshwar Dayal and India's Ambassador to Jordan, IS Chopra.[7]

Later that evening, President Dr Radhakrishnan called on the Jordanian King and accompanied him to the State Banquet that he was hosting in the King's honour. As was the practice, floral decorations adorned the Grand Open Staircase, the Ashok Hall and the State Dining Room. The PBG, in resplendent winter

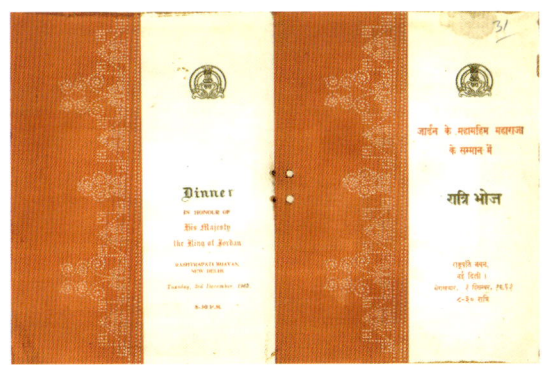

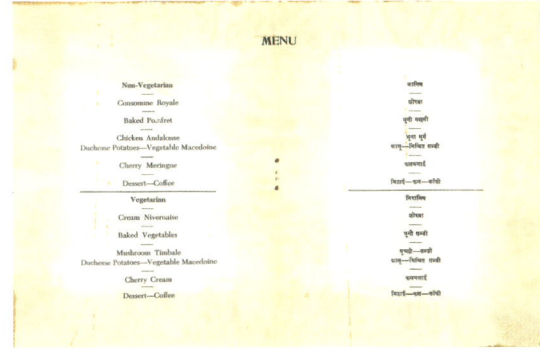

Menu of the banquet held in honour of King Hussein in December 1963.

(L-R): Indira Gandhi, Prime Minister Nehru, Vice President Dr Zakir Husain, King Hussein and President Dr Radhakrishnan at Rashtrapati Bhavan in December 1963. Credit: PD

uniform, lined the walkway from the Grand Open Staircase to the Ashok Hall. The whole ambience was one of stately elegance.

Guests arrived by 8.15 pm and were conducted to the Ashok Hall by the *aides–de–camp* (AsDC). At 8.35 pm, President Dr Radhakrishnan and King Hussein, escorted by the AsDC and MSP, arrived under the central arch of the Ashok Hall, where they stood to attention while the band played the national anthems of both Jordan and India. Following this, the waiting guests - who stood in a horse-shoe formation with their wives on their right - were introduced to the Indian President and the Jordanian King. The banquet began after introductions were over.

A special menu was prepared for the banquet. The non–vegetarian fare included *Consommé Royale, Baked Pomfret, Chicken Andalouse, Duchesse Potatoes, Vegetable Macedoine* and *Cherry Meringue*. The vegetarians began their meal with *Cream Nivernaise*, followed by *Baked Vegetables, Mushroom Timbale, Duchesse Potatoes, Vegetable Macedoine* and *Cherry Cream*.

After the dinner, and before the dessert and coffee were served, the Indian President proposed a toast to the King of Jordan. In his speech, President Dr Radhakrishnan commented on Jordan's history and described King Hussein as a unique blend of past and present. He said, "So you represent history of centuries. You also represent modernism. You were at Harrow and Sandhurst, centres of intellectual learning and military training. You are a good pilot and a good photographer. That shows how very modern you are. With that modernised outlook you are trying to improve the conditions in your country, modernise your country so to say without losing your fidelity to the fundamentals of Islam."[8]

President Dr Radhakrishnan also referred to the common goals of India and Jordan to build peace saying, "War is our greatest enemy. We must all become partners in the quest for peace; stand by one another, not in enmity, not in arming ourselves but in trying to protect the vital interests of humanity."[9]

Complimenting the King on his unflinching commitment to improving the lives of his countrymen, the President spoke of the long future that lay before the King. Adding a touch of humour, he said, "You are a man of great courage, great adventure. You have youth on your side, not like me, an old man here, very tired."[10] The Jordanian national anthem was played before King Hussein replied.

Beginning with measured modesty, the King said, "Sir, no matter how hard I may try, I must admit failure to express what I feel and what I have felt ever since this morning when I arrived in this dear land."[11] Referring to Jordan, he said, "We are a small country, but we have hopes of a better future. We are little in number but we

President Dr Radhakrishnan delivering banquet speech at Rashtrapati Bhavan. Seated opposite is King Hussein. (December 1963). Credit: PC

have the ideals and principles which all free men all over the world hold dear. We hope that out of Jordan and in Jordan we can set a good example for others, how a people can work and surmount obstacles despite the fact that these obstacles may be formidable."[12]

The Jordanian King also commented on the commonalities of both the countries, their problems and hopes, saying, "There are many similarities between us, the two countries, the problems we face and the hopes we have. In Jordan we are also trying to build a future based on the best that we can retain from our past and the best that we can gain from the experiences of others. We feel that this is the way, and is and has been the case here. We are also proud of the friendly ties that exist between us and the good relations that exist between us. We know that these relations will grow stronger with the passage of time."[13]

Thanking President Dr Radhakrishnan, Hussein concluded, "You inspired me and brought new strength into me...no matter how difficult one might find life, one should stick to one's principles and what one believes in... Sir, [I] find it a privilege meeting such a great scholar, who is at the same time as modest as you are and as dedicated as you are to the service of your great nation."[14] The Indian national anthem was played after King Hussein's address. After the dinner, the Jordanian guests were ushered to their suites/rooms.

The next day, on December 4, Hussein visited a "community development project near Delhi," and later attended a Civic Reception.[15] He also attended a reception at the Ashoka Hotel hosted by the Jordanian Ambassador.[16] On December 5, the King watched a thrilling polo match between the Cavaliers and the Delhi Polo Club, organised in his honour at the Jaipur Polo Ground. President Dr Radhakrishnan accompanied King Hussein and, to their delight, it was a keenly fought match with the Cavaliers trouncing Delhi Polo Club by 6–3.[17] The King also visited the Indian Agricultural Research Institute, the National Physical Laboratory and the National Museum in Delhi the same day.[18]

Later, at 8.30 pm, King Hussein hosted a dinner in honour of President Dr Radhakrishnan at the Ashoka Hotel. At the reception, he proposed a toast to the Indian leader and said, "We have been very, very impressed with all we have seen, not only the great progress that has been made in all fields, in science and development. The progress is remarkable but what has interested us most is the people's dedication, their ability to work, their desire to improve and their faith in the leadership of this country."[19]

In words that partly betrayed his emotions, King Hussein said, "I will carry back to my Jordanian family news of what I have seen and my impressions. I know they will be very interested. I will tell them, we had a great deal in common although we are a small country and at some distance."[20] Concluding his address, King Hussein thanked the Indian President, the Prime Minister, and the people of India for their warm and cordial hospitality.

In his reply to the King's toast, President Dr Radhakrishnan said that he appreciated the King's kind words, and lauded him as a "man of great courage and conviction determined not merely to improve the conditions of life in Jordan but of the whole Arab world and in the whole of humanity."[21] The Indian President concluded by raising a toast to the health of the King of Jordan.

The next day, on December 6, King Hussein departed for Palam Airport on his visit to other cities in the country. The President and the King drove in the cars from the President's Garage and reached the airport at 9.20 am. After inspecting a Guard of Honour, His Majesty bade farewell to the President, Vice President, Prime Minister and others, before embarking on his tour.

A grand *Bharat Darshan* (India tour) spanning 10 days, from December 6–15, had been carefully planned for the King of Jordan. His first stop was Agra where he and his entourage visited the Taj Mahal and the old city of Fatehpur Sikri before embarking for Dehradun. The King, an alumnus of Sandhurst, lunched with cadets at the Indian Military Academy on December 7.

The Gir Forest in Gujarat, abode of the majestic Asiatic Lion, was the next halt. After they had landed at Keshod Airport, the royal party was taken on a safari ride through the Gir forests. Bangalore, in the State of Mysore (now Karnataka), was the next stop.

On December 11, the King and his entourage landed in Madras to visit the home of Dravidian art and culture. King Hussein visited the Shore Temples in Mahabalipuram and travelled to Nagarjunasagar. The royal party's next halt was Hyderabad. Here, on December 12, King Hussein attended a convocation ceremony.

The last stop of the Indian tour was Bombay where the King and his entourage landed on December 14, at 11.30 am. Arriving in an IAF Super Constellation from Hyderabad, the King was received by the Governor of Bombay, HK Chainani; the Chief Minister of Bombay, VP Naik and the Chief Secretary to the State Government, NT Mone, amongst others.

Starting a whirlwind tour of the western metropolis, the King and his entourage first visited the Atomic Energy Establishment in Trombay. Later in the day, King Hussein addressed the Indo-Arab Society at the Radio Club. In his address, the King commended the Society on its remarkable work in promoting closer relations between India and the Arab world. To commemorate the special occasion, the President of the Society, Dr Rafiq Zakaria, presented a "silver salver" to the Guest of Honour.[22] Later in the day, the Governor hosted a banquet in honour of the King of Jordan at Raj Bhavan.

On the last day of his visit to India, December 15, the King started with a tour of the ancient rock caves of Elephanta. Later he went on board the INS Mysore of the Western Naval Command. His Majesty was received by Rear Admiral AK Chatterji and Captain KK Sanjana, Commanding Officer of INS Mysore and was given a 21-gun salute. A plaque engraved with the flagship's crest was presented to the King.[23]

That evening, the Arab community of Mumbai hosted a dinner in honour of King Hussein at which the Governor and his wife were also present. At the dinner, the King said that he had brought with himself the friendship of the Jordanian people and that he "will take back tomorrow" India's "friendship to them."[24] He praised the Indians and drew parallels to the peoples of the two countries and hoped for better bilateral relations. At the dinner, he was gifted a venerable, hand-written *Quran* and two books in Arabic. After dinner, the King's final engagement in Mumbai, to which he was accompanied by the Governor of Maharashtra, was a visit to an Indian Film Exhibition.[25]

The next day, on December 16, King Hussein-bin-Talal and his entourage left for Tehran at 11.00 am by the Swissair DC-8. Before leaving, the Chief Minister of Bombay presented him an album containing 25 photographs of His Majesty's visit to Bombay.[26] The Deputy Principal Information Officer, PD Murti, also presented the King another album that contained photographs of His Majesty's visits to other parts of India. As the King departed, he thanked his Indian hosts in Mumbai for their warm hospitality.

On the same day, the King sent President Dr Radhakrishnan a telegram thanking him for the "hospitality and sincerity" with which the Government of India and the people received him throughout the country. He said that he would return to Jordan with the "richest memories" of the spontaneous and genuine friendship of people of India" towards his country. He earnestly hoped that his "visit may have helped to further promote the ties of friendship and understanding" between the peoples of the two nations.

He also extended an invitation to the Indian President to visit Jordan and hoped that he would accept it so that "the Government and the people of Jordan may tender some of the affection and hospitality which" they had "met throughout" their stay in India.[27] President Dr Radhakrishnan replied to the telegram the very next day, communicating his delight that the King had a "useful time" in India. He said, "We are grateful to you for your kind invitation to visit Jordan. We shall certainly let you know when a suitable opportunity arises."[28] He also communicated his best wishes to the King and the people of Jordan.

King Hussein also sent a telegram thanking the Indian Prime Minister, Jawaharlal Nehru, expressing his deep appreciation for the friendship that the Prime Minister had shown him. Prime Minister Nehru replied to the Jordanian King thanking him for his kind words, and expressed his appreciation for Hussein's "devotion to the cause of peace and to the welfare of the Jordanian people."[29]

The 13-day State Visit by King Hussein strengthened Indo-Jordanian relations. A joint communiqué issued at the end of the visit declared India's readiness "to co-operate with Jordan in furtherance of His Majesty's plans for the social and economic development of the country."[30] The communiqué further declared Jordan's support of India's position against Chinese aggression, and also articulated Delhi's "understanding and appreciation of the Palestine problem."[31]

King Hussein-bin-Talal ruled Jordan for another 36 years, surviving perhaps the maximum number of attempts on the life of a ruler. In one instance, an assistant cook at the palace tried to poison him but gave himself away when he tested his plan on 16 palace cats, killing them all.

The King died of cancer on February 7, 1999. He was 63.

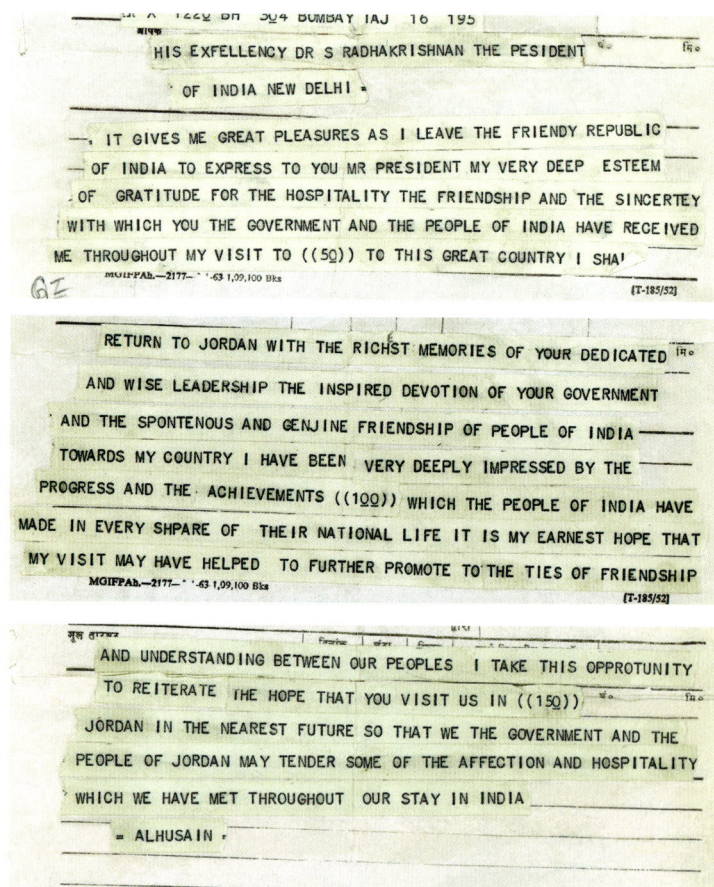

Telegram of thanks from King Hussein to President Dr Radhakrishnan.

Notes

[1] Avi Shlaim, Lion of Jordan: *The Life of King Hussein in War and Peace* (London: Penguin, 2008), p. 1.

[2] "King Hussein of Jordan," *The Telegraph*, February 8, 1999, accessed April 3, 2015, http://www.telegraph.co.uk/news/obituaries/royalty-obituaries/7136625/King-Hussein-of-Jordan.html.

[3] "The Boy King," *Time*, April 2, 1956, accessed June 1, 2015, http://content.time.com/time/subscriber/printout/0,8816,862061,00.html.

[4] "Warm Welcome to Jordan King in Delhi," *The Times of India* (New Delhi), December 4, 1963, p. 1.

[5] Ibid.

[6] Records, President's Secretariat, Rashtrapati Bhavan, File No. 15(9)/63.

[7] "Warm Welcome to Jordan King in Delhi," p. 1.

[8] Ministry of External Affairs (1995), Government of India, MEA Library, Foreign Affairs Records 1963 Volume IX, accessed April 13, 2015, www.mealib.nic.in/?pdf2551?000.

[9] Ibid.

[10] Ibid.

[11] Ibid.

[12] Ibid.

[13] Ibid.

[14] Ibid.

[15] "Warm Welcome to Jordan King in Delhi," p. 1.

[16] Ibid. 1

[17] "Jordan King Treated to Thrilling Polo," *The Hindustan Times* (New Delhi), December 6, 1963, p. 10.

[18] "King Hussein," *The Times of India* (New Delhi), December 6, 1963, p. 9.

[19] Ministry of External Affairs (1995), Foreign Affairs Records 1963 Volume IX.

[20] Ibid.

[21] Ibid.

[22] "Jordan King Calls for Arab Unity," *The Times of India* (New Delhi), December 15, 1963, p. 7.

[23] "King Hussein Given Warm Welcome on INS 'Mysore'," *The Times of India* (New Delhi), December 16, 1963, p. 1.

[24] Ibid.

[25] Ibid.

[26] "King Hussein's Visit Ends," *The Times of India* (New Delhi), December 17, 1963, p. 5.

[27] Records, President's Secretariat, File No. 15(9)/63.

[28] Ibid.

[29] Ibid.

[30] "Continued Indian Aid Assured: Joint Communiqué," *The Times of India* (New Delhi), December 17, 1963, p. 5.

[31] Ibid.

The Prime Minister and Crown Prince of Kuwait, Sheikh Sabah Al-Salim Al-Sabah, arrived on a State Visit to India from November 17– 28, 1964. During this 12–day trip, he stayed in the capital for four days. He spent the remaining days, travelling to different parts of the country.

Born in the year 1913, the Crown Prince was the youngest son of Salim Al-Mubarak Al-Sabah, the 9th ruler of Kuwait. The Crown Prince took active part in governance only at the age of 40, when he became President of the Police Department under the kingship of his half-brother Abdullah Al-Salim Al-Sabah, the 11th ruler of Kuwait. He then served as Foreign Minister of Kuwait from June 1961. He later became Prime Minister of Kuwait on February 2, 1963, and it was in this capacity that he visited India. The Prince would go on to become the 12th ruler of Kuwait in 1965, after his brother, Abdullah's death.

Visit of

H.R.H. Sheikh Sabah Al-Salim Al-Sabah

Prime Minister and Crown Prince of Kuwait

India and Kuwait had cordial relations, from the time the latter ceased to be a British protectorate and became independent in 1961. India was one of the first countries to establish diplomatic ties with Kuwait and their relations grew. On its part, Kuwait had supported India on many occasions. Notable among these was its support for India during the Chinese aggression of 1962 and its opposition to China's nuclear tests in 1964. Both countries also had strong economic ties. Interestingly, "until 1961 Indian Rupee was the legal tender in Kuwait."[1] It was thus to further strengthen the bilateral relations between the two countries that the Indian Prime Minister extended an invitation to the Prime Minister and Crown Prince of Kuwait to visit India.

On November 17, 1964, a special Kuwait Air Force Boeing, carrying the Prime Minister of Kuwait, landed at Palam Airport at 12.00 noon. The Crown Prince was accompanied by a group of high-ranking officials, including his Minister of State for the Affairs of the Council of Ministers, Abdul Aziz Hussain.

As the visiting Prime Minister alighted, he was greeted by the thunderous sound of a 21–gun salute and a full ceremonial welcome. He was received at the airport by Prime Minister Lal Bahadur Shastri, the Mayor of Delhi, Bawa Bachittar Singh, the Military Secretary to the President (MSP), Major General DGR Rajwade who represented the President of India, Dr Sarvepalli Radhakrishnan and a host of Cabinet Ministers and diplomatic officials. The Kuwaiti Prime Minister was presented an Inter-Services Guard of Honour.

Prime Minister Shastri welcomed the Crown Prince, hailing the historical ties between the two countries. He also hoped that the Prince would see India's efforts towards dealing with her "manifold problems to ensure" that its people lead "a better and happier life."[2]

Facing page:
Prime Minister Prince Al-Sabah (left)
in conversation with President Dr Radhakrishnan
at Rashtrapati Bhavan
in November 1964. Credit: PC

In reply to Prime Minister Shastri's address, the visiting dignitary said, "With all the values of Indian and Kuwaiti friendship, I greet you my dear friend , and have the honour to convey the greetings of my Emir, H. H. Sheikh Abdulla al Salim al Sabah, and the people of Kuwait to the people, Government and leaders of great India."[3]

Before he left the airport, he spoke to members of the press and said, "Our two countries have strong historical affiliations which characterised our relations with fruitful co-operation, friendliness, affection and mutual understanding. I am confident that with the leaders of India we shall foster our co-operation and cement the extremely friendly relations existing between our countries."[3]

The visiting delegation, then, drove to Rashtrapati Bhavan in two Cadillacs and other guest cars from the President's Garage. The Crown Prince sat in the same car as Prime Minister Shastri and was "cheered by thousands lining the 10-mile route from the airport to Rashtrapati Bhavan."[4] On their arrival at Rashtrapati Bhavan, the dignitaries were warmly received by the MSP. Thereafter, they were conducted to their respective suites/rooms.

The Crown Prince stayed in the Dwarka Suite, Abdul Aziz Hussain in the Nalanda Suite and Adel Jarrah in the Himalaya Suite. The Military Attachés shared the Tagore Bedroom. The rest of the entourage stayed in the Dakshin, Pepsu, Neelam, Godavari and Mysore Bedrooms.

Shortly after the arrival of the delegation at Rashtrapati Bhavan, the Prime Minister visited *Rajghat* and *Shantivana*, the *samadhis* of Mahatma Gandhi and Jawaharlal Nehru respectively to pay his homage. Later in the afternoon, he met Prime Minister Shastri at his residence on 10, Janpath. In the evening, the Kuwaiti Prime Minister met the Indian Foreign Affairs Minister, Swaran Singh.

Later that night, at 8.30, Prime Minister Shastri hosted a banquet in honour of the Kuwaiti Prime Minister at Rashtrapati Bhavan.

(R-L): Prince Al-Sabah with Prime Minister Lal Bahadur Shastri at Rashtrapati Bhavan in November 1964. Credit: PD

Prime Minister Lal Bahadur Shastri (left) with Prince Al-Sabah at Rashtrapati Bhavan in November 1964. Credit: PD

Prince Al-Sabah (left) with Foreign Minister of India, Sardar Swaran Singh, during cultural event at Rashtrapati Bhavan in November 1964. Credit: PD

The Ashok Hall and Banquet Hall were beautifully decorated for the occasion. The services of the Sikh Regimental Centre Band were requisitioned and they played a medley of songs. After an elaborate meal, Prime Minister Shastri delivered his banquet speech and welcomed his Kuwaiti counterpart and his entourage. He highlighted the cordial relationship between India and Kuwait, and praised the economic development of Kuwait, which he observed, was higher than that of New York. The Prime Minister expressed optimism at the possibility of both countries establishing joint ventures. He singled out for praise, Kuwait's treatment of the Indian diaspora, who were extended "complete freedom of occupation."[5] The Prime Minister also expressed his gratitude for Kuwait's support of India during the Chinese aggression in 1962. Concluding his address, Prime Minister Shastri said, "May I once again thank Your Highness for your kind visit and may I say that we will continue to work for peace in the world and it is a happy augury that we see eye to eye with each other on many important and vital matters."[6] He then raised a toast to the "health of the Crown Prince and Prime Minister of Kuwait."[7]

Replying to Prime Minister Shastri's address, the Prime Minister of Kuwait Al-Sabah thanked his host, for extending him an invitation to the "great nation of India", which, was a matter of "great pleasure and privilege."[8] He also thanked Prime Minister Shastri for his kind

UNOFFICIAL TRANSLATION

His Excellency Dr. Sarvepalli Radhakrishnan,
President of the Indian Republic.

Your Excellency,

It gives me a great pleasure to see the bonds of friendship between our two countries getting firmer and the good relations luckily subsisting between the Indian people and all the Arabs, becoming more strongly established.

True, the kind invitation directed by your esteemed Government to His Excellency the Prime Minister and Crown Prince, Shaikh Sabah Al-Salim Al-Sabah, had the best effect with us. We have entrusted him to express to your Excellency in person our warmest hearty greetings and great appreciation for the amazing efforts you have been exerting for the construction of your great country and the achievement of welfare and plenty for your friendly people.

Indeed, this visit is a good initiative and a blessed step tending to promote fruitful co-operation with your friendly country in all spheres of life, definitely to the mutual advantage of both peoples. Further, in this context, it pleases me to extol your country's exalted attitude in supporting all just issues as well as the attainment of legal rights by all peoples leading ultimately to maintain the most deeply desired and sought peace.

Lastly, while our hearts are full of hope that the sincere efforts of men of good will towards the good of mankind would be crowned with success, we at the same time, wish your Excellency continued good health and happiness and your great people all progress and prosperity.

(sgd.) Abdulla Alsalim Alsabah.

Unofficial translation of letter of goodwill from Emir Abdulla Al-Salim Al-Sabah to President Dr Radhakrishnan.

words, which he would "cherish and store as a very dear souvenir."[9] Expounding upon the old trade relations between the two countries, he opined that such trade routes were valuable for the "spiritual and cultural products generating from human conduct." He also endorsed the importance of friendship concluding that, "we don't forget any expression of friendship but cherish it in our hearts forever with love and devotion." Ending his brief address, he raised a toast to the Prime Minister of India, Lal Bahadur Shastri.[10]

Coffee and fruits were served after the speeches. The guests were then escorted to the Ashok Hall, where they were treated to a dance and musical recital.

The next day, November 18, the visiting Prime Minister called on President Dr Radhakrishnan at 12.30 pm in the Morning Room at Rashtrapati Bhavan. Both leaders exchanged pleasantries over light refreshments. The Crown Prince also handed over a letter, written in Arabic, from the Emir of Kuwait. The letter spoke about the warm bonds of friendship between the two countries that had further been strengthened by the Indian Government's invitation to the Prime Minister of Kuwait. The Emir wished the Indian President "good health and happiness," and "progress and prosperity" for the people of India.[11]

President Dr Radhakrishnan, later on, replied to the Emir's letter saying that it was a pleasure to receive the honoured dignitaries from Kuwait. He expressed the hope that the visit had "helped to strengthen further the existing bonds of friendship between our two countries."[12] He also hoped that the "visit of the Crown Prince will be a precursor of the State visit of Your Highness to India."[13]

Later, President Dr Radhakrishnan hosted a luncheon in honour of the Kuwaiti Prime Minister. Guests, who were invited for lunch, were escorted to the Yellow Drawing Room, while the President and the Kuwaiti Prime Minister were engaged in discussions. At 1.00 in the afternoon, the Indian President and the Kuwaiti Prime Minister proceeded to the Yellow Drawing Room, where they were introduced to the guests. Fifteen minutes later, dignitaries and guests proceeded to the Grey Dining Room for lunch. The Sikh Regimental Centre Band played light music during the one-hour meal. After lunch, the Crown Prince proceeded to his suite.

That evening, a Civic Reception was held at the Red Fort in honour of the Prime Minister of Kuwait. Reading out the welcome address, the Mayor of Delhi, Bachittar Singh, commented on the commonalities in the approach of the two countries on international issues. The Mayor lauded Kuwait for its "highly developed system of social welfare," and also expressed "gratification" on the state of the well-being of the Indian diaspora in that country.[14] Replying to the address, the Crown Prince thanked Delhi for the warm reception. He recalled the ideals of Pandit Nehru and Mahatma Gandhi, and stated that these very principles were the "basis of Kuwait's declared policy at home and in the international field."[15] While speaking at the reception, the Prince also announced a donation of Rs 1 lakh to the Nehru Memorial Fund.

Reply of President Dr Radhakrishnan to goodwill letter from Emir Abdulla.

Prime Minister Shastri took the opportunity to convey his gratitude to Kuwait for its willingness to help developing economies including India's. Prime Minister Shastri humorously mentioned that so great was the cordiality between the two nations that he had even "got himself invited to Kuwait without waiting for an invitation."[16] The Crown Prince was gifted "an intricately carved ivory canoe at this reception."[17]

The Crown Prince also attended another reception later, hosted the Jamiat-Ulema-i-Hind. The Jamiat-Ulema-i-Hind, one of the primary Islamic organisations in India, was founded in the year 1919. Speaking at the reception, the Crown Prince "urged the Indian Muslims to serve their country and religion as true followers of Islam."[18]

The next day, November 19, the Indo-Arab Society held a reception in honour of Kuwait's Crown Prince. Dr Syed Mahmud, President of the Society, welcomed the Prince and talked about the not merely cordial but "intimate" relationship that India and Kuwait shared with each other. Speaking on the occasion, the Prince expressed happiness about the "overwhelming" welcome accorded to him in India, and said that he would preserve it as a "precious souvenir."[19] He added that his interactions with the Indian leaders were "fruitful", and were conspicuously characterised by "friendliness, affection and mutual understanding."[20] He had rich words of praise for India's support for the Arabs in Algeria and Suez.

Two days later, on November 21, at 8.50 in the morning, the Kuwaiti Prime Minister left Rashtrapati Bhavan for Palam Airport to embark on a tour of other cities of the country, including Aligarh, Agra, Bangalore, Poona and Bombay. The Crown Prince was given a full ceremonial send-off, including a Guard of Honour at the airport. The Indian Prime Minister, Cabinet Ministers and the MSP, amongst others bade him farewell. The aircraft took off at 9.30 am bringing an end to the Crown Prince's stay in Delhi.

After spending 12 days in the country, the visiting Prime Minister left for Kuwait on November 28, 1964, from Bombay's Santa Cruz Airport. The Chief Minister of Maharashtra, VP Naik, and several members of the consular corps saw him off. Before he boarded the flight, the visiting Prime Minister expressed his appreciation for the "kindness and hospitality" shown to him during his stay in India.[21]

A joint communiqué was issued in New Delhi on November 29, 1964, after the Prince had returned to Kuwait. It referred to the enriching experience of the Crown Prince and his entourage, during their stay in India, which helped them to further understand and appreciate Indian culture. It also dealt with the discussions between the Prince and Prime Minister Shastri on various issues, ranging from development to international politics. The visiting Prince had expressed the hope that differences between India and Pakistan would be resolved soon without any external interference. The communiqué ended on the note that Prime Minister Shastri had gladly accepted Kuwait's invitation to visit the country.[22]

On November 24, 1965, the Crown Prince succeeded his brother to become the Emir of Kuwait. His rule continued until December 31, 1977, when he died of cancer. He was 64.

Notes

[1] Ministry of External Affairs (2014), Government of India, "India–Kuwait Relations", accessed May 05, 2015, http://www.mea.gov.in/Portal/ForeignRelation/Kuwait__December_2014.pdf

[2] "Close Ties with India: Kuwait P.M. Gratified," *The Times of India* (New Delhi), November 18, 1964, p. 7.

[3] Ibid.

[4] Ibid.

[5] Ibid.

[6] Ministry of External Affairs (1995), Government of India, MEA Library, Foreign Affairs Records 1964, Volume X, accessed May 25, 2015, http://mealib.nic.in/?pdf2552?000

[7] Ibid.

[8] Ibid.

[9] Ibid.

[10] Ibid.

[11] Ibid.

[12] Records, President's Secretariat, Rashtrapati Bhavan, File No. 15(13)/64.

[13] Ibid.

[14] Ibid.

[15] Indo-Kuwait Talks Soon to Evolve Guiding Principle," *The Hindustan Times* (New Delhi), November 19, 1964, p. 9.

[16] Ibid.

[17] "The Proof of Cordiality," *The Hindustan Times* (New Delhi), November 19, 1964, p. 9.

[18] "Indo-Kuwait Talks Soon to Evolve Guiding Principle," *The Hindustan Times* (New Delhi), November 19, 1964, p. 9.

[19] "Reception for Crown Prince," *The Hindustan Times* (New Delhi), November 19, 1964, p. 9.

[20] "Kuwaiti Premier is Gratified," *The Times of India* (New Delhi), November 20, 1964, p. 4.

[21] Ibid.

[22] "Kuwait PM flies home", *The Times of India* (New Delhi), November 27, 1964, p. 8.

[23] Ministry of External Affairs (1995), Foreign Affairs Records 1964, Volume X

Maharaja Padma Shumshere Jung Bahadur Rana of Nepal was amongst the first leaders of a nation to be received at Government House (now Rashtrapati Bhavan), after India gained independence in 1947. This visit in March 1948 was, however, different from those of other foreign dignitaries, as he chose not to reside at Government House during his stay in Delhi.

The visit to Delhi came in response to an invitation from India's first Prime Minister, Jawaharlal Nehru. It was extended after the Ministry of External Affairs and Commonwealth Relations (EA&CR) had received information that the Maharaja was contemplating retirement and wanted to settle down in Ranchi (presently in the Indian state of Jharkhand). Before settling down, he had planned an extensive tour of India and also expressed a desire to "pay an informal visit to Delhi towards the end of February or early March to meet H.E. the Governor-General and Prime Minister."[1]

The invitation from Prime Minister Nehru was sent to the Maharaja on December 18, 1947. The communication read: "I have learnt with much regret of your Highness' decision to retire from office for reasons of health, and I understand that Your Highness will be visiting Calcutta for medical treatment and will thereafter reside at Ranchi... I need hardly assure you that the Government of India and I personally will do all in our power to meet Your Highness' wishes in respect of facilities for your journey and your residence at Ranchi... I shall be most happy if Your Highness will include a visit to Delhi in your programme to give me an opportunity of meeting you."[2]

Visit of

H.H. Padma Shumshere Jung Bahadur Rana

Maharaja of Nepal

Following the invitation, a letter from the EA&CR was sent to Colonel DH Currie, Military Secretary to the Governor-General (MSGG), informing that the Maharaja would arrive in Delhi on March 12, and would depart on March 19. If convenient to the Governor-General, the Maharaja would like to call on him at Government House, on either March 17, 18 or 19.[3]

Born in 1882 to Maharaja Bhim Shumshere, who was later succeeded by his uncle, Juddha Shumshere Rana, Padma Shumshere Jung Bahadur Rana came from a line of nine Rana rulers and assumed the hereditary office of Prime Minister of Nepal on November 29, 1945.[4] Prior to this, he served as Commander-in-Chief of the Nepal Army, and also held the post of Honorary Colonel in the British Army. As Prime Minister, he was the Supreme Commander-in-Chief of the Nepal Armed Forces.

The Maharaja had desired to usher in democratic reforms in Nepal. He advocated the liberalisation of his country, and pushed for a new constitution that would give more rights to the people. The proposed constitution had envisaged the establishment of a democratic governing structure, including the creation of a bicameral legislature at the Centre.[5] Other far-reaching changes proposed in the new constitution, framed with the

Facing page:
(L-R): Princess Rama, Lady Mountbatten, Maharaja Padma, Governor-General of India Lord Mountbatten and Maharani of Nepal at Government House (now Rashtrapati Bhavan) in March 1948. Credit: PD

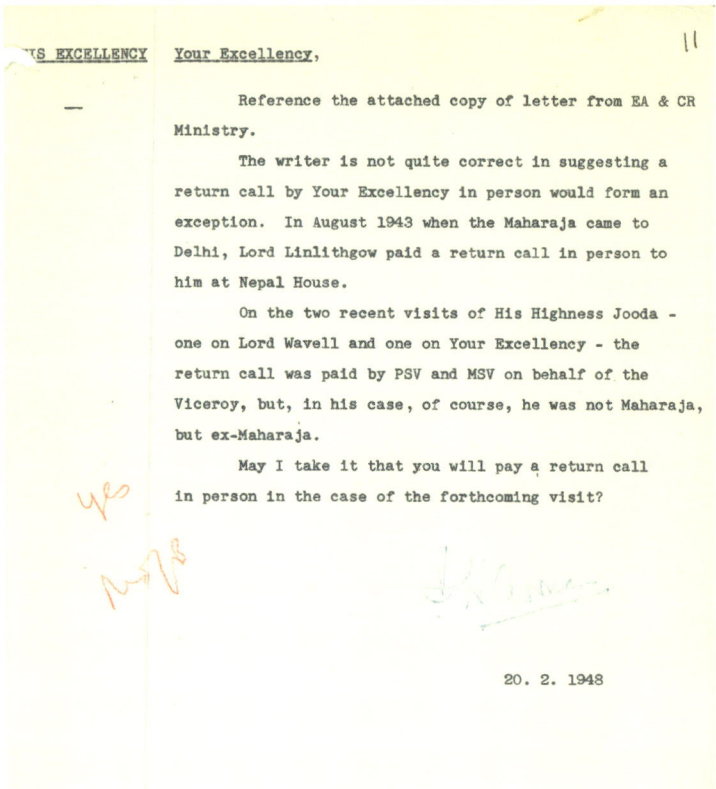

Your Excellency,

Reference the attached copy of letter from EA & CR Ministry.

The writer is not quite correct in suggesting a return call by Your Excellency in person would form an exception. In August 1943 when the Maharaja came to Delhi, Lord Linlithgow paid a return call in person to him at Nepal House.

On the two recent visits of His Highness Jooda - one on Lord Wavell and one on Your Excellency - the return call was paid by PSV and MSV on behalf of the Viceroy, but, in his case, of course, he was not Maharaja, but ex-Maharaja.

May I take it that you will pay a return call in person in the case of the forthcoming visit?

20. 2. 1948

Communication on the return call on Maharaja of Nepal by Lord Mountbatten and accepted by him with minutes in red on left.

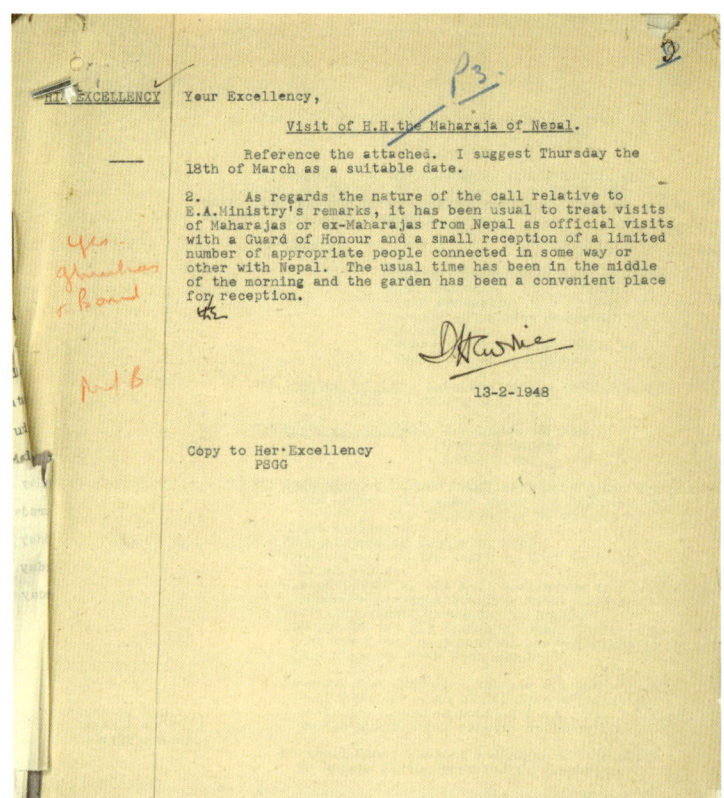

Your Excellency,

Visit of H.H.the Maharaja of Nepal.

Reference the attached. I suggest Thursday the 18th of March as a suitable date.

2. As regards the nature of the call relative to E.A.Ministry's remarks, it has been usual to treat visits of Maharajas or ex-Maharajas from Nepal as official visits with a Guard of Honour and a small reception of a limited number of appropriate people connected in some way or other with Nepal. The usual time has been in the middle of the morning and the garden has been a convenient place for reception.

13-2-1948

Copy to Her Excellency
PSGG

Approval (in red on left margin), accorded by Lord Mountbatten for presentation of Guard of Honour for Maharaja Padma.

help of Indian advisors, included the provision of adult franchise and an independent judiciary.

At the end of January 1948, however, a week before he was scheduled to announce the constitutional reforms, the Maharaja abdicated his position as Prime Minister on grounds of ill-health. Announcing that he had to consult physicians in India, a time-consuming process, he decided that it was in the best interests of his country, if he retired in favour of his brother, Mohan Shumshere Jung Bahadur Rana.

Before the Maharaja arrived in India, protocol officials were locked in extended parleys to decide if the visit would be termed a State Visit. The EA&CR Ministry, in the meantime, informed Colonel Currie that they were deliberating the issue and only after they had heard from the Indian Ambassador to Nepal, would the Governor-General's Secretariat be informed of the formalities to be followed during the visit.

The Governor-General, however, was not one who countenanced protracted bureaucratic delays in decision making. He quickly laid the issue to rest approving a proposal contained in a memo from Colonel Currie which read: "it has been usual to treat visits of Maharajas or ex-Maharajas from Nepal as official visits with a Guard of Honour and a small reception of a limited number of appropriate people connected in some way or other with Nepal."[6] The memo was approved by Lord Mountbatten with the noting: "Yes" "[sic]" "& Band."[7]

A related issue that engaged the EA&CR Ministry was whether the Governor-General of India should pay a return call on the Maharaja. An Under Secretary at the Ministry wrote to the MSGG suggesting that the Governor-General pay a return call on the Maharaja in person. The letter added that though strictly according to protocol, the Governor-General did not need to return the call, "an exception might be made and special honour shown to Maharaja Padma, as he has been extremely helpful over the retention by India of Gurkha troops."[8]

The Military Secretary, however, disagreed with the Ministry of EA&CR in suggesting that a return call by the Governor-General would "form an exception." In a note to the Governor-General, he drew a parallel between this occasion and the time when, in 1943, Lord Linlithgow had paid a return call on the Maharaja of Nepal in person at Nepal House. The note dated February 20, 1948 sent by Colonel Currie was approved without reservation by Lord Mountbatten with a simple "Yes," putting to rest issues which would have perhaps, engaged the analytical minds of the Ministry of EA&CR for many days.[9]

Another matter that engaged Lord Mountbatten's attention was of the presents to be given to the Maharaja. When an earlier note was sent to him on this subject, the Governor-General queried the MSGG asking, "We have already given him full dress photos in silver frames – What can we give now?"[10]

Maharaja Padma inspecting a Guard of Honour in Forecourt at Government House (now Rashtrapati Bhavan) in March 1948. Credit: PD

Maharaja Padma escorted by military staff to Durbar Hall, Government House (now Rashtrapati Bhavan) in March 1948. Credit: PD

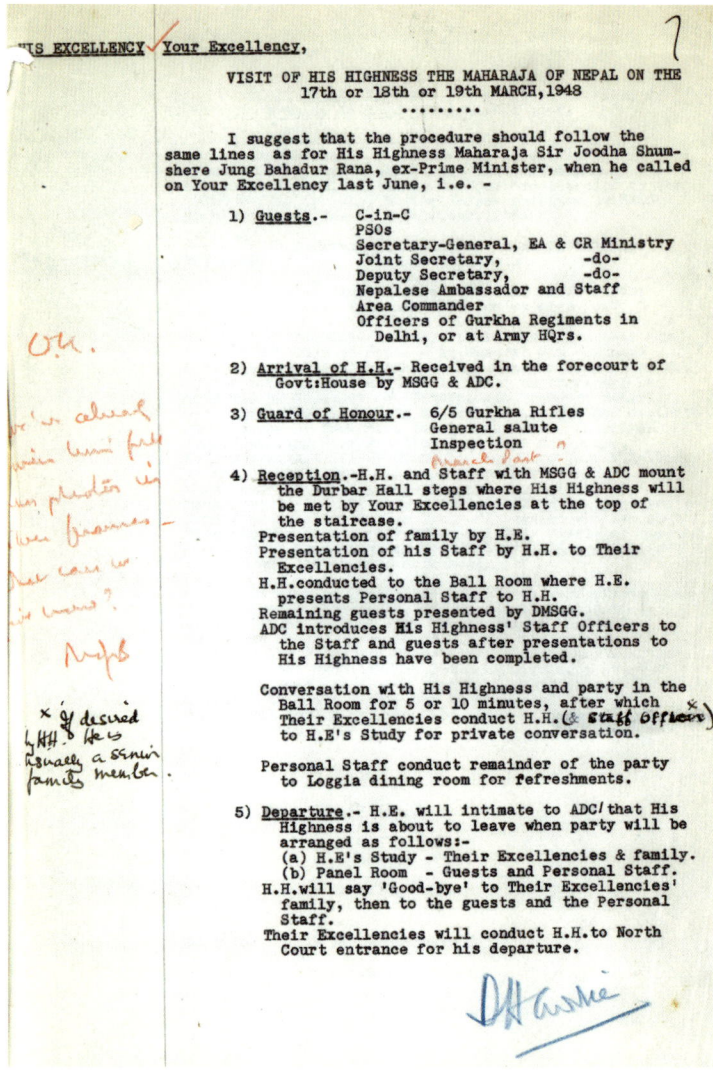

The MSGG received the Maharaja on behalf of the Governor-General after taking special permission from Lord Mountbatten. Besides, a representative of the Prime Minister; HVR Iyengar, Secretary General of the Ministry of EA&CR, its Joint Secretary, PA Menon and Under Secretary, VMM Nair and the Chief Commissioner of Delhi received the Maharaja.

Elaborate arrangements had been made in Government House to ensure that the royal visitor was received with the pomp and ceremony his title demanded. The details of the programme had been very carefully prepared and personally approved of by the Governor-General.

It was, as always, a highly synchronised programme. By 11.30 am, the Personal Staff of the Governor-General were on duty, and the men from The President's Bodyguard were in position at the Durbar Hall steps, passages and the Ballroom. By 11.45 am, a select group of guests, who had been chosen to attend the reception ceremony at Government House, trickled in from the North Entrance. They were escorted to the Ballroom through the North Marble Staircase. There they were received by the Deputy Military Secretary to the Governor-General (DMSGG).

At 10 minutes to noon, the Governor-General; the Nepalese Ambassador; Princess Rama; Rani Bhuban Rajya Lakshmi Sahiba, a Nepalese aristocrat and wife of the Raja Sahib of Khetri; and HVR Iyengar and his wife arrived. They were escorted to the entrance of the Durbar Hall, where they awaited the arrival of Lord and Lady Mountbatten. Lady Brabourne, Lady Pamela Mountbatten, daughters of the Governor-General and Lady Brecknock[13] also assembled at the same location.

At five minutes to noon, Lord Mountbatten, splendidly attired in a dark blue monkey jacket, with his sword in its scabbard, and the Star of India and the Nepalese Star shining proudly on his breast, joined those who had already assembled at the entrance to the Durbar Hall. The Governor-General was accompanied by his wife, Edwina. Outside, in the sun and in absolute quiet, stood an Inter-Services Guard of Honour and an Inter–Services Band at the rear.

At 12 noon, the gates of Government House swung wide open welcoming the royal motorcade. The cars drove into the Forecourt via the North Sunken Road and came to a halt at a point opposite to where the Guard of Honour was positioned. The Maharaja "dismounted" from the car and was received by the MSGG and an aide-de-camp (ADC). He was presented a Guard of Honour by the 6/5 Gurkha Rifles which gave him a "General Salute" while the band played Nepal's national anthem.

After the Maharaja had inspected the Guard of Honour, he was escorted up the wide, shallow steps to the Durbar Hall, where he was warmly received by the waiting dignitaries. Lord Mountbatten presented Lady Brabourne and Lady Pamela Mountbatten, Lady Brecknock and their Personal Staff to the Maharaja. Thereafter, the visiting dignitary presented his staff members to the Governor-

Note on arrangements for the Maharaja's visit to Government House (now Rashtrapati Bhavan) as approved by Lord Mountbatten vide minutes in red on left margin.

The MSGG recommended that it would be appropriate that "separate photographs of Your Excellencies in silver frames bearing Your Excellencies' new Gold Monograms should be given to Lt. General His Highness Maharaja Sir Padma Shumshere Jung Bahadur Rana when he calls on Your Excellencies."[11] His Highness Sir Juddha Shumshere Jung Bahadur Rana had sent the Governor-General presents on the occasion of his silver wedding anniversary. The Governor-General had in return sent a silver Cigarette Box and silver Flap jack from Edwina Mountbatten to Her Highness, General Juddha's wife besides photo frames of Lord and Lady Mountbatten.

After obtaining the Governor-General's approval, the date of the Maharaja's visit to Government House was fixed for March 18, 1948. The Maharaja arrived at New Delhi Railway Station from Calcutta by a special train on the morning of March 12, 1948, and alighted at the ceremonial platform.[12] This was a private visit, and accordingly, there was no Guard of Honour at the Railway Station.

(L-R): Lord and Lady Mountbatten, Maharani of Nepal and Maharaja Padma climbing the steps to the Durbar Hall of Government House (now Rashtrapati Bhavan) in March 1948. Credit: PD

Maharaja Padma (left) with Prime Minister Nehru at the latter's residence, Teen Murti Bhavan, in March 1948. Credit PD

General. Next to be introduced were the Nepalese Ambassador, Princess Rama, Rajkumari Bhuban, and the Iyengars.

The Maharaja was then escorted to the Ballroom by uniformed *aides-de-camp* (AsDC). Here 19 select guests, including Brockman, Private Secretary to the Governor-General (PSGG), and Lady Currie were introduced by the Governor-General to the Maharaja. Other guests, in the meanwhile, were escorted by the Deputy Comptroller, Governor-General's Household (DCGGH) to the Ballroom where they were introduced by the DMSGG.

Thereafter, Lord and Lady Mountbatten and the Maharaja spent about 10-15 minutes in conversation in the Ballroom. Following this brief interaction, the Maharaja, Lady Brabourne, Lady Pamela Mountbatten and Lady Brecknock, the Nepalese Ambassador, his family and General Krishna Shumshere Jung Bahadur Rana (who was accompanying the Maharaja) were all conducted to the Governor-General's Study. After the remaining guests left the premises via the Viceroy's Staircase, the Maharaja bade the House Party (Lady Brabourne, Lady Pamela Mountbatten and Lady Brecknock) goodbye.

Lord and Lady Mountbatten then escorted the Maharaja to the North Entrance, where the Presidential Rolls-Royce, (assigned to him) was stationed. The motorcade left for the Nepalese Embassy on Barakhamba Road. It was followed by a police escort and a Humber II.

At 2.55 pm, the Governor-General left Government House in his Rolls Royce for the Nepalese Embassy to make a return call on the Maharaja. Accompanied by the PSGG and MSGG, this return call by the Governor-General was brief. Lord Mountbatten, dressed in a monkey jacket sporting the Star of India and the Nepal Star, returned to Government House at 3.20 pm.

The Nepalese Ambassador hosted a dinner at the Nepalese Embassy, in honour of the visiting Maharaja, in the evening. Notable dignitaries who attended the event included the "Governor-General and Lady Mountbatten, Pandit Nehru, Sardar Baldev Singh, diplomatic representatives of various countries and a large gathering of distinguished Indians."[14]

Maharaja Padma Shumshere left New Delhi by a special train from the ceremonial platform of the station at 8.35 pm on March 19, 1948.

He passed away on April 11, 1961, near Calcutta.[15] He was 78.

Notes

1 Records, President's Secretariat, Rashtrapati Bhavan, File No. V–II/41.

2 Ibid.

3 Ibid.

4 "Nepal's New Premier," *The Times of India* (New Delhi), December 1, 1945, p. 1.

5 "Liberal Rule for Nepal," *The Times of India* (New Delhi), February 11, 1948, p. 1.

6 Records, President's Secretariat, File No. V–II/41.

7 Ibid.

8 Ibid.

9 Ibid.

10 Ibid.

11 Ibid.

12 "Nepal Premier in Delhi," *The Times of India* (New Delhi), March 19, 1948, p. 6.

13 There were no details regarding Lady Brecknock in the documents of Rashtrapati Bhavan. However, from the website (http://www.wherwell.net/ lady–brecknock.htm), she has been referred to as the cousin of Lady Mountbatten.

14 "Nepal Premier to Leave Today," *The Statesman* (New Delhi), March 19, 1948, p. 4.

15 Harris M. Lentz, *Heads of States and Government: A worldwide Encyclopaedia of Over2,300 Leaders, 1945 through 1992* (London: Fitzroy Dearborn Publishers, 1995), p. 573.

The maximum number of times that Rashtrapati Bhavan has had the honour of hosting a Head of State/ Government has been in the case of Maharaja Mahendra Bir Bikram Shah Dev, the 9th King of the Shah dynasty of Nepal.[1] He was, in fact, one of the two Heads of States (the other being President Josip Broz Tito of Yugoslavia) to have stayed at Rashtrapati Bhavan, as the honoured guest of four Indian Presidents – Dr Rajendra Prasad, Dr Sarvepalli Radhakrishnan, Dr Zakir Husain and VV Giri.

Prince Mahendra was born to King Tribhuvan and Queen Kanti on June 11, 1920, in a defining period of Nepal's history. He spent his early life under house arrest in his palace during the reign of the Rana dynasty that had come to power after the Kot massacre in 1846. Consequently, Crown Prince Mahendra was home-schooled with little formal instruction. Yet, he was a polyglot, fluent in Nepali, Hindi, English, Sanskrit and Urdu and had a gift for poetry.[2]

Prince Mahendra was coronated on May 2, 1956. He had grown up to be a man with leadership qualities. Writing about the Crown Prince's qualities, *The Statesman* said that Prince Mahendra, though "young, looks wiser than his years, seems to keep an open mind on most issues and has the interest of his country close at heart."[3]

King Mahendra had many great attributes. Though he was described as a shy, slender and rather short man, given to wearing prescription glasses, he was "an excellent rider at an early age."[4] He was also described as "a sensitive poet by inclination, a statesman by necessity."[5]

November 1955
June 1958
July 1960
August 1961
August 27–31, 1963
May 1964
November 25 to December 18, 1965
August 26–27, 1970

Visits of

H.M. Maharaja Mahendra Bir Bikram Shah Dev

of Nepal

As a King, Mahendra had taken several initiatives. He enlisted international support for the development of his country, stuck in a "medieval economy."[6] He introduced many social and political reforms, notable amongst them was the 'Panchayat System,' a form of indigenous democracy which he felt was more suited to Nepal's political system. He made special efforts to be in touch with his people. He undertook extensive tours of his country, on foot accompanied by 2000 people, and travelled from village to village, and learning more about the villagers. He blessed them, something that the people valued immensely as the King is considered to be an incarnation of the Hindu God 'Vishnu' in Nepal.[7]

The November 1955 Visit

The King also took active interest in his nation's foreign policy, as he was well aware of Nepal's unique geopolitical location between two large countries and worked towards establishing its neutrality vis-à-vis China and India.

Before King Mahendra's accession, Nepal had diplomatic relations with only four countries in the world – India, Britain, USA and France. Described as "a man who

Facing page:
(L-R): King Mahendra Bir Bikram Shah Dev (second) with Queen Ratna (partially obscured) and President Dr Prasad at Rashtrapati Bhavan in July 1960. Credit: PC

would rather listen to others than talk himself,"[8] one of the better attributes of a mature foreign policy strategist, the King worked tirelessly to increase Nepal's diplomatic presence in a number of countries including Pakistan, China and the Soviet Union. To shake away its perceived isolation, Nepal also joined the United Nations in 1955 and the Non-Aligned Movement in 1961. The establishment of links with the outside world were no mean achievements, given Nepal's long history of relative international isolation and "dependence on outside assistance."[9]

King Mahendra was aware of the warm and cordial relationship Nepal had with India. Consequently, his first visit to India came in November 1955, less than a year after he had ascended the throne as King of Nepal. It was a six-week long visit during which he travelled the length and breadth of the country to understand what his nation could learn from India. He is said to have remarked upon his return, "If I can put into practice all that I learnt and saw in India my visit there can be said to be successful."[10]

The June 1958 Visit

In 1958, the King of Nepal decided to stop-over in New Delhi for a day, on his way to Moscow for a three-week long State Visit. Though his brief halt was termed as private visit, King Mahendra and Queen Ratna Rajya Laxmi Rana Shah, whom heal most always travelled, stayed at Rashtrapati Bhavan as State Guests. It was in the summer of 1958, two days into the month of June, when the flight carrying the royal couple and a delegation of 30 high-ranking officials touched down at New Delhi's Safdarjung Airport. Prime Minister Jawaharlal Nehru, Members of the Cabinet and the Service Chiefs, received the Nepalese royal couple.[11]

Later in the day, Prime Minister Nehru called on the King and Queen at Rashtrapati Bhavan. They discussed issues concerning international affairs and matters of mutual interest. The meeting was followed by lunch. The next day, the royal couple met President Dr Rajendra Prasad for tea. In the evening, the Prime Minister of India hosted a dinner in honour of the visiting King and Queen.[12] The following day, June 4 in the morning, his visit to India ended and King Mahendra departed for the Soviet Union in a special plane dispatched by the Soviet Government.[13]

The July 1960 Visit

Rashtrapati Bhavan had the honour of hosting the royal couple of Nepal again in July 1960. Though this too was a private visit, India welcomed the visiting dignitaries with all the pomp and grandeur associated with a ceremonial State Visit.[14]

It, however, came at a time of political turbulence In Nepal. The Kingdom had its first Parliamentary elections in 1959, in which the Nepali Congress Party emerged victorious. However, democracy could not be sustained for long. Eighteen months after the elections,

on December 15, 1960, King Mahendra dismissed the Cabinet, dissolved the elected Parliament and assumed personal rule.[15]

The Prime Minister of Nepal, Bishweshwar Prasad Koirala, and other Ministers were arrested while the King charged the Nepali Congress Party of "misusing [sic] authority to serve the party interests, dislocating and paralysing governmental authority, imperilling the national unity, and failure to introduce economic reforms."[16] He further assumed the Chairmanship of a "new Council of Ministers"[17] that he appointed.

As a "King by birth and a democrat by faith,"[18] the ruler explained his actions as being motivated by his determination "to save Nepal from corrupt practices and ensure the smooth working and resuscitation of the democratic system in times to come."[19] His means, he asserted, would be a system of "guided democracy."[20]

This visit materialised when the King and the Queen decided to spend a fortnight in Kashmir on a private visit on their way home after a 3-month long world tour.[21] On arrival at the airport, they were given a State Reception at the airport by the Government of Kashmir.

After spending 10 sunny, pleasant days in Srinagar, the royal couple came to New Delhi on the morning of July 20, 1960 and were received with the ceremonies associated with a State Arrival.[22] The couple and their young son, 10-year-old Prince Dhirendra, spent four days in Delhi before departing for Darjeeling, en route to Kathmandu.

The airport was decorated with the flags of the two countries. After the magnificently uniformed Services Band played the national anthems of both countries, King Mahendra took the salute of the Inter-Services Guard of Honour. On their arrival, the splendidly attired couple were presented bouquets and garlands by an excited crowd and many bowed low acknowledging the King's divine and the couple's royal status. At the airport, the King spoke to the correspondents and expressed his gratitude to the President of India, the Prime Minister, the Government and the people for the warm welcome accorded to him. "It gives me great pleasure," he said, "to be in the Capital of friendly India once again after three months' visit abroad."[23]

A little after noon the next day, the King met President Dr Prasad informally in the latter's study for 40-minutes.[24] Their discussions were reportedly centred on the King's recent foreign trip, especially his visit to the United States. Later that day, the President hosted a lunch in honour of the King and Queen. In the evening, Bhagwan Sahay, India's former Ambassador to Nepal held a dinner in honour of the royal guests. The King and Queen's other engagements included a meeting with Ellsworth Bunker, the US Ambassador to India, and a meeting with Pandit Govind Ballabh Pant, India's Union Home Minister.[25] The King also enjoyed a film show at Rashtrapati Bhavan's private theatre the day before he left.[26]

The strength and vibrancy of the bilateral relationship were

Vice President Dr Radhakrishnan (left) with King Mahendra at Rashtrapati Bhavan in August 1961. Credit: PC

particularly evident during this visit. The multiple times the King referred to India as a "friendly nation," and three meetings that the Prime Minister of India had with the King[27] despite it being a private visit, was testimony to the close relations that the two nations shared.

The August 1961 Visit

King Mahendra returned to New Delhi at the end of August 1961 as a State Guest. He was travelling with his wife, Queen Ratna, and Crown Prince Dhirendra (who was home on vacation from Eton), as well as the Foreign Minister Dr Tulsi Giri, *en route* to Belgrade for the "neutral Summit conference" that was to begin on September 1, 1961. The Belgrade Conference was expected to address major international issues of the time including the Berlin crisis, the Angola crisis and the Bizerte dispute. The royal family had planned to arrive in India on August 28 and proceed to Belgrade the following day.[28]

On August 28, as scheduled, the royal couple arrived at Palam Airport in their personal plane, to a ceremonial reception. They were received by the Vice President, Dr Radhakrishnan; Prime Minister Nehru and the Mayor of Delhi amongst others. The Mayor of Delhi, Sham Nath, garlanded the King in swathes of marigolds as a 21-gun salute boomed in welcome. After the reception, the royal family drove to Rashtrapati Bhavan, where

they stayed in its Guest Wing.[29]

This was, however, a short visit. Nevertheless, King Mahendra found time to hold an hour-long press conference, described as an "informal chat" at the Embassy of Nepal on the second day of his visit.[30] He spoke about matters relating to the detention of former Prime Minister BP Koirala, border issues with China, the issue of the ownership of Mount Everest and the new "*Panchayat System*" he had introduced. He emphasised that the Government and the people of Nepal had the "friendliest" feelings for India.[31] "It would be wrong to say," he said, "that there was any anti-Indian feeling in his country merely because some excited people had said something or wrote against India."[32]

He also answered questions from the press with great finesse. Given to asking leading questions, one journalist questioned whether the King found Prime Minister Nehru friendlier now. He replied that "he had always found Mr Nehru very friendly" and added humorously, "but this time he is more friendly."[33]

The August 1963 Visit

Between 1961 and 1963, there were many bilateral visits between India and Nepal. India's Home Minister, Lal Bahadur Shastri visited Nepal in March 1963 on a "goodwill mission."[34] During the visit, Shastri also extended an invitation to King Mahendra to

(L-R): King Mahendra Bir Bikram Shah Dev, President Dr Radhakrishnan and Queen Ratna at Rashtrapati Bhavan in August 1963. Credit: PC

visit India, which the King accepted.[35]

Responding to the invitation, King Mahendra arrived in India for 13 days, from August 27, 1963. This visit was given particular importance by both nations. On the eve of the visit, Government of India released a publication entitled, "Cooperation for progress in Nepal."[36] It had messages from the President of India and the Prime Minister on the common bonds that exist between the two nations and the close ties that they maintain.

Prime Minister Nehru's message stressed that friendly cooperation between India and Nepal would "continue to grow and benefit the peoples of both the countries."[37] President Dr Radhakrishnan too wrote in the same vein and stressed on the bond of friendship and understanding, based on a common cultural heritage that existed between India and Nepal.[38]

Almost in reciprocation, *The Commoner*, Kathmandu's oldest English daily, published a three-column editorial on its front page, welcoming King Mahendra's visit to New Delhi beginning the following day. "We are certain" the editorial read, "that he [King Mahendra] would make it clear to India that we of Nepal are not among those who will ever betray a friend or see a friend betrayed."[39]

With this near euphoric build-up, King Mahendra and Queen Ratna arrived at Delhi's Palam Airport on August 27, 1963, to a "warm" welcome. They were greeted by President Dr Radhakrishnan, Prime Minister Nehru and other senior officials of the Government of India.[40]

The President of India, in his welcome speech at the airport, complimented the visiting dignitary on the recent social reforms that he had introduced in Nepal. He described them as "great steps towards the emancipation of the people of Nepal."[41] King Mahendra in his reply expressed his appreciation and satisfaction in the manner in which India was trying to understand Nepal's problems.[42]

After the reception at the airport, the King and the Queen drove to Rashtrapati Bhavan in a Presidential motorcade, accompanied by President Dr Radhakrishnan.[43] Shortly after their arrival, the royal couple, accompanied by Dr Tulsi Giri, Prime Minister of Nepal and his wife, paid a courtesy call on the Indian President. Prime Minister Nehru called on King Mahendra on the evening of August 27, 1963.[44]

Later the same evening, a State Banquet was hosted by President Dr Radhakrishnan in honour of Their Majesties in the grand Banquet Hall of Rashtrapati Bhavan. It was attended by almost a hundred guests including Vice President, Dr Zakir Husain; Prime Minister, Jawaharlal Nehru; Cabinet Ministers and Service Chiefs.[45] The fare on offer at the banquet was an elaborate four-course meal prepared by the kitchen of Rashtrapati Bhavan. On the menu were delicacies like *Mulligatawny Soup* and *Fish and Cabbage Paupiettes*. An *Oriental preparation of Chicken/Vegetables with Potato Croquettes and Green Peas* on the side formed the main course. The meal ended with *Fruit Chantillyas* dessert.[46]

Following the grand meal, President Dr Radhakrishnan proposed a toast in honour of King Mahendra and Queen Ratna. In his banquet speech, the President underlined the importance of the reforms introduced in Nepal and how they would promote equality

(Seated, R-L): Queen Ratna, President Dr Prasad and King Mahendra at Rashtrapati Bhavan in May 1964. Credit: PC

in the country. He added that there was a further need to make a disciplined effort, promote education and create public awareness until the reforms make a difference in reality.

In his reply, King Mahendra underscored the importance of Indo-Nepal relations. India and Nepal had, he said, "lived together in peace and amity since ages past and we adhere to our long cherished belief that this historical relationship between our two countries can be further strengthened."[47]

The second day of the trip began with a visit to *Rajghat* where the couple paid their respects at Gandhi's *samadhi* and signed the Visitors Book. Later, the Defence Minister of India, YB Chawan, called on the King at Rashtrapati Bhavan. In the afternoon, Home Minister Lal Bahadur Shastri held discussions with the King for about 30-minutes. King Mahendra later met Prime Minister Nehru for an hour-and-a-half, before having lunch en suite.[48] The meeting covered topics ranging from the completion of India-aided projects, to further economic assistance to Nepal.[49]

The busy day ended with King Mahendra inaugurating an exhibition of Nepalese contemporary paintings and home-crafts arranged by the Council of Nepalese Affairs at the India International Centre. The King and Queen also attended a reception hosted in their honour by the All India Indo-Nepal Friendship Association. Several Indian Ministers, Members of Parliament, diplomats, leaders of political and social organisations attended the reception.[50]

Their Majesties were to leave for Srinagar on the morning of

August 30, 1963. They were, however, forced by bad weather, to return to Delhi shortly after take-off. Their visit to Srinagar had to wait for the following day. President Dr Radhakrishnan, Vice President Dr Zakir Husain, Prime Minister Nehru, Indira Gandhi, members of the diplomatic corps and Chiefs of the three Services bid the distinguished guests goodbye at Palam Airport on the morning of August 31. They returned to Delhi on September 8, accompanied by the *Sardar-i-Riyasat*, Dr Karan Singh. The couple, however, drove to the Nepalese Embassy as their State Visit had ended when they left Delhi on August 31. They flew to Israel the next morning.

It was yet another successful and enjoyable visit for the royal couple. The King gave expression to his sentiment when he told the assembled pressmen before he left for Srinagar, that memories of the reception and hospitality accorded to him and the Queen would remain evergreen in his mind.[51]

The May 1964 Visit

On May 17, King Mahendra arrived in India on a day's private visit, accompanied by Queen Ratna, two of their daughters and the King's sister. King Mahendra met with Prime Minister Nehru after which he and his family departed for West Germany.

King Mahendra and Queen Ratna were in Germany when the news reached them that Jawaharlal Nehru had passed away on May 27, 1964, just 10 days after they had met him. As their programme in Germany could not be altered, the royal couple rerouted their return journey to spend two days in Delhi before leaving for Kathmandu.

The flight carrying the royal couple landed at New Delhi's Palam Airport on the night of June 17, 1964. King Mahendra was received by Minister of State for Foreign Affairs, Lakshmi Menon. Shortly after arriving in New Delhi, King Mahendra said that Pandit Nehru's mantle had fallen on the able shoulders of Lal Bahadur Shastri, who had succeeded Pandit Nehru as Prime Minister. He further added that under the new Prime Minister's leadership, Nepal looked "forward with confidence to the continued improvement and strengthening of Indo–Nepalese bonds of friendship."[52] The King recalled the role played by Prime Minister Nehru in promoting Indo–Nepal relations and also his international stature and said that the late Prime Minister was "not only the best friend of Nepal but also a great world statesman."[53] They laid a wreath at Nehru's *Samadhi* at *Shantivana*, and later met Indira Gandhi and offered their condolences on the death of her father.

The November 1965 Visit

War broke out between India and Pakistan in the summer of 1965. Disturbed by this eruption of hostilities, King Mahendra penned identical letters to the Presidents of both countries, appealing for peace, while strongly maintaining Nepal's neutrality.[54]

In a gesture of Nepal's continuing goodwill towards India, King Mahendra and Queen Ratna arrived in New Delhi on a four-week visit on November 25, 1965. He came with a large entourage that included his Foreign Minister. The visit also sought to serve another purpose. King Mahendra planned to undertake a *tirthyatra*, visiting 20 temples across India.[55]

As the royal couple's special aircraft landed at Palam Airport, a 21-gun salute boomed in welcome. As they alighted from the aircraft, they were welcomed by President Dr Radhakrishnan, Vice President Zakir Husain, Prime Minister Shastri, Mayor of Delhi, Chief of Protocol (COP) and the Military Secretary to the President (MSP) Major General GS Gill. Thereafter, the King inspected an Inter-Services Guard of Honour. Following this, the assembled Ministers, Members of Parliament and diplomats were introduced to the King and Queen by the COP.[56] The King was then led to especially erected enclosure at the airport where a group of select invitees were introduced to the royal couple.

Delivering his customary speech at the airport, President Dr Radhakrishnan welcomed the King and Queen and noted the interdependent nature of bilateral ties between India and Nepal. He assured the King of India's continued political and economic assistance. In his reply, King Mahendra thanked the President for his invitation and also conveyed "the best wishes of the Nepalese people to the people of India."[57]

King Mahendra and his entourage then drove to Rashtrapati Bhavan in a grand motorcade. The King and the President were seated in a Mercedes Benz and the Prime Minister and the Queen in a Cadillac. As the motorcade reached Vijay Chowk, the President's Bodyguard (PBG) on their magnificent steeds, escorted the motorcade to Rashtrapati Bhavan.

The motorcade arrived at the Forecourt at 4.20 pm. The PBG branched off as the cars came to a stately halt. The King of Nepal was received by the MSP. The Personal Staff of the President, dressed in their Blue Patrol jackets, blue overalls, resplendent in their full medals, sashes, swords and aiguillettes, stood to attention in the corridors of Rashtrapati Bhavan. The President then introduced his Personal Staff to the King, after which the guests were escorted to the Guest Loggia for refreshments. Later, the King and Queen were escorted to the Dwarka Suite through the corridors lined with sowars of the PBG holding lances and dressed in full ceremonial uniforms with knee-high boots. The personal standard of King Mahendra was flown atop the Guest Wing. Sentries were specially posted to keep the corridors clear of unauthorised people for the duration of the King's stay. The entourage stayed at Rashtrapati Bhavan.

At 5.15 pm, the King and Queen of Nepal called on President Dr

King Mahendra (left) with President Dr Radhakrishnan at Rashtrapati Bhavan in May 1964. Credit: PC

(L-R): King Mahendra (second), Queen Ratna and President Dr Radhakrishnan at Rashtrapati Bhavan in November 1965. Credit: PC

Radhakrishnan in the Morning Room. They were escorted to the venue by the *aides-de-camp* (AsDC). After exchanging pleasantries, the President and the visiting dignitaries were conducted to the Yellow Drawing Room, where the President's Personal Staff and the King's delegates had congregated and were waiting to be introduced to the principals. After the introductions and light refreshments, the gathering dispersed at 5.45 pm to get ready for the State Banquet that was hosted later that evening.

At 8.20 pm, the President of India paid a return call on the King and Queen in their suite. And at 8.32 pm, accompanied by three AsDC, they were escorted to the Ashok Hall via the Guest Corridor. The *sowars* of PBG stood as sentinels, as the three dignitaries walked to the central arch of the Ashok Hall. After they came to a halt under it, the band struck up the national anthems of both countries

in succession. Thereafter, the guests, who had arrived earlier and were standing in horseshoe formation, "with wives to the right", were introduced to the King, Queen and the Indian President. The gathering then moved to the Banquet Hall for a scrumptious feast. After the last course, the *khidmatgars* (butlers), as per instructions, cleared the tables and left the Hall. The President of India then raised a toast to His Majesty the King of Nepal.[58]

Proposing the toast, President Dr Radhakrishnan said that India was desirous of assisting Nepal in its development. He said, "you are trying to develop the economy of your country. In that we should like to be of some little assistance to you as a mere illustration of economic cooperation between growing countries."[59] The President described Nepal as India's "good and friendly neighbour." Replying to the toast, King Mahendra said that Nepal had immense respect for

August 10, 1970.

Your Majesty,

I understand that Your Majesty will be passing through Delhi enroute to Europe on August 26. May I say that Your Majesty would be most welcome to stay in Rashtrapati Bhavan. Although I have to be in South India on a tour to Hyderabad, I do hope that Your Majesty will make use of Rashtrapati Bhavan which will be a matter of great pleasure and satisfaction to us all. The Vice-President will be in New Delhi throughout.

Also, it would be our pleasure and privilege if Your Majesties could accept our invitation to be our guests on the return journey when Your Majesties land in Bombay.

I avail myself of this opportunity to renew to Your Majesty the assurances of my highest esteem.

Yours sincerely,

Sd. V.V. Giri

His Majesty
Shri Shri Shri Shri Shri
Maharajadhiraja Mahendra Bir Bikram Shah Deva,
King of Nepal,
KATHMANDU.

DS(N)

PS may be informed of the arrangements

12.8

Letter from President VV Giri to King Mahendra inviting him to "stay" at Rashtrapati Bhavan.

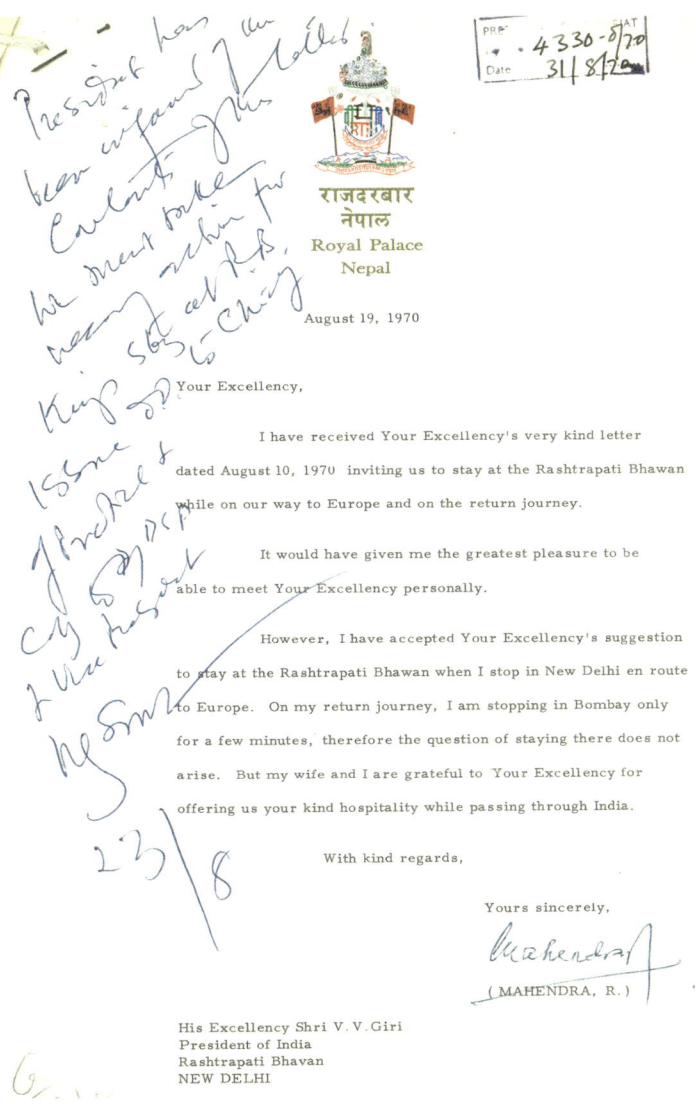

राजदरबार
नेपाल
Royal Palace
Nepal

August 19, 1970

Your Excellency,

I have received Your Excellency's very kind letter dated August 10, 1970 inviting us to stay at the Rashtrapati Bhawan while on our way to Europe and on the return journey.

It would have given me the greatest pleasure to be able to meet Your Excellency personally.

However, I have accepted Your Excellency's suggestion to stay at the Rashtrapati Bhawan when I stop in New Delhi en route to Europe. On my return journey, I am stopping in Bombay only for a few minutes, therefore the question of staying there does not arise. But my wife and I are grateful to Your Excellency for offering us your kind hospitality while passing through India.

With kind regards,

Yours sincerely,

(MAHENDRA, R.)

His Excellency Shri V.V.Giri
President of India
Rashtrapati Bhavan
NEW DELHI

Letter of acceptance from King Mahendra to stay at Rashtrapati Bhavan.

India and its peace loving tradition.[60] After the banquet, the visiting dignitaries or the House Party as they are termed, were conducted to their respective suites. The other invitees were escorted to their vehicles by the President's Personal Staff.

On the afternoon of next day, November 26, the Prime Minister of India hosted a luncheon in honour of the royal guests in the Grey Dining Room at Rashtrapati Bhavan. Guests, who arrived at the South Court via the South Sunken Road, were conducted to the Yellow Drawing Room by the Rashtrapati Bhavan staff. The Prime Minister arrived at 12.50 pm and received the King and Queen of Nepal who arrived five minutes later. After the assembled guests were presented to the principals, the distinguished guests and invitees were escorted to the Grey Dining Room where they sat according to a pre-arranged table plan for lunch. At 2.50 pm, the lunch ended and the Prime Minister took leave of his guests and departed for his residence.

On November 27, the Indian Prime Minister met the King of Nepal, without aides. The meeting was held at the Embassy of Nepal and lasted for 45 minutes. It was followed by a meeting with the Indian Minister for External Affairs, Swaran Singh. Thereafter, King Mahendra had lunch with the Indian Prime Minister at the Embassy.

The royal couple hosted a dinner in honour of the President of India the next evening at 8.30 at the Ashoka Hotel. President Dr Radhakrishnan left Rashtrapati Bhavan at 8.29 pm from the North Court. Six minutes later, he alighted at the Hotel where he was received by the King and Queen. The three of them were then escorted to the Lounge where the other members of the entourage were waiting for the President, King and Queen. The entire group was then conducted to the Banquet Hall for dinner.

The royal couple left on their *tirthyatra* early the next day. At 8.30 am, the President, conducted by ADC–I, went to the Dwarka Suite from where, eight minutes later, he escorted the King and Queen, to the South Court. The Presidential motorcade left for Palam Airport at 8.40 am. At the airport the King was given a ceremonial send-off that included a Guard of Honour. Before boarding the plane, he bade farewell to the Prime Minister, Cabinet Ministers, the Vice President and the President of India.

The royal couple returned to Kathmandu on December 18, 1965, after their *tirthyatra*.[61]

The August 1970 Visit

In 1970, President VV Giri had sent an invitation to the Nepalese royal couple to stop over in New Delhi, while they were *en–route* to Europe and also on their return journey. Extending the invitation, President Giri wrote, "May I say that Your Majesty would be most welcome to stay at Rashtrapati Bhavan... Although I have to be in South India on a tour to Hyderabad, I do hope that Your Majesty will make use of Rashtrapati Bhavan... The Vice President will be in New Delhi throughout."[62]

The President also invited the royal couple to be his guests on their return journey from Europe. He wrote, "It would be our pleasure and privilege if Your Majesties could accept our invitation to be our guests on the return journey when Your Majesties land in Bombay."[63] King Mahendra accepted the invitation to stay at Rashtrapati Bhavan en route to Europe, but regretted his inability to visit Delhi on his return journey. His plane was scheduled to stop in Bombay only for a few minutes.[64]

King Mahendra arrived at New Delhi's Palam Airport at 4.25 pm on August 26, 1970, aboard Royal Nepal Airways flight 205. He was accompanied by his wife, their son Dhirendra and an entourage of seven.[65] The Vice President of India, Gopal Swarup Pathak, received him at the airport. This visit focused on the signing of a new treaty between the two countries on trade and transit. A delegation of high officials and Ministers from Nepal had already arrived in India a few days before, to begin the preparatory work.[66]

Later that evening, the Vice President hosted a banquet in honour of the King and the Queen. After the main courses were served, a toast was raised to the health of the royal couple and the friendship between India and Nepal. After the banquet, the royal couple was treated to a classical dance performance and musical programme in Rashtrapati Bhavan.[67]

The next day, the King met Prime Minister Indira Gandhi at Rashtrapati Bhavan for bilateral talks that lasted a little over an hour. The meeting took place without any aides. A number of outstanding issues were ironed out[68] in this "very useful"[69] meeting. Prime Minister Indira Gandhi then hosted a lunch for the royal couple in Rashtrapati Bhavan.[70] The King departed for London at 11.30 pm, on August 27, 1970, on board Air France flight 193, leaving Indian soil for the last time.[71]

King Mahendra's multiple visits and the days spent 'under the dome' helped further strengthen Indo–Nepal relations.

King Mahendra passed away on January 31, 1972. He was 52. Queen Ratna, now referred to as "former Queen mother", is 87.[72]

Notes

[1] From the various public sources, it is understood that King Mahendra Bir Bikram Shah Dev had visited India in 1955, 1958, 1960, 1961, 1962, 1963, 1964, 1965 and 1970. Only the 1955, 1958, 1960, 1961, 1963, 1965 and 1970 visits have been covered as the documents relating to other visits were not traceable. Even with regard to the visits covered, the files regarding some of them were incomplete. Some only had a sheet or two. Hence, the details of such visits were pieced together from public sources. In regard to some such visits, it was not possible to definitely confirm the dates on which the King stayed at the Rashtrapati Bhavan and therefore, only the months in which the visits have occurred have found mention in this chapter.

[2] Nepal Trading Corporation, *The Citizen King: Biography of Mahendra Bir Bikram Shah Deva The Ruler of Nepal* (New Delhi: Nepal Trading Corporation, 1959), p. 17.

[3] Nepal Trading Corporation, *The Citizen King*, p. 23.

[4] Y.G. Krishnamurti, *His Majesty King Mahendra Bir Bikram Shah Dev: An Analytical Biography* (Bombay: The Nityan and Society, 1963), p. 20.

[5] "Diplomacy: The Student King," *Time*, May 9, 1960, accessed May 18, 2015, http://content.time.com/time/subscriber/article/0,33009,897442,00.html.

[6] "Nepal: The King & Koirala," *Time*, February 3, 1961, accessed May 18, 2015, http://content.time.com/time/subscriber/article/0,33009,872040,00.html.

[7] "Diplomacy: The Student King," *Time*.

[8] Nepal Trading Corporation, *The Citizen King*, p. 17.

[9] Rishikesh Shaha, *Three Decades and Two Kings* (1960–1990): Eclipse of Nepal's Partyless Monarchic Rule (New Delhi: Sterling Publishers, 1990), p. 7.

[10] Nepal Trading Corporation, *The Citizen King*, p. 39.

[11] "Premier Meets King of Nepal," *The Times of India* (New Delhi), June 3, 1958, p. 1.

[12] Ibid.

[13] "King of Nepal to Visit Delhi," *The Times of India* (New Delhi), May 24, 1958, p. 9.

[14] "Warm Welcome to Mahendra," *The Hindustan Times* (New Delhi), July 21, 1960, p. 1.

[15] Hasan Askari Rizvi, "*Party Politics in Nepal,*" in *Nepal: Government and Politics*, ed. Verinder Grover, 207–227. (New Delhi: Deep and Deep Publications, 2000), 219.

[16] Ibid.

[17] "Nepal King Heads New Government," *The New York Times*, December 27, 1960, p. 9.

[18] Nepal Trading Corporation, *The Citizen King*, p. 18.

[19] "Nepal King Heads New Government," p. 9.

[20] "Nepal's King Plans 'Guided Democracy,'" *The New York Times*, January 6, 1961, p. 2.

[21] "King Mahendra," *The Times of India*, New Delhi, 9 July 1960, p. 6.

[22] "Four-Day "Private" Visit to Capital," *The Times of India* (New Delhi), July 21, 1960, p. 1.

23 "Warm Welcome to Mahendra," p. 1.

24 "Nepal King Confers with Dr. Prasad," *The Hindustan Times* (New Delhi), July 22, 1960, p. 10.

25 "Nehru Calls on Nepal King," *The Hindustan Times* (New Delhi), July 22, 1960, p. 13.

26 "Nehru, Mahendra Meet Again," *The Hindustan Times* (New Delhi), July 23, 1960, p. 1.

27 "Mahendra and Nehru Confer," *The New York Times*, July 24, 1960, p. 20.

28 "Nepalese King to Lead Team," *The Times of India* (New Delhi), August 5, 1961, p. 8.

29 "PM Discusses World Issues with King Mahendra and U Nu," *The Hindustan Times* (New Delhi), August 29, 1961, p. 13.

30 "Nepal to be Firm with China on Everest Issue," *The Hindu* (New Delhi), August 30, 1961, p. 1.

31 Ibid.

32 "No Anti-Indian feeling in Nepal, King Mahendra Says," *The Hindustan Times* (New Delhi), August 30, 1961, p. 1.

33 "Nepal to be firm with China on Everest Issue," p. 1.

34 "Mr. Shashtri's Mission," *The Times of India* (New Delhi), March 4, 1963, p. 6.

35 "King and Queen of Nepal to Visit India Soon," *The Times of India* (New Delhi), March 8, 1963, p. 10.

36 "Indo-Nepalese Ties," *The Times of India* (New Delhi), August 27, 1963, p. 9.

37 Ibid.

38 Ibid.

39 "Mahendra's Visit to India," *The Times of India* (New Delhi), August 27, 1963, p. 9.

40 "India & Nepal Must Live in Amity," *The Hindu* (New Delhi), August 29, 1963, p. 1.

41 Ibid.

42 Ibid.

43 Ibid.

44 Ibid. p. 7.

45 Ibid.

46 Records, President's Secretariat, Rashtrapati Bhavan

47 Ibid.

48 "Nehru Calls on King," *The Hindu* (New Delhi), August 29, 1963, p. 7.

49 "Nepal's Problems," *The Hindu* (New Delhi), August 30, 1963, p. 1.

50 Ibid.

51 "Kashmir Trip Postponed," *The Times of India* (New Delhi), August 31, 1963, p. 1.

52 "King Mahendra in Delhi," *The Hindu* (New Delhi), June 18, 1964, p. 1.

53 "Mahendra Hopes for Better Ties with India," *The Hindustan Times* (New Delhi), June 18, 1964, p. 1.

54 "Nepal, Neutral, Already Hurt by Big Neighbours' Conflict," *The New York Times*, September 10, 1965, p. 14.

55 K. Rangaswami, "Warm welcome to Nepal King in Delhi," *The Hindu* (New Delhi), November 26, 1965, p. 1.

56 Ibid.

57 Ibid.

58 Records, President's Secretariat, Rashtrapati Bhavan, File no. 15 (8)/70.

59 Ministry of External Affairs (1995), Foreign Affair Records 1965, Government of India, MEA Library, Foreign Affairs Records 1961, Volume VII, accessed May 28, 2015, http://mealib.nic.in/?pdf2553?000.

60 Ibid.

61 "India's Stand on Conflict with Pak," *The Hindu* (New Delhi), November 28, 1965, p. 1.

62 Records, President's Secretariat, File no. 15 (8)/70.

63 Ibid.

64 Ibid.

65 Ibid.

66 "King Mahendra's Stress on Transit," *The Times of India* (New Delhi), August 27, 1970, p. 1.

67 Records, President's Secretariat, File no. 15 (8)/70.

68 "Indo-Nepali Differences Now Narrow," *The Times of India* (New Delhi), August 28, 1970, p. 1.

69 "Mahendra, PM Talks 'Useful'," *The Hindustan Times* (New Delhi), August 29, 1970, p. 1.

70 Records, President's Secretariat, File no. 15 (8)/70.

71 Ibid.

72 Bhuvan Sharma, "Solitary Life," *Nepali Times*, accessed on May 17, 2015, nepaltimes.com/news.php?id=17847#.Vga=du0Pmqqko

Liaquat Ali Khan, Pakistan's first Prime Minister, arrived in New Delhi on a six-day State Visit, on April 2, 1950. He was the first Head of Government of his country to visit India. The visit came barely three years after both nations were born amidst large-scale violence and communal carnage.

Liaquat Ali Khan was born on October 1, 1895 to a wealthy landed family in Karnal (now in the state of Haryana, India). His family held the title of 'Nawab', whose landed assets, he was fond of reminiscing, were something he left behind to move to Pakistan.[1] Prime Minister Khan was often called "Nawabzada Liaquat Ali" or simply "Nawabzada," meaning the son of a Nawab. His father Nawab Rustam Ali Khan, "whose wealth and standing had become proverbial in Karnal,"[2] was pre-eminent in his locality, which was also home to certain Persian nobles who had settled there since the reign of Shah Jahan.

Visits of
H.E. Mr Liaquat Ali Khan
Prime Minister of Pakistan

Liaquat Ali Khan was educated at the Aligarh Muslim University, Exeter College in Oxford and the Middle Temple in London. He was a lawyer by education and an active politician in the Muslim League in British India. He also served as Finance Minister in the Interim Government before independence.

Liaquat Ali was an early proponent and ardent supporter of Pakistan, who worked tirelessly with Jinnah to make the Muslim nation a reality. He became Pakistan's first Prime Minister, Defence Minister and Minister of Commonwealth and Kashmir Affairs. His legacy is seen as the consolidation of the State of Pakistan.

Though after 1947 there was no war between India and Pakistan until the 1960s, relations between the two nations continued to be strained.

As a gesture of goodwill, Indian President Dr Rajendra Prasad extended a personal invitation to Prime Minister Liaquat Ali Khan and his delegation to reside at Government House as State Guests during their stay in Delhi. The invitation was extended through the Military Secretary to the President (MSP), Colonel B Chatterjee. It was immediately accepted and Prime Minister Khan sent a reply thanking the President and added, "I shall be happy to stay with you while in Delhi."[3]

The April 1950 Visit

Prime Minister Liaquat Ali Khan landed at New Delhi's Palam Airport at 11.35 am in a private Viking aircraft that flew the flags of both India and Pakistan as a gesture of goodwill. The Prime Minister of India, Jawaharlal Nehru, welcomed his distinguished guest with a warm handshake and then introduced him to the other dignitaries. The MSP, who represented the President; and the High Commissioners of Pakistan, UK, Canada, Australia and Ceylon, were also at the airport.[4]

Facing page:
Prime Minister Liaquat Ali Khan (left)
with President Dr Prasad
at Government House
(now Rashtrapati Bhavan) in
April 1950. Credit: PC

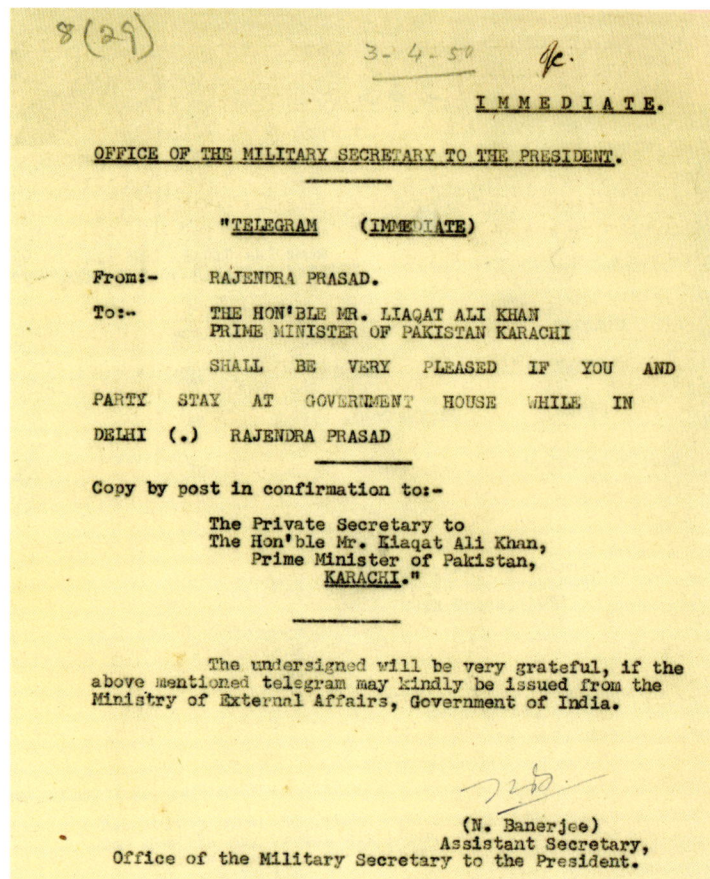

*Telegram from President Dr Prasad to Prime Minister Liaquat Ali
inviting him to stay at Government House (now Rashtrapati Bhavan).*

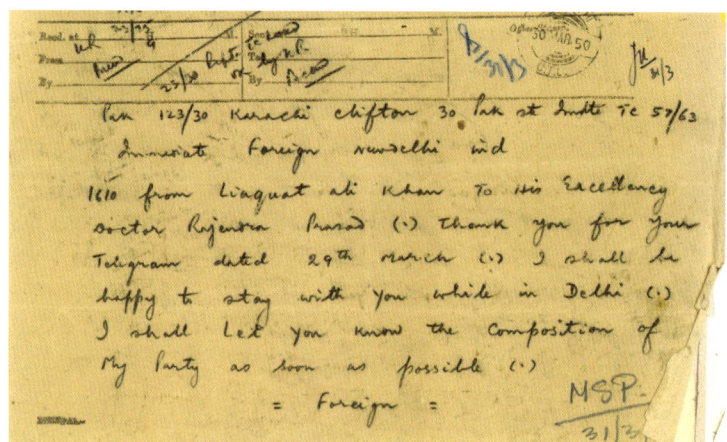

*Telegram of acceptance from Prime Minister Liaquat Ali to stay
at Government House (now Rashtrapati Bhavan).*

The two Prime Ministers then posed for photographs and answered questions from the press. When asked about his journey, Prime Minister Khan, who had taken off from Karachi 15-minutes late, replied that he had a pleasant journey but that he could have "done it quicker." Unwilling to accept that his old friend Liaquat Ali Khan could make even an innocuous fault such as this, Pandit Nehru smilingly interjected and said, "No, you have arrived very punctually."[5]

The Pakistani Prime Minister's entourage included Siddique Ali Khan, Political Secretary to the Prime Minister and a former Member of the Indian Central Assembly before independence. Many of those who had come to welcome Prime Minister Khan were his old friends with whom he chatted, before leaving for Government House with the rest of his delegation.[6]

A stately Humber, bearing testament to the continued weakness of Indians for high-end British engineering, brought Prime Minister Khan and Prime Minister Nehru from the airport to Government House, amidst tight security. Members of his entourage followed in a Buick and a Pontiac, while his Personal Staff and stenographer brought up the rear in a Station Wagon. The Pakistani Prime Minister and members of his office disembarked at the North Court, while his domestic staff alighted at the South Court.[7]

On arrival, the Pakistani Prime Minister was received by the Deputy Military Secretary to the President (DMSP), Major Mohammed Yunus Khan; the Comptroller, President's Household (CPH) and an *aide-de-camp* (ADC). He was then escorted to the President's Study, while the accompanying Pakistani officials were conducted to the Morning Room.

President Dr Rajendra Prasad graciously received Prime Minister Khan in his Study. The Pakistani Prime Minister was followed by Prime Minister Nehru who had not left his guest's side since he had received him at the airport. He was then escorted to the Morning Room, where he presented his officials to the President. In keeping with protocol, the MSP presented President of India's Personal Staff to Prime Minister Khan. Thereafter, the Pakistani delegation was escorted to their respective suites/rooms by the staff.[8]

Prime Minister Liaquat Ali Khan stayed in the Irwin Suite. Secretary General, Chaudhary Muhammad Ali stayed in the Reading Suite; Foreign Secretary, M Ikramullah in the Birdwood Suite and Chief Secretary, East Bengal, Aziz Ahmed, in the Clive Suite.

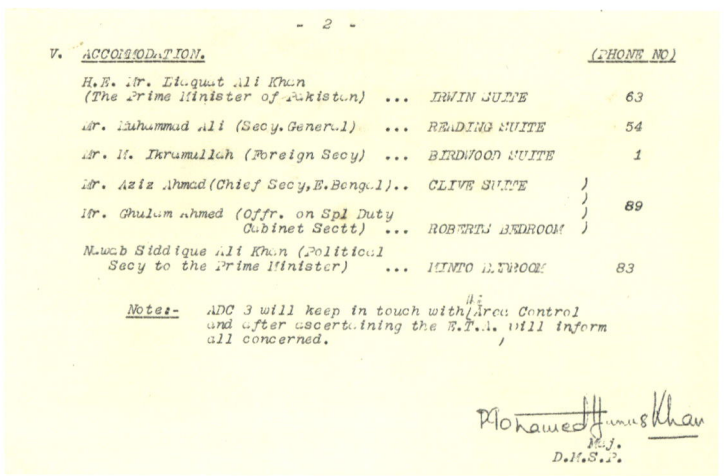

Room Allocation Plan.

In the afternoon, both Prime Ministers had a formal meeting at the Government House.[9] It lasted over two hours during which a host of issues was discussed. Chief among them were the problems in Bengal, which was witness to recent communal clashes. Procedures for further talks also came up for deliberation.[10]

The issues were contentious and defied easy agreement. Nevertheless, there was optimism in several quarters that the personal relations of the two leaders may help iron out even the seemingly irreconcilable differences. *The New York Times* opined that Prime Minister Nehru and Prime Minister Khan had frequently played bridge together during the pre-Partition days and that the renewal of the old "bridge table atmosphere" would complement the settlement between India and Pakistan.[11]

After the meeting of the two leaders, Prime Minister Khan visited *Rajghat* accompanied by Muhammad Ali, Ikramullah Khan and Mohammad Ismail. They were escorted by the Chief of Protocol (COP), BK Kapoor and Colonel B Chatterjee. Prime Minister Khan placed two wreaths of flowers on Mahatma Gandhi's *samadhi* and observed two minutes silence.[12] On his way back to the Government House, Prime Minister Khan stopped for a while at his old residence, which then housed the Pakistan High Commission.[13]

Later that evening, in an unusual gesture,[14] the President hosted a regal State Banquet in honour of Prime Minister Khan at the grand Banquet Hall in Government House. The departure from the norm of a Heads of State hosting banquet for their counter parts only was testimony to the importance India attached to this visit. It was also reflective of the personal bonds that the leaders of the two nations shared. The banquet was attended by the Pakistani delegation, the Pakistani High Commissioner to India and the Indian High Commissioner to Pakistan, Members of the Indian Cabinet and other dignitaries.[15]

Most of the next day, April 3, was spent by the delegates of both nations in discussions. Late that afternoon, Prime Minister Khan spent some time at the National Museum, housed in the State Room of Rashtrapati Bhavan. He evinced interest in the various artefacts on display.[16] In the evening, Prime Minister Nehru hosted a dinner at his residence, Teen Murti Bhavan, for his Pakistani counterpart. The invitees included many of Prime Minister Nehru's Cabinet Members.[17]

After the day-long meetings, a joint communiqué was issued that night by the Indian Prime Minister's Secretariat. It outlined the areas of agreement between the two sides. It also entrusted to both Governments, the responsibility for the security and protection of the minorities by punishing those engaging in violence, for compensating and rehabilitating victims, for recovering looted property and abducted women and punishing rumourmongers.[18]

(L-R): Prime Minister Nehru, Prime Minister Liaquat Ali Khan and President Dr Prasad at Government House (now Rashtrapati Bhavan) in April 1950. Credit: PC

Prime Minister Liaquat Ali Khan (left) and President Dr Prasad at Government House (now Rashtrapati Bhavan) in July 1950. Credit: PC

The next day, the Prime Ministers of India and Pakistan held discussions for over two hours. The main agenda of the talks was the setting up of an efficient machinery to implement the agreement they had reached to restore confidence in the minorities.[19]

Prime Minister Khan received two deputations of prominent Muslim leaders at Government House on April 4. One was headed by Nawab Ismail Khan, the Nawab of Chattari and the other was led by Maulana Hifzur Rahman, General Secretary of the Jamait-ul-Ulema-i-Hind. He assured them of his utmost efforts in finding a solution to the problems faced by the minorities.[20]

That evening, Prime Minister Khan met President Dr Prasad who was scheduled to leave for Bombay the following day. The meeting, which took place in Government House, lasted over 45 minutes.[21]

On April 5, Prime Minister Khan had lunch with Prime Minister Nehru and Deputy Prime Minister Patel at Government House, where the three discussed salient points to be included in the agreement that was being drafted. The luncheon meeting lasted for two-and-a-half hours. As an understanding between the two sides was taking longer than expected, Prime Minister Khan extended his stay for three days for reaching an agreement and signing it.[22]

Finally, an agreement was reached after intense and detailed deliberations that lasted over a week. The joint Indo-Pakistan declaration on the protection of minorities, called the Liaquat-

Nehru Pact, or the Delhi Pact, was finally signed on April 8, 1950, at Government House at 2.00 pm.[23] Under the Pact, the two Governments undertook to safeguard the rights of the minorities in their respective countries, prevent "offences against persons and property," punish offenders and prevent "propaganda against the territorial integrity of both countries" and take action against those who engage in such propaganda.[24] Further, the Pact provided for the return of property to refugees who went back to their homes or to help in their rehabilitation.[25]

Prime Minister Liaquat Ali Khan flew back to Karachi the same day. He talked to the press for three minutes before boarding the Viking aircraft at Palam Airport around 3.00 pm. He said he hoped to visit Delhi again soon and expressed happiness at the agreements that the two Prime Ministers had reached. When a press correspondent queried if he were happy with the visit, Prime Minister Khan replied, "Don't I look it?" Prime Minister Nehru; MSP Colonel Chatterjee; the UK High Commissioner, Sir Archibald Nye; the High Commissioner of Pakistan, Mohammed Ismail, and other high officials saw the Pakistani Prime Minister off.[26]

Several political analysts concluded that the meetings were a remarkable success as the Nehru-Khan Pact provided security for millions in both countries. It also paved the way for further discussions on even more contentious issues. Within two days of his return to Pakistan, on April 10, 1950, Prime Minister Khan made a statement in the Pakistan Constituent Assembly regarding the agreement and said, "I look upon this agreement as the precursor of a new understanding between India and Pakistan."[27]

The July 1950 Visit

Three months later, Prime Minister Liaquat Ali Khan returned to Delhi in the humid month of July. This time, he hoped to resolve the Kashmir dispute.

Prime Minister Khan landed in Delhi "around noon" on July 20, 1950.[28] He was warmly received at the airport by the MSP, Colonel Chatterjee who represented the President, Prime Minister Jawaharlal Nehru, the High Commissioners of Pakistan, Australia, Canada and Ceylon– just as he had been three months ago. Prime Minister Khan was accompanied by the Secretary General of the Pakistan Government, Muhammad Ali; Joint Secretary, Ministry of Kashmir Affairs, Mahomed Ayub; Secretary to the Prime Minister, Hamid and his Personal Assistant.[29]

After inspecting a Guard of Honour presented by the Indian Air Force, Prime Minister Khan talked to the press. His replies reflected a sense of optimism, not very often expressed in the guarded replies of Heads of Governments visiting foreign nations. When asked if he expected the talks to succeed, he replied, "we hope to solve everything and you see that rain is always a good sign", referring to the heavy showers that had poured over Delhi barely a few hours before his arrival.[30] He felt that the Delhi Pact, signed on his previous visit, was working "splendidly." The Pakistani leader was evidently in a good mood. When a correspondent asked what he had got back from his recent trip to the US, he replied, tongue-in-cheek, "I got myself back."[31]

Transport arrangements from the airport were also similar to those made during his previous visit, with vehicles for the visiting dignitaries coming from the President's Garage. A Humber brought Prime Minister Khan and the MSP who was escorting him, to Government House. The rest of the delegation rode in a Buick and a Pontiac while the Pakistani Prime Minister's Personal Assistant, staff members and baggage followed in a Station Wagon.[32]

The CPH received Prime Minister Khan at the North Court. He was then escorted to the President's Study where the two leaders had an informal meeting. The rest of the delegation was escorted to the pleasant Morning Room, which has a blue ceiling and a splendid view of the fountains in the Mughal Gardens. President Dr Prasad

(L-R): Prime Minister Khan, Sir Owen Dixen (UN Mediator for Kashmir) and Prime Minister Nehru at talks at Government House (now Rashtrapati Bhavan) in July 1950. Credit: PC

and the Pakistani Prime Minister were thereafter escorted to the Morning Room and formally introduced to the officials of each side.[33] The introductions were followed by refreshments.

Later, the President's Personal Staff escorted the visiting dignitaries to their respective suites/rooms. Prime Minister Liaquat Ali Khan stayed in the Irwin Suite, Muhammad Ali in the Birdwood Suite and Mahomed Ayub in the Lytton Bedroom.[34]

There was no specific agenda for the talks that began in right earnest at 4.00 pm on July 20 and which lasted 150-minutes. The discussions were also attended by Sir Owen Dixon, who was appointed as the mediator by the United Nations.[35] These were the third round of discussions between the two countries on Kashmir.[36]

The President of India along with the former Governor-General, C Rajagopalachari, now Central Minister without Portfolio, had tea with the three delegates that evening. Prime Minister Nehru also hosted a dinner in honour of his Pakistani counterpart later that night. The talks continued the next day from 10.00 am to 1.00 pm and resumed at 4.30 pm for two more hours.[37]

Prime Minister Khan later attended a reception hosted in his honour by the Pakistani High Commissioner in India. Members of the diplomatic corps, Indian Cabinet Ministers and other senior dignitaries were present.[38] On July 22, the tripartite talks, now in their third day, lasted another five hours taking the total duration of the Nehru–Liaquat–Dixon conference to a staggering 12 and a half hours.[39]

In the evening, President Dr Rajendra Prasad hosted a State Banquet in honour of the Prime Minister of Pakistan. The President, on his arrival at the grand Ball Room, was joined by Prime Minister Khan and Prime Minister Nehru. Guests included Sir Owen Dixon, Ministers of the Government of India, senior officials of the Ministry of External Affairs and "States Ministry." They were formally presented to President Dr Prasad and the Prime Minister of Pakistan in the Ball Room that sported the national flags of India and Pakistan. After introductions were over, the guests were conducted to the Banquet Hall. At the banquet,[40] the President of India was seated between the Prime Minister of Pakistan and Sir Owen while Prime Minister Nehru sat opposite President Dr Prasad.[41]

The tripartite talks continued for another two days, but no solution was in sight even after 17 and a half hours of marathon discussions.[42] As the issues had proved to be intractable, the talks were declared inconclusive in the afternoon of July 24, 1950, and the next round of discussions was scheduled in Karachi a month later.

A joint communiqué was issued the same day that sought to keep the hopes of a solution alive. It said that some aspects of the problem needed further examination and hence, the conference was being adjourned.[43]

This visit of the Pakistani Prime Minister had yielded no tangible results even after almost four days of hectic parleys. Prime Minister Khan was scheduled to leave for Karachi the next day, and what remained of the day was spent on meeting Indian leaders. Soon after the conference, he met with the Minister of Industry and Supply, HK Mahtab.[44] He also called on the President of India that evening and bid him farewell.

The Pakistani Prime Minister left for Karachi in the morning of July 25, 1950. On reaching Mauripur airfield in Karachi, he told an eagerly awaiting press, "*Nishastam O Guftum Wa Barkhastam*" – an old Persian proverb that translates as, "we met, we discussed and we dispersed."[45] The stalemate led to a gap of three years before any Head of State from Pakistan visited India again.

Government House was the venue for most of the discussions that were held between Prime Minister Nehru and Prime Minister Khan as it was for the delegation level talks. The Indian President's house became a home away from home for the visiting Pakistani delegation. Only this time they were visitors in a nation that had been theirs as well, barely three years ago.

Liaquat Ali Khan was assassinated on October 16, 1951 at a public meeting in Rawalpindi. He was conferred the title of "*Shaheed–e– Millat*" – "Martyr of the Nation." He was 56.[46]

Notes

1 "Pakistan: The Glory of Moguls," *Time*, May 8, 1950, accessed April 10, 2015, http://content.time.com/time/subscriber/article/0,33009,812405-1,00.html.

2 Mohammed Reza Kazimi, *Liaquat Ali Khan: His Life and Work* (Karachi: Oxford University Press, 2003), p. 6.

3 Records, President's Secretariat, Rashtrapati Bhavan, File No. 103 CER.

4 "Nehru–Liaquat Ali talks Begin," *The Hindustan Times* (New Delhi), April 3, 1950, p. 1.

5 Ibid.

6 Ibid.

7 Records, President's Secretariat, File No. 103 CER.

8 Ibid.

9 "Declare Pakistan Democratic State," *The Times of India* (New Delhi), April 3, 1950, p. 1.

10 "Nehru–Liaquat Ali talks begin," p.1.

11 Robert Trumbull, "Pakistan's Chief in India for talks," *The New York Times*, April 3, 1950, p. 15.

12 "Liaqat Ali's Visit to Rajghat," *The Hindu* (New Delhi), April 3, 1950, p. 4.

13 "Nehru–Liaqat Ali Talks", *The Hindu* (New Delhi), April 3 1950, p. 4.

14 Usually official banquets are hosted by Government leaders only for their visiting counterparts.

15 "Minorities' Problem Dominates Delhi Talks," *The Times of India* (New Delhi), April 3, 1950, p. 1.

16 "Delhi Talks Progress," *The Hindu* (New Delhi), April 4, 1950, p. 4.

17 Ibid.

18 "Progress in Delhi Talks," *The Times of India* (New Delhi), April 4, 1950, p. 1.

19 "Protection of Minorities," *The Hindu* (New Delhi), April 5, 1950, p. 4.

20 Ibid.

21 Ibid.

22 "Final Draft Likely Today," *The Hindustan Times* (New Delhi), April 6, 1950, p. 1.

23 "Minorities Pact Signed," *The Times of India* (New Delhi), April 9 1950, p. 1.

24 Ministry of External Affairs (2012), Government of India, MEA Library, "India–Pakistan Relations", accessed June 25, 2015, http://mea.gov.in/Images/pdf/India-Pakistan-std.pdf.

25 Ibid.

26 "Minorities Pact Signed," p.1.

27 Ziauddin Ahmad, *Shaheed–e–Millat: Liaquat Ali Khan, Builder of Pakistan* (Karachi: Royal Book Company, 1990), p. 239.

28 Records, President's Secretariat, File No. 103 CER.

29 "Delhi Pact Working Splendidly," *The Hindu* (New Delhi), July 21, 1950, p.1.

30 Ibid.

31 Ibid.

32 Records, President's Secretariat, File No. 103 CER.

33 Ibid.

34 Ibid.

35 "Tripartite Talks on Kashmir," *The Times of India* (New Delhi), July 21, 1950, p. 1.

36 "Nehru, Liaquat Ali Open Kashmir Talk," *The New York Times*, July 21, 1950, p. 9.

37 "Delhi Talks on Kashmir," *The Hindu* (New Delhi), July 22, 1950, p. 4.

38 Ibid.

39 "Kashmir Talks," *The Hindu* (New Delhi), July 23, 1950, p. 1.

40 This time, it appears that there were no banquet speeches. The MEA website only has banquet speeches since 1955. None of the newspapers of the day after the banquet reported anything about it. *The Hindustan Times* and *The Hindu* carried news of the banquet on July 23, 1950, two days after the banquet. There was, however, no reference to any speeches.

41 "President's Banquet," *The Hindu* (New Delhi), July, 23, 1950, p. 1.

42 "Talks on Kashmir Prove Abortive," *The Hindustan Times* (New Delhi), July 25, 1950, p.1.

43 "Kashmir Talks Inconclusive," *The Times of India* (New Delhi), July 25 1950, p. 1.

44 "Talks on Kashmir Prove Abortive," p. 1.

45 "Mr. Liaquat Ali Back in Karachi," *The Times of India* (New Delhi), July 26, 1950, p. 7.

46 "62nd death Anniversary of Liaquat Ali Khan today," *The News*, October 16, 2013, accessed May 12, 2015, http://www.thenews.com.pk/article-122687-62nd-death-Anniversary-of-Liaquat-Ali-Khan-today.

Pakistan's third Prime Minister, Mohammed Ali Bogra landed in India on August 16, 1953 at 7.30 pm on a four-day State Visit. It was his first visit to India and the second by a Pakistani Prime Minister.

Born on October 19, 1909, in Bogra, East Pakistan, Mohammed Ali Bogra graduated from Presidency College, Calcutta. He joined politics at an early age and was elected as a legislator from Bogra at the age of 28. After Pakistan's independence, he served as his country's Ambassador to Burma, its High Commissioner to Canada and later as the Ambassador to the United States. Thereafter, in April 1953, he was appointed Prime Minister by Governor-General Ghulam Mohammed.

Visits of
H.E. Mr Mohammed Ali Bogra
Prime Minister of Pakistan

Mohammed Ali Bogra's visit was of critical importance for both countries, as it came at a crucial time when both India and Pakistan were struggling to find a common solution to the Kashmir dispute. Prime Minister Nehru and Prime Minister Bogra had met twice earlier. The first time was in June, during the Commonwealth Prime Minister's Conference held in London in 1953. The second was in the following month when Prime Minister Nehru visited Karachi. Both meetings failed to yield any solution to the Kashmir issue. Prime Minister Bogra's visit to India, a month later, however, raised hopes of a thaw in relations and the prospects of a settlement of the differences between the two nations looked brighter.

The 1953 Visit

The Pan American Boeing 377 Strato-clipper carrying the Pakistani Prime Minister and his entourage, landed at Palam Airport at 7.30 pm to a very warm welcome. Indian Prime Minister Jawaharlal Nehru received the visiting dignitaries along with a host of Indian dignitaries. They included Vijayalakshmi Pandit; the Military Secretary to the President (MSP), Major General Chatterjee; and the Pakistani High Commissioner to India, Ghazanfar Ali Khan.[1] Prime Minister Bogra was accompanied by his wife, Begum Mohammed Ali; his Foreign Minister, Muhammad Zafrullah Khan and a group of high-ranking officials. India's High Commissioner to Pakistan, Mohan Sinha Mehta, was also part of his entourage.[2] After the introductions, the Pakistani Prime Minister was presented an Inter-Services Guard of Honour. The presentation was a special gesture as Prime Minister Bogra had arrived "after nightfall."[3]

A crowd of 20,000 people had also congregated at the airport to catch a "fleeting glimpse of the Pakistani Prime Minister."[4] The crowd was visibly excited to the see the visiting dignitary and gave expression to it by chanting, "Muhammad Ali *Zindabad*."[5] The crowd was so overcome by exuberance that the police found it difficult to maintain order. *The*

*Facing page:
President Dr Prasd (left) with
Prime Minister Mohammed Ali Bogra
at Rashtrapati Bhavan in
August 1953. Credit: PC*

(L-R): Foreign Minister of Pakistan Zafrullah Khan, Vijayalakshmi Pandit, Begum Hamida Mohammed Ali, President Dr Prasad, Prime Minister Mohammed Ali Bogra and Prime Minister Nehru at Rashtrapati Bhavan in August 1953. Credit: PC

New York Times even reported that more "than 5,000 persons broke through cordons of police at the airport and nearly mobbed the Pakistan leader."[6] The perceived breach of security led to sudden changes in the reception plan at the airport. It was decided that the visiting dignitary would acknowledge the greetings of the people from an open jeep. Accordingly, Prime Minister Bogra, his wife and Prime Minister Nehru got into the vehicle and went around waving to the cheering crowd that continued to shout, "Muhammad Ali Zindabad." The people threw garlands and wreaths at the jeep as it reached near them and the Pakistani Prime Minister often extended his hand and those amongst the crowd that could reach him, shook it with vigorous excitement.

After nearly 45 minutes at the airport, the Prime Minister and his delegation were driven to the Rashtrapati Bhavan. On their arrival, they were received by the officials of the President's Secretariat and escorted to the Guest Wing. As was the practice, Prime Minister Bogra, who was the head of the delegation, stayed at the Irwin Suite. After spending a short time in his suite, Prime Minister Bogra called on the Indian President Dr Rajendra Prasad. Later that night, he met with Prime Minister Nehru and reportedly discussed programmes for the following days over a "quiet dinner."[7]

The next day, on August 17, the Pakistani Prime Minister laid a wreath at the *samadhi* of Mahatma Gandhi's at *Rajghat*. He also took a "photograph of the *samadhi* and its surroundings."[8] From *Rajghat*, Prime Minister Bogra headed to Parliament House. Here he witnessed the proceedings of the Lower House for some time from the President's Box."[9] On seeing the visiting Prime Minister, the Members of Parliament loudly cheered him and he graciously acknowledged the greetings with a bow.

After returning to Rashtrapati Bhavan, Prime Minister Bogra met the President for approximately 30-minutes. The visiting Prime

Minister thereafter had lunch with India's Education Minister, Maulana Abul Kalam Azad. He then visited Rajendra Nagar which was a refugee colony. In particular, he visited Salaan High School and he spent nearly 15-minutes.He donated Rs 500 "to the school management for distribution of sweets to the children."[10]

The visits were followed by formal talks between the two Prime Ministers that aimed towards finding a solution to the Kashmir problem. *The Times of India* reported that definite progress was made during this meeting, and that the two leaders agreed to work towards an early settlement.[11] The Pakistani Prime Minister however, pointed out that it was "advisable not to be unduly optimistic."[12]

Later that evening, President Dr Prasad held a reception in the Mughal Gardens at Rashtrapati Bhavan in honour of the visiting Premier. Indian Cabinet Ministers and members of the diplomatic corps were among the more than 500 guests were invited to the reception. However, in what someone described as a good "sign from the heavens," it began raining no sooner than Prime Minister Bogra and President Dr Prasad arrived at the venue, and many dignitaries took cover beneath the trees till the downpour subsided. After this rather unusual reception, Prime Minister Bogra, his wife and Zafrullah Khan dined with Vijayalakshmi Pandit.[13]

The next couple of days were largely consumed by intense bilateral discussions. The only major break from them was on August 19 when Prime Minister Mohammed Ali Bogra was given a grand Civic Reception at the *Diwan–i–Khas* of the Red Fort. Prime Minister Nehru accompanied his Pakistani counterpart for the reception.

The entire route from Rashtrapati Bhavan to the Red Fort was lined by "enthusiastic crowds" that cheered the motorcade of the leaders as it drove by. At the venue of the reception too, the enthusiasm to see Prime Minister Bogra was no less. A sudden drizzle did nothing

President Dr Prasad (second from right on the right row) with Prime Minister Mohammad Ali Bogra of Pakistan (seated opposite) and Prime Minister Nehru on his right along with other dignitaries at a Luncheon at Rashtrapati Bhavan in August 1953. Credit: PC

to dampen the excitement of the 10,000 people, including ministers and diplomats, who had gathered at the Red Fort. The Pakistani Prime Minister was demonstrably moved by the warmth of his welcome and he described it as "warm, cordial and exuberant."[14] His sentiments were expressed in words that were evocative of the past. He said, "I feel that I am in no foreign country and I am no stranger among you" and that Delhi has "given me a right royal reception and I shall cherish this memory for the whole of my life."[15] Following the reception, Prime Minister Bogra visited the Jama Masjid, Nizamuddin *Dargah*[16] and the *Chausathi* Hall.

At the end of the four-day visit, a joint press communiqué was released by both Prime Ministers on August 20. It concluded with an appeal to the media and political leaders that they should desist from "words and actions which promote discord between the two countries."[17] The visiting Prime Minister also declared that the objective of his visit to India was "partially fulfilled."[18] He returned to Pakistan on the morning of August 21, 1953.

Following the Nehru-Bogra talks, there were signs of gradual improvement in the ties between India and Pakistan. It was evident in the series of cricket matches played between them, in the agreement on property-related matters and the "partial restoration of railway communications between the two countries."[19] However, this phase was also marked by sporadic violence, especially the incident at Nekowal in Jammu where the Pakistani Border Police attacked Indian civilians resulting in 12 deaths.[20]

The contentious Kashmir issue however, continued to fester and no agreement was reached with regard to the plebiscite's administrator. It was in this context that the Pakistani Prime Minister arrived in India on his second visit.

The 1955 Visit

Pakistan Prime Minister Bogra and his entourage landed at the Palam airport, at 9.00 am on May 14, 1955. On his arrival, he was warmly received by Prime Minister Jawaharlal Nehru and the Chief of Protocol (COP). The MSP, Major General Yadunath Singh welcomed the Prime Minister on behalf of the President. Thereafter, Prime Minister Bogra was presented an Inter-Services Guard of Honour. After the presentation, the Pakistani Prime Minister was escorted to a specially erected *shamiana* where the select invitees were introduced to the visiting dignitary.

This time Prime Minister Bogra came with his second wife, Begum Aliya Mohammed Ali and 14 delegates. They included his Minister for the Interior, Major General Iskander Mirza and his wife Begum Mirza; Cabinet Secretary of Pakistan, Aziz Ahmed; Director-General of Radio Pakistan, ZA Bokhari; and Public Relations Officer, Douglas. Major-General Iskander Mirza would later, in 1956, become the first President of Pakistan.

After the reception at the airport, the Pakistani delegation drove to Rashtrapati Bhavan. Prime Minister Bogra, his wife and the MSP who was escorting them, drove in a Humber, an elegant British automobile from the President's Garage. Major General Iskander Mirza and his wife followed in an Oldsmobile accompanied by an *aide-de-camp* (ADC) of the President.

At the Rashtrapati Bhavan, Prime Minister Bogra and his wife stayed in the Irwin Suite and the Birdwood Sitting Room respectively. Major General Mirza and his wife stayed in the Reading Suite. Aziz Ahmed stayed in the Clive Bed Room and the Wellesley Sitting Room.

At 10.30 that morning, Prime Minister Bogra called on the Indian President Dr Prasad. At the meeting, Pakistani Prime Minister handed over a personal letter from the Governor-General of Pakistan, Malik Ghulam Mohammed, addressed to the Indian President. The letter communicated that the Governor-General was unable to make the trip himself owing to ill health.

At 11.30 am, "within two hours of his arrival... Mohammed Ali Bogra plunged into discussions with Mr. Nehru on Kashmir and other outstanding Indo–Pakistani problems."[21] The meeting at Pandit Nehru's residence continued for over 100 minutes. It was also attended by India's Home Minister, Govind Ballabh Pant and Member of Parliament, Maulana Abul Kalam Azad; and Pakistan's Interior Minister, Major General Iskander Mirza. The two Prime Ministers discussed several issues ranging from the Kashmir dispute to the Nekowal incident. During the meeting, the Pakistani Prime Minister expressed deep regret over the incident and promised the severest action against any personnel found guilty by the United Nations' observers.[22]

In view of the importance of the talks between the two leaders, the social engagements of Prime Minister Bogra were kept to a minimum. He managed to, however, have lunch with Pandit Nehru that day at 1.15 pm at the latter's residence. At 7.00 pm Prime Minister Bogra met the Indian Vice President, Dr Radhakrishnan

at his residence on 2, King Edward Road, following which he had a 'quiet dinner' with the High Commissioner of Pakistan at Hardinge Avenue.

On the next day, May 15, at 10.00 am, Prime Minister Bogra again met the Indian Prime Minister for a little over 100 minutes. During the meeting, the leaders discussed issues relating to external influences that affected Indo–Pak bilateral ties. Besides, they exchanged views on the transfer of enclaves between India and Pakistan, and the mass exodus from both sides of the border, especially from East Pakistan.[23]

Later at 7.00 pm, the Indian President hosted a grand 'At Home' at the Mughal Gardens in honour of the visiting Pakistani Prime Minister. As was the practice for such receptions, elaborate arrangements were made. The garden was elegantly lit up and the water rising high from the energised fountains added to the spectacular ambience of the setting enveloped by the amber glow of the disappearing sun. The well-known Bombay Sappers Band was positioned in the garden to play light music.

The guests arrived via the South Sunken road. They alighted at the South Court where they were received by the *aides-de-*

(L-R): Begum Aliya Mohammed Ali, President Dr Prasad and Prime Minister Mohammad Ali Bogra at Rashhtrapati Bhavan in May 1955. Credit: PD

camp (AsDC), Lieutenant Gajraj Singh and Major Tara Singh and escorted to the Mughal Gardens. The special invitees, however, arrived via the Main Gates and alighted in the North Court. They were conducted to the Yellow Drawing Room where they were introduced to the Prime Minister of Pakistan and the President of India. After the introductions, the distinguished guests were escorted to the Mughal Gardens where they joined the other guests who had arrived at the venue in advance. In the background, the Bombay Sappers' Band played a medley of light music to the delight of the 500 odd guests invited for the occasion.[24] In the grand setting, the guests exchanged pleasantries and cheerfully chatted with the visiting Pakistani delegates.

The talks between the two Prime Ministers resumed the next day. The meeting lasted for around two hours. Though it was the third successive day of talks, the two sides could make no significant progress in resolving the outstanding issues confronting them.

The two leaders could only agree, that the communiqué they planned to issue, "should be very carefully drafted to avoid any impression being created" that India and Pakistan "had broken or ended negotiations."[25]

At the end of the fourth day, however, there was a significant breakthrough. Agreements were reached on reducing border tensions. After the conclusion of the meetings, a joint press communiqué was issued. In it, the two countries expressed hope of resuming talks at a later stage after fully considering the various issues that had been discussed during the meetings.[26]

The Prime Minister of Pakistan left for his country on the morning of May 18, 1955. At the airport, while speaking to the press correspondents, Prime Minister Mohammed Ali Bogra compared the issue of Kashmir to that of a chronic disease, which could not be treated by overnight cures.[27] He also expressed satisfaction with the progress of the negotiations.

(L-R): Prime Minister Nehru (second), Begum Aliya Mohammed Ali and Prime Minister Bogra in Mughal Gardens at Rashtrapati Bhavan in May 1955. Credit: PC

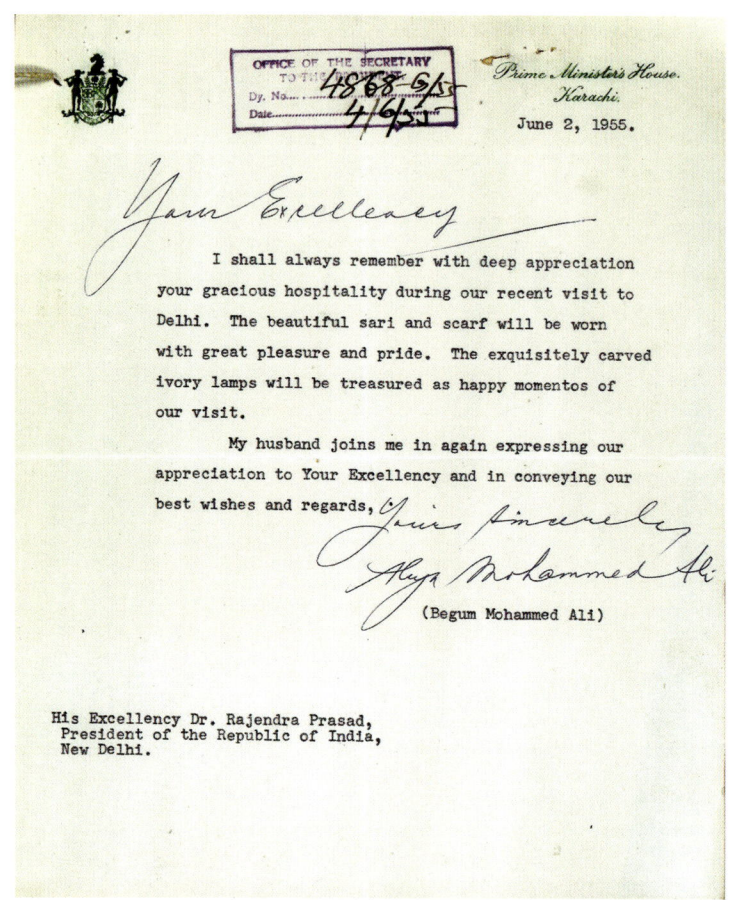

Letter of thanks from Begum Mohammed Ali to President Dr Prasad.

The hospitality extended by India during the visit had evidently pleased the Prime Minister and his wife in particular. It was apparent in the personal letter that Begum Aliya Mohammad Ali wrote to President Dr Rajendra Prasad on June 2, 1955 from Karachi. In the letter, she thanked the President for the "gracious hospitality," the gift of a scarf and a *sari* that was presented to her, which she said would be "worn with great pleasure and pride."[28] She also thanked him for the "exquisitely carved ivory lamps" that would be "treasured as happy mementos [*sic*]" of their visit to India.[29]

Prime Minister Bogra demitted office on August 11, 1955 as he was unable to form the Government after the 1955 elections. The former Prime Minister, "known for his excessive praise of everything American,"[30] later served as his country's Ambassador to the US from November the same year. In 1962, he was appointed Foreign Minister of Pakistan and continued to hold this post till his death on January 23, 1963. He was 53. Begum Aliya Mohammed Ali died on February 16, 2014. She was 90.

Notes

[1] S. Mulgaokar, "Mr. Ali Overwhelmed by Delhi Reception," *The Times of India* (New Delhi), August 17, 1953, p. 1.

[2] John P. Callahan, "Big Crowd Greets Pakistani in India," *The New York Times*, August 17, 1953, p. 1.

[3] Mulgaokar, "Mr. Ali Overwhelmed by Delhi Reception," p. 1.

[4] Ibid.

[5] Ibid.

[6] Callahan, "Big Crowd Greets Pakistani in India," p. 1.

[7] Mulgaokar, "Mr. Ali Overwhelmed by Delhi Reception," p. 1.

[8] S. Mulgaokar, "'Definite Progress' on Kashmir Issue," *The Times of India* (New Delhi), August 18, 1953, p. 7.

[9] Ibid.

[10] Ibid.

[11] Ibid., p. 1.

[12] "Nehru and Ali Open Parley on Kashmir," *The New York Times*, August 18, 1953, p. 4.

[13] Mulgaokar, "'Definite Progress' on Kashmir Issue," p. 7.

[14] "Delhi Citizens' Reception to Mr. Ali," *The Times of India* (New Delhi), August 20, 1953, p. 7.

[15] Ibid.

[16] *Dargah* is an Islamic shrine of a saint especially a Sufi.

[17] S. Mulgaokar, "Plebiscite in Kashmir State is Agreed Upon," *The Times of India* (New Delhi), August 21, 1953, p. 1.

[18] S. Mulgaokar, "Kashmir Issue May be Solved in a Year," *The Times of India* (New Delhi), August 21, 1955, p. 7.

[19] "Direct Talks to Settle Kashmir Dispute," *The Times of India* (New Delhi), May 14, 1955, p. 1.

[20] Ministry of External Affairs (1955), Government of India, MEA Library, Annual Reports 1955–56, accessed May 15, 2015, http://mealib.nic.in/?2386?000.

[21] "Nehru–Ali Talks Open in Delhi," *The Times of India* (New Delhi), May 15, 1955, p. 1.

[22] *Selected Works of Jawaharlal Nehru (2001)*, 1 February–31 May 1955 – Series 2, Volume 28, Jawaharlal Nehru Memorial Fund, New Delhi, p. 246.

[23] Ibid.

[24] Records, President's Secretariat, Rashtrapati Bhavan, File No. 204.

[25] *Selected Works of Jawaharlal Nehru* (2001), p. 259.

[26] A.M. Rosenthal, "Talk on Kashmir Ends Hopefully," *The New York Times*, May 19, 1955, p. 11.

[27] Ibid.

[28] Records, President's Secretariat, File No. 204.

[29] Ibid.

[30] Robert J. McMahon, *The Cold War on the Periphery: The United States, India, and Pakistan* (New York: Columbia University Press, 1994), p. 162.

On January 25, 1955, Malik Ghulam Mohammed, Governor-General of Pakistan, arrived in New Delhi on a three-day visit which, in his own words, was "purely for goodwill."[1] The next day he participated in India's Republic Day celebrations becoming one of the first foreign Heads of State to do so.

A Kakazai Pathan, Malik Ghulam Mohammed was born in Lahore in Punjab on August 29, 1895.[2] After graduating from Aligarh Muslim University, he started a successful career in accounting. In 1945, Ghulam Mohammed co-founded Mahindra & Mohammed – a steel company in Mumbai with two brothers – JC and KC Mahindra. The company as founded did not, however, survive the partition of India. Ghulam Mohammed went on to become Pakistan's Finance Minister in 1947 and later its Governor-General. The company thus lost one of its founders and was renamed Mahindra & Mahindra. It is today one of India's leading automobile manufacturers.[3]

Visit of
H.E. Mr Malik Ghulam Mohammed
Governor–General of Pakistan

In 1951, Ghulam Mohammed was appointed Governor-General after Prime Minister Liaquat Ali Khan was assassinated. Afflicted by infantile paralysis when he was middle-aged, Governor-General Malik Ghulam Mohammed often kept ill-health. By 1951, his condition had worsened, though his influence in Pakistani politics remained astonishingly strong. An article published in *The Times of India*, two days before the Pakistani Governor-General arrived in India, echoed his preeminent position in Pakistan politics. It wrote, "The guiding mind [of Pakistan] lies in the frail twisted body of Ghulam Mohammed whose eyes apparently, noting nothing, miss nothing."[4] An editorial in the same newspaper commented that events in Pakistan were evidence of the "supreme and predominant position"[5] of the Governor-General.

The visit received global attention.[6] No formal talks had been scheduled, though a high-level delegation accompanied Governor-General Malik Ghulam Mohammed on the visit. It included Major General Iskander Mirza, Minister for the Interior and Khan Abdul Jabbar Khan, Minister for Communications, popularly known as Dr Khan Sahib[7] who was the elder brother of Khan Abdul Gaffar Khan, known as Frontier Gandhi.

Before his departure on January 25, 1955, Governor-General Malik Ghulam Mohammed spoke to the press in Karachi and said, "I have personally very close association with India – I mean pre-partition India – and these associations cannot be wiped out by the passage of time. I have a deep regard for the progress of both countries and shall try my best to promote a settlement and understanding between them."[8]

At 12 noon, a motorcade comprising an Oldsmobile, various guest cars and luggage Lorries departed Rashtrapati Bhavan for Palam Airport. Twenty minutes later, a

Facing page:
(L-R): President Dr Prasad with Governor-General Malik Ghulam Mohammed at Palam Airport, Delhi in January 1955. Credit: PC

Governor–General Malik Ghulam and President Dr Prasad exchanging greetings at Rashtrapati Bhavan in January 1955. Credit: PC

Buick followed along with a Rolls Royce that drove the President of India and his *aide–de–camp* (ADC) to the airport. An extra Packard was also sent and an escort car, which transported the Inspector of Police.[9]

At 12.45 pm, a special British twin–engine, short–range Vickers VC–1 Viking aircraft carrying the Governor–General of Pakistan and the Pakistani Minister of Communications touched down at Palam Airport's VIP bay. The aircraft was flying the flags of India, Pakistan as well as the Governor–General's own standard as a special gesture. General Iskander Mirza, accompanied by his wife, was to arrive separately at 8.20 pm from Karachi.

A 21–gun salute boomed in welcome as Governor–General Malik Ghulam Mohammed alighted from the aircraft, the sound of the guns mixing with the cheers of the crowds assembled at the airport. Immaculately dressed in a grey *sherwani*, with a deep red rose in its buttonhole, Governor–General Malik Ghulam Mohammed was warmly received by the President of India, Dr Rajendra Prasad. Prime Minister Nehru, who was an "old friend," of the Governor-

General,[10] Cabinet Ministers, Chiefs of the three Services, and members of the diplomatic corps were also at the airport to welcome the Pakistani leader.

Governor–General Ghulam Mohammed took the salute presented by an Inter–Services Guard of Honour, but was unable to inspect the parade on account of his frail health. As he was too fatigued to walk to the enclosure where the special invitees were assembled, they walked in file and were introduced to the Governor–General.

The reception at the airport was not ordinary. The Ministry of External Affairs had issued 600 admission cards for the arrival ceremony. [11] They included 200 for the press and 200 special cards for the arrival ceremony. There was a buzzing and excited crowd of Sikhs, Hindus and Muslims who carried garlands of flowers to welcome the Governor–General. A foreign newspaper wrote that so infectious was the enthusiasm that "it was difficult to remember that the two countries had been at loggerheads for years."[12]

Though Governor–General Malik Ghulam Mohammed was visibly exhausted, he summoned enough energy to address the

Tour Booklet of Governor–General sent from Pakistan.

press at the airport. Queried if the political climate was favourable for settling outstanding problems confronting the two nations, the Governor-General replied, "I am a man of goodwill. I have faith in me."[13] Further, he expressed faith and confidence in the Indian Prime Minister to solve problems and said, "I have more faith in Jawaharlal than you have."[14] He was, nevertheless, willing to hold official talks should the opportunity arise.[15] After this brief interaction, the distinguished delegation drove to the Rashtrapati Bhavan along the roads lined by crowds that were anxious to get a glimpse of the Pakistani leader.

After reaching Vijay Chowk, the Rolls Royce carrying the two Heads of State, turned into the stately gates of Rashtrapati Bhavan and drove through the South Sunken Road to the South Court. Here, a detachment of the 1st Battalion of the Guards Regiment waited to present the Governor-General with a Guard of Honour. Governor-General Malik Ghulam Mohammed's poor health, however, prevented him from inspecting it. Instead, after the national anthems of both countries had been played, the President of India conducted a visibly tired Governor-General to his specially appointed suite.[16]

Rashtrapati Bhavan had taken a great deal of care to ensure that the Governor-General was made as comfortable as possible during his stay 'under the dome.' On the evening of Sunday, January 23, 1955, Colonel SN Raza, Military Secretary to the Governor-General had arrived in Delhi on a BOAC flight. An Oldsmobile from the President's Garage had brought Colonel Raza to Rashtrapati Bhavan. The next day, an advance team arrived in Delhi at 7.45 pm on an Indian Airlines Corporation Service flight from Karachi. They had several rounds of discussion with Rashtrapati Bhavan officials on the arrangements to be made for the Governor-General's visit. The attention to detail was also meticulous as was the liaising between the officials of India and Pakistan. It also resulted in the sharing of the programme booklet prepared by the nation of a visiting Head of State/Government for the first time with India.

After detailed deliberation, it was decided that the Governor-General should be accommodated on the ground floor of the Guest Wing. This decision was taken to save the Governor-General of the additional effort required to come down to the ground floor every time he left for engagements and return to it after they were over. He was therefore allotted the Dufferin Suite and the Elgin Bedroom on the ground floor in lieu of the lavishly appointed Dwarka Suite situated on the first floor where Heads of State/Government usually stay.

Every requirement of the Governor-General was met by Rashtrapati Bhavan. As was desired by the Pakistan officials, a wooden bed, standing not more than one foot from the ground was provided for the Governor-General. A wheelchair was also kept on stand-by at all times and a nurse or personal attendant was placed on call at all hours of the night and day.[17]

The rest of Governor-General's entourage was accommodated in the various suites/rooms in Rashtrapati Bhavan according to their seniority. Dr Khan Sahib stayed in the Minto Bedroom; Mohammed Ali, the Finance Minister, in the Reading Suite and Major General Iskander Mirza and his wife in the Birdwood Suite.[18]

After arriving in his room, Governor-General Malik Ghulam Mohammed had a quiet lunch. His first official engagement was at *Rajghat*.

RASHTRAPATI BHAVAN, NEW DELHI

			Phone.
Ground Floor			
H.E. the Governor-General of Pakistan. ...	{ Dufferin Suite ...		31
	{ Elgin bed room ...		
Capt. Nawabzada Azmat Khan }	Ava bed room	...	123
Capt. Saeed Ahmed Khan } ...			
Colonel A. Rahman	Ava sitting room	...	122
First Floor			
The Hon'ble Dr. Khan Sahib	Minto bed room	...	83
The Hon'ble Mr. Mohd. Ali	Reading Suite	...	54
Shri C. Rajagopalachari	Irwin Suite	...	63
The Hon'ble Major-General Iskander Mirza and Mrs. Mirza.	Birdwood Suite	...	1
Second Floor			
Mr. Farrukh Amin }	Lytton bed room	...	114
Dr. A. H. Akhtar }			
Colonel S. N. Raza }	Stanley bed room	...	109
Mr. In am Mohd. }			
Miss R Borel	Goschen bed room	...	104
Mr. S. Wahajuddin Ahmed	Napier bed room	...	...

Room Allocation Plan.

As the cavalcade of cars drew up at *Rajghat*, the crowd of onlookers who had gathered in the vicinity, cheered the visitors with shouts of "Dr Khan Sahib *Zindabad*" and "Ghulam Mohammed *Zindabad*."[19] At 4.30 pm the Governor-General laid a wreath at Mahatma Gandhi's *samadhi*.

The Governor-General placed a giant wreath made of green, red and white flowers on the *samadhi*, and stood before it for a while in reverential silence.[20] Though, frail in body, he did not use a wheel-chair while he went to the *samadhi*, but he could not do without it on the way back.[21] Dr Khan Sahib and the Pakistan High Commissioner to India, Raja Ghaznafar Ali Khan also placed wreaths at the memorial.[22] Dr Khan Sahib was, in fact, a star attraction at the venue and the crowds which had gathered the *Rajghat* gave him a resounding welcome. Some of them could not suppress their excitement on seeing him and broke through the police cordon to reach the Pakistani leader. Many touched his feet, while the police struggled to control the "exuberant mass."[23]

From *Rajghat*, the visitors drove to Jamia Millia Islamia University. During the drive, Governor-General Malik Ghulam Mohammed spoke to Indian officials and offered, rather charmingly, to send marble from Pakistan to lay on the floor of Gandhi's *samadhi* and its precincts.[24]

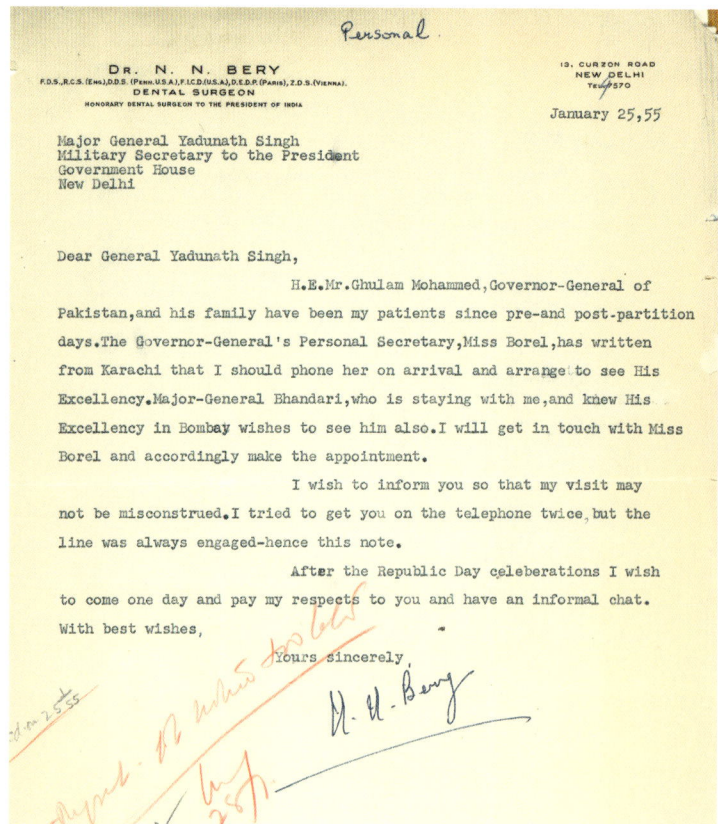

Letter from Dr NN Bery requesting an audience with Governor-General.

Jamia Millia Islamia was beautifully decorated giving it a festive appearance. There were colourful banners and flags fluttering in the breeze all over the vast compound of the university. The Governor-General also attended a reception organised by the university in his honour. He spoke at the reception and expounded the cause of Indo-Pak unity. He exhorted the university to continue its work for unity between the two countries and lay the foundation for their friendship. He said, "The people of our two countries have suffered much in the past; they have lost in lives, in property and in women during that madness; the time has now arrived when we should learn to forget the bitterness of the past; hatred destroys and love builds... I assure you that I shall do my very best to see that our differences are resolved and that we live as extremely good and friendly neighbours."[25]

At the university, the Governor-General also paid his respects at the mausoleum of Dr MA Ansari, who was a valiant freedom fighter and a close associate of Mahatma Gandhi. He still had old friends at the university. After laying flowers at Dr Ansari's mausoleum, he stayed to have tea with his friends and catch up on old times.[26]

So pleasant had been his meeting with his old friends, that the drive back to Rashtrapati Bhavan brought back memories of yet another one, BK Kaul, Deputy Secretary, Economic Affairs. Disregarding his fatigue, he took a detour to Kaul's house, dropping by unexpectedly to spend an hour with the friend.[27]

Indeed, the Governor-General's circle of friends in India was large. If there was any evidence required, the flood of requests received prior to his arrival for an audience, bore testimony to this fact.

One such letter came from Dr NN Bery, a dental surgeon who had been the Governor-General's dentist before Partition. Dr Bery wrote to Major General Yadunath Singh, Military Secretary to the President (MSP), on January 25, requesting to be granted some time with the Governor-General for himself and another old acquaintance, Major General Bhandari. He stated in the request that, "The Governor-General's Personal Secretary, Miss Borel, has written from Karachi that I should phone her on arrival and arrange to see His Excellency."[28] Unfortunately, Dr Bery had left it too late and his request could not be fitted into the Governor-General's tight schedule.

Governor-General Ghulam Mohammed returned to Rashtrapati Bhavan just in time to attend a State Banquet that the Indian President hosted in his honour. By 8.00 pm, the lights and fountains in the Mughal Garden were switched on making the ambience warm and welcoming. Loudspeakers had been installed so that everyone present could hear the addresses of both Heads of State.

The President's Bodyguard (PBG) stood to attention in the corridors and staircases and the Personal Staff were attired in crisp, starched uniforms. The large State Room[29] of Rashtrapati Bhavan was dressed up for the occasion, with pots and vases containing the myriad-hued flowers of the fast approaching spring. Flags of India and Pakistan hung from the walls signalling that the function was indeed as formal as receptions for Heads of States are.

The first guests arrived by 8.20 pm and reached the South Court via the South Sunken Road. They were received by the President's Personal Staff, at the north entrance of the West Subway and conducted to the State Room. At 8.25 pm, the President of India was escorted to the Dufferin Suite from where he accompanied the Pakistani Governor-General to the State Room.

The two leaders walked across the corridor through the Southeast door and came to a stop under the central arch in the large State Room. Thereafter, the national anthems of both countries were played in succession. The MSP, Major-General Yadunath Singh, then presented the guests to the two Heads of State. After introductions were over, the guests were conducted to the Banquet Hall for dinner led by the Indian President and the Governor-General, while the Navy Band played "March."[30]

The invitees to the banquet from the Indian side included Prime Minister Jawaharlal Nehru, Members of the Cabinet, Dr MS Mehta, the Indian High Commissioner to Pakistan and heads of diplomatic missions. The invitees from the visiting side included Major General Iskander Mirza, his wife, Begum Mirza, Dr Khan Sahib and Raja Ghaznafar Ali Khan, Pakistan High Commissioner to India.

After a splendid dinner, both Heads of State raised a toast to each other and their countries. President Dr Prasad welcomed the Governor-General in Hindi, referring to the "common background and a common experience" that the two nations shared, he emphasised that this could "provide the foundation for enduring friendship and understanding" between the two of them and no problem "would not be capable of solution in a spirit of friendliness and understanding."[31] Commenting on the visit of the Governor-General, President Dr Prasad said, "May I express the hope that you will find time later to pay us a longer visit so that we might have an opportunity of showing you something more of New India."[32]

Governor-General Ghulam Mohammed delivering banquet speech at Rashtrapati Bhavan. Seated opposite is President Dr Rajendra Prasad and on his left is Vice President Dr Radhakrishnan. (January 1955). Credit: PC

Replying to President Dr Prasad's warm words of welcome, the Pakistani Governor-General raised his glass and said, "Since my arrival here I have been deeply moved by your kind hospitality, and I thank Your Excellency for it... I am no stranger to this great country of yours, nor are most of my countrymen. In the freedom of this sub-continent, the peoples of India and Pakistan worked shoulder to shoulder, and it is due to their sacrifices that we enjoy the blessings of freedom today." He hastened to add that as the problems facing both countries were similar, "The ideal time has now come to prove sincerely that the basic and major points of dispute can be mutually solved without delay... The time for action is now...people will not wait."[33]

The banquet lasted till 10.00 pm, and the Indian Navy Band played carefully selected pieces of music until the last guests left the Banquet Hall. *Shehnai* players, the All India Radio Orchestra were also present in the Banquet Hall and they also played a medley of songs while the banquet was in progress. As the *khidmatgars*

(butlers) came in to clear the dishes, the Governor-General bid the guests goodbye, before being escorted to his apartment on the ground floor. He had to wake up early to attend the Republic Day Parade on the following day.

A bright and sunny dawn ushered in India's fifth Republic Day. The arrangements were flawless. The ceremonial arrival of the two Heads of State to the special rostrum on Rajpath was particularly rehearsed and meticulously planned as this time, it would not just be the Indian President who would be riding to Kingsway in a horse-drawn carriages.

The programme began at 9.30 am. All the invitees had arrived almost 30 minutes earlier. Amongst the high dignitaries to arrive early was the Prime Minister of India. After arriving at the Saluting Base, he was seen in a jovial mood, laughing genially with a group of school children. An observant correspondent from The Hindustan Times captured the essence of the moment and wrote, "Who were happier – the Prime Minister or the children – it was not easy to say."[34]

President Dr Prasad (right) with Governor-General Ghulam Mohammed arriving at Rashtrapati Bhavan in State Coach in January 1955. Credit: PC

The President of India, flanked by his regal bodyguards, arrived at the venue at 9.30 am in the Presidential State Coach. He was received by Prime Minister Nehru, who led him to the special "red and gold chair glittering in the sun."[35] The national flag was hoisted, and a 31-gun salute boomed to mark the celebratory occasion.

It was a grand spectacle and as the band struck up the national anthem, the President took the salute in the impressive setting. India's Republic Day Parade had already gained world fame for the unity and diversity of the nation that the programmes on the occasion personified. *The New York Times* wrote that it was "as modern as the self-conscious movie extras from Bombay and as ancient as the leaping dances of the tribesmen from Assam."[36]

Caparisoned Indian elephants, splendid in ceremonial gold and decorated right down to the tips of their trunks, lumbered down the parade route, drawing huge cheers from the crowd. Unfortunately, this regal spectacle was somewhat marred when the sound of a dozen French-manufactured jets flying overhead panicked the pachyderms. They stopped dead in their tracks in alarm, and then made a wild dash for the side-lines. Fortunately, they chose to merely huddle together until the noise of the jets had faded, rather than run amok through the crowd.[37]

There was much discussion about the time that the Governor-General should arrive for the celebrations as well as the mode of transport that he may use to reach the venue. Prime Minister Nehru had opined that the Governor-General should arrive in a carriage-in-four, escorted by lancers, a little before the President. The Governor-General of Pakistan, however, arrived towards the end of the first half of the parade, at 10.15 am and was welcomed by the newly-appointed Defence Minister, Dr Katju.[38]

At 4.00 pm, that day, the President of India hosted a reception for Governor-General Malik Ghulam Mohammed in the cheerful Morning Room at Rashtrapati Bhavan. With its blue ceiling, white trimmings and splendid view of the Mughal Gardens, the Morning Room was the ideal locale for the gathering. Several invitees attended the elegant reception. After this function, Governor-General Ghulam Mohammed was escorted to his suite where he rested had a quiet dinner.[39]

The next day was relatively free of official engagements. Governor-General Malik Ghulam Mohammed spent the morning en suite, before leaving for a luncheon at the Education Minister, Maulana Azad's home. The lunch was an informal and leisurely affair even though the Kashmir conundrum was briefly discussed. Dr Khan Sahib, Major-General Iskander Mirza, Choudhury Mohammed Ali, and Raja Ghaznafar Ali Khan also attended the lunch.[40]

In the evening, a special show of folk dances was organised in the Governor-General's honour at the National Stadium. A Station Wagon from the President's Garage brought the advance party first. It was followed by a Commer Van that ferried a special wheelchair and a "handle chair"[41] for the ailing Governor-General. A Humber, a Buick and an Ambassador arrived next carrying members of President Dr Prasad's family.

Governor-General Ghulam Mohammed arrived at the venue in a Rolls Royce, which was followed by another Buick, and a Packard with his Personal Staff. The President's family and the Governor-General were conducted to the President's Box before the programme. The show started at 6.15 pm and continued for another two-and-a-half hours until 8.45 pm, though arrangements were in place for the Governor-General to leave whenever he chose to.[42]

The President of India had organised a dinner for the Governor-General at Rashtrapati Bhavan that evening. Major-General Iskander Mirza, Dr Khan Sahib, Choudhury Mohammed Ali, Dr Radhakrishnan, C Rajagopalachari and Sardar Swaran Singh were some of the invitees. President Dr Prasad presented the Governor-General with an "ivory model of the Qutub Minar and an autographed photograph"[43] of himself as remembrances of his visit to India.

While the Governor-General was busy with his programmes, Dr Khan Sahib visited the refugee colonies in Faridabad. Here a crowd of "over 20,000" refugees from the Frontier Province gave him a grand reception. He was received in "traditional *Pathan* style" with "firing guns and beating drums".[44] Thereafter, he travelled to rehabilitation centres visiting Khan Market on Humayun Road and Abdul Ghaffar Market in Karol Bagh and, the two markets that were named after Dr Khan Sahib and his brother respectively. Highly impressed by the successful functioning of the centres, Dr Khan Sahib remarked in a lighter vein that, "it was because all of them were Pathans and were from the Frontier."[45]

The short but extremely successful trip of Pakistan's Governor-General came to an end on the morning of January 28. By 8.00 am, baggage had been loaded onto the lorry waiting in the South Court. A Station Wagon and an Oldsmobile from the President's Garage drove the Governor-General's entourage to the airport.

At 8.50 am, President Dr Prasad went to the Dufferin Suite from where he escorted the Governor-General to the South Court. Here Governor-General Ghulam Mohammed was accorded a Guard of Honour while a band played the national anthems of both countries.[46]

After the 'parade' came to 'Order Arms,' a Rolls Royce pulled up. It drove the President and the Governor-General to New Delhi's Palam Airport. By 9.00 am, Governor-General Ghulam Mohammed had said goodbye to his temporary residence 'under the dome.'

The farewell "was as touching and colourful as the reception was warm and grand."[47] The President, Vice President, Prime Minister, Cabinet Ministers and Members of the Indian Parliament bade him farewell as did a number of his personal friends.[48] The bonhomie of "old boys' reunion" delayed the Governor-General's Viking aircraft for 30-minutes,[49] but nobody seemed to care or even notice. After inspecting the Guard of Honour, just before he boarded the aircraft, Governor-General Ghulam Mohammed put an arm around Prime Minister Nehru and said, "We must settle all the outstanding disputes between us. You must pave the way for it. God bless you."[50]

As the plane took off, 21-guns boomed in salute to what had been a very successful and last visit by the gracious Head of State. His entire entourage did not, however, return with the Governor-General. Dr Khan Sahib, a cricket enthusiast, chose to stay back as he and his wife were to travel to Lahore from India to watch a cricket match. Dr Khan Sahib then became the target of a group of pressmen who bombarded him with a barrage of questions, but he was not one to easily fall prey to questions. He parried all of them but chose to answer one. The question was – had he "bowled or batted" during the visit? Khan Sahib's reply was that he had batted as well as bowled.[51]

Upon his arrival in Karachi, he sent a message of thanks to the President of India, expressing his gratitude for the hospitality and kindness he had received in India. In it, he expressed the hope that his visit would foster close relations between the two nations and said, "promote understanding and bring our countries closely together."[52]

The visit had evidently helped ease the tension that was spawned by the bitter communal carnage that followed the Partition of India. On reaching Karachi, the Governor-General told the press that the "climate is now more suitable for settlement of Indo–Pakistan disputes than ever before."[53]

Later that year, on October 6, 1955, Governor-General Malik Ghulam Mohammed was forced by ill-health to resign. He died almost a year later, in Karachi, on August 29, 1956. He was 61.[5]

From His Excellency the Governor-General of Pakistan.
To His Excellency the President of India.

I wish on my departure from India to thank you wholeheartedly for your hospitality and your kindness. I was deeply touched by your kind regards for me and pray to God for your continued good health and for the prosperity of the people of India. I sincerely hope that my visit to India might help to promote understanding and bring our countries closely together. I was glad to see the marked progress which India has made and I again wish Your Excellency peace, happiness and prosperity.

I shall be grateful if my sincere thanks are conveyed to the Government and people of India.

With kindest regards from Ghulam Mohammed.

Message of thanks from Governor–General Malik Ghulam to President Dr Prasad.

Notes

1 "Better Indo–Pakistan Relations," *The Times* (London), January 29, 1955, p. 5.

2 Harris M. Lentz, *Heads of States and Governments: A Worldwide Encyclopaedia of Over 2,300 Leaders, 1945 through 1992* (London: Fitzroy Dearborn Publishers, 1995), p. 606.

3 "Malik Ghulam Muhammad," accessed June 3, 2015, http://www.pakistanherald.com/profile/malik-ghulam-muhammad-1177.

4 "Men, Matters and Memories: Ariel's," *The Times of India* (New Delhi), January 23, 1955, p. 8.

5 "Welcome," *The Times of India* (New Delhi), January 25, 1955, p. 6.

6 "Pakistani to Visit India," *The New York Times*, January 15, 1955, p. 3.

7 Records, President's Secretariat, Rashtrapati Bhavan, File No. 209.

8 "Indo–Pakistan Relations," *The Hindu* (New Delhi), January 25, 1955, p. 8.

9 Records, President's Secretariat, File No. 209.

10 "Pakistan Governor Invites Indian Talks," *The New York Times*, January 26, 1955, p. 12.

11 Records, President's Secretariat, File No. 209.

12 "Pakistan Leaders in Delhi Ovation on Arrival," *The Times* (London), January 26, 1955, p. 7.

13 "Pak G.–G. Calls for Peace and Tolerance," *The Times of India* (New Delhi), January 26, 1955, p. 13.

14 Ibid.

15 "Pakistan Governor Invites Indian Talks," p. 12.

16 Records, President's Secretariat, File No. 209.

17 Ibid.

18 Ibid.

19 "Pak G.–G. Visits Rajghat," *The Times of India* (New Delhi), January 26, 1955, p. 13.

20 Ibid.

21 "Full Faith in Nehru," *The Hindustan Times* (New Delhi), January 26, 1955, p. 1.

22 "Pak G.–G. Visits Rajghat," p. 13.

23 Ibid.

24 Ibid.

25 "Ghulam Md.'s Speech at Jamia Millia," *The Hindustan Times* (New Delhi), January 26, 1955, p. 16.

26 "Pak G.–G. Visits Rajghat," p. 13.

27 "Ghulam Md.'s Speech at Jamia Millia," p. 16.

28 Records, President's Secretariat, File No. 209.

29 The Large State Room is the Ashok Hall. The new nomenclature was seen used only during this visit. Why this change was effected is not clear from the records.

30 Records, President's Secretariat, File No. 209.

31 Ministry of External Affairs (1995), Government of India, MEA Library, Foreign Affairs Records 1955, Volume I, accessed June 4, 2015, mealib.nic.in/?pdf2543?000.

32 Ibid.

33 Ibid.

34 "Colourful Republic Day Parade in Delhi," *The Hindustan Times* (New Delhi), January 17, 1955, p. 14.

35 Ibid.

36 A.M. Rosenthal, "Indian Elephants and Jets Parade," *The New York Times*, January 27, 1955, p. 7.

37 Ibid.

38 "Colourful Republic Day Parade in Delhi," p. 14.

39 Records, President's Secretariat, File No. 209.

40 "The Kashmir Problem," *The Hindu* (New Delhi), January 28, 1955, p. 8.

41 Records, President's Secretariat, File no. 209.

42 Ibid.

43 "Goodwill Generated by Pak G.-G.'s Visit," *The Times of India* (New Delhi), January 28, 1955, p. 1.

44 "Climate Propitious for Settlement," *The Hindustan Times* (New Delhi), January 29, 1955, p. 12.

45 Ibid.

46 Records, President's Secretariat, File no. 209.

47 "Climate Propitious for Settlement," p. 12.

48 Ibid.

49 "Mr. Nehru Leaves Delhi in Lively Mood," *The Times* (London), January 29, 1955, p. 5.

50 "Mr. Ghulam Mohd.," *The Hindu* (New Delhi), January 29, 1955. p. 7.

51 "Climate Propitious for Settlement," p. 1.

52 Records, President's Secretariat, File no. 209

53 Better Indo–Pakistan Relations," p. 5.

54 Lentz, Heads of States and Governments, p. 606.

It was a balmy September day in 1958, when the seventh Prime Minister of Pakistan, Malik Sir Feroz Khan Noon, arrived in Delhi on a two-day visit.

Malik Feroz Khan Noon was born in Lahore on May 7, 1893, to an affluent family in the Punjab. After completing his early education in Lahore, he went to England from where he graduated in history from Oxford University in 1916 and later successfully passed his Bar-at-Law examinations. After practicing at the Lahore High Court, he joined politics and was appointed Minister of Health and Education in the "Punjab Legislative Assembly."[1] Thereafter, he served as High Commissioner of India to the Court of St. James from 1936-41, when he was knighted.

On his return, Feroz Khan Noon became the first Indian to be allocated the defence portfolio in the Viceroy's Council. After independence, he became the Chief Minister of the Punjab Province in Pakistan. Thereafter, he served as Pakistan's Foreign Minister, before becoming Prime Minister on December 16, 1957.

Visit of
September 9–11, 1958

H.E. Malik Sir Feroz Khan Noon
Prime Minister of Pakistan

Prime Minister Noon visited India the next year. The visit, however, came at a time when relations between the two countries were not at their best. Tensions had, however, somewhat eased with the election of Noon as Prime Minister who opposed war with India terming it as "nothing short of lunacy"[2] and attacked his country's opposition parties for taking such extreme stances.[3] He hoped that a political solution could be found to settle the differences between the two countries and undertook the trip to India with this objective.

A Pakistan Air Force Viscount, carrying Prime Minister Noon and his Austrian-born wife, Begum Viqarun Nisa Noon, along with a 22-member entourage, landed at Palam Airport on September 9, 1958 at 11.20 am. A host of dignitaries, including Indian Prime Minister Nehru and other Cabinet Ministers welcomed the Pakistani Prime Minister at the airport.

The welcome was followed by the presentation of a Guard of Honour. Speaking at the airport, after he had inspected the Guard of Honour, Prime Minister Noon said, "For me to be in Delhi is a happy occasion. It is a happy occasion to renew old acquaintances. I hope we will achieve the purpose for which we have come."[4]

After the ceremonial reception, the two Prime Ministers, Noon and Nehru, drove to Rashtrapati Bhavan in an open convertible Cadillac. Crowds that had gathered all along the roads and streets cheered the motorcade as it sped past. A closed Cadillac, a DeSoto, a Dodge and four other guest cars followed the convertible.

On their arrival at the Rashtrapati Bhavan, the Pakistani delegation was received by the Comptroller, President's Household (CPH). The President's Bodyguard, in their

Facing page:
Prime Minister Noon (left)
with President Dr Prasad
at Rashtrapati Bhavan in
September 1958. Credit: PC

(L-R): Begum Noon, Prime Minister Nehru and Prime Minister Noon at Palam Airport, New Delhi, in September 1958. Credit: PD

resplendent uniforms lined the way from the alighting point to the Guest Wing of Rashtrapati Bhavan, where select members of the delegation were to be accommodated. Prime Minister Noon and Begum Noon stayed in the Dwarka and Nalanda Suites respectively. The Secretary to the Ministry of Foreign Affairs and Commonwealth Relations of Pakistan, MSA Baig, stayed in the Tagore Suite on the ground floor of the Presidential palace; the Secretary to the Ministry of Defence, MM Khurshid was accommodated in the Himalaya Suite; the Chief Secretary of West Pakistan, SF Hassan was allotted the Dakshin Bedroom and the Chief Secretary of East Pakistan, Hamid Ali was to stay in the Pepsu Bedroom. Other rooms – Godavari, Pratap, Mysore, Neelam and Gautam – accommodated various other members of the entourage. Amongst those who stayed at Rashtrapati Bhavan was Sultan Ahmed, the "Personal Servant" of the Prime Minster. The rest of the delegation was accommodated at Hotel Ashoka.

Security inside Rashtrapati Bhavan was augmented for the Pakistani Prime Minister. Two armed orderlies, dressed in plain clothes, were stationed outside the Dwarka Suite. While one of the orderlies would remain outside the Suite's main door, the other was to accompany the Prime Minister during his "movements within the house."[5]

At 12.30 pm, the Pakistani Prime Minister started his official visit with a trip to *Rajghat* where he laid a wreath on the *samadhi* of Mahatma Gandhi. Thereafter, he returned to Rashtrapati Bhavan for a quiet lunch en suite.

Around 4.00 pm, Prime Minister Noon met with Prime Minister Nehru to discuss matters of mutual concern at the latter's residence at Teen Murti Bhavan. The talks lasted for nearly two–hours–and–45–minutes. Though neither side revealed any details of the discussions, the press reported that the meetings were more promising than those Prime Minister Nehru had held with the Prime Ministers of Pakistan over the last eight years.[6]

While Prime Minister Noon was engaged in official talks, Begum Noon had other plans. This was communicated by the Chief of Protocol (COP) to the Deputy Military Secretary to the President (DMSP), Lieutenant Colonel Ghufran. A request was made to the DMSP, to make special arrangements for Begum Noon to go for shopping and sightseeing while Prime Minister Noon conferred with Pandit Nehru. The DMSP in turn wrote to Lajwanti Yunus, wife of Mohammed Yunus who was a freedom fighter. He had migrated to India after the partition and was later inducted into the Indian Foreign Service by Prime Minister Nehru. A resident of 13, Willingdon Crescent, Lajwanti Yunus was requested to join Begum Noon for tea at 4.30 pm and later accompany her on the outing. A similar request was also made to Rani Harnarain Singh, wife of Major General Harnarain Singh, Military Secretary to the President (MSP).

Following talks with the Indian Prime Minister at Teen Murti Bhavan, Prime Minister Noon drove back to Rashtrapati Bhavan. At 7.00 that evening, the Pakistani High Commissioner, Mian Ziauddin hosted a reception, which he had originally planned only for Prime Minister Noon. Perhaps, someone in the Pakistani High

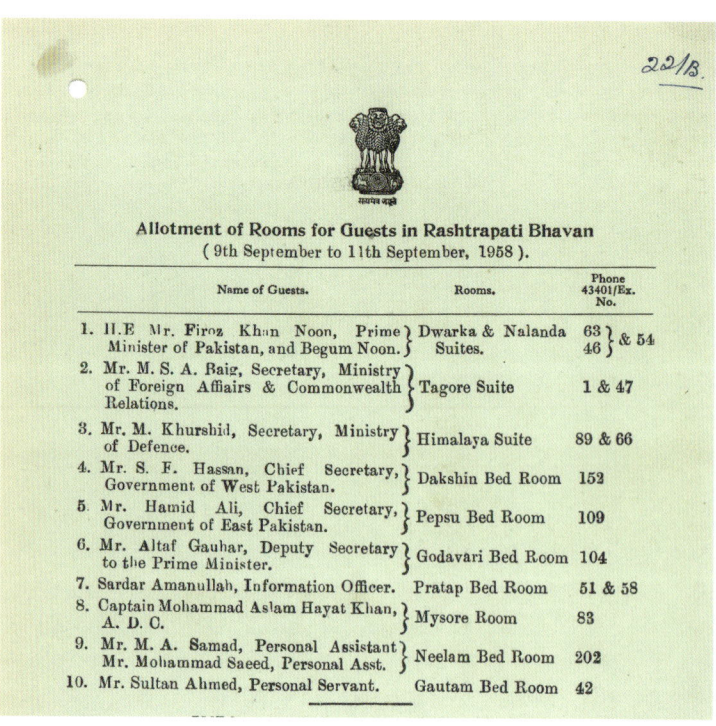

Room Allocation Plan.

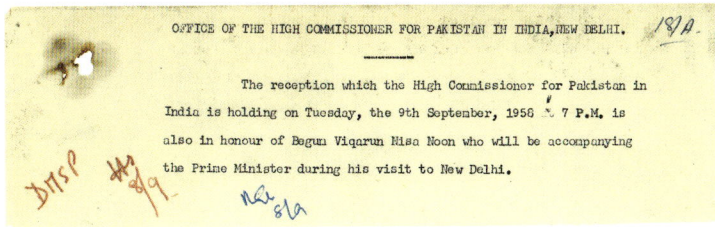

Note from the Pakistan High Commissioner confirming that the reception was also in honour of Begum Noon.

and prominent citizens had gathered at Hyderabad House, the former palace of the *Nizam* of Hyderabad. At the reception, Pandit Nehru and Prime Minister Noon chatted amiably while the large group of photographers who were present captured the moment for posterity.[7]

Neither Prime Minister Noon nor h is wife stayed at the reception too long. By 8.15 pm, the motorcade was on the move again, this time to 16, Golf Links, where Sohan Lal, a Member of the Legislative Assembly of Uttar Pradesh and the former Chairman of the Lahore Electricity Supply Company, was hosting a dinner for the Prime Ministerial couple. This was a far smaller, more select affair, with only some 30 invitees on the guest list, including Sardar Swaran Singh and SK Patil. A delicious buffet was served on the lawns, and the Prime Minister and his wife spent some time chatting with guests before leaving for Rashtrapati Bhavan.

Early next morning, at 9.00, Prime Minister Noon started the day by laying the foundation stone of the Chancery Building of the Pakistan High Commission in New Delhi. After this ceremony, he met with Pandit Nehru for talks at Teen Murti Bhavan. The discussions were confined "to methods of avoiding fresh outbreaks, such as the recent ones along East Pakistan's frontier with the Indian states of West Bengal and Assam and territory of Tripura."[8] No communiqué was issued just yet, but officials did hint that

Commission had made an embarrassing slip–up or Begum Noon may not have initially planned to accompany her husband to the reception. Soon, however, a typed strip of paper was hastily sent to Rashtrapati Bhavan stating that "The reception which the High Commissioner for Pakistan in India is holding on Tuesday, the 9th September, 1958 at 7 P.M. is also in honour of Begum Viqarun Nisa Noon." The venue of the reception was also shifted from the originally planned venue at 8/B, Harding Avenue (now Mathura Road), where it was to be held on the lawns behind the residence of the Pakistani High Commissioner to India, to Hyderabad House.

Nearly 500 invitees, including the Prime Minister of India, Union Ministers, members of the diplomatic corps, senior Government officials, Members of Parliament, Counsellors

(Front row, R-L): Prime Minister Nehru, Vice President Dr Radhakrishnan, Begum Noon, Speaker of Lok Sabha Ayyangar and Prime Minister Noon (extreme left) at Parliament House in September 1958. Credit: PD

Prime Minister Noon would not return to Karachi empty handed. Prime Minister Nehru, in fact, was rather optimistic about the outcome of the talks, telling reporters, "I think our talks have largely succeeded."[9] On the other hand, Prime Minister Noon was less forthcoming and was not prepared to reveal what was on his mind. All he said before his departure was, "I will talk in Karachi."[10]

With the talks over, Prime Minister Noon returned to Rashtrapati Bhavan, and called on President Dr Rajendra Prasad at 12.30 pm. The two leaders had lunch together in the stately Grey Dining Room with a few select invitees. The list of invitees were restricted to the Prime Minister of India, Defence Minister, Deputy Minister of External Affairs, the Foreign Secretary, the Commonwealth Secretary, the COP, the High Commissioner of Pakistan, the Deputy High Commissioner of Pakistan, the Secretary to the President and the MSP.

After spending a while in his suite after lunch, Prime Minister Noon left for Parliament House, where a tea party was hosted in his honour at 5.30 pm on the lawns by the Chairman of the Rajya Sabha, and the Speaker of the Lok Sabha. Later in his memoirs, Prime Minister Noon recounted, "I [was] met with much cordiality in Delhi, especially in the Parliament House reception. The then Vice President of India, Shri Radhakrishnan, was there and all the Ministers, including Pandit Pant, who had made a special effort to come in spite of bad health."[11] Later that night, Prime Minister Noon dined with Pandit Nehru at the latter's residence.

The meetings between Pandit Nehru and Prime Minister Noon had resulted in some positive outcomes. Agreements were reached on certain issues on the border disputes which seemed intractable. The repudiation of force by both sides as a means of settlement of the disputes was in itself a success. The talks on the whole were held in an atmosphere of cordiality as could be expected "in the light of the long personal acquaintance of these two men."[12]

The next morning on September 11, 1958, at 9.00, Prime Minister Noon and his entourage departed for Palam Airport, where a special aircraft was waiting to take them back to Karachi. Speaking to media correspondents at the airport, before boarding the flight, Prime Minister Noon described the talks he had had with his Indian counterpart as "Very useful."[13] After a ceremonial send-off, Prime Minister Noon emplaned for Karachi at 9.30 am.

Though the two-day bilateral talks between Prime Minister Noon and Prime Minister Nehru were conducted behind closed doors, they culminated in a joint communiqué that was issued on September 11. It stated that agreements were reached on the settlement of most of the border disputes in the eastern region, which included the exchange of several strips of territories "with a view to removing causes of tensions."[14]

(L-R): Prime Minister Noon, President Dr Prasad and Begum Noon at Rashtrapati Bhavan in September 1958. Credit: PC

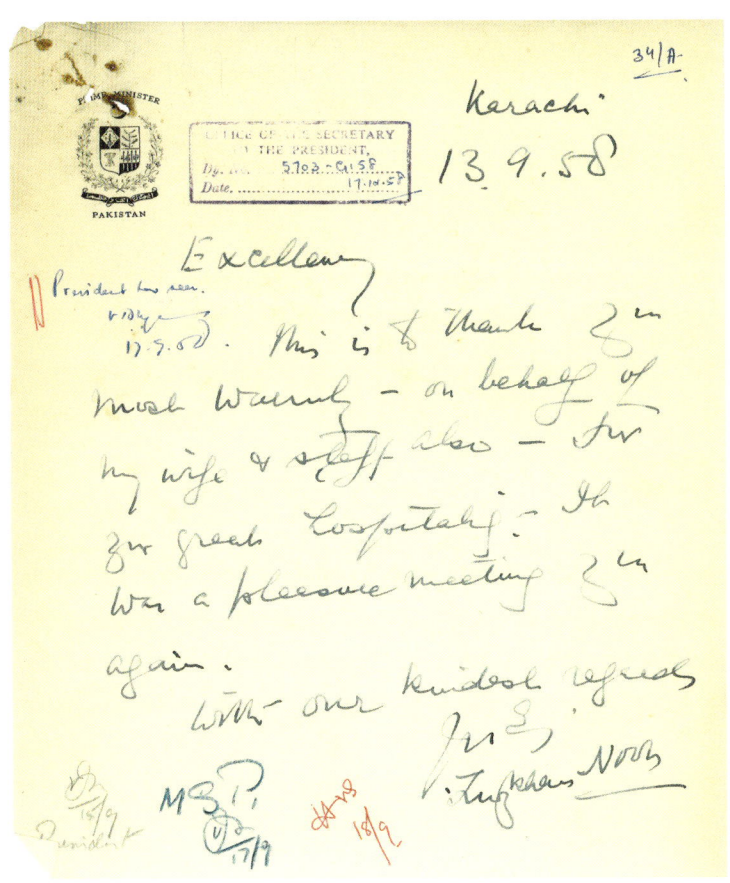

A hand-written letter of thanks from Prime Minister Noon to President Dr Prasad.

In his memoirs, Prime Minister Noon wrote that, "The Noon–Nehru pact...was a success, as all outstanding boundary disputes of East Pakistan were settled."[15] Commenting on Pandit Nehru, he wrote of him as a "great patriot, self-sacrificing, highly polished and polite, he was honest and fair in administering public affairs."[16]

In an unusual gesture Prime Minister Noon sent the Indian President, Dr Rajendra Prasad a hand-written letter within two days of his reaching Karachi. In the letter Prime Minister Noon thanked the President "most warmly – on behalf of my wife and staff also – for your great hospitality."[17] Prime Minister Noon had also left a gift for the MSP, Major General Sardar Harnarain Singh, who wrote to the High Commissioner requesting him to convey his "sincere thanks" to the Pakistani Prime Minister.

Feroz Khan Noon's tenure as Prime Minister of Pakistan came to an abrupt end on October 7, 1958, almost a month after his India visit, when martial law was enforced in the country. Feroz Khan Noon died on December 9, 1970. He was 77. Begum Viqarun Nisa died on January 16, 2000. She was 80.

Notes

[1] Harris M. Lentz, *Heads of States and Governments: A Worldwide Encyclopaedia of Over 2,300 Leaders, 1945 through 1992* (London: Fitzroy Dearborn Publishers, 1995), p. 612.

[2] Vera Micheles Dean, *New Patterns of Democracy in India* (Cambridge: Harvard University Press, 1959), p. 200.

[3] Elie Abel, "Pakistani Leader Visits India Today," *The New York Times*, September 9, 1958, p. 6.

[4] "Nehru–Noon Talks on Border Issues Begin in Delhi," *The Hindustan Times* (New Delhi), September 10, 1958, p. 1.

[5] Records, President's Secretariat, Rashtrapati Bhavan, File No. 30/CER/63.

[6] Elie Abel, "Pakistani Opens Talk With Nehru," *The New York Times*, September 10, 1958, p. 17.

[7] Ibid.

[8] "Nehru–Noon Talks End in Cordial Aura," *The New York Times*, September 11, 1958, p. 5

[9] Ibid.

[10] Ibid.

[11] Feroz Khan Noon, *From Memory* (Lahore: Ferozsons, 1966), p. 286.

[12] "India–Pakistan Agreement," *The New York Times*, September 11, 1958, p. 24.

[13] "Nehru and Noon," *The New York Times*, September 14, 1958, p. 166.

[14] Ibid.

[15] Noon, *From Memory*, p. 287

[16] Ibid.

[17] Records, President's Secretariat, File No. 30/CER/63.

On the sunny winter morning of November 4, 1957, a special Air Vietnam Plane landed at New Delhi's Palam Airport at 10.30, bringing the first President of the Republic of Vietnam, Ngo Dinh Diem, on a four-day 'goodwill' visit. Known as "a resilient, deeply religious Vietnamese nationalist,"[1] President Diem's talks with Prime Minister Jawaharlal Nehru were expected to strengthen relations between the two countries.

Ngo Dinh Diem was born on January 3, 1901, to a Minister's family serving Emperor Thanh Thai's Government.[2] Raised as a devout Catholic, Ngo Dinh Diem received his primary education at Hue, and later joined the Civil Service. In the year 1933, he was appointed the Minister of Interior in the Government of Emperor Bao Dai, but resigned within two months of assuming charge in opposition to "the French colonial government."[3] During the years that followed he refused offers to join various Governments including that of Ho Chi Minh's. He finally changed his mind and was appointed Prime Minister under the Bao Dai Government. Ngo Dinh Diem sponsored a referendum, and replaced Bao Dai to become the first President of the Republic of Vietnam on October 26, 1955.[4]

Visit of

H.E. Mr Ngo Dinh Diem

President of the Republic of Vietnam

Both India and South Vietnam shared many common features. Both were agricultural economies and "recognised the significance of closer relations between the two countries"[5] despite certain differences in the context of the Cold War. It was in this context that the Government of India extended an invitation to President Ngo Dinh Diem to visit India. Prime Minister Nehru had also visited South Vietnam in 1954 and President Diem received him personally at the airport.

President Diem landed at Palam Airport in Delhi at half past 10 in the morning, flying directly from Saigon. His special aircraft was escorted to Delhi from Aligarh by "eight Indian Air Force Vampire jets."[6] As the wheels of the Presidential aircraft descended for landing, the jets sheared off in perfect formation and with equally perfect synchronisation. President Diem was accorded a full ceremonial welcome.

President Dr Rajendra Prasad, Prime Minister Jawaharlal Nehru, Cabinet Members and members of the diplomatic corps, received the elegantly dressed Vietnamese President. Conspicuous by their absence were the "communists."[7]

After President Dr Prasad received President Diem, the Indian Prime Minister introduced the visiting dignitary to his Cabinet Members. Thereafter, the magnificently turbaned band of the Rajputana Rifles Regimental Centre (RRRC) played the national anthems of both countries. President Diem later inspected the Guard of Honour on the tarmac. This was followed by the customary speeches at the airport. Speaking on the occasion, President Dr Prasad welcomed President Diem and his entourage,

Facing page:
President Diem (left) and
President Dr Prasad at Rashtrapati Bhavan in
November 1957. Credit: PD

President Diem (seated in centre), with President Dr Prasad to his right and Prime Minister Nehru to his left (all in rear row) arriving in the Forecourt at Rashtrapati Bhavan in November 1957. Credit: PD

laying emphasis on the common links between India and Vietnam, and the similar aspirations of the peoples of both countries. He remarked that every country in the world should "be free to mould its destinies with goodwill towards all others and work according to its own genius for its prosperity."[8]

Describing President Dr Prasad as a "venerated symbol of the Indian nation,"[9] President Diem recalled Indian Prime Minister Nehru's visit to Vietnam three years ago, and Vice President Dr Radhakrishnan's more recent visit. He added that India had left "an indelible imprint on Asian thought."[10] Hundreds of Civil Servants, who were given a few hours off from work, also witnessed the arrival ceremony of the visiting Head of State.

After the ceremonial reception, President Diem drove to Rashtrapati Bhavan in an open Cadillac, along the roads that were lined with the fluttering flags of both countries. He was seated with President Dr Prasad to his right and Prime Minister Nehru to his left. Members of President Diem's entourage followed in an Oldsmobile and a DeSoto from the Indian President's Garage. From Vijay Chowk onwards, where the cavalcade arrived at 11.00 am, it was the President's Bodyguard (PBG), dressed in their ceremonial best that escorted the motorcade towards its ultimate destination.

Rashtrapati Bhavan did not, as usual, spare any efforts to make the Vietnamese President's stay and his first visit to India memorable. Thorough rehearsals were held all day on November 2, 1957, to ensure that protocol was strictly followed. Major General Sardar

Harnarain Singh, Military Secretary to the President (MSP), had issued instructions, as he normally did on such occasions, to restrict movement in the South Wing so as to ensure cleanliness and avoid any kind of noise when the distinguished guests were in residence.[11]

Security was tightened in Rashtrapati Bhavan during President Diem's stay. A detailed memo was sent by BL Chhiber, Deputy Superintendent of Police at Rashtrapati Bhavan, to the concerned officials regarding the security measures to be taken at Rashtrapati Bhavan during the visit. On his instructions, uniformed men were posted along the fountain, from the iron fencing of the main gate, right up to the Forecourt, and in front of the Southeast and Northeast Wings. This was also done to facilitate the staff of Rashtrapati Bhavan to witness the movement of the cavalcade, should they wish to, without causing any disruption.

Men were posted on the first floor verandas of the Southeast and Northeast Wings to stop people from peeping out of the windows, during the movement of the visitors.[12] The MSP was also unequivocal in his advisory to MK Vellodi, Secretary, Planning Commission and Secretary, Cabinet Secretariat, whose office was located on the Southern flank of the Rashtrapati Bhavan. "It is only for a short time," he explained in a memo to Vellodi, "but it cannot be helped. I hope this would be understood by all who are working with you."[13]

Traffic from the South Sunken Road was stopped at 8.45 sharp on the morning of November 4, 1957. Mounted sentries had been posted at the main gates by the Commandant of The President's

President Diem (second from left) with President Dr Prasad at Rashtrapati Bhavan in November 1957. Credit: PD

in the elegant Dwarka Suite while other members of his entourage were housed in the Tagore Suite, Himalaya Suite, Dakshin Room, Pepsu Room, Mysore Room, Godavari Room, Neelam Bedroom and Gautam Bedroom.[15]

After spending a short while in his suite, President Diem called on the Indian President for tea. Though President Diem was fluent in French, he was not as comfortable with English necessitating the presence of an interpreter at the meeting. During discussions, President Diem expressed a desire to read some Gandhian literature for a greater understanding of the philosophy of the Father of the

Bodyguard, from 8.00 am to 5.00 pm every day for the duration of the visit.

After his arrival at the wide and imposing gravelled Forecourt of Rashtrapati Bhavan, President Diem got into an open Jeep that was flying the Vietnamese flag. He inspected a special Guard of Honour presented by The President's Bodyguard and the 4th Guards Battalion.[14] The entourage was then driven to the South Court, where they alighted and were escorted to their accommodation.

The Vietnamese delegation consisted of 30 people, of whom 10 were accommodated at Rashtrapati Bhavan. President Diem stayed

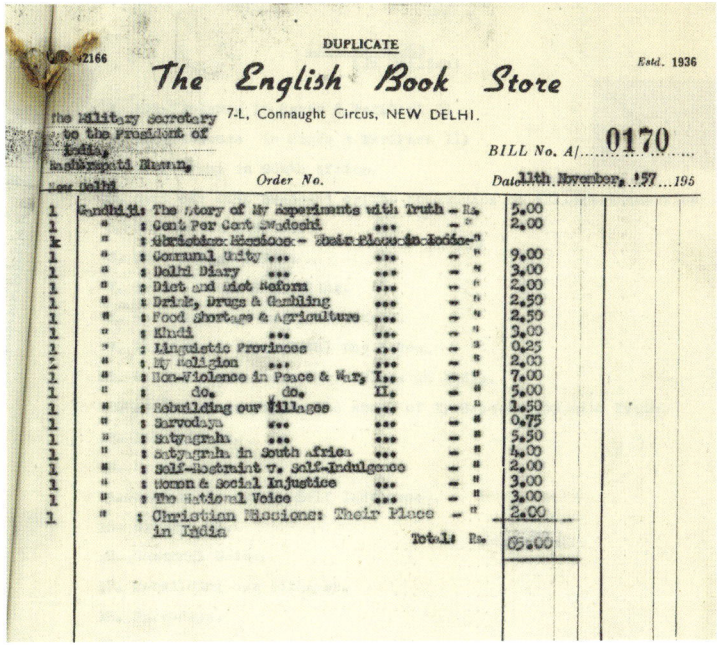

Bill of the English books purchased as presents for President Diem.

Nation. The *aides-de-camp* (AsDC) of the President sprung into action immediately. A flurry of memos were exchanged urging the immediate purchase of two sets of the Mahatma's complete works, one in English and one in Hindi. The Hindi books were ordered from *Sasta Sahitya Mandal*, while the English books were ordered from the English Book Store in Connaught Circus.

Little did anyone in the office of the MSP realise that the princely sum of Rs 94 incurred for the purchase of the literature would later become something of a bone of contention. The bills for the books were sent to the Ministry of External Affairs (MEA) after the books had arrived and had been placed in the Dwarka Suite. Records at the President's Secretariat, however, revealed that the protocol officials of MEA disclaimed all knowledge of the bills and the need to reimburse the amount.[16]

That evening, at 6.00, the Indian Prime Minister called on President Ngo Dinh Diem in the Dwarka Suite and the two leaders spent an hour in discussions. While this meeting was in progress,

Allotment of Rooms for Guests in Rashtrapati Bhavan

(4th November, 1957 to 6th November, 1957)
and
(8th November, 1957 to 9th November, 1957).

Name of Guests.	Rooms.	Phone 43401/Ex. No.
1. His Excellency Mr. Ngo Dinh, Diem President of the Republic of Vietnam.	Dwarka Suite	63
2. Mr. Vu Van Mau, Secretary of State for Foreign Affairs.	Tagore Suite	1
3. Mr. Pham Dang Lam, Secretary General, Secretariat of State for Foreign Affairs.	Himalaya Suite	89/66
4. General Van Thanh Cao.	Dakshin Room	152
5. General Mai Huu Xuan, ADC to his Excellency the President.	Pepsu Room	109
6. Mr. Vo Van Hai, Chief of the Special Cabinet of His Excellency the President.	Mysore Room	83
7. Mr. Ton That Thien, Press Officer to the Presidency.	Godavari Room	104
8. Captain Nguyen Duc Xich, Security Officer. 9. Lieut. Pham Van Thao, Security Officer.	Neelam Bedroom	202
10. Mr. Nguyen Van Dien, Stenographer.	Gautam Bedroom	42

Room Allocation Plan.

senior Vietnamese officials met with their counterparts and other concerned officers from India. The session was presided over by MK Vellodi. The focus of the discussions was on the achievements of the First Five Year Plan, especially in the field of agriculture and the objectives of the Second Five Year Plan. More such discussions and sessions especially focused on the technical aspects of planning were held during the stay of the Vietnamese delegation.[17]

Later, President Diem, accompanied by President Dr Rajendra Prasad, travelled from Rashtrapati Bhavan to Vietnam House on 24, Prithviraj Road, where the Consul General of the Republic of Vietnam hosted a reception at 7.00 pm in the honour of the visiting President. Select invitees included the President of India, the Vice President, Prime Minister and members of the Indian Cabinet. After the reception, President Diem returned to Rashtrapati Bhavan and had dinner en-suite. Later at 9.30 pm, a special performance of the timeless saga of "Heer Ranjha"[18] was staged at Rashtrapati Bhavan for the visiting President and his delegation.[19]

President Diem's schedule started early the next day. After breakfast, he travelled to *Rajghat*, where he laid a wreath on the *samadhi* of Mahatma Gandhi, but the homage was not without its uncomfortable moments. When the Head of State had arrived at the venue, it suddenly occurred to the Indian officials that there were neither flowers nor a wreath that could be laid on the *samadhi*. President Diem who was known for his politeness, waited patiently while officials scampered hither and yon to organise flowers and arrange for a wreath to quickly end a dilemma that, however, lingered. The hunt only ended when an exasperated

official located a flower vendor on the pavement outside *Rajghat*. Much to the delight of the vendor, his entire stock was virtually snapped up saving the protocol officials' further blushes.[20]

From *Rajghat*, President Diem drove to the Indian Agricultural Research Institute, the National Physics Laboratory, Cottage Industries Emporium and Kashmir Emporium before retiring to have lunch with a select gathering in his suite at Rashtrapati Bhavan. As time was short, he had earlier invited senior Indian officials for a luncheon meeting. The invitees included SK Patil, Minister for Irrigation and Power; SK Dey, Minister for Community Development and VT Krishnamachari, Deputy Chairman of the Planning Commission.[21]

The Catholic Association of New Delhi had planned a reception in honour of President Diem at St. Columba's Grounds, Alexandra Place (Now *Goldakkhana*) at 5.00 pm. Since President Diem was a Head of State, there were several layers of approvals required and protocols had to be adhered to.

The reception was short, as President Diem had to be at the Indian Council of World Affairs at Sapru House at 6.15 pm. He arrived at the venue on time and used this platform to convey his feelings regarding the reunification of Vietnam. He stated that while he was in favour of reunification, it could not be at the cost of sacrificing liberty.

Taking questions from an eager audience after his speech, President Diem was equally categorical in blaming the communists, the French and the Geneva Accords for the division of Vietnam. He said that two conditions had to be fulfilled for the reunification

President Dr Prasad (left) with President Diem at Rashtrapati Bhavan in November 1957. Credit: PC

President Diem delivering banquet speech at Rashtrapati Bhavan. Seated opposite him is President Dr Prasad. Seated second, on the left of President Dr Prasad is Prime Minister Nehru. (November 1957). Credit: PD

of Vietnam. The first was that the, "democratic institutions in Vietnam must be consolidated"[22] and the second was that North Vietnam should "give up the methods of terrorism and have respect for dignity of the human personality."[23]

Later that evening, a State Banquet was hosted by the President of India in honour of President Diem in the Banquet Hall. President Diem arrived for the banquet in traditional Vietnamese attire. As was customary after the two Presidents reached the Ashok Hall, the national anthems of both the nations were played. Thereafter, the invitees were introduced to the Presidents and later escorted to the Banquet Hall.

As was the practice at banquets, after the dinner, the host, President of India spoke. President Dr Prasad welcomed President Diem warmly and referred to him as the Head of State of a country like India, which had gained independence after a long period of domination by foreign powers. He spoke of the geographical proximity between the two nations, as well as their mutual aspirations and concerns. Underscoring India's goodwill towards South Vietnam, President Dr Prasad concluded his speech with the hope that President Diem's visit would strengthen the historic connections between their respective countries.

The Vietnamese President was evidently touched by the speech. He replied to the welcome address, reading from a speech neatly written on a piece of paper. Speaking clearly into the large microphones that had been placed in front of the Head of State, he said, "Your invitation has given me the opportunity to come at long last on a pilgrimage to your great country, the cradle of one of the oldest and most wondrous civilisations of history, whose present development is the focus of attention of the world, especially for Asian peoples."[24] In a move to reflect a certain identity of thought with Indian philosophy, President Diem quoted Vice President Dr Radhakrishnan and said, "greatness and material prosperity is not everything: it is not an end but a means which, if properly utilised, would permit the liberation of man from economic subjection."[25] Thereafter, he raised a toast "to the health of President Dr Rajendra Prasad, to the prosperity of India and to Indo-Vietnamese friendship."[26]

On November 6, 1957, President Diem visited a community project at Baraut on the outskirts of the city. Thereafter, he attended a luncheon hosted by Prime Minister Nehru, and laid out on the expansive lawn of his residence at Teen Murti Bhavan.

After the luncheon, President Diem had an hour-long meeting from 4.00–5.00 pm at the Planning Commission. Later he travelled to Azad Park, where a Civic Reception was held in his honour. The President's Secretariat too lent a helping hand with the function. On a request from the office of the Secretary of New Delhi's Town Hall, DMSP, Lieutenant Colonel M Ghufran sent a 'ceremonial chair' for the use of President Diem.

The reception was a grand affair and was also attended by the Prime Minister of India. President Diem spoke at the occasion and said that he was moved and impressed by what he called, "the vibrant heart of India."[27] He expressed his wonderment at the reconstruction activities underway in Delhi and earnestly wished for the city's prosperity and growth.

Prime Minister Nehru, too, spoke on the occasion and said that "the people of India are renewing their friendship with the Vietnamese people which dates back to centuries."[28] Emphasising the need for nations that have even different systems and policies to promote goodwill, he said, "nations, irrespective of their ideologies and systems of government, can live together in peace only by pursuing a policy based on friendship and goodwill towards one another."[29]

Towards the end of the reception, as a token of remembrance, President Diem was presented an exquisitely worked and detailed Kashmiri carpet. In return, he too offered a gift of a traditional Vietnamese work of lacquer with motifs of banana leaves skilfully detailed over it.[30]

In the evening, President Ngo Dinh Diem hosted a dinner at Vietnam House, which was attended by the Indian President, Vice President and the Prime Minister. Reiterating his stance on various political issues, President Diem declared that the foremost endeavour of his Government was the "reunification of Vietnam."[31] He also reaffirmed his declared policy that South Vietnam would not seek talks with the communist regime of North Vietnam, until the latter learnt to value the freedom and dignity of the people.

After dinner, President Diem and his entourage left for Nangal by a special train, from the ceremonial platform at New Delhi Railway Station. After a day's visit to the town, they visited Agra. President Diem and his entourage returned to New Delhi at 10.00 pm on November 8, 1957. That night, Prime Minister Nehru and President Ngo Dinh Diem issued a joint communiqué.[32] It stated that the leaders of both nations had decided "to continue and increase the cooperation between their two countries in the pursuit of their common goal of economic and social advancement of their people. They are resolved to continue to work, in their respective spheres, for the maintenance of peace in the world and understanding between nations."[33] However, the communiqué made no reference to the reunification of Vietnam.

On the morning of November 9, 1957, a Cadillac of the President of India took the President of Vietnam from Rashtrapati Bhavan to Palam Airport. President Diem's entourage followed in a DeSoto, an Oldsmobile and other guest cars. At the airport, President Diem was conducted to a special *shamiana* from where he held a press conference before his departure. Addressing assembled pressmen, he

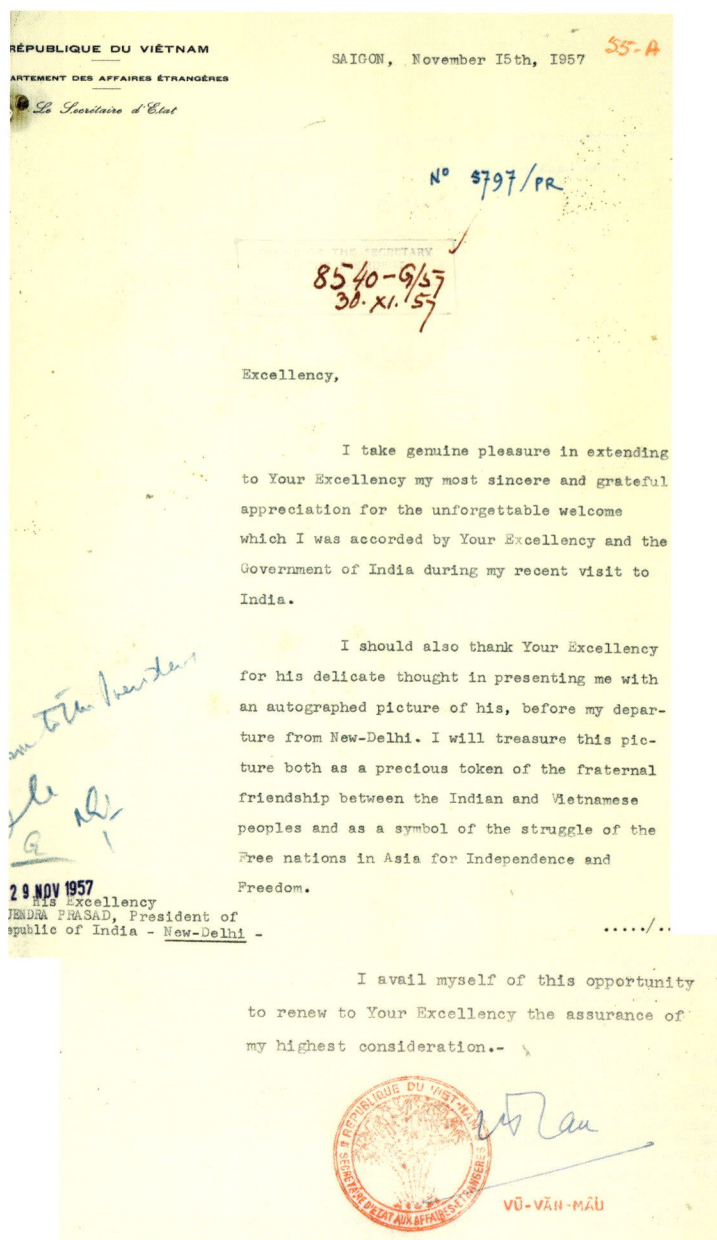

Letter of thanks from President Diem to President Dr Prasad.

clarified that South Vietnam would not allow foreign military bases or troops on its soil. He explained that even though South Vietnam was not a member of SEATO, its geographic location was covered by the organisation.[34]

After the press conference, President Diem took leave of the Ministers and officials, who were present at the airport to bid him farewell. He was also presented a ceremonial Guard of Honour. President Dr Rajendra Prasad then walked his Vietnamese counterpart to the waiting aircraft.

During the stay of the Vietnamese delegation in India, the Government of India presented its members several gifts. President

Diem was presented an ivory boat in the shape of a peacock, a set of books personally autographed by Prime Minister Jawaharlal Nehru, 12 pounds of Indian coffee beans and six pounds of Indian cashew nuts. They were discreetly placed in his room by the DMSP on the advice of the MEA.[35]

President Diem was evidently pleased and happy with his visit to India. He was particularly delighted by the warm hospitality that he received. In a letter he thanked President Dr Prasad for what he said was an "unforgettable welcome" that he received in India and the "delicate thought" in presenting him with an autographed picture of his. President Diem also sent his autographed photo to the President of India and it was received on November 29, 1957.

Almost six years to the day of his arrival in India, Ngo Dinh Diem and his brother Ngo Dinh Nhu, were arrested, shot and bayoneted to death on November 2, 1963. He was 62.

Notes

[1] "The Beleaguered Man," *Time*, April 4, 1955, accessed May 4, 2015, http://content.time.com/time/subscriber/article/0,33009,866120,00.html.

[2] Harris M. Lentz, *Heads of States and Governments: A Worldwide Encyclopedia of Over 2,300 Leaders, 1945 through 1992* (London: Fitzroy Dearborn Publishers, 1995), p. 827.

[3] Ibid.

[4] Lentz, Heads of States and Governments, p. 827.

[5] "Mr. Diem Arrives in Delhi Today," *The Times of India* (New Delhi), November 4, 1957, p. 3.

[6] "Indians Give Ngo a Warm Welcome," *The New York Times*, November 5, 1957, p. 11.

[7] Ibid.

[8] "Mr. Diem in Delhi," *The Hindu* (New Delhi), November 5, 1957, p. 4.

[9] Ibid.

[10] "Indelible Imprint on Asian Thought," *The Times of India* (New Delhi), November 5, 1957, p. 1.

[11] Records, President's Secretariat, Rashtrapati Bhavan, File No. 30/CER/6.

[12] Ibid.

[13] Ibid.

[14] Ibid.

[15] Ibid.

[16] Ibid.

[17] "Experts' Talks with Planning Officials," *The Hindu* (New Delhi), November 6, 1957, p. 5.

[18] A tragic love story originally written in 1766 by Waris Shah, a Punjabi Sufi Poet of Chisti order.

[19] Records, President's Secretariat, File No. 30/CER/6.

[20] "Forgotten Flowers," *The Hindustan Times* (New Delhi), November 6, 1957, p. 1.

[21] Records, President's Secretariat, File No. 30/CER/6.

[22] "Division of Vietnam," *The Hindustan Times* (New Delhi), November 6, 1957, p. 1.

[23] Ibid.

[24] Ministry of External Affairs (1995), Government of India, MEA Library, Foreign Affairs Records 1957, Volume III, accessed April 23, 2015, http://mealib.nic.in/?pdf2545?000.

[25] Ibid.

[26] Ibid.

[27] "Prodigious Efforts by Indians," *The Times of India* (New Delhi), November 7, 1957, p. 5.

[28] *Selected Works of Jawaharlal Nehru 2009*, 1 November – 31 December 1957 – Series 2, Volume 40, Jawaharlal Nehru Memorial Fund, New Delhi, p. 624.

[29] Ibid.

[30] "Prodigious Efforts by Indians," p. 5.

[31] "Reunification of Viet Nam," *The Times of India* (New Delhi), November 7, 1957, p. 5.

[32] "Vietnamese Leader and Nehru End Talk," *The New York Times*, November 9, 1957, p. 4.

[33] Ministry of External Affairs (1995), Foreign Affairs Records, Volume III.

[34] "Diem Leaves for Saigon," *The Hindu* (New Delhi), November 10, 1957, p. 4.

[35] Records, President's Secretariat, File No. 30/CER/6.

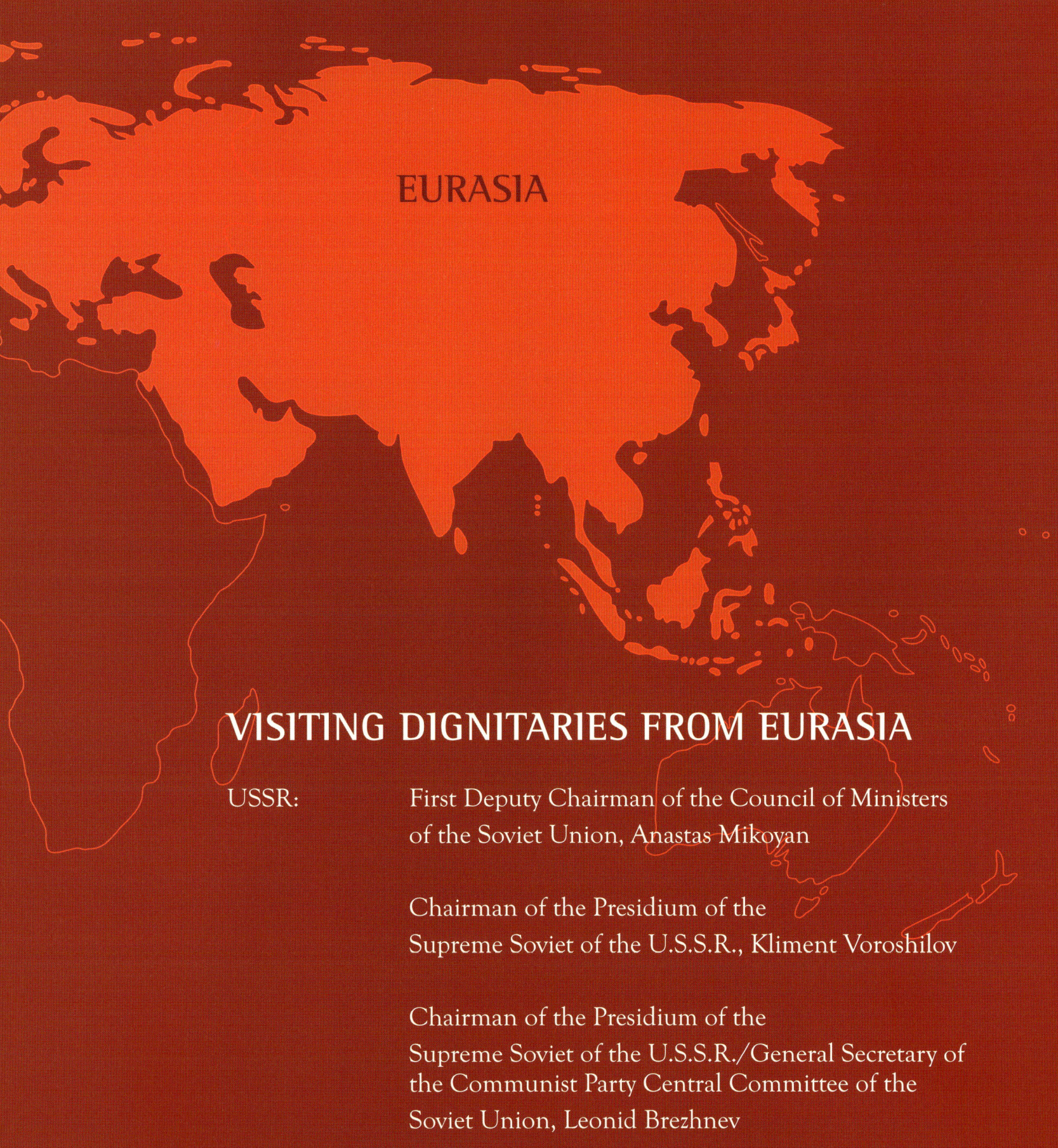

EURASIA

VISITING DIGNITARIES FROM EURASIA

USSR: First Deputy Chairman of the Council of Ministers
          of the Soviet Union, Anastas Mikoyan

          Chairman of the Presidium of the
          Supreme Soviet of the U.S.S.R., Kliment Voroshilov

          Chairman of the Presidium of the
          Supreme Soviet of the U.S.S.R./General Secretary of
          the Communist Party Central Committee of the
          Soviet Union, Leonid Brezhnev

It was in the spring of 1956, that Rashtrapati Bhavan welcomed the First Deputy Chairman of the Council of Ministers of the USSR, Anastas Ivanovich Mikoyan, on his first State Visit to India. He arrived in New Delhi on a four-day visit from Karachi, where he was a guest at a function on March 23, in which Pakistan declared itself an Islamic Republic.

Reputed to have spanned the Soviet political horizon between "Ilyich and Ilyich" (the patronymic of both Lenin and Brezhnev), Mikoyan spent over four long decades at the top of the Soviet political hierarchy.[1] Such was his political acumen that he was credited with the ability to "walk through the Red Square on a rainy day passing between the drops of water and coming out dry."[2]

Anastas Mikoyan was born in the village of Sanahin in Russian Armenia (present-day northern Armenia) on November 25, 1895, as the older of two siblings. He came from humble origins. His father was a carpenter and his mother a rug-weaver. Though Mikoyan's parents lived ordinary lives, both their sons gained world fame - Anastas as a leading political figure in erstwhile USSR and Artem as an aeronautical engineer who co-founded the design bureau that rolled out the world-famous MiG fighter aircraft.

Visits of

H.E. Mr Anastas Mikoyan

First Deputy Chairman of The Council of Ministers of The USSR

As a young man, Mikoyan won laurels as a skilful diplomat during Lenin's time by working with the people whose families had been ravaged by massive famines in southern Russia in the early 1920s. By the time he was 26-years-old, he was elected to the Central Committee of the Russian Communist Party. It was here that he was immediately noticed and befriended by Joseph Stalin. In the power struggle that followed Lenin's death in 1924, Mikoyan supported Stalin who gave him the post of People's Commissar for External and Internal Trade and also made him a Candidate Member in the Party's Politburo.

After Joseph Stalin's death in 1953, Mikoyan came into his own. In the power struggle that ensued, Khrushchev rewarded him by giving him the post of First Deputy Chairman of the Council of Ministers of the USSR or the First Deputy Premier of the USSR. In the backdrop of this political churning, the USSR needed to establish international credibility and Mikoyan, "the Kremlin's agile Armenian,"[3] was seen as just the man to present his nation's credentials to leaders across the globe. It was as the First Deputy Chairman of the Council of Ministers of the USSR that Mikoyan visited India in March 1956.

The 1956 Visit

First Deputy Chairman Mikoyan's arrival was scheduled on March 26, 1956. The day was both propitious and portentous as by next sunrise, it would be a day special to most Indians–*Holi*, the day of the festival of colours.

Facing page:
First Deputy Chairman Mikoyan (left)
with President Dr Prasad
at Rashtrapati Bhavan in
March 1956. Credit: PD

During this festival, those who do not stay indoors are fair game for those who roam the city, looking for an opportunity to splash people with coloured water or smear them with powders of all imaginable colours. The First Deputy Chairman's arrival at this time, therefore, placed those in charge of protocol in a dilemma. It was certainly not safe for the Soviet leader to be moving around the city without running the danger of being splashed with colours. The overcautious and worried protocol officers played safe and scheduled all of First Deputy Chairman's more important courtesy calls which involved leaving Raisina Hill, after March 27.

The Soviet leader and his 39-member 'goodwill' team landed at Palam Airport in Delhi on March 26, 1956, a little after 10.45 am in two special Ilyushin aircraft.[4] On his arrival, he was received by the Union Minister of Commerce and Industry, TT Krishnamachari; Minister in the Ministry of External Affairs, Syed Mahmud and Deputy Minister for External Affairs, AK Chanda,[5] Indira Gandhi and other senior Indian officials[6] in what *The New York Times* called, in tongue-in-cheek humour, with "un-Holi-like dignity".[7]

The theme of the visit was – "Indo-Soviet economic co-operation."[8] It seemed most appropriate for the time, as it was in the early 1950s that the foundation of the strong Indo-Soviet relations across a wide spectrum of issues was laid. Of them, economic relations were amongst those that were accorded the highest priority.

Addressing the press at the airport, the First Deputy Chairman, who spoke in Russian, said, "I am very glad to set foot on the friendly soil of the peace-loving Indian nation."[9] Reflecting on how the Russian people viewed Indian leaders, he recalled Nehru's earlier visit to the USSR and said that the Indian Prime Minister

had won the hearts of the Soviet people with his charm. After his address to the press at the airport, the First Deputy Chairman drove to Rashtrapati Bhavan in an Oldsmobile, while members of his entourage followed in guest cars.

The contingent that accompanied the Soviet leader was large and included a lady, Madam Ekaterina Petrovna Burilina. There were not enough rooms at Rashtrapati Bhavan to accommodate all of them and this issue came up for some discussions. In a memo, CJ Munsiff, Deputy Chief of Protocol (DCOP) advised the Deputy Military Secretary to the President (DMSP), Colonel M Ghufran, to accommodate as many members as possible, preferably that most members should be accommodated on a twin-sharing basis. He, however, quickly realised that there was a real danger of his advice being taken rather literally and he hastily added, "Except, of course, Madam Ekaterina Petrovna Burilina, who will have to be given a room to herself."[10] Finally, after assessing the accommodation available at Rashtrapati Bhavan, the First Deputy Chairman and 10 members of his 39-strong entourage stayed at Rashtrapati Bhavan. Others were divided variously between the Oberoi Maidens, the Cecil, the Claridges, the Ambassador and Mr Fonseca's in Golf Links.

As regards security, the concerned agencies augmented it for the First Deputy Chairman. In addition to the existing security, an armed officer was provided for his personal protection by the Assistant Director of the Intelligence Bureau, Ministry of Home Affairs.[11]

The first day of the Soviet leaders stay in Delhi was fairly relaxed. After the airport ceremony, there were no engagements before the

First Deputy Chairman Mikoyan (left) with President Dr Prasad at Rashtrapati Bhavan in March 1956. Credit: PC

informal lunch that was organised at Rashtrapati Bhavan. The formal engagement for the day was the First Deputy Chairman's meeting with the Indian Prime Minister at his residence, Teen Murti Bhavan, at 4.00 pm.

Discussions between Prime Minister Nehru and the First Deputy Chairman lasted three hours with NR Pillai, the Secretary General of the Ministry of External Affairs and MA Menshikov, the Soviet Ambassador to India, in attendance.[12] Though no official communiqué was issued after the meeting, both the national and international media reported that the talks centred around topics like the changes that were taking place in the Soviet Union in the post-Stalin era, Indo-Soviet economic cooperation and global affairs.[13] After the meeting, the Soviet leader stayed on for dinner which was served at 8.30 pm. The extended stay gave the two leaders more time to discuss issues of mutual interest.

The next day, March 27, was *Holi*. The weather was perfect and as *The New York Times* wrote, it was a day when it was impossible to have much on the mind except fun.[14] Rashtrapati Bhavan too reflected the mood and was witness to some regulated fun.

The morning saw the Indian Prime Minister Nehru and his daughter, Indira Gandhi arrive to call on the First Deputy Chairman and President Dr Rajendra Prasad. But they came with *gulal* (colour that is applied on people during *Holi*).

It was a fine sunny morning, and to match the balminess of the day, the Deputy Premier had dressed in a light blue summer suit. He was evidently dressed for meetings that were scheduled until lunch with Ministers and officers of the Ministries of Commerce and Industry and Steel. But his departure was interrupted by Pandit Nehru who arrived in clothes soaked in rainbow-hued water. His laughter and sense of fun indicated that he was not one to miss out on the merriment that this festival had to offer. Nehru greeted the Soviet leader, exchanged *Holi* greetings and daubed a *tilak* (a spot of colour worn on the forehead) of *gulal* on the First Deputy Chairman's forehead, unmindful and ignoring the fact that the visiting dignitary was ready to leave for a series of meetings. The Soviet leader was not one to miss out on the fun either.

The expression of spontaneous warmth in the daubing of the *tilak* on the First Deputy Chairman was not lost on the Soviet leader. The spirit of the day was infectious and the visibly pleased visiting dignitary requested a photographer who was rendering the moment tangible for a print of the photo he had taken.[15]

After the colourful start to the day, there were meetings with TT Krishnamachari and the Minister for Works, Housing and

(R-L): First Deputy Chairman Mikoyan and Prime Minister Nehru (third from right) enjoying Holi at Rashtrapati Bhavan in March 1956. Credit: PD

Supply, Swaran Singh; Minister for Commerce, DP Karmarkar; Minister for Industry, N Kanungo and other officials of the Government of India. The meetings had positive outcomes. India received assurances that Soviet Union would increase its imports from India to liquidate their collected rupee credits, which was important for India to have a healthy balance of payment position.[16] The meeting also drew up a tentative list of items including vegetable oils, pepper, oilseeds, tea, shoes, shellac, and minerals that the Soviet Union would import in higher quantities.[17] It also reviewed the progress in the completion of the Bhilai Plant.[18] Later, the First Deputy Chairman met the Minister for Natural Resources, KD Malaviya[19] and stopped to call on the Vice President at his residence on 2, King Edward Road (now Maulana Azad Road).

That evening, the Soviet leader attended a reception held in his honour by the Ambassador of the USSR at its Embassy on Curzon Road. Elegantly dressed in a well-cut evening jacket, he answered questions from several journalists present at the reception. The questions were mainly related to the post-Stalin political system in the USSR.[20]

The same day at 8.30 pm, a dinner was hosted in honour of the visiting dignitary at the grand Banquet Hall in Rashtrapati Bhavan by TT Krishnamachari. In his banquet address, the Soviet leader

reiterated that his country was happy to extend all economic support to India's development. He also added that the Soviet Union did not intend to export goods that India could manufacture herself, as it would create competition for their indigenous products.[21] Dinner was followed by a cultural programme held in Rashtrapati Bhavan's private theatre.

Early on Wednesday, March 28, the First Deputy Chairman paid his respects to the Father of the Nation by placing a wreath on his *samadhi* at *Rajghat*.[22] At 9.30 am, he attended a meeting held by the Planning Commission in the Committee Room at Rashtrapati Bhavan.[23] The Soviet Ambassador, MA Menshikov; the Deputy Chairman of the Planning Commission, VT Krishnamachari; the Minister for Planning, GL Nanda; Finance Minister CD Deshmukh as well as members and senior officers of the Planning Commission were also present.[24]

During the meeting, the Soviet leader took questions which he answered with disarming frankness and simplicity. Later he held talks with the Indian Finance Minister, CD Deshmukh and Home Minister, Pandit GB Pant at the latter's residence.

After the meeting, President Dr Rajendra Prasad hosted a lunch in honour of the visiting dignitary in the Grey Dining Room. No

First Deputy Chairman Mikoyan (seen in side profile) at a lunch hosted by President Dr Prasad (seated opposite, facing and first from right) at Rashtrapati Bhavan. Also seen in picture (facing) is Prime Minister Nehru (third from right). (March 1956). Credit: PD

(L-R): Prime Minister Nehru (second), President Dr Prasad, First Deputy Chairman Mikoyan, Vice President Dr Radhakrishnan (second to the left of Soviet leader) and other dignitaries at Rashtrapati Bhavan in March 1956. Credit: PC

sooner was lunch over than the Soviet leader received a request from Nehru for a meeting. On receipt of the request, the First Deputy Chairman who was scheduled to meet Maulana Azad, cancelled the programme and met the Prime Minister. Both leaders discussed the outcomes of the various discussions the Soviet leader had with Indian Cabinet Ministers.[25]

At 5.30 that evening, the visiting dignitary attended a reception organised in his honour by the Minister for Parliamentary Affairs, Satya Narayan Sinha, at Parliament House. At the reception, Harindranath Chattopadhyaya, Member of First Lok Sabha and younger brother of Sarojini Naidu, welcomed the Soviet leader with a poem. It described Indians and Soviets as brothers and how cooperation between them could promote world peace. The English translation of the poem read:

> *"Leave, O leave, all frustration,*
> *Now that Indians and Soviets are brothers,*
> *Now that the Dharma Chakra and the Red Flag fly together,*
> *And we both sing the same song of world peace,*
> *Leave, O leave this frustration,*
> *Our goal shall remain one, which none dare shake;*
> *Though our paths may be different,*
> *And the colours of our flags may be different,*
> *When we come together,*
> *We fly our flags together."*[26]

First Deputy Chairman Mikoyan, in his address, complimented the Speaker of the Lok Sabha, M Ananthasayanam Ayyangar, on the smooth, but rather authoritative manner in which he conducted the proceedings. Speaking via an interpreter, the visiting dignitary added good-humouredly, "Dictator" to which a visibly embarrassed Ayyangar blurted, "No, I am a democrat". Loud gales of laughter rocked the House, as the First Deputy Chairman amusedly reassured the flustered Speaker that he could well be termed a "democratic dictator!"[27]

As the day drew to a close, the Soviet leader hosted a farewell dinner for his Indian hosts. The venue was Hyderabad House where a select group of invitees including the Prime Minister, Cabinet Ministers and senior diplomats attended.

Next morning, at 8.30, First Deputy Chairman Anastas Mikoyan boarded a twin-engine Illyushin-14 aircraft to Agra to see the famous Taj Mahal, before stopping in Calcutta prior to his departure from India. TT Krishnamachari, Syed Mahmud, Indira Gandhi and some senior Ministers bade him farewell at the airport.[28] A group of Soviet children who were at the airport garlanded the Soviet leader and presented him bouquets in a symbolic gesture of friendship.

Addressing the media before boarding his flight, an emotional First Deputy Chairman said, "I had heard and read a great deal about India, but what I saw here I did not imagine. I carry away with me unforgettable impressions about India and her great people."[29] He folded his hands before the assembled crowd, in the universally known gesture of *Namaste*, before turning and walking up the gangway and into the aircraft.

His first visit to India successfully over, the Soviet leader departed for Rangoon on a State Visit from Calcutta on March 30.

The 1964 visit

Nearly eight years later, on June 20, 1964, the First Deputy Chairman of the Council of Ministers of the Soviet Union, Anastas Mikoyan returned to India on his second visit. It was a two-day trip and he was en route to Jakarta, with an 11-member parliamentary delegation.[30]

At 11.30 am[31] a gleaming Soviet Ilyushin aircraft carrying the Soviet leader and his entourage touched down at New Delhi's Palam Airport. He was received, much like his last visit, by TT Krishnamachari, now Finance Minister of India; officials of the Ministry of External Affairs and heads of Communist missions. This time, however, the diplomatic representatives of China and North Korea were conspicuous by their absence reflecting the brewing tension between the Soviet Union and these countries.[32]

First Deputy Chairman Mikoyan was visibly pleased to be back in India and opined thus on his arrival: "It will always be pleasant to be here," he told the pressmen assembled on the tarmac.[33] The mood in the country, however, was sombre. Jawaharlal Nehru had passed away barely a month before.

Two days were too short for the visit of an eminent leader from an important nation. Consequently, the schedule of the Soviet leader was very hectic. During his brief stay, he met with several Indian leaders including President Dr Radhakrishnan; Prime Minister Lal Bahadur Shastri and the Finance and Defence Ministers. On arrival, he met the President at Rashtrapati Bhavan. He then met Indira Gandhi and conveyed his personal condolences on the passing of her father, whom he later described as "a great son of India."[34]

After his meeting with Indira Gandhi, the Deputy Premier held talks with TT Krishnamachari. His mission was to communicate to the Indian Finance Minister the Soviet desire to help India implement its Fourth Five Year Plan and assist in establishing a steel plant in Bokaro. Thereafter, he met with the Defence Minister, YB Chavan and discussed the decision taken in 1962 to co-produce – through technology transfer – the Mikoyan-Gurevich MiG-21 supersonic jet fighter aircraft.

On the last day of his visit, the First Deputy Chairman paid tribute to Mahatma Gandhi and laid a wreath at his *samadhi*.[35] From there, he travelled to *Shantivana*, Jawaharlal Nehru's *samadhi*, where the leader paid his respects to the late Prime Minister. The Deputy Premier then met Prime Minister Lal Bahadur Shastri for nearly 70-minutes at the External Affairs Ministry and discussed a wide range of subjects; from the Soviet Union's policy on Kashmir, to the situation in Laos and future economic collaboration between India and the USSR.[36]

Following the meeting, the Soviet leader attended a luncheon that was hosted in his honour by the Prime Minister at Rashtrapati Bhavan. The Invitees included TT Krishnamachari, Gulzarilal Nanda, YB Chavan, C Subramaniam and Humayun Kabir.[37] Later that afternoon, the Soviet delegation met the Speaker of the Lok Sabha for tea. Over tea, the Speaker extended an invitation to the Soviet delegation to make an official visit to India next winter. The same night, the First Deputy Chairman and his delegation of 11-members left for Jakarta[38].

By the middle of 1964, there was a change in the political leadership of the Soviet Union. By 1965, Mikoyan was forced to retire and live out the remainder of his life writing his memoirs.

Mikoyan passed away on October 21, 1978. He was 82.

Notes

[1] "Prominent Russians: Anastas Mikoyan," accessed June 18, 2015, http://russiapedia.rt.com/prominent-russians/politics-and-society/anastas-mikoyan/

[2] Ibid.

[3] Ibid.

[4] John P. Callahan, "Pakistan Rejects Soviet Aid Offers," *The New York Times*, March 27, 1956, p. 11.

[5] "New Direction of Soviet Policy," *The Hindu* (New Delhi), March 27, 1956, p. 5.

[6] A.M. Rosenthal, "Mikoyan Arrival No Indian Splash," *The New York Times*, March 27, 1956, p. 12.

[7] Ibid.

[8] "Mr. Mikoyan to Stay for Week in India," *The Times of India* (New Delhi), March 24, 1956, p. 1.

[9] "New Direction of Soviet Policy," p. 5.

[10] Records, President's Secretariat, Rashtrapati Bhavan, File No. 274 (1956).

[11] Records, President's Secretariat, File No. 274 (1956).

[12] "New Direction of Soviet Policy," p. 5.

[13] "Nehru-Mikoyan Talks," *The Times of India* (New Delhi), March 27, 1956, p. 1.

[14] Rosenthal, "Mikoyan Arrival No Indian Splash," p. 12.

[15] "President & Premier Join in Fun," *The Times of India* (New Delhi), March 28, 1956, p. 8.

[16] "Russia to Buy More from India," *The Times of India* (New Delhi), March 28, 1956, p. 1.

[17] "Indian Oils & Minerals on Soviet Import List," *The Times of India* (New Delhi), March 25, 1956, p. 1.

[18] "Russia to Buy More from India," p. 1.

[19] "Mikoyan's Meeting with Nehru," *The Hindustan Times* (New Delhi), March 27, 1956, p. 14.

[20] A.M. Rosenthal, "Mikoyan Admits Stalinist Unrest, but Says 'Cult' will be Broken," *The New York Times*, March 28, 1956, p. 18.

[21] "Russia to Buy Indian Manufactured Articles," *The Hindustan Times* (New Delhi), March 29, 1956, p. 1.

[22] Rosenthal, "Mikoyan Arrival No Indian Splash," p. 12.

[23] "Talks with Planning Commission," *The Hindu* (New Delhi), March 29, 1956, p. 4.

[24] "Wide Disparity in Soviet Personal Incomes," *The Times of India* (New Delhi), March 29, 1956, p. 1.

[25] Ibid.

[26] "Mikoyan's Visit to Lok Sabha," *The Hindu* (New Delhi), March 29, 1956, p. 4.

[27] "India's Speaker Praised," *The Times of India* (New Delhi), March 29, 1956, p. 7.

[28] "Hopes of Stronger Indo-Soviet Ties," *The Hindustan Times* (New Delhi), March 30, 1956, p. 12.

[29] Ibid.

[30] "Mikoyan is in New Delhi," *The New York Times*, June 21, 1964, p. 9.

[31] "Mikoyan for Delhi," *The Times of India* (New Delhi), June 19, 1964, p. 9.

[32] "Mikoyan Sees TTK and Chavan," *The Times of India* (New Delhi), June 21, 1964, p. 7.

[33] "MiG Project will be Established Soon–Mikoyan," *The Hindustan Times Weekly* (New Delhi), June 21, 1964, p. 9.

[34] "Moscow will Help Us Follow Nehru's Policy," *The Times of India* (New Delhi), June 22, 1964, p. 7.

[35] "Moscow will Help Us Follow Nehru's Policy," p. 1.

[36] Ibid.

[37] Ibid.

[38] Ibid.

Kliment Efremovich Voroshilov, Chairman of the Presidium of the Supreme Soviet of the U.S.S.R., arrived in India on January 20, 1960, on a 16-day State Visit. Chairman Voroshilov was originally scheduled to visit India in 1959, but it had to be cancelled due to reasons of his ill health.[1] Instead, a Soviet goodwill delegation headed by Andrey Andreyev, Member of the Presidium of the Supreme Soviet of the U.S.S.R. was sent to India from February 24 - March 12, 1959.[2]

Kliment Voroshilov was born on February 4, 1881, in the Bakhmut district of present-day Ukraine. He joined the Bolshevik faction of the Russian Social Democratic Labour Party in 1904. Following the Russian Revolution of 1917, he joined the Red Army and later became a Commissar of Internal Affairs. He aligned himself with Joseph Stalin, and the two rose together quickly through the ranks of the Soviet Military. In 1953, Kliment Voroshilov was appointed Chairman of the Presidium of the Supreme Soviet Republic, a post he held for seven years until May 1960, and it was in this capacity that he undertook the visit to India from January 20 - February 6, 1960.

Visit of

January 20 to February 6, 1960

H.E. Mr Kliment Efremovich Voroshilov

President of the Supreme Soviet of the U.S.S.R.

President Voroshilov arrived at noon on the cold wintry afternoon of January 20, in a special four-engine, turboprop Ilyushin-18 Soviet aircraft, which landed at New Delhi's Palam Airport. A group of 18 British-manufactured Indian Air Force Hawker Hunter fighter jets escorted his plane from Ambala (a city in the neighbouring state of Haryana).

The aircraft had taken off from Tashkent, carrying the Soviet President and his 70-odd strong delegation, including his daughter-in-law, N Voroshilova. The visit was considered important, and the Government of India underscored its symbolism. It included the dispatch of the one-and-a-half-dozen fighter aircraft, a number which is perhaps the highest ordered to the sky for such escort duties.

Elaborate arrangements were also made for the visit. In the run-up to the arrival of the Soviet President, All India Radio (AIR), the national public service broadcaster, aired short talks on Marshal Voroshilov's life by the Ambassadors of both countries.[3] Official preparations for the arrival ceremonies too had begun as early as January 16. Security and protocol officers carried out full dress and technical rehearsals along the route the motorcade was to take.[4] The MEA also undertook the unprecedented step of circulating an advisory listing the correct pronunciations of the names of the 16 senior delegates, stating, "it always creates a good impression on visitors to hear their names pronounced correctly."[5]

A 21-gun salute, fired by the Field Regiment of the Territorial Army, boomed in welcome as the Soviet aircraft touched down. The 78-year-old Marshal Voroshilov alighted the steps, smiling and waving to an excited crowd, looking fit for a man known to be frail in health. President Dr Rajendra Prasad, Prime Minister Jawaharlal Nehru,

Facing page:
(Standing, L-R): President Dr Prasad, President Voroshilov and Prime Minister Nehru arriving at Rashtrapati Bhavan in January 1960. Credit: PC

(R-L): President Dr Prasad (second) with President Voroshilov at Rashtrapati Bhavan in January 1960. Credit: PC

the ambassadors of various countries, the Mayor of Delhi Trilok Chand Sharma and several other dignitaries welcomed Marshal Voroshilov.[6] Thereafter, the Soviet leader was escorted to the special enclosure, where the select invitees were introduced to him. By the time the introductions ended, President Voroshilov had so many garlands and ropes of flowers around his neck that they almost weighed the leader down. Among those who had welcomed him were a group of Russian children, dressed in immaculate white dresses. The children who were delighted to see their leader presented him with bouquets. Nearly 4000 people who had gathered at the airport despite the cold weather enthusiastically cheered the Soviet leader.

After exchanging pleasantries with guests in the special enclosure, the Soviet President was conducted to the Saluting Dais by the Chief of Protocol (COP) of the Ministry of External Affairs (MEA). Prime Minister Nehru who walked to the dais, arm-in-arm with Madame Voroshilova, followed him.[7] The Soviet leader was thereafter accorded an Inter-Services Guard of Honour while the Rajasthan Rifles Band played *Light of Foot*[8] in the background.[9]

Speaking in Hindi, President Dr Prasad warmly welcomed President Voroshilov, and said, "In your present visit, we see the fulfilment of a long cherished wish of ours, that the President of a great and friendly country...would spend some days in our midst."[10] President Voroshilov, speaking in Russian, replied, "The Soviet people sincerely wishes the sun of mutual friendship to shine upon our countries and warm the hearts of their peoples." He smiled, as he looked around at the large crowd gathered across the tarmac, and said, "*Hindi–Rusi, bhai–bhai*"[11] (Indians and Russians are brothers).

After the ceremonial welcome at the airport, the Russian entourage was escorted to the waiting motorcade. Marshal Voroshilov and his daughter-in-law drove to Rashtrapati Bhavan in a blue convertible Cadillac, the same car used by President Eisenhower nearly a month earlier. Seated with them was the Indian President. Two open Cadillacs, a DeSoto and eight other 'guest cars' brought up the rear, carrying the remaining members of the Russian delegation. A Jeep, a Fargo Lorry and a truck drove behind the motorcade, bearing the baggage of the visiting dignitaries.

The ceremonial route to Rashtrapati Bhavan was the same, through which virtually all Heads of State travelled. New Delhi had become accustomed to greeting foreign dignitaries, and *The New York Times* noted that the capital city had "established a routine for it."[12] Large crowds had gathered along the route and greeted President Voroshilov with cries of "*Zindabad*," "*Jai Hind*"

President Voroshilov proceeding to inspect a Guard of Honor in the Forecourt at Rashtrapati Bhavan in January 1960. Credit: PD

and "*Hindi–Rusi bhai-bhai*" as the motorcade passed by.[13] The crowds were so large that it took more than an hour to traverse the ceremonial the 12-mile route.

Nine motorcycle outriders from the Army, Navy and Air Force escorted the Presidential motorcade to Rashtrapati Bhavan. As it arrived at Vijay Chowk, the President's Bodyguard (PBG) escorted it in ceremonial formation to the Rashtrapati Bhavan.

The officials of Rashtrapati Bhavan had made meticulous arrangements to welcome the Soviet leader. Red carpets were laid along the gravel pathways leading to the ceremonial *shamiana*. A Saluting Dais had been erected for President Voroshilov in the Forecourt to enable him to inspect the Guard of Honour and take the salute. For the second time on the same day, he was bestowed with an honour and recognition very seldom extended.

As the motorcade entered the Forecourt, the PBG separated in perfect synchronisation, and the Cadillac came to a majestic halt in front of the *shamiana*. The Military Secretary to the President (MSP) then escorted Marshal Voroshilov to the Saluting Dais. He then took the salute as an Inter-Services Band played the national anthem of the Soviet Union. Descending from the dais, Marshal Voroshilov inspected the impressive Guard of Honour from a Jeep bearing his standard.

Once the ceremony was over, the Cadillacs took the guests to the South Court, which had been beautifully decorated with *rangoli*

– colourful patterns made on the floor, symbolising a traditional welcome for guests. In another warm and personal gesture, the Indian President's grandchildren received the Marshal and the delegation with an *aarti*-ceremony. Marshal Voroshilov was then conducted to the Guest Loggia by the Comptroller, President's Household (CPH) for refreshments. Other guests were ushered to their suites by the *aides–de–camp* (AsDC).

The Marshal stayed in the regal Dwarka Suite, FR Kozlov, the First Deputy to the Chairman of the Council of Ministers and his wife stayed in the Nalanda Suite and President Voroshilov's daughter-in-law stayed in the Mysore Room. Other senior members who stayed in Rashtrapati Bhavan included Madame YA Furtseva, Deputy to the Supreme Soviet and VV Kuznetsov, First Deputy to the Minister of Foreign Affairs. As soon as the Marshal arrived at the Rashtrapati Bhavan, the Soviet President's house flag was flown above the Guest Wing.

As the Soviet delegation was unusually large, all the members of the entourage could not be accommodated at the Rashtrapati Bhavan. Alternate arrangements were made for them in the nearby hotels. The delegation members, however, preferred to stay at the Rashtrapati Bhavan, as there was a certain prestige attached to being accommodated along with the principal delegates in the Guest Wing. This was also the sense of many of the Personal Staff attached to the President in the decades immediately after India's independence. For instance, Commodore (Retired) JP Syal, an ADC from 1955 to 1956 told the author, that he had observed that delegations even preferred to stay two to a room rather than shifting to other accommodations outside Rashtrapati Bhavan.[14] The same seemed to be the preference of the delegation accompanying the Soviet leader. Consequently, 36 members of the entourage were accommodated in 10 rooms, while 28 others shared six rooms.[15] Despite these arrangements, all the members could not be accommodated at Rashtrapati Bhavan. The less senior of them, acquiesced with great reluctance, to being accommodated at Hyderabad House, Ashoka Hotel and Janpath Hotel.

While the President's Secretariat was grappling with the unusually large delegation, MEA made yet another request for accommodation at the Rashtrapati Bhavan. AK Nag, the Deputy Chief of Protocol, addressed a letter to Lieutenant Colonel CS Reddy, Deputy Military Secretary to the President (DMSP), requesting him to accommodate the visiting Vice-Chancellor of Austria, Dr Pitterman and his delegation at Rashtrapati Bhavan. The request had to be politely declined and the Austrian dignitaries were accommodated in Hyderabad House instead.[16]

The importance of the visit and the large number of delegates staying at the Rashtrapati Bhavan necessitated the augmentation of both the support and the security staff. The strength of the household staff was increased and a number of additional *khidmatgars* (butlers) and waiters were deployed to cope with the requirements of the large delegation. Eighty-four plainly dressed constables and 66

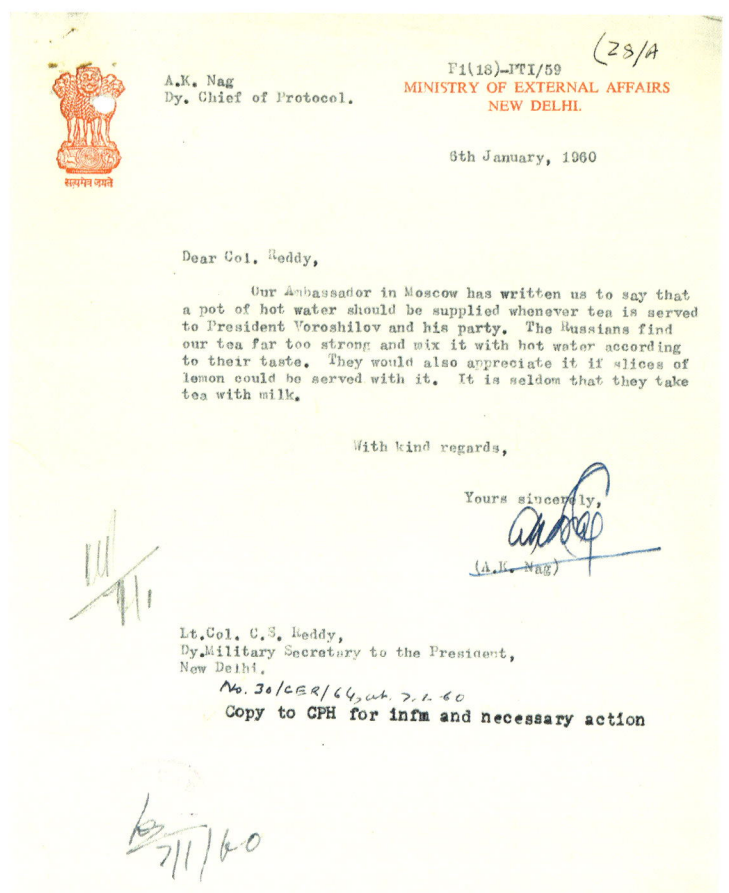

A.K. Nag
Dy. Chief of Protocol.

F1(18)-PTI/59 (28/A

MINISTRY OF EXTERNAL AFFAIRS
NEW DELHI.

6th January, 1960

Dear Col. Reddy,

Our Ambassador in Moscow has written us to say that a pot of hot water should be supplied whenever tea is served to President Voroshilov and his party. The Russians find our tea far too strong and mix it with hot water according to their taste. They would also appreciate it if slices of lemon could be served with it. It is seldom that they take tea with milk.

With kind regards,

Yours sincerely,

(A.K. Nag)

Lt.Col. C.S. Reddy,
Dy.Military Secretary to the President,
New Delhi.

No. 30/CGR/64, dt. 7.1.60
Copy to CPH for infm and necessary action

MEA's communication on provision of tea for visiting delegation.

Ministry of External Affairs
...
VISIT OF PRESIDENT VOROSHILOV.
—

Since it always creates a good impression on visitors to hear their names pronounced correctly, the following correct pronunciations may kindly be noted :

Name & Designation.	pronounced as
1. H.E. Mr. K.E. VOROSHILOV, Chairman of the Presidium of the Supreme Soviet, USSR.	"Varasheelov" (The stress is on 'i')
2. Mrs. N.I. VOROSHILOVA, Daughter-in-law of H.E. Mr. K.E. Voroshilov.	"Varasheelava" (The stress is on 'i' and 'a').
3. H.E. Mr. F.R.KOZLOV, First Deputy Chairman of the Council of Ministers, USSR.	"Kaz-Lauv" (The stress is on the second 'O').
4. Mrs. A.K.KRASNOVA, wife of H.E. Mr. F.R. Kozlov.	"Kraasnovaa" (The stress is on the two 'aa').
5. Mme. Ye.A.FURTSEVA, Deputy of the Supreme Soviet, USSR.	"Foor-tseva" (The stress is on 'u' and 'a'. 'TS' is to be pronounced as 'Z' in MOZART)
6. H.E. Mr. IVAN ALEXANDROVICH BENEDIKTOV, Ambassador of USSR in India and his Interpreter.	(The stress is on the two 'ee' and 'd' is soft.)
7. Mr. KUZNETSEV, First Deputy Foreign Minister, USSR.	"Kuz-net-sov" (The stress is on 'o' and 't' is soft as in TAMASHA).
8. Mr. N.N. DANILOV, Deputy Minister of Culture, USSR.	"Daneelov" (The stress is on 'i' and 'd' is soft as in DUNIYA).
9. Mr. A.I. Imamov, Minister of Culture, Tadjik, USSR.	"Imaamov" (Stress is on 'a').
10. Mr. A.M.MARKOV, Member of the Collegium of the Ministry of Health, USSR.	"Maarkof" (The stress is on 'a').
11. Mr. V.I.LIKHACHEV, Head of the South Asia Division, Ministry of Foreign Affairs.	"Li-kha-chov" (The stress is on 'a' and 'o').
12. Mr. A.B. ROMANOV, Member of the Union of Journalists, USSR.	"Ramanof" (The stress is on 'a' and 'o').
13. Mr. V.B.SPANDARYAN, Head of the Eastern Division of the Ministry of Foreign Trade, USSR.	"Is-pan-daryaan" (The stress is on last 'a').
14. Mr. V.I.AVILOV, Deputy Head of	"Aveelof" (The stress is on

Advisory on correct pronunciation of the names of the delegates.

uniformed men were posted at Rashtrapati Bhavan, under the command of the Deputy Superintendent of Police. The Russian Embassy had also deputed a representative at the Enquiry Office to identify any Russian national who may want to meet the Premier. As many of the additional staff pressed into service, were from the Central Public Works Department wing of the President's Estate, the Deputy Superintendent of Police, BL Chhibber carried out a special check of their antecedents.[17]

Further, a contingent of the PBG, including mounted guards, was deployed to complement the security arrangements made by the Delhi Police. Special tents with *kanats*[18] were pitched for the men of the PBG. Provisions of long mirrors, beds, tables, chairs, dressing tables, heaters, a telephone etc. were made for them by the President's Secretariat.

The Household division of the President's Secretariat had to also augment their staff. Their work had also increased manifold and some of the advisories that were received regarding the visit did not make their duty any easy.

The Indian Ambassador to Moscow had written to the MEA, which in turn communicated to the President's Secretariat that hot water should be supplied to the Soviet delegation whenever tea was served. The communication said, "The Russians find our tea far too strong...and they mix it with hot water according to their taste. They would also appreciate it if slices of lemon could be served with it."[19] Though it was a rather innocuous advisory and seemingly simple to fulfil, in actuality, it meant that hot water had to be provided to nearly three dozen members, on demand. This required that water had to be continuously kept on the boil, and butlers positioned in readiness at the small kitchenette in the Guest Wing, which was designed and equipped to serve only a delegation quarter of the size, of the one staying at that time at Rashtrapati Bhavan. The instructions certainly challenged the well-experienced household staff of the President's Secretariat, but they braced to the task taking turns to rest.

After the Russian dignitaries had settled down in their suites/rooms, lunch was served at 1.30 pm *en suite*. At 5.00 pm, President Voroshilov, FR Kozlov, YA Furtseva and VV Kuznetsov called on the President in his Study. The dignitaries were escorted by the MSP, along the corridors that were lined by the men of the PBG in their resplendent uniforms. After a brief exchange of greetings, the AsDC escorted the distinguished guests to the Yellow Drawing Room where the Marshal's delegation was introduced to President Dr Prasad.

In a rather charming gesture, Madame Furtseva and FR Kozlov, who had accompanied the Marshal greeted the President in Hindi, much to the amusement of all present. Thereafter, tea and light refreshments were served.[20] During tea, Marshal Voroshilov extended President Dr Prasad, an invitation to visit Moscow that summer. The President happily accepted this invitation. Later, the Soviet leader held talks with Prime Minister J Nehru, who called on him at 6.00 pm in the Sitting Room of the Dwarka Suite. He was later joined by Secretary General External Affairs Ministry, NR Pillai; Foreign Secretary, S Dutt and Indian Ambassador to Moscow, KPS Menon.[21] After the talks were over, the dignitaries attended a State Banquet hosted in President Voroshilov's honour by President Dr Prasad.

Banquets held in the opulent Banquet Hall are invariably a glittering and elaborate affair. Flower pots and vases were carefully arranged along the corridors and staircases leading from the Guest Wing to the Ashok Hall, imparting a splash of colour to the area. The tall strapping men of the PBG, in their full ceremonial uniforms, gripping lances and standing to attention, were in position all along the route. Personal Staff of the President were in attendance, dressed immaculately in Blue Patrols, black coats, trousers and black shoes. The fountains and the lights in the Mughal Gardens were switched on at half past seven. They brought the Gardens to life, with the droplets of water from the beautiful Victoria Regia Lily-shaped fountains glistening in the rays of light from coloured bulbs. Two sets of microphones were also installed in the Banquet Hall for the principals to make their speeches.

Guests arrived by quarter past eight at the South Court via the South Sunken Road for the banquet, which was scheduled to begin 15 minutes later. They were conducted to the Ashok Hall to wait for the House Party (the invitees who were not from outside the Rashtrapati Bhavan).

The President left his apartment for the Dwarka Suite, shortly before the banquet began, preceded by AsDC 1 and 2. From there, he escorted his guest, Marshal Voroshilov, to the Ashok Hall via the Guest Corridor on the first floor. As soon as the dignitaries reached the central arch of the Ashok Hall, they halted and the Sikh Regimental Centre Band played the national anthems of both the countries in succession. The guests, who had assembled in a horseshoe formation, were then introduced to the Soviet President, after which everyone moved to the Banquet Hall for dinner. Prime Minister Jawaharlal Nehru, Indira Gandhi, senior Ministers of the Cabinet, the Chief Justice of India, members of the Soviet entourage and diplomats were amongst distinguished invitees who attended the banquet. In all, nearly a hundred invitees attended the banquet that evening.[22]

The menu was specially drawn up. It included select vegetarian and non-vegetarian delicacies. The non-vegetarians had *Fried Prawns* and *Hyderabadi Biryani*, while the vegetarians had delicacies that included *Vegetable Croquettes*, *Plum Kofta Curry* and *Italian Potatoes*.

Dessert was a *Gateau*, after which coffee was served. While dinner was being served, the band, heard but unseen in the gallery, played the "*Slow Valse, Tango, Valse* and *Troop*".

After the main courses, President Dr Prasad gave his banquet speech. He spoke of the friendly bilateral relations that India and the USSR shared and the common goals that they steadfastly pursued for the establishment of world peace. He said, "On our own horizons, we unfortunately face new problems but I can assure Your Excellency that we remain resolute and are determined to seek peaceful solutions in our traditional spirit of negotiation and conciliation." The Indian President, however, did not raise a toast at the end of his speech. [23],

In his reply, Marshal Voroshilov reiterated the friendship that both the countries cherished and praised India's struggle for independence and Prime Minister Nehru's leadership of the country prior to and since independence. He observed, "Life has shown, and we note this with gratification, that the relations that have so happily taken shape between our countries are exceedingly useful both to the Soviet Union and Indian peoples." He then raised a toast to the health of the President, the Prime Minister, and all the guests and to "peace and to unshakeable friendship among all the nations of the world."[24]

After the banquet got over at 10.00 pm, guests moved to the Ashok Hall where AIR had organised an elaborate, perfectly choreographed dance and music recital. Nearly 130 artistes and accompanists had practised select *Bharatnatyam*, *Mohiniattam*, *Kathak* and *Kuchipudi* dances for days, under the keen eyes of Indira Gandhi, who had worked diligently to put the grand performance together.[25]

President Dr Prasad (standing, on right) delivering banquet speech at Rashtrapati Bhavan. Seated opposite to him is President Voroshilov. (January 1960). Credit: PD

President Voroshilov greeting artists after cultural programme at Rashtrapati Bhavan. On extreme left is Prime Minister Nehru. (January 1960). Credit: PD

The seating of the guests, too, was carefully planned. Marshal Voroshilov sat between the Indian President and Prime Minister. Indira Gandhi sat next to Madame YA Furtseva and FR Kozlov was seated next to the Indian President.[26] The enthralling performances received a standing ovation, following which the curtain came down for the night.

The next morning, President Voroshilov left Rashtrapati Bhavan at 8.45 after an early breakfast. Dressed in a dark blue suit and sporting a felt hat, the Marshal laid a wreath at Mahatma Gandhi's memorial. He then planted a sapling and said, I am happy to plant this tree of Soviet–Indian Friendship... May this friendship grow with the tree."[27]

The waiting motorcade then took the Soviet leader to the World Agriculture Fair. President Voroshilov was welcomed by Panjabrao Deshmukh, the Minister for Agriculture in the triangular lawn in front of the Defence Pavilion. The general public was not allowed entry for the duration of President Voroshilov's visit but photographers and pressmen covered the event extensively. The President was all praise for the tools and machines that were on display in a section of the "India Today" pavilion.[28]

Next on the agenda, was a visit to the All India Fine Arts and Crafts Society Hall at Old Mill Road (now known as *Rafi Marg*). Here, President Voroshilov saw a Svetoslav Roerich exhibition. The famous painter's work had been arranged in four galleries on the ground floor and in the basement. Roerich and a number of officials greeted the Marshal, who spent the better part of half-an-hour examining the paintings.[29]

On returning to Rashtrapati Bhavan, Marshal Voroshilov held meetings with the Prime Minister of India and Members of the Planning Commission in the Panelled Room. Prime Minister Nehru then hosted a lunch in the Soviet President's honour at his residence at Teen Murti Bhavan. After a leisurely lunch, the President visited the Qutub Minar and Humayun's Tomb, before he returned to Rashtrapati Bhavan.

At 5.00 pm, President Voroshilov left Rashtrapati Bhavan for a second visit to the World Agriculture Fair. This time he was accompanied by President Dr Prasad. The leaders saw the Soviet Pavilion and witnessed a specially arranged song and dance programme organised in President Voroshilov's honour by the Soviet Ambassador.[30] Here, too, the Soviet President stressed the importance of the peaceful cooperation and friendship between the two nations.[31]

On Friday, January 22, President Voroshilov was up for breakfast at 6.00 am to be in Ajronda village in Gurgaon District (presently in the state of Haryana) by 8.00 am to visit community development projects. The Soviet leader expressed a keen interest in the fine varieties of wheat, barley and potatoes being grown on land, which had, until six years ago, been barren. When he was told that the yield of potatoes was about 300 *maunds*[32] per acre, he said thoughtfully, "that is not much."[33]

As President Voroshilov was enquiring about the crops, a man pulled a potato plant out by its roots to show it to the Marshal. It visibly irritated the Soviet President who snapped, "You are not a cultivator. I can say from your manner of plucking the plant that you are one of those who know only how to eat potatoes but not how to grow them."[34] However, a smile returned to the President's face when he witnessed a *bhangra* dance especially staged for him by the villagers. After the colourful dance performance, a visibly pleased Soviet leader went around shaking hands much to the delight of the officials and villagers.

At 11.00 am, the President left Ajronda for Palam Airport. A Soviet Tupolev-104 jetliner flew him to Agra from where he returned by 4.30 pm and drove straight to Rashtrapati Bhavan in the President's Cadillac. He returned from Agra early, as he had to witness the "Beating Retreat," that is held three days after the Republic Day celebrations but was specially organised that evening for the Soviet President. The special show was staged, as MEA had informed that the Marshal would be away in Bangalore on January 29, the day when the event is traditionally held. The hour-long ceremony showcased 22 of the finest bands from the Indian Army, Navy and Air Force, dressed in their splendid regalia.[35]

President Voroshilov hosted a banquet at the Ashoka Hotel later that evening in honour of President Dr Prasad. The President of India joined his Soviet counterpart in the ante-room of the Banquet Hall, and both Heads of State stood to attention as the national anthems of both their countries were played. In his speech, the Soviet President noted that peace is "extremely necessary for India and all the States...for developing their economies." In his reply, the

Indian President said that he hoped that "the world, weary of war and fear of armed conflict" would give peace a chance and Indo-Soviet cooperation would grow in industry and agriculture.[36] After the banquet, at 10.15 pm, the 78-year-old Marshal concluded what had been a busy day for him.

Plans for the next two days had included trips to Raipur, Bhilai and Chandigarh but were cancelled due to Marshal Voroshilov's indisposition. The remaining Soviet delegation, however, went ahead with the planned schedule.[37]

By January 24, President Voroshilov's health had improved enough to enable him to attend a Civic Reception held in his honour by the Delhi Municipal Committee at the Red Fort. President Voroshilov arrived via the Lahore Gate, accompanied by Prime Minister Nehru. He was received by the Mayor of New Delhi, Trilok Chand. Marshal Voroshilov was visibly pleased to see that a 10,000-strong crowd had gathered for his reception and waved at them. Prime Minister Nehru conducted President Voroshilov around the beautifully decorated *Diwan-i-Aam*, where Mughal rulers had once held court to hear public complaints. Speaking at the reception, the Soviet President had rich words of praise for Prime Minister Nehru for his "untiring efforts" in defence of peace, which he asserted, "had won him great respect throughout the world."[38] Prime Minister Nehru who also spoke at the reception singled out the economic assistance that the

President Dr Prasad (second from left) greeting President Voroshilov at Rashtrapati Bhavan in January 1960. Credit: PD

Soviet Union was extending to India for special reference, and thanked Marshal Voroshilov for his nation's continued support. He also underscored the "love and respect" the nations shared. At the end of the reception, the Russian leader was presented a gift of an ivory casket containing five ivory elephants of different sizes and the Soviet leader smilingly accepted the memorabilia.[39]

Marshal Voroshilov spent most of the next day, January 25, in the Dwarka Suite. In the evening, he attended an 'At Home' that was to have been hosted by the President of India, on the lush green expanse of the Mughal Gardens. However, President Dr Prasad could not host the function as planned, as he had to be at the bedside of his sister, Bhagwati Devi, who was critically ill and passed away later that evening. In view of this personal tragedy that the President had to grapple with, Prime Minister Nehru stepped in and hosted the 'At Home'. The President, however, desired to keep the news of his sister's death a secret to prevent any disruptions in the Republic Day programme that fell on the following day.[40] Later that evening, the Indo-Soviet Cultural Society held a reception in President Voroshilov's honour at the Imperial Hotel.

Early next morning, the Soviet President met President Dr Prasad and conveyed his personal condolences. President Dr Prasad, however, did not permit his personal grief and tragedy to interfere with the role he had to perform as India's Head of State on Republic Day.[41]

Dressed in a black *sherwani*, President Dr Prasad arrived in his black State Coach drawn by six caparisoned horses and was escorted by the mounted contingent of PBG. Prime Minister Nehru received him at the Rajpath saluting base. A 31-gun salute boomed, as President Dr Prasad unfurled the Indian tricolour, which was followed by the playing of the country's national anthem.

The President of India took the salute as different contingents marched past. A cultural pageant ended the Republic Day Parade. President Voroshilov, who had arrived earlier after leaving Rashtrapati Bhavan at 9.05 am[42] and was seated in a special enclosure, appeared visibly delighted at the splendid display of military might and Indian culture. Other special guests at the event included the Nepalese Prime Minister, BP Koirala and the Maharajkumar of Sikkim.[43]

The Soviet President began the second leg of his visit to India the next day. He left for Bombay from where he travelled on to Bangalore, Madras and Calcutta. He was warmly received in every city. The Soviet leader also took time to visit Kathmandu during his trip and returned to Delhi on February 5, a day before his State Visit to India ended. Later that day, he broadcast a speech to the Indian nation from Studio No. 8 of the All India Radio. In his address, he emphasised once again the strength of Indo-Soviet friendship and said, "The friendship between our peoples serves the cause of strengthening peace...throughout the

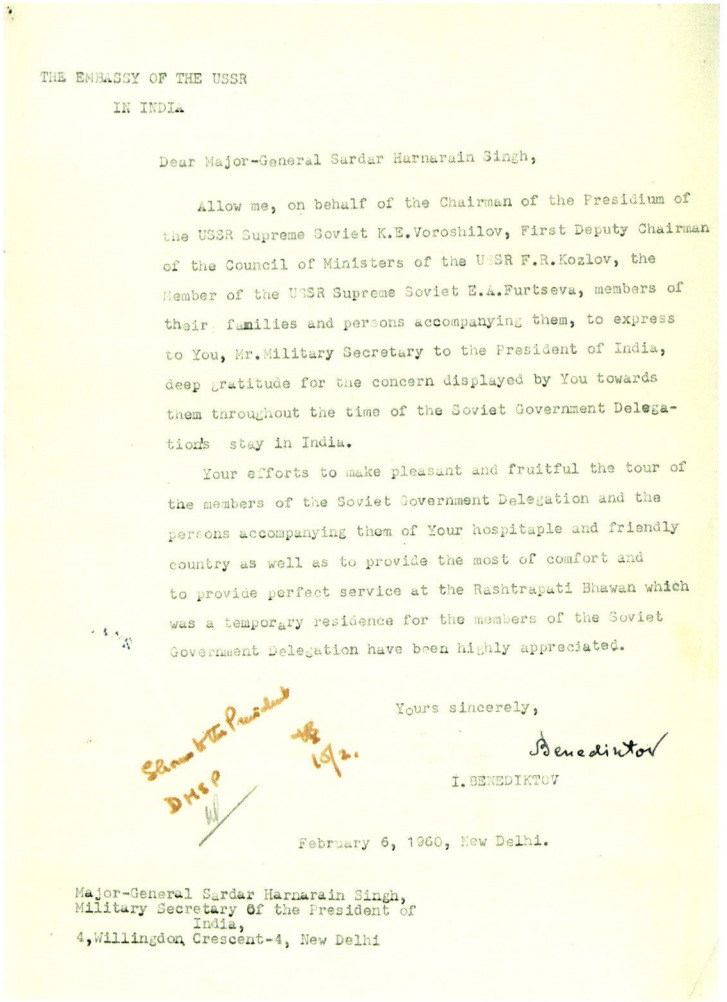

Letter of thanks from the Embassy of the USSR to MSP, Major General Harnarain Singh.

world." He praised India for its growing international prestige and its achievements.[44]

As dawn broke over Delhi on February 6, at 5.30 am, the President of India and his AsDC escorted the Soviet delegation to the South Court. From there, the visiting delegation drove in a motorcade comprising three Cadillacs, a Dodge and a DeSoto, with two Fargo vans to Palam Airport.

President Voroshilov drove to the airport in a Cadillac with the Indian President and Prime Minister and reached by 5.45 am. The President, Prime Minister, diplomats, Cabinet Ministers and other guests bade him farewell at the airport. He was given a full ceremonial send-off including a 21-gun salute. He warmly shook hands with all the dignitaries who bid him farewell and boarded the same Ilyushin aircraft that had flown him to New Delhi. By 6.00 am, President Voroshilov was airborne, taking with him, the fond memories of his visit to India.

Later that day, the MEA issued a joint communiqué in which both nations reaffirmed their faith, sincerity and commitment to resolving all disputes peacefully. In it, they also called for the "prohibition of thermo-nuclear weapons and other means of mass destruction."[45]

After his departure, the Soviet Ambassador to India, Ivan Benediktov sent a thank you note on behalf of the Chairman of the Presidium of the Supreme Soviet, KE Voroshilov and others to the MSP, Major General Harnarain Singh. It read, "Allow me...to express to you...deep gratitude for the concern displayed by you towards them throughout the time of the Soviet Government delegation's stay in India. Your efforts to make pleasant and fruitful the tour of the members of the Soviet Government delegation and the persons accompanying them... have been highly appreciated."[46]

In May 1960, Voroshilov's request to retire was accepted, and Leonid Brezhnev took over the reins of power. Kliment Voroshilov died in Moscow on December 2, 1969. He was 87.

Notes

[1] "Voroshilov is Ill," *The New York Times*, February 15, 1959, p. 15.

[2] Records, President's Secretariat, Rashtrapati Bhavan, File No. 30/CER/64.

[3] "Voroshilov is a Hero of Soviet Union," *The Hindustan Times* (New Delhi), January 20, 1960, p. 4.

[4] Records, President's Secretariat, File No. 30/CER/64.

[5] Ibid.

[6] "Warm Welcome for M. Voroshilov in New Delhi," *The Times of India* (New Delhi), January 21, 1960, p. 1.

[7] "Soviet President in Delhi," *The Hindu* (New Delhi), January 21, 1960, p. 1.

[8] *Light of Foot* is a popular marching tune in the Commonwealth countries.

[9] "Soviet President in Delhi," p. 1.

[10] Ibid.

[11] Ibid.

[12] Paul Grimes, "High Soviet Aides Begin Indian Visit," *The New York Times*, January 21, 1960, p. 5.

[13] "Desire for Peace Basis of Indo-Soviet Ties," *The Hindustan Times* (New Delhi), January 21, 1960, p. 1.

[14] Commodore (Retired) JP Syal (2015), telephonic interview by Dr Thomas Mathew, New Delhi, May12, 2015.

[15] "Not Many Protocol Problems," *The Hindustan Times* (New Delhi), January 21, 1960, p. 1.

[16] Records, President's Secretariat, File No. 30/CER/64.

[17] Ibid.

[18] "*Kanat*" is a Hindi word that refers to the walls of a tent.

[19] Records, President's Secretariat, File No. 30/CER/64.

[20] "Not Many Protocol Problems," p. 1.

[21] "Nehru Calls on Voroshilov," *The Hindu* (New Delhi), January 21, 1960, p. 5.

[22] "Border Dispute with China," *The Times of India* (New Delhi), January 21, 1960, p. 1.

[23] Ministry of External Affairs (1995), Government of India, MEA Library, Foreign Affairs Records 1960, Volume VI, accessed May 21, 2015, http://mealib.nic.in/?pdf2548?000

[24] Ministry of External Affairs (1995), Foreign Affairs Records 1960, Volume VI

[25] Records, President's Secretariat, File No. 30/CER/64.

[26] Ibid.

[27] "Wreath Placed at Samadhi," *The Times of India* (New Delhi), January 22, 1960, p. 9.

[28] "Soviet Leader Visits Agriculture Fair," *The Times of India* (New Delhi), January 22, 1960, p. 9.

[29] "Invitation to Artist," *The Times of India* (New Delhi), January 22, 1960, p. 9.

[30] Records, President's Secretariat, File No. 30/CER/64.

[31] Valmiki Choudhary, ed., *Dr. Rajendra Prasad: Correspondence and Select Documents, Volume 21* (January 1960 – February 1963) (New Delhi: Allied Publishers Limited, 1992), p. 377.

[32] Indian unit of weight measurement, 1 *maund* is approximately 38 kgs.

[33] "Mr. Voroshilov Visits Village in Punjab," *The Times of India* (New Delhi), January 23, 1960, p. 7.

[34] "Cultivator and his Ways," *The Times of India* (New Delhi), January 23, 1960, p. 7.

[35] "Beating of the Retreat," *The Times of India* (New Delhi), January 23, 1960, p. 7.

[36] Valmiki Choudhary, ed., *Dr. Rajendra Prasad: Correspondence and Select Documents, Volume 21* (January 1960 – February 1963), p. 377.

[37] "Mr. Voroshilov Indisposed," *The Times of India* (New Delhi), January 24, 1960, p. 1.

[38] "Russian Readiness to Disarm Completely," *The Times of India* (New Delhi), January 25, 1960, p. 1.

[39] "Russian Readiness to Disarm Completely," p. 1.

[40] "Dr. Prasad Bereaved," *The Times of India* (New Delhi), January 28, 1960, p. 3.

[41] "Spectacular Parade in New Delhi," *The Times of India* (New Delhi), January 28, 1960, p. 7.

[42] Records, President's Secretariat, File No. 30/CER/64.

[43] "Spectacular Parade in New Delhi," p. 7.

[44] Valmiki Choudhary, ed., *Dr. Rajendra Prasad: Correspondence and Select Documents, Volume 21* (January 1960 – February 1963), p. 379

[45] Ministry of External Affairs (1995), Government of India, MEA Library, Foreign Affairs Records 1960, Volume VI.

[46] Records, President's Secretariat, File No. 30/CER/64.

Leonid Ilyich Brezhnev, the longest-serving leader of the Soviet Union after Stalin, paid three visits to India. His first trip was the longest: December 15-29, 1961. His second visit was from November 26-30, 1973, and the third, from December 8-11, 1980. Interestingly, every time India received the Soviet leader, it was a more powerful Brezhnev that the nation welcomed.

The Soviet leader was born on December 19, 1906, to a steel worker's family in Kamenskoye [now Dniprodzerzhynsk] in present-day Ukraine. He joined Komsomol in 1923, which according to Brezhnev shaped his world outlook, attitude to the policies of the Government and to the Party.[1] Brezhnev studied to become a qualified metallurgical engineer and graduated at the top of his class. After completing his studies, he devoted his full time to politics attaining an almost iconic status.

A local paper chose to describe him as, "The son of a worker, he has himself worked at the factory as a stoker and a fitter...he was our best party organiser... And he was at the top of his class...this young engineer has the makings for achieving much."[2] Brezhnev's singular achievement, however, was not in the field of engineering, but in politics, where his career reached its zenith.

Visits of

H.E. Leonid Brezhnev

Chairman of the Presidium of the Supreme Soviet of the U.S.S.R./General Secretary of the Communist party Central Committee of the Soviet Union

Brezhnev's political rise was rapid. By the Second World War, he had climbed the political ladder to become an important regional leader. During the War, he served as Political Commissar and this brought him in contact with Khrushchev, who became his mentor.

Rising swiftly within the party hierarchy, Brezhnev was promoted as Member of the Central Committee of the Communist Party of the Soviet Union (CPSU) and a candidate member of the Politburo in 1952. When his mentor, Khrushchev, succeeded Stalin, Brezhnev's fortunes changed and he was re-elected to his earlier position in the Central Committee and the Politburo - a position which he had lost.

In 1960, a year prior to his first visit to India, Brezhnev was appointed Chairman of the Presidium of the Supreme Soviet. Four years on, he became the General Secretary of CPSU, making him the most powerful official in the country, though in protocol he came after the Chairman of the Presidium (Head of State) and the Premier (Head of Government).

In 1976, he became the Marshal of the Soviet Union, making him the only party functionary in the country, after Stalin, to hold the rank. One year later, Brezhnev was elected Chairman of the Presidium of the Supreme Soviet, becoming the first person in the history of the Soviet Union to simultaneously hold the top positions in the Party and the State.

Facing page:
President Brezhnev (left)
with President Dr Prasad
at Rashtrapati Bhavan
in December 1961. Credit: PC

The 1961 Visit

President Brezhnev's first visit to India in December 1961 was arranged at short notice. It expectedly led to some anxious moments, impelling officials to sacrifice their holidays and work overtime to make elaborate arrangements for this important visit by the Head of State of a friendly superpower. The finalisation of the programme itself entailed considerable time and hectic parleys.

Prior to the visit, Soviet officials had communicated a list of do's and don'ts while fixing President Brezhnev's programme in India. Among them was the request not to crowd his itinerary as he was not in the best of health. It was further advised that programmes were not to be scheduled before 9.00 in the morning and that small functions at odd places should be avoided. The advisory was clear about the places President Brezhnev wished to avoid and those that he preferred to visit.

Places already visited by Soviet dignitaries in previous visits to India were to be avoided. What he wished to see included, "Indian village life and something of our [Indian] old cultural life"[3] and a visit to Calcutta, besides the Vizag Port, where equipment from the Soviet Union landed for "assisted projects in India."[4] The President's desire to address the Indian Parliament was also communicated. These advisories were carefully deliberated by New Delhi and all attempts were made to comply with them to the extent possible.

Despite earnest efforts by Indian officials, the Soviet President's itinerary could not be organised entirely as desired by Moscow. There were particularly two programmes that could not be arranged for him. The first was the address to the Parliament. It was not feasible as the Parliament had already been adjourned for the year. The second was his visit to the Vizag Port. The city did not have secure and comfortable lodgings befitting a Head of State. It led the Chief Secretary of Hyderabad to explicitly request the Foreign Office not to include it in the itinerary.[5]

The detailed advisories also restricted New Delhi's freedom to draw up President Brezhnev's programme in India. The programme was ultimately finalised after detailed discussions with the Soviet side. It entailed considerable time and consequently, the programme was only ready shortly before the arrival of the Soviet leader in India.

The President of the Soviet Union and his entourage landed in Delhi from Tashkent on December 15, 1961. He arrived in a four-engine Russian Ilyushin Il-18 that was escorted for the last 50-miles by eight fighter jets of the Indian Air Force in a regal display of pomp, grandeur and power. The number of jets escorting the plane was, however, 10 less than those that had escorted President Eisenhower's plane to Delhi two years ago. A perfectly synchronised 21-gun salute boomed in welcome just as the wheels of the Soviet leader's aircraft touched the runway at Palam Airport at 3.00 in the afternoon.

The Soviet President had arrived accompanied by a 30-member delegation. Amongst them were the Supreme Soviet Chairman of Kirghiz, TK Kulatov; the Deputy Foreign Minister, YA Malik; the Chief of Foreign Office South Asia Division, VI Likhachev and the Soviet Ambassador to India, IA Benediktov. A party of four Soviet press representatives had arrived in advance to cover the visit.

The duty of receiving the Soviet President fell on the Indian Vice President, Dr Sarvepalli Radhakrishnan, as President Dr Rajendra Prasad was indisposed and his doctor had restricted his physical activities "to the very minimum."[6] The Indian Prime Minister, Jawaharlal Nehru, Cabinet Ministers, several other dignitaries and thousands of people were at the airport to welcome the Soviet leader. After Vice President Dr Radhakrishnan welcomed President Brezhnev at the foot of the stairs, the Mayor of Delhi, Sham Nath, did the honours by garlanding him and presenting a bouquet to Madame Viktoria Petrovna Brezhneva.[7]

After formal introductions, President Brezhnev was escorted to the Saluting Dais. He then inspected an Inter–Services Guard of Honour. This was followed by the welcome speech by Vice President Dr Radhakrishnan. He said in an obvious reference to the visit of Khrushchev and Bulganin in 1955 that the relations between the two countries "have been considerably strengthened by the visit of our leaders to your country and your leaders to our country."[8]

President Brezhnev matched Vice President Dr Radhakrishnan's expression of cordiality and said, "Stepping on the ancient soil of India, we first of all wish to convey best wishes for the happiness and prosperity of the great Indian people from the people of the Soviet Union."[9] He reciprocated the calls for peace stating that the friendship between the Soviet Union and India is, "above all, a friendship of two peace-loving States, hundreds of millions of citizens of which are standing for peace, freedom and independence of all nations."[10]

After the arrival ceremony, the Soviet President and his entourage drove to Rashtrapati Bhavan along the 12-mile ceremonial route, in a grand motorcade of 21 cars. Service and police outriders flanked the Soviet leader's car. The motorcade also included police cars and press agency cars, amongst others.

President Brezhnev was seated next to Vice President Dr Radhakrishnan in the stately Mercedes provided by the President's Secretariat. Thousands that had lined the route decorated with coloured banners, festoons and hundreds of flags of India and the USSR, cheered the Soviet leader as the motorcade passed by. People showered flower petals on the Soviet leader, schoolchildren greeted him with enthusiasm and President Brezhnev graciously "returned the greetings with *namaste*."[11]

When the motorcade reached Vijay Chowk, the resplendently dressed President's Bodyguard (PBG), on their equally impressive steeds, received the President of the Soviet Union with a grand salute and escorted the motorcade to the Forecourt of Rashtrapati Bhavan. The cars crawled to a stop at the alighting point as the

(L-R): Vice President Dr Radhakrishnan (third) with President Brezhnev at Rashtrapati Bhavan in December 1961. Credit: PC

PBG branched off. The Soviet dignitaries were warmly received by the Military Secretary to the President (MSP), Major General Sardar Harnarain Singh.

The Vice President then introduced President Brezhnev to the Personal Staff on duty who had lined up inside the corridor. They were dressed in blue patrol jackets and overalls, replete with sashes and aiguillettes and glittering with medals, and swords hung at their sides. Thereafter, Vice President Dr Radhakrishnan escorted President Brezhnev to the Guest Loggia where light refreshments were served. All the guests were then escorted to their respective rooms and suites. The Guest Wing also flew the personal standard of the President of the Soviet Union.

In keeping with protocol, President Brezhnev stayed in the regal Dwarka Suite and Madame Brezhneva in the Nalanda Suite. Besides them, 14 members of the delegation stayed at Rashtrapati Bhavan. TK Kulatov, Chairman of the Presidium of the Supreme Soviet Union stayed in the Himalaya Suite; YA Malik, Deputy Minister for Foreign Affairs in the Bombay Bedroom and VI Likahchev, Chief of South Asia Division of the Foreign Ministry, in the Godavari Bedroom. Eight of the remaining members who stayed at the Rashtrapati Bhavan were accommodated two to a room. The rest of the delegation stayed at the Ashoka Hotel and Hyderabad House.

After the dignitaries had comfortably settled into their suites/rooms 'under the dome', the President of the USSR and Madame Brezhneva paid a courtesy call on the Vice President at 5.00 pm, in the Morning Room. All three dignitaries were then conducted to the Yellow Drawing Room where President Brezhnev introduced his delegation to Vice President Dr Radhakrishnan. President Brezhnev then returned to his suite escorted by the Deputy Military Secretary to the President (DMSP), Lieutenant Colonel CS Reddy and an *aide-de-camp* (ADC).[12]

Later that evening, Vice President Dr Radhakrishnan hosted a grand State Banquet in honour of the Soviet President. It was an elaborate affair for which the President's Secretariat had made meticulous arrangements. Tables were arranged near the South Court, where the guests alighted for them to place their hats. The halls, rooms and passages being used in connection with the banquet were elegantly decorated. Floral arrangements lent colour to the Ashok Hall, the Guest Loggia, the Banquet Hall and the Grand Open Staircase. The garden lights were switched on at 7.00 pm and the amber glow of the setting sun shimmered the waters of the fountains that formed drops as they fell. At the Banquet Hall, four sets of microphones were installed in the Banquet Hall for use by the dignitaries and one set was specially earmarked for All India Radio.

ALLOTMENT OF ROOMS.

Name of Guests.	Rooms.	Phone 35321/Ex. Nos.
H.E. Mr. L. I. Brezhnev, President of the Presidium of the Supreme Soviet of the Union of Soviet Socialist Republics. Madame L. I. Brezhneva	Dwarka and Nalanda Suites	63 & 46 & 54
H.E. Mr. T.K. Kulatov, Chairman of the Presidium of the Supreme Soviet of the Kirghiz SSR	Himalaya Suite	89 & 66
H.E. Mr. Y. A. Malik, Deputy Minister for Foreign Affairs of the USSR.	Bombay Room	114
H.E. Mr. I. V. Arkhipov, Deputy Chairman of the State Committee for External Economic Relations under the Council of Ministers of the USSR.	Pepsu Room	109
Mr. V. I. Likhachev, Chief of South Asia Division of the Ministry of Foreign Affairs of the USSR.	Godawari Room	104
Mr. K. U. Chernenko, Chief of the Secretariat of the Chairman of the Presidium of the Supreme Soviet of the USSR.	Dakshin Room	152
Mr. G E. Tsukanov, Assistant of Chairman of Presidium of the Supreme Soviet of the USSR.	Partap Room	51
Mr. S. S. Eriskovsky, Chief ADC of Chairman of Presidium of the Supreme Soviet of the USSR. Mr. A. Y. Riabenko, ADC of Chairman of Presidium of the Supreme Soviet of the USSR.	Tagore Room	47
Mr. Y. N. Vinogradov, Interpreter. Mr. Nikolai G. Rodionov, Doctor.	Mysore Room	83
Mr. O. A. Krokhalev, Interpreter. Mr. A. S. Bychkov, Senior Official of the President of USSR.	Neelam Room	202
Mrs. Mariya Andeevna Epifanova, Attendant. Mrs. E. Sergueevna Kuzichkina, Cook.	Gautam Room	42

Room Allocation Plan.

It was a high profile visit and many clamoured to be invited. The pressure on the Ministry of External Affairs (MEA) delayed the finalisation of the suggestive guest list causing the President's Secretariat which is responsible for the organisation of the banquet some anxious moments. Frequent reminders from Rashtrapati Bhavan to MEA were also of no avail. The Chief of Protocol (COP), SK Banerji, regretted the delay in a letter dated December 12, 1961, stating that President Brezhnev's visit had been finalised a week before his arrival and hence the External Affairs Ministry "did not find it physically possible to prepare the guest list earlier."[13]

A request was also received from royalty for inclusion in any function associated with the State Visit. The Secretary to the *Sardar-i-Riyasat*, Jammu and Kashmir, Iqbal N Dewan, wrote to the MSP intimating him that the Maharaja and Maharani of Kashmir, Dr Karan Singh and Yasho Rajya Lakshmi, would be in Delhi from December 14–20 in this connection. The letter stated that they had visited the USSR in 1959 at Khrushchev's invitation and that the President of India might want to include them in one of the functions connected with President Brezhnev's visit as a sign of reciprocity. The request was granted.[14]

According to tradition, Vice President Dr Radhakrishnan called on President Brezhnev in the sitting room of the Dwarka Suite to escort the Soviet leader and Madame Brezhneva to the banquet. The Vice President had left his residence 2, Maulana Azad Marg, at 7.30 pm accompanied by ADC-1 for the Rashtrapati Bhavan. He was received by the MSP who escorted him to the Dwarka Sitting Room. After exchanging greetings, the Vice President accompanied President Brezhnev and Madame Brezhneva to the Ashok Hall, along the corridors and stairs lined by the *sowars* of the PBG.

The Sikh Regimental Centre Band struck the chords of the national anthem of the USSR followed by India's, as the distinguished guests stood to attention under the central arch of the Ashok Hall. The large panelled mirrors and the magnificent tiered chandeliers added glitter and grandeur to the evening. The assembled guests were then introduced to President Brezhnev and Vice President Dr Radhakrishnan by the COP and the MSP. The invitees thereafter moved to the Banquet Hall for dinner at 8.20 pm. The meal included a fare of select dishes. President Brezhnev's personal cook had also worked alongside the finest chefs of Rashtrapati Bhavan to prepare the dishes.

After serving the courses of a delicately prepared meal, the *khidmatgars* (butlers) cleared the tables and left the hall as instructed in advance. The Vice President then proposed a toast. Reading his written speech, Vice President Dr Radhakrishnan said: "Friendship is the thing which we want most in the present world. After all when we come to think of it, we find that there is not such vital differences as to justify any kind of military conflict between the great powers. We are all interested in the rapid industrialisation of our countries. We are also interested in establishing social justice."[15]

Vice President Dr Radhakrishnan praised President Brezhnev for his stand on disarmament, comparing it to Lenin's teachings. He added, "I have no doubt that in your efforts for achieving peace, for overcoming the obstacles of fear, anger, hatred and jealousy, you will find us co-operating with you to the utmost extent to which we can."[16] Vice President Dr Radhakrishnan then raised his glass and toasted to the health of President Brezhnev and Madame Brezhneva. The band, which had been playing select Indian music during the meal, struck up the national anthem of the USSR.

The Soviet President, in his reply, thanked the Indian Vice President for his kind words and said, "From the first moment of our stay in India, we, if I may put it this way, found ourselves captured by your hospitality. This is the rare case when captivity is pleasant."[17] President Brezhnev also commented on the friendly relations between India and the Soviet Union terming them more than mere traditional commonalities. He added that they were predicated on the common advocacy for peace. President Brezhnev concluded saying, "May this friendship develop and strengthen for the good of our peoples, for the benefit of the world peace."[18] President Brezhnev then raised his glass to toast the health of the Indian President, Dr Prasad, wishing for his speedy recovery, and to the health of Vice President Dr Radhakrishnan and Prime Minister Nehru. The national anthem of India followed. After the speeches, the *khidmatgars* (butlers) returned to serve coffee and fruits.

The banquet was followed by a cultural programme showcasing India's rich diversity. It was presented by the artistes of the Song and Dance Division of All India Radio, for which elaborate arrangements, including the provision of special sound equipment, had been made in the Ashok Hall.

The day following his arrival began with a visit to *Rajghat* where President Brezhnev laid a wreath of pink and white roses at Mahatma Gandhi's *samadhi* and observed a minute's silence. He then proceeded to plant a tree in the compound before returning to Rashtrapati Bhavan.

He spent the pleasant winter afternoon in a meeting at Teen Murti Bhavan, the residence of the Indian Prime Minister. The meeting had originally been scheduled to take place at Rashtrapati Bhavan, but the venue was changed at the last minute.

Prime Minister Nehru and President Brezhnev discussed various important issues that included "disarmament, the German question, colonialism and world peace."[19] The talks lasted nearly two hours. At the meeting, President Brezhnev reportedly also delivered a "personal message from the Soviet Premier Khrushchev to Mr Nehru."[20] Another round of meetings was scheduled for later during the visit.

In the evening, the Soviet President visited the Indian Industries Fair, accompanied by the Indian Minister for Industries, Manubhai Shah and the Soviet Ambassador, Ivan Benediktov. President Brezhnev was evidently impressed with the exhibition-display that he told cameramen, "Don't photograph me, instead, photograph these beautiful things," pointing towards a stunning *zari* work.[21]

President Brezhnev also went around the "Our India" pavilion, where he evinced great interest in Indian costumes, musical instruments, and models from the Khajuraho and Konark temples.[22] At the venue, the Secretary of the Fair, Chentsal Rao, gifted an ivory bedside lamp to the Soviet President. Madame Brezhneva was also presented with "a beautiful Banaras silk scarf with jari [*zari*] work."[23] After a quiet dinner in his suite, the Soviet President retired for the day.

The next morning, President Brezhnev left on an extensive tour of India that took him to Agra, Bombay, Ankleshwar, Baroda, Calcutta, Madras, Mahabalipuram and Jaipur. While on this tour, President Brezhnev celebrated his 55th birthday on December 19, in Ankleshwar, in the State of Gujarat. President Dr Rajendra Prasad and Prime Minister Nehru conveyed their greetings to the Soviet President.[24] The birthday was spent visiting the oilfields that were "being developed in collaboration with Soviet oil technicians."[25]

On December 26, while he was returning to Delhi from Calcutta, the Soviet leader took a little detour to visit the forts of Jaipur and Amber. He also undertook an "exciting" elephant ride with his wife, their first experience. At the end of it, an enraptured Soviet President flaunted his knowledge of *Hindustani* by virtually shouting *shukria* (thank you) when he left.[26]

The Soviet guests returned to Delhi about half-an-hour before noon. As advised by the Soviet officials, President Brezhnev's engagements for the last two days had been kept to a minimum. They were largely confined to talks between him and Prime Minister Nehru, taking forward the somewhat inconclusive discussions that the two leaders had already had on December 16. The talks that continued for over 40-minutes were proclaimed to be a success. Prime Minister Nehru then hosted a lunch for the Soviet President.[27]

A Civic Reception was organised in President Brezhnev's honour at the Red Fort in the evening of the next day. At the reception, Pandit Nehru hailed President Brezhnev's support for India's action in Goa and claimed, "even our critics who are angry with us will appreciate our position when they get to know the full story of Goa."[28] Taking a concordant stance, President Brezhnev in his reply said that the action in Goa was "something inevitable, something historic."[29]

The next day was not hectic. The first engagement was scheduled for 6.00 in the evening. It was a farewell address broadcast on All India Radio. In his address, President Brezhnev reiterated his support for Goa's liberation and referred to Indo-Soviet collaboration. He was also appreciative of the people of India and he said that this tour had given him a glimpse of how "'the diligent people of India' live and work."[30]

President Brezhnev's last engagement in India was a banquet that he hosted in honour of the President of India, Dr Rajendra Prasad, at the Ashoka Hotel at 8.30 pm. He had accepted the invitation and attended the banquet.[31]

President Brezhnev departed for Moscow on December 29, 1961 at 10.00 am and was given a ceremonial farewell at the airport. Speaking to correspondents at the airport, President Brezhnev remarked: "Wherever I met the India [sic] people, in towns and villages, there were manifestations of the Indian people's friendship for the Soviet people."[32] He then inspected an Inter-Services Guard of Honour while the national anthems of both countries were played.

As the Chairman of the Presidium of the Supreme Soviet Union boarded his plane to Moscow, a 21-gun salute was fired in his honour.[33] In a gesture testifying to the success of the visit, President Brezhnev sent a message from aboard his Ilyushin-18, thanking the President, the Vice President and the Prime Minister for their hospitality. The message ended with the words, "I wish happiness and prosperity for the wonderful people of the republic of India."[34]

Indo-Soviet relations continued to strengthen buoyed by this historic visit. India became a recipient of larger developmental aid from the Soviet Union. Meanwhile, President Brezhnev continued to rise in the party hierarchy and in 1964, became General Secretary of the Communist Party of the Soviet Union, succeeding Khrushchev.

The 1973 Visit

Leonid Brezhnev's second visit came at a crucial phase in India's history and when Indo-Soviet relations were at their acme. India had emerged victorious in the Bangladesh War of 1971 and two years had not even passed since. The unflinching support that the Soviet Union extended India to Delhi during the crisis was still fresh in the people's mind.

The fact that under General Secretary Brezhnev's leadership, Moscow had neutralised the US "tilt" towards Pakistan had also got wide publicity. As Henry Kissinger wrote in his memoirs, The White House Years, the Soviet Union gave "diplomatic support to India's maximum demands, airlifting military supplies, and pledging to veto inconvenient resolutions in the UN Security Council."[35] In addition, as scholars have written, General Secretary Brezhnev had "deep feelings of affection and sympathy"[36] towards India. No phase in the history of the ties between India and the Soviet Union can, therefore, legitimately compete with this period, to be described as the golden phase in the two nations' bilateral relations.

General Secretary Brezhnev's arrival at this juncture, therefore, made scholars describe his visit as one by "an old and sincere friend."[37] Ironically, however, it could not be declared a State Visit. It was termed as a "friendly official" visit, for Brezhnev, the all-powerful General Secretary of the CPSU, did not have the *de-jure* title of a Head of State or Head of Government. This prevented India from extending him the ceremonial welcome reserved for Heads of States. Consequently, adhering to protocol, the President of India was not at the airport to receive the Soviet leader. Yet there was no doubt in minds of the Indian leaders that they were dealing with a more powerful leader albeit with a less impressive title.

The arrangements made by the Soviet side for the visit were also of an unprecedented scale. Notable amongst them were the special arrangements made for the coverage of the visit. Soviet officials went to extraordinary lengths to ensure live television coverage of the visit; the first ever for a visiting dignitary to India. A special earth station was set up at the television training centre, 20 km from Palam by 60 Soviet technicians. The earth station was directly connected through micro-wave links with mobile vans with bowl-shaped antennas completing the link. A mobile van was also parked at Rashtrapati Bhavan for the live coverage of General Secretary Brezhnev's select programmes. Besides the provision of live telecast, arrangements were also made for the live broadcast of the programmes of the Soviet leader in two languages.[38] The Soviet print media was fed by over two dozen journalists including those from the Soviet national news agency TASS who had already arrived in India.

(L-R): General Secretary Brezhnev (second) sharing lighter moments with President Giri at Rashtrapati Bhavan. Soviet Foreign Minister, Gromyko (on right of General Secretary Brezhnev), looks on. (November 1973). Credit: PD

General Secretary Brezhnev landed at Palam Airport at 11.00 am on November 26, 1973. This time he came in a four-engine Ilyushin Il-62 aircraft, successor of the Il-18 that he had arrived in 12 years ago. As General Secretary Brezhnev's aircraft touched down, he was given a 21-gun salute, usually reserved for visiting Heads of State, in an evident departure from the strict protocol norms.

Prime Minister Indira Gandhi, her Cabinet colleagues and other senior officials were at the airport to receive him. The reception was exuberant and the large congregation of people welcomed the Soviet leader with cries of "Comrade Brezhnev, *Druzhba*"[39] (friend Brezhnev) throughout the arrival ceremony at the airport.

In her welcome address, Prime Minister Indira Gandhi, described the Soviet leader as a "distinguished leader of a great and friendly country."[40] In his reply, General Secretary Brezhnev remarked that his visit was aimed at "further consolidation of friendship and expansion of co-operation between India and Russia."[41]

The welcome had perceptibly pleased the visiting dignitary. The press noted that General Secretary Brezhnev was smiling throughout the entire 39-minute reception at the airport. This prompted a newspaper correspondent to ask the wife of a senior diplomat, how the Soviet leader could be smiling continuously over such a long period. She replied, "Comrade Brezhnev created a smiling record today." The newspaper headlined the story, "Smile that broke all records."[42]

After the welcome ceremony, the Soviet leader drove to Rashtrapati Bhavan in a six-door, bulletproof Mercedes Benz. Seated next to him was Prime Minister Indira Gandhi. It was a long motorcade of 32 cars and nine press cars apart from outriders. The streets along the route to Rashtrapati Bhavan were bedecked with arches of flowers and the hundreds of flags, festoons and banners gave the city a festive look. Thousands had gathered along the roads to greet General Secretary Brezhnev and they shouted slogans in Hindi, Punjabi, Urdu and English welcoming the Soviet leader.[43] In Connaught Circus, people had waited since 9.00 am and they showered petals as the motorcade passed by. Special arches were erected in the city and thousands of posters were stuck on its walls welcoming him. At several places, children broke into *bhangra*[44] at the sight of the motorcade. Under the headline, "Delhi goes gay to greet Brezhnev," *The Times of India* described the reception the Soviet leader received as a "welcome unsurpassed in recent years for its spontaneous popular enthusiasm."[45]

Thirty-five splendidly attired men of the PBG, astride their magnificent horses, escorted the Soviet Leader's motorcade in a colourful procession from Vijay Chowk. Seventeen of them preceded the vehicles and an equal number followed while two horsemen flanked either side of General Secretary Brezhnev's limousine. Another division of 13 men awaited the arrival of the dignitaries at the Rashtrapati Bhavan Forecourt.

On his arrival, the Soviet leader was greeted by the MSP, Major General Amreek Singh, at the South Court of Rashtrapati Bhavan. He was then introduced to the Personal Staff of the President of India who stood in the corridors in their blue jackets arrayed with medals. Prime Minister Gandhi and General Secretary Brezhnev were thereafter escorted to the Dwarka Suite, where the Soviet leader was to stay. On arrival at the suite, they were served refreshments.

The Soviet leader had arrived with a large and high-powered delegation. It was estimated by *The New York Times* to be around

General Secretary Brezhnev's motorcade climbing the gradient leading to Rashtrapati Bhavan in November 1973. Credit: PD

(R-L): Prime Minister Indira Gandhi (second) with General Secretary Brezhnev at a cultural programme at Rashtrapati Bhavan in November 1973. Credit: PD

300 and consisted of "journalists, cameramen and security staff as well as economic and political officials"[46] making it the largest delegation for a State Guest staying 'under the dome'. The senior members of the delegation included Politburo members Andrei Gromyko and Dinumuhammed Kunatev amongst other senior functionaries. From amongst the delegated, 13 were accommodated in Rashtrapati Bhavan according to their seniority.

Though General Secretary Brezhnev did not hold any significant position in the Soviet Government or the State, the visit had a strong economic agenda. Many agreements were planned to be concluded primarily to assist India in the implementation of its Fifth Five Year Plan. Officials of the Soviet Union had also arrived in advance to hold discussions and finalise economic agreements. The Soviet Deputy Prime Minister, Nikolai Baibakov had also landed in Delhi, prior to the arrival of General Secretary Brezhnev to give finishing touches to the agreements drafted by the officials of both countries.[47] Baibakov had held meetings with Planning Minister DP Dhar and Finance Minister YB Chavan. The Soviet Deputy Foreign Minister Pegov, who had also arrived earlier, held meetings with PN Dhar, the Indian Prime Minister's Secretary and Kewal Singh, the Foreign Secretary.

While hectic parleys of the advance team were in progress, Rashtrapati Bhavan geared itself to host the important delegation and make arrangements for the frequent meetings, arrivals and departures of Indian leaders calling on their Soviet counterparts staying 'under the dome'. The most important task before the Rashtrapati Bhavan officials was to ensure that the stay of the important leader and

his delegation was as comfortable as possible. To ensure this, all advisories received communicating the preferences of the Soviet guests were diligently complied with, though some of them were obviously inapprehensible.

One such request was for placing a "*Lifebuoy*" brand soap in every room, even though Rashtrapati Bhavan was famous for sparing no effort to provide the best of toiletries to visiting guests. The reason why this particular brand of soap, amongst the cheapest available in the market at the time, was specifically identified was enough to perplex even the best in the hospitality business. Needless to say the Comptroller, President's Household (CPH) was bewildered as well. Nevertheless, he ensured that every room, including the Soviet leaders, had a cake of *Lifebuoy*, in addition to top brand soaps, in each room.

Another request from the Soviet side was to provide thick curtains on both sides of the Dwarka Suite to ostensibly minimise the noise level in the room. It once again intrigued the President's Secretariat staff. Rashtrapati Bhavan is located on a vast property that has no thoroughfares. It was virtually turned into a fortress every time a State Guest came calling or chose to stay in Rashtrapati Bhavan. In any case, considerable space separates the Suite and the nearest public road which also leads to the President's Estate. The traffic is extremely thin and no heavy vehicles, except with special permission, are allowed to ply on it. As a matter of abundant precaution, special instructions were issued during the stay of dignitaries prohibiting anyone from peering out of windows or making noise. A request was also received for at least two good electric irons, ironing boards and for the switch in the Nalanda Sitting Room to be covered with a "box."[48]

Advisory on food preferences was also received by the President's Secretariat. It included the placing of medium–sized tins of pineapple, guava and grape juices in the refrigerators in all the rooms. The advisory also contained a security component. Specific requests were received for chicken, mutton and fish to be examined by a doctor before being served. Samples were to be kept in the presence of a security officer and a member of the delegation especially tasked with laboratory examination.[49]

Amongst the advisories received was one that specifically related to the Soviet leader's food preferences. It was received by the Ministry of External Affairs which communicated it to the President's Secretariat. The advisory stated that General Secretary Brezhnev preferred herring with boiled potatoes, salads without mayonnaise or spices as snacks, fresh cabbage soup and borscht, lean meat and fruit salad for meals. On receipt of this special advisory, the CPH swung into action and cooks in Rashtrapati Bhavan rehearsed the preparation of these dishes. The advisory also mentioned that General Secretary Brezhnev only drank *Tsinandali* and *Mukuzani* dry wines and *Borzhomi* and *Narzan* mineral water. These were adequately stocked with a little help from the MEA.

This time the security and other arrangements for the Soviet leader and his delegation were also more elaborate. The President's

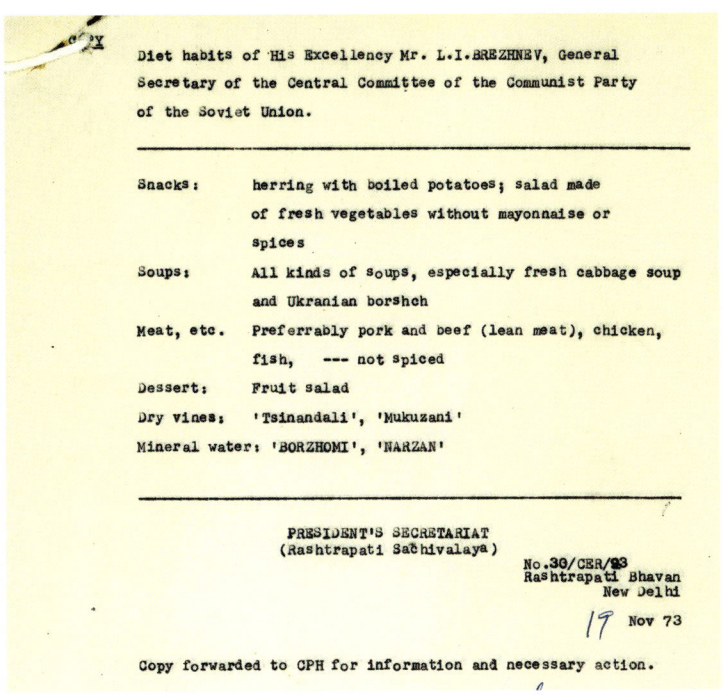

Advisory on dietary preferences of General Secretary Brezhnev.

Secretariat took special measures in consultation with Soviet officials and Indian security agencies. One Soviet adjutant and one security attendant accompanied General Secretary Brezhnev at all times. A Soviet security officer, dedicated to General Secretary Brezhnev's security, was posted at the Reception Office of Rashtrapati Bhavan; while two security officers and one diplomatic officer, essentially an interpreter, were posted at the telecommunications office. In light of the numerous incidents of letter bombs that were being sent around the world, the Post Master of the Rashtrapati Bhavan Post Office had been instructed not to send any *dak*[50] to the Soviet dignitaries directly but forward it to the Soviet Embassy or to the Soviet officers at the Enquiry Office.

Separate communication set-up was also installed for the Soviet delegation. An advance team had installed it in the Neelam and Gautam Bedrooms on the second floor of the Guest Wing. A telephone exchange was also established to secure communication among the delegates who were accommodated outside the Bhavan. A large array of equipment was specially flown in from the Soviet Union for the visit. It included 20 tonnes of equipment and they came in crates that were so huge that it took seven trucks to transport them to Rashtrapati Bhavan.

A team of doctors had also arrived from the Soviet Union to attend to General Secretary Brezhnev. After consultation with the President's physician, special arrangements were made to cater to meet any medical emergency. The working hours of the Rashtrapati Bhavan Post Office were changed to keep it open from 6.00 am to 11.00 pm, during the stay of the Soviet delegation. Instructions were issued to the tele-printer office to be kept open beyond office hours.

The plethora of instructions issued by the President's Secretariat for this important visit also led to some interesting use of the English language. The CPH was so determined to ensure that the boiler was kept running to provide hot water round the clock. To communicate that there should be no disruption in the services, he let his military lexicon creep into a letter addressed to the Executive Engineer, President's Estate Division. His communication read: "Boiler may please be commissioned round the clock to obliterate the inconvenience to the Guests."[51]

In the afternoon of the day he arrived, General Secretary Brezhnev laid wreaths on the *samadhis* of Mahatma Gandhi, Pandit Jawaharlal Nehru and Lal Bahadur Shastri. He also planted a *Chilka* sapling in the *Rajghat* compound, just as he had done 12 years ago.[52] He was pleased to see that the sapling he had planted in 1961 had now grown into a tall tree. Before he signed the Visitors' Book at the *Samadhi* of the father of the nation, General Secretary Brezhnev wrote, "With deep respect for the memory of the great son of the Indian people – Mahatma Gandhi."

Official discussions between Prime Minister Indira Gandhi and General Secretary Brezhnev began later in the afternoon; six hours after the delegation's arrival. The two leaders first met for 35-minutes in the Prime Minister's office before joining the delegations from their respective countries in the Conference Hall of South Block. This round of discussions lasted nearly three hours. Indo-Soviet bilateral relations and international issues were the major focus of the discussions.[53]

Later that evening, Prime Minister Gandhi hosted a "glittering" State Banquet in honour of the Soviet leader at the grand Banquet Hall of Rashtrapati Bhavan. At 7.50 pm, Prime Minister Gandhi, dressed in a "beige coloured silk sari"[54] escorted General Secretary Brezhnev who wore a "dark blue suit,"[55] to the banquet. The national anthems of both countries were played after the dignitaries reached the central arch of the Ashok Hall. This was followed by the introduction of the guests who had assembled in a horse-shoe formation, with their wives to their right. The guests included members of the Soviet delegation and a hundred invitees from the Indian side comprising of senior Cabinet Ministers, the Speaker of the Lok Sabha and the three Service Chiefs amongst others.

After the introductions, the dignitaries were escorted to the Banquet Hall. The fare at the dinner was primarily Indian. It included *Cream Doieldieu, Vol-Au-Vent, Tandoori Chicken with Kabab, Naan, Cauliflower-Bhujia, Stuffed Tomato, Green Peas, Mixed Salad, Papad, Achar* and *Chutney*, fruits, dessert and coffee.[56]

After the main courses, Prime Minister Gandhi delivered her banquet speech. Speaking in Hindi, she lauded the Soviet leader for his personal contribution towards promoting "the growth of Indo-Soviet relations during the past decade."[57] Prime Minister Gandhi, in an attempt to remove misconceptions about the Indo-Soviet Treaty of Friendship signed in 1971, commented that it was "not aimed at any other country, its intention and its effect

General Secretary Leonid Brezhnev addressing Civic Reception at Red Fort, Delhi, in November 1973. Credit: PD

is to strengthen the forces of peace and stability in the world."[58] General Secretary Brezhnev, in his reply, agreed with the Indian Prime Minister and hailed the Treaty as being of "outstanding international importance", whose "beneficial effect on the entire situation in Asia is becoming increasingly obvious."[59]

After the Banquet, the Soviet dignitaries were treated to a dance and music recital presented by renowned artistes of the *Sangeet Kala Akademi* in the Ashok Hall. Performances included group song and dances in the Indian classical styles of *Kathak, Manipuri* (*Ras*) and *Bharatnatyam* (*Tillana*).[60]

The next day, General Secretary Brezhnev called on the President of India, VV Giri, in the Morning Room of Rashtrapati Bhavan. The meeting lasted almost an hour. After the call on, Prime Minister Gandhi arrived with her granddaughter, Priyanka Gandhi, who wanted to meet the Soviet leader.[61] General Secretary Brezhnev and Prime Minister Gandhi had an almost two-hour long private discussion. Later, President Giri hosted a lunch for General Secretary Brezhnev in the lawns of the Mughal Gardens. Besides the Soviet delegation, guests included the Vice President of India, Dr Radhakrishnan; Prime Minister Gandhi; select Members of Parliament and some Central Ministers.[62]

A Civic Reception was held in the evening at the Red Fort to honour of the Soviet General Secretary. Speaking from a canopied rostrum to a big crowd gathered on the open ground, General Secretary Brezhnev declared that Indo-Soviet friendship would "last for centuries."[63] The speech, delivered in Russian and translated in "chaste Hindi by a Russian interpreter"[64] continued for over 90 minutes. The crowd, however, became restless and the police had to restrain "those who tried to drift away."[65]

The third day of the visit was almost consumed by political deliberations. On the next day, November 29, the visiting Soviet

leader had no scheduled engagements till 4.00 pm. There was, however, a surprise visitor for the Secretary Brezhnev in the morning. It was Rahul Gandhi who came calling accompanied by his grandmother, Prime Minister Indira Gandhi. The 'unusual' visitor had brought for the Soviet leader an even more unusual gift; one straight from his heart. It was a "talking bird", a *mynah* and Secretary Brezhnev warmly accepted it.[66]

The lunch that day was a quiet affair for General Secretary Brezhnev. Later, he met Prime Minister Indira Gandhi for official talks which lasted nearly two hours. The evening was reserved for his address to the Indian Parliament which he had missed during his last trip to India in 1961. At 6.05 pm, General Secretary Brezhnev addressed the Parliament of India in the Central Hall of Sansad Bhavan. The address was broadcast and telecast live.[67] The President's family members also heard the address from the President's Box.

The later part of the evening was reserved for the signing of four bilateral agreements. The venue chosen for the event was the Ashok Hall. Prime Minister Gandhi wearing a cream-striped, red-bordered sari with a matching cream blouse and General Secretary Brezhnev in a formal blue suit and red tie were there to sign the main agreements.[68]

The most important agreement signed was the 15-year agreement for further development of economic and trade co-operation. Other agreements included a consular convention, cooperation between the State Planning Committee of the USSR and the Indian Planning Commission and a protocol to the 15-year agreement providing for the immediate shipment of petroleum and petro-chemical products etc. The agreements were signed by General Secretary Brezhnev and Prime Minister Gandhi, Andrei Gromyko and Swaran Singh and Nikolai Baibakov and DP Dhar in the Ashok Hall in the presence of four Indian Ministers and other senior officials.

General Secretary Brezhnev's visit ended on November 30, 1973, around noon. The motorcade left Rashtrapati Bhavan at 11.20 am and drove through Freeman's Avenue, South Avenue, Willingdon Crescent, Sardar Patel Road, Gurgaon Road and Parade Road to the Technical Area of Palam Airport. General Secretary Brezhnev was accorded a traditional ceremonial farewell before his departure for Moscow.

The importance of this visit, coming as it did after the 1971 India-Pakistan War, underscored the strong relations existing between the two nations. The visit further strengthened the already robust ties between the two countries.

The 1980 Visit

President Brezhnev's third visit to India came after a gap of seven years, in December 1980. This time, he came as the most powerful party functionary of the Soviet Union and its Head of State.

President Brezhnev was now, however, a physically weak man and frail in health. The signs were unmistakable.

In view of his poor health, several special arrangements were made by the Rashtrapati Bhavan officials to cater to his medical requirements.

President Brezhnev and his 200-member entourage arrived at Palam Airport on December 8, 1980, at 11.00 am by a special Il-62 and were extended a full ceremonial welcome. His arrival was announced by the booming sound of the 21-gun salute and unlike in the 1973 visit, the President of India, N Sanjeeva Reddy was present to welcome him as soon as he set foot on Indian soil. Thereafter, President Brezhnev proceeded to the Saluting Dais when the national anthems of both the nations were played. The circumstances surrounding his visit too were different this time.

The Soviet intervention in Afghanistan in 1979 had substantially increased the threat to President Brezhnev's life. Responding to the situation, Soviet officials flew in with their cars for the use by their President despite India's offer to provide a limousine from the Indian President's garage for the visiting dignitary. They were so unrelenting with regard to security of their leader that the Soviet side also flew in a driver for the car that President Brezhnev would use during the visit. The only concession that they made was that the Soviet cars would travel in India with India's national crest. Five of these crests were accordingly sent to the Protocol Division of the Ministry of External Affairs.[69]

After being introduced to the dignitaries in the special enclosure, President Brezhnev travelled to Rashtrapati Bhavan in the "bullet-proof Mercedes Benz especially flown in from Moscow," flanked by four security cars.[70] Seated beside President Brezhnev was the President of India. The only other occupant, beside the Soviet driver, was an interpreter. The motorcade included a Mercedes 600, a Mercedes 350 and two baggage vans from the President's Garage.

As during his previous two visits, the roads were decorated with the flags of both countries and flower arches dotted the roads. There were crowds of people all along the streets waiting to catch a glimpse of the 74-year-old Soviet Head of State.

The mounted lancers of PBG escorted the motorcade from Vijay Chowk. By 11.55 am, the dignitaries alighted at the South Court of Rashtrapati Bhavan where they were received by the MSP, Major General GS Jamwal. President Reddy personally escorted the Soviet General Secretary to the Dwarka Suite where President Brezhnev stayed as he had done on his previous two visits.

Fifteen senior delegates of the entourage were allotted suites in Rashtrapati Bhavan according to their seniority. Foreign Minister Gromyko stayed in the Nalanda Suite, First Deputy Chairman of the USSR Council of Ministers IV Arkhipov was accommodated in the Himalaya Bedroom and AY Ryabenko and VT Medvedev in the Tagore Bedroom.

After arriving at the Rashtrapati Bhavan, he had lunch in his suite, and thereafter, President Brezhnev paid a courtesy call on President Reddy in his study. Later, President Brezhnev met Prime Minister Gandhi for approximately 50 minutes, and exchanged preliminary views on the prevailing international situation.

(Seated, facing, L-R): Foreign Minister Gromyko, President Reddy and President Brezhnev at Rashtrapati Bhavan in December 1980. Credit: PC

Later that day, at 7.30 pm, President Reddy hosted a State Banquet in honour of the Soviet President. After the national anthems and formal introductions, the dignitaries were escorted to the Banquet Hall. President Reddy was seated between Foreign Minister Gromyko and Deputy Premier Arkhipov, while President Brezhnev was flanked by Prime Minister Gandhi and Vice President Hidayatullah.

The menu for the banquet was elaborate and had been finalised after considerable deliberations. It consisted of a delectable mix of both non-vegetarian and vegetarian dishes – *Smoked Pomfret, Hussaini Kabab, Paneer Cutlets, Paneer Khara Korma, Swiss Charlotte,* followed by dessert and coffee.

In his banquet speech, President Reddy welcomed President Brezhnev and praised his work in promoting peace and cooperation.

He stated that any external interference in the region would cause a grave threat to peace and stability, and India would always "remain opposed to any form of intervention, covert or overt, by outside forces in the internal affairs of the region."[71] President Reddy ended his speech expressing the hope that the Soviet leader's visit would bring peace and stability to Asia and the world.

Replying to President Reddy's speech, President Brezhnev focussed on bilateral relations delving on the mutual respect and trust that the Indians and Soviets shared with one another, carefully steered clear of any reference to Afghanistan. He was, however, critical of the West accusing it of whipping up the arms race. He concluded by raising a toast to the President, Prime Minister and "to the success and prosperity of the friendly and great India; and to a lasting peace an [sic] Earth!"[72] The arrival of the President and

President Brezhnev (third from left) with President Reddy at Rashtrapati Bhavan in December 1980. Credit: PC

Table Plan of the State Banquet.

the distinguished guests, formal introductions, the toast and speeches at the banquet were telecast on *Doordarshan* as well as on Soviet television.[73]

The next day, December 9, President Brezhnev and Prime Minister Gandhi met for a fresh round of discussions on the Afghan issue, but failed to come to a common conclusion. Prime Minister Indira Gandhi had, however, in very clear terms, communicated to President Brezhnev that Soviet actions in Afghanistan had security implications for India.[74]

Unusually, President Brezhnev did not go to *Rajghat* during this visit. When the press enquired about this deviation from the tradition, his office remarked that President Brezhnev's practices were in line with the "general custom followed in all countries that a head of state goes to a mausoleum and pays his respects on his first visit. During subsequent visits, wreaths can be placed on his behalf."[75]

As during the previous two visits, the Soviet leader was given a Civic Reception. This time it was not held at a public venue. Though Red Fort was originally selected as the venue for the reception, it was changed at the last moment to Vigyan Bhavan on account of security concerns. The reception was held at 12.45 pm; only select invitations were issued and the gathering was deliberately kept small. In their speeches, both President Brezhnev and Prime Minister Indira Gandhi focussed on the mutual trust that existed between the two countries. Commenting on the strong relations that the two nations shared, Prime Minister

Prime Minister Indira Gandhi delivering banquet speech at Rashtrapati Bhavan. President Brezhnev is on her right. (December 1980). Credit: PD

PROGRAMME
SIGNING CEREMONY
INDO-SOVIET DOCUMENTS
10th December, 1980.

Joint Indo-Soviet Declaration, to be signed by :
INDIRA GANDHI,
Prime Minister of the Republic of India

L. I. BREZHNEV,
General Secretary of the Central Committee of the CPSU, Chairman of the Presidium of the Supreme Soviet of the USSR.

Agreement on Economic and Technical Cooperation between the Republic of India and the Union of Soviet Socialist Republics

to be signed by :
INDIRA GANDHI,
for the Republic of India.

L. I. BREZHNEV,
for the Union of Soviet Socialist Republics.

Trade Agreement between the Republic of India and the Union of Soviet Socialist Republics

to be signed by :
PRANAB MUKHERJEE,
Minister of Commerce and Steel & Mines

I. V. ARKHIPOV,
First Deputy Chairman of the Council of Ministers of the USSR.

Protocol on Cooperation in the field of cinematography to be signed by :
VASANT SATHE,
Minister of Information & Broadcasting

F. T. YERMASH,
Chairman of the State Committee of the USSR for Cinematography.

Programme of Cultural, Scientific and Educational Exchanges between the Republic of India and the Union of Soviet Socialist Republics from January 1, 1981 to December 31, 1982.

to be signed by :
MIR NASRULLAH,
Additional Secretary,
Ministry of Education & Culture

N. P. FIRYUBIN,
Deputy Minister of Foreign Affairs of the USSR.

Programme of Agreement Signing Ceremony.

Gandhi remarked that the agreements on vital issues between both countries "outweigh" their differences.[76]

The next day, the two countries signed a number of bilateral agreements and a "Joint Declaration" in the Ashok Hall of Rashtrapati Bhavan. The former included a Trade Agreement between the Republic of India and the Union of the Soviet Socialist Republic that was signed, on behalf of India, by President Pranab Mukherjee, who was then the Minister of Commerce and Steel and Mines.[77] The Joint Declaration stated that "outstanding issues in Asia and the world as a whole can and should be resolved by peaceful means so as to enable the countries of the region to devote their energies to the task of national development."[78]

Later that day, President Brezhnev addressed the Indian Parliament. He arrived at the Parliament to a standing ovation.[79] He spoke in Russian, which was simultaneously translated by an interpreter. In his address he pitched for a system collective security in Asia. President Brezhnev emphasised that the "friendship" between the two nations was a "common asset" of both the nations and that their relations "have stood the test of time."[80] Parliamentarians thumped their desks and clapped as the Soviet leader spoke. Rashtrapati Bhavan helped organise the event. It sent six low-back ceremonial chairs and 200 "black chairs" to Sansad Bhavan for the event and they were to be "returned immediately after the function is over."[81]

This four-day visit ended with a banquet hosted by President Brezhnev at the Soviet Embassy in New Delhi in honour of the Indian President and the Prime Minister. A special invitation, with the message written in both Russian and Hindi, was sent to President Reddy who accepted the same. President Reddy left Rashtrapati Bhavan at seven minutes to eight that night and was received at the Embassy by President Brezhnev. The two dignitaries were then conducted to the Reception Hall where the rest of the guests joined them.[82] The invitees included Prime Minister Gandhi, senior officials and Ministers.[83]

В ЧЕСТЬ ЕГО ПРЕВОСХОДИТЕЛЬСТВА
Господина Н. САНДЖИВА РЕДДИ, ПРЕЗИДЕНТА РЕСПУБЛИКИ ИНДИЯ,
и ЕЕ ПРЕВОСХОДИТЕЛЬСТВА Госпожи ИНДИРЫ ГАНДИ,
ПРЕМЬЕР-МИНИСТРА РЕСПУБЛИКИ ИНДИЯ

ГЕНЕРАЛЬНЫЙ СЕКРЕТАРЬ ЦК КПСС,
ПРЕДСЕДАТЕЛЬ ПРЕЗИДИУМА ВЕРХОВНОГО СОВЕТА СССР
ЛЕОНИД ИЛЬИЧ БРЕЖНЕВ

просит *Е. П. г-на Нилам Санджива Редди*

пожаловать на обед в среду, 10 декабря 1980 года, в 20 часов.

Посольство СССР   Просьба ответить
Дели Шантипатх, Чанакьяпури   тел.: 615875

भारत गणराज्य के राष्ट्रपति महामहिम श्री नीलम संजीव रेड्डो
तथा भारत गणराज्य की प्रधान मंत्री परमश्रेष्ठ श्रीमती इन्दिरा गांधी
के सम्मान में

सोवियत संघ की कम्युनिस्ट पार्टी की केंद्रीय समिति के महासचिव,
सोवियत समाजवादी जनतंत्र संघ के सर्वोच्च सोवियत
के अध्यक्ष-मंडल के अध्यक्ष ल॰ इ॰ ब्रेझनेव
बुधवार, १० दिसंबर को संध्या ८००० बजे
राज-भोज के लिये पधारने का
H.E. Mr. Neelam Sanjiva Reddy
से निवेदन करते हैं।

दिल्ली स्थित सोवियत संघ का राज-दूतावास
शांति पथ, चाणक्यपुरी
सूचनार्थ निवेदन
फ्रोन : ६१५८७५

Special invitation to President Reddy for the banquet hosted by President Brezhnev at the Soviet Embassy.

Prime Minister Indira Gandhi (centre right) and President Brezhnev (center left) during the Agreement Signing Ceremony at Rashtrapati Bhavan in December 1980. Credit: PD

The next day, President Reddy and President Brezhnev met in the Yellow Drawing Room at 11.58 am. After an exchange of pleasantries, they left for the airport. The President's Personal Staff stood in the corridors and bid the visiting dignitaries farewell. The ceremonial motorcade that headed to the airport followed the same formation as it had when it arrived.

Thousands of people had gathered to see the Soviet General Secretary and they shouted slogans like, "*Lal salam*," "*Hindi–Rusi bhai–bhai.*"[84] President Brezhnev was seen off by President Reddy, Prime Minister Gandhi, Members of Parliament and various Ministers amongst others

At 12.45 that afternoon, President Brezhnev and his entourage left India for the last time. A full ceremonial farewell that included a Guard of Honour and a 21-gun salute together with the national anthems of both nations being played, underscored and reflected the respect and affection India had for a man under whom the USSR "stood by India."[85]

The visit of the Soviet Head of State reaffirmed the cordial and strong relations existing between the two nations. The Ministry of External Affairs described the visit as "a valuable opportunity of reaffirming the strength and vitality of Indo–Soviet relations."[86]

President Brezhnev continued as the Head of Government of the Soviet Union for another two years. On November 10, 1982, he died of a heart attack after making his last public appearance at the October Revolution anniversary celebrations that had taken place just three days earlier. He was 75. Madame Viktoria Brezhneva died in 1995. She was 87.

Notes

1 Academy of Sciences of the USSR, *Leonid I. Brezhnev: Pages from His Life* (New York: Simon and Schuster, 1979), p.10.

2 Ibid., p. 1.

3 Records, President's Secretariat, Rashtrapati Bhavan, File No. 30/CER/137.

4 Ibid.

5 Ibid.

6 Ibid.

7 "Big Welcome at Airport," *The Hindustan Times* (New Delhi), December 16, 1961, p. 1.

8 "Warm Welcome to Brezhnev in Delhi," *The Times of India* (New Delhi), December 16, 1961, p. 1.

9 "Big Welcome at Airport," p. 8.

10 Ibid.

11 Ibid.

12 Records, President's Secretariat, File No. 30/CER/137.

13 Ibid.

14 Ibid.

15 Ministry of External Affairs (1995), Government of India, MEA Library, Foreign Affairs Records, 1961, Volume VII, accessed April 13, 2015, http://mealib.nic.in/?pdf2549?000

16 Ibid.

17 Ibid.

18 Ibid.

19 "Brezhnev and Nehru Confer," *The Hindu* (New Delhi), December 17, 1961, p. 1.

20 "Brezhnev and PM discuss World Issues," *The Hindustan Times* Weekly (New Delhi), December 17, 1961, p. 1.

21 "Brezhnev, Nehru Visit Indian Industries Fair," *The Hindustan Times Weekly* (New Delhi), December 17, 1961, p. 5.

22 Ibid.

23 "Brezhnev Has Talks With Nehru," *The Times of India* (New Delhi), December 17, 1961, p. 1.

24 "Brezhnev Hails Progress of Indian Oil Industry," *The Times of India* (New Delhi), December 20, 1961, p. 8.

25 Ibid.

26 "Brezhnev Enjoys Elephant Ride," *The Times of India* (New Delhi), December 26, 1961, p. 9.

27 "Brezhnev–Nehru Talks Continue," *The Times of India* (New Delhi), December 28, 1961, p. 9.

28 "Nehru Hails Soviet Support on Goa," *The Times of India* (New Delhi), December 28, 1961, p. 9.

29 Ibid.

30 "Goa Action Just and Legitimate," *The Times of India* (New Delhi), December 29, 1961, p. 1.

31 Records, President's Secretariat, File No. 30/CER/137.

32 "Soviet President Bids Adieu to India," *The Times of India* (New Delhi), December 30, 1961, p. 8.

33 Ibid.

34 Ibid.

35 Henry Kissinger, *White House Years* (London: Simon & Schuster, 2011), pp. 885–886.

36 Academy of Sciences of the USSR, Leonid I. Brezhnev, p. 214.

37 Academy of Sciences of the USSR, Leonid I. Brezhnev, p. 222.

38 "Live TV Coverage of Brezhnev's Visit," *The Times of India* (New Delhi), November 26, 1973, p. 5.

39 "Warm Welcome to Brezhnev," *The Statesman* (New Delhi), November 27, 1973, p. 1.

40 Ibid.

41 Ibid.

42 "Smile That Broke all Records," *The Times of India* (New Delhi), November 27, 1973, p. 1.

43 "Flowers and Dance Greet Brezhnev," *The Times of India* (New Delhi), November 27, 1973, p. 5.

44 A folk dance of Punjab.

45 "Delhi Goes Gay to Greet Brezhnev," *The Times of India* (New Delhi), November27, 1973, p. 1.

46 "India and Soviet Agree to Solidify Links," *The New York Times*, November 28, 1973, p. 3.

47 Prithvis Chakravarti, "Big Welcome Awaits Brezhnev as Soviet Leader Arrives Today," *The Hindustan Times* (New Delhi), November 26, 1973, p. 1.

48 Records, President's Secretariat, Rashtrapati Bhavan, File No. 30/CER/93.

49 Ibid.

50 *Dak* is a Hindi word that means post.

51 Records, President's Secretariat, File No. 30/CER/93.

52 "Homage at Samadhis of Gandhi, Nehru," *The Hindustan Times* (New Delhi), December 27, 1973, p. 1.

53 "Indo–Soviet Ties A Model," *The Statesman* (New Delhi), November 27, 1973, p. 1.

54 "Glitter & Spice at Banquet," *The Statesman* (New Delhi), November 27, 1973, p. 1.

55 Ibid.

56 Ibid.

57 Ministry of External Affairs (1995), Government of India, MEA Library, Foreign Affairs Records 1973, Volume XIX, accessed May 29, 2015,http://mealib.nic.in/?pdf2561?000.

58 Ibid.

59 Ibid.

60 "Glitter & Spice at Banquet," p. 1.

61 "Soviet Leader Meets Giri," *The Times of India* (New Delhi), November 28, 1973, p. 7.

62 "Lunch with President," *The Times of India* (New Delhi), November 28, 1973, p. 7.

63 "Brezhnev Call for Collective Security Plan in Asia," *The Times* (London), November 28, 1973, p. 6.

64 "USSR Will Stand by India," *The Statesman* (New Delhi), November 28, 1973, p. 1.

65 "Brezhnev Call for Collective Security Plan in Asia," p. 6.

66 "Gift of Mynah," *The Times of India* (New Delhi), November 30, 1973, p. 7.

67 "Address to M.P.s to be Broadcast," *The Times of India* (New Delhi), November 28, 1973, p. 1.

68 "Indira, Brezhnev Sign 15-year Economic and Trade Pact," *The Times of India* (New Delhi), November 30, 1973, p. 1.

69 Records, President's Secretariat, Rashtrapati Bhavan, File No. 30/CER/255(80).

70 "Surprise Change in Motorcade Route," *The Hindu* (New Delhi), December 9, 1980, p. 1.

71 Ministry of External Affairs (1995), Government of India, MEA Library, Foreign Affairs Records 1980, Volume XXVI, accessed May 29, 2015, http://mealib.nic.in/?pdf2568?000.

72 Ibid.

73 Records, President's Secretariat, File No. 30/CER/255(80).

74 G.K. Reddy, "As Long As the U.S. and Pak. Complicate Matters We Will Stay...: Brezhnev," The Hindu (New Delhi), December 10, 1980, p. 1.

75 "Car Flown in from Russia," *The Times of India* (New Delhi), December 9, 1980, p. 1.

76 "Indo-Soviet Harmony, Outweighs Differences'," *The Hindu* (New Delhi), December 10, 1980, p. 9.

77 Records, President's Secretariat, File No. 30/CER/255(80).

78 Ministry of External Affairs (1995), Foreign Affairs Records 1980, Volume XXVI.

79 "Standing Ovation for Brezhnev," *The Hindustan Times* (New Delhi), December 11, 1980, p. 14.

80 "Ties With India Unchanged: Brezhnev," *The Times of India* (New Delhi), December 11, 1980, p. 13.

81 Records, President's Secretariat, File No. 30/CER/255(80).

82 Ibid.

83 "Return Banquet," *The Times of India* (New Delhi), December 11, 1980, p. 1.

84 "Affectionate Send-Off," *The Times of India* (New Delhi), December 12, 1980, p. 1.

85 K.P.S. Menon, *Memories and Musings* (New Delhi: Allied Publishers Private Ltd., 1979), p. 264.

86 External Publicity Division, Ministry of External Affairs, Government of India, "President Leonid Brezhnev visits India: December 8 TO 11, 1980," MEA-50|XP (Press)|1|81

EUROPE

VISITING DIGNITARIES FROM EUROPE

CZECHOSLOVAKIA: Prime Minister Viliam Siroky

NORWAY: Prime Minister Einar Gerhardson

POLAND: Prime Minister Jósef Cyrankiewicz

UK: Earl Clement Attlee
                               Queen Elizabeth II

YUGOSLAVIA: President Josip Tito

The Prime Minister of Czechoslovakia, Viliam Siroky, first visited India from January 3-16, 1958. This 12-day State Visit was a part of a longer tour to South and South-East Asia. Though it was called a "goodwill visit,"[1] the trip also had an economic agenda. India was in talks with Czechoslovakia, for technical and financial assistance to set up a large foundry in Ranchi, in the present day Indian State of Jharkhand. It was to be established as a part of a Russian-designed heavy machine building project.[2]

India and Czechoslovakia shared warm and cordial relations even though Czechoslovakia was a member of the Warsaw Pact and India was a founding member of the non-aligned movement that opposed the division of the world into antagonistic blocs and the creation of military alliances of the Cold War.

These differences notwithstanding, both countries recognised the need to create an environment conducive to economic cooperation. Their views on disarmament and world peace were more congruent than the apparent divergence. India was keen to further strengthen bilateral relations with Czechoslovakia. The visit of Prime Minister Siroky was seen primarily, as an event facilitating economic cooperation.

Viliam Siroky was born on May 31, 1902, in a railway worker's family, in the erstwhile Kingdom of Hungary. He started working on the railroads at the age of 15, and soon became familiar with Hungarian workers' politics. However, Viliam Siroky's real entry into the world of politics began when he joined the Social Democratic Party as a supporter of the revolutionary left wing movement.

Visit of

H.E. Mr Viliam Siroky

Prime Minister of Czechoslovakia

As a co-founder of Bratislava's Communist Party that subscribed to Marxist ideology, Viliam Siroky was elected to the Czechoslovak Parliament in 1935.[3] He fled to France and later to the Soviet Union when the Nazis occupied Czechoslovakia, returning to join "the underground to oppose the German-controlled Fascist Government in Slovakia."[4]

After Czechoslovakia's liberation, Viliam Siroky rapidly rose through the political ranks becoming the Foreign Minister in 1950. During his tenure as the Foreign Minister, he altered the vector of his country's foreign policy and brought it in "closer alignment with the Soviet Union."[5] Viliam Siroky became Prime Minister of Czechoslovakia on March 21, 1953, and it was in this capacity that he visited India. He landed at the Indian Air Force (IAF) Station, Palam, Delhi, on January 3, 1958, on the hour at 2.00 pm after a six-and-a-half hour flight from Moscow.[6]

The Prime Minister, who was travelling aboard the latest Russian-built, twin-engine Tupolev Tu-104 Czech Airlines jet aircraft, stepped off the plane to a warm welcome. The first to greet him was Prime Minister Jawaharlal Nehru. The other dignitaries present at the Airport, included Food Minister Ajit Prasad Jain, Defence Minister

Facing page:
Prime Minister Viliam Siroky (left)
with President Dr Prasad
at Rashtrapati Bhavan
in January 1958. Credit: PC

(R-L): Prime Minister Viliam Siroky with Prime Minister Nehru at Rashtrapati Bhavan. Indira Gandhi is on extreme left. (January 1958). Credit: PD

Krishna Menon and the Czechoslovak Ambassador to India, Jiri Mosek. The President of India was represented by his Military Secretary, Major General Harnarain Singh.[7]

A group of Czechoslovak children, dressed in white shirts and blue shorts, holding the flags of both India and Czechoslovakia and carrying bouquets, welcomed their Prime Minister in a warm display of affection. Prime Minister Viliam Siroky was visibly delighted to see them. The Prime Minister received their floral offerings, with a broad smile, patted their cheeks and shook hands with them. He then proceeded to inspect a Guard of Honour presented by an Inter–Services contingent.[8]

Speaking at the airport, Prime Minister Nehru welcomed the Czech Prime Minister by recalling the fond memories he had of his own visit to Czechoslovakia three years back. He said that the visiting Prime Minister too would have similar experiences in India. Addressing Prime Minister Siroky directly, Prime Minister Nehru said, "Wherever you go, you will be welcomed with affection and you will see that our people love your country and people."[9]

Prime Minister Siroky replied to Prime Minister Nehru's words of welcome, and said, "Stirred with emotion of profound happiness, we are stepping upon the soil of India, the land of millennial history, and magnificent culture."[10] He declared that, "his visit would strengthen not only the traditional friendship between

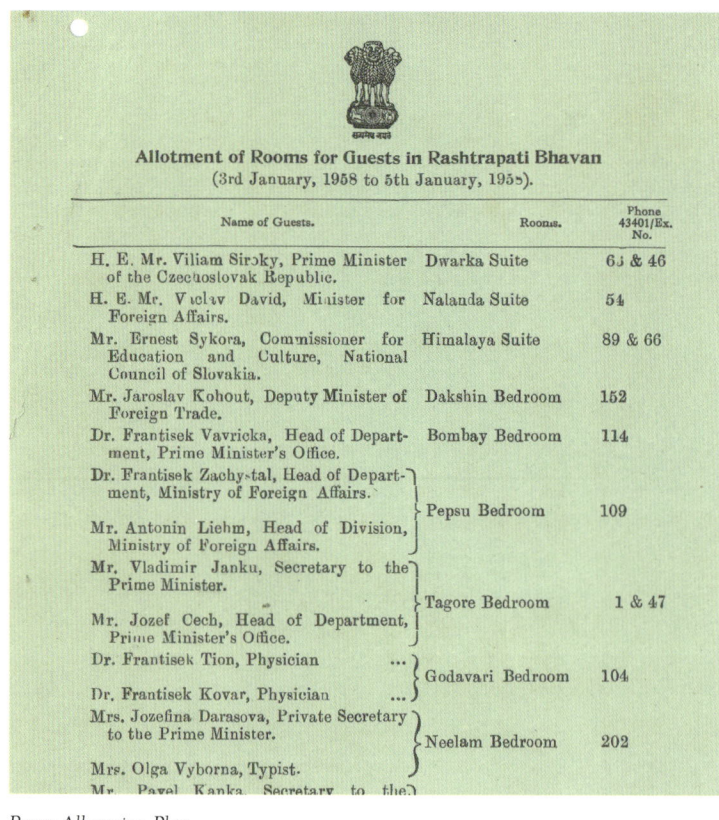

Room Allocation Plan.

(*Front row, L-R): President Dr Prasad, Prime Minister Viliam Siroky and Indian Defence Minister Krishna Menon at Rashtrapati Bhavan in January 1958. Credit: PD*)

the Czechoslovak Prime Ministers rode in an open Cadillac, while the rest of his entourage followed in a green Cadillac, a DeSoto, an Oldsmobile and other cars from the President's Garage.[13] A huge crowd had gathered all along the nine-mile route leading to Rashtrapati Bhavan and they cheered the Czechoslovak Prime Minster as his motorcade drove past. The crowd was especially thick near the Secretariat building and greeted Prime Minister Siroky enthusiastically.[14]

The Czechoslovak entourage consisted of 28 members including Foreign Minister, Vaclav David; Commissioner for Education and Culture, National Council of Slovakia, Ernest Sykora; Deputy Minister of Foreign Trade, Jaroslav Kohout and the Indian Ambassador to Czechoslovakia, JN Khosla.[15] On their arrival at Rashtrapati Bhavan, the Comptroller, President's Household (CPH), the Deputy Military Secretary to the President (DMSP), and members of the President's Staff greeted them. Prime Minister Siroky stayed in the Dwarka Suite and Vaclav David in the Nalanda Suite. Other members of the entourage were first escorted to the Yellow Drawing Room, where refreshments were served. After refreshments, 13 members of the visiting Prime Minister's entourage staying in Rashtrapati Bhavan, were escorted to their respective suites/rooms.

India and his own country but the cause of peace."[11] Prime Minister Siroky also wished the people of India "happiness and success" in the new year of 1958.[12]

After the ceremonial welcome and the speeches, Prime Minister Siroky and his entourage left for Rashtrapati Bhavan. The Indian and

Shortly after his arrival, Prime Minister Siroky met Prime Minister Nehru at the latter's residence at Teen Murti Bhavan. During

Prime Minister Viliam Siroky (facing, third from left), at lunch in Mughal Gardens at Rashtrapati Bhavan. Seated opposite (fourth from left) is President Dr Prasad. Seated right of Prime Minister Siroky is Prime Minister Nehru. (January 1958). Credit: PD

(Front row, R-L): President Dr Prasad, Prime Minister Siroky and Prime Minister Nehru in the Mughal Gardens at Rashtrapati Bhavan in January 1958. Credit: PD

their meeting which *The Times of India* described as "serious,"[16] they discussed issues of common interest including disarmament and the creation of an "Atom Free" zone in Europe.[17] From the Czechoslovak side, its Foreign Minister, the Commissioner for Education and Culture, and its Ambassador to India were present at the discussions. The Secretary General in the Ministry of External Affairs (MEA), NR Pillai and the Indian Ambassador to Czechoslovakia assisted Prime Minister Nehru at the talks.[18]

The meeting lasted for about 75-minutes, and was conducted "through an interpreter." The media reported that an understanding was reached at the meeting on Czechoslovakia's financial and technical support to the Indian "foundry-forge project."[19] It was reported that foreign exchange to the tune of Rs 16 crore (of the project cost of Rs 30 crore) would be met by Czechoslovakia.[20]

The next day, January 4, Prime Minister Siroky visited *Rajghat* at 9.00 am, and laid a wreath at the *samadhi* of Mahatma Gandhi. The Czechoslovak Prime Minister then called on the Vice President, Dr Radhakrishnan, at his residence on 2, King Edward Road (now Maulana Azad Road). He later visited the National Physical Laboratory and the Indian Agricultural Research Institute. On the afternoon of the same day, Prime Minister Siroky called on President, Dr Rajendra Prasad, at Rashtrapati Bhavan and had lunch with him.

That evening at 8.30, a State Banquet was hosted at Rashtrapati Bhavan by Prime Minister Nehru in honour of Prime Minister Siroky, for which 90 guests were invited. Those who attended the banquet included Vice President Dr Radhakrishnan, Union Ministers and members of the diplomatic corps.

The arrangements made for the banquet were, as usual, grand. The corridors and staircases leading from the Guest Wing to the Ashok Hall were specially decorated and had exquisite flower arrangements. The men of the PBG, in their full ceremonial winter uniforms, lined the passages used by the visiting delegation. At the break of dusk, the lights and beautiful fountains of the Mughal Garden were switched on, adding to the beauty of the view from the Ashok and Banquet Halls.

The Personal Staff of the President conducted both the Prime Ministers separately to the Ashok Hall, where they received the guests at the entrance. After the guests had arrived, they were conducted to the Banquet Hall.

After the main courses were served, Prime Minister Nehru proposed a toast to the visiting Prime Minister. In his speech, he welcomed Prime Minister Siroky and acknowledged the "friendly co-operation" of his country in building India.[21] Prime Minister Nehru also spoke at length about the dangers that armament race spawned, and said, "I think that the first duty before all of us and every country and more especially those who happen to be in positions of some authority is to work for peace."[22]

In his reply, the Czechoslovak Prime Minister referred to the similarities in the policies of both nations on international issues. He echoed Prime Minister Nehru's view on world peace, and said that both "India and Czechoslovakia were endeavouring for, and would continue to devote all their strength to the prevention of both small and great wars so that humanity could finally 'enter a happy age of peace, free from any fear.'"[23] He also appealed for "a consistent application of the principles of peaceful co-existence and an extensive development of economic and cultural co-operation among nations."[24] Prime Minister Siroky concluded his speech by saying that he would do everything necessary to strengthen friendly ties between the two countries. After the banquet, the guests were treated to a 60-minute dance and music recital, especially organised for the visiting delegation.

The next day, on January 5, Prime Minister Siroky visited a community project in Baraut, in the Meerut district of the neighbouring state of Uttar Pradesh. He "had a look at rural India" for the first time, and was impressed by what he saw.[25] He appreciated the self-improvement work undertaken by the villagers and in a gesture of friendship, presented them with a tractor made in Czechoslovakia. The villagers reciprocated, by gifting Prime Minister Siroky, a "small hatchet made in the village."[26]

That afternoon, Prime Minister Siroky had lunch with the Czechoslovak Ambassador to India at Rashtrapati Bhavan. At half past four that afternoon, the visiting Prime Minister attended a reception at Hyderabad House, where he was presented with a flower vase and a brass plate. The reception had been hosted in his honour by the Indo–Czechoslovak Association.

Later that evening, the Czechoslovak Prime Minister also attended a Civic Reception, held in his honour, at the historic Red Fort. Hundreds of people had lined the five-mile route, and "lustily cheered" at the sight of both Prime Ministers travelling together.[27] The route from the entrance of the Red Fort to the *Diwan–i–Khas* had been "tastefully decorated by floral cones and fluorescent tubes."[28] Coloured lights on trees and hedges imparted a festive look to the reception. A total of 6,500 invitation cards had been sent out, and the attendance was large. The dignitaries who attended included President Dr Prasad and Defence Minister Krishna Menon. The two Prime Ministers were warmly greeted on their arrival at the venue and the Czechoslovak Prime Minister was welcomed with garlands. The event began with a welcome song by a group of girls from Municipal schools across the capital.[29]

The visiting Prime Minister greeted the enthusiastic audience, through an interpreter, with words chosen to convey the warmth of his feelings. But the interpreter, somewhat literally, translated his "warm greetings" in Hindi as, "*garam garam salaam*"[30] (In Hindi *garam* means hot and *salaam* means greetings). In saying so, the interpreter ended up conveying Hot Hot Greetings, instead of

the warm greetings extended by the visiting Prime Minster to the audience. The crowd, perhaps understanding the spirit of the Prime Minister's greetings, responded with loud cheers and applause.

Prime Minister Siroky commented on the friendly ties between India and Czechoslovakia that dated back "deep into past history."[31] Decrying the creation of Cold War military blocs, he supported India's position against antagonistic alliances and said that the "Simultaneous abrogation of both the Warsaw Treaty and the Atlantic Pact would be a real step towards peace."[32] Elaborating on the issue, he expressed his support for the creation of a 'neutral zone' in Central Europe. The President of the Municipality, RN Aggarwal, presented a carpet to the visiting dignitary of behalf of the citizens of Delhi.[33]

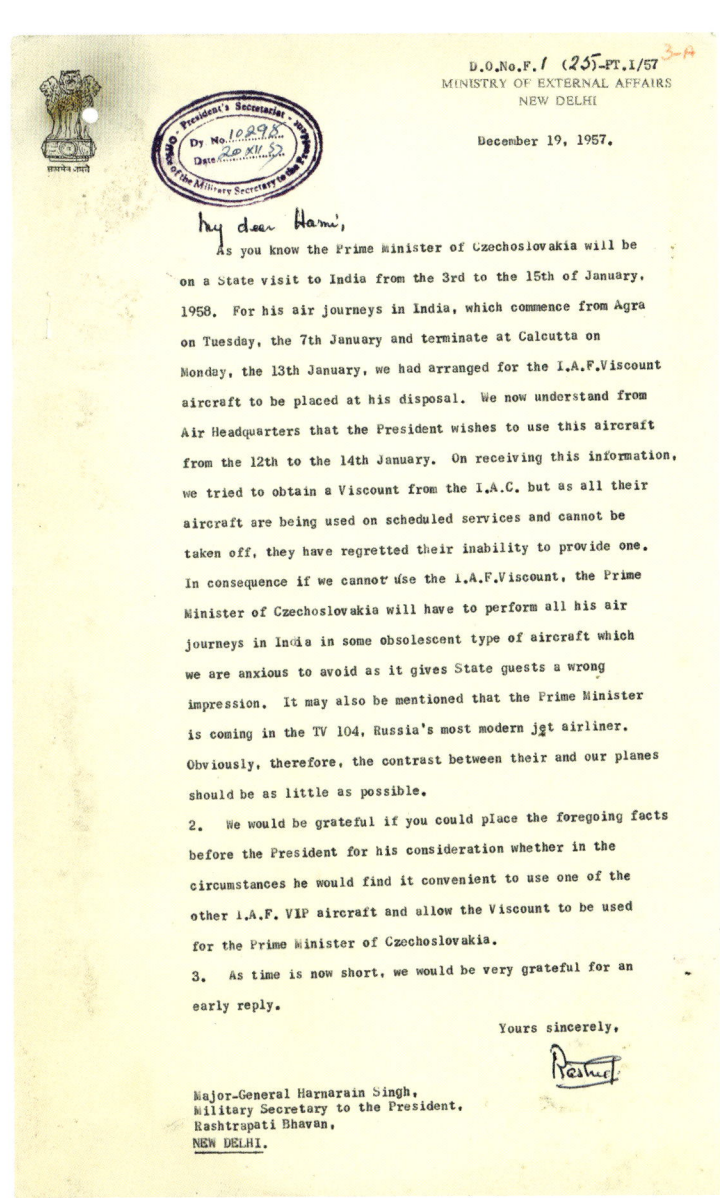

Letter from MEA requesting the President's aircraft for Prime Minister Siroky.

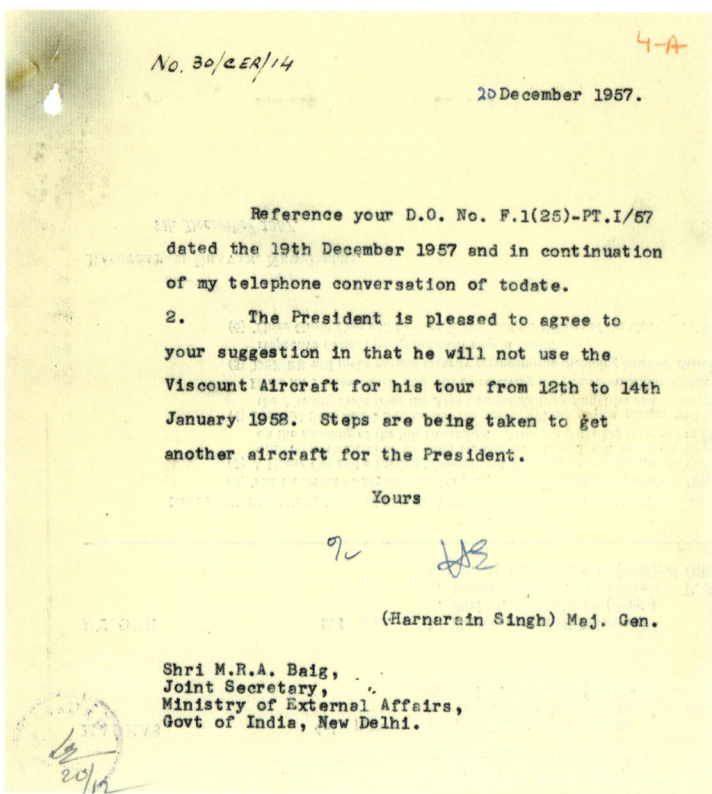

No. 30/CER/14

4-A

2o December 1957.

Reference your D.O. No. F.1(25)-PT.I/57
dated the 19th December 1957 and in continuation
of my telephone conversation of todate.

2.   The President is pleased to agree to
your suggestion in that he will not use the
Viscount Aircraft for his tour from 12th to 14th
January 1958. Steps are being taken to get
another aircraft for the President.

Yours

(Harnarain Singh) Maj. Gen.

Shri M.R.A. Baig,
Joint Secretary,
Ministry of External Affairs,
Govt of India, New Delhi.

President's approval for use of his aircraft for Prime Minister Viliam Siroky.

During the course of the day, a joint statement was issued by the Prime Ministers of both countries echoing their sentiments on disarmament and the need to abandon weapons of mass destruction. Both leaders also expressed their regret that China was not appropriately represented in the United Nations. The two Prime Ministers also communicated their satisfaction on the conclusion of agreements regarding the foundry-forge project and the extension of a grant of "$63,000,000 loan [to India] for the construction of a foundry at Ranchi" by the Czechoslovak Government.[34]

In the evening, at half past eight, Prime Minister Siroky hosted a banquet at the Ashoka Hotel for his hosts. Vice President Dr Radhakrishnan, Prime Minister Nehru, several Cabinet Ministers and many Parliamentarians attended the event. At the banquet, Prime Minister Siroky "proposed a toast to the President" and followed it by a toast to the Vice President and Prime Minister Nehru.[35] Addressing the invitees, he conveyed his "profound satisfaction at the course and results" the two countries had achieved during the past three days.[36] In his reply, Vice President Dr Radhakrishnan raised a toast to "Mr. Siroky and to the prosperity of the people of Czechoslovakia and to world peace."[37]

After the banquet, the Czechoslovak delegation left for Nangal at 11.00 pm by special train from the ceremonial platform at the New Delhi Railway Station. He was given a private send-off.[38] Arriving in Nangal, the next morning, on January 6, 1958, at quarter past

nine, he visited the Bhakra Dam. The Czechoslovak Prime Minister was immensely impressed by the reservoir, which he described as "the battle-ground for peace."[39]

Surprised at the size of the dam, Prime Minister Siroky told the Indian Ambassador, JN Khosla, who was accompanying him on the tour that he had "ever been too modest." He said, "You have never told us that you have such wonderful projects in hand in your country."[40] He added, "You are certainly going ahead at a faster pace than we are doing in our country."[41]

Prime Minister Siroky left for Agra the same night, by train on the hour at 9.00. Despite his hectic schedule, the Prime Minister showed no signs of fatigue and visited several historic places in Agra, including Itmad-ud-Daula's tomb, the Agra Fort, and the Taj Mahal, which he later described as a "dream in white marble."[42] Prime Minister Siroky left for Bombay at 3.00 in the afternoon of January 7, where he spent two days.

The aircraft that he would use for travel within India came up for some serious discussions between the MEA and the President's Secretariat.

Normally the Indian Air Force provides aircraft from its VIP squadron for visiting Heads of States to travel within the country. A difficulty, however, arose this time as the President, Dr Prasad, had intimated in advance that he would be travelling by the same IAF Viscount, that had been proposed for Prime Minister Siroky's use by the MEA. The possibility that the Viscount may not be available for the use of the visiting Prime Minister caused consternation in the MEA. Faced with this dilemma, MRA Baig, the Chief of Protocol (COP), wrote to the MSP, making an impassioned plea, soliciting the consideration of the President to use another aircraft. He added that if the Viscount was not available, then Prime Minister Siroky would be forced to travel in some "obsolescent type of aircraft" and it This would also give the visiting Prime Minister, who had arrived in a Tu-104, "Russia's most modern jet airliner" an opportunity to "contrast between their and our planes."[43] The President agreed with the MEA's suggestion, and thus, the Czechoslovak Prime Minister flew in the IAF Viscount, India's best aircraft at the time.

Prime Minister Siroky was given a 'rousing reception' on his arrival in Bombay. He visited several places including the famous Aarey Milk Colony, the Atomic Energy Establishment, the *Khadi* Emporium and Handloom House. At the Civic Reception hosted in Kamla Nehru Park, he famously referred to Bombay as "one of the most beautiful [cities] in Asia."[44]

On January 9, at 9.00 am Prime Minister Siroky left for Poona where he was accorded a warm reception. His six-hour stay in the city included a visit to the Central Water and Power Research Station and lunch at the National Defence Academy.[45] From Poona, he went to Bangalore in the afternoon, where he was shown around the Hindustan Aircraft Factory and the "Rail Coach section of the HAL."[46]

The Czechoslovak Prime Minister's visit to the Indian Telephone Industries impressed him so much that he wrote in the Visitor's book, "We congratulate your workers, engineers, electricians and management for the results you have achieved thus far. The organisation of work is remarkable... We wish all the people of India much success in their industrial development."[47]

On January 11, Prime Minister Siroky arrived in Madras to a tumultuous welcome. He visited "the Central Government's Rs eight-crore giant integral coach factory in Perambur."[48] He reached Calcutta, his final stop in India, on January 13. In a farewell message recorded on All India Radio, he characterised the Indian people as having a "desire for peace and friendship among nations and a determination to secure overall development of the great power of Asia–India."[49]

After spending two weeks in India, Prime Minister Viliam Siroky left for Cambodia via Rangoon in the early hours of January 16. About a fortnight later, on February 2, 1958, *en route* to Prague from Colombo, Prime Minister Siroky halted overnight in India and stayed at the Rashtrapati Bhavan once more.

Viliam Siroky continued as Prime Minister of Czechoslovakia until 1963. He died on October 6, 1971. He was 69.

Notes

[1] "Civic Reception," *The Times of India* (New Delhi), January 4, 1958, p. 8.

[2] "Mr. Siroky in Delhi," *The Times* (London), January 1, 1958, p. 12.

[3] "Czech Premier arrives in Delhi today," *The Hindustan Times* (New Delhi), January 3, 1958, p. 4.

[4] Harris M. Lentz, *Heads of States and Governments: A Worldwide Encyclopaedia of Over 2,300 Leaders, 1945 Through 1992* (London: Fitzroy Dearborn Publishers, 1995), p. 216.

[5] Ibid.

[6] "Promotion of Peace," *The Hindu* (New Delhi), January 4, 1958, p. 6.

[7] "Mr. Siroky in New Delhi," *The Times of India* (New Delhi), January 4, 1958, p. 7.

[8] Ibid.

[9] "'Atom Free' Zone in Europe," *The Hindustan Times* (New Delhi), January 4, 1958, p. 12.

[10] Promotion of Peace," p. 6.

[11] Ibid.

[12] "Mr. Siroky in New Delhi," p. 7.

[13] Records, President's Secretariat, Rashtrapati Bhavan, File No. 30/CER/14.

[14] "Mr. Siroky in New Delhi," *The Times of India*, (New Delhi), January 4, 1958, p. 7.

[15] Ibid.

[16] "Indo–Czech Talks Begin in Delhi," *The Times of India* (New Delhi), January 4, 1958, p. 1.

[17] "'Atom Free' Zone in Europe," *The Hindustan Times* (New Delhi), January 4, 1958, p. 1.

[18] Ibid.

[19] Ibid.

[20] "'Atom Free' Zone in Europe," p. 12.

[21] "Disarmament is problem No. I," *The Hindustan Times* (New Delhi), January 5, 1958, p. 13.

[22] Ibid., p. 1.

[23] Ibid., p. 13.

[24] Ibid.

[25] "Abrogation of Warsaw Pact," *The Times of India* (New Delhi), January 6, 1958, p. 9.

[26] Ibid.

[27] Ibid.

[28] "Abrogation of Warsaw Pact & N.A.T.O. Urged," *The Hindustan Times* (New Delhi), January 6, 1958, p. 1.

[29] Ibid.

[30] "Abrogation of Warsaw Pact & N.A.T.O. Urged," p. 1.

[31] Ibid.

[32] Ibid.

[33] Ibid.

[34] "India Obtains Czech Loan," *The New York Times*, January 5, 1958, p. 7.

[35] "Further Indo–Czech Co-operation," *The Hindustan Times* (New Delhi), January 6, 1958, p. 1.

[36] Ibid.

[37] Ibid.

[38] Records, President's Secretariat, File No. 30/CER/14.

[39] "Czech Premier at Nangal," *The Times of India* (New Delhi), January 7, 1958, p. 7.

[40] Ibid.

[41] Ibid.

[42] "Czech Premier Calls for Banning Nuclear Tests", *The Times of India* (New Delhi), January 9, 1958, p. 1.

[43] Records, President's Secretariat, File No. 30/CER/14.

[44] "Czech Premier Calls for Banning Nuclear Tests," p. 1.

[45] "Move for No-War Pact Hailed," *The Times of India* (New Delhi), January 10, 1958, p. 5.

[46] "Industries in Bangalore," *The Hindu* (New Delhi), January 11, 1958, p. 8.

[47] Ibid.

[48] "Aid with Strings Criticised," *The Times of India* (New Delhi), January 12, 1958, p. 12.

[49] "Indo–Czech Ties Stressed", *The Times of India* (New Delhi), January 17, 1958, p. 8.

As the grey and foggy winter settled over Delhi in the November of 1958, Rashtrapati Bhavan readied itself to host Einar Henry Gerhardsen, the Prime Minister of Norway. He arrived in India on a two-week visit, on 27th of the month and it marked the first-ever visit by a Prime Minister of his country to India or to Asia for that matter.[1]

Affectionately referred to as "*Landsfaderen*"[2] (Father of the Fatherland), the longest-serving Prime Minister of Norway, Einar Gerhardsen, was born in Asker on May 10, 1897. He was one of four children born to working-class parents in Oslo. Einar Gerhardsen had little formal schooling and studied only for seven years.[3] Thereafter, he took up odd jobs and subsequently became a road worker. In 1919, he joined the Labour Party's youth organisation and in 1922 started his long career as a paid Union Representative of the road workers. Early in life itself, he earned the reputation as a man of impeccable honesty that he even paid for the stamps he used on his personal letters.[4] He soon rose in public life.

Visit of

H.E. Mr Einar Gerhardsen

Prime Minister of Norway

By the Second World War, he had become the Mayor of Oslo. During the Nazi occupation, he was ousted from public office. He simply went back to mending roads wearing his overalls during the day but devoted his nights to organising resistance against the occupation.[5] He played an active part in the movement to free his country from foreign occupation and facilitated the formation of the Nygaardsvold Government (Norwegian government in exile during the War under Prime Minister Johan Nygaardsvold) and the monarchy in exile.[6] He was, arrested for his role in the resistance movement and sent to the camps in Grini in Norway and Sachsenhausen in Germany.[7] After the end of the War, his Labour party was swept to power in the election held in Norway in late 1945. On November 5, the "rugged, rock-like" Gerhardsen became the Prime Minster heading the youngest Cabinet.[8] He continued as the Prime Minister for nearly two decades. These following two decades came to be referred to as the 'Gerhardsen era' in Norwegian politics.[9]

The "Grand Old Man of Norwegian socialism"[10] was Prime Minister for almost 17 years. Although Prime Minister Gerhardsen identified reconstruction as the most important task after the War, he also nudged the Norwegian society towards a socialist direction. Despite making the biggest strides in reaching pre-war industrial levels in Western Europe,[11] the Gerhardsen years saw the idea of a Welfare State consolidate in Norway.

India and Norway shared a warm relationship since the establishment of diplomatic relations in 1947. Prime Minister Gerhardsen's socialistic policies brought him ideologically close to India, which was also striving to find a middle path between capitalism and the communist model of socialism. Norway extended assistance to India

Facing page:
President Dr Prasad (left) greeting
Prime Minister Einar Gerhardsen
at Rashtrapati Bhavan
in November 1958. Credit: PC

Prime Minister Gerhardsen inspecting a Guard of Honour at Palam Airport, New Delhi, in November 1958. Credit: PD

in its quest for development, especially in areas where its expertise was well recognised, as in the field of fisheries. The joint Indo–Norwegian Fisheries Project established in the State of Kerala as early as in the spring of 1953 was a model of this cooperation.[12]

Prime Minister Gerhardsen landed at Palam Airport from Karachi, a little after 5.00 on the chilly evening of November 27, 1958, in a specially chartered Indian Airlines Corporation Viscount.[13] He was accompanied by his wife, Werna Gerhardsen who was also a Labour Party politician. The Prime Minister of India, Jawaharlal Nehru; some of his Cabinet colleagues; the Military Secretary to the President (MSP), Major General Sardar Harnarain Singh; senior Government officials and a crowd braving the cold extended him and his delegation a warm welcome.[14]

Thereafter, he inspected a Guard of Honour and was then formally introduced to the dignitaries who had congregated in a special enclosure. The Norwegian Prime Minister did not, however, make the customary speech which visiting Heads of States/Government did, at the airport. Instead he issued a statement.[15] In it, he said, that back home "we look upon India as a vital exponent of the democratic idea in Asia."[16] Referring to Prime Minister Nehru's international fame, the statement said, "in Norway they [Norwegians] had come to know Prime Minister Nehru as a champion of peace and easing of world tension. Rarely had any foreign statesman been received in Oslo with such warmth and admiration as was Mr Nehru."[17]

The statement added that India and Norway were dedicated to "a constructive international policy which may secure a peaceful future for the world."[18]

After the welcome ceremony at the airport, Prime Minister Gerhardsen drove to Rashtrapati Bhavan in the Indian President's Cadillac, in a motorcade that comprised a green Cadillac, an open Cadillac, a DeSoto, other cars and baggage Lorries. The visiting delegation was received at Rashtrapati Bhavan by the Comptroller, President's Household (CPH) and the Personal Staff who were dressed in red coats/frock coats complete with medals. Their attire included overalls, swords and sashes and red turbans or caps. The visiting delegation was then conducted to their respective apartments.[19]

Since it was not a very large entourage, all the members were accommodated in the Guest Wing of Rashtrapati Bhavan. According to tradition, Prime Minister Gerhardsen, as the Head of the Norwegian delegation, stayed in the Dwarka Suite. His wife, Werna Gerhardsen stayed in the Nalanda Suite. Halvard M Lange, Foreign Minister of Norway and his wife stayed in the Tagore Suite; Frithjof Jacobsen, the Director of the Political Department of the Foreign Ministry stayed in the Bombay Bedroom; Einar Diesen, Chief Editor of *Aftenposten*, Norway's largest newspaper, was accommodated in the Pepsu Bedroom. Other members of the delegation were earmarked rooms according to their seniority.[20]

On his first morning in India, Prime Minister Gerhardsen visited *Rajghat* and paid his respects at the *samadhi* of Mahatma Gandhi. The visiting Prime Minister, accompanied by his Foreign Minister, Lange, then called on Prime Minister Nehru. The meeting, which included the Indian Ambassador to Norway, the Secretary-General of the External Affairs Ministry and the Foreign Secretary, lasted about an-hour-and-a-half. The leaders were understood to have discussed international issues.[21]

Later that afternoon, the Norwegian Prime Minister addressed the Members of India's Parliament, in the Central Hall of Sansad Bhavan. Prime Minister Gerhardsen said that he felt strange, that the representative of one of the smallest democratic countries in the world should be addressing representatives of the largest. This opportunity, he said was an honour and a privilege for him.[22]

In his brief address, he complimented India's development and cultural advancement, which, he opined, would shape Asian and world events.[23] Prime Minister Gerhardsen also referred to the work of the Norwegian fishery experts in Kerala, and said that he was happy his country was sharing its know-how in this field with India.[24] He concluded by conveying to the Parliament, his "best wishes for a happy and peaceful future for the people of India."[25]

Allotment of Rooms for Guests in Rashtrapati Bhavan
(27th November to 1st December, 1958).

Name of Guests.	Rooms.	Phone 43401/Ex. No.
1. H.E. Mr. Einar Gerhardsen, Prime Minister of Norway. 2. Mrs. Gerhardsen.	Dwarka and Nalanda suites	63 & 54
3. H.E. Mr. Halvard Lange, Foreign Minister of Norway. 4. Mrs. Lange.	Tagore suite	1 & 47
5. Mr. Frithjof Jacobsen, Director of the Political Department of the Foreign Ministry.	Bombay bed room	114
6. Mr. Einar Diesen, Chief Editor of the " Aftenposten ".	Pepsu bed room	109
7. Mr. Per O. Proitz, First Secy. of the Ministry.	Godavari bed room	104
H.E. Mr. Andre Malraux and Mrs. Malraux.	Himalaya Suite	89 & 66

IMPORTANT TELEPHONE NUMBERS

Name.	Designation.	Telephone Nos.	
		Residence.	Office.
RASHTRAPATI BHAVAN.			
1. Major-Genl. Sardar Harnarain Singh.	Military Secretary to the President.	43401/169	35954
2. Lt.-Col. S. S. Maitra	Surgeon to the President	43401/38	43401/35
3. Lt. - Col. Harnath Singh.	Comptroller, President's Household.	43401/19	42913 43401/30
4. Lt.-Col. M. Ghufran	Deputy Military Secretary to the President.	43401/31	43401/23
5. Capt. Joginder Singh	Guests' ADC ...	43401/79	43401/9 & 10
6. Mrs. M. Mabert ...	Housekeeper ...	43401/33	...
7. Reception Office ...	..	...	43401/105
			43401/28

Room Allocation Plan.

The Vice President of India and Chairperson of the Rajya Sabha, Dr Sarvepalli Radhakrishnan thanked the Norwegian Prime Minister for extending his country's assistance to develop India's fisheries.[26]

That evening, Prime Minister Gerhardsen was accorded a grand Civic Reception at the *Diwan–i–Khas* of the Red Fort. Though the weather was inclement and it was drizzling, it did not dampen the enthusiasm of the large crowds who had gathered for the reception.[27] Aruna Asaf Ali, Mayor of Delhi, welcomed Prime Minister Gerhardsen on behalf of the citizens. She praised Norway for its advancement in science and technology, and for conceiving the idea of the sovereignty of the people as early as 1814. She also emphasised that both India and Norway had won their freedom by non–violent means. Prime Minister Nehru, in his address, complimented Norway and also spoke about its development assistance to India.[28]

The Norwegian Prime Minister was graciously acknowledging the compliments he and his country had received. He reminded everyone that the modern man was overwhelmed by technology and it increasingly makes him to lose contact with the past. He urged people to draw inspiration from the Red Fort and said of India, "If there is a paradise on earth, it is here, it is here."[29] Speaking about how he felt to be in India, he said, "Our visit here has been a tremendous experience which we shall never forget."[30] The Mayor presented the Norwegian Prime Minister with a silver *surahi* and a pair of exquisitely carved fruit bowls; Werna Gerhardsen was given a *zari* scarf embroidered in the famous Benaras style. As a return gift, Prime Minister Gerhardsen presented the Mayor a fine cut–glass bowl.[31]

The long day, however, was not over yet. The Prime Minister of India hosted a grand State Banquet for his Norwegian counterpart and Werna Gerhardsen at Rashtrapati Bhavan. The Ashok Hall, the Banquet Hall and areas that were to be used in connection with the banquet were readied for the event. For the recording of the speeches, two sets of microphones were installed in the Banquet Hall in addition to the one positioned by All India Radio. The President's Bodyguard, in their knee-high boots and red overcoats had lined the route from the Guest Wing to the Ashok Hall. The Garden Superintendent energised all the fountains in the Mughal Gardens, besides brilliant floral decorations along the corridors, staircases and in the Ashok Hall. The Gorkha Regimental Centre Band was tasked to play music from the gallery of the Banquet Hall.[32]

Invitees arrived at the South Court via the South Sunken Road and were conducted to the Ashok Hall by the officials of the President's Secretariat. Special tables were provided for guests to keep their hats and coats and a car call system was installed to hail vehicles after the banquet. The host, Pandit Nehru, arrived early at the Ashok Hall. He was followed by, the Gerhardsens and the Norwegian delegation. Thereafter, both the Prime Ministers and Werna Gerhardsen received the guests at the entrance to the Ashok Hall.

Prime Minister Nehru delivering banquet speech at Rashtrapati Bhavan. Prime Minister Gerhardsen is seated opposite. (November 1958). Credit: PD

They included the Chief Justice of the Supreme Court, Cabinet Ministers and select members of the diplomatic corps amongst others. In addition, those, whose names figured in the list of invitees prepared in advance for possible inclusion in parties to be hosted in the Norwegian Prime Minister's honour, were extended invitation. They included India's Ambassador to Norway, Maharao Madan Singh Ji and the Minister of Food and Agriculture, AP Jain.[33]

After the guests arrived at the Ashok Hall, they were escorted to the Banquet Hall and had seated according to a carefully prepared table plan. After dinner Pandit Nehru addressed the guests and proposed a toast to the "Prime Minister of Norway and Madam Gerhardsen."[34] He referred to his own visit to Norway a–year–and–a–half ago and said that the simplicity and friendliness of the people of that country he had experienced had affected his thinking and his heart. Referring to India, he clarified to the Norwegian Prime Minister that what he had seen during his visit so far, the Red Fort, Parliament House, and Rashtrapati Bhavan were not really India. He said that the Indians were very simple people and even lacked basic necessities of life. The country, however, did have "some kind of basic strength or value" which has kept it going.[35]

In his reply, Prime Minister Gerhardsen admitted that he and his Foreign Minister, Lange, had been looking forward to visiting India "with the keenest expectation" ever since Prime Minister Nehru had invited them during his visit to Norway. He romanticised India and said, "In their old story–books Norwegian children got to know India as the strange and distant land of fairy-tale. It was so far away that one imagined that a flying carpet would be the only possible conveyance with which to reach it. India, we learnt, was the country with the world's highest mountains, with jungles and vast plains, with elephants and tigers, with temples and enchanting buildings such as the Taj Mahal. And above all it is the land of eternal sunshine and warmth. To people, in a land of ice and snow such as Norway this, perhaps, more than anything else, made India the land of fairytales."[36]

Speaking on the issue of nuclear weapons, he said that "The world today is living in the shadow of the catastrophe which a nuclear war would mean. We all know what is at stake. It is quite natural that India has been particularly committed to the work of international disarmament and the easing of tension. This work is truly in the spirit of Mahatma Gandhi... The important thing in my view is that our two countries are working towards the same goal, even though we do not always choose to follow the same road towards the goal." He concluded his speech by raising a toast to the Prime Minister of India and to "friendship between Norway and India."[37] The gala dinner was followed by a cultural programme of dance and music.

Prime Minister Gerhardsen spent most of the following day seeing the changing face of India and holding discussions with Indian leaders and senior functionaries of the government. He, however,

(L-R): Prime Minister Gerhardsen (second) with Prime Minister Nehru at Rashtrapati Bhavan in November 1958. Credit: PD

began his day by inspecting the proposed site for the Norwegian Embassy. Thereafter, he visited the Indian Agricultural Research Institute, the nation's premier organisation for agricultural research, education and extension. Later in the afternoon, he had lunch with Pandit Nehru at his Teen Murti Bhavan residence. The two Prime Ministers were joined by PN Sapru, Member of the Rajya Sabha; Maranatha Chandrasekhar, Member of the Pay Commission; Hans Olav, the Norwegian Ambassador to New Delhi and the Maharao of Kutch, India's Ambassador to Norway.[38] After lunch, Prime Minister Gerhardsen met Members of the Planning Commission and held discussions on various economic issues. Subsequently, he called on Vice President Dr Radhakrishnan and later visited the "India 1958" exhibition.[39]

The next day, on November 30, Prime Minister Gerhardsen went to the Ballabgarh Community Project in Gurgaon, escorted from Rashtrapati Bhavan by two officers of the Community Project.[40] After the visit, the Norwegian Prime Minister called on the President of India, Dr Rajendra Prasad and had lunch with him. Later in the day, he went on a sightseeing trip of Delhi. The evening saw him attend a reception hosted in his honour at Hyderabad House by the Ambassador of Norway to India.[41]

On December 1, Prime Minister Gerhardsen embarked on a tour of some of the cities of India. When he left Rashtrapati Bhavan, he was bid farewell by its staff who was dressed in their ceremonial

red tunics, overalls, with their swords, sashes, medals and caps, just as they had been on arrival. The baggage of the delegation was sent an hour in advance by the Transport Superintendent. The Prime Minister and his delegation left Delhi at 10.30 am from Palam Airport after a ceremonial send-off.[42]

The visiting Prime Minister made a short visit to Agra and Bhuj. Thereafter, he went on to Bangalore and Cochin, spending two days each in both the cities. From Cochin, the Norwegian delegation arrived at Aurangabad and spent two days exploring the famed Ajanta and Ellora Caves. Thereafter, the Norwegian Prime Minister and his delegation arrived in Bombay by a special IAF plane. On their arrival, they were received by Chief Minister YB Chavan and the Consul-General for Norway amongst others. A Guard of Honour was presented by a detachment of the Indian Navy.[43] At Bombay, the visiting dignitaries visited the atomic energy establishment and the Aarey Milk Colony.[44] Prime Minister Gerhardsen was demonstrably impressed by the standard of the Aarey Milk Colony. He commented that it was in the same league as any other dairy development project in the world.

On December 11, the day of his departure from India, Prime Minister Gerhardsen held a press conference, in which he fielded questions on a variety of topics, from India's industries to its relations with Red China. Replying to questions from the press, he reiterated his country's stand on nuclear weapons and re-affirmed that Norway

(Seated L-R): Werna Gerhardsen, Speaker of the Lok Sabha Ayyangar, Vice President Dr Radhakrishnan and Prime Minister Gerhardsen at Parliament House in November 1958. Credit: PD

would not make nuclear weapons as it was beyond her means. He added that despite being a member of NATO, his country would not allow any nuclear weapons on its soil except when it perceived a direct threat. He also lauded the "skill and direction" of India's industries "as modern as in any other part of the world."[45]

On December 11, at 5.05 pm Prime Minister, Einar Gerhardsen, was given a ceremonial send off as he departed for Karachi from the Bombay airport. He was presented a Guard of Honour by an Indian Naval detachment. The Labour Minister of Bombay, Shantilal Shah;

aide-de-camp to the Governor of Bombay and senior Government officials, together with members of the diplomatic corps, bid the Prime Minister farewell. After a warm hand-shake, Prime Minister Gerhardsen boarded an IAC plane that took him to Karachi.[46]

Prime Minister Einar Gerhardsen led his country as its Head of Government until 1965. He, however, continued to serve in the *Storting*, the Norwegian Parliament, till he retired from politics in 1972.[47] He died on September 19, 1987 in Oslo. He was 90. Werna Gerhardsen died on January 11, 1970. She was 57.

Notes

[1] "Maintenance of Peace," *The Hindu* (New Delhi), November 30, 1958, p. 9

[2] "Einar Gerhardsen," *Norwegian Encyclopaedia*, accessed May 20, 2015, https://snl.no/Einar_Gerhardsen.

[3] Peter Kerr, "Einar Gerhardsen Dies at 90; Led Norway as Welfare State," *The New York Times*, September 20, 1987, accessed May 21, 2015, http://www.nytimes.com/1987/09/20/obituaries/einar-gerhardsen-dies-at-90-led-norway-as-welfare-state.html

[4] "Norway: End of an institution," *Time*, August 30, 1963, accessed May 20, 2015, http://content.time.com/time/magazine/article/0,9171,940710,00.html.

[5] "Brutal Fact," Time, March 15, 1948, accessed May 20, 2015, http://content.time.com/time/magazine/article/0,9171,940710,00.html.

[6] "Einar Gerhardsen," www.regjeringen.no, accessed May 21, 2015, https://www.regjeringen.no/nb/om_regjeringa/tidligere/departementer_embeter/embeter/statsminister-1814-/einar-henry-gerhardsen/id463396

[7] Kerr, "Einar Gerhardsen."

[8] "With the stream," *Time*, November 12, 1945, accessed May 20, 2015, http://content.time.com/time/magazine/article/0,9171,792512,00.html.

[9] Ibid.

[10] "Norway: an end to Labor," *Time*, September 24, 1965, accessed May 20, 2015, http://content.time.com/time/magazine/article/0,8816,834351,00.html.

[11] "Brutal Fact", *Time*.

[12] Helge Pharo, "Altruism, Security and the Impact of Oil: Norway's Foreign Economic Assistance Policy, 1958–1971", *Contemporary European History* (Volume 12, Issue04, 2003) p.530 accessed May 20, 2015, Doi: http://dx.doi.org/10.1017/S0960777303001401

[13] "Delhi Policy hailed," *The Times of India* (New Delhi), November 28, 1958, p. 1.

[14] "Arrival in Delhi," *The Hindu*, (New Delhi), November 28, 1958, p. 1.

[15] "Delhi Policy hailed," p. 1.

[16] "Arrival in Delhi," p. 1.

[17] Ibid.

[18] "Delhi Policy hailed," p. 1.

[19] Records, President's Secretariat, Rashtrapati Bhavan, File No.30/CER/70

[20] Ibid.

[21] "Civic Reception to Norwegian Premier," *The Hindustan Times* (New Delhi), November 29, 1958, p. 5.

[22] "Promotion of Peace," *The Hindu* (New Delhi), November 29, 1958, p. 1.

[23] "Short Address to M.P.s," *The Times of India* (New Delhi), November 29, 1958, p. 1.

[24] "Common Outlook on Peace," *The Hindustan Times*, November 29, 1958, p. 1.

[25] "Promotion of Peace," p. 1.

[26] "Common Outlook on Peace," *The Hindustan Times*, November 29, 1958, p. 1.

[27] Ibid.

[28] "Civic Reception to Norwegian Premier", p. 5.

[29] Ibid.

[30] "Short Address to M.P.s," p. 1.

[31] Ibid.

[32] Records, President's Secretariat, File No.30/CER/70.

[33] Records, President's Secretariat, File No.30/CER/70.

[34] Ministry of External Affairs (1995), Government of India, MEA Library, Foreign Affairs Records 1958, Volume IV, accessed May 6, 2015, mealib.nic.in/?pdf2546?000.

[35] Ibid.

[36] Ibid.

[37] Ibid.

[38] "Meeting with planning body," *The Times of India* (New Delhi), November 30, 1958, p. 7.

[39] Ibid.

[40] Records, President's Secretariat, File No.30/CER/70.

[41] "Mr. Einar Gerhardsen", *The Times of India* (New Delhi), December 2, 1958, p. 9

[42] Records, President's Secretariat, File No.30/CER/70

[43] "Warm Welcome Accorded to Norwegian Premier," *The Times of India*, December 10, 1958, p.9.

[44] Records, President's Secretariat, File No.30/CER/70.

[45] "Norwegian Premier Lauds Indian Industries," *The Times of India* (New Delhi), December 12, 1958, p

[46] "Departure for Karachi," *The Times of India* (New Delhi), December 12, 1958, p. 5

[47] Kerr, "Einar Gerhardsen."

The first official bilateral visit between India and Poland was in June 1955, when Indian Prime Minister, Jawaharlal Nehru visited Warsaw. Two years later, the Prime Minister of Poland, Józef Cyrankiewicz paid a return visit to India,[1] from March 24 to April 3, 1957, as a part of his extended Asia tour[2].

Józef Cyrankiewicz belonged to the generation of European leaders whose lives and personalities were shaped by the Second World War. He was born on April 23, 1911, in the south eastern Polish city of Tarnow. He came from a family of intellectuals and graduated from the Jagiellonian University.[3] Later, in 1935, he became an organiser in the Polish Socialist Party.[4]

When the Second World War broke out in 1939, Józef Cyrankiewicz joined the army and was taken prisoner by the invading German troops.[5] He, however, managed to escape and joined the resistance movement fighting the occupation forces. He was recaptured and interned at Auschwitz. In the camp, he actively participated in the underground resistance movement.[6]

Visit of

H.E. Mr Józef Cyrankiewicz

Prime Minister of Poland

After the War, Józef Cyrankiewicz returned to active politics and rose rapidly through the party ranks. He was elected General Secretary of the Central Executive Committee of the Polish Socialist Party in 1945 and two years later, became the Prime Minister of Poland.

Prime Minister Cyrankiewicz had initially planned to visit India in 1956, a year after Pandit Nehru's visit to Poland. The dates had been finalised and both sides had completed necessary preparations for the visit. It did not, however, materialise and was rescheduled to early 1957.

Prime Minister Józef Cyrankiewicz arrived in India on a 10-day State Visit on March 24, 1957 landing at Palam Airport at 4.00 in the evening. As Prime Minister Cyrankiewicz descended from the aircraft, he was warmly welcomed by the cries of crowds cheering "Indo-Polish Friendship *Zindabad*".[7] Prime Minister Nehru, Indira Gandhi, VK Krishna Menon, the Services Chiefs, Central Ministers, members of the diplomatic corps and representatives of various welfare organisations in the city received the Polish leader.[8] In addition, 200 lorry-loads of people[9] were also at the airport to welcome the Polish leader who was accompanied by his wife, Madame Nina Andrycz Józef Cyrankiewicz, and an entourage of 23 members.

After formal handshakes, Prime Minister Józef Cyrankiewicz and his wife were garlanded by groups of children who sang songs of welcome.[10] The Polish Premier then took the salute of a hundred-strong Inter-Services Guard of Honour, before proceeding to a specially erected rostrum from where the two Prime Ministers addressed the gathering.

Facing page:
(L-R): Madame Nina Cyrankiewicz,
President Dr Prasad and
Prime Minister Józef Cyrankiewicz
at Rashtrapati Bhavan in
March 1957. Credit: PC

Pandit Nehru, in his welcome speech, expressed the hope that this visit would pave the way for closer relations between the two nations. In a lighter vein, Pandit Nehru recalled that when Prime Minister Cyrankiewicz had landed in India *en route* to Burma on March 17, a week back, he had told him that it was very hot in Delhi and later confided that "Rangoon and Cambodia" were "hotter." Referring to this incident, Prime Minister Nehru told the Polish Prime Minister, "You have [now] a greater appreciation of the climate of Delhi."[11]

A visibly pleased Polish Prime Minister in his reply, expressed his delight at the welcome he was accorded. He said, "I thank you very much for your magnificent reception to me and to the delegation accompanying me. We hope that during our visit we will be able to see and learn of your great achievements."[12]

After the reception at the airport, the Polish Prime Minister and his wife, accompanied by the Indian Prime Minister and Indira Gandhi, drove to Rashtrapati Bhavan in an open black Cadillac through the city that was festooned to welcome the Polish leader.[13] On their arrival at Rashtrapati Bhavan, the Prime Minister and his delegation were welcomed by officers of the President's Secretariat and escorted to their respective suites/rooms.

Prime Minister Cyrankiewicz and his wife, Nina Cyrankiewicz stayed in the Dwarka Suite. It was unlike most Heads of States/Heads of

Room Allocation Plan.

Governments who normally preferred to stay in the Dwarka Suite while their spouses occupied the neighbouring Nalanda Suite. Nine members of the delegation were accommodated in the Guest Wing of Rashtrapati Bhavan. They included Karol Kuryluk, Minister of Culture and Art, who stayed in the Nalanda Suite and Eugeniusz Stawinski, Minister of Small Scale Industry, who stayed in the Tagore Suite. The rest of the delegation was accommodated in Hyderabad House.

Rashtrapati Bhavan had made all the necessary arrangements for the visit. As was the practice, the Rashtrapati Bhavan Post Office was instructed to be kept open for extended hours, to ensure that the Polish delegation could make use of the facilities as and when required. Elaborate security arrangements for the visiting delegation were made by the Military Secretary to the President (MSP), Major General Yadhunath Singh. Circulars were issued barring peeping from office windows and the number of personnel in front of the South Wing was reduced to a minimum.[14]

According to the programme that was drawn up, Prime Minister Cyrankiewicz was scheduled to meet Pandit Nehru on the day of his arrival at 6.30 pm. The meeting was, however, postponed to the next day. The Prime Minister instead preferred to stay indoors for the rest of that evening and ended the day with a quiet dinner at 8.30 pm *en suite*.

The next day began early. After breakfast, Prime Minister Cyrankiewicz left Rashtrapati Bhavan at 9.00 am for *Rajghat*, where he paid respects at Mahatma Gandhi's *samadhi*. After laying a wreath at the memorial, Prime Minister Cyrankiewicz took an unplanned detour to Teen Murti Bhavan, Prime Minister Nehru's residence. It was an informal visit, and the Indian Prime Minister was delighted to receive Prime Minister Cyrankiewicz, who got an opportunity to see the Bhavan's beautifully landscaped garden and the Indian Prime Minister's pet white tiger cubs, *Raja* and *Rani*.[15]

After the visit to Teen Murti Bhavan, Prime Minister Cyrankiewicz travelled the short distance to 2, King Edward Road (now Maulana Azad Road), where he met Vice President Dr Radhakrishnan. The meeting lasted an hour, after which the Polish Prime Minister spent rest of the morning, visiting the National Physical Laboratory and the Indian Agricultural Research Institute. He returned to Rashtrapati Bhavan and after lunch and a rest, attended a reception hosted by the Indo-Polish Cultural Association at 5.00 pm.[16]

The reception was held in the dining hall of Hotel Janpath, a short distance from Rashtrapati Bhavan. The Prime Minister of India, members of the diplomatic corps, Government officials and Members of the Association were present on the occasion. *The Hindustan Times Weekly* reported Prime Minister Cyrankiewicz asserting "that friendship was not an abstract notion and it grew out of mutual understanding and goodwill."[17]

By 6.00 pm, Prime Minister Cyrankiewicz was on the move again, this time travelling with his wife and Prime Minister Nehru to the

(L-R): Prime Minister Nehru (second), Madame Nina Cyrankiewicz, President Dr Prasad and Prime Minister Józef Cyrankiewicz at Rashtrapati Bhavan in March 1957. Credit: PC

Red Fort for a Civic Reception organised by the Delhi Municipal Committee. Thousands of people had lined the route and they cheered the leaders as the motorcade of the Polish leader passed. The entire route from Janpath to the ramparts of the Red Fort was tastefully and colourfully decorated. The Mughal fort too was illuminated with colourful lights.

At the reception, Prime Minister Cyrankiewicz addressed the 10,000-strong gathering in Polish, which was simultaneously translated into English. In the speech, he drew parallels between the reception that Prime Minister Nehru had received when he visited Warsaw in June 1955, and his visit to India. He said that in India, he and his delegation felt "the same warmth, enthusiasm and sympathy."[18] The reception too had its light moments. Perhaps, in a spontaneous exhibition of Indian geniality, during the function, an over-enthusiastic member of the Municipal Committee emerged unannounced and unexpectedly presented Prime Minister Cyrankiewicz with a long garland and a carpet which an amused Polish Prime Minister was seen sportingly carrying under his arm.[19]

Later that evening, Prime Minister Nehru hosted a State Banquet at 8.30 pm, in honour of the Polish Prime Minister. This was hosted

in the Banquet Hall of Rashtrapati Bhavan. The Vice President of India, Cabinet Ministers and members of the diplomatic corps were among the 120 invitees that attended the function.[20]

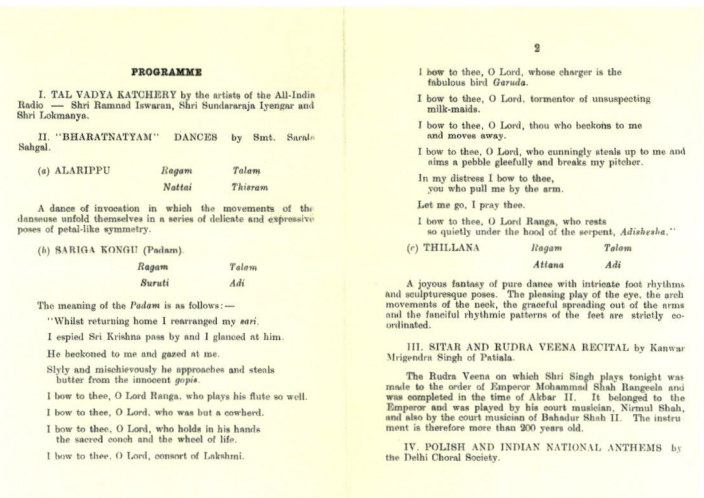

"Programme" of the Dance and Music Recital in honour of Prime Minister Cyrankiewicz

Prime Minister Nehru arrived at Rashtrapati Bhavan 15 minutes in advance and was conducted to the Dwarka Suite from where he escorted the Polish Premier and his wife to the Ashok Hall. Guests, who had arrived at the South Entrance of the West Subway via the South Court, were guided to the Yellow Drawing Room where they congregated. They were later conducted to the Ashok Hall after the two Prime Ministers had reached there. The national anthems of both countries were played and thereafter, the guests were formally introduced to the Prime Ministers. Following the introductions, the dignitaries were escorted to the Banquet Hall, where they enjoyed an elaborately laid out fare. After the banquet, the distinguished guests were treated to a programme of traditional Indian classical dance and music.

The recital began with the rendition of classical music by the artistes of All India Radio. This was followed by a classical *Bharatnatyam* dance, which focussed on the *Raas* associated with Krishna and was performed by danseuse Sarala Sahgal. Next were the *rudra veena* and *sitar* performances which particularly delighted the guests. The former was of particular significance as it was played by maestro Kanwar Mrigendra Singh of Patiala on a 200-year-old instrument that once belonged to Emperor Akbar II, Bahadur Shah Zafar's father, who had ruled in India in the early 19th century. The last to perform was the Delhi Choral Society which sang the Polish and Indian national anthems, much to the delight of the guests.[21]

The morning of March 26 was deliberatively kept flexible to give the Prime Minister Cyrankiewicz the choice to hold talks or go for sightseeing. He chose the former and had two-hour discussions with the Indian Prime Minister on national and international issues. The subjects discussed included the strengthening of bilateral relations and issues related to the three-nation armistice supervision group in Indochina, in which India, Poland and Canada were represented.[22]

At 12.30 pm, Prime Minister Cyrankiewicz called on the President of India, Dr Rajendra Prasad at Rashtrapati Bhavan and later had lunch with him. One of the main highlights of the visit was reserved for the evening—it was the address of the Polish Prime Minister to the Members of Parliament (MPs) in the Central Hall of Sansad Bhavan. On his arrival at the venue, he was warmly received by the Chairman of the Rajya Sabha, Dr Radhakrishnan. Thereafter, Prime Minister Cyrankiewicz and his wife were escorted to the President's Box to watch the proceedings of the House. As soon as they reached the special enclosure, they were greeted by loud cheers from the well of the House. Later, the Polish Prime Minister addressed the MPs. Speaking in his deep baritone voice, he explained his country's new foreign policy vector. He said that Poland had now "fully returned to the ideas of sovereignty, democracy and socialism."[23] Elaborating on this aspect, he said that he would strive for solidarity with other socialist nations on the basis of "full independence, equality of partners and non-interference in internal affairs."[24]

At 6.30 pm, Prime Minister Cyrankiewicz addressed the Indian Council of World Affairs at Sapru House. He spoke at great length to an audience of nearly 900 people and justified Poland's membership in the Warsaw Pact asserting that it was to neutralise what he said were the threats it faced from West Germany. Later that evening, the visiting Prime Minister hosted a banquet at the Ashoka Hotel for his Indian hosts. Nearly two hundred guests attended the function and they included the Vice President of India, Prime Minister, MPs, members of the diplomatic corps and other prominent citizens. Special security arrangements were made at the venue and along the routes demarcated for the motorcades. An armed reserve was discreetly deployed at the hotel to cater to any contingency.[25]

On the morning of March 27, which was his last day in Delhi, Prime Minister Cyrankiewicz and Prime Minister Nehru issued a joint statement calling on the 'big powers' to give up nuclear and thermo-nuclear testing. The communiqué also referred to the Indo-Polish Cultural Agreement signed on the same day, which provided for the countries to cooperate in the field of education, science and culture. Both Prime Ministers also reaffirmed their faith in the Panchsheel Agreement and declared that it was the ideal method to resolve disputes.[26]

Thereafter, Prime Minister Cyrankiewicz left Delhi for his tour of select cities of the country. Prior to his departure, the Polish Prime Minister recorded an address to the nation at the All India Radio studio. He spoke for 45-minutes in Polish and the speech was translated into Hindi. In his address, the Prime Minister Cyrankiewicz called for strengthening the bonds of friendship between the two countries as both nations stood for the "cause of liberty and progress."[27] He marvelled at the enthusiasm with which development was being pursued in India, and drew parallels with Poland's own struggle with the past and its efforts to break free from it and forge a brighter future. These common ideals, he said, were enough to "bridge the differences of climate and culture as well as the discrepancy between your great country of 400 million inhabitants and the small Polish nation."[28]

After the recording, at 12 noon, Prime Minister Cyrankiewicz returned to Rashtrapati Bhavan for his last meal 'under the dome', which he had with his wife in the Dwarka Suite. The Polish Prime Minister and his delegation then departed for New Delhi Railway Station from where a special train took the visiting dignitaries to Sonepat. Prime Minister Nehru and other officials saw the leader off from the ceremonial platform of the railway station. At Sonepat, the visiting Prime Minister and his entourage visited various community development projects.[29]

Thereafter, Prime Minister Cyrankiewicz travelled to Nangal, Agra, Bangalore, Bombay and arrived in Calcutta on April 1, 1957. The Polish Ambassador to India, Jerzy Grudzinski and India's Ambassador to Moscow and Poland, KPS Menon, accompanied the Prime Minister on his tour.

In the early hours of April 3, Prime Minister Cyrankiewicz and his wife drove to Dum Dum Airport in an open car. Crowds, which had gathered on the streets, cheered the leader who acknowledged their greetings by standing up and waving as the motorcade passed by.

At the airport, the Polish Prime Minister inspected a Guard of Honour presented by a detachment of the Jammu and Kashmir Battalion.[30] He was thereafter given a warm send–off by the Indian Ambassador to Poland, Ministers of West Bengal and other dignitaries. Prime Minster Cyrankiewicz and his entourage left for Hanoi in a Special Indian Airlines aircraft.

Józef Cyrankiewicz remained Prime Minister until 1970. He held the ceremonial post of the President of his country for the next two years and later also served as Chairman of the Polish Peace Committee from 1973 to 1986. He died on January 20, 1989. He was 77. Nina Andrycz Cyrankiewicz died on January 31, 2014. She was 101.

Notes

[1] From the various public sources, it is understood that Cyrankiewicz had visited India in 1957 & 1960. Only the 1957 visit has been covered as the documents relating to other visits were not traceable.

[2] Polish Premier Arrives In Delhi on Way To Burma," *The Times of India* (New Delhi), March 18, 1957, p. 1.

[3] "100th Anniversary of the Birth of Joseph Cyrankiewicz–"eternal premiere" of" PRL," April 23, 2011, accessed May 15, 2015, http://naukawpolsce.pap.pl/aktualnosci/news,381531,100-rocznica-urodzin-jozefa-cyrankiewicza---wiecznego-premiera-prl-u.html.

[4] Harris M. Lentz, *Heads of States and Governments: A Worldwide Encyclopaedia of Over 2,300 Leaders, 1945 through 1992* (London: Fitzroy Dearborn Publishers, 1995), p. 644.

[5] Andrzej Krajewski, "Joseph Cyrankiewicz, or how to end the idealists," Newsweek, May 3, 2011, accessed May 15, 2015, http://historia.newsweek.pl/jozef-cyrankiewicz--czyli-jak-koncza-idealisci,75928,1,1.html.

[6] Ibid.

[7] "Polish Premier in Delhi," *The Hindustan Times* (New Delhi), March 25, 1957, p. 7.

[8] "Polish Premier in Delhi," *The Hindu* (New Delhi), March 25, 1957, p. 5.

[9] "Poland's Premier in Delhi," *The Times of India* (New Delhi), March 25, 1957, p. 1.

[10] "Polish Premier in Delhi," *The Hindu*, p. 5.

[11] "Polish Premier in Delhi," *The Hindustan Times*, p. 7.

[12] "Polish Premier in Delhi," *The Hindu*, p. 5.

[13] Records, President's Secretariat, File No. 1(24)-Pt I/56

[14] Ibid.

[15] "Bonds of Friendship with India Stressed," *The Hindustan Times Weekly* (New Delhi), March 26, 1957, p. 12.

[16] Ibid.

[17] Ibid.

[18] Ibid.

[19] Ibid., p. 1.

[20] Ibid., p. 12.

[21] Records, President's Secretariat, File No. 1(24)-Pt I/56

[22] "Polish Premier in New Delhi," *The New York Times*, March 25, 1957, p. 6.

[23] "New Political Trend in Poland Explained," *The Hindustan Times* (New Delhi), March 27, 1957, p. 1.

[24] Ibid.

[25] Records, President's Secretariat, File No. 1(24)-Pt I/56

[26] "Nehru–Cyrankiewicz Statement," *The Hindustan Times* (New Delhi), March 28, 1957, p. 1.

[27] "Indo-Polish Friendship," *The Hindustan Times* (New Delhi), March 20, 1957, p. 5.

[28] Ibid.

[29] "Nehru–Cyrankiewicz Statement," p. 1.

[30] "Ensuring Peace in World," *The Times of India* (New Delhi), April 4, 1957, p. 11.

In the winter of 1956, India welcomed Lord (Clement Richard) and Lady (Violet) Attlee as State Guests, though the former was neither a Head of State nor a Head of Government. He was, however, a special guest. He was the former Prime Minister of Britain who had "presided over the decolonisation of India, Pakistan, Burma, Ceylon and Jordan, and saw the creation of the State of Israel upon Britain's withdrawal from Palestine."[1] Lord and Lady Attlee were on a three-week visit from October 11 to November 3, 1956, at the invitation of the Indian Prime Minister, Pandit Jawaharlal Nehru.

This was not Lord Attlee's first visit to India. Most notable amongst them were his previous visits were those in 1928 and 1929, as a member of the Simon Commission.

Visit of
Earl Clement Richard Attlee

October 11 to November 3, 1956

Clement Attlee, son of a solicitor, was born on January 3, 1883 in the County of Surrey. He studied at the prestigious University of Oxford and later trained as a lawyer. For a brief time, Attlee worked at a charitable club at London's East End in 1906, which gave him a first-hand experience of the poverty and deprivation that plagued the slum children of the area. In what would seem like a paradigm shift, this experience radically changed Attlee's political views from that of a conservative to a socialist.[2] Referring to this radical transformation, the magazine, Time wrote that Attlee was a "staunch Tory until he visited a London slum. The squalor turned the young lawyer into a social worker and socialist."[3] The transformation was striking. As his future polices would bear testimony, "his service and residence in the East End formed his socialist and political base."[4] In the year 1908, he joined the Independent Labour Party and rose quickly through the ranks evidencing his political dexterity.

When the First World War broke out, he joined the military as a Captain and was later promoted to the rank of Major. These few years in the military earned Attlee the reputation of being an effective and efficient leader.[5] After the War, he successfully contested for the post of Mayor of Stepney in 1919. Sixteen years on, he was appointed Leader of the Independent Labour Party in 1935 and held the position for the next two decades. From 1942 to 1945, Attlee served as Deputy Prime Minister in Churchill's Cabinet before becoming Prime Minister on July 26, 1945 and served in that capacity for a little over six years until 1951, when the Labour Party was defeated.

On October 11, 1956, Lord and Lady Attlee arrived at Santa Cruz Airport in Bombay, by BOAC Flight 774, on what can be described as a pleasure trip. The Chief Minister of Bombay, Morarji Desai, received them. The other dignitaries who welcomed the visiting guests included the Mayor of Bombay, SA Kader; Sheriff Dalip Singh; UK's Deputy High Commissioner in Bombay, HA Twist and Chief

Secretary of Maharashtra, MD Bhansali.[6] Speaking to reporters at the airport, Lord Attlee recalled his yesteryears when he had visited Bombay, and smilingly told the press, "I am a small man now."[7]

After the ceremonies at the airport, Lord and Lady Attlee drove to Raj Bhavan where they stayed as guests of the Governor of Bombay.[8] In the evening, a Civic Reception was hosted at the Town Hall by the Bombay Municipal Corporation in honour of Lord and Lady Attlee. The Governor, Chief Minister, Mayor, Chief Justice of Bombay, Speaker of the Bombay Legislative Assembly, Ministers of the State Government, Municipal Councillors, Members of the Consular Corps, Members of the Legislative Assembly and prominent businessmen were present at the occasion.[9]

At the reception, Salebhoy Abdul Kader, Mayor of Bombay, introduced Attlee as "the Prime Minister of the United Kingdom, who was instrumental in ushering in Indian independence."[10] In his welcome address, he described the visiting guest as "an able statesman, a great Parliamentarian and, above all, a gentleman and a friend of our country, who has left on his work the imprint of his personality, integrity of character and a high sense of justice."[11]

Replying to the Mayor's address, Lord Attlee, in his first public address of this visit, called India, a "protagonist of democracy and good government in Asia" and went on to add that Bombay was "a meeting place of the East and the West."[12] At the reception, Lord Attlee was presented with the welcome address in a sandalwood casket etched with an ivory inlaid pattern, as a token of remembrance of the event.

Later that evening, the Governor of Bombay hosted a welcome dinner at Raj Bhavan in honour of the visiting dignitary. Invitees on the occasion included the Chief Minister of Bombay, Chief Justice of Bombay, Governor of Assam, and representatives of the Commonwealth countries, amongst others.[13]

Next morning, on October 12, Lord Attlee and his wife began their "personal" tour of India. Their first stop was Jamnagar, a city on the western coast of Gujarat. The *Rajpramukh*[14] of Saurashtra, the Jam Saheb of Nawanagar and the Chief Minister of Saurashtra, Rasiklal Parikh received them. Lord and Lady Attlee "visited the Research Institute, Juvan Shivanji Library and the Jain temple."[15] A Civic Reception was also held in their honour and was presided over by the *Rajpramukh* of Saurashtra.

After travelling to Rajkot from Jamnagar, the couple were back in Bombay on the evening of October 13. The next day, Lord and Lady Attlee visited the famous Aarey Milk Colony, which was established in 1949 as a pioneer project to process milk for Bombay. Lord Attlee was evidently impressed by the project and he said that it "represented an outstanding example of foresight and imagination."[16] Before leaving the Colony's premises, the couple planted an almond tree in the garden. Later in the day, the Bombay branch of United Kingdom Citizens Association held a reception in honour of the distinguished guests.

That evening, the Press Guild of India organised a dinner in honour of Lord and Lady Attlee at the Taj Mahal Hotel. During this event, Lord Attlee congratulated India on having a "strong, independent and vigorous press full of variety."[17] He further expressed the hope that Indian newspapers would maintain this feature and not develop a monotonous tendency like the newspapers in the UK. Commenting on the need for a lively press, Lord Attlee added that it would "keep politicians alert, active and alive to their duty."[18] This event ended Attlee's stay in Bombay. The next day, at a quarter past eight in the morning, Lord and Lady Attlee emplaned for Madras.

The Attlees spent October 15-19, rediscovering Madras. The city reminded Attlee of the demonstrations that were held against the Simon Commission in the late 1920s. Addressing a civic meeting in Madras, in the presence of the city's Mayor, Lord Attlee said that he was "happy to make friends with those who waved black flags against him years ago."[19]

Lord Attlee's notable engagements in Madras included attending a meeting of the Rotary Club in the city and a visit to Madras University on October 18. Addressing the meeting at the Rotary Club, Attlee spoke about the Indian Industry and said, "it seems to me you have got the right kind of balance – balance between heavy and light industries, between industry and agriculture, between industry and social service and between production and spending."[20] The same day, the University had organised a special convocation to honour Lord Attlee, awarding him the Honorary Degree of Doctor of Laws. Speaking on the occasion, Attlee remarked that a fraternity existed amidst the universities of the world, and that this fraternity was one of the "strongest bulwarks of peace."[21]

On October 20, Lord and Lady Attlee landed in Calcutta, where they stayed for a day. On their arrival, they had a meeting with the Chief Minister of West Bengal, Dr BC Roy, after which the couple went sightseeing. They also visited a refugee women's co-operative home, *Udaya Villa*, in Kamarhatty where the handicrafts impressed them so greatly that they signed the Guest Book stating: "There is much variety in the designs and the work seems to us to be a very high standard."[22]

In Calcutta, Lord Attlee met the Indian Prime Minister, Pandit Nehru on October 21. The venue of the meeting was Raj Bhavan and it lasted for about half-an-hour.[23] Lord Attlee had forgotten his glasses in the VIP room at Vishakhapatnam airport. They were, later, flown to him in Calcutta and were restored towards the end of his meeting with Pandit Nehru.

Lord Attlee's next stop was India's most populous State, Uttar Pradesh (UP). Travelling in an Indian Airlines Corporation (IAC) plane, Lord and Lady Attlee arrived at Amausi Airport in Uttar Pradesh. The Governor of the State, KM Munshi and his wife Lilavati warmly received them. Also present at the airport were the Chief Minister of UP, Dr Sampurnan and the State Legislative Assembly's leader of Opposition, Genda Singh.[24]

The couple stayed at Government House during their two-day visit and witnessed the proceedings in both Houses of the Uttar Pradesh Legislature. Lord Attlee also addressed the UP Legislature, conveying the greetings of the Commonwealth Parliamentary Association to the legislators. He was in praise of India's contributions to maintaining world peace. His speech also highlighted the importance of the opposition in a democratic nation and asserted that it had the huge responsibility of "constructive criticism."[25]

After spending two days in UP, the couple travelled to the capital city of Delhi. The IAC plane carrying the distinguished guests landed at Safdarjung Airport at 4.10 on the evening of October 23, 1956.[26] In a break with protocol, Indian Prime Minister Nehru was at the airport to receive Lord Attlee and his wife. Others present at the airport were the Indian Ambassador to the United Nations,

VK Krishna Menon; Secretary-General for External Affairs, Raghavan Pillai; Commonwealth Secretary, MJ Desai and the Polish Ambassador to India, Jerzy Grudzinski, along with other diplomatic officers from Britain, Ceylon and Canada.

Appreciating the gesture, Lord Attlee told the media that the people of India had been extremely warm and welcoming all along the tour.[27] After the reception at the airport, Lord and Lady Attlee drove to Rashtrapati Bhavan in a Cadillac, while the Deputy Military Secretary to the President (DMSP) followed them in a DeSoto.[28] The large crowd that had gathered outside the airport to catch a glimpse of the visiting guests enthusiastically cheered Lord and Lady Attlee.

On arrival at Rashtrapati Bhavan, the couple were warmly received by the *aide-de-camp* (ADC) to the President and welcomed with all

(L-R): Prime Minister Nehru receiving Lord and Lady Attlee at Palam Airport, New Delhi, in October 1956. Credit: PD

ceremonial tradition. They stayed in the resplendent Dwarka Suite. President Dr Rajendra Prasad was away on a four–day visit to Nepal when the foreign visitors arrived and consequently, they could call on the Indian Head of State only after he returned on October 25.

It was, however, suggested by the Deputy Chief of Protocol, Commander CJ Munsiff that Lord and Lady Attlee could call on the President on the evening of October 23, subject to his convenience. However, the DMSP Lieutenant Colonel Ghufran informed Commander Munsiff that the President was on tour, and hence the meeting was rescheduled and fixed for 12.30 pm on October 25.

At a quarter past six in the evening, Lord Attlee called on the Prime Minister, and later had dinner at Rashtrapati Bhavan. The next day, October 24, Lord Attlee visited All India Radio (AIR) at 10.00 am, where he recorded a message that was broadcast that night. In his broadcast, Lord Attlee thanked the Government and people of India for the warm welcome he had received. He was also impressed by India's pluralistic society and said that the nation had "dynamic governments and they can make bold experiments."[29] He illustrated by citing the examples of the Milk-Farm in Bombay, the railway carriage works he had seen in Madras the reforms that were being carried out in Indian villages and more. He also congratulated Prime Minister Nehru on the leadership he was providing the nation and praised the free and fair General Elections in India.[30]

At AIR, the Director General gifted Lord Attlee with a souvenir comprising "an album of records of Mahatma Gandhi's prayer meeting speeches,"[31] after which Lord Attlee proceeded to a lunch held in his honour by the High Commissioner of Ceylon. In the evening, around 6.30, Lord Attlee addressed the Indian Council of World Affairs and ended the day after dinner with Prime Minister Nehru.

The next morning was kept free for the couple to go sightseeing. Later, in the afternoon at 12.30, Lord Attlee called on President Dr Prasad. Following this informal 20-minute meeting, the dignitaries had lunch together. Pandit Nehru and some Union Cabinet Members also attended the lunch.[32] The next day, October 26, at 8.40 am, the Attlees left for the Pink City of India, Jaipur, where the Maharaja of Jaipur held a grand reception for the couple.

Lord Attlee also attended a United Nations Day meeting that day where he was the Chief Guest. On this occasion, he raised concerns over the use of nuclear weapons. Talking about their repercussions, he said, "our civilisation may go down as civilisations have gone down in the past."[33]

Lord and Lady Attlee returned to Delhi from Jaipur by car on October 27. The distinguished guests then went to Kashmir, termed as 'paradise on earth' by the Mughals, where they spent the next three days. It was autumn in Kashmir. It was perhaps the best time to be in the state and the couple enjoyed the cool Himalayan climate and the splendid vistas.

The couple, thereafter, proceeded to Chandigarh, Nangal and Agra before heading back to Delhi on November 2. Lord and Lady Attlee left for Karachi on November 3, 1956. IAC Flight 441, carrying the couple left Safdarjung Airport at 9.15 am, bringing to a close, their three-week holiday in India.

Lord Attlee died on October 8, 1967. He was 84. Lady Attlee had passed away three years earlier, on June 7, 1964. She was 68.

Lord and Lady Atlee with Prime Minister Nehru (Centre) at Rashtrapati Bhavan in October 1956. Credit: PD

(R-L): Lord and Lady Atlee with Union Minister Krishna Menon and USSR Ambassador Menshikov (shaking hands) at Rashtrapati Bhavan in October 1956. Credit: PD

Notes

[1] Jak Brown, "Past Prime Ministers: Clement Attlee Labour 1945–1951," accessed on May 3, 2015, https://www.gov.uk/government/history/past-prime-ministers/clement-attlee.

[2] Zoe Dare Hall, "Clement Attlee: Veteran of Gallipoli who went on to become Prime Minister," The Telegraph, February 1, 2014, accessed May 3, 2015, http://www.telegraph.co.uk/history/world-war-one/inside-firsta-world-war/part-six/10608029/clement-attlee-gallipoli.html.

[3] "World: The Egalitarian Example," *Time*, October 20, 1967, accessed May 3, 2015 http://content.time.com/time/subscriber/article/0,33009,902111,00.html.

[4] Jerry Hardman Brookshire, Clement Atlee (Manchester University Press, 1995), p. 35.

[5] Brown, "Past Prime Ministers"

[6] "Reception to Attlees," *The Times of India* (New Delhi), October 12, 1956, p. 9.

[7] Ibid.

[8] "Bombay Tribute to Lord Attlee," *The Times* (London), October 12, 1956, p. 9.

[9] "Protagonist of Democracy," *The Times of India* (New Delhi), October 12, 1956, p. 9.

[10] Ibid.

[11] Ibid.

[12] Ibid., p. 1.

[13] "Party at Raj Bhavan," *The Times of India* (New Delhi), October 12, 1956, p. 9.

[14] *Rajpramukhs* were appointed Governors of certain provinces and states of India from 1947 until 1956.

[15] "Reception to Earl Attlee," *The Times of India* (New Delhi), October 13, 1956, p. 7.

[16] "Milk Colony Praised," *The Times of India* (New Delhi), October 15, 1956, p. 3.

[17] "High Standard of Indian papers," *The Times of India* (New Delhi), October 15, 1956, p. 3.

[18] Ibid.

[19] "Madras Welcome to Earl Attlee," *The Times of India* (New Delhi), October 16, 1956, p. 3.

[20] "India's Plan, Well Balanced," *The Times of India* (New Delhi), October 20, 1956 p. 6.

[21] "Varsities' Role stressed," *The Times of India* (New Delhi), October 20, 1956 p. 6.

[22] "Lord Attlee at Refugee Women's Home," *Hindusthan Standard* (New Delhi), October 23, 1956, p. 9.

[23] "Nehru's Discussion with Attlee," *Hindusthan Standard* (New Delhi), October 23, 1956, p. 9.

[24] "Contribution to World Peace," *The Times of India* (New Delhi), October 23, 1956, p. 5.

[25] Ibid.

[26] Records, President's Secretariat, Rashtrapati Bhavan, File No. 258.

[27] "Earl Attlee in Delhi," *The Hindu* (New Delhi), October 24, 1956 p

[28] Records, President's Secretariat, File No. 258.

[29] "A Nation on the Move," *The Hindu* (New Delhi), October 25, 1956, p. 4.

[30] Ibid.

[31] Ibid.

[32] "Attlees Call on President," *Hindusthan Standard* (New Delhi), October 27, 1956, p. 3.

[33] "Need to control Hydrogen Bomb stressed," *The Times of India* (New Delhi), October 28, 1956, p. 10.

The second half of 1960 and particularly its last months were unusually busy for the staff of Rashtrapati Bhavan. Queen Elizabeth II and Prince Philip, The Duke of Edinburgh, were to arrive in the first month of the following year and time seemed too short to complete all the preparations to give the royal couple a befitting welcome.

The visit had not taken long to finalise. In May 1960, on the side-lines of the Commonwealth Prime Ministers' Conference, held in London, Pandit Nehru discussed the possibility of the visit with the Queen. No sooner had he returned from the London conference and conferred with President Dr Rajendra Prasad, than a formal invitation was sent to the Queen on May 31. The invitation declared that for the President, the Government and the people of India, it "will be a privilege to welcome"[1] Her Royal Majesty and His Royal Highness to India.

The reply did not take long to arrive. By early June, the Queen and her husband had accepted the invitation, sending Delhi into a tizzy on the preparations to be made to receive, for the first time in independent India, the monarch of a nation that had ruled the country for over 200 years. It was as if Britain's erstwhile subjects did not know how to welcome the royals. The last royal visit to India had been that of Queen Elizabeth II's grandparents, King George V and Queen Mary, who had held the grand Delhi Durbar in 1911 to proclaim themselves Emperor and Empress of India. The memories of that visit were, however, too distant to offer any relevant clues to organise a visit almost five decades later.

January 21 to March 2, 1961
November 17–26, 1983
October 12–17, 1997

Visit of

H.M. Queen Elizabeth II &
H.R.H. Prince Philip, Duke of Edinburgh

The Queen's visit was important for several reasons. The visit was a grand symbolic gesture. While in India, she was expected to discuss the friendly ties between the two countries, focussing on the history they shared and how relations could be further strengthened. She is the most significant monarch amongst her contemporaries and is also the Head of the Commonwealth.

'Lilibet', as she was called within the family, was born on April 21, 1926, to the Duke and Duchess of York, who later became King George VI and Queen Elizabeth. Little Lilibet was no ordinary child. At a very young age itself, she exhibited signs of suitability for her future role. As a biographer of the Queen revealed, Winston Churchill, the Britishwartime Prime Minister had formed a similar opinion of her. When the Prime Minister reportedly met the two-year-old, he sensed "an air of authority and reflectiveness astonishing in an infant."[2] However, before wielding her majestic authority as Queen of England, she would be sequestered within the royal confines for most of her adolescent life. She was home-tutored, and unlike her younger sister Margaret, had little exposure to the outside world.

Facing page:
(L-R): Queen Elizabeth II,
President Dr Prasad and
Prince Philip at Rashtrapati Bhavan in
January 1961. Credit: PC

```
RASHTRAPATI BHAVAN
NEW DELHI

                                    31st May 1960

Your Majesty,

            I am happy to learn from my Prime Minister,
who has just returned from the Commonwealth Prime Ministers'
Meeting, that he has spoken to Your Majesty about the
possibility of your visiting India.  I now have very great
pleasure in extending to Your Majesty and to His Royal
Highness the Duke of Edinburgh a warm and cordial invitation
to pay a visit to India at any suitable time in the coming
winter season.  To me, as well as to the Government and the
people of India, it will be a privilege to welcome Your
Majesty and His Royal Highness in our country, and it is my
earnest hope that you will find it convenient to accept this
invitation.

            I avail myself of this opportunity to express
to Your Majesty and to His Royal Highness the Duke of
Edinburgh my best wishes for your personal welfare as well
as the assurances of my high esteem and constant friendship.

                                    Your good friend,


                                    Rajendra Prasad
                                    PRESIDENT OF INDIA.

Her Majesty Queen Elizabeth II,
      Buckingham Palace,
            LONDON.
```

Invitation from President Dr Prasad to Queen Elizabeth II and Prince Philip.

Princess Elizabeth's quiet family life ended soon after her grandfather, King George V, died in 1936. King Edward VIII, who, before the end of the year, abdicated the throne to marry a twice-divorced American, succeeded him. Thereupon, Princess Elizabeth's father ascended the throne as King George VI. Since then, the blue-eyed Princess was fettered with protocols and precedents, as she was being groomed to be her father's successor. Queen Elizabeth's life has always been one of paradoxes, a pompous display on the outside, and a quiet inside.[3] At the age of 34, when she visited India for the first time, she had "on her own appointed Macmillan as the Prime Minister,"[4] and was experienced in the affairs of state.

The 1961 Visit

The officials at Rashtrapati Bhavan worked feverishly for several months preparing for the visit. Every minute aspect was deliberated in detail and advance action taken to ensure that the Queen felt at home during her stay at Rashtrapati Bhavan, the erstwhile residence of the Viceroys regal enough to house the royals.

Discussions between the Queen's staff and various officers of the Indian Government started early. Several advisories were received by the President's Secretariat on the impending visit. They were detailed and left nothing to conjecture.[5] Virtually everything, from the music she liked to her dislike of armchairs at the dining table, was meticulously listed. And the President's Secretariat acted on each of them.

Her preference of music-*the marching tunes* by Souza and Alfort; operettas and musical theatres by Gilbert and Sullivan and Rogers and Hammerstein; light classical and ballet music by Tchaikovsky[6] was carefully noted by the President's Secretariat. These details were shared with the bands identified for possible deployment during the visit. As the preferences were available in advance, it gave the bands sufficient time to practice the tunes.

The logistical arrangements to be made for the visit, however, tested the ingenuity of the President's Secretariat. The Queen was bringing with her three six-foot high wardrobes that had to be kept standing while being transported.[7] Major Milbank, a Member of the advance party from Buckingham Palace had cautioned that the Queen's wardrobe was "a closely guarded secret."[8] These two instructions precluded the possibility of shifting of the contents of the wardrobes to manageable containers. It was, therefore, a Hobson's choice for the President's staff, and a way had to be found to transport the wardrobes standing. The predicament, however, was that there was neither any such transportation in the ownership of the President of India, nor was there any that he could commandeer, large enough to transport the wardrobes as advised.

The Deputy Chief of Protocol (DCOP), JS Teja approached the civil airlines, Indian Airlines Corporation (IAC) for assistance but they had no solution to offer. As an alternative, Teja then suggested that the Ministry of Defence be approached for such Lorries. That suggestion too could provide no relief as they only had open Lorries. Finally, Lorries were requisitioned and covered with "tarpaulin and canvas cloth," fulfilling the tall order.[9]

No effort was also spared to ensure the flawless handling and identification of the baggage of the royal entourage. A meeting was held by the Ministry of External Affairs (MEA), at the level of the DCOP, and it was decided to use colour coded tags on the luggage transported by "*Royal Britannia*" and "*Support Britannia*" aircraft. The Queen's baggage was attached with "light green" tags and that of the Duke, with "green with a blue corner" markers. The baggage of the Queen's entourage was attached with "Yellow" tags making identification and separation of baggage easy for special handling where required.

The advisory received from Buckingham Palace regarding her food and beverage preferences was, however, more elaborate than others. It informed that the Queen would prefer cooked breakfast and this was specifically noted by the chef and communicated to the cooks.

There was, however, one advisory that was rather perplexing as it informed that the Queen drank dry tea and, that it would be

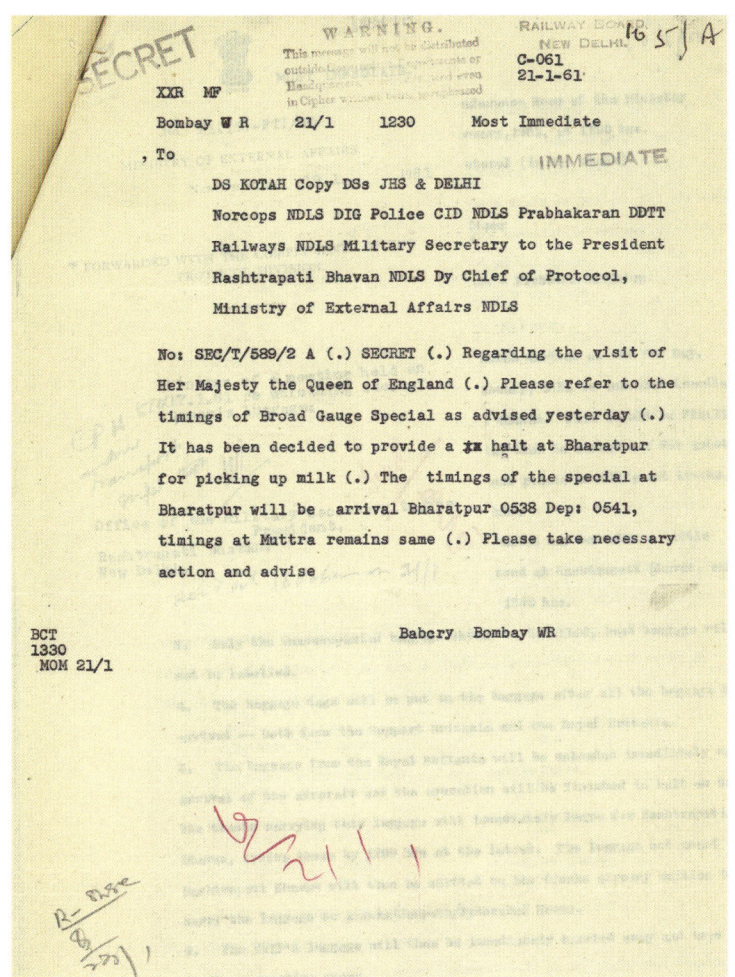

Special arrangements for "picking up" milk for the visit of "Her Majesty the Queen of England."

Proposed Menus for Her Majesty Queen Elizabeth II and Party

21-1-1961 — LUNCH
Mango Cocktail
Baked Prawns - Salad
Chicken Maryland
Potatoes - Cabbage
Pineapple Tutpari
Cheese and Biscuits
Dessert - Coffee
Fruits

BANQUET
Hors D'Oeuvre
Almond Soup
Fish Paupiette - Salad
Roast Goose
Mint Potatoes - Green Peas
Cauliflower
Meringue Basket
Croutes Emerson
Dessert - Coffee

22-1-1961 — BREAKFAST
Cornflakes / Quaker Oats
Kidney Grilled
Eggs to order
Ham - Bacon
Toast-Jam-Marmalade-Honey
Fruits
Tea - Coffee

25-1-1961 — LUNCH
Grape Fruit
Eggs Florentine
Mixed Grill
Potatoes - Cauliflower Salad
Cold Ham - Chicken Salad
Fruit Trifle
Cheese and Biscuits
Dessert - Coffee

DINNER
Cream Nivarnaise
Fish Orly
Tomato Sauce
Roast Spring Chicken
Roast Potatoes - Peas
Chocolate Souffle
Dessert - Coffee

26-1-1961 — LUNCH
Cherry Cocktail
Fish Gratin
Pork Chops
Finger Potatoes - Cabbage
Cold Duck - Mutton Salad
Parfait Praline
Cheese and Biscuits
Dessert - Coffee

27-1-1961 — BREAKFAST
Cornflakes / Quaker Oats
Fish Cakes
Eggs to order - Bacon
Toast-Jam-Marmalade-Honey
Fruits
Tea - Coffee

LUNCH (out)

DINNER
Artichoke Soup
Fish Grilled - Salad
Guinea Fowl Italian
Potatoes - Beans
Cream Diplomat
Dessert - Coffee

28-1-1961 — BREAKFAST
Cornflakes / Quaker Oats
Grilled Sausages
Eggs to order - Bacon
Toast-Jam-Marmalade-Honey
Fruits
Tea - Coffee

LUNCH
Eggs Lorraine
Mutton Casserole
Potatoes-Brinjals Farcie
Gular Kababs
Cold Chicken - Ham Salad
Fruit Ritz
Cheese and Biscuits

"Proposed Menu" for Queen Elizabeth II during her stay at Rashtrapati Bhavan.

---

brought from Buckingham Palace. It was not known why tea had to be sourced from London, when India was one of the largest producers and perhaps, of some of the best quality tea in the world. Though not directly connected with Queen's preference of food and beverages, special request was also received to permit the Queen's page, Bennett and the Duke's valet, Candy to attend on the royals during lunches, though they would not be serving.

With so many advisories on the Queen's food and beverage preferences, it was not easy for Rashtrapati Bhavan to prepare the menus for the visiting dignitary. The British High Commission, however, helped ease the anxiety by sending it a suggestive menu daily. The President's Secretariat also geared up for the occasion and selected the best cook, under whose overall charge and watchful eyes, the food for the royals would be prepared. The choice was not however, difficult. The mantle fell on Safir Hussain, who had honed his culinary skills serving six former Viceroys to India and two culinary experts assisted him.[10]

Besides, the Government of India had taken action on its own to ensure that nothing but the best was served to the Queen.

Attention to detail was so punctilious that food items were sourced from locations where the best was available. Government did not hesitate to deploy its resources for their transportation. The wide reach of the Indian Railways came in handy for the procurement of one such item – fresh milk. The railway authorities issued instructions for the train "Broad Gauge Special" to make a special three-minute halt in Bharatpur, a town situated nearly 200 kilometres south of Delhi, to pick up fresh milk every day during the stay of the royals at Rashtrapati Bhavan.[11]

One of the items contained in the advisory also specifically mentioned that the Queen would only accept bouquet and not garlands and her dislike of armchairs at the table. A request was also received to provide a hot plate and an electric kettle in the breakfast room. The requirement of a heavy and a light ironing board too found place in the communication received from the Buckingham Palace. All these advisories were complied with. One communication also clarified the Duke's full designation as "H.R.H. The Prince Philip Duke of Edinburgh."[12]

The Dwarka Suite, which had been earmarked for the Queen, also got a makeover. It was refurbished to give it the ambience of old

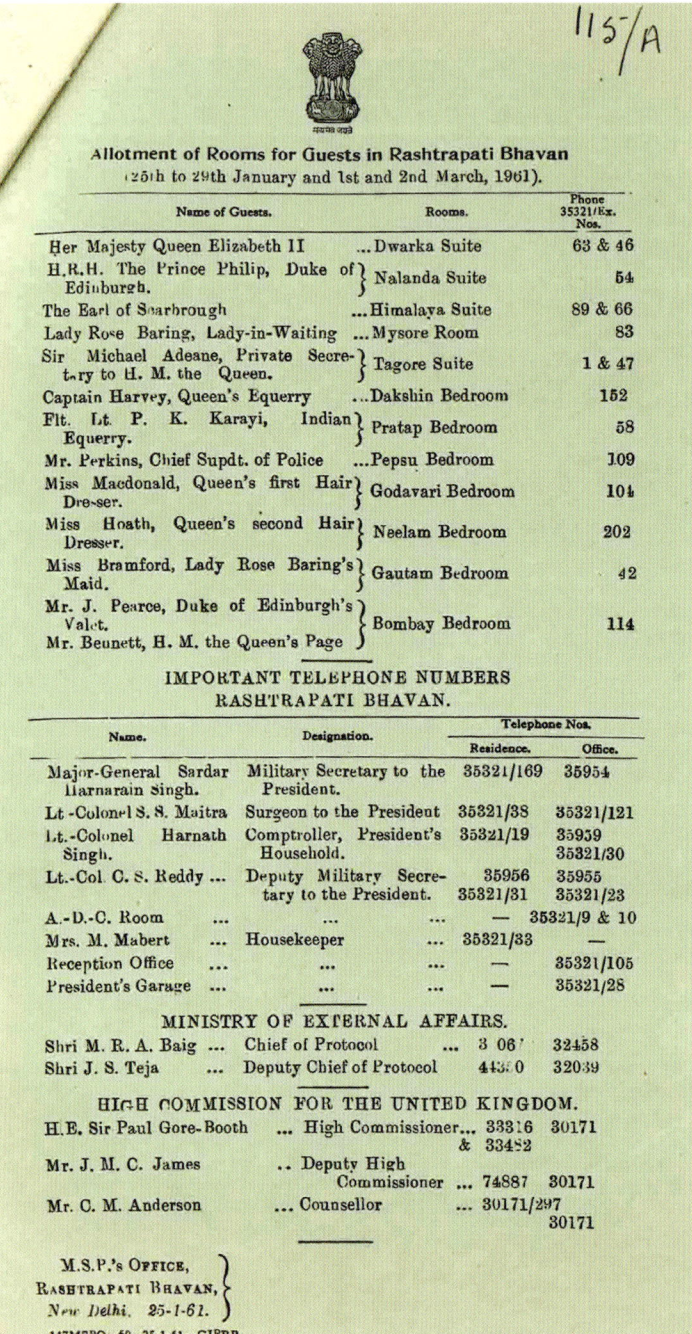

115/A

Allotment of Rooms for Guests in Rashtrapati Bhavan
(25th to 29th January and 1st and 2nd March, 1961).

Name of Guests.	Rooms.	Phone 35321/Ex. Nos.
Her Majesty Queen Elizabeth II	...Dwarka Suite	63 & 46
H.R.H. The Prince Philip, Duke of Edinburgh.	Nalanda Suite	54
The Earl of Scarbrough	...Himalaya Suite	89 & 66
Lady Rose Baring, Lady-in-Waiting	...Mysore Room	83
Sir Michael Adeane, Private Secretary to H. M. the Queen.	Tagore Suite	1 & 47
Captain Harvey, Queen's Equerry	...Dakshin Bedroom	152
Flt. Lt. P. K. Karayi, Indian Equerry.	Pratap Bedroom	58
Mr. Perkins, Chief Supdt. of Police	...Pepsu Bedroom	109
Miss Macdonald, Queen's first Hair Dresser.	Godavari Bedroom	104
Miss Hoath, Queen's second Hair Dresser.	Neelam Bedroom	202
Miss Bramford, Lady Rose Baring's Maid.	Gautam Bedroom	42
Mr. J. Pearce, Duke of Edinburgh's Valet. Mr. Bennett, H. M. the Queen's Page	Bombay Bedroom	114

IMPORTANT TELEPHONE NUMBERS RASHTRAPATI BHAVAN.

Name.	Designation.	Telephone Nos. Residence.	Office.
Major-General Sardar Harnarain Singh.	Military Secretary to the President.	35321/169	35954
Lt.-Colonel S. S. Maitra	Surgeon to the President	35321/38	35321/121
Lt.-Colonel Harnath Singh.	Comptroller, President's Household.	35321/19	35959 35321/30
Lt.-Col. C. S. Reddy ...	Deputy Military Secretary to the President.	35956 35321/31	35955 35321/23
A.-D.-C. Room ...	... ...	—	35321/9 & 10
Mrs. M. Mabert ...	Housekeeper ...	35321/33	—
Reception Office ...	... ...	—	35321/105
President's Garage ...	... ...	—	35321/28

MINISTRY OF EXTERNAL AFFAIRS.

Shri M. R. A. Baig ...	Chief of Protocol ...	3 06?	32458
Shri J. S. Teja ...	Deputy Chief of Protocol	443?0	32039

HIGH COMMISSION FOR THE UNITED KINGDOM.

H.E. Sir Paul Gore-Booth	... High Commissioner...	33316 & 33452	30171
Mr. J. M. C. James	.. Deputy High Commissioner ...	74887	30171
Mr. C. M. Anderson	... Counsellor ...	30171/297	30171

M.S.P.'s Office,
Rashtrapati Bhavan,
New Delhi. 25-1-61.
147MSPO—60—25-1-61—GIPRB.

Room Allocation Plan.

world British aristocracy, said Dooj Prakash, a retired member of the Household Staff. Several items were brought from Government House, Simla, for the purpose. These items included a sofa-set, a bed, carpets and a special chair for the Queen to relax in.[13] A "wireless link" was also installed in the Dwarka Suite to enable the Queen to be in touch with London.

Records of the President's Secretariat also reveal that security arrangements made for the royal couple were unprecedented. Uniformed men were posted near the main gate on both sides of the

Jaipur Column and the precincts of the Forecourt when the couple arrived. This area was also sanitised and kept clear of unauthorised people and onlookers were strictly prohibited from crossing sentry points on the South and North Sunken Roads. A special enquiry officer was assigned on duty from 6.00 am until the Queen and the Duke of Edinburgh retired for the night.

The lawns on the south side of the Guest Wing and on the east and west corners were manned by armed orderlies in plain clothes. Similar arrangements were made near 'sensitive' areas like the spiral steps leading to the ground floor, which were close to the lift for general use near the marble staircase on the ground floor. The Deputy Superintendent of Police, Rashtrapati Bhavan, augmented the surveillance and security measures on the roof and in the basement of Rashtrapati Bhavan.

The announcement of the Queen's visit also revived the nostalgia of those who had served the British royalty in the past. An old *khidmatgar* (butler) called Mohammed Ibrahim Khan from Nasik, a city in the State of Maharashtra, who had served King George V at the 1911 Durbar and over 70 years, wrote to Lieutenant General GW Pike, Vice Chief of the Imperial General Staff. In the letter, he offered his "services for the dining room and going out ceremonies" during Queen Elizabeth's visit to India.[14]

On receipt of this request, Lieutenant General Pike took up the matter with the British High Commissioner who wrote to HRA Baig, Chief of Protocol (COP), to give the *khidmatgar* "some modest employment connected with the Queen's forthcoming visit to India." The High Commissioner had also attached an extract of the letter he had received from Lieutenant General Pike. The extract revealed that the request of Ibrahim Khan was to give him, "a chance to serve the Queen in 'some humble capacity' as he served her grandfather nearly fifty years ago." However, Khan's wishes could not be accommodated as he was too old in age to be assigned specific duties during the Queen's visit.[15]

As the day approached, India went to great lengths to showcase its unrivalled heritage, to extend its much-celebrated Indian hospitality and to demonstrate how important the visit was for the nation. Thousands of Tricolours and Union Jacks were fixed on newly erected poles all along the streets of Delhi. The roads were thoroughly cleaned and electric light bulbs were hung on virtually every tree in the city. The scramble to 'light up' was so frenetic that it led to a scarcity of light bulbs and electrical equipment in the capital.[16]

Such was the enthusiasm of the Indian Government that the President and the Prime Minister frequently surprised officials and workers with site visits to personally supervise the arrangements for the Queen. Prime Minister Nehru is reported to have personally overseen the protocol to be followed when the Queen travelled in the open carriage.[17] Vijaya Lakshmi Pandit, the sister of Prime Minister Nehru, and then the High Commissioner to UK, also took personal interest in the visit. She deputed an Air Force officer to Buckingham Palace to learn its protocol.[18] The President even personally inspected the Dwarka Suite, the only known instance where any President had done so before the arrival of a State Guest. After his inspection, the room was "sealed" for security reasons.[19]

Security arrangements in the city were also made on a mammoth scale. Six thousand policemen were pressed into duty for the big day. Several new roads were also built to facilitate crowd movement. The arrangements were so extensive, far-reaching and elaborate that in seven months Delhi wore a somewhat different look to give the royals "one of the greatest welcomes that India has ever given a visitor."[20]

The excitement associated with the visit infected not only the officialdom but also the private institutions. Many of them gave their employees a free day to join the lakhs of people who were keen to at least get a glimpse of the Queen and the Duke. Some even went further. Delhi Floorings Private Limited, for instance, declared the day of the arrival as a paid holiday to allow its workers to join in the welcome.[21] The eagerness to be in Delhi on the day of the arrival of the Queen stretched the existing transport infrastructure in the city and adjoining areas. To manage the surging demand, Indian Railways ran at least seven special trains to the capital.

On January 21, 1961, Delhi awoke early. It was *Basant Panchami*, the traditional festival that heralds the onset of spring. The Queen was arriving that day, and as the early morning mist quickly yielded to sunshine, it seemed that good weather too would greet the Queen.

Around 11.00 am, the Royal Britannia, a VC-10 aircraft, flying the Queen's new personal flag, a royal blue field bearing the crowned initial "E" set within a ring of stemmed gold roses, touched down at Palam Airport. Queen Elizabeth II wearing "an ice-blue dress and coat of satin gabardine, a matching petal hat and a three row string of pearls,"[22] and her consort, The Prince Philip, Duke of Edinburgh alighted to the booming sound of a 21-gun salute and a rousing welcome by huge cheering crowds.

President Dr Prasad, Prime Minister Nehru, and several other dignitaries greeted the royals on their arrival. The Queen was presented a 150-strong Inter-Services Guard of Honour. The Queen was thereafter introduced to the dignitaries present at the airport as the Sikh Regimental Centre Band played the "*Voice of the Guns*".[23]

In his welcome speech at the airport, President Dr Prasad declared that the centuries of association between India and Britain had left "an abiding influence" on the "minds" of the people and the nation's "institutions." He added that independent India shared with Britain "certain common aims, international goodwill and international peace being, perhaps, the most important of them."[24]

The Queen responded to the Indian President and said, "I am thrilled to be here,"[25] expressing in these five words an innocent excitement conveying her delight abjuring the measured words that reigning monarchs normally utter. This struck an immediate chord with the crowds. She expressed the hope that her visit would demonstrate the respect and friendship that existed between the two countries and among nations of the Commonwealth and said, "To all in India I bring a greeting of goodwill and affection from the British people."[26]

Queen Elizabeth then drove the 13-mile distance to Rashtrapati Bhavan with the President, in a black, convertible six-door Mercedes-Benz customised and imported from Germany for this visit.[27] They were followed by a Cadillac that ferried Prime Minister Nehru and the Duke of Edinburgh. For the better comfort of the guests, four "dunlop cushions" were discretely placed in the luxury cars by an *aide-de-camp* (ADC) before the vehicles left the garage for the airport.[28]

An estimated 1.5 million people eager to catch a glimpse of the youthful monarch packed the ceremonial route. They had come in all conceivable forms of transport that reflected the face of India of the early 1960s. *The New York Times* reported that there were hundreds of wooden carts parked near the airport, and many of the oxen and camels had British flags hung like bibs around their necks.[29] The crowds cheered as the motorcade passed by and the Queen gracefully acknowledged their greetings.

As the motorcade reached Janpath, a 'Welcome' sign written with marigolds and a carpet of flowers greeted the royal couple. When the procession of cars reached Vijay Chowk, The President's Bodyguard (PBG) dressed in their red and black winter uniforms, took over command and the outriders escorting the vehicles branched off. The eagerness to get a closer look at the Queen was

Queen Elizabeth II delivering banquet speech at Rashtrapati Bhavan. Seated opposite is President Dr Prasad and to Queen's right is Prime Minister Nehru. (January 1961). Credit: PC

so insuperable that the crowds broke through the security cordon and surged towards the car. The PBG, mounted on their horses, however, kept the restless crowd at bay and managed to clear the way for the motorcade.[30]

The excitement connected with the visit was, however, of a different nature for the security officials. There were intelligence reports that there could be anti-imperialist demonstrations during the Queen's visit. But, there were none. The exuberance of the people in greeting the Queen all along the ceremonial route doused the apprehensions of such demonstration. As a biographer of the Queen wrote, the country seemed too busy welcoming its guests.[31] *The New York Times* reported that Indians who had once welcomed Queen Elizabeth's grandfather, King George V as their ruler, "hailed Queen Elizabeth II as their friend and equal."[32]

At the Rashtrapati Bhavan too, a special welcome awaited the Queen. It was not the usual reception. The President's grand daughters had flown in specially to give a personal touch to the welcome. When Queen Elizabeth and her consort arrived at Rashtrapati Bhavan, the girls gave them a traditional welcome. They applied vermilion on the foreheads of the royal couple and offered flowers from a silver salver.[33] After this reception, the Queen and the Duke were introduced to the President's family and his Personal Staff who were neatly attired in starched White Patrols. The Personal Staff then escorted the royal couple and their entourage to their accommodation.

The entourage of the Queen, besides the Duke, included 34 other members headed by the Lord Chamberlain and the Earl of Scarborough, Sir Roger Lumley. The Queen had also come with a sizeable contingent of her Personal Staff. It included the Lady of the Bedchamber, two Women of the Bedchamber, the Queen's Private Secretary, Press Secretary, Captain of the Queen's flight, a Medical Officer and the Treasurer to the Duke of Edinburgh's Household.[34]

The Queen stayed in the Dwarka Suite, the most elegant and well-appointed of all the suites in Rashtrapati Bhavan. Prince Philip stayed in the neighbouring Nalanda Suite. The other suites/rooms were earmarked for the visiting dignitaries according to their seniority.

The Queen and her husband began their tour of India with a visit to *Rajghat* at 4.15 pm, where they laid a wreath of 500 white roses on Mahatma Gandhi's *Samadhi* and observed a minute's silence. At the *Rajghat*, the Queen planted a pine sapling between a flowering magnolia and a mango tree that had been planted by President Eisenhower and President Dr Rajendra Prasad respectively.[35] Before the royal couple left the monument, *Rajghat* Samadhi Committee presented books to them. These included five books on Mahatma Gandhi and a model of the Yeravada spinning wheel, named after the jail in Pune where Gandhiji invented the wheel during his internment.[36]

After the visit to the *Rajghat*, at 5.30 pm, a press reception was arranged for the Queen in Rashtrapati Bhavan's Durbar Hall. It was attended by 135 press representatives from various countries.

It lasted one hour and gave the journalists an opportunity to meet the royals. During the reception, the Queen and the Duke "moved among the assembled newspapermen and talked to most of them."[37] The easy manner in which the Queen interacted with the press prompted *The Statesman* to write that the Queen was a "gracious listener and her sense of humour was conspicuous."[38]

Later that evening, President Dr Prasad hosted a State Banquet in honour of the royal guests. It was not like the banquets usually hosted at Rashtrapati Bhavan and entailed many things new. Ithad a distinct class of its own. Virtually everyone, from the President downwards, played a part in its conduct.

The invitation for the banquet too was unique. It was made of specially designed *bhojpatra*[39]. Encased in a "wooden scroll lined with silk inside,"[40] the intricate designs on the card and on the scroll were made by hand by the artists of Rashtrapati Bhavan. In an unusual gesture, the President took it upon himself and delivered the card personally to the royal couple.[41]

The banquet, not unnaturally, attracted the attention of the prominent citizenry of the country,many of whom yearned to be invited for the grand evening. Among the several requests received were those from the *Raja of Kurundwad* and the *Nawab of Rampur*, who asked to be included in the various events that would be attended by the Queen. Several of these requests could not be acceded to as the guest lists for all such events particularly for the banquet, were decided in advance.

The banquet began at 8.30 pm. The Queen was most elegantly attired in a white dress with a train of iridescent lace embroidered with pearls, crystals and diamonds. A ruby and diamond necklace along with a matching bracelet and earrings completed the ensemble. She also chose to wear the 19th century Russian fringe diamond tiara[42] which was presented to Queen Alexandra on her 25th wedding anniversary in 1880 and later passed on to Queen Mary, Queen Elizabeth's grandmother.[43]

The menu was carefully selected and was almost entirely a European fare. The first course was *Hors d'oeuvres*, followed by an *Almond Soup*. The salad was *Fish Paupiette* while the main course comprised the choicest delicacies – *Roast Goose, Mint Potatoes, Green Peas and Cauliflower*. Desserts were a *Meringue Basket* and *Croutes Emerson*.

After the main courses were served, President Dr Prasad delivered his banquet speech. He welcomed the distinguished guests reminding them that the banquet was being held on *Basant Panchami* and highlighted the importance of the ties that linked India with the United Kingdom. He emphasised the strengths of the Commonwealth and said, "the visit of Your Majesty will further strengthen and enrich the friendship" shared by the two countries. He further observed that British influence in India is evident in the "English language, literature" Indian laws etc. and hence Queen Elizabeth would in many ways feel at home.[44] The President concluded his speech by raising a toast "to the health of Her Majesty, Queen Elizabeth Head of the Commonwealth, and that of His Royal Highness, the Duke of Edinburgh."[45]

The toast was followed by the Queen's speech in which she expressed her eagerness to explore India and remarked that President Dr Prasad had done a fine job of leading the country for over 10 years with "dignity and distinction."[46] She added that while she hoped India continued to progress into the future, it should not discard its traditions and legacy which are amongst the best in the world. The Queen acknowledged India's needs and potentialities, and assured it of assistance from Britain and the other Commonwealth countries and said, "I am sure that in combining scientific and technological progress with the ancient Indian values of toleration, compassion and wisdom, India will be an example to the world. May God aid you in your task."[47]

The State Banquet was followed by a dance and music recital specially put together for the distinguished guests. The performances included *Manipur Raas*, a Bengali folk song, a group dance by a team from Tagore's Shantiniketan and a brief *shehnai* recital by the legendary Ustad Bismillah Khan.

The next morning at 10.00, the royal couple attended an hour–long Sunday Mass at the Cathedral Church of Redemption along with the Indian President. The royal couple later departed for Jaipur.

An elegantly dressed Queen made a grand entry into the Pink City seated beside the Maharaja of Jaipur on a bejewelled elephant. The pachyderm was the best and the biggest that could be marshalled and the spectacle was reminiscent of the pomp and extravagance with which emperors welcomed visiting monarchs. Though expressing initial diffidence at riding an elephant that perhaps could not distinguish between a royal and a commoner, the Queen was soon seen smiling from the comfort of her 'high' seat. The procession ended at the inner courtyard, where women of the Jaipur Palace applied a ceremonial *tilak* on the foreheads of their distinguished guests.

The grand show had also frayed some sensitivities. The then Governor of Rajasthan, Gurumukh Nihal Singh, wrote to the Secretary to the Government of India, V Viswanathan, expressing his disappointment over the prominent role that the Maharaja was getting to perform in the affairs connected with the visit of the Queen. He stated that any public ceremonial procession through the streets of the city should have been presided over by the Governor of the State, and not the Maharaja who held no official status.[48]

The royal guests returned to Delhi on January 25 at 9.30 am, arriving by the 'President's Special' train at the Ceremonial platform of the

Queen Elizabeth II and President Dr Prasad arriving in State Coach for Republic Day Parade on 26 January 1961. Credit: PC

New Delhi Railway Station. At 4.00 in the evening of that day, an 'At Home' reception was organised on the Central Lawns of Rashtrapati Bhavan in honour of the Queen and the Duke. It was another grand affair and the rush to be invited for the event proved very challenging for the President's Secretariat. The requests from foreign diplomats to be invited for the At Home were virtually no less. Since the invitee list was unusually large, special arrangements were made for the senior diplomats to arrive for the function to help them avoid the long queues expected at the common entrances to the Mughal Gardens. They were invited as "Special entry guests" and congregated in the Yellow Drawing Room from where they were conducted to the central lawn of the garden.

The event, as expected, proved to be daunting and a nightmare for the security agencies. The guests came for the reception in unprecedented numbers and there were 8000 of them.[49] Even for Rashtrapati Bhavan which is used to a couple of thousands for an At Home functions, the number this time was too huge for comfort. The challenge was to prevent eager guests from getting too close to the Queen and the Duke. To discourage invitees from milling around the Guest of Honour in the hope of being photographed in the same frame, an instruction was issued to photographers to only take pictures during the time of her arrival and departure. This and other special instructions to prevent eager crowds from forming around the Queen were to little avail. The rush to be seen near the Queen was virtually unstoppable. Despite all the precautions and security arrangements put in place, the President's Personal Staff had to form a cordon around the visiting dignitary to keep eager crowds at bay.

The 'At Home', despite the organisational nightmare that it proved to be, was a resounding success. The Queen, dressed in a pink and blue taffeta and wearing a hat of multi-coloured flowers, mixed freely with the guests. She talked to various groups who were cleared in advance. They included the UK citizens serving with the Government of India and members of YMCA. Seventy special invitees, who were separately briefed the previous day, were also presented to the Queen. After the At Home, the Queen left for the Ashoka Hotel where she attended a costume parade at 7.00 pm.[50]

The next day was Republic Day and the Queen was to participate in the celebrations. While almost all the connected issues were resolved, there was one–relating to the side on which the Queen would be seated while travelling to the Saluting Base- that defied easy resolution. It became a subject of extensive deliberations between the COP, MRA Baig, and the Military Secretary to the President (MSP), Major General Sardar Harnarain Singh. It was suggested by Baig that the Queen could be seated on the right hand side of the President of India as they travelled to the saluting base.

The suggestion that the Supreme Commander of the Armed Forces and the first citizen of the nation be seated on the left of a guest when he drove to take the salute on India's Republic Day did not find favour with many. They opined that on this important national day, the President of India should not be seen as occupying a position less important than a foreign guest, especially one who represented a nation from which India had gained independence after a long struggle. The MEA, however, continued to maintain that it would be appropriate for the President to be seated on the left of the Queen. It reiterated its stand in a letter dated January 5, 1961, addressed to the MSP and opined that "it will be quite in order if she sits on the right of the President."[51] The President accepted the advice of MEA.

The next day, January 26, 1961, the Queen witnessed India's Republic Day celebrations as the Guest of Honour. The event included a mammoth parade and a gala procession. *The New York Times* reported that there were over a lakh people who had congregated to witness the event.[52] After the Parade, the Queen met members of various voluntary groups at 4.00 pm, at the reception hosted by the President of India in the gardens of Rashtrapati Bhavan. Those she met included members of the Delhi Women's Association, nationals of the United Kingdom (UK) with the United Nations agency, Army officers, UK citizens serving with the Government of India, important clergymen, Tenzing Norgay and his daughters.[53]

A photograph of the Queen and the Duke sent to Ahmed Din by Private Secretary to the Queen. (1961).

20/A.

at Lahore.

13th February, 1961

Dear Mr. President,

I see from our programme that on
1st March - the last night of our stay in India -
it is arranged that we should dine privately
in our rooms at Rashtrapati Bhavan.

It would give much pleasure to my
husband and me if you would join us on this
occasion.   I have also invited the Prime Minister
and Mrs Indira Gandhi.   May we hope to have your
company ?

Yours sincerely

Elizabeth R

The President of India.

Queen's invitation to Dr Prasad for dinner at Dwarka Suite.

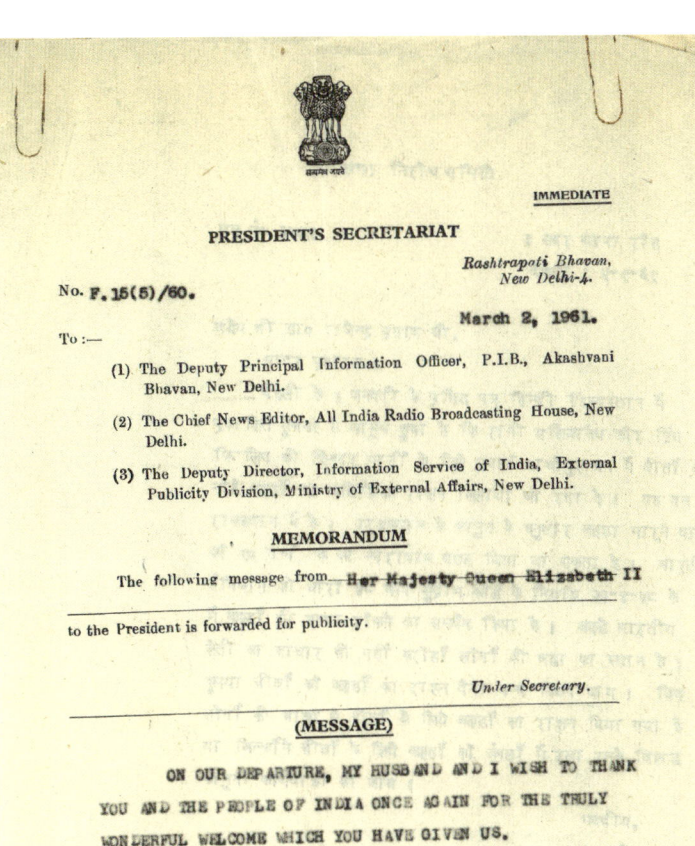

IMMEDIATE

PRESIDENT'S SECRETARIAT

Rashtrapati Bhavan,
New Delhi-4.

No. F. 15(5)/60.

March 2, 1961.

To :—

(1) The Deputy Principal Information Officer, P.I.B., Akashvani
Bhavan, New Delhi.

(2) The Chief News Editor, All India Radio Broadcasting House, New
Delhi.

(3) The Deputy Director, Information Service of India, External
Publicity Division, Ministry of External Affairs, New Delhi.

MEMORANDUM

The following message from ~~Her Majesty Queen Elizabeth II~~

to the President is forwarded for publicity.

Under Secretary.

(MESSAGE)

ON OUR DEPARTURE, MY HUSBAND AND I WISH TO THANK
YOU AND THE PEOPLE OF INDIA ONCE AGAIN FOR THE TRULY
WONDERFUL WELCOME WHICH YOU HAVE GIVEN US.

Message of thanks from Queen Elizabeth II to President Dr Prasad.

BUCKINGHAM PALACE

March 20th 1961.

Dear Mr. President,

Our visit to India is now over and
I would like to assure you that my husband and
I will retain the happiest recollections of the
busy days spent in your country.

It was a wonderful experience, full of
heart-warming affection from the Indian people
and with many opportunities of seeing the life
and problems in all the four corners of a vast
land.

You yourself were so very kind to us
when we stayed with you for the first week and I
do thank you for making us feel so much at home.

The whole journey was a very memorable
one and we shall always remember our welcome and
our tour with great pleasure.

Yours sincerely,

Sd/- Elizabeth R.

Letter of thanks from Queen Elizabeth II to President Dr Prasad
received through the UK High Commission.

The next day began with President Dr Prasad's grandchildren calling on the Queen at 9.45 am in the Dwarka Sitting Room. Thereafter, the royal couple visited the All India Institute of Medical Sciences (AIIMS) and attended the National Cadet Corps Rally at the Indian Air Force Sports Ground.

On January 28, the Queen and the Duke of Edinburgh visited the Cottage Industries Emporium in Delhi. Even this was not treated as a usual visit by a Head of State, desirous of seeing the traditional art and crafts of the country, as many had done since India gained independence. To ensure that the Queen would miss nothing of the best of India's traditional products and that the arrangements were flawless, Prime Minister Nehru personally visited the emporium and oversaw the arrangements.

The Queen arrived at the emporium on the hour at 10 in morning. She was shown some of the traditional products that were stocked in the various outlets. On behalf of the All India Handicrafts Board, the Emporium presented the Queen with a gold brocade *sari* which had taken the famous artisans of Surat nearly four months to complete.[54] Another of the presents to the Queen was a "2 ft. high model of Qutab Minar carved out of a complete ivory tusk."[55]

In the afternoon of the same day, at 4.30, a Civic Reception was held for the Queen and the Duke of Edinburgh at the Ramlila Grounds. *The Hindustan Times* reported that at a cost of Rs one lakh, it was the most expensive reception ever accorded to a visiting foreign dignitary.[56] About five lakh people attended it.[57]

The Queen arrived at the venue wearing a peach-coloured dress and a fur stole to a rapturous welcome. A visibly moved Queen stood on the white sandstone pavilion and addressed the cheering crowd who had occupied virtually every inch of the available space to get a closer view of the dignitary. "All around, as far as the eye could see, were people perched on the roofs of mud houses, on Government bungalows and on office buildings."[58] She thanked the citizens of Delhi for the memorable welcome. She added that her wonderful experience in India and the happy atmosphere during her visit was another proof of the spirit that existed amongst the countries in the Commonwealth.[59] The Queen ended her speech in Hindi saying, "*Apke hardik swagat ke liye bahut bahut shukriya* (many many thanks for your hearty welcome)," and "rendered it well, in correct accent."[60] Prime Minister Nehru also spoke at the reception and reminded the Queen about the enthusiastic welcome that the people of Delhi gave her. He said "No King or Emperor, could have given you the welcome that republicans of Delhi have given you."[61]

The royal couple made short visits to Agra, Udaipur and Ahmedabad, before flying off to Pakistan, where they stayed from February 1–16. They visited several Indian cities like Benaras, Bangalore, Madras and Calcutta on their return. From Lahore, the Queen sent invitations to President Dr Prasad, Pandit Nehru and Indira Gandhi to join them for dinner in her private suite at Rashtrapati Bhavan on the last day of their stay. The Indian President communicated his acceptance.

On February 18, 1961, in Calcutta (now Kolkata), the Queen attended the Queen Elizabeth II Cup races at the Race Course. The tradition of royal visitors attending the races here was set by King Edward VII when he was Prince of Wales and was followed by George V both in his capacity as Prince of Wales and then again as King Emperor. Queen Elizabeth II continued the tradition. Later that evening, the Queen attended a reception at the Royal Calcutta Turf Club given by the UK residents, whose congregation was the largest in Calcutta than in any other town or city in India.

During her stay, the Queen received several gifts. These included a collection of Indian stamps presented to her for her son, the Prince of Wales, by the Minister of Transport and Communication, Dr Subbarayan and the Philatelic Officer of Posts and Telegraph Department, TN Mehta;[62] a portrait of the Queen drawn on a *peepal* leaf and a hank of *khadi* yarn. The Government of India presented her with magnificent sandalwood carving of a scene from the *Mahabharata* which was personally presented by President Dr Prasad. Silks and brocades were some other gifts. Prime Minister Nehru presented a soft *pashmina* blanket to Prince Philip.[63]

The month-long visit also included a trip to Nepal where the royal couple stayed from February 26–28.

In a fine gesture by the Queen, on March 1, 2015, a day before her departure, she met the staff of the President's Household and thanked them for making her stay comfortable. Syed Din, son of Ahmed Din, a *khidmatgar* attached to the Dwarka Suite, fondly remembers that his father had been gifted a signed photograph of the royal couple. He proudly said that it was a present by the Queen given as recognition of the good service that he had rendered.[64] The Queen also met the Tour Staff, Police Officers of the Delhi Area and a few other people on the suggestion of the British High Commissioner.

In the evening, The Queen made a farewell broadcast over All India Radio (AIR) from a room close to the Dwarka Suite. The Queen had prohibited anyone from entering the room during the broadcast. She cleared her throat a few times and then went on air at 8.30 pm. She addressed millions of Indians and thanked them for the "kindness" she and her husband had received in India. She had rich words of praise for India's unflinching commitment to the ideals of democracy, and said, "No one can fail to recognise that this country is dedicated to bringing about, within a democratic framework, a better, richer, and happier life for every citizen."[65] She also added that her visit demonstrated "that the new Commonwealth which came into being in 1947 was firmly based in the hearts and minds of the people."[66]

On March 2, 1961, at around 9:45 am, the PBG lined the South Court as Queen Elizabeth and Prince Philip left Rashtrapati Bhavan for Palam Airport accompanied by the President. The royal guests proceeded in state, and were given a ceremonial farewell at the airport. They boarded the flight for Tehran at 10.30 am.

The same day, the President of India received a message from the Queen, thanking him and the people of India for the welcome and hospitality extended to her throughout the stay in the country. Five days after she left India, the Queen received a special gift. It was "an hour long colour documentary film" on the royal visit to India specially made by the Films Division of the Union Ministry of Information & Broadcasting. It was presented to the Queen on March 8, 1961, at Buckingham Palace.[67]

At a later date, on March 27, 1961, a letter from the Queen to President Dr Prasad reached Rashtrapati Bhavan. In it, she thanked the Indian President for the "wonderful experience, full of heart-warming affection from the Indian people" she and the Duke had in India, and said that those memories would remain with her forever.[68]

The visit of the Queen marked an important chapter in the history of independent India, for it exemplified India's willingness to move beyond its colonial past and share friendly ties with the UK. It was also one of the longest visits by a foreign Head of State to India.

The 1983 Visit

The Queen's second visit to India, in 1983, came after a long gap of 22 years. A lot had changed since her last visit. India had made significant progress in the field of industry, infrastructure, and technology and indeed had become the world cricket champion in June of the same year. The Queen herself, now 57, was older but radiated the same charm that had captured the fascination of millions of Indians during her last visit. As on the previous occasion, she was accompanied by her husband, Prince Philip, the Duke of Edinburgh. Unlike the previous five-week visit, this trip would, however, last no more than nine days.

A month before the Queen's arrival, an advance team headed by Deputy Private Secretary to the Queen, Sir William Heseltine, arrived in India to give finishing touches to her programme. It was decided that the Queen would arrive in Delhi, but would also visit Hyderabad and Pune. A decision was also taken to give adequate publicity to the visit.

A request was received by the President's Secretariat on the accommodation required for the delegates who would be accompanying the royal couple. This list included a request for Sir Philip Moore, Private Secretary to the Queen, to be accommodated in the Himalaya Suite. This, however, did not find favour with the

Queen Elizabeth II with President Giani Zail Singh at Rashtrapati Bhavan. Also seen behind, to the right of the Queen, is Prince Philip. (November 1983). Credit: PC

President's Secretariat as the room was reserved for dignitaries of the rank of a Minister, and Sir Moore, unfortunately, did not qualify as

Queen Elizabeth II delivering banquet speech at Rashtrapati Bhavan. Seated opposite is President Giani Zail Singh. Seated on right of the Queen is Prime Minister Gandhi. (November 1983). Credit: PC

one. Finally, however, India's traditional philosophy of *Atithi Devo Bhava* surmounted the technical restriction and Sir Philip Moore stayed in the comfort of the Himalaya Suite.

The Royal Secretariat also requested permission to open a temporary office in the Guest Wing Loggia of Rashtrapati Bhavan. This was granted and all necessary facilities like infrastructural support etc. were extended by Rashtrapati Bhavan.[69] The Dwarka Suite was specially refurbished for the Queen's stay. From curtains to furniture, everything was changed to give the place a "Vice regal decor."

(L-R): Prince Philip, Prime Minister Gandhi and Queen Elizabeth II at Rashtrapati Bhavan in November 1983. Credit: PC

The Bhavan had already been acquainted with the Queen's preferences for drinks and meals, along with those of the Duke of Edinburgh's. The advisory on Queen's preferences was less elaborate this time than what was communicated during the 1961 visit. It indicated that she would prefer a simple three-course meal for the day. There was no special advisory on her likes or dislikes, except for her dislike for uncooked shellfish. Prince Philip's preferences were similar to those of the Queen's, with the minor difference that he was not partial to strawberries. The Queen preferred gin and tonic while the Prince favoured beer. All these aspects were carefully noted by the CPH and arrangements were made accordingly.

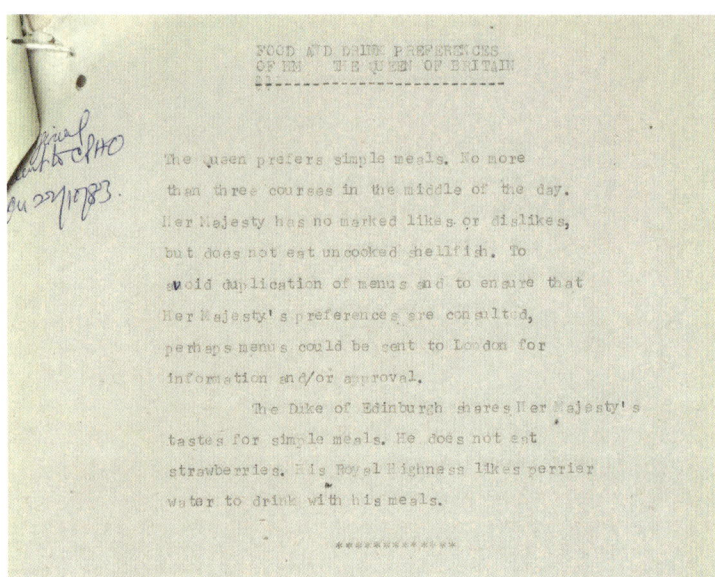

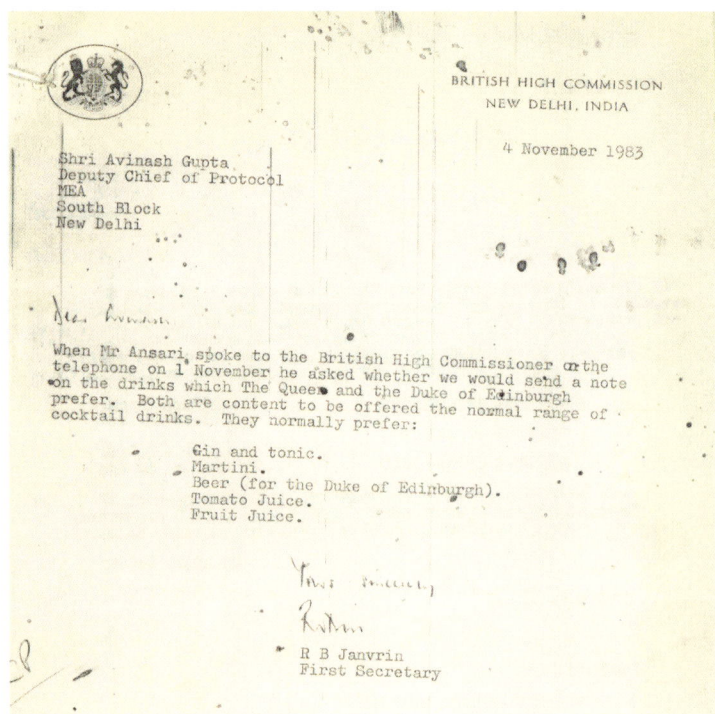

Advisories on food and drink preferences of Their Excellencies.

Queen Elizabeth II presenting the 'Order of Merit' to Mother Teresa in the Mughal Gardens at Rashtrapati Bhavan in November 1983. Credit: PC

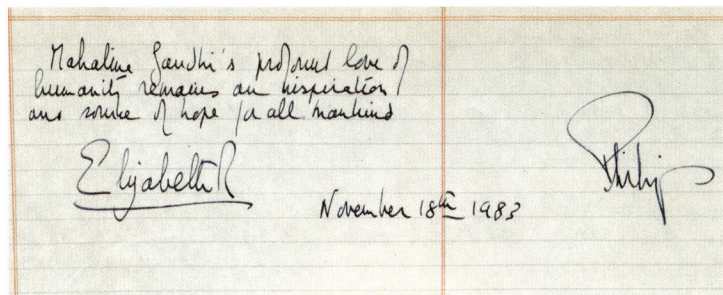

Mahatma Gandhi's profound love of humanity remains an inspiration and source of hope for all mankind

Elizabeth R   November 18th 1983   *Philip*

Comments of Queen Elizabeth II and Prince Philip in Visitors' Book at Rajghat.

The British Broadcasting Corporation (BBC) had also requested permission in advance for filming the building and the interior suites that had been especially refurbished for the Queen. They followed the visit closely and even filmed the Queen and Prime Minister Gandhi in the Mughal Gardens later in the tour for a "Christmas film."[70]

The people too once again got ready to welcome the Queen. On the day of her arrival, November 17, 1983, Delhi wore a festive appearance. Several arches made of flowers were erected along the ceremonial route, giving the otherwise busy city a fresh vibrant look. Life-sized portraits of Queen Elizabeth and Prince Philip were put up at road intersections.[71]

Queen Elizabeth II landed at Palam airport in New Delhi on the hour at 12.00 noon by a US made special Lockheed Tristar aircraft

of the Royal Air Force, The Astral Rose. After the plane came to a halt in the alighting zone, the Queen, "immaculately dressed in a pink and white dress with a matching hat," alighted from the royal jetliner smiling.[72] She was accorded a full ceremonial welcome with the traditional 21-gun salute and a Guard of Honour. The special guests gathered there were then introduced to the Queen.

After reception at the airport, she drove to Rashtrapati Bhavan in a six-door, bulletproof Mercedes, seated next to President Giani Zail Singh. Though the motorcade was to take the ceremonial route, there was a last minute change necessitated by a massive rally that was being taken by *Ekatmata Yagna Yatra*, a religious revival movement, near the Central Secretariat. Consequently, the cavalcade had to take the contingency route through Parliament Street. After reaching the Parliament House, the Queen and the Indian President shifted to an open convertible limousine for the remaining short drive to the Rashtrapati Bhavan.

The rally also compelled in a change of the Queen's scheduled programme on the first day of her arrival. The religious rally had attracted more than 40,000 people and there were traffic jams and roads were full of people. In view of this, it was reasoned that it may be difficult to sanitise and clear the route for the Queen to visit the *Rajghat* on her first day in India,[73] as normally Heads of States do.

As the visit to *Rajghat* was postponed, she had a light schedule on the first day in Delhi. The programmes were limited to formal calls. Her first call on was on the President in his renovated Study. At 4.00 pm, the Vice President of India paid a call on the Queen in the

The 7th Commonwealth Heads of Government Meeting (CHOGM) held in New Delhi in November 1983. Credit: PD

(R-L): Sonia Gandhi being introduced to Queen Elizabeth II. To Sonia's right is Rajiv Gandhi. Seen behind left of the Queen is President Giani Zail Singh (partially obscured) and behind (right) is Chief of Protocol, Hamid Ansari. (November 1983). Credit: PC

The menu for the banquet was carefully chosen and included a mix of European and Indian delicacies. For non-vegetarians there was *Pomfret Normande, Chicken Parisienne, Kabab Platter, Chicken Malai Kabab, Mutton Bott Kabab* and *Reshmi Kabab*.[75] The vegetarian menu consisted of *Mushroom Florentine* as a starter, followed by *Dauphina Potato, Vegetable Jardinière,* "Vegetable Platter, *Vegetable Shammi Kabab, Vegetable Shaslik* and *Arbi Kabab.*"[76]

After the dinner, the junior butlers cleared the tables and President Singh proposed a toast to the visiting dignitaries. He extended a warm welcome to the royal guests on behalf of the people and the Government of India. He referred to the international issues that were bedevilling prospects of peace and stability in the world. The imperative need for disarmament as a measure to reduce tension between the East and West was one of the highlights of his speech. He said that the Governments of India and the UK should "increasingly work together to spread the message of peace, understanding and cooperation throughout the world."[77] Concluding his speech, President Singh raised a toast to the "health and happiness" of the royal couple.[78]

In her response, Queen Elizabeth referred to the common ties between India and the UK. She made singular reference to the common threads of history that bind the two nations. She expressed confidence in the prowess of the historical ties to bridge the difference between the two nations and said, "Outsiders may wonder why an island people living on the Western edge of Europe should have a deep affinity with this great country in Southern Asia, with such a wide gulf in size, distance, climate, race, religion, economy and culture. But we know that in spite of the differences the gap can be bridged, for we have an association based on shared history."[79] She added that the association between the two countries should be strengthened not "only for our own advantage but for the

Morning Room of Rashtrapati Bhavan. Later that evening, Prime Minister Indira Gandhi called on the Queen and had a 40-minute meeting in the same room. After the official call on meetings, the Queen visited the British High Commission for a reception to meet the Commonwealth Press Union.

Later that evening, President Singh hosted a State Banquet in honour of the Queen and her consort. As usual, elaborate arrangements were made for the banquet. The Grand Open Staircase, Ashok Hall, Upper Loggia, Banquet Hall and the South Entrance of the West Subway were specially decorated with beautiful flower arrangements. The PBG also lined the corridors from the Guest Wing to the Ashok Hall. The lights and fountains of the Mughal Gardens were switched on. Tables had been placed near the alighting point for guests to keep their hats. A special arrangement was made in the South Drawing Room to accommodate the large number of journalists and photographers who had come to cover the event. It was equipped with loudspeakers and special seating arrangements for the press corps.

At five minutes past eight in the evening, the President of India, escorted by the MSP and ADC-I, called on the Queen and the Duke of Edinburgh in the Dwarka Sitting Room. After a brief exchange of pleasantries, the President escorted the Queen and the Duke of Edinburgh to the Ashok Hall. For the banquet, Queen Elizabeth "wore an evening dress of pale blue silver lace, over pale blue organza." The jewellery was a matching set that included her Russian diamond tiara,[74] the same that she had worn during her 1961 visit to India.

As the three halted under the central arch of the Hall, the band played the national anthems of both countries. The guests, who had arrived via the South Sunken Road and were waiting for the House Party, were then introduced to the royal couple. After the round of introductions, they were conducted to the grand Banquet Hall.

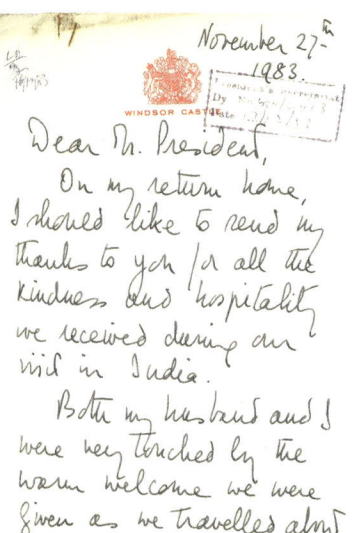

Hand-written letter of thanks from Queen Elizabeth II to President Zail Singh.

benefit of our restless and imperfect world."[80] She then raised a toast to the Indian President and "to the prosperity and happiness of the Indian people."[81]

The first programme of the next day, November 18, was the visit to *Rajghat*. She arrived at the monument and placed a wreath at Gandhi's *samadhi*. After laying the wreath, she penned in the Visitors' Book that Gandhi remains the beacon of hope for the people. She wrote, "Mahatma Gandhi's profound love of humanity remains an inspiration and source of hope for all mankind."[82]

Thereafter, Queen Elizabeth walked around the compound, and located the sapling that she had planted 22 years ago and observed that it had "grown into a tall pine tree"; and a legend on its side read: "Pinus Longifolia: Planted by Her Majesty Queen Elizabeth II on January 21, 1961."[83] She then went on a tour of the Red Fort, followed by a visit to St Thomas School on Mandir Marg at 11.30 am. She also met the High Commissioners of the Commonwealth countries in the afternoon, and had lunch with Indira Gandhi at her residence.

In the evening, the Queen and the Duke of Edinburgh visited the Delhi War Graves Cemetery in Delhi Cantonment, "where they laid wreaths specially flown in from the United Kingdom."[84] Following the ceremony, the royal couple witnessed an enthralling equestrian performance by the PBG in the Forecourt of Rashtrapati Bhavan. An extra brass band had been attached to Rashtrapati Bhavan for the event. By the evening, around 7.00, the royal couple left for Hyderabad, where they would stay at Rashtrapati Nilayam, the Indian President's official retreat where he spends around two weeks every year.

The next day, the royal couple visited several places including Bharat Heavy Electricals Research and Development Establishment and the International Crop Research for Semi-Arid Tropics (ICRISAT) headquarters in Hyderabad. The Queen looked delighted to see that scientists from 21 different countries were working to increase India's food productivity. She also visited tourist spots including the Qutab Shahi Tombs and the Golconda Fort.

The following day, November 20, was the royal couple's 36th wedding anniversary. The Queen started her day by attending a service at the Holy Trinity Church in Hyderabad.[85] President Singh sent her a bouquet congratulating the couple on their special day. The Queen sent a letter thanking him. Later, she visited Devara Yamjal village, almost 13 kms away from Hyderabad.[86]

The next morning, the royal couple emplaned for Pune, where they visited the National Defence Academy at Khadakvasla, and had lunch with the cadets. After a five-hour stay, the Queen and her husband returned to Delhi. At around nine that evening, the Queen hosted a gala reception at the British High Commissioner's residence, in honour of her Indian hosts. The Chief Guest at the reception was the President of India, Giani Zail Singh. Others present included Vice President M Hidayatullah and Prime Minister Gandhi.[87] One of the special invitees was India's cricket legend, the 'Little Master' Sunil Gavaskar, who had equalled "Sir Don Bradman's record of 29 Test centuries"[88] merely 19 days before the Queen began her visit.

The Queen's visit coincided with the 7th Commonwealth Heads of Government Meeting that began on November 23. This was the first time this meeting was held in India and the presence of the Queen, the Head of the Commonwealth, enhanced the importance of the meeting. On its first day, the Queen and the Duke of Edinburgh hosted the "Queen's glittering banquet"[89] at Hyderabad House for the Heads of the Commonwealth Governments. It was a special menu and the fare was prepared by Chefs who had been specially flown in from Britain. The dinner menu was European with *Traite Saumonee Galleini* served as an appetiser, followed by *Salle D'agneau Bordelaise* and *Broccoli Glace Feves a La Crèmeas* main course.[90]

For the next few days, until her departure, Queen Elizabeth was busy attending to her duties as the Head of the Commonwealth. Heads of Governments also called on her at Rashtrapati Bhavan. Prince Philip, however, had a separate schedule. He visited several places including the Indian Institute of Technology (IIT), Delhi; the Gir Lion Sanctuary in Gujarat and the city of Bombay.

On November 24, Queen Elizabeth presented the "insignia of the Order of Merit" to Mother Teresa for her dedication to helping the underprivileged. The "Order of Merit" is a distinction that can only be held by 24 people at any given time. It was conferred on Mother Teresa at a ceremony held in the Mughal Gardens outside the Yellow Drawing Room at Rashtrapati Bhavan[91] Former President Dr Radhakrishnan had also received the award in 1963.

As the visit neared its end, Queen Elizabeth presented her hosts with a set of 30 Acron Computers. In a letter dated November 2, 1983, and addressed to MH Ansari, then Chief of Protocol (presently, the Vice President of India), the British High Commission offered to "provide training in the United Kingdom to staff who might be involved in using these micro-computers."[92]

The Queen and the Duke of Edinburgh departed for London on the morning of November 26, from Palam Airport after a ceremonial farewell.

The visit was a grand success, and in an unusual gesture, signifying her satisfaction and happiness on her visit to India, the Queen penned a personal letter to the President, from Windsor Castle on November 27, 1983. The letter contained sentiments of appreciation for the Indian hospitality. The Queen thanked the President and wrote: "We shall always have the happiest memories of our stay in Delhi and in Hyderabad." After her last visit, too, she had in a letter expressed similar sentiments to the Indian President. But this time, the letter was handwritten in comparison to the one sent in 1961, which did not contain the signature of the Queen, but was only forwarded by the British High Commissioner, who said he had been "commanded" to do so.[93]

The 1997 Visit

In 1997, the Queen arrived in India on her third visit to the country, more than two decades after her first visit in 1961. The purpose of this visit was to participate in the commemoration celebration of 50 years of India's independence. The week long visit began on October 12.

As on the previous two visits, the President's Secretariat had made elaborate arrangements for her stay 'under the dome'. An advance party led by the Queen's Deputy Private Secretary, Robin Janvrin had inspected the Guest Wing and the other places on the Queen's itinerary as early as in July.

All the various officers of the President's Secretariat were instructed to give the Rashtrapati Bhavan a facelift. The Guest Wing was the first to get a makeover. Its precincts were tidied up and beautified. The storage space near the Wing was cleared for the visit. The DMSP personally intervened and wrote to the Executive Engineer, President's Estate Division, to remove the pile of old furniture close to the Guest Wing as it presented "an ungainly sight."[94]

The Garden Superintendent got all the flowerpots painted and new plaques were fixed next to the plants in the Mughal Garden. The Under Secretary for Co-ordination ensured that all roads that had been damaged in cable-laying work were resurfaced. The

Forecourt steps got a thorough scrubbing and screens matching the surrounding ambience were placed where required. As during the previous visit, the Royal Household Office was set up in the Guest Loggia. The President's Secretariat provided the best revolving chairs and computer tables from its inventory to set up the office.

The Queen and the Duke landed at Indira Gandhi International Airport (Indian Air Force Technical Area) at 9.30 pm on October 12, 1997, in a British Aerospace 146 aircraft from Karachi. The Queen emerged from the aircraft "wearing a red hat (to match the red carpet treatment she received) and a multi-coloured floral print dress."[95] She was welcomed by the Minister of State for External Affairs, Kamla Sinha; the British High Commissioner, Sir David Gore-Booth; Foreign Secretary of India, K Raghunath and India's High Commissioner to the Court of St James, LM Singhvi. Neither the President, nor the Prime Minister were there as the practice of according visiting Heads of States a ceremonial welcome at the airport had been discontinued by this time.

After the formal introductions, the Queen was driven in a limousine to Rashtrapati Bhavan. On their arrival, the royal couple was received by the Deputy Military Secretary to the President (DMSP), Colonel DS Ahlawat, in the South Court. The guests were then conducted to their respective suites by the President's Household Staff. The Queen, according to protocol, stayed in the Dwarka Suite

Queen Elizabeth II with President Narayanan at Rashtrapati Bhavan in October 1997. Credit: PC

(L-R): President Narayanan receiving Queen Elizabeth II and Prince Philip at Rashtrapati Bhavan in October 1997. Credit: PC

and the Duke in the Nalanda Suite, just as they had during their last two visits. The rest of the delegation stayed in various suites/ rooms according to their seniority.

The next morning at 10.00, the Queen was given a ceremonial welcome at the Forecourt of Rashtrapati Bhavan. The royal couple was escorted to the venue through Gate No. 7 of Rashtrapati Bhavan. The motorcade then drove through a part of the erstwhile ceremonial route via Willingdon Crescent, Rajpath and Vijay Chowk to reach Rashtrapati Bhavan. At the main gate, they were received by the PBG and escorted to the Forecourt in a ceremonial formation. As the motorcade reached the Jaipur Column, the ceremonial guard branched off into two detachments and a 21-gun salute was fired at a frequency of one round every two-and-a-half seconds welcomed the Queen.

The royal couple alighted where the Viceroy's Court, as the gravelled path was known, meets the Forecourt and were welcomed by the President of India, KR Narayanan, Prime Minister IK Gujral and select Cabinet Ministers. The Queen was then escorted to the special platform from where she took the salute. The national anthems of the two countries were played after which the Queen was presented a 150-strong Inter-Services

Guard of Honour. Thereafter, she was introduced to the special invitees who were lined in a single row in a separate enclosure.

Immediately afterwards, the Queen and the Duke of Edinburgh left for *Rajghat* via India Gate and laid wreaths on the *samadhi* of Mahatma Gandhi. Later, at 11.20 am, the royal couple called on President Narayanan and his wife, Usha, in the North Drawing Room of Rashtrapati Bhavan. The four then departed for the National Museum to inaugurate an exhibition titled "*The Enduring Image*" that was held in collaboration with the British Museum. As *The Hindu* described, the event "put into action the oft-repeated statement of Britain and India being 'old friends and modern partners.'"[96]

The Prime Minister of India, IK Gujral, called on the Queen around 1.00 in the afternoon at Hyderabad House. The meeting lasted half-an-hour and the Prime Minister then hosted a lunch in honour of the British monarch at the same venue. Later that afternoon, the Queen paid a visit to the British High Commission and met the staff there. A media reception was also hosted at the High Commission. The Vice President of India, Krishan Kant and his wife Suman Kant, called on the Queen after she returned to Rashtrapati Bhavan in the late afternoon. The short meeting took place in the South Drawing Room at 4.15 pm.

MUSIC TITLE	Vegetable Consomme
	*
	Mushroom Florentine
	*
OCCASIONAL	Paneer Tikka, Vegetable Seekh Kabab,
MARCHE MILITAIRE	Baby Uttapam with Coconut Chutney
(ORPUS SL. NO.1)	Gobhi Musallam
	Malai Kofta Curry
BANDITENSTRAICHE	Stuffed Tomatoes
	Aubergine with Yoghurt
LO, HERE THE GENTLE-LARK	Beans & Baby Corn
	Dal Bukhara
VAISHNAVO JANATO	Vegetable Pulao
ENGLISH FOLK SONG	Plain Roti/ Baby Naan/Parantha
(FOLK SONGS FROM SOMERSET)	Cucumber Raita
	Salad with French Dressing
JAYO STUTE	Papad - Pickle
	*
YAMAN	Lemon Souffle
	Rasmalai
SYMPHONY NO. 1	Jalebi
(VIVACE)	*
ABIDE WITH ME	Fresh Fruits
	*
	Coffee/Tea
	Cheese Assortment

(Left): Music played at the banquet held in honour of Queen Elizabeth II at Rashtrapati Bhavan. (Right): Menu of the banquet.

A State Banquet was hosted by President Narayanan and his wife for the Queen and the Duke of Edinburgh at 8.00 in the evening in the Banquet Hall of Rashtrapati Bhavan. The President and the First Lady arrived in the Dwarka Sitting Room at 7.50 pm, escorted by the DMSP, MSP and two AsDC. They then escorted their guests to the Ashok Hall, via the Guest Wing Corridor, which had been decorated specially for the event. The *sowars* of the PBG lined the corridor, standing to attention, holding their lances firmly in their hands. As the procession halted under the central arch of the Ashok Hall, the national anthems of the UK and India were played.

Invitees to the banquet were then introduced to the royal couple, after which the principals and the guests moved to the Banquet Hall where they were seated in accordance with a carefully prepared table plan.

A Naval Orchestra of 35 including a band master, played light music from the band gallery of the Banquet Hall while dinner was being served. They played "*Marche Militaire*", "*Banditenstraiche*", "*Lo, here the gentle–lark*", "*Vaishnava Janato*", "English folk Song",

"*Jayo Stute*", "*Yaman*", "*Symphony No. 1 (Vivace)*", and "*Abide with Me*" while liveried butlers served an elaborate meal consisting of *Chicken Consommé, Fish Florentine, Seekh Kabab, Stuffed Tomatoes, Vegetable Pulao, Cucumber Raita, Rasmalai*, fresh fruits, coffee and an assortment of cheeses.

Just before the coffee was served, the *khidmatgars* cleared the tables and left the room. The President of India then gave a speech. He began by welcoming the Queen and her consort to India, reminding the gathering of the reason for their visit. He said, "Your gracious presence amongst us at this time brings back to us memories of the sense of liberation and reconciliation that pervaded the first days of our independence." President Narayanan outlined briefly the progress India had made since 1947, and said, "Your Majesty, India today is a country throbbing with change and great expectations. Our greatest achievements...to have built up a democratic system." He then described India's contribution to international peace and stability through non–alignment and the promotion of peace and harmony. He concluded by raising a toast to the Queen and the Duke of Edinburgh, for their happiness and to the peace and prosperity of the UK and "the enduring friendship and co-operation" between the two countries.[97]

The Queen replied to the toast saying, "If countries in the region share a goal, and understand that by working together they give themselves a better chance of achieving it, then historical hostilities can be buried for good."[98] She also acknowledged the difficult past that India and the UK shared and referred to the Jallianwala Bagh massacre of 1919. She termed it as a "distressing example" of some of the "difficult episodes" in the two nations' history and said, "but history cannot be rewritten however much we might sometimes wish otherwise. It has its moments of sadness, as well as gladness. We must learn from the sadness and build on the gladness."[99] Coffee and fruits were served after which the banquet ended.

The next day, the royal couple departed for Amritsar at 10.30 in the morning from the Palam Air Force Station. This segment of the visit had resurrected some of the bitter memories of the British rule in India and there was opposition to the Queen visiting the site of the most gruesome killings of unarmed civilians by British troops in India. Newspapers carried articles describing protests in Punjab and Delhi against the Queen visiting the site, though in some areas, the opposition was less strident. Tempers, however, cooled after her banquet speech and a demonstration, by people representing the families of those killed in 1919 was called off a few hours before her scheduled departure. They declared that "they had felt vindicated by the speech in New Delhi."[100]

The Queen visited Jallianwala Bagh, laid a wreath at the memorial and observed 30-seconds of silence. She also visited *Harmandir Sahib* or the Golden Temple, the holiest of Sikh shrines. By 3.00 in the afternoon, she was back at Rashtrapati Bhavan. The British High Commissioner hosted a reception for the Queen and the Duke of Edinburgh in the evening.

On October 15, the Queen had a "farewell *tete-a-tete* with the President" in the Yellow Drawing Room at Rashtrapati Bhavan.

The Duke had, however, left for Ahmedabad earlier in the day. At the meeting, the President presented the Queen with a photo album containing pictures taken during her visit to India. He also extended her another invitation to visit India. The two leaders also discussed the Commonwealth Heads of Government Conference that was scheduled to be held in Edinburgh soon.[101]

The Queen took leave of the President after thanking him, the people and the Government of India for the famed Indian hospitality extended to her yet again.[102] The President's Staff lined up and bade farewell to their guest near the South Court Entrance. A Guard of Honour was presented by a detachment of 4 Bihar Regiment on the north side of the Jaipur Column near the main gates.

The Queen then left for Pragati Maidan where she opened an exhibition titled "*Towards 2000*" which centred around Indo-British partnership. She then went to the British Council and the Brotherhood House after lunch at the British High Commissioner's residence.

Later in the afternoon, she visited the Delhi War Graves Cemetery in Delhi Cantonment and laid a wreath at the memorial there. Thereafter, she drove directly to the Air Force Station, Palam at 5.40 pm from where she left for Chennai. Prime Minister Gujral and members of the Cabinet saw her off at the airport. She spent the next two days in the southern States of Tamil Nadu and Kerala.

In Chennai, the Queen went to the renowned MGR Film City for the launch of *Marudanayagam*, a Tamil film by the popular film personality, Kamal Haasan.[103] She also visited the famed Kalakshetra Foundation, one of the most reputed academies for Indian classical music and dance. The Queen also went to Kanchipuram, Sriperambudur and to Kochi, in Kerala.

Queen Elizabeth II left India on October 18, 1997, at 1.25 in the afternoon after a successful visit.

Elizabeth II continues at the Queen of the United Kingdom of Great Britain and Northern Ireland and the Head of the Commonwealth. She is 89. The Prince Philip, Duke of Edinburgh, is now 94.

Notes

(Endnotes)

1 Records, President's Secretariat, Rashtrapati Bhavan, File No. 30/CER/116.

2 Sally Bedell Smith, *Elizabeth the Queen: The Woman Behind the Throne* (London: Penguin, 2012), p. 2.

3 Robert T. Elson, "A Person Apart, Bounded by Precedent," *Life*, March 6, 1964, Vol. 56, No. 10, p. 93

4 Society for the Study of State Governments, *Journal*, Volume 3-4, Pennsylvania State University, 1970, p. 52.

5 Elson, "A Person Apart, Bounded by Precedent," p. 93.

6 Records, President's Secretariat, File No. 30/CER/116.

7 Ibid.

8 "Queen Leaves for Tour of India Today," *The Hindustan Times* (New Delhi), January 20, 1961, p. 1.

9 Records, President's Secretariat, File No. 30/CER/116.

10 "Big Welcome Awaits the Queen," *The Hindustan Times* (New Delhi), January 21, 1961, p. 1.

11 Records, President's Secretariat, File No. 30/CER/116.

12 Records, President's Secretariat, File No. 30/CER/116.

13 Dooj Prakash (2015), personal interview by Dr Thomas Mathew, New Delhi, April 9, 2015.

14 Records, President's Secretariat, File No. 30/CER/116.

15 Ibid.

16 "Illuminations for Queen," *The Hindustan Times* (New Delhi), January 17, 1961, p. 3.

17 Balwant Raj Kapoor, *My Days at Rashtrapati Bhavan* (New Delhi: Jnanada Prakashan, 2013), p. 31.

18 Ibid, p. 30.

19 "The President will present Banquet card," *The Hindustan Times* (New Delhi) January 20, 1961, p. 1.

20 P. Grimes, "India Hails Queen in Huge Welcome," *The New York Times*, January 22, 1961, p. 3.

21 Records, President's Secretariat, File No. 30/CER/116.

22 Dermot Morrah, ed., *The Queen's visit: Elizabeth II in India and Pakistan* (London: Asia Publishing House, 1961), p. 56.

23 Ibid., p. 57.

24 Grimes, "India Hails Queen," p. 3.

25 Ibid.

26 Ibid.

27 Kapoor, My Days at Rashtrapati Bhavan, p. 31.

28 Records, President's Secretariat, File No. 30/CER/116.

29 Grimes, "India Hails Queen," p. 3.

30 "Delhi Makes a Festival of it," *The Statesman* (New Delhi), January 22, 1961, p. 3.

31 Sarah Bradford, *Queen Elizabeth II: Her Life in Our Times* (London: Viking,2012), p. 23.

32 Grimes, "India Hails Queen," p. 3.

33 "Vermilion for the Queen," *The Hindustan Times* (New Delhi), January 15, 1961, p. 1.

34 P. Dasgupta, "Elaborate Arrangements for Great Reception," *The Times of India*, January 20, 1961, p. 7.

35 Ibid.

36 "Queen pays honour to Gandhi," *Chicago Tribune*, January 22, 1961, p.6. , accessed December 16, 2014, http://archives.chicagotribune.com/1961/01/22/page/6/article/queen–pays–honor–to–gandhi.

37 "Queen talks and listens at Reception," The Sunday Statesman (New Delhi), January 22, 1961, p. 3.

38 Ibid.

39 Thin strips of the bark of the Himalayan Birch processed and made suitable for writing and was very popular in India in the ancient and middle ages.

40 "The President will present Banquet Card," p. 1.

41 Ibid.

42 "Close Indo–British ties emphasized," *The Statesman* (New Delhi), January 22, 1961, p. 3.

43 "Dress of Pale Blue Silver," *The Hindustan Times* (New Delhi), November 18, 1983, p. 4.

44 Records, President's Secretariat, File No. 15(5)/60.

45 Ministry of External Affairs (1995), Government of India, MEA Library, Foreign Affairs Records 1961, Volume VII, accessed May 28, 2015, http://mealib.nic.in/?pdf2549?000.

46 Ibid.

47 Ibid.

48 Records, President's Secretariat, File No. 15(5)/60.

49 "8000 at President's reception", *The Statesman* (New Delhi), January 26, 1961, p. 9.

50 Records, President's Secretariat, File No. 30/CER/116.

51 Ibid.

52 "Queen Joins in Marking India's Republic Day," *The New York Times*, January 27, 1961, p. 5.

53 Records, President's Secretariat, File No. 30/CER/116.

54 "Nehru Visits Emporium," *The Hindustan Times*, January20, 1961, p. 3.

55 Ibid.

56 "Most Expensive Reception," *The Hindustan Times*, January 20, 1961, p. 3.

57 "Special Ties Bind UK and India," *The Hindustan Times* (New Delhi), January 29, 1961, p. 1.

58 "Memorable Delhi Civic Reception for Queen," *The Statesman* (New Delhi), January 29, 1961, p. 1.

59 "India–UK ties example to world, Says Queen," *The Hindustan Times* (New Delhi), January 29, 1961, p. 4.

60 "Special Ties Bind U.K. And India," *The Hindustan Times* (New Delhi), January 29, 1961, p. 1.

61 "Memorable Delhi Civic Reception for Queen," p. 1.

62 Records, President's Secretariat, File No. 15/5/60.

63 Ibid.

64 Syed Din (2015), personal interview by Dr Thomas Mathew, New Delhi, April 5, 2015.

65 Morrah, The Queen's visit, p. 44.

66 Ibid.

67 "Warm send-off to the Queen after a memorable visit," *The Hindustan Times* (New Delhi), March 3, 1961, p. 1.

68 Records, President's Secretariat, File No. 30/CER/116.

69 "India Dusts off Past For the Queen's Visit," *The New York Times*, November 17, 1983, accessed May 23, 2015, http://www.nytimes.com/1983/11/17/world/india-dusts-off-past-for-the-queen-s-visit.html.

70 Records, President's Secretariat, File No. 30/CER/9(83).

71 Ibid.

72 G.K. Reddy, "Queen Arrives to a Glittering Welcome," *The Hindu* (New Delhi), November 18, 1983, p. 1.

73 "Hindu Rally Rivals Turnout For Queen on Arrival in India," *The New York Times*, November 18, 1983, accessed May 23, 2015, http://www.nytimes.com/1983/11/18/world/hindu-rally-rivals-turnout-for-queen-on-arrival-in-india.html?pagewanted=print.

74 "Dress of Pale Blue Silver, p. 4.

75 "Feast Fit for a Queen," *The Hindustan Times* (New Delhi), November 18, 1983, p. 1.

76 Ibid.

77 Ministry of External Affairs (1995), Government of India, MEA Library, Foreign Affairs Records 1961, Volume VII, accessed May 23, 2015, http://mealib.nic.in/?pdf2571?000.

78 Ibid.

79 Ibid.

80 Ibid.

81 Ibid.

82 Ibid.

83 Ibid.

84 "Equestrian Show for Queen," *The Times of India* (New Delhi), November 19, 1983, p. 1.

85 "Queen has a Quiet Day," *The Times of India* (New Delhi), November 21, 1983, p. 9.

86 "Royal Visitor to Get a Glimpse of Indian Rural Life," *The Hindu* (New Delhi), November 18, 1983, p. 10.

87 "Queen Hosts Reception," *The Hindustan Times* (New Delhi), November 22, 1983, p. 7.

88 "Royal Wish to Meet Gavaskar," *The Hindustan Times* (New Delhi), November 19, 1983, p. 1.

89 "Queen's Glittering Banquet," *The Hindustan Times* (New Delhi), November 24, 1983, p. 1.

90 Ibid.

91 "Order Presented to Teresa," *The Hindustan Times* (New Delhi), November 25, 1983, p. 1.

92 Records, President's Secretariat, File No. 30/CER/9(83).

93 Ibid.

94 Records, President's Secretariat, File No. V–11012/21/97–CER.

95 "Queen gets a warm welcome," *The Hindustan Times* (New Delhi), October 13, 1997, p. 1.

96 "Ceremonial welcome for Queen Elizabeth," *The Hindu* (New Delhi), October 14, 1997, p. 1.

97 Ministry of External affairs, Government of India, MEA Library, Foreign Affairs Records 1997, Volume XLIII, accessed May 5, 2015, http://mealib.nic.in/?pdf2585?000.

98 Mahendra Ved, "Queen's insistence on J&K Surprises Observers," *The Times of India* (New Delhi), October 14, 1997, p. 10.

99 John F. Burns, "In India, Queen Bows Her Head Over a Massacre in 1919," *The New York Times*, October 15, 1997, accessed May 5, 2015, http://www.nytimes.com/1997/10/15/world/in-india-queen-bows-her-head-over-a-massacre-in-1919.html.

100 Ibid.

101 Records, President's Secretariat, File No. V–11012/21/97–CER.

102 "Queen inaugurates industrial expo," *The Hindu* (New Delhi), October16, 1997, p. 13.

103 "Rare Pic: Silver-Screen Stars Moment with queen," June 14, 2013, accessed May 7, 2015, http://www.gulte.com/movienews/17975/Rare-Pic-Silver-Screen-stars-moment-with-Queen.

When Yugoslavia's President Josip Broz Tito landed in India on December 16, 1954, on a three-week visit, it was reported that he was the first foreign Head of State[1] to set foot on the soil of independent India.[2] In all likelihood, he was also the first foreign Head of State to stay at the Rashtrapati Bhavan. By 1974, President Tito had visited India six times in 20-odd years, creating another record for the maximum number of State Visits by the Head of State of a non-neighbouring country.

Tito, as he is popularly known, is often remembered as one of the greatest leaders of the Second World War. He was born on May 7, 1892, in Croatia to a family of peasants, as the seventh of the 15 children of his parents.

Tito grew up as a normal child of his times. There was no early indication that he would, one day, become the President of his country and a leader of world stature. Two years after he had completed his elementary education, 15-year-old Tito joined a locksmith as an apprentice. In the year 1913, he was conscripted to the Austro-Hungarian Army, and a year later, he fought against the Serbs, as a Sergeant Major in the First World War.

December 16, 1954 to January 6, 1955
January 13-19, 1959
October 20-25, 1966
January 22-27, 1968
October 16-20, 1971
January 24-29, 1974

Visits of

Marshal Josip Broz Tito

President of The Socialist Federal Republic of Yugoslavia

Tito was badly wounded in the war and was captured by Russia. His internment in the country of his captors, first as a prisoner and then as a supporter of the Bolshevik Movement, transformed him from a soldier into a revolutionary.[3] After his return to Croatia, in 1920, he became an active participant of the Communist Party of Yugoslavia (CPY).

In 1928, he became the Zagreb Branch Secretary of the CPY, but was arrested the same year, and tried in court for his "illegal" communist activities and sent to jail. He spent the time of his internment to further the modest education he had received in his village. He studied extensively the political and economic subjects that were related to his philosophy.[4] Following his release, Tito worked from the Soviet Union for more than a year as a Politburo Member of the CPY. It was during this time that he assumed the pseudonym "Tito" that the world knows him by.

Tito gradually rose up the political hierarchy, becoming Secretary General of the CPY in 1937. When the Second World War broke out and Germany occupied Yugoslavia, Tito headed the resistance movement which liberated large portions of his country from the occupation forces. Towards the end of the war, on March 6, 1945, he became Prime Minister of Yugoslavia.

In 1953, Tito was elected President of the country. As the President, he led his country by "the extraordinary, almost instinctive, comprehension of the realities of Yugoslavia and of world politics, plus a capacity for bold decision."[5] Pursuing

Facing page:
President Tito (left)
with President Dr Prasad in
Mughal Gardens at Rashtrapati Bhavan in
December 1954. Credit: PC

the policy of non-alignment along with Pandit Nehru, the two leaders developed a deep personal bond and became its prominent articulators.

The 1954 Visit

President Tito's first visit to India came in the month of December 1954. It was a grand affair. Unlike other leaders who visited India, the Yugoslavian President chose to arrive by sea. The 15-day voyage was undertaken on the 5,000-ton Presidential yacht named "*Galeb*,"[6] meaning "seagull" in Croatian. This 117-metre-long vessel was powered by two fiat diesel engines and was often used by the leader on his foreign journeys.[7]

The yacht was escorted by two destroyer ships of the Yugoslavian Navy.[8] Accompanying President Tito were several high level dignitaries including Vice President Aleksander Rankovic; Member of the Executive Council and Secretary of the State of Foreign Affairs, Koca Popovic; Member of Federal Executive Council and Chairman, Executive Council of the People's Republic of Serbia, Jovan Vaselino; Member of the Federal Executive Council and Vice Chairman, Executive Council of the People's Republic of Croatia, Ivan Krajacic; Secretary General to the Yugoslavian President, Joza Vilfan and Commander-in-Chief, Yugoslav Navy, Major General Milan Zezelji amongst others.[9] The Indian Ambassador to Yugoslavia, Rajeshwar Dayal, was also part of the entourage.

President Tito's dramatic arrival in his yacht was matched by India's equally spectacular and majestic welcome. India deployed three Indian destroyer ships – the "*Godavari*", "*Ganga*" and "*Gomati*"– 10-miles into the Arabian Sea to receive the Yugoslavian President.[10] An article in *The New York Times* wrote that "A destroyer squadron went out into the Arabian Sea to meet his ship and a formation of four-engined bombers wheeled overhead."[11]

At 8.00 in the morning when the Indian destroyers met the Yugoslavian ships, the thunderous sound of "*Godavari's*" 21-gun salute in honour of President Tito filled the air. This was accompanied by the flight of Indian Air Force planes which soared past the ships adding a deafening roar to the boom of the guns. Approximately thirty minutes past the hour, "*Galeb*" fired a national salute, which was "returned by the battery at Castle Barracks."[12]

As the Yugoslavian ship dropped anchor in Bombay harbour, several Indian dignitaries including the Military Secretary to the President (MSP), Major General B Chatterjee, who was representing the Indian President Dr Rajendra Prasad; the Governor of Bombay, Mangaldas Pakvasa; the Chief Minister of Bombay, Morarji Desai; Deputy Minister of the External Affairs Ministry, AK Chanda and the Chief of Protocol (COP), IS Chopra, boarded the "*Galeb*" to call on the visiting Head of State. President Tito, then, boarded a "special motor-launch"[13] which took him to the Gateway of India, where another elaborate welcome awaited him.

The visit of the Yugoslavian President had generated considerable interest in Bombay. Thousands of city dwellers had gathered to catch a glimpse of the visiting President. The security arrangements were, however, so tight that none could get close to the Yugoslavian leader. Describing the scene, *The New York Times* wrote, "There were outer police cordons, inner cordons and inner-inner cordons."[14]

As soon as the President arrived at the Gateway, the Army Battery fired a 21-gun salute. Marshal Tito, resplendent in his grey-medalled uniform, was ceremoniously received by the MSP and other dignitaries, who had earlier called on him on board his yacht. The Mayor of Bombay, Dahyabhai Patel and Sheriff MN Dalal, welcomed President Tito with garlands.

This was followed by *Hejslovenia* (the national anthem of Yugoslavia) and *Jana Gana Mana* (the national anthem of India). The President's Colour that was first presented to the Navy in 1951 was "dipped in salute to the distinguished Head of a foreign State."[15] As was customary for visiting Heads of State, Marshal Tito inspected the Guard of Honour, presented by the Indian Navy, as 11 Liberator bombers flew past.[16] In keeping with Western traditions, Marshal Tito saluted the officers of the Navy all through the inspection.

President Tito spent six-and-a-half odd hours in Bombay. During this short time, he visited the 1200-year-old Elephanta Caves. Admiring the archaeological marvel, President Tito evinced keen interest in the frescos depicting "the marriage of Lord Shiva and Parvati" as well as in Shiva's dance.[17] After spending half-an-hour at the Caves, the Yugoslavian President returned to the Gateway of India, where he was again accorded a Naval Guard of Honour. He then visited the Naval dockyard and attended a reception "aboard the Indian Navy Flagship Delhi"[18] before proceeding to the Governor's House for lunch and rest.

President Tito left for Delhi from Bombay Central Station. The MSP, the Governor, the Mayor, several Ministers, the Service Chiefs and the Chief Minister were at the station to bid President Tito goodbye. Before his departure, the Mayor once again garlanded a delighted President Tito who commented, "This is a beautiful thing, and you win people with it. I like it."[19] A Guard of Honour was also presented by the Bombay Armed Police to the President.

The President then embarked on a 850-mile journey Delhi at 4.00 pm on a special 12-coach train powered by two engines. It was one of the longest trains in India at that time. Two drivers, one guard and 40 attendants were specially handpicked by the Indian Railway for the journey. *The Hindu* reported that this special train had "the most modern air conditioned coaches besides being luxuriously furnished."[20] It also had a cinema, library and a bar.[21] The "[c]rockery, cutlery and linen" that were used on the train had been especially flown in from England by the Government of India.[22] The Government also waived prohibitory laws for President Tito to enable him to enjoy his Slivovitz (Yugoslavian Plum Brandy) on the train – a gesture, *The New York Times* called a "special present" by a "dry state" (Bombay State).[23] Another special freight train of eight wagons chugged behind President Tito's special train, carrying the visiting party's luggage. A pilot train with security personnel was ahead of the President's special train.[24]

If President Tito's welcome in Bombay was majestic, his welcome in Delhi was no less splendid. The scale of preparations in Delhi for President Tito's arrival was virtually unmatched. The ceremonial platform in New Delhi Railway Station was exquisitely decorated with flowers, and flags of India and Yugoslavia. A red carpet was spread out to welcome the guests.

All the top Indian leaders were there to receive him. The dignitaries included the President, Dr Rajendra Prasad, Vice President Dr Radhakrishnan and Prime Minster Pandit Nehru. The attire of the dignitaries also reflected the importance attached to the welcome ceremony. President Tito was handsomely dressed in an "egg shell blue, tastefully trimmed with scarlet and gold"[25] military uniform. The Indian dignitaries too were formally dressed in "black *achkan* coats and tight white trousers"[26] leading *The Times* to comment, "There was hardly a *dhoti* to be seen."[27]

When President Tito arrived at the ceremonial platform on December 17, 1954, at 4.00 pm, the national anthems of both nations were played. This was followed by a 21–gun salute after which a Guard of Honour was presented to the Yugoslavian President.

Before he left for Rashtrapati Bhavan, President Tito spoke to the media and commented on the worldview of India. He said that India was known as a "peace–loving nation and one endowed with lofty moral qualities" and added that the people of India would never "shed the blood and tears of other nations for their selfish ends."[28] He further said, "I am convinced that our stay in India and our meetings and talks with President Prasad, Prime Minister Nehru and the other leaders will be of great benefit to both the countries."[29]

It was not only officialdom who had turned up at the station to receive and welcome President Tito. A large gathering of more than 5,000 people had also congregated outside the station. After the reception, President Tito left for Rashtrapati Bhavan in an open limousine accompanied by President Dr Rajendra Prasad. The motorcade passed through Connaught Place and Queensway (now Janpath) *en route* to Rashtrapati Bhavan. Crowds had gathered all along the roads and they shouted "*Marshal Tito Zindabad,*" to which President Tito responded by waving his hand.[30] As the ceremonial motorcade reached Vijay Chowk, the President's Bodyguard (PBG) in yet another imperial style and tradition, escorted it to Rashtrapati Bhavan.

On his arrival at Rashtrapati Bhavan, President Tito had a brief, informal chat with President Dr Rajendra Prasad. Thereafter, the Indian President escorted his Yugoslavian counterpart to the magnificent Dwarka Suite. Other members of the entourage were accommodated in Rashtrapati Bhavan according to their ranks. In the evening, Prime Minister Nehru called on President Tito for a brief meeting. Later, President Tito travelled to Teen Murti Bhavan and the leaders had their "first round of informal talks" at the Prime Minister's residence over a "quiet dinner." President Tito then returned to Rashtrapati Bhavan for the day.[31]

Prime Minister Nehru (left) with President Tito at Rashtrapati Bhavan in December 1954. Credit: PC

President Tito raising a toast at the banquet in his honour at Rashtrapati Bhavan. Seated to his right are Indira Gandhi and Vice President Dr Radhakrishnan. (December 1954). Credit: PD

The next day, December 18, President Tito visited *Rajghat* and laid a wreath made of red, white and blue flowers representing the colours of the national flag of Yugoslavia,[32] on the *samadhi* of Mahatma Gandhi. After observing a two-minute silence, President Tito took pictures of the memorial and planted "an *Asoka* sapling" in the compound.[33]

President Tito's schedule for the morning included visits to the Red Fort and Jama Masjid. At 11.00 am, he had a two-hour private meeting with Prime Minister Nehru. Though details of the meeting were not released, the two leaders were reported to have discussed issues of "peaceful coexistence."[34]

That afternoon, President Tito and President Dr Rajendra Prasad had lunch at Rashtrapati Bhavan. Thereafter, the Yugoslavian President witnessed an enthralling "polo match and mounted sports" at the Race Course Grounds.[35] The President's Secretariat added some more items to the sporting event. A musical ride by the PBG, massed bands and the display of Beating Retreat[36] added to the attractions at the Race Course Grounds. President Tito met the Indian Prime Minister once more, that evening and conferred privately with him for an hour.

At 8.30 pm, President Dr Prasad hosted a grand State Banquet for President Tito. It was laid out with great care and aplomb in the Banquet Hall of Rashtrapati Bhavan. After the main courses,

President Dr Rajendra Prasad proposed a toast to President Tito and lauded the role he had played in the Second World War. Emphasising the importance of President Tito's visit, the Indian President reiterated that the Yugoslavian President's "visit to India will undoubtedly help in strengthening the friendship between the two countries to their mutual advantage and for the promotion of peace and understanding among nations."[37]

President Tito, in his reply, commended India's role "in the establishment and maintenance of world peace."[38] In consonance with the hope expressed by the President Dr Prasad, President Tito underlined that the common goals pursued by both countries had formed a "solid basis for the strengthening of ties," and held the two nations together in "links of the warmest friendship."[39]

The next morning, President Tito got a glimpse of rural life in India, when he visited Nathupur, Rasoi, and Badhkhalsa villages in Sonepat, some 25 miles outside Delhi. When he arrived at the villages, the inhabitants welcomed President Tito by showering petals of roses and marigolds and garlanding him with accompanying cries of "*Marshal Tito Ki Jai*."[40]

In Badhkhalsa village, he said that there was much in common between the peoples of both countries as India and Yugoslavia were primarily agricultural economies. At Nathupur, the villagers presented him with "baskets of sweets made of *gur* [jaggery], raisins, almonds and other nuts."[41] The President was so delighted by the welcome that emulating the habit of a villager, he tried his skill at chewing on a sugarcane stick. A demonstration of the game of *kabaddi* was also staged for him and according to newspaper reports, he thoroughly enjoyed it.[42]

Later in the day, a Civic Reception was held in President Tito's honour at the *Diwan-i-Khas* in the Red Fort. He drove from Rashtrapati Bhavan to the venue in an open limousine. Along the route, huge crowds cheered President Tito's motorcade. On his arrival at the venue, the national anthems of both countries were played. Thereafter, RN Agarwal, President of the Delhi Municipal Committee, and the host of the event, welcomed President Tito, remarking that his visit was an event of global significance.

Replying to the welcome address, the Yugoslavian President thanked and praised India for the warm welcome that he had been receiving here. He described Delhi as a "symbol of the vitality, of the creative power and the freedom loving spirit of the whole Indian nation."[43] He once again reiterated that both India and Yugoslavia shared the goal of maintaining world peace. He further expressed the hope that his visit would strengthen the relations between the two nations. At the reception, President Tito was presented "an exquisite ivory work- a folding screen," a copy of the welcome address inscribed on "silk brocade" and a copy of the book, *Tito ki Kahani* (the story of Tito), a Hindi translation of the biography of the leader authored by Vladimir Dedijer.[44] In the evening, the Yugoslavian President visited All India Radio Station, where he recorded a message that was broadcast later. In his message, he emphasised the core features of non-alignment, particularly non-interference and peaceful co-existence which formed the cornerstone of both countries' foreign policy. He added, "On the basis of this principle of co-existence, our two countries are endeavouring to develop the broadest possible measure of co-operation with the widest number of States."[45] The Yugoslavian President was also the Guest of Honour at a dinner hosted by Pandit Nehru at his Teen Murti Bhavan residence that evening.

Much of the morning of the next day, December 20, had been booked for sightseeing. President Tito, accompanied by his Vice President Aleksander Rankovic, visited "Delhi University, Miranda House, Jamia Millia and Kasturba Niketan, the displaced children's home in Lajpat Nagar."[46] He also visited the Qutub Minar and was impressed by its marvellous architecture.

In the afternoon, Vice President Dr Radhakrishnan hosted a Reception in honour of the Yugoslavian leader at the Mughal Gardens of Rashtrapati Bhavan. President Dr Rajendra Prasad, PM Nehru, several Parliamentarians and over 2,500 guests attended the event.[47]

(L-R): President Tito, Vice President Dr Radhakrishnan and President Dr Prasad being escorted by AsDC for 'At Home' in Mughal Gardens at Rashtrapati Bhavan in December 1954. Credit: PC

President Tito (left) and President Dr Prasad trying their hand at music at Rashtrapati Bhavan in December 1954. Credit: PC

That evening, President Tito met Prime Minister Nehru. This was an informal meeting that lasted almost 75-minutes. President Tito also hosted a banquet at Hyderabad House in honour of his Indian hosts. Proposing a toast to President Dr Rajendra Prasad, Prime Minister Nehru and the other Indian leaders present, President Tito underlined the need to improve the living standards of the people as this, he said, was a pre-requisite for peaceful co-existence. President Dr Rajendra Prasad agreed with President Tito's observation in his reply and proposed a toast to the Yugoslavian President and his colleagues.

On December 21, at 9.00 am, President Tito and Prime Minister Nehru attended a magnificent air show at Palam Airport. This was being staged by the Indian Air Force in honour of the Yugoslavian President. Air Marshal Mukherji received the guests, and a contingent of 150 Air Force personnel presented a Guard of Honour. After the impressive show, President Tito congratulated the officers on their fine performance, and shared a cup of tea with them at the Officers' Mess.

President Tito addressed the Indian Parliament later in the day. Dressed in a "simple civilian suit,"[48] and accompanied by Pandit Nehru and Vice President Dr Radhakrishnan, President Tito stepped into Parliament to continuous applause. Welcoming the distinguished guest, Vice President Dr Radhakrishnan said that both "India and Yugoslavia were engaged in the high enterprise of building a social and economic democracy."[49] He added that India shared President Tito's faith in coexistence.

In his address to Parliament, President Tito delved on various subjects, ranging from peaceful co-existence to non-interference in the internal affairs of other nations. He opined that adherence to the UN Charter could be a possible way to reduce tensions in the world and re-affirmed his position on pursuing the policy of non-alignment in the bipolar world. He concluded his speech, thanking the Indian Government and the Indian people for the warm welcome extended to him and his delegation.

Later, a reception was held at Hyderabad House by the Yugoslavian Ambassador in honour of President Tito. It was attended by approximately 1000 people, including President Dr Prasad, Vice President Dr Radhakrishnan and Prime Minister Nehru.

On December 22, President Tito left Delhi on an extensive tour of India. On the same day, a joint statement signed by Prime Minister Nehru and President Tito was issued. The statement, besides reaffirming the friendly ties between the two countries, declared the two leaders' strong beliefs in the basic tenets of Panchsheel, the "Five principles of coexistence."[50] They also cleared the air of the speculation that a "third force" was being considered in the context of the creation of the two blocks by the US and USSR.[51]

On his extensive tour, he visited several places including Nangal, Simla, Gwalior, Calcutta, Madras and Cochin. In Gwalior, then known for its tiger population, President Tito spent a good eight hours in the jungles of Shivpuri, shooting tigers. Interestingly, the Government of India had cancelled all shooting licenses, so that when President Tito sighted a tiger, he would "have no competition in bagging it."[52] This time ironically, the Yugoslavian President known to be a "passionate hunter,"[53] did not carry a rifle with him. He merely shot six of them with his camera for his photo album.[54]

President Tito left for Rangoon aboard the "*Galeb*" on January 6, 1955.

The 1959 Visit

President Tito's second visit to India was in 1959, four years after his first visit. The seven-day tour from January 13-19, unlike his previous, was described as an "unofficial" visit.[55] Nevertheless, President Tito was accorded all the honours "normally accorded to a visiting chief of state."[56]

President Tito once again arrived aboard his Presidential yacht the "Galeb." As was done during his last visit, India sent its naval destroyers to welcome him. The "*Ganga*", "*Godavari*" and "*Yamuna*" greeted the "*Galeb*" 15 miles away from the Madras Harbour, with a booming 21-gun salute.[57]

This time the Yugoslavian President was accompanied by his wife Madame Jovanka Broz. She was 30 years his junior and a '*heroine*' of Yugoslavia's fight against the occupying Nazis. Other members of his entourage included the Under Secretary of State for Foreign Affairs, Veljko Micunovic and the Secretary General of the President's Office, Leo Mates.

President Tito's second visit was a part of his larger tour to South-East Asia. He had come to India from Burma. On arrival, he was once again welcomed with all the fanfare and protocol. After the reception, President Tito and his entourage proceeded to Raj Bhavan from where, after a brief halt and lunch, they travelled to Mahabalipuram, a tourist centre 37 miles away from Madras. In the evening, the Governor of Madras hosted a State Dinner in honour of the Yugoslavian President.

The next morning, January 14, President Tito and his entourage left for Delhi in a Yugoslavian Air Transport DC-6 aircraft, escorted by eight Indian Air Force jets. At the airport, President Tito was warmly welcomed by President Dr Prasad, who had cancelled his

President Tito (left) with President Dr Prasad at Rashtrapati Bhavan in January 1959. Credit: PC

scheduled visit to Bombay, to personally receive the visiting Head of State. Vice President Dr Radhakrishnan, Prime Minister Nehru and other dignitaries were present to welcome the Yugoslavian President. A full ceremonial welcome was accorded and it included a 21-gun salute and an Inter-Services Guard of Honour. As *The New York Times* wrote, India greeted President Tito "as an old and cherished friend."[58]

After a brief welcome address at the airport, President Tito was escorted to Rashtrapati Bhavan in an open car accompanied by President Dr Prasad and Vice President Dr Radhakrishnan. Another car carrying Madame Broz, Pandit Nehru and Indira Gandhi immediately followed it.

At Rashtrapati Bhavan, President Tito was received in the South Court by officials of the President's Secretariat. The PBG in their resplendent uniforms had lined the route from the South Court through the staircase to the corridor leading to the Guest Wing on the southern side of the building. Following tradition, President Tito stayed in the Dwarka Suite and Madame Broz in the Nalanda Suite. Other members of the delegation stayed in allocated suites/rooms, according to their seniority.

Soon after his arrival in Delhi, President Tito went to *Rajghat* and laid a wreath on Mahatma Gandhi's *samadhi*. Later in the day, he called on President Dr Prasad. In the evening, Prime Minister Nehru called on the Yugoslavian President at Rashtrapati Bhavan, and the two leaders had an hour-long discussion. President Dr Prasad hosted a State Banquet for the visiting Yugoslavian President that evening.

Speaking at the banquet, President Dr Prasad first welcomed President Tito and Madame Tito. He specially welcomed the latter, as she was visiting India for the first time. He further elaborated on the common goals of the two countries and said, "It is not necessary for me to recount here on this occasion all the common factors that bring our two countries closer. I should, however, briefly mention that neither of our two countries is affiliated to any military blocs, and this fact alone makes it easier for us to understand each other better and to work together for the furthering of peace."[59]

In his reply, President Tito thanked the President, Prime Minister and the Government for the warm welcome accorded to him though he was on an unofficial visit. He said, "Allow me first of all to thank you for the extraordinary welcome you and the Government of India headed by Prime Minister Nehru have accorded to us…We are on an informal visit this time and therefore the cordial reception which has been extended to us demonstrates even more and to a full extent the friendship and mutual understanding between the peoples of our countries."[60] He further elaborated on the strong bilateral ties between India and Yugoslavia. Striking an optimistic note, he remarked that the combined efforts of peace-loving forces, that included both India and Yugoslavia, would "succeed to save mankind from the disaster of a new war."[61] Concluding his short address, President Tito proposed a toast to the health of President Dr Prasad and to the prosperity of the nation. Following the banquet, the visiting dignitaries were treated to an impressive dance and music programme, after which they proceeded to their respective suites/rooms.

The next day on the morning of January 15, President Tito, accompanied by Prime Minister Nehru, visited the Delhi Cantonment Parade Ground to witness the Army Day Parade. President Tito was dressed in an "attractive light blue uniform"[62] and the two leaders were received at the venue by the Defence Minister, VK Krishna Menon.

Much of President Tito's day was spent in conferring with Prime Minister Nehru, privately at Rashtrapati Bhavan. Prime Minister Nehru met the Yugoslavian leader twice and held discussion for a total of over four hours. The talks culminated in a communiqué, which was released on January 16. It referred to the discussions between the two leaders on subjects ranging from international issues in Europe and Asia to bilateral ties between India and Yugoslavia. It further reaffirmed the two leaders' faith in non-alignment.

That evening, President Tito went to the "India-1958" exhibition and spent over 90-minutes visiting the different pavilions. He was particularly impressed to see the "maps and models showing India's irrigation projects at the power and irrigation pavilion."[63]

Madame Broz had a different itinerary for the day. At the time when her husband was busy holding private discussions with Prime Minister Nehru, she travelled to Agra to see one of India's finest marvels, the Taj Mahal. She also visited the Agra Fort, *Itmad-ud-Daula's Tomb* and Fatehpur Sikri, and returned to Delhi in the evening. President Tito and his wife dined with Prime Minister Nehru at his residence later that evening.

On January 16, President Tito and his entourage left on a two-day visit to Hyderabad. At the end of the visit, they flew to Madras where President Tito boarded a special train for a visit to Madurai and Tiruchirappalli,[64] the former, renowned for its famous Meenakshi Temple and the historic Tirumalai Naik Palace. The visiting delegation was received warmly at both these places. *The New York Times* reported that the temple elephants at the Meenakshi Temple "raised their trunks in salute as President Tito of Yugoslavia and his wife arrived at the temple,"[65] where he made a contribution of Rs 1000. On January 19, President Tito boarded his yacht and set sail for Ceylon.

President Tito's visit to India resulted in the strengthening of the two nations' political and economic ties. The continuity in India's policy of non-alignment by Prime Minister Lal Bahadur Shastri after Prime Minister Nehru's death in 1964, and later by Pandit Nehru's daughter, Indira Gandhi, who succeeded Prime Minister Shastri, formed the cornerstone of the close ties between India and Yugoslavia. It was this foreign policy of non-alignment that became the reason for President Tito's third visit to India, from October 20-25, 1966.

The 1966 Visit

A Tripartite Summit meeting between India, Egypt and Yugoslavia was held in New Delhi. To attend this meeting, the Yugoslavian President accompanied by his wife, Madame Jovanka Broz, arrived in India on October 20, 1966, with a 29-member entourage. Unlike his two previous visits, this time President Tito arrived in a Russian Aeroflot Ilyushin 18, and landed at Palam Airport at 9:30 am.

President Dr Radhakrishnan and Prime Minister Indira Gandhi personally received President Tito at the airport. He was accorded a ceremonial welcome that included a 21-gun salute and an Inter-Services Guard of Honour. Thereafter, he left for Rashtrapati Bhavan in a ceremonial motorcade.

This time, only select members of President Tito's entourage were accommodated at Rashtrapati Bhavan. This was because President Nasser and a part of his delegation were scheduled to arrive that evening and stay at the same venue. President Tito stayed in the Dwarka Suite and Madame Broz in the Nalanda Suite. Other suites

assigned to members of President Tito's entourage included the Tagore Bedroom, the Mysore Bedroom and the Pratap Bedroom.

It was indeed very rare for two Heads of States to be staying at Rashtrapati Bhavan at the same time. This cast heavy responsibility on the officials of the President's Secretariat, particularly the *khidmatgars* (butlers) and the kitchen staff. To cope with the increased work, their strength was augmented. Considerable time was spent preparing different menus for two delegations from two different continents, each with different dietary preferences. For instance, the Egyptian delegation primarily preferred dry meat items, a taste that the European delegation did not share.

With the staff at Rashtrapati Bhavan ready to meet any request from the two leaders and their delegations, it appeared that things were completely under control. However, nobody had imagined that there would be a demand for a hairdresser. Thus, when the External Affairs Ministry suddenly conveyed a request from the Embassy of Yugoslavia for a "dressing saloon" for Madame Broz,[66] it sent the staff at Rashtrapati Bhavan into a tizzy. Not to be found wanting

Tripartite (India, Yugoslavia and Egypt) meeting at the Committee Room of Rashtrapati Bhavan. Prime Minister Gandhi is seated on the right (near the lamp). Seated (facing, on third right from centre), is President Nasser. President Tito is obscured in photo. (October 1966). Credit: PC

in their hospitality, the officials quickly located a hairdresser, procured the necessary equipment and ensured that everything was in readiness to meet any request from Madame Broz.[67]

The following four days were reserved for tripartite talks between Prime Minister Indira Gandhi, President Nasser and President Tito. Most of these meetings were held in the Panel Room at Rashtrapati Bhavan. President Tito, however, could not attend to all his other programmes.

President Tito's doctor had advised to "relieve President [Marshal Tito] of over-strain."[68] In view of this, the planned Civic Reception for President Tito at the Red Fort and a return call by President Tito on the Indian President had to be cancelled. His itinerary too was trimmed to give him sufficient rest between scheduled meetings.

On October 21, at 8.30 pm, a gala Banquet was organised in honour of Josip Broz Tito, President of Yugoslavia; Gamal Abdel Nasser, President of the United Arab Republic and Madame Broz.

At the banquet, President Dr Radhakrishnan, described both the Heads of State as "friends of this country" who he said had come to India to "cooperate in the task of securing peace." He then elaborated on the relevance of non-alignment in the context of the superpower rivalry and said though it has been characterised

as "negative in appearance," it is "positive in content" affording to nations "the independence to decide every issue on its merits and not led by any other interests." He complimented President Tito for "tempering communism with democracy" and raised a toast to the "health of President Tito, Madam Tito and President Nasser."[69]

President Tito, in his reply, appreciated the warm welcome he and his delegates received in India. He specifically thanked President Dr Radhakrishnan for what he said were "words that reflect the sincere friendship" between India and Yugoslavia. He further added that relations between the two nations had strengthened across its entire spectrum and expressed the hope that it would be reinforced. Referring to the relevance of the non-aligned movement, he said that its existence was imperative to avoid further conflict and that there were new opportunities for "the activity of peace-loving forces." Concluding his speech, he raised a toast to President Dr Radhakrishnan, Prime Minister Gandhi, President Nasser and "the happiness and wellbeing of the Indian people and to peace in the world."[70]

During President Tito's stay in Delhi, Madame Broz Tito had many separate programmes. While the Yugoslavian President was engaged in official talks, Madame Broz visited various places. Her itinerary included the Cottage Industries Emporium, the Qutub Minar, the National Museum and the International Dolls' Museum. Later, presumably persuaded by his wife, the couple visited the Red Fort and watched the well-known "Son et Lumiere" held there. The couple also visited the Nehru Memorial Museum on the evening of October 23, 1966. It was reported that they spent time looking at the "pictures, writings and personal belongings"[71] of Pandit Nehru who was "a great friend of the Titos."[72]

While no concrete agreements were reached during the tripartite talks, all three leaders re-affirmed their commitment to the non-alignment policy. At 9.00 am on October 25, 1966, President Tito departed for Belgrade from Palam Airport. He was given a full ceremonial send-off that included a Guard of Honour and a 21-gun salute.

The 1968 Visit

The Yugoslavian President visited New Delhi again in January, 1968. This visit was of a special significance. President Tito and the Soviet Premier AN Kosygin were to be Guests of Honour at India's 19th Republic Day celebrations. In addition, it came at a time when the war in Vietnam was escalating and the involvement of the super powers in the local conflict had become an issue of agitated deliberation among non-aligned countries.

On this visit as well, President Tito was accompanied by his wife, Madame Jovanka Broz and a large delegation of 35 members. The President and his entourage arrived by a Soviet made Ilyushin 18 aircraft. They landed at Palam Airport at 3.00 pm on January

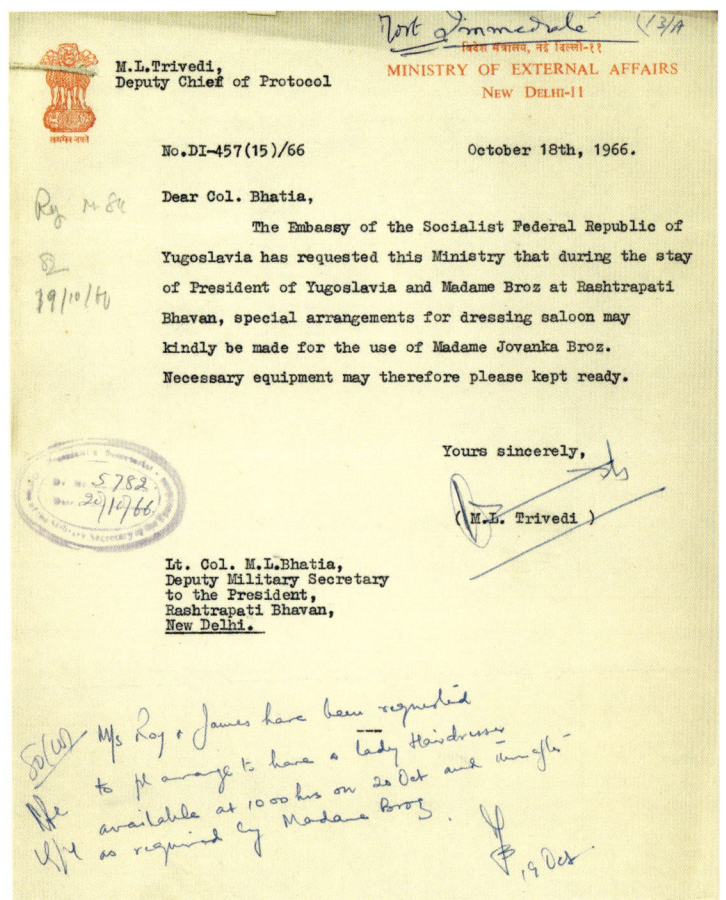

Letter from MEA regarding Madame Tito's special request for a dressing saloon.

22, 1968, to a ceremonial reception. President Dr Zakir Husain, Prime Minister Indira Gandhi and some Cabinet members and other dignitaries received the visiting delegation.

In his welcome address, President Dr Zakir Husain recalled the close bonds of friendship that existed between Pandit Nehru and President Tito. He lauded President Tito for his personal contribution towards non-alignment and said, "We, in India, feel proud and privileged to be partners with you in our common dedication to these ideals."[73] In his reply, President Tito thanked the President of India for the very cordial reception and expressed his happiness over the strengthening relations between the two countries.

After the programme at the airport, an impressive motorcade brought the Yugoslavian leader and his delegation to Rashtrapati Bhavan where they stayed in its various suites and rooms according to their seniority. Later that evening, Prime Minister Indira Gandhi called on President Tito at Rashtrapati Bhavan and had a 25-minute discussion with him. This was followed by a State Banquet hosted by the President of India for his visiting counterpart.

The next morning, the Yugoslavian President visited the *samadhis* of Mahatma Gandhi and Pandit Nehru at *Rajghat* and *Shantivana*

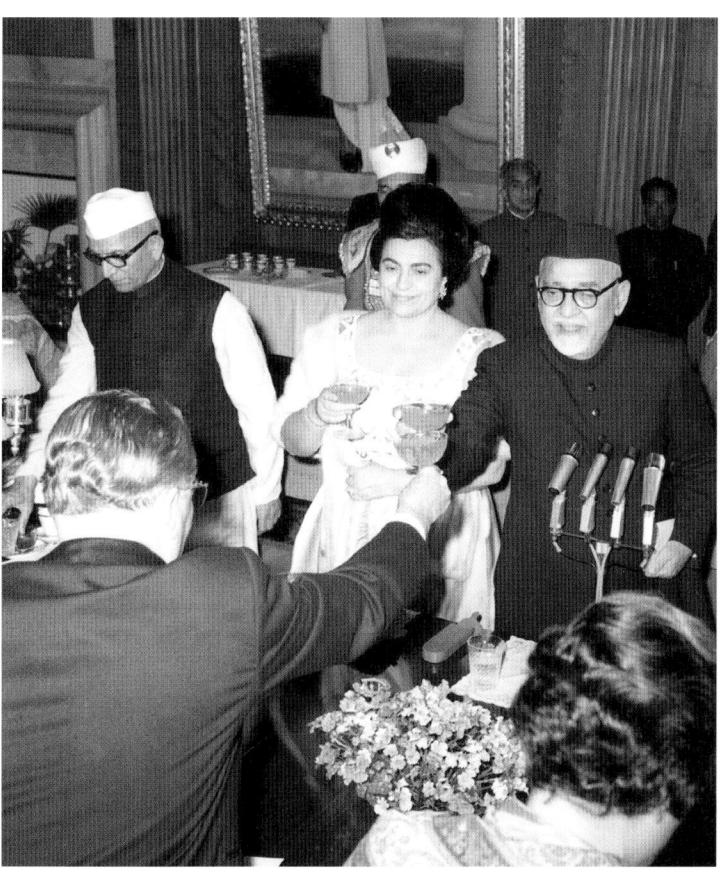

Marshal Tito (with back to the camera) and President Dr Husain (extreme right facing) exchanging toast at the banquet at Rashtrapati Bhavan. Also seen to the right of President Dr Husain is Madame Jovanka Broz. (January 1968). Credit: PD

respectively. The later part of the day was consumed by official talks. The Yugoslavian President and the Indian Prime Minister held talks for nearly three hours, over two sessions, discussing various international issues, most prominent among them being the Vietnam War and the West Asia crisis. The leaders also discussed India-Pakistan relations. Several other important meetings were also held that day and bilateral issues with trade relations dominated the talks. The day concluded with a private dinner hosted by Prime Minister Indira Gandhi for the Yugoslavian leader.

Over the next two days, Tito visited Bhopal in Madhya Pradesh. Madame Broz, however, preferred to travel to Bombay, Aurangabad and other places of tourist interest.

The Yugoslavian President returned to Delhi to attend India's 19th Republic Day. This was a programme that was not on the original schedule of the visiting dignitary. President Tito was scheduled to depart for Addis Ababa on January 24, but it was rescheduled so that he could attend the celebrations. This was done at the request of Prime Minister Indira Gandhi, with whom he shared a great rapport.[74]

Preparations were made on a grand scale for the January 26 celebrations. Official festivities for the day included a military parade and a display of India's "military machinery", amongst other things.[75] President Tito was seated with Prime Minister Indira Gandhi and Premier Kosygin, amidst thousands of spectators – all of whom watched the show with great interest.

The Yugoslavian President and his entourage left India for Addis Ababa, Ethiopia, the next morning, on January 27. He was given a ceremonial send-off that included an Inter-Services Guard of Honour and a 21-gun salute.

By mid-1971, India was faced with the exodus of refugees from East Pakistan, now Bangladesh. The Bengali-speaking population from East Pakistan was fleeing to India in droves, in the face of repression by the Pakistan military. To deal with the crisis, it was important for India to have the support of Yugoslavia, which was a founding member of the Non-Aligned Movement and one of India's closest partners. It was in this context that President Tito's fifth visit to India, from October 16-20, 1971, took place.

The 1971 Visit

Late President Dr Zakir Husain, during his visit to Yugoslavia in June 1968, had extended an invitation to Marshal Tito and Madame Broz to visit India. The invitation was cordially accepted, but no formal dates were fixed at that time.

On August 11, 1971, President of India, VV Giri, renewed it and sent the President of Yugoslavia, Josip Tito, a formal invitation to visit India. This invitation was accepted and on October 16, 1971, President Tito arrived in India with his wife and a 30-member delegation. The delegation included the Head of the Cabinet of the Supreme Commander of the Armed Forces, Lieutenant General

(Front row, L-R): President Tito, President VV Giri and Madame Jovanka Broz at Rashtrapati Bhavan in October 1971. Credit: PC

```
TO HIS EXCELLENCY
MR. V.V. GIRI
PRESIDENT OF THE REPUBLIC OF INDIA
NEW DELHI.


        LEAVING THE TERRITORY OF FRIENDLY INDIA, I WISH TO
EXPRESS ONCE AGAIN MY WARMEST THANKS FOR THE WONDERFUL
RECEPTION AND CORDIAL HOSPITALITY.  THESE FEW DAYS THAT WE
HAVE SPENT IN YOUR MIDST, AMONG OUR/FRIENDS, WE SHALL RETAIN
IN A VERY PLEASANT MEMORY.  THE TALKS WE HAD WERE, THIS TIME
TOO, REALLY FRIENDLY, OPEN, AND USEFUL, AND I AM CONVINCED
THAT THEY WILL CONTRIBUTE TO THE STRENGTHENING OF FRIENDSHIP
AND COOPERATION BETWEEN YUGOSLAVIA AND INDIA.  I AVAIL
MYSELF OF THIS OPPORTUNITY TO EXPRESS MY BEST WISHES FOR YOUR
GOOD HEALTH AND PERSONAL HAPPINESS AND FOR NEW SUCCESSES TO
THE FRIENDLY PEOPLE OF INDIA  IN THEIR CREATIVE WORK.


                            JOSIP BROZ TITO.
```

Telegram of thanks from President Tito to President VV Giri.

Bruno Vulotic and *aide-de-camp* to the President, Colonel Andjelko Valter, amongst others.

The special aircraft carrying the Yugoslavian President landed at Palam Airport at 5.40 pm. He had come from Tehran where he attended the 2,500[th] Anniversary of the Persian Monarchy. President VV Giri, who also attended the same event, had timed his return to Delhi early enough to be at the airport, to welcome President Tito. However President Giri could manage to arrive in just 20-minutes before his Yugoslavian counterpart.

As President Tito alighted from the plane to the booming sound of a 21-gun salute, he was warmly greeted at the airport by President Giri, Vice President GS Pathak and Prime Minister Indira Gandhi. He was then presented a Guard of Honour. This time, however, the usual practice of welcome speeches was dispensed with.

After the reception at the airport, the Yugoslavian President drove to Rashtrapati Bhavan. Large crowds had lined the ceremonial route and they cheered the Yugoslavian leader as his motorcade passed by.

At Rashtrapati Bhavan, as in the past, Marshal Tito stayed in the Dwarka Suite, while members of his entourage were allotted other suites/rooms. After a quiet dinner en suite, the visiting President retired for the evening.

The next morning, as was the customary practice, President Tito visited *Rajghat* and *Shantivana* where he laid wreaths on Mahatma Gandhi's and Jawaharlal Nehru's *samadhis*. Later that morning, he called on President VV Giri. The Indian Vice President GS Pathak also called on Marshal Tito during the day. That night at

8.30, President VV Giri hosted a grand banquet in honour of his Yugoslavian counterpart.

In his banquet speech, President Giri made a particular reference to the growing economic and political cooperation between the two countries. Through the words spoken at the banquet, he apprised President Tito of the problems in East Pakistan and said that it required the immediate attention of the world community. On India's response to the crisis, he said that Delhi was firm in its resolve to assist in the "restoration of the human rights and fundamental freedoms of the people of East Bengal."[76]

The next two days of President Tito were primarily spent on discussions with the Indian Prime Minister on issues concerning the humanitarian problems caused by the increasing number of Bengali-speaking East Pakistanis seeking refuge in India.

The Yugoslavian President left India for Cairo on October 20, at 9.30 am. He was accorded a ceremonial send-off at the airport. Soon after his departure, a joint communiqué was issued which declared Yugoslavia's support for India. The communiqué stated that Yugoslavia "shared India's deep concern over the serious social and political tensions engendered in India, and the strains placed on India's economy, by many millions of refugees."[77]

The visit was highly successful from an Indian standpoint, for it reassured India of Yugoslavia's continued friendship and support. President Tito, in a personal telegram addressed to the Indian President, expressed his "warmest thanks for the wonderful reception and cordial hospitality."[78] He remarked that the talks were friendly, open and useful, and would "contribute to the strengthening of friendship and cooperation between Yugoslavia and India."[79]

The 1974 Visit

President Tito's sixth and final visit to India came in the month of January 1974. He was on a six-day State Visit,[80] from January 24-29, during which he again stayed as a State Guest at Rashtrapati Bhavan. The main purpose of this visit, as reported by *The Times of India*, was to receive the Nehru Memorial Award for International Understanding.[81]

There were other issues that President Tito and PM Indira Gandhi were keen to discuss. The Arab-Israeli conflict of 1973 and the US policy in the Middle East had resulted in an oil embargo against some countries in the West. It had also adversely impacted both India and Yugoslavia. It was reported that during this visit, President Tito was "likely to press for an early Non-aligned Summit to consider the changing international situation as also the implications of the oil crisis for developing countries."[82]

In the six days that he was in India, President Tito was also the Guest of Honour, for the second time, at India's 25th Republic Day Parade. Several bilateral talks with Prime Minister Indira Gandhi were also held during this visit. The joint communiqué

(L-R): President Tito, President VV Giri and Madame Jovanka Broz at Rashtrapati Bhavan in October 1974. Credit: PC

issued referred to the wide range of subjects discussed by the two leaders. They included, the strengthening of bilateral relations, closer cooperation amongst non-aligned countries, and the urgency to resolve the West Asian crisis. On January 29, 1974, President Tito departed India for Dhaka. He was given a ceremonial send-off.

As a Head of State who had stayed 'under the dome' on all his six visits, President Tito had become a familiar face to the *khidmatgars*. Several of them had the privilege of serving the Yugoslavian leader. One of them, Abdul Majid, was Head Butler at the time and he had served President Tito and Madame Broz at Rashtrapati Bhavan in 1968, 1971 and 1974, their last three visits to India. He recalled with nostalgia, the friendly demeanour of President Tito and Madame Broz Tito. He reminisced that whenever he served the distinguished couple, they never failed to thank him with a smile and were quite

President VV Giri (left) and President Tito in State Coach leaving Rashtrapati Bhavan for Republic Day Parade on 26 January 1974. Credit: PC

(R-L): President Giri, Madam Jovanka Broz Tito and President Tito arriving for 'At Home' in the Mughal Gardens at Rashtrapati Bhavan in January 1974. Credit: PC

pleased with the service at Rashtrapati Bhavan. In fact, Majid had become such a familiar face with the couple that he was selected to be the couple's personal butler during their tour to Hyderabad in 1959.[83]

Majid also told the author that whenever Heads of State or important leaders stayed at Rashtrapati Bhavan, the CPH ensured that everything possible was done to make their stay as comfortable as possible. He said that on several occasions, many Heads of State and various leaders shared their deep

appreciation for the services rendered by the butlers and other staff at Rashtrapati Bhavan.

Josip Broz Tito, a revered war veteran in his country as some described him, died in office on May 4, 1980, after serving as the President of his country for almost four decades. He was 87. Representatives of 122 States were present at his funeral, which the BBC described as a "roll call of world leaders."[84]

Jovanka Broz Tito died in Belgrade on October 20, 2013. She was 88.

Notes

1 "Marshal Tito Visits India," *The Hindu* (New Delhi), December 17, 1954, p. 7.

2 However, *The New York Times*, December 17, 1954 reported that Marshal Tito was the "first non–Asian head of state to visit independent India." *The Times* (London), December 18, 1954 reported that Tito was the "first head of a European State to pay a formal visit to the Republic."

The Times (London), December 18, 1954 reported that Tito was the "first head of a European State to pay a formal visit to the Republic."

3 Suresh Kumar Jain, "Tito–The Artisan Who Defied Kremlin," *The Times of India* (New Delhi), December 12, 1954, p. 8.

4 Fitzroy Maclean, "Tito: A Study," *Foreign Affairs*, vol.28, no.2, January 1950, p. 232.

5 John C. Campbell, "Tito: The Achievement and the Legacy," *Foreign Affairs*, vol.58, no.5, Summer 1980, p. 1055.

6 A.M. Rosenthal, "Bombay Acclaims Tito on Arrival," *The New York Times*, December 17, 1954, p. 8.

7 Galeb was used by Marshal Tito for the first time in 1952 in Podgora where he conducted an inspection of boats from its deck. Galeb was in his service for 27 years sailing 86,062 nautical miles over the Adriatic and other seas on political missions. By Tito's death in 1980, "Galeb" had played host to 102 world statesmen. Amongst the leaders entertained on Galeb were India's Prime Ministers Pandit Jawaharlal Nehru and Indira Gandhi.

8 "Grand Welcome Await Marshal Tito," *The Times of India* (New Delhi), December 16, 1954, p. 1.

9 "Marshal Tito Visits India," *The Hindu* (New Delhi), December 17, 1954, p. 7.

10 "Grand Welcome Await Marshal Tito," p. 1.

11 Rosenthal, "Bombay Acclaims Tito on Arrival," p. 8.

12 "Marshal Tito to be Given 21–Gun Salute," *The Times of India* (New Delhi), December 10, 1954, p. 7.

13 Ibid.

14 Rosenthal, "Bombay Acclaims Tito on Arrival," p. 8.

15 "Marshal Tito Visits India," p. 7.

16 "Large Crowds Line Bombay Roads," *The Times of India* (New Delhi), December 17, 1954, p. 3.

17 Ibid.

18 Ibid.

19 Ibid., p. 1.

20 "Marshal Tito Visits India," p. 7.

21 Ibid.

22 Ibid.

23 "Rosenthal, "Bombay Acclaims Tito on Arrival," p. 8.

24 "Large Crowds Line Bombay Roads," p. 3.

25 "Viceregal Splendour Recalled," *The Times* (London), December 18, 1954, p. 5.

26 Ibid.

27 Ibid.

28 "Yugoslavia and India," *The Hindu* (New Delhi), December 18, 1954, p. 2.

29 Ibid.

30 "President Receives Marshal Tito," *The Hindustan Times* (New Delhi), December 18, 1954, p. 12.

31 Ibid.

32 "Tito Pays Homage at Rajghat 'Samadhi'," *The Hindustan Times* (New Delhi), December 19, 1954, p. 1.

33 Ibid.

34 "Tito and Nehru Confer on 'Peaceful Coexistence'," *The New York Times*, December 19, 1954, p. 3.

35 "Tito Pays Homage at Rajghat 'Samadhi'," p. 1.

36 Ibid.

37 "Promotion of Peace," *The Hindu* (New Delhi), December 19, 1954, p. 4.

38 Ibid.

39 Ibid.

40 "Visit to Community Block Near Delhi," *The Hindustan Times* (New Delhi), December 20, 1954, p. 5.

41 Ibid.

42 Ibid., p. 6.

43 "Symbol of Country's Spirit," *The Hindustan Times* (New Delhi), December 20, 1954, p. 5.

44 Ibid.

45 "Similar Approach to World Problems," *The Hindustan Times* (New Delhi), December, 1954, p. 5.

46 "Tito Goes Round Delhi," *The Hindustan Times* (New Delhi), December 21, 1954, p. 4.

47 Ibid.

48 "Equality Among Nations Urged," *The Hindustan Times* (New Delhi), December 22, 1954, p. 1.

49 Ibid.

50 "Indian Basis of Coexistence," *The Times* (London), December 24, 1954, p. 5.

51 A.M. Rosenthal, "'3D Bloc' Spurned By Nehru and Tito," *The New York Times*, December 24, 1954, p. 2.

52 "Tiger Insurance for Tito," *The New York Times*, December 28, 1954, p. 16.

53 Raymond H. Anderson, "Giant Among Communists Governed Like a Monarch," *The New York Times*, May 5, 1980, p. A12.

54 "Tito 'Shoots' Six Tigers," *The New York Times*, December 29, 1954, p. 3.

55 Elie Abel, "India Greets Tito as an Old Friend," *The New York Times*, January 15, 1959, p. 4.

56 Ibid.

57 "Marshal Tito Arrives in Madras," *The Times of India* (New Delhi), January 14, 1959, p. 1.

58 Elie Abel, "India Greets Tito as an Old Friend," p. 4.

59 Ministry of External Affairs (1995), Government of India, MEA Library, Foreign Affairs Records 1959, Volume V, accessed May 10, 2015, http://mealib.nic.in/?pdf2547?000.

60 Ibid.

61 Ibid.

62 "PM Takes Salute at Colourful Army Day Parade," *The Hindustan Times* (New Delhi), January 16, 1959, p. 5.

63 "Nehru–Tito Talks on Germany," *The Hindustan Times* (New Delhi), January 16, 1959, p. 12.

64 Marshal Tito's Indian Tour," *The Times of India* (New Delhi), December 29, 1958, p. 1.

65 "Elephants Salute Tito," *The New York Times*, January 19, 1959, p. 17.

66 Records, President's Secretariat, Rashtrapati Bhavan, File No. 30/CER/210(III).

67 Ibid.

68 Ibid.

69 Ministry of External Affairs (1995), Government of India, MEA Library, Foreign Affairs Records 1971, Volume V, accessed May 10, 2015, http://mealib.nic.in/?pdf2554?000.

70 Ibid.

71 "Visit to Nehru Museum," *The Times of India* (New Delhi), October 24, 1966, p. 1.

72 Ibid.

73 Ministry of External Affairs (1995), Government of India, MEA Library, Foreign Affairs Records 1968, Volume XIV, accessed May 10, 2015, http://mealib.nic.in/?pdf2556?000.

74 "Many of World's Notables Are Making New Delhi a Crossroads," *The New York Times*, January 25, 1968, p. 8.

75 Terence Smith, "Kosygin and Tito See Indian Parade," *The New York Times*, January 27, 1968, p. 2.

76 Ministry of External Affairs (1995), Government of India, MEA Library, Foreign Affairs Records 1971, Volume V, accessed May 10, 2015, http://mealib.nic.in/?pdf2547?000.

77 Tito Supports India on Pakistani Crisis," *The New York Times*, October 21, 1971, p. 4.

78 Records, President's Secretariat, File No. 206(3)-GI/71.

79 Ibid.

80 "Tito Calls for Steps to Ensure Peace," *The Statesman* (New Delhi), January 25, 1974, p. 1.

81 "Warm Welcome for Tito in Delhi," *The Times of India* (New Delhi), January 25, 1974, p. 1.

82 "Tito Wants Early Summit," *The Statesman* (New Delhi), January 24, 1974, p. 1.

83 Abdul Majid (2015), personal interview by Thomas Mathew, New Delhi, April 5, 2015.

84 "The Legacy of Yugoslavia's Marshal Tito," *BBC News*, April 26, 2010, accessed June 4, 2015, http://news.bbc.co.uk/2/hi/europe/8636034.stm.

NORTH
AMERICA

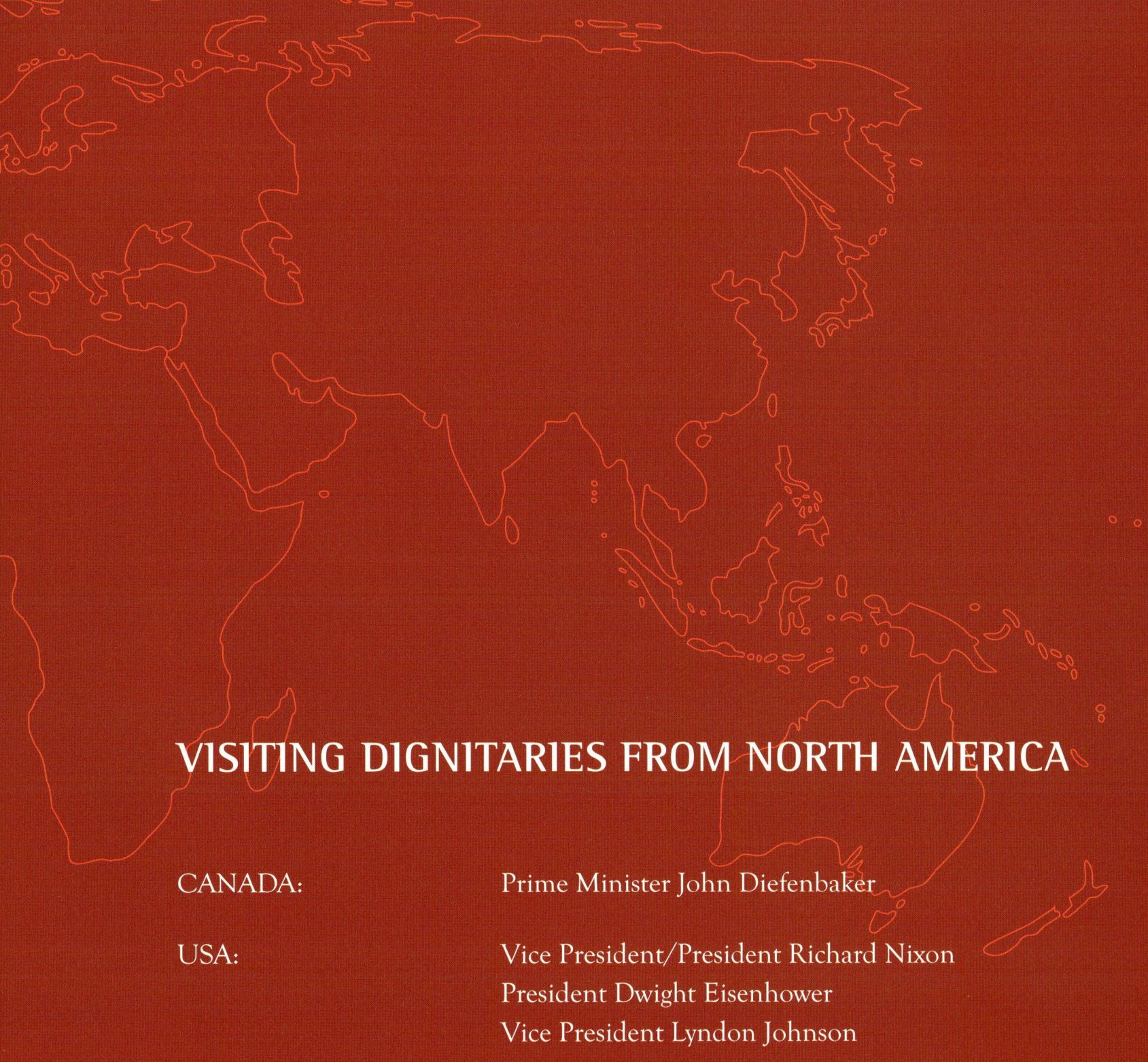

VISITING DIGNITARIES FROM NORTH AMERICA

CANADA: Prime Minister John Diefenbaker

USA: Vice President/President Richard Nixon
                   President Dwight Eisenhower
                   Vice President Lyndon Johnson

271

The Canadian Prime Minister, John George Diefenbaker's visit to India for six days, from November 18-24, 1958, was of great significance for the nation. India had gained Independence only a decade before and was actively seeking foreign collaboration and technology to build its industrial base. Canada was a notable Western nation that was willing to extend such assistance despite the two nations' political differences. Importantly, Canada was assisting India in building its first nuclear reactor (CIRUS) at Bhabha Atomic Research Centre. It was also a "substantial contributor to the financing of India's first and second Five Year Plans."[1]

At the international level too, India and Canada shared the goal of achieving peace through economic prosperity. As an adjunct to this policy, Canada had invested in the Colombo Plan, an initiative of Commonwealth countries to assist fellow nations to improve their living standards. These shared perceptions promoted closer relations between the two nations. In view of Canada's support for India's development plans and its common approach to issues of peace, India's Prime Minister Jawaharlal Nehru had accorded particular importance to the visit.

Visit of

November 18-24, 1958

H.E. Mr John George Diefenbaker

Prime Minister of Canada

Dief, as he was popularly called, was born on September 18, 1895, in the province of Ontario, Canada. His father, William Diefenbaker, was a teacher of History and Politics, and had a considerable influence on his initial political disposition. Dief, however, grew up to be a leader and a Progressive Conservative politician, removed from the liberal political beliefs of his father.

When pursuing his Master's degree from a local university, Dief responded to his patriotic calling during the First World War and enlisted in the army in 1916. He became a Lieutenant "in the Infantry of the Active Militia."[2] In the war, he suffered injuries, though the exact circumstances that led to it have been a cause of some debate. After his return in 1917, Dief became a lawyer in 1919, and practiced law for over a decade, during which he developed a close relationship with the Conservative Party and pursued his political career with determination. The Canadian Government's archival record on Dief also underscores this aspect of his character. It states, "Diefenbaker's political career is a lesson in determination and tenacity."[3]

Dief's first electoral victory came in 1940, when he was chosen to represent the Lake Centre constituency in the House of Commons. In 1956, he became the leader of the Progressive Conservatives, and by the next year, he had led his party to victory in the general elections, breaking a 22-year-old Liberal grip on power, to become the 13th Prime Minister of Canada. As Prime Minister, he was bold in his decisions and did not shy away from pursuing new policies. It was evident in his support for the rights of the aboriginal community in Canada which resulted in the first-ever induction of an

Facing page:
(L-R): Olive Diefenbaker, President Dr Prasad and Prime Minister Diefenbaker at Rashtrapati Bhavan in November 1958. Credit: PC

aborigine to the Senate. He was also the first Prime Minister of his country to induct a woman in the Cabinet as a Minister.

On the evening of November 18, 1958, a special plane carrying Prime Minister John Diefenbaker, his wife, Olive Diefenbaker and an entourage of 14 people, landed at Palam Airport from Pakistan. Members of Diefenbaker's delegation included his brother, Elmer Diefenbaker, and his Counsellor for the Department of External Affairs, HB Robinson.

A warm welcome awaited the Canadian Prime Minister and his delegation. As Prime Minister Diefenbaker disembarked from the aircraft, it was a visibly cheerful Prime Minister Nehru who welcomed his Canadian counterpart. Prime Minister Nehru then introduced Prime Minister Diefenbaker to the dignitaries who included the Mayor of Delhi and various Cabinet Ministers present at the airport. The introductions were a delightful sight. Prime Minister Diefenbaker, who was over six feet tall, bent gracefully to shake hands with his Indian hosts.

After the introductions, he was presented an Inter-Services Guard of Honour, before Prime Minister Nehru made his traditional welcome speech. Prime Minister Diefenbaker was so impressed by the welcome, that in an impromptu reply to Prime Minister Nehru's speech, he said, "I must say how deeply touched I am by the warmth of the welcome and the numbers that have turned up."[4]

After the reception at the airport, Prime Minister Diefenbaker and his entourage travelled to Rashtrapati Bhavan in a ceremonial motorcade, which included a closed green Cadillac, an open Cadillac, a DeSoto, and a number of other cars belonging to the President's Garage. At Rashtrapati Bhavan, the visiting dignitaries were warmly received and escorted to their respective suites. Prime Minister Diefenbaker and his wife stayed in the Dwarka and Nalanda Suites respectively. The Tagore Suite, Dakshin Bedroom, Bombay Bedroom, Pepsu Bedroom, Godavari Bedroom, Mysore Bedroom and Neelam Bedroom accommodated other members of the entourage.

Later that evening, Prime Minister Diefenbaker visited the exhibition, "India 1958," which showcased India's economic progress since its Independence. The exhibition comprised of nearly 300 pavilions, and had stalls divided over 22 centres. Impressed by it, Prime Minister Diefenbaker was later quoted as saying: "It [the exhibition] showed in an unmistakable manner something of the greatness of India's future, something of the principles to which she adhered and something of that abiding dedication to the maintenance of peace not only in India but throughout the world."[5]

The next day, as the sun brightened the winter day, Prime Minister Diefenbaker and his wife visited *Rajghat* and placed a wreath on Mahatma Gandhi's *samadhi*. He then called on the Indian Prime Minister at his residence at Teen Murti Bhavan, and had discussions for almost an hour and a half. Indian Foreign Secretary S Dutt and the Canadian High Commissioner Chester Ronning

were present at the meeting. Olive Diefenbaker had a separate programme. While her husband was closeted in discussions with Prime Minister Nehru, she visited Lady Irwin College and the Cottage Industries Emporium.

The couple returned to Rashtrapati Bhavan from their respective locations in the afternoon and called on the President of India, Dr Rajendra Prasad. Soon thereafter, at 1.00 pm, the Canadian Prime Minister and his wife were escorted to the stately Banquet Hall for lunch, which President Dr Rajendra Prasad had especially hosted in honour of the visiting Prime Minister. The President hosting lunch for a Head of Government was a departure from the norm, as usually Heads of State are hosts only to their counterparts. This departure, once again, was testimony to the importance that the Indian Government had attached to the visit.

Approximately 60 invitees including Prime Minister Jawaharlal Nehru, Finance Minister Morarji Desai, Indira Gandhi, the members of the Canadian delegation, the daughter of the Canadian High Commissioner[6] and Minister for Community Development, SK Dey, attended the lunch. Several Commonwealth High Commissioners and the Ambassadors of the United States and France were also among the honoured invitees.[7]

After lunch, Prime Minister Diefenbaker retired to his room to rest and prepare for a press conference that was scheduled to be held at 4.00 pm at Vigyan Bhavan. Speaking to correspondents during the conference, Prime Minister Diefenbaker shared details of his visit to Pakistan. Replying to a question, the Canadian Prime Minister opined that the military regime in Pakistan would not in any way hamper the Commonwealth's promotion of democracy.[8] He clarified his stand on Kashmir's plebiscite, which he thought had been misconstrued, and added that India and Pakistan needed to sort out their issues on a bilateral-negotiating platform.[9] Much to the delight of the Indian leaders, Prime Minister Diefenbaker publicly spoke about Canada's wish to assist India in its Five Year Plan.

The conference lasted for over an hour. Busy as it may have been, the events of the day were far from over. In the evening at 6.00, Prime Minister Diefenbaker was accorded a grand Civic Reception at the *Diwan-i-Khas* of the Red Fort. Olive Diefenbaker and Prime Minister Nehru accompanied the Canadian Prime Minister to the reception. The venue had been specially lit up and decorated for the occasion. The services of a Police Band were also requisitioned for the event. The programme began with playing of the national anthems of Canada and India. Thereafter, the Mayor of Delhi, Aruna Asaf Ali, welcomed the distinguished guests hailing Canada as a "'flourishing democracy' devoted to the pursuit of peace among nations."[10] Prime Minister also addressed the gathering and lauded Canada for its "assistance for building the India-Canada reactor near Bombay, the re-equipping of the Indian railway system and the execution of various electricity generation schemes."[11] After Prime Minister Nehru's address, Aruna Asaf Ali presented Prime

(L-R): Olive Diefenbaker, Prime Minister Nehru and Prime Minister Diefenbaker (immediately behind Prime Minister Nehru), at Rashtrapati Bhavan in November 1958. Credit: PD

traditions. He especially highlighted the role of municipalities in sustaining democratic practices.[14] After the Civic Reception, the dignitaries returned to Rashtrapati Bhavan.

Later that evening, at 8.30, Prime Minister Nehru hosted a banquet in honour of the Canadian Prime Minister and his wife. Elaborate preparations were made for the banquet by Rashtrapati Bhavan. The Gorkha Regimental Centre Band played the music, while vases and pots filled with flowers imparted a splash of colour to the stately Open Staircase, Ashok Hall, Banquet Hall and the Cinema Hall.

The Prime Ministers of India and Canada arrived at the Ashok Hall at ten past eight, and stood at the entrance to receive the guests. They then moved to the Banquet Hall, where, after dinner and before coffee was served, Prime Minister Nehru proposed a toast to Queen Elizabeth II of Great Britain. The toast to the Queen of England was necessitated by Canada's membership of the Commonwealth and its pledging of sovereignty to the Queen which made her the Head of State of the country. In contrast, though India was also a member of the international body of erstwhile British colonies, it had chosen to be a Republic.

After Prime Minister Nehru's toast, the Gorkha Band played the national anthem of the United Kingdom, *God Save the Queen*. Prime Minister Diefenbaker then proposed a toast to the President of India, which was followed by *Jana Gana Mana*, India's national anthem. It was followed by the addresses of both the Heads of Governments.

Minister Diefenbaker a copy of the welcome address printed on silk and "framed in gold lace,"[12] besides two silver vases and a *zari* scarf to Olive Diefenbaker.[13] Speaking at the reception, Prime Minister Diefenbaker elaborated on the pillars of his foreign policy which he said were the pursuit of peace and adherence to democratic

Prime Minister Diefenbaker (facing, second from right) at banquet at Rashtrapati Bhavan. On his left is Indira Gandhi. Third from right (opposite Prime Minister Diefenbaker) is Prime Minister Nehru. (November 1958). Credit: PD

First to speak was Prime Minister Nehru, who in a carefully worded address, welcomed the Canadian Prime Minister and his wife as "friends", and not as mere representatives of their country.[15] Prime Minister Nehru referred to Canada's immense contribution in making India a part of the Commonwealth and said, "it may not be perhaps improper for me to say something that might be considered secret" that "it was the Canadian representative at the Prime Ministers' Conferences in London who helped us greatly in finding a way out in this new position because we were anxious, in spite of being a Republic, to continue in that close relationship."[16]

Prime Minister Diefenbaker's quest for peace was singled out by Prime Minister Nehru for praise. He elaborated and said, "When these problems are discussed, these great problems of the world today, peace and war and problems of disarmament, all kinds of formulae are evolved and discussed. It has often struck me that the problem really has no doubt to be dealt with by experts, politicians, scientists and others. But perhaps the basic thing is the psychological approach and not purely the political approach, the approach of trying to win over the other party, trying to be friends with the other party."[17]

The Canadian Prime Minister's reply was equally moving and had a distinct personal touch. He said that he and his wife were deeply gratified by the warm reception that they had been accorded in India. He departed from the usual scripted lines of a banquet speech and struck a personal and endearing note surprising all present by wishing Indira Gandhi, whose birthday it was that day. He wished her saying, "May I say this, Sir... There is somebody sitting not too far away from me – I hope she will pardon me saying this – no matter how long ago her birthday was, I hope she would never pass over 21. And to her the warmest of good wishes and congratulations. May the next year be still happier."[18] Before ending his address, Prime Minister Diefenbaker lauded India's efforts in ensuring freedom and rights to all its citizens and added, "Anything we can do to cooperate in that regard, I can assure you will be done,

(L-R): Olive Diefenbaker (second), Prime Minister Nehru and Prime Minister Diefenbaker at a cultural programme at Rashtrapati Bhavan in November 1958. Credit: PD

Prime Minister Diefenbaker (standing, second from left), with Olive Diefenbaker (fifth from left) and Prime Minister Nehru (circled) with the artists at Rashtrapati Bhavan in November 1958. Credit: PD

Programme of the cultural show held at Rashtrapati Bhavan.

because after all we are joined together in a fellowship, the like of which the world has not seen."[19] After the banquet, the dignitaries were escorted to the "Cinema Hall"[20], where they were treated to a scintillating performance of music and dance, organised by the All India Radio. The performances included *Khamas, Kirat–Arjuna, Kashmiri* Group Song, *Natanamadinar, Sarod* Recital, *Tabla Tarang,* Night in Gujarat and *Mohini Attam.*[21]

On November 20, the next day, Prime Minister Diefenbaker and his wife were up early. After a quick breakfast in the suite, they departed for New Delhi's Palam Airport, from where they boarded a special Indian Air Force plane for Kotah, Rajasthan. Away from the hustle-bustle of the capital, their visit to Kotah, located on the banks of the River Chambal and famous for its palaces and gardens, was primarily for pleasure. They also went on a "Big Game Shoot"[22] (tiger–shoot) in the afternoon "hosted by the Maharajah of Kotah."[23] This event, though suggested as a form of entertainment, was the cause of some concern for some of the members of the visiting delegation. Prime Minister Diefenbaker's advisers were especially chary of the negative impact his image could suffer if he actually shot a tiger or "worse if he was 'eaten' by a tiger."[24] The Canadian Prime Minister, however, went ahead with the programme, and much to the relief of his advisers, there was no trophy that he could bag. They returned to the Kotah Palace for a night's stay.

The next morning, the Diefenbakers emplaned for Agra, where they visited the Taj Mahal. By late afternoon they were back in Delhi. The same evening, Prime Minister Diefenbaker visited Lok Sabha where the Chairman of the Rajya Sabha and the Speaker of the Lok Sabha hosted an 'At Home' in his honour. After this, the Canadian Prime Minister addressed Members of Parliament (MPs) in the Central Hall.

Introducing Prime Minister Diefenbaker to the Parliamentarians, the Indian Vice President Dr Radhakrishnan hailed him as the "Prime Minister of a country which was older in democracy and from whom India had to learn a great many things as a young democracy."[25] He added that India and Canada shared close ties that were demonstrated on several occasions at the meetings of the multilateral fora or their creations, like the Commonwealth, the Colombo Plan, and the Far Eastern Commission.

Prime Minister Diefenbaker's address to the Members of Parliament was notable for its grace and conviction. In an inspiring speech, he spoke about the "trust and fraternity" that defined his relations with Prime Minister Nehru and that of his country with India, despite their differences.[26] Further, he pledged his nation's support to the Colombo Plan as a part of his nation's policy to support less developed countries.

He also defended his country's support of NATO, stating that it was only a "defensive organisation."[27] To drive home the point that this was the premise on which it had joined the military alliance. In statesman-like words, Prime Minister Diefenbaker appreciated India's policy of non-alignment.[28] His address was well received by the MPs who gave him a standing ovation.

On the next day, the Chancellor of Delhi University, Vice President Dr Radhakrishnan conferred on Prime Minister Diefenbaker an Honorary Degree of Doctor of Laws. India's Prime Minister, Jawaharlal Nehru and Vice Chancellor of the University, Dr VKRV Rao, were amongst the distinguished invitees who attended the function that was held at the University, by its. After receiving the honour, Prime Minister Diefenbaker who seldom let a moment for humour pass, said, "I came to India as a student, and I seem to have graduated quickly."[29]

Later at 3.00 pm, the Canadian Prime Minister met with the members of the Planning Commission to discuss the industrial progress the two countries had made. While her husband was holding talks, Olive Diefenbaker met Indira Gandhi for tea.

Prime Minister Diefenbaker and his wife Olive chose to spend the first half of Sunday, November 23, for sightseeing. This was followed by lunch at Prime Minister Nehru's residence at Teen Murti Bhavan. Prime Minister Nehru also took this opportunity to discuss Canada's assistance for India's Second Five Year Plan to which Prime Minister Diefenbaker is reported to have responded positively.

On Monday, November 24, the Canadian Prime Minister ended his trip to India. He and his entourage left Delhi at 8.00 am, flying to Colombo on a three-day visit. The Mayor of Delhi, Members of Parliament, officials, ministers and members of the diplomatic corps were present to bid him farewell at the airport.[30]

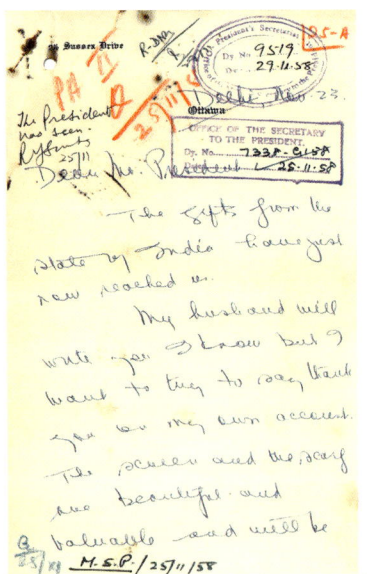

Hand–written letter of thanks from Olive Diefenbaker to President Dr Rajendra Prasad.

The visit of Prime Minister Diefenbaker was highly successful and it further strengthened India–Canada relations. As future events bore evidence, Prime Minister Diefenbaker and his wife, Olive Diefenbaker, were evidently touched by the warmth and the personal touch of the Indian hosts. This prompted Olive Diefenbaker to break with tradition and send a touching handwritten letter from 24 Sussex Drive, Ottawa, the official residence of the Canadian Prime Minister to the Indian President Dr Rajendra Prasad. In it, she thanked the President for what she said was the, "privilege of staying" at Rashtrapati Bhavan and for the "wonderful and kindly care" that was given to them. She described the experience as something which was "unforgettable."

John Diefenbaker was politically active until 1978. He suffered a stroke and passed away the next year, on August 16, 1979, one month shy of 84 years. Olive Diefenbaker died on September 22, 1976. She was 74.

Notes

1 "Diefenbaker hints at Pakistani shift," *The New York Times*, November 20, 1958, p. 3.

2 Arthur Slade, *John Diefenbaker: An Appointment with Destiny* (Quebec: XYZ Publishing, 2001), p. 10.

3 "The Right Honourable John George Diefenbaker: Biography (1895–1979)," accessed May 16, 2015, https://www.collectionscanada.gc.ca/primeministers/h4-3331-e.html.

4 "Canadian Premier in Delhi," *The Times of India* (New Delhi), November 19, 1958, p. 1.

5 "Canadian Help Lauded," *The Times of India* (New Delhi), November 20, 1958, p. 7.

6 The available record does not mention the High Commissioner's daughter by name. The records also do not ascertain the Canadian High Commissioner as one of the invitees to the lunch. However, in all probability he was an invitee as he was present in most of the official talks.

7 Records, President's Secretariat, Rashtrapati Bhavan, File No. 30/CER/68.

8 "Early Return to Democratic Ways," *The Times of India* (New Delhi), November 20, 1958, p. 7.

9 "Advent of Military Regimes in W. Asia," *The Hindu* (New Delhi), November 20, 1958, p. 1.

10 "Civic Address Presented," *The Hindu* (New Delhi), November 20, 1958, p. 6.

11 "Canadian Help Lauded," p. 7.

12 "Civic Address Presented," p. 6.

13 Ibid.

14 Ibid.

15 Ministry of External Affairs (1995), Government of India, MEA Library, Foreign Affairs Records 1958, Volume IV, accessed May 16, 2015, http://mealib.nic.in/?pdf2546?000.

16 Ibid.

17 Ibid.

18 Ibid.

19 Ibid.

20 Records, President's Secretariat, File No. 30/CER/68.

21 Ibid.

22 Ibid.

23 Ryan M. Touhey, *Conflicting Visions: Canada and India in the Cold War World, 1946–76* (Vancouver: University of British Columbia Press, 2015), p. 133.

24 Ibid.

25 "Membership of Atlantic Pact," *The Hindu* (New Delhi), November 22, 1958, p. 1.

26 "Common Aim with India," *The Times of India* (New Delhi), November 22, 1958, p. 7.

27 "Membership of Atlantic Pact," p. 1.

28 Ibid.

29 "Honorary Degree Conferred," *The Hindu* (New Delhi), November 23, 1958, p. 5.

30 Records, President's Secretariat, File No. 30/CER/68.

Richard Milhous Nixon, the 36th Vice President of the United States of America, visited India in 1953. Sixteen years later, in 1969, he returned as the 37th President of his country. On both these visits, he stayed at the Rashtrapati Bhavan. Famous for his sharp political acumen and keen grasp of the complex geopolitical dynamics of the Cold War, his visits drew world attention. Both his trips to India too were during crucial phases in world history and no less important in India's.

Richard Nixon was born in California in the year 1913. The second of five boys born to a grocery owner, his early life was marked by financial hardship and a somewhat troubled childhood. He was later quoted as saying, "We were poor, but the glory of it was, we didn't know it."[1]

Visits of

H.E. Mr Richard Nixon

The Vice President/President of The United States of America

Nixon never let his family's poor financial circumstances either dampen his ambitions or hinder his education. He pursued his studies with vigour and achieved outstanding academic success. He also developed exceptional debating skills. He continued his higher studies and pursued Law from the renowned Duke University. In his final year of law, he became the President of the Duke Bar Association. When World War II broke out, he joined the US Navy. Soon after the end of the War, he chose to contest elections to the House of Representative in 1946 and emerged victorious. Four years later, he was elected to the Senate from his home state of California.[2]

Displaying extraordinary determination, he rose rapidly through the maze of US politics and became the only leader of his country to be elected twice as both the Vice President and the President. He first became Vice President, when he was nominated as the running mate of General Eisenhower in the 1953 presidential election. When Eisenhower won the White House, Nixon, 39, became the second youngest holder of the office of the Vice President in US history.

The 1953 Visit

On November 29, 1953, Vice President Nixon landed in Madras with his wife, Patricia Nixon, who normally accompanied her husband on foreign visits. They arrived from Ceylon in a US Air Force Dakota plane on a visit that the Vice President said, had no declared agenda. He said so to media correspondents on arrival at Madras airport and added that he hoped to convey the 'goodwill' that average Americans had for the Indian nation.[3]

Vice President Nixon's decision to begin his tour from Madras was a departure from the normal practice of leaders on State Visits who arrive in the capital of the nation they are visiting. He did it with the reason of seeing more of India and meeting

Facing page:
(L-R): Patricia Nixon, President Dr Prasad
and Vice President Richard Nixon in
Mughal Gardens at Rashtrapati Bhavan in
December1953. Credit: PC

C Rajagopalachari, India's first Indian Governor-General and then Chief Minister of the State.

At Madras, Vice President Nixon met C Rajagopalachari and their talks reportedly covered international problems, including those of "mutual interest" to the two countries. The talks apparently pleased the visiting dignitary who remarked, "he talked more than I. He was talking much to my benefit."[4] The Vice President was so highly impressed and influenced by Rajagopalachari that he described him as an "infinitely wise man." The meeting was also sufficient for Vice President Nixon to disagree with Paul Hoffman's (he had supervised the Marshall Plan), portrayal of Rajagopalachari as "one of the world's most gifted men" describing it as "an understatement."[5] He wrote: "[Rajagopalachari] had such a dramatic effect on me that I used many of his thoughts in my speeches over the next several years."[6]

The next day, November 30, Vice President Nixon visited Bangalore, where his programme included a tour of the Hindustan Aircraft Factory, which he described as a "striking symbol of the progress that is in store for India in the future."[7] He also met the Chief Minister of Mysore (now the State of Karnataka), Hanumanthaiah, with whom he discussed several issues including the policy that the US should follow in Asia. The US Vice President then returned to Madras the same day and left for Delhi, this time in a Constellation military transport aircraft. Before leaving Madras, however, he did not fail to tell journalists about his engagements and the impressions he had gathered during his stay in the city. In statements that revealed his satisfaction over the first leg of the visit a perceptibly relaxed Vice President Nixon, shared jokes with journalists about how both Rajagopalachari and he had tried to govern their respective countries. He told them that the Chief Minister had succeeded while he had failed.[8] Striking a chord that was sure to please his local hosts, the Vice President, who had the "knack" of saying the "right things"[9] remarked that "he wished to come back some time to Madras to see its beach."[10]

During his four-day visit to New Delhi, Vice President Nixon stayed at Rashtrapati Bhavan as the guest of India's first President, Dr Rajendra Prasad. When the Vice President and his entourage arrived at Palam Airport in Delhi, the Military Secretary to the President (MSP), Major General B Chatterjee welcomed him on behalf of the President of India. The Chief of Protocol (COP), IS Chopra, received him on behalf of the Government of India.

Vice President Nixon began his programme in Delhi on December 1, by laying a wreath on the *samadhi* of Mahatma Gandhi. Thereafter, Vice President Nixon accompanied by US Ambassador George V Allen, met Pandit Nehru at the External Affairs Ministry, where they held discussions for nearly 20-minutes. The stated objective of the meeting was to personally convey President Eisenhower's greetings to Prime Minister Nehru.

The Vice President's programme for the day included a meeting with about 500 US Embassy staffers and those connected with the Mission. He also attended a pre-lunch reception at the Ambassador's residence, which was attended by the Indian Vice President, Dr Sarvepalli Radhakrishnan; Members of Parliament; heads of the diplomatic corps and other dignitaries. In the evening, the Indian Vice President hosted a welcome reception in honour of his visiting counterpart.

Patricia Nixon, meanwhile, had a separate itinerary. While her husband was involved in the affairs of the state, she visited the Cottage Industries Emporium on Queens Way (now Janpath), the 'Harijan Colony' (now named Valmiki Sadan) on Reading Road (now Mandir Marg) where she distributed sweets to the children of the settlement and the Indian Co-operative Union Community centres in Jhandewalan in Karol Bagh.[11] She also presented a cheque of $ 500 to Indira Gandhi on behalf of the veterans of the former China, India and Burma theatres, towards the aid of Indian children.[12] In the afternoon, the President of India hosted Vice President Nixon and his wife to tea. Later that evening, the couple attended a reception hosted by the Indian Vice President.

The next day, December 2, on the hour at six in the evening, Vice President Nixon had a formal meeting with the Prime Minister of India, Pandit Nehru. It lasted for two hours and the leaders exchanged views on world politics. Though the discussions were termed confidential, Vice President Nixon himself described it as, "highly packed".[13] After his talks, he reportedly commented that Nehru was very "eloquent and an ardent advocate of his point of view" and did most of the talking as the US Vice President was "anxious to get the Prime Minister's views,"[14] communicating, perhaps, that there were several issues on which the two did not agree.

It was obvious that on the political front, there were differences of opinion on the recognition of Communist China, the US arms aid to Pakistan and a possible military agreement between Pakistan and the US. These agreements did not, however, detract Prime Minister Nehru from admitting to the consonance of interests at the fundamental level between the two countries. Referring to his meeting with Vice President Nixon, Pandit Nehru said that there was "no basic chasm" between India and the United States.[15]

It was not all work for the US Vice President. Despite their busy schedule, the American Vice President and his wife squeezed enough time out on December 2, to visit some of the villages in Sonepat, located around 25 miles north of Delhi. They had left in the early hours of the day and arrived to a warm welcome by the villagers. During this visit, Vice President Nixon presented a steel plough to a resident farmer, named Dharam Singh.[16] He also "took a turn at ploughing a new furrow in Singh's freshly turned field."[17]

The general impression of the visit was that it provided an opportunity for the "friendly airing" of differences between the two nations. The obvious political differences did not affect the warm and affection with which the people of India receive visiting dignitaries. *The New York Times* echoed these perceptions and wrote

(L-R): President Dr Prasad, Vice President Nixon and Patricia Nixon sitting in Mughal Gardens at Rashtrapati Bhavan in December1953. Credit: PC

that "it is safe to say that the Vice President must have left India convinced that the Indian people's friendliness toward Americans is in reality deep and positive" and that "No people are more responsive to friendship than the Indians."[18]

The next day, December 3, Vice President Nixon addressed a joint session of Parliament. When he arrived for the address, Vice President Dr Radhakrishnan extended the US leader a "very cordial welcome." In his speech, he requested his US counterpart to convey India's greetings and good wishes to the US President to which the Members of Parliament (MPs) responded by "loud and prolonged" cheers.[19]

During his half hour address, the visiting dignitary underscored the commonalities between the two countries and said, "The air you breathe here is free, there is tolerance of religion, freedom of speech, freedom of the press, justice under law and a dedication to the ways of peace."[20] Vice President Nixon also expressed his country's vital interest in India continuing to be "independent, free and strong economically and every other way" and that US support would "generously be provided to assist" Indian Government "in the programme that they have developed to accomplish those purposes."[21] This assurance was welcomed by the MPs with loud cheers.[22]

The next day, December 4, Vice President Nixon left for Kabul. Before departure, he expressed his admiration for India, which he remarked, had all the signs of a nation with a great potential. He gave expression to this perception and said, "In every village I went and every place that I visited, there is a dedication on the part of the people to make all the sacrifices that are necessary to deal with India's problems. That element is a major factor which assures India's progress in the future."[23]

The Times too, referred to the education of the US Vice President about India and Asia and about what they stood for. The newspaper wrote, "It is also generally agreed that the [Nixon] displayed a receptiveness and percipience which would prevent him from repeating errors sometimes made by Western visitors in assessing the forces at work in Asia to day and the leadership of them."[24]

Richard and Patricia Nixon were seen off at the airport by the MSP Major General Chatterjee on behalf of the Indian President, and the COP, IS Chopra. Others who bade farewell included US Embassy officials, the Ambassadors of Iran, Iraq and Afghanistan and the High Commissioner of Canada.[25]

There were several opinions that newspapers voiced on the visit. *The Times* commented that it may have educated the US Vice

IMPORTANT TELEPHONE NUMBERS			
Name	Designation	Telephone Nos.	
		Office	Residence

RASHTRAPATI BHAVAN

Name	Designation	Office	Residence
Dr. Nagendra Singh	Secretary to the President	374930 375321/11	374723 375321/36
Shri V. Phadke ...	Deputy Secretary to the President.	376677 375321/112	387559 375321/56
Shri A. M. Abdul Hamid.	Press Secretary to the President.	376535 375321/120	376922
Major-General Amreek Singh.	Military Secretary to the President.	376754 375321/22	374665 375321/169
Lt.-Col. M. L. Bhatia	Deputy Military Secretary to the President & Comptroller, President's Household.	372959 375321/30 & 373955 375321/23 76255/86	376956 375321/55
Dr. Harbans Lal	Surgeon to the President	375321/121	387810 375321/38
A.-D.-C. Room ..		375321/9&10	
Mrs. M. Mabert ...	Housekeeper		375321/33
Reception Office ..		375321/105	
President's Garage		375321/28	

MINISTRY OF EXTERNAL AFFAIRS

Name	Designation	Office	Residence
Shri Prithi Singh	Chief of Protocol	372520	376842
Capt. D. F. Pereira, I.N.	Deputy Chief of Protocol	372039	42187

ALLOTMENT OF ROOMS		
Name of Guests	Rooms	Phone 76255 Ext. Nos.
H.E. Mr. Richard M. Nixon, President of the United States of America.	Dwarka Suite— Bed Room / Sitting Room	80 / 79
Mrs. Nixon.	Nalanda Suite— Bed Room / Sitting Room	78 / 78-A
H.E. Mr. Emil Mosbacher, Chief of Protocol. Mrs. Mosbacher.	Bombay Bed Room	71
Dr. Henry Kissinger, Assistant to the President.	Dakshin Bed Room	72
Mr. H. R. Haldeman, Assistant to the President. Col. James D. Hughes, Armed Forces Aide to the President.	Tagore Bed Room	76&77
Mr. John Whitaker, Secretary to the Cabinet. Mr. Dwight L. Chapin, Special Assistant to the President.	Mysore Bed Room	75
Mr. Ronald L. Ziegler, Press Secretary.	Pepsu Bed Room	70
Miss Rose Mary Woods, Personal Assistant to the President.	Himalaya Bed Room	69
Dr. Walter Tkach, White House Physician. Mr. William Lake.	Godavari Bed Room	81

Room Allocation Plan.

President on the dynamics of the situation in India and Asia and how to appreciate them. The newspaper wrote, "It is also generally agreed that he [Nixon] displayed a receptiveness and percipience which would prevent him from repeating errors sometimes made by Western visitors in assessing the forces at work in Asia to-day and the leadership of them."[26]

The evaluation of the outcome of the visit was too no different. The overwhelming assessment was that it provided both nations an opportunity for the "friendly airing" of their differences. The apparent divergence in their perception on many issues and subjects, however, did not impair the warmth and affection with which the Indian people greeted Vice President Nixon and the feeling of goodwill they have for America. *The New York Times* echoed these perceptions. It wrote that "It is safe to say that the Vice President must have left India convinced that the Indian people's friendliness toward Americans is in reality deep and positive" and that "No people are more responsive to friendship than the Indians."[27]

A keen traveller by nature, Richard Nixon visited India as a private citizen in 1967, reportedly to deepen his understanding of Asia. But this was not to be his last visit.

The 1969 Visit

In 1960, John F Kennedy defeated Nixon in the US Presidential elections. Two years on, he ran for Governor of California and again lost. A deeply disappointed Nixon vowed to quit politics. Yet he continued to be one of the most well-known politicians of the US.[28] It was not long before he changed his mind and plunged back into active politics.

In a spectacular comeback, Nixon won the Presidential election in 1968. Within a year, President Nixon, then 56, visited India on July 31, 1969, on a 22-hour trip, the shortest ever by an American President. With this visit, however, he became the only US leader to visit India as Vice President and President of his country.

The visit also came at a time of great significance for mankind; on the 10th day of the man's landing on the moon. This feat had not only captured the imagination of the peoples and nations around the world, it virtually set their emotions on fire and India was one nation that signified it, perhaps, more than any other did. They could not believe that any one could set foot on moon. To the people of India, the moon is intertwined with its culture, including astrology, which millions believe in. The news of the landing understandably so ignited their desires that they sent over 1000 sent telegrams to the US Embassy expressing their eagerness to either

President Nixon's motorcade climbing the gradient to Rashtrapati Bhavan in July 1969. Credit: PC

travel to the moon or buy land there. One enterprising Indian from Baroda went to the extent of sending a telegram to the US Ambassador to India, Kenneth Keating, for the allotment of a 370 sq. metre plot "in the vicinity of the Sea of Tranquillity."[29] This led the US President to later quip to Keating, "Don't accept all of them. I have some candidates of my own."[30]

US Air Force One, carrying President Nixon and his delegation, touched down at Palam Airport on July 31, 1969, at 12.30 pm. A 21–gun salute echoed as the dignitaries alighted the ladder to a warm welcome by the Acting President of India, Mohammad Hidayatullah. Prime Minister Indira Gandhi, Cabinet Members, the three Service Chiefs and other dignitaries also received President Nixon.

President Nixon (left) with the Acting President Hidayatullah at Rashtrapati Bhavan in July 1969. Credit: PC

President Nixon's entourage included the US Ambassador, Kenneth B Keating; COP, Emil Mosbacher; National Security Assistant to the President, Dr Henry Kissinger; Cabinet Secretary, John Whitaker and 25 others. About 200 members of the White House Press had also arrived separately in two commercial aircrafts.[31]

After a warm reception, Prithi Singh, the Indian COP, escorted the visiting President to the Saluting Base, where he inspected a Guard of Honour presented by a 150-strong Inter-Services contingent. Thereafter, President Nixon was escorted to the President's Box, where the special invitees to the reception were introduced to the visiting dignitary.

In his welcome speech at the airport, Acting President Hidayatullah opined that President Nixon's visit was yet another step in bringing the two countries together. He also lauded the US President for the successful execution of the Apollo 11 Mission.

In his reply to the welcome speech of the Acting President, the US President thanked him for his kind words. He further recalled his visit to India in 1953 as the Vice President of his country when Pandit Nehru was the Prime Minister. The US President said that his Government's political objectives were the same as that of the late Pandit Nehru, to have a "generation of uninterrupted peace."[32]

The ceremonial reception at the airport concluded smoothly without any disruption that rain, which was forecast, threatened to cause. As July is usually the wettest of all months in Delhi, contingency plans were, however, drawn up for both the arrival and departure ceremonies, though they were not easy to finalise. As it was concluded that rain was imminent, the Indian Foreign Secretary and the American Ambassador took upon themselves the responsibility of drawing up the plan and decided that the arrival and departure ceremonies would be held in the Durbar Hall in case of inclement weather. They identified the Hall for the two Presidents to deliver their customary speeches and for the introductions of the Indian Cabinet Ministers, special invitees and the heads of foreign missions to President Nixon. Similar contingency plan was also made for the departure ceremony. These were communicated by the COP to the MSP.

The plan was for the Indian President and the Prime Minister to pick up the US President and Patricia Nixon and bring them straight to Durbar Hall in the event of rain. This had to be modified and the use of the Durbar Hall had to be shelved because of its poor acoustics, lack of air-conditioning or even fans. The Ashok Hall was selected instead, as it also has two separate covered entrances that could provide separate access to the invitees and the two Presidents to arrive in procession. To the relief of the Indian officials, particularly those of Rashtrapati Bhavan, they did not have to implement the contingency plan as the weather forecast proved to be inaccurate. It rained only after President Nixon left the Indian soil, prompting the US President to quip, "I'll be called Nixon the rainmaker."[33]

After the addresses at the airport, the guests travelled to Rashtrapati Bhavan in a ceremonial motorcade. This time, the Indian President was seated to the left of his US counterpart in President Nixon's Presidential Lincoln Continental, a bulletproof limousine specially flown in from the US. Nine Inter-Services outriders and four security outriders flanked President Nixon's limousine. Pushpa Shah, the wife of the acting President and Patricia Nixon drove behind in a Rolls Royce, accompanied by a cavalcade of over a dozen other vehicles. Thousands of men, women and children had gathered to cheer the American President.

In the Cantonment area, President Nixon himself tapped the bulletproof glass of his car and ordered the Secret Service to stop his limousine, as he saw nearly 700 girls from Loreto Convent and over 1200 boys and girls of St. Mary's School lining the route to welcome him. The US President and the First Lady stepped out to greet the children and Patricia Nixon presented four pens embossed with their names to be given to the "Sisters" at the convent. Near Teen Murti Bhavan, the US President got down with the Acting Indian President and shook hands with people who had "enthusiastically stretched out their arms for a handshake."[34]

During this visit, security for the US President was elaborate and unprecedented. The Home Ministry had also drawn up special rules and instructions for the security of the visiting dignitary over and above what were laid down in the 'Blue Book' that contains detailed security instructions for the protection of the Indian President and Prime Minister.

Security "fears" raised by the US Secret Service almost jeopardised the planned traditional Imperial rectangular formation in which the President's Bodyguard (PBG) escorts a visiting Head of State

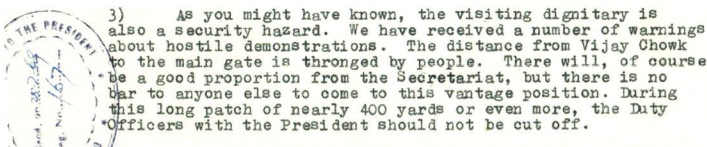

*Extract from the letter of a senior intelligence functionary intending
to communicate that Nixon is a security risk. He, however,
ended up communicating the opposite, that Nixon was "a security hazard."*

from Vijay Chowk as the motorcade slowly climbs the gentle slope to Rashtrapati Bhavan through its regal gates. The fears led to a flurry of activity and exchange of correspondence between security agencies, COP Prithi Singh and MSP Major General Amreek Singh.

The Secret Service was, however, insistent that they have the final word when it came to the security of the US President. They were reluctant to deviate from the plan of an escort car manned entirely by US officials and another provided by the Government of India to closely follow, at all times, the visiting President's car, as was agreed to in discussions with the Ministry of External Affairs and Ministry of Home Affairs. This arrangement was considered important, as it was perceived that several thousands of people would gather on both sides of South and North Block as the motorcade covered the 400 yards from Vijay Chowk to Rashtrapati Bhavan and this

could prove to be a security hazard. They were apprehensive of the possibility of "over enthusiastic" crowds stepping on to the road and getting close to the motorcade as they had, when Prime Minister Alexei Kosygin of USSR had traversed the same route a year earlier. Reports that there could be "hostile" demonstrations against President Nixon only exacerbated their worries.

The ensuing parleys had evidently exhausted many and exposed some raw nerves. The letters to resolve the impasse carried some amusing errors. One such letter written by a senior intelligence functionary, attempting to describe the security threat that the US President faced, ended up conveying the opposite that, "the visiting dignitary is also a security hazard."[35] Fortunately, in the hectic confabulations, nobody took notice of the *faux pas*.

The same official had not evidently placed any premium on finesse in communication either. He was insistent on a change in the planned formation of the PBG contingent as it escorted the motorcade of the US President from Vijay Chowk. Wanting to communicate that the cars of Pushpa Shah and the Indian Prime Minster should proceed in a block without being separated by horses, he wrote that if the plan of PBG remained unchanged, "Mrs Nixon and Mrs Gandhi" would be able to "only see the back of the horses."[36]

The deadlock was finally resolved with the intervention of the Secretary to the President, Dr Nagendra Singh, who decided that

President Nixon (centre, with back to the lamp) at official talks at Rashtrapati Bhavan. On the left of President Nixon is Henry Kissinger. (August 1969). Credit: PC

the car with the two Presidents would have behind it five mounted officers, two in each row with one horse behind them. Flanking them would be the escort duty cars. The car carrying Pushpa Shah and Patricia Nixon would be positioned behind the five mounted officers with regimental flags, behind which would be the car of the Prime Minister with the rest of the mounted horses to its rear.

As the President's motorcade approached Rashtrapati Bhavan, a group of 200 people belonging to the Communist Party of India (CPI) and the Indian-Vietnam Friendship Association, protested against Washington's Vietnam policy. They, however, failed to dampen the celebratory mood of the occasion. It rather showcased the vibrancy of India's pluralistic society and democracy, in the right to dissent.

After reaching Rashtrapati Bhavan, President Nixon called on the Acting President Mohammad Hidayatullah at 1:40 pm in the cheerfully painted Morning Room. The two Presidents exchanged pleasantries for nearly 20-minutes over light refreshments, after which both Heads of State were conducted to their respective rooms by their *aides-de-camp* (AsDC).The US President stayed in the well-appointed Dwarka Suite for his one-night stay 'under the dome', which was linked by radio-telephone to the White House, while Patricia Nixon occupied the equally beautiful Nalanda Suite. Rashtrapati Bhavan accommodated 14-members of the delegation. The rest had to be content with the less majestic ambience of Ashoka Hotel.

The timing of the visit was least propitious from the weather point of view. July is also hot and sultry, making it perhaps the most oppressive month to be visiting Delhi. The foreign media accompanying the Presidential delegation and those from India trailing him were up for some hard times. The US Embassy's frantic search for 10 air-conditioned buses for the foreign journalists met with little success. After a desperate hunt, they were able to get hold of only three and many unfortunate members of the press had to swelter in the remaining seven non-air conditioned buses.[37]

The enthusiastic hunt of some journalists for liquid refreshments to quench their thirst after their rather demanding road journey trailing the President to Rashtrapati Bhavan, ended up in a "large bowl containing a yellowish liquid." An enterprising journalist led the way helping himself to a large drink from the bowl and others followed shortly thereafter. When their parched mouths and taste buds had regained their sensitivity, someone enquired about the rather "funny" taste of the drink, to which a bearer nonchalantly replied that the bowl contained the water that had been used to wash ice cream spoons.[38]

The US President's schedule was packed. In less than an hour after his meeting with the Indian President, President Nixon and his delegation held talks with Indian Prime Minister, Indira Gandhi, and her delegation for nearly two-and-a-half hours in the Panel Room at Rashtrapati Bhavan. The three major subjects discussed were related to Vietnam, India-Pakistan relations, and

Asian security.[39] On the Indian side, participants included the Indian Ambassador to the US, Ali Yavar Jung; the Secretary of the Foreign Trade Ministry, KB Lall; the Special Secretary from the Department of Economic Affairs, Dr IG Patel, and other Joint Secretaries and Director-rank officials of the Government. US officials who were part of the discussion included Ambassador Kenneth Keating, Dr Henry Kissinger, Joseph J Sisco and Morris J Williams, amongst others.

Soon after the meeting, President Nixon departed for *Rajghat* where he laid a wreath at the *samadhi* of Mahatma Gandhi and returned to Rashtrapati Bhavan at 5.50 pm. Thirty minutes later, India's Acting President called on the US President at the sitting room of the Dwarka Suite.

While her husband was engaged in the affairs of the state, Patricia Nixon, had a separate itinerary. She visited Chattarpur village on the outskirts of Delhi and spent 45-minutes there. Students of the local Government Secondary School, playing fifes and drums, warmly welcomed the First Lady, who was dressed in pink when she arrived at the village. The villagers, too, were visibly excited to receive the First Lady of the US and they expressed it in their rustic, but endearing style. The event was not without its amusing moments that the US press captured with interest.

The New York Times wrote that when the First Lady was introduced to the villagers who were told that "The honourable lady visiting them was from America, a country that had recently conquered the moon," they misinterpreted the introduction to mean that she was "the lady from the moon."[40] As word spread of the unique visitor, there was a rush of villagers to take a look at the "lady from the moon." The villagers were demonstrably very pleased with the visit that they did not forget to give her a parting gift as if to say, thank you for coming to the village. It was the kind of memorabilia that the First Lady may never have received before or since as a token of affection: a "basketful of eggs."[41]

At 8.30 pm, Acting President Hidayatullah hosted a State Banquet in honour of President Nixon. It was a gala event and the dinner was "magnificent"[42] as President Nixon himself chose to describe it later. After the main courses were served, Acting President Mohammad Hidayatullah proposed a toast to the US President. In his address that followed, he described President Nixon's tour as "a journey in quest of peace,"[43] undertaken with the desire to promote closer relations and friendship between the two countries. The Acting President, however, politely but unequivocally, added that closer relations could not be at the expense of India's independence. He further said that India would not abandon its non-aligned policy, assuring at the same time that its policy was rooted in its "determination to remain independent and to exist in peace and friendship with others."[44] The Acting President concluded his address hoping that the US President and the First Lady would visit India again, for a longer duration.

THE WHITE HOUSE

WASHINGTON

September 5, 1969

Dear General:

Let me express my deep appreciation and sincere gratitude for the outstanding work done by you and your staff during President Nixon's visit. The preparation and attention to detail are a credit to your leadership. I felt honored to have the opportunity to work so closely with you, Lt. Col. Bhatia and the other Military Aides to the President. Please express my appreciation and congratulations for a job well done.

Sir, I trust that you have received notification that the packages were delivered. They were mailed the day after my arrival in Washington -- I was glad to do this for you.

Sincerely yours,

Ronald H. Walker
Presidential Advance Man

Major General Amreek Singh
Military Secretary to the President
4, President's Estate
New Delhi, India

P.S. I sure miss the mango ice cream.

Ronald H Walker, Presidential Advance Man, missing India's "mango ice cream."

President Nixon, in his reply to Acting President Hidayatullah's toast, thanked his Indian host for his gracious words, and stressed the need for peace in the region. The American President recalled his visit to *Rajghat* earlier during the day and remarked that it was his privilege to pay homage to "a great man of peace."[45] President Nixon noted that the ongoing situation required a different kind of peace, one that not only recognises "many threats to peace, but also the many dimensions of peace."[46] Respecting India's policy of non-alignment, he said, "We respect India's policy of non-alignment, its determination to play its role in the search for peace in its own way. What matters is not how peace is preserved, but that it be preserved."[47]

After the toast, fruits and coffee were served, and the dignitaries were then conducted to the Ashok Hall for a 30-minute cultural programme by 38 artistes that had been organised by the Song and Drama Division, Ministry of Information and Broadcasting. The performances selected were India's popular dances, *Bharatnatyam, Hindola* and *Shahi Mehfil, Kathak, Pung Cholam* and *Odissi*.[48] The curtains came down on the day's events around 10.15 pm.

The programme for the next day began early at 8.30 am with the Indian Prime Minister and the US President meeting with their advisers in the Panel Room at Rashtrapati Bhavan. The meeting lasted for an hour-and-a-half. At 10.10 am, the American President and his entourage departed for Palam Airport, where he was given a ceremonial send-off.

The Acting President Mohammed Hidayatullah and his wife bade farewell to the President and Patricia Nixon at the airport. Prime Minister Indira Gandhi, the Mayor of Delhi and his wife and other dignitaries also bid the US President and First Lady good-bye.

In his farewell speech, President Nixon declared that his talks with the Indian Prime Minister and President had been "most helpful in establishing a new channel of communication, a new attitude with regard to the relations between our two countries."[49]

Every minute detail of the visit was meticulously planned and executed by Rashtrapati Bhavan and the Government. Perhaps, the postscript of the letter written by Ronald Walker, who was part of President Nixon's entourage, to the MSP from the White House, said it all. It read, "I sure miss the mango ice cream"[50] communicating once again that Indian hospitality and friendliness was unmatched, just as *The New York Times* had said in 1953 after Nixon's visit as Vice President, "No people are more responsive to friendship than the Indians."[51]

President Richard Nixon died on April 22, 1994. He was 81. Patricia Nixon had died almost a year earlier on June 22, 1993 at the same age – the day after their 53rd Wedding Anniversary. Their younger daughter, Julie is married to President Eisenhower's grandson, David.

Notes

1 Jonathan Aitken, *Nixon: A Life*, (London: Weidenfeld & Nicolson, 1993), p. 12.

2 Richard Nixon, *The Memoirs of Richard Nixon: Volume I* (New York: Warner Books, 1978), p. 95.

3 "Mr. Nixon in Delhi," *The Hindu* (New Delhi), December 1, 1953, p. 5.

4 "Mr. Nixon Says He Has No Diplomatic Deal To Sell," *The Times of India* (New Delhi), November 30, 1953, p. 1.

5 Nixon, *The Memoirs of Richard Nixon*, p. 162.

6 Ibid.

7 "U.S. Opposition to Colonialism," *The Hindu* (New Delhi), December 1, 1953, p. 9.

8 "Mr. Nixon," p. 1.

9 Nixon, *The Memoirs of Richard Nixon*, p. 166.

10 "U.S. Opposition," p. 9.

11 "IKE's Greetings Conveyed to Mr. Nehru," *The Times of India* (New Delhi), December 2, 1953, p. 1.

12 Ibid.

13 "Mr. Nixon Meets Premier," *The Times of India* (New Delhi), December 3, 1953, p. 7.

14 Ibid.

15 "Nixon and Nehru," *The New York Times*, December 1, 1953, p. 16

16 "Mr. Nixon Visits Project Area," *The Times of India* (New Delhi), December 3, 1953, p. 5.

17 Ibid.

18 "Nixon and Nehru," p. 16.

19 "U.S.A. Vitally Interested in Free India's Future," *The Hindustan Times* (New Delhi), December 4, 1953.p. 12.

20 Ibid.

21 Ibid., p. 1.

22 "Basic U.S. Policy Aimed at Securing Peace," *The Times of India* (New Delhi), December 5, 1953, p. 7.

23 Ibid.

24 "End of Mr. Nixon's visit to India," *The Times* (London), December 5, 1953, p. 5.

25 "Military Aid to Pakistan," *The Hindu* (New Delhi), December 5, 1953, p. 6.

26 "End of Mr. Nixon's visit to India," *The Times* (London), December 5, 1953, p. 5.

27 "Nixon and Nehru," p. 16

28 Heron Marquez, *Richard M Nixon* (Minneapolis, MN: Lerner Publications Company, 2003), p. 9.

29 "Nixon's visit: Indo-Pak ties may be discussed," *The Times of India* (New Delhi), July 30, 1969, p. 11.

30 "Economic aid to India: Nixon's assurance," *The Times of India* (New Delhi), August 2, 1969, p. 10.

31 Records, President's Secretariat, Rashtrapati Bhavan, File No. 30/CER/266

32 "Nixon Sets for himself Nehru's goal of peace," *The Times of India* (New Delhi), August 1, 1969, p. 1.

33 "Nixon Remarks on return," *The New York Times*, August 4, 1969, p. 14.

34 "Warm Airport Welcome," *The Hindustan Times* (New Delhi), August 1, 1969, p. 9.

35 Records, President's Secretariat, File No. 30/CER/266

36 Ibid.

37 Schanberg, "New Delhi Polishes Up," p. 14.

38 "The drink that tasted funny," *The Hindustan Times* (New Delhi), July 31, 1969, p. 3.

39 "Nixon, PM Review Asian Scene," *The Hindustan Times* (New Delhi), August 1, 1969, p. 1.

40 K. Kasturi Rangan, "Mrs. Nixon's Visit to Village Is Joyous," *The New York Times*, August 1, 1969, p. 14.

41 Ibid.

42 "India has great future, feels Nixon," *The Times of India* (New Delhi), August 2, 1969, p.1.

43 Office of the Federal Register National Archives and Records Service General Service Administration, Public Papers of the Presidents of the United States: Richard Nixon, Containing the Public Messages, Speeches, and Statements of the President, 1969 (Washington: United States Government Printing Office, 1971), p. 591.

44 Ibid., p. 594.

45 Ibid., p. 591.

46 Ibid., p. 592.

47 Ibid.

48 Records, President's Secretariat, File No. 30/CER/266.

49 The National Archives of the United States, Public Papers of the Presidents of the United States, p. 596.

50 Records, President's Secretariat, File No. 30/CER/266.

51 "Nixon and Nehru,"p. 16.

It was in the cold winter month of December 1959, that Dwight David Eisenhower, the first President of the United States of America to visit India, arrived on a five-day tour. The chill of the winter month did not, however, dampen the spontaneous exuberance and warmth of the reception, for the welcome was in the words of Pandit Nehru, "from the heart."[1]

A highly decorated Second World War General, the former Supreme Commander of the Allied forces in Europe and the 34th President of the United States, undertook the trip influenced by the mystery that he had conjured up of the region after Prime Minister Nehru's visit to the US in 1956. Describing the yearning to see India after Pandit Nehru's visit, President Eisenhower said, "I was so intrigued by the picture he [Nehru] painted of the region, its people and their aspirations that my desire to see that country for myself became stronger."[2] The President would also later write that "India has been a source of fascination to me for many years."[3]

Visit of

H.E. Dwight Eisenhower

President of the United States of America

Dwight D Eisenhower, known famously as "Ike", a childhood nickname that stuck all his life, was born in Texas in 1890. He was one of six sons born into a family of poor means that left him virtually nothing in worldly possessions.

At the age of 20, he joined the US Military Academy at West Point. After an illustrious career in the Armed Forces, he threw his hat into the political ring to emerge as the Republican contender for The White House. He won the elections on debut in 1952, with an impressive 83.2% of the electoral vote. He surpassed this feat in the next Presidential election in 1956 by nearly three more percentage points winning The White House for the second time. He was also to become one of the 13 Presidents in the US' 239-year history to serve two full terms. His popularity rating at home was also not something many US Presidents could match and he received the second highest average Gallup rating[4] any incumbent has had since the end of the War.

President Eisenhower was fond of travelling and the induction of three new Boeing 707s into the Presidential fleet towards the end of 1958 made his "travel so easy and comfortable."[5] It enabled him to undertake, with comparative ease, long overseas journeys travelling to 28 countries in the last two years of his Presidency in comparison to just six in the previous six years.

The President's propensity to tour was also based on his conviction that in order to win friends, there was no "substitute for personal contact" which furthers "understanding and good will."[6] The 11-nation tour that included India was one among those undertaken towards the end of his second term to serve the declared objective of strengthening ties with the 'Free World.' An adjunct to this objective

Facing page:
President Eisenhower (centre)
with President Dr Prasad in
Mughal Gardens at Rashtrapati Bhavan in
December 1959. Credit: PD

was Washington's perceived need to dispel notions that US policies were 'Europe-First.' President Eisenhower's visit to India achieved several of these objectives.

The five-day visit, the second longest by any US President, was not only remarkable for the imprint he left on the leaders of the country, but also for the goodwill that he was able to generate in the people of India. The visit had many high points. It had all the trappings reserved for a monarch, from caparisoned elephants to large, petal-throwing crowds that had gathered in admiration of arguably the most powerful man in the world.

The addresses, speeches and statements made by the US President and leaders of India during the visit reflected the recognition of the common values on which the foundation of both nations rested. While Indian leaders made references to the US President as a leader committed to the pursuit of peace, President Eisenhower's remarks barely concealed the lure of the mystery that a huge and diverse India presented.

The US President began his visit to India landing at Palam Airport, half-an-hour behind schedule, on December 9, at 5.10 pm. He had travelled in his customised Boeing 707 Stratoliner, the first jet aircraft to be used to transport a US President by the Presidential Airlift Group. An elite group of 18 Indian Air Force Hunter jets escorted his plane.

President Eisenhower came down the flight of stairs to the deafening sound of a 21-gun salute and the lusty cheers and applause of a huge crowd of nearly 25,000 people who had gathered at the airport to welcome him. He was enthusiastically received by his Indian counterpart, President Dr Rajendra Prasad, and thereafter introduced to Vice President Dr Radhakrishnan. Prime Minister Pandit Nehru, who had himself arrived late, after being caught in severe traffic snarls caused by the unprecedented movement of lakhs of people jostling for vantage positions to get a glimpse of the US President, greeted President Eisenhower warmly. Thereafter Prime Minister Nehru's daughter, Indira Gandhi; the Mayor of Delhi, Trilok Chand Sharma; the Indian Ambassador to the US, MC Chagla; the US Ambassador to India, Ellsworth Bunker and his wife Harriet, and several others were introduced to the President.

After the US president received the Guard of Honour and had received the greetings of VIPs and other dignitaries in a special enclosure, the Indian President addressed the gathering. He welcomed the US President as a "messenger of peace". President Eisenhower replied in his characteristic style, gesticulating as he spoke and matched the sentiments expressed by his Indian counterpart saying, "As I set foot on the soil of India, I am fulfilling a cherished wish, held for many years...[that] I would come back to India while I was still President."[7]

As a soldier, President Eisenhower who was perhaps less familiar with what a struggle that abjures violent methods could achieve heaped praise on India's extraordinarily peaceful freedom movement. He recalled how it had won the world's admiration. In words that were not without political significance, he affirmed that the leaders of the United States stood together with those of India in their common quest for peace.

On a personal level, he made known his desire to explore the fascinating facets of the country during this visit. Referring to Pandit Nehru's book, *Discovery of India*, which is a treatise on Indian history, culture and philosophy, he said that he hoped that during his short stay he would be able to make his own "personal discovery" of the country.[8]

After the airport ceremony, President Eisenhower stepped into an open blue Cadillac, which bore the *Ashoka Emblem*. The car was a gift from the King of Saudi Arabia.[9] It was the first and only time in all the six US Presidential visits so far, that a US President had travelled in an open car from the airport to Rashtrapati Bhavan. Escorted by 11 outriders, the US President was flanked on his right by President Dr Rajendra Prasad and on his left by Prime Minister Pandit Nehru on the 13-mile drive.

The city was dressed up as if it were in the midst of a festival, with decorative lights and fancy banners that proclaimed the arrival of the dignitary. The entire route from Palam Airport to Rashtrapati Bhavan was lit by hundreds of fluorescent lights and flags of both nations fluttered from every lamp post and pole along the way.

Security was tight and over 600 policemen were deployed to regulate the traffic from Palam Airport to Rashtrapati Bhavan. Police personnel in plain clothes were positioned at various places to watch the crowds. 'Roof-watchers' stood on buildings and other security men scoured the route of the Presidential motorcade.

A huge crowd of one-and-a-half million people including men, women and children had been gathering all along the route from Palam Airport to Rashtrapati Bhavan since the morning, just to catch a glimpse of the US President. The crowd was so restless that a US newspaper chose to headline the story as, "India greets President in Mass Demonstration."[10] The excitement and sheer size of the large crowds caused *Universal International News* to describe it as, "the throng is the biggest seen in India," adding that it was "the most important single stop-over in his itinerary."[11]

Several of those in the huge crowds that had come to see the visiting President had travelled in trucks, bullock-carts, camel-carts and *tongas* (usually a two-wheeled horse drawn cart). The Northern Railways had also lent a helping hand by arranging special trains on December 9 for people coming from around the capital.[12]

The million-plus people who had lined the route the US President was going to take were not disappointed. To their delight, President Eisenhower waved to the cheering crowds taking off his hat and holding it high in one hand in his own inimitable style as if to say thank you. He was soaking in the adulatory greetings as the 24-car convoy slowly moved along the ceremonial route to shouts of "*Prince of Peace Zindabad*."[13] The roads could hardly contain the swelling crowds. Kitchner Road (now Sardar Patel Marg) had a congregation of villagers led by "*panchas*" (members of a *gram panchayat*[14] in a village), bearing the banners of their *panchayats*.

The immediate route to Connaught Place was especially bedecked to receive the President. Fruit and flower-laden arches were erected on Irwin Road (now Baba Kharak Singh Marg). The motorcade took 45-minutes to drive past Delhi's iconic market centre, Connaught Place. The crowd was at its thickest here and the convoy was greeted with tumultuous applause. Welcome tunes blared out and people showered roses, jasmines and marigolds on the President's car. At several places, Pandit Nehru collected garlands that were also being thrown on the car, and passed them on to the US President.

Such was the enthusiasm of the crowd that it rendered the elaborate arrangements the traffic police had made quite ineffective. The city plunged into chaos and huge traffic jams restricted the motorcade's progress to a snail's pace. Even the hundreds of policemen, especially deployed, took hours to untangle the traffic mess. Sensing that the hapless police were having little success in managing the crowds, Pandit Nehru tried his skill at traffic management but this too met with little success.

The last leg of the journey was not without incidents either. People, in some cases 10-deep, had already gathered on either side of Vijay Chowk. They included many VIPs, Members of Parliament and foreigners.[15] The crowd was so overcome by excitement that when somebody shouted, "Look at President Eisenhower" all eyes turned to the road only to see what turned out to be a life-sized picture of the President being hawked by some enterprising person.

All along the route, the reception the US President received was so phenomenal, that one newspaper described it as a "fabulous spectacle"[16] that "deeply impressed"[17] President Eisenhower who communicated his sentiments to both President Dr Rajendra Prasad and Prime Minister Nehru. The "enthusiasm and spontaneity

President Eisenhower with both hands raised (circled) with Prime Minister Nehru on his left, surrounded by exuberant crowd in Connaught Place, New Delhi, in December 1959. Credit: US Embassy

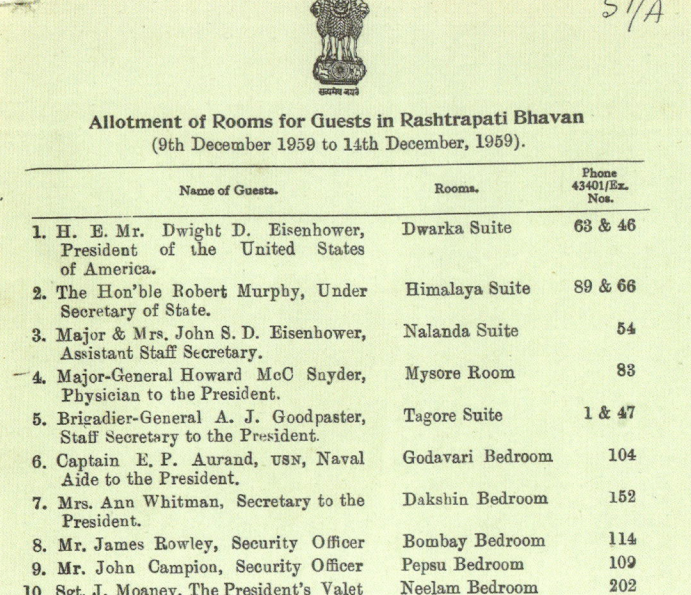

Allotment of Rooms for Guests in Rashtrapati Bhavan
(9th December 1959 to 14th December, 1959).

Name of Guests.	Rooms.	Phone 43401/Ex. Nos.
1. H. E. Mr. Dwight D. Eisenhower, President of the United States of America.	Dwarka Suite	63 & 46
2. The Hon'ble Robert Murphy, Under Secretary of State.	Himalaya Suite	89 & 66
3. Major & Mrs. John S. D. Eisenhower, Assistant Staff Secretary.	Nalanda Suite	54
4. Major-General Howard McC Snyder, Physician to the President.	Mysore Room	83
5. Brigadier-General A. J. Goodpaster, Staff Secretary to the President.	Tagore Suite	1 & 47
6. Captain E. P. Aurand, USN, Naval Aide to the President.	Godavari Bedroom	104
7. Mrs. Ann Whitman, Secretary to the President.	Dakshin Bedroom	152
8. Mr. James Rowley, Security Officer	Bombay Bedroom	114
9. Mr. John Campion, Security Officer	Pepsu Bedroom	109
10. Sgt. J. Moaney, The President's Valet	Neelam Bedroom	202

Room Allocation Plan.

moved" the President so much that he told reporters that this was something they should "write about."[18]

The response of the people to the visit was unprecedented. There were so many flowers, bouquets, garlands and masses of petals thrown at the car that one newspaper wrote, "It was flowers all the way."[19] By the time the motorcade reached Rashtrapati Bhavan, it had a foot deep mass of roses, jasmines and marigolds.

The confusion that reigned supreme on the roads later persuaded the Government of India to constitute a committee under BN Jha, Union Home Secretary, to recommend steps to prevent such recurrences. The report, amongst other changes, led to the building of an alternate route to the airport and major modifications in the procedure of handling State Visits.[20]

If the welcome that President Eisenhower received along the ceremonial route was unusual, another one, more special, awaited him when he stepped down at the South Court at Rashtrapati Bhavan. Waiting here were President Dr Prasad's four grand-daughters who presented bouquets to the visiting President. One of them carried two oil lamps on a platter and after performing an *aarti*,[21] she showered President Eisenhower with rose petals.[22] Meanwhile, a Hindu priest chanted hymns from the *Vedas* in the background to ward off the 'evil eye' and to bestow prosperity on the US President.

After the ceremony, President Dr Prasad linked arms with the US President and escorted him into Rashtrapati Bhavan and to the Dwarka Suite[23] where he was given Sanca Coffee in the Sitting Room. The President's entourage consisted of nearly 100-members, which was large for those days. It included his son and Assistant Staff Secretary, Major John SD Eisenhower

No.30/CER/99, dated 21.11.59.

THE FOLLOWING ARE THE PREFERENCES OF HIS EXCELLENCY THE PRESIDENT OF AMERICA.

FOOD As far as possible fatty foods to be avoided. He is fond of steak and indulges in large quantities of fresh fruits (likes mangees) at all times. He prefers fruit to be kept in his room so that he can eat in between meals. He also prefers buckets of Ice in his room, in case there is no Frigidaire in his room.

The President prefers De-Cafanized Cofee (SANCA) E.A.Ministry is trying to arrange to get about three tins and during all meals he prefers to drink Special Barley water which he is going to bring from America. Khalassis should be warned that he be served with this water even during Banquet.

The President likes Scotch Whisky (Chivas-Regal, Dimple Scotch or Black Dog)

MEDICAL. Oxygen cylinders should be handy. As already discussed please earmark an Ambulance to stand-by.

GENERAL. The President does not wish flowers to be put in his Bedroom.

He would like a 110-Volt plug point for his Dry Shaver.

Sd/- C.S.Reddy.
Lt.-Col.
21.11.59.

Surgeon
C.P.H.

Communication on "preferences" of President Eisenhower.

and his wife Barbara Eisenhower; the President's Press Secretary, James C Hagerty and Under Secretary of State, Robert Murphy. The visiting delegation was escorted to the Yellow Drawing Room for light refreshments. They were later taken to their respective suites.

The Himalaya Suite was allotted to Robert Murphy and the Nalanda Suite to Major John SD Eisenhower and his wife Barbara Eisenhower. Seven others were accommodated in Rashtrapati Bhavan, their rooms assigned according to their seniority. Following usual practice, the US President's 'House Flag' was flown on the flag mast on top of the Guest Wing from the morning of December 10. In addition, two mounted *sowars* (horsemen) kept ceremonial guard at the main entrance of Rashtrapati Bhavan throughout the US President's stay.

Every arrangement for the President and his entourage was reviewed to make the visit unique and give it a personal touch. This did not go unnoticed and one senior US Government official remarked that the arrangements were "splendid."[24]

Every advisory received from the US authorities was diligently followed, especially the President's likes and dislikes. The responsibility for ensuring compliance rested on the shoulders of the Comptroller, President's Household (CPH). The usual practice of placing fresh flowers to impart a splash of colour to the Dwarka Suite and to give the room a welcome touch was dispensed with as the President did not fancy flowers in his room.

The items not available in India were procured with a little help from the Ministry of External Affairs (MEA) so that Rashtrapati Bhavan did not lack in anything. There was enough "Scotch whisky" particularly the brands listed in the advisory – "Chivas Regal, Dimple Scotch or Black Dog"[25] that the President liked. "Buckets of ice in the room," were constantly replenished. Fresh fruit was deliberately stocked in plenty as it was advised that the President "indulges in large quantities of fresh fruit (like mangoes) at all times" and that they be kept in his room so that he could "eat in between meals."[26]

Special arrangements were made to cater to the President's preference for steak and "de-cafanized coffee (Sanca)." Since this brand was not locally available, the MEA lent a helping hand in procuring two tins of it. As advised, "fatty foods" were also avoided. Since the visiting President preferred to drink "special barley" water, it was brought from the US.

The electrical wing of Rashtrapati Bhavan worked overtime. Among the several special arrangements made for the visit, was the provision of a 110-volt connection in the Dwarka Suite so that the President could use his 'dry shaver.' The wing also lent equipment to the US Signal Corps, eliciting the special gratitude of the Commander, George J McNally, who in a letter to the Chief of Protocol (COP), MRA Baig, appreciated the services of Hargopal Singh, Chief Electrician at Rashtrapati Bhavan. In the letter, he complimented the Chief Electrician for not only cooperating with the US team by lending them "technical assistance but went much further by lending" the US staff "the electrical equipment necessary" for the visit.[27] These extensive arrangements resulted in a virtual makeover of Rashtrapati Bhavan prompting *The Times of India* to refer to it as the "Little White House."[28]

Since the President and his delegation had arrived late in the evening, there was no official programme scheduled for the rest of the day. It left the President free to spend his first night in India

President Eisenhower (left) with President Dr Prasad at Rashtrapati Bhavan in December 1959. Credit: PC

Scouts and Guides presenting a scarf to President Eisenhower at Rashtrapati Bhavan. Seen behind, to the President's right, is Prime Minister Nehru. (December 1959). Credit: PD

·having a "quiet dinner" with around eight people in his private dining room (Tagore Sitting Room).

The next morning at 9.30, President Eisenhower left for *Rajghat* where he placed a wreath at Mahatma Gandhi's *samadhi*. Though Delhi does not wake up particularly early on winter mornings, a surprisingly large crowd had gathered near the venue braving the morning chill, clapping and cheering as the President came out of his car "dressed in a steel grey suit."[29] Two members from his party, holding a wreath made of 500 freshly picked red, pink and white roses, led the President to the *samadhi*. The President also planted a *Magnolia grandiflora* sapling (known in India as *champa*) that blossoms in spring and has large white fragrant flowers.[30]

On his return to Rashtrapati Bhavan, President Eisenhower called on President Dr Rajendra Prasad who received the visiting dignitary at the entrance to his Study at 9.40 am.[31] Also present were MC Chagla, Indian Ambassador to the US and Ellsworth Bunker, the US Ambassador to India. After spending about 15-minutes together, the two leaders went for a walk through the Mughal Gardens escorted by President Dr Prasad's aides. The Personal Staff of the two Presidents stood in two rows, "on the green velvety lawns moistened by the morning dew."[32] President Eisenhower introduced his son, Major John Eisenhower, James Hagerty, Major General Howard Snyder and others to President Dr Prasad. The Indian President's Personal Staff was then introduced to President Eisenhower.

A specially erected *shamiana* provided shade to a select few as they sat sipping tea and listening to President Eisenhower talk about his experience in India so far, including the reception he had received at the hands of the people.

At 10.30 am, Prime Minister Nehru and President Eisenhower met in the Dwarka Suite without aides. Their discussions lasted 75-minutes. The international situation, particularly the easing of Cold War tensions, dominated the talks. India–China relations also figured prominently in their deliberations.

Later, at Rashtrapati Bhavan, President Eisenhower met representatives of the Bharat Scout and Girl Guides. The "scouts and guides gave a salute to Eisenhower at the outer gate of Rashtrapati Bhavan,"[33] after which the President inspected their "patrols" and asked them the age–criteria by which they were classified as "scouts", "guides", "*bulbuls*" and "cubs."[34]

On behalf of the Bharat Scouts and Girl Guides, a purple *khadi* scarf bearing the Association's insignia was tied around President Eisenhower's neck by Scout Anil and Guide Meena, both aged 13. In a brief speech, President Eisenhower thanked the group for the honour, and promised to send an autographed message for them later.[35]

After a 10-minute meeting with the Scouts and Guides, President Eisenhower attended a lunch hosted in his honour by Prime Minister Nehru at his residence, Teen Murti Bhavan. Before the lunch that was laid out in the garden, under ornate canopies from Tibet, both leaders conferred once more. This time it was for an hour and they were accompanied by their senior aides, Murphy, US Assistant Secretary of State; Bunker, US Ambassador to India; NR Pillai, Secretary General of the Ministry of External Affairs and MC Chagla, Indian Ambassador to the US.[36] The Indian Vice President, Dr S Radhakrishnan; the Home Minister, Pandit GB Pant; the Finance Minister, Morarji Desai; Ambassadors from the South American countries and Members of the Indian Parliament were among the 40 invitees selected to attend the lunch.

It was a "simple five-course" meal which included Indian dishes like *Kashmiri Pulao, Cucumber Raita* and *Orange Khir*.[37] The menu, however, ignored the advice of the US President's doctor, "forbidding experimentation"[38] with President Eisenhower's diet. It was also his first opportunity to taste the famous Indian dish, *Tandoori Chicken*.[39]

The occasion also provided President Eisenhower his first opportunity to interact informally with Indian Ministers and officials and enjoy some lighter moments. It was an opportune time as well, to refer to the elephant motif that was carved on the ivory woggle and presented to the US President earlier in the day by the Scouts and Guides. The President was told that in India the elephant is traditionally viewed as the harbinger of peace and good health. This piece of information had evidently pleased President Eisenhower as it was and is also the symbol of the Republican Party to which he belonged. A visibly pleased US President was soon seen passing around his party's boutonniere which he fished out of his pocket.

After lunch, at 5.00 pm, the President addressed a joint session of the Indian Parliament. Welcoming President Eisenhower, the Vice President of India, Dr Sarvepalli Radhakrishnan, referred to him as the "servant of a new and nobler world" expressing that the US could expect "India's whole-hearted co-operation in his attempts to secure peace."[40] Stressing the fundamental threads of "equality, respect for law, individual dignity, social justice and progress," Vice President Dr Radhakrishnan said that the "bond of shared ideals is stronger than military pacts."[41]

As President Eisenhower rose to speak, the hall reverberated with loud cheers and thunderous clapping. The President's speech too did not disappoint the excited Members of Parliament, as he began his address with the words, "I bring to this nation of 400 million assurances from my own people that they feel the welfare of America is bound up with the welfare of India. America shares with India the deep desire to live in freedom, human dignity and peace with justice."[42]

Stressing the common foreign policy objectives of both nations, he underlined the need to expand democracy and fight "political subjection, racial inequality, [and] economic misery."[43] He also appreciated India's courage in battling the several odds that the nation had confronted since its independence.

Eschewing Cold War terms, he projected America's belief in democracy and freedom. He also called for greater understanding between India and the US. The President used this platform to advocate his vision of pursuing "controlled, universal disarmament" as a path to obliterate the world's fear, suspicion and prejudice in the international order to achieve greater peace.[44] It was a brief exposition of US policy. When he concluded his address, Members of Parliament broke into another round of rapturous applause. The President's speech was so well received that a newspaper headline referred to it as President Eisenhower's transformation, "From Peace Messenger to Freedom Crusader."[45]

The evening of the day was reserved for a glittering banquet in honour of the visiting President. The preparations for this event were carefully made over several days.

At 8.30 pm, the appointed time, the Indian President in his *bandhgala* and *churidar* and the US President in his suit and bow tie with two *aides-de-camp* (AsDC) constituting the front, arrived at the grand Ashok Hall. As they walked in slow measured steps, and stopped at the central arch of the Hall, the Sikh Regimental Centre Band, which was positioned in the band gallery, played first the national anthem of the USA and then that of India. After the national anthems, the COP, MRA Baig introduced the invitees to the two Presidents.

The guests included Vice President Dr Radhakrishnan, Prime Minister Jawaharlal Nehru, Indira Gandhi, select members of the Council of Ministers, heads of diplomatic missions and Chiefs of the three Services amongst others. Among the prominent citizens invited were Acharya Kripalani, his wife Sucheta Kripalani, GD Birla and CD Deshmukh.[46]

After introductions were over, the two Presidents and the invitees were conducted to the Banquet Hall. A sumptuous fare of Turkish[47] delights and Indian delicacies like "*Raisin Pulao, Plum Kofta Curry* and *Alu-Dum*"[48] followed. After the main courses, the President of India delivered his banquet speech before proposing a toast. In his address, President Dr Prasad once again welcomed President Eisenhower and recalled that Prime Minister Nehru had had the privilege of visiting the US twice, in 1949 and 1956. He emphasised the shared values and common goals of both nations and said, "Our two Republics have a common faith in democratic institutions and the democratic way of life and are dedicated to the cause of peace and freedom... We wish to learn from you and to enlist your co-operation and sympathy in the great task we have undertaken in our own country."[49]

President Dr Prasad's address was notable for the chord it struck with the US President. He thanked President Eisenhower for his inspiring speech earlier at Parliament, and remarked that his visit came "at a very, very opportune moment in history" and hoped that the "visit will bear all the fruit."[50] At a personal level, President Dr Prasad hoped that while in India the US President would get a glimpse of India's changing face.

President Eisenhower matched his host's sentiments. In his reply, he thanked the Indian President for the "over-generosity of the remarks" about the US and himself. He said that even though he had hardly spent 24 hours in India, it seemed like an "unforgettable experience."[51] He was eloquent in his praise of India and said, "In a scant twenty-four hours, the strength of India's spirit, which seems to me to be compounded of faith, dedication, courage and love of country, has been borne in upon me in a most remarkable way. It is a spirit which will not be denied – no one who has felt it could fail to be uplifted by it."[52]

The US President also returned the personal compliments he had received at the hands of his Indian counterpart in equal measure. Referring to President Dr Prasad, he said, "And you, Sir, are the Head of a great Republic. To its present world position you have contributed much. Distinguished lawyer, devoted fighter for independence, and President of India fashioned out of years of struggle and now advancing in the light of a grand vision, yours is a life upon which man may look with satisfaction and a feeling of accomplishment."[53]

After concluding his address, President Eisenhower raised a toast to the health of the Indian President and his wife. The banquet ended with fruits and coffee.

Following the grand dinner, the two Presidents retired to the Ashok Hall, where they were treated to a scintillating dance performance and music recital organised by All India Radio. *Bharatnatyam* by Kamala Laxman; *Manipuri Raas* and *Maibi* by Thambal Devi, Tondon Devi, Savitri Devi and Ibetombi Devi; *Bhatiali* Songs by Nirmalendu Chowdhury; *Garba* by Chitra Dholakia and others; *Kurathi* by Vyjayanthimala, and *Odissi* by Indrani Rehman kept the audience riveted. An elegant booklet in a shade of red that was especially printed for Rashtrapati Bhavan explained the various performances with brief write-ups on the artistes. This gave the visiting delegation a microcosmic picture of the various Indian dances.

Early next morning on December 11, President Eisenhower and Ambassador Bunker visited the newly built US Chancery. From there, President Eisenhower left for the University of Delhi at 9.20

President Eisenhower (left) and President Dr Prasad being escorted to the State Banquet by AsDC at Rashtrapati Bhavan in December 1959. Credit: US Embassy

am where he was conferred with an Honorary Degree of Doctor of Laws.

At 1.00 pm, the visiting dignitary hosted a lunch in honour of President Dr Rajendra Prasad at the US Ambassador's residence. In the evening, both Presidents visited the World Agriculture Fair, which was declared open to the public by President Dr Prasad. After about an-hour-and-a-half both Presidents returned to Rashtrapati Bhavan where the US President had a quiet dinner en suite.

An 'At Home' was hosted the next day, December 12, by the Indian President in honour of his counterpart. After the guests had arrived, the two Presidents stepped out of the Morning Room accompanied by two AsDC, Military Secretary to the President (MSP), the Staff Officer of the President of the USA, two Honorary AsDC and the President's Bodyguard (PBG). The procession proceeded to the Central Lawn, which was bathed in the amber glow of the setting winter sun. Here they took their assigned positions with the flags behind them. The band struck up the national anthems of the two countries, the *Star Spangled Banner* followed by *Jana Gana Mana*.

As the reception progressed, President Eisenhower was introduced to select Indian invitees, while President Dr Prasad met with some American guests. Sometime into the function, the rush to have a *darshan*[54] of the US President was so "frenzied" and "frenetic" that the two leaders were literally mobbed. Newspapers quickly drew comparisons between the visits of Khrushchev and Marshal Tito and concluded that neither had experienced anything like this. The episode was dramatically described as an event in which "President Eisenhower was taken prisoner in Rashtrapati Bhavan today!"[55]

The insistence of the invitees to have a *darshan* was so unrelenting that a coffee table was hurriedly brought out upon which the US President clambered, waving his hands to greet excited and restless admirers. National anthems were played again when the two Heads of State departed from the venue. After the reception, President Eisenhower made an unscheduled visit to "Dr Prasad's suite where he spent some time with his grandchildren."[56] President Eisenhower also visited President Dr Prasad's *puja* room.[57] The two thereafter went on a stroll through different parts

President Eisenhower delivering banquet speech at Rashtrapati Bhavan. Seated opposite is President Dr Prasad. Seated on the right of President Eisenhower is Indira Gandhi. (December 1959). Credit: PD

(Seated, R-L): President Dr Prasad and President Eisenhower during 'At Home' Reception in Mughal Gardens at Rashtrapati Bhavan in December 1959. Credit: PD

Minister with flowers, garlands and bouquets.[60] The welcome was so enthusiastic that "when the President alighted at the Taj, he emerged out of a three-foot-high heap of flowers."[61] The US President and Pandit Nehru posed for several photographs, much to the delight of the gathered crowd.

The visiting dignitaries spent around 30-minutes at the Taj Mahal, which was bathed in sunlight, with Pandit Nehru acting as a guide. Reminiscing about his childhood days, President Eisenhower told Pandit Nehru how, "As a little boy in his farming state of Kansas he had read of the beautiful Taj." He remarked that this was "one of the things that I wanted most to see on this trip."[62] A visibly impressed American President commented on the architecture saying that, "It is one architect I would not quarrel with."[63] As a memento of his visit to Agra, the Government of Uttar Pradesh presented him with some finely embroidered bedspreads.

After his visit to the Taj Mahal, the President flew to the Balwant Vidyapeeth Rural Institute in a helicopter and thereafter to Laramda - a small village with 835 people, seven miles away from the Taj. President Eisenhower, who arrived in "a cream-coloured open convertible"[64] with Pandit Nehru sitting beside him, was accompanied by his son and daughter-in-law. The entire village was spruced up for the occasion with the villagers dressed in their best attire. About 10,000 people from Agra and the nearby villages had gathered to cheer the dignitaries.

The President was "shown the village poultry, piggery, cow-shed and the *Panchayat Garh*."[65] While in the village, Pandit Nehru invited the President to visit the house of Tikam Singh, *Pradhan* of the *Panchayat*.[66] Tikam Singh's 17-year-old son presented a garland to the President. Departing from their scheduled travel plans, the President and the Prime Minister then flew to Fatehpur Sikri, but despite this detour, they still managed to return to Delhi in time for lunch.

In the evening, there was a Civic Reception at the Ramlila Grounds that President Eisenhower had to attend. The Government had evidently put its might behind the organisation of the event. Prime Minister Nehru had visited the grounds himself and spent over half-an-hour checking the arrangements for the rally.

The grounds had been "reconditioned", the entire place was illuminated, multi-coloured lights were strung up on trees, the Turkman Gate was lit up and four welcome arches had been erected.[67] The route from Rashtrapati Bhavan to the Ramlila Grounds had been "decorated with rows of the US Stars and Stripes and the Indian Tricolour" along with festoons and banners.[68]

President Eisenhower arrived at the venue to a hero's welcome.[69] It was the high point of his direct interaction with the people of India. As he rose to reply to the Civic Address from a rostrum built to resemble a South Indian temple, the President was visibly overwhelmed by the loud cheers from the masses that numbered over a million.

of Rashtrapati Bhavan. After covering some ground, President Dr Rajendra Prasad escorted the US President to the Dwarka Suite.

Later that evening, President Eisenhower hosted a dinner for the Prime Minister of India at the US Ambassador's residence. Dinner, at 8.30 pm and was a 'black tie' event. It was attended by "no more than 23 guests."[58] The invitees included Indira Gandhi, VKRV Rao, MC Chagla, General Thimayya, Rajkumari Amrit Kaur and the Secretary General of the External Affairs Ministry, NR Pillai.[59] The dinner ended with an hour-long talk between Prime Minister Nehru and President Eisenhower.

On Sunday, December 13, the American President began his day by attending a prayer service at the famous Cathedral Church of the Redemption located on the 'quiet Church Lane' near Rashtrapati Bhavan. It had, during pre-independence days, served as the church of the Viceroys.

In perhaps what was a display of the bonhomie that had developed between President Dr Rajendra Prasad and the US President, the former, a practising Hindu, accompanied President Eisenhower to church. Ellsworth and Harriet Bunker as well as Father Earnest John, who was the priest at the Cathedral Church of the Redemption, received them. After the nearly 55-minute prayer service, President Eisenhower left for Agra accompanied by Prime Minister Nehru. This too was an unusual gesture. It was not normal for the Prime Minister to accompany a foreign Head of State, especially on trips outside the capital.

The reception at the Kheria Aerodrome in Agra was remarkable. Thousands of people thronged the entire route to the Taj Mahal, showering the vehicle carrying the President and the Prime

Speaking directly to the Indian people, President Eisenhower made a moving plea for a closer understanding and trust between the two countries. He quoted Mahatma Gandhi on several occasions to point out the commonalities shared by the two nations. In his words, "Between the first largest democracy on earth, India, and the, second largest, America, lie 10,000 miles of land and ocean. But in our fundamental ideas and convictions about democracy we are close neighbours. We ought to be closer."[70]

President Eisenhower referred to India's march towards economic prosperity and advocated the need for "private investment" in realising this prosperity. Concluding his address, the US President said that India was, "becoming one of the greatest investment opportunities of our time – an investment in the strengthening of freedom, in the prosperity of the world."[71] Before the function ended, President Eisenhower was presented with some samples of Indian handicrafts as a token of friendship and good wishes from the people of India.[72]

The sheer magnitude of the reception was so impressive that the President's Press Secretary, Hagerty, later told newsmen that, "The President thinks that this was the greatest tribute he ever received. He had seen large crowds, but the largest he had seen until today was at the Trafalgar Square in London on the V–Day in 1945. The President thinks the Ramlila Grounds crowd was even larger."[73] Several others, including Indira Gandhi and Pandit Nehru commented that the crowd was the biggest ever seen at the Ramlila Grounds.[74]

Later in the evening, President Eisenhower broadcast his farewell remarks on All India Radio. It was a touching adieu. He expressed his reluctance to leave the country and also spoke extensively about the commonalities and the common objectives shared by India and

President Eisenhower at Civic Reception at Ram Lila Grounds, Delhi, in December 1959. Credit: US Embassy

the US. "To develop a country in which every man and woman may have the opportunity, in freedom, to work out for himself, in his own way, a rich and satisfying life; a country in which, as Abraham Lincoln said, Government is of the people, by the people, and for the people."[75] President Eisenhower concluded by thanking the people of India for their warm welcome and wished them "good fortune and success."[76]

The visit of the President had generated so much goodwill that by the penultimate day of his stay, scores of gifts had poured in. Those presented by the Government of India included ivory and sandalwood carvings, silver tea sets and Benaras brocades. Amongst the presents sent for the President's wife, Mamie Eisenhower, were a brocade *sari* and stole.

The principal gift from President Dr Prasad to the American President was a beautiful carving in sandalwood and snow-white ivory. It was perhaps as unusual in size as the importance India had attached to the visit. The gift was as large as an office desk and the carving depicted a battle scene from the epic *Mahabharata* where Karna's chariot is stuck in the mud. The three characters in the carving, Karna, Krishna and Arjuna were worked in ivory whilst the chariot was made of sandalwood.[77]

Besides the Government's presents, several gifts had reached the American President during his stay in India. One of these was a pair of shoes from Mohamed Usman H Fazlur Rehman, proprietor of Fazal Boot House in Jodhpur. He entreated the MSP to present, on his behalf, to the "Worthy President of the United States of America the pair of shoes, which we have specially prepared for him." He added that Jodhpur shoes were "renowned all over the world" and the shoes sent that were "prepared for the Visiting Dignitary" were "unstiched [*sic*]"[78] with embroidery work on velvet.

The next day, December 14, was when President Eisenhower was due to depart. He left early for Palam Airport accompanied by President Dr Rajendra Prasad and Prime Minister Nehru. He was given a rather quiet farewell – there was neither any gun salute nor a Guard of Honour. He had requested this to be a "quiet affair" as he did not "wish to disturb anyone."[79]

At 6.00 am, President Eisenhower bid goodbye to a nation that had received him with unmitigated warmth, after what Prime Minister Nehru referred to as a "pilgrimage of peace."[80] As the US Assistant Secretary of Commerce, Henry Kearns, chose to describe, it was a "magnificent reception for President Eisenhower" that was "appreciated by all Americans."[81]

It was indeed a reception by a million-plus Indians, the size of which was or has never been seen since, with the possible exception of the visit of Queen Elizabeth II in 1961.

President Eisenhower (second from right), admiring his gift from President Dr Prasad (first from right) at Rashtrapati Bhavan in December 1959. Credit: PC

Dooj Prakash, former employee, President's Secretariat, assigned to open the door of the car for President Eisenhower.

FAZAL BOOT HOUSE
BAZAR GIRDIKOT
JODHPUR.

JODHPUR,
7th December, 1959.

Dear Sir,

His Excellency Mr. Eisenhower, President, United States of America will be visiting our Country from the 9th of this month. On this memorable visit, it behoves us all to accord him a rousing reception. We, who live at some distance from Delhi, can think of presenting him with a befitting local industrial product as a token of our respect and good-will for him. Jodhpur Shoes are renowned all the world over for their artistic beauty and softness. We prepare shoes with our hands and the shoes which we have prepared for the Visiting President is unstiched one with embriodery work on Valvet. It is our home product.

We shall feel greatly obliged if you will be kind enough to present on our behalf to the Worthy President of United States of America, the pair of shoes, which we have specially prepared for him and which we send in this parcel and request His Excellency to favour us by accepting the same. We hope and believe that he will be pleased to appreciate this pair of shoes as a specimen of Indian Craftmanship.

Thanking you.

The Military Secre-
tary to the President,
India,
Rastrapati Bhawan,
NEW DELHI.

Yours faithfully,

(Mohamed Usman H. Fazlur Rehman)

PROPRIETOR

Request of Fazlur Rehman from Jodhpur to present a pair of hand-crafted shoes to President Eisenhower.

THE FOREIGN SERVICE
OF THE
UNITED STATES OF AMERICA

American Embassy
New Delhi, India,
December 17, 1959

My dear Colonel Reddy:

Thank you for the list of Rashtrapati Bhavan personnel who should be remembered for their excellent services during President Eisenhower's visit. Here are forty-one medallions which our President wanted them to have.

Best regards to you,

Sincerely yours,

Edward P. Maffitt

Edward P. Maffitt
Counselor for Political Affairs

Enclosure:

41 medallions

Communication from US Embassy dispatching special medallions to Rashtrapati Bhavan staff.

After the President's return to the US, a flood of thank you letters poured in. There was only one letter that he had personally signed and it was unusual for the levels of hierarchy it sought to reach. The letter was to PL Mehta, Inspector General of Police, Delhi, thanking him personally for the security and general arrangements made by the Delhi Police and the admirable job his men had done in managing the huge crowds during the President's tours in Delhi.[82] The letter was perhaps expressing the indelibility of his impressions of the sheer size, magnitude and exuberance of the reception he had received in the capital.

If the crowds that greeted the US President charmed him, he also charmed many of the Rashtrapati Bhavan personnel who worked to make the visit a success. Dooj Prakash, who worked in the President's Household, still has nostalgic memories of the visit. He had opened and shut the door of President Eisenhower's car when he left Rashtrapati Bhavan for the last time. He remembers how the President lowered the car's window to shake his hand and say thank you. Fifty-six years on, the memory still lingers and Prakash demonstrates the way the President warmly shook his hand.[83]

Forty-four medallions were sent for the personnel at Rashtrapati Bhavan, whom President Eisenhower wanted to be remembered for their excellent service. The President's grandchildren also received certificates.

President Dwight D Eisenhower died on March 28, 1969. He was 78.

Notes

[1] "Mission of President Eisenhower," *The Times of India* (New Delhi), December 10, 1959, p. 10.

[2] Dennis Kux, *India and the United States: Estranged Democracies, 1941–1991* (Washington DC: National Defence University Press, 1993), p. 164.

[3] Dwight D. Eisenhower, *The White House Years, Waging Peace, 1956–1961* (London: Heinemann, 1966), p. 113.

[4] "Presidential Approval Ratings – Gallup Historical Statistics and Trends," *Gallup*, accessed on May 12, 2015, http://www.gallup.com/poll/116677/presidential-approval-ratings-gallup-historical-statistics-trends.aspx.

[5] Daniel P. Franklin, *Pitiful Giants: Presidents in Their Final Terms* (London: Palgrave Macmillan, 2014), p. 213.

[6] Department of State, U.S. Government, Office of the Historian, Foreign Relations of the United States, 1958-1960, Volume V, American Republics, Document 337, December 1, 1959, Washington "Letter From President Eisenhower to President Lopez Mateos,"accessed on April 5 2015, https://history.state.gov/historicaldocuments/frus1958-60v05/d337.

[7] "U.S. Stands With India in Common Quest for Peace," *The Times of India* (New Delhi), December 10, 1959, p. 9

[8] Ibid.

[9] Balwant R. Kapoor, *My Days at Rashtrapati Bhavan: The Memoirs of an Air Force ADC to President Dr. Rajendra Prasad* (New Delhi: Jnanda Prakashan (P&D), 2013), p. 20.

[10] "India greets President in Mass Demonstration," *The Cornell Daily Sun* (Ithaca), Volume LXXVI, 10 December 1959 accessed June 5, 2015, http://cdsun.library.cornell.edu/cgi-bin/cornell?a=d&d=CDS19591210-01&e=--------20--81----ginger+sun-----#

[11] "General Eisenhower as a World War II officer and the U.S. President," accessed June 5, 2015, http://www.criticalpast.com

[12] "Delhi Given New Look: U.S. President's Visit," *The Times of India* (New Delhi), December 5, 1959, p. 9.

[13] Zindabad is a Hindi word meaning "long live."

[14] *Gram Panchayat* is a village council.

[15] "Eisenhower arrives in Delhi," *The Hindu* (New Delhi), December 10, 1959, p. 1.

[16] "Crowds Line Route," *The Times of India* (New Delhi), December 10, 1959, p. 1.

[17] "Unique Welcome to U.S. President," *The Times of India* (New Delhi), December 10, 1959, p. 1.

[18] "Crowds Line Route," p. 1.

[19] Ibid.

[20] According to the Report of the Committee on Traffic Arrangement for Special Occasions in Delhi, 1960, from the Ministry of Home Affairs, Government of India, a road connecting Shanti Path to Gurgaon Road via Vasant Vihar through Rao Tula Ram Marg was specially built as an alternate path to the airport.

[21] *Aarti* is a traditional form of Indian welcome extended to guests. In this, the guest is garlanded and vermillion is applied on the forehead with the tip of the thumb. It is performed as an act of veneration and love.

[22] "Eisenhower arrives in Delhi," p.12.

[23] Ibid.

[24] From the letter dated February 1, 1960 by U.E. Baughman, Chief, U.S. Secret Services to Major General Sardar Harnarain Singh, MSP, Records, President's Secretariat, Rashtrapati Bhavan, File No. 30/CER/99.

[25] Records, President's Secretariat, File No. 30/CER/99.

[26] Ibid.

[27] Ibid.

[28] "Unique welcome to U.S. President," p. 1.

[29] "Leader's Homage to Mahatma Gandhi," *The Times of India* (New Delhi), December 11, 1959, p. 7.

[30] Ibid.

[31] "Courtesy Call on Dr. Prasad," *The Hindu* (New Delhi), December 11, 1959, p. 1.

[32] Ibid.

[33] "Scouts and Guides Greet IKE," *The Hindu*, 12 December 1959, p. 1.

[34] Ibid.

[35] Ibid.

[36] "Nehru–Eisenhower Talks Begin," *The Hindu* (New Delhi), December 11, 1959, p. 1.

[37] "IKE Likes Tandoori Chicken," *The Hindustan Times* (New Delhi), December 11, 1959, p. 1.

[38] "Elephant Intrigues GOP Man," *The Hindustan Times* (New Delhi), December 11, 1959, p. 1.

[39] "IKE Likes Tandoori Chicken," p. 1.

[40] "American Desire for Genuine, Controlled Disarmament," *The Times of India* (New Delhi), December 11, 1959, p. 6.

[41] Ministry of External Affairs (1995), Government of India, MEA Library, Foreign Affairs Records 1959 Volume V, accessed April 3, 2015, http://mealib.nic.in/?pdf2547?000.

[42] Ibid.

[43] Ibid.

[44] Ibid.

[45] "From Peace Messenger to Freedom Crusader," *The Hindustan Times* (New Delhi), December 14, 1959, p. 1.

[46] "Ike likes Tandoori Chicken," p. 1.

[47] Kapoor, *My Days at Rashtrapati Bhavan*, p. 20.

[48] "IKE Likes Tandoori Chicken," p. 1.

[49] Ministry of External Affairs (1995), Government of India, MEA Library, Foreign Affairs Records 1959 Volume V.

[50] Ibid.

[51] Ibid.

[52] Ibid.

[53] Ibid.

[54] The Hindi word darshan means to pay respects.

[55] "Aides Guard Ike, Prasad in Party Crush," *The Hindustan Times* Weekly (New Delhi), December 13, 1959, p. 1.

[56] Ibid.

[57] "Mr. Eisenhower and Mr. Nehru Hold Further Talks," *The Times of India* (New Delhi), December 13, 1959, p. 1.

[58] "PM Dines with Eisenhower," *The Hindustan Times Weekly* (New Delhi), December 13, 1959, p 1.

[59] Ibid.

[60] "President Chats with Worker," *The Times of India* (New Delhi), December 14, 1959, p. 7.

[61] Ibid.

[62] "Ike's Dream Come True at Seeing Taj," *The Hindustan Times* (New Delhi), December 14, 1959, p. 1.

[63] Ibid.

[64] "Big Welcome Accorded," *The Times of India* (New Delhi), December 14, 1959, p. 7.

[65] Ibid.

[66] Ibid.

[67] "All Waiting to Join Ike Rally," *The Hindustan Times Weekly* (New Delhi), December 13, 1959, p. 1.

[68] Ibid.

[69] "His Biggest Crowd," *The Hindustan Times* (New Delhi), December 14, 1959, p. 1.

[70] "India Marches to a Great Destiny," *The Times of India* (New Delhi), December 14, 1959, p. 7.

[71] Ibid.

[72] Ibid.

[73] "His Biggest Crowd," p. 1.

[74] "India, U.S. Must Come Closer," *The Hindustan Times* (New Delhi), December 14, 1959, p. 1.

[75] "Reluctant to Leave India, Says Mr. Eisenhower," *The Times of India* (New Delhi), December 14, 1959, p. 6.

[76] Ibid.

[77] Records, President's Secretariat, File No. 30/CER/99.

[78] Why the shoes were unstitched remains a mystery. But the most rational explanation may be that they were unaware of the shoe size of the President and would have expected him to have it stitched according to his size.

[79] Records, President's Secretariat, File No. 30/CER/99.

[80] "World Impact of Ike Trip Hailed By Nehru," The Florence Times (Alabama), December 12, 1959, accessed on April 5, 2015, https://news.google.com/newspapers?nid=1842&dat=19591212&id=CyUsAAAAIBAJ&sjid=S-54FAAAAIBAJ&pg=2180,4823146&hl=en.

[81] Records, President's Secretariat, File No. 30/CER/99.

[82] "Delhi Police Thanked," The Times of India (New Delhi), December 18, 1959, p. 11.

[83] Dooj Prakash began working in the Government House (now Rashtrapati Bhavan), in 1944 and retired in 1992. He lives in Rashtrapati Bhavan with his son who works in the Household Section of the President's Secretariat.

Lyndon Baines Johnson, the 37th Vice President of the United States of America, landed in India on May 18, 1961, on a two-day State Visit. He was under instructions from President John F Kennedy, to undertake a tour of seven South-East and South Asian countries, to enlist support for Washington's Cold War strategic plans to counter the USSR and China.

Among the seven countries, India was particularly identified for the visit for its potential to be a counter-weight against the People's Republic of China.[1] It was the second visit by a US Vice President to India after Richard Nixon's visit in 1953.

Lyndon Johnson was born on August 27, 1908, in Stonewall, a town in Texas to Samuel Ealy Johnson Jr and Rebekah Baines Johnson. He had an uneasy childhood and faced financial difficulties that forced him to take up chores and odd jobs. However, he did not let these hardships hinder his education and completed his graduation in 1930.

Visit of

H.E. Mr Lyndon Johnson

Vice President of The United States of America

His introduction to politics occurred when he was appointed Legislative Secretary to the Texas Democratic Congressman, Richard Kleberg, in 1931. He served in this capacity for over three years and resigned from the post to accept an offer from President Roosevelt in a programme initiated by him and was appointed as the Texas Director of the National Youth Administration (NYA). Lyndon Johnson was just 26 and this appointment made him the State's youngest director.[2]

In 1936, he resigned from the post and in the next year, contested the election to the US House of Representatives. He won handsomely and served in the house for 12 years. During the Second World War, he took a leave of absence from Congress to serve in the US Armed Forces and earned a Silver Star, the third highest gallantry award. In 1948, he was elected to the Senate and became its youngest Minority Leader five years later and served in the House for 12 years.

Fortunes changed for Lyndon Johnson when he was selected as the running mate of Kennedy, the Democratic nominee for the 1960 US Presidential elections. With Kennedy's victory, Lyndon Johnson became the Vice President of the United States.

Vice President Johnson arrived on his only visit to India, accompanied by his wife Claudia Alta Taylor or 'Lady Bird' as she was popularly known, after her nursemaid gave her the nickname,[3] and an entourage of 33 and a press party of 31 members. They landed in New Delhi at 02.30 pm. He arrived in a special American four-engine, red and silver Air Force Boeing 707 jet, two hours behind schedule.[4] At the airport, Vice President Johnson alighted to a warm and cordial welcome. Vice President Dr Radhakrishnan, Prime Minister Jawaharlal Nehru, Cabinet Ministers, senior civil and military officers and heads of diplomatic missions received him at the airport. He was accorded a full ceremonial reception with an Inter-Services Guard of Honour.

Facing page:
Vice President Johnson (left)
with Vice President Dr Radhakrishnan
at Rashtrapati Bhavan in
May 1961. Credit: PD

The scorching summer sun, however, cut short the welcome ceremony at the airport. Vice President Johnson too delivered a short speech but appealed that its duration may not be misconstrued and said, "I hope my brevity will not be considered a lack of interest."[5] In his address, he conveyed the warm regards of US President Kennedy and said, "I can tell you that our President is intensely interested in your country, and its future."[6] Vice President Johnson also hastened to add that as the representative of his President, he was visiting India to listen and learn.

In his brief speech, he also recalled the role played by Mahatma Gandhi in securing India's freedom through peaceful means. He said that India's independence was achieved through "the path of peace – the path of your greatest man."[7]

After the ceremonial welcome, Vice President Johnson and the entourage were driven to Rashtrapati Bhavan in a Mercedes Benz, an open Cadillac, two other Cadillacs, a Plymouth and other cars provided by the President's Garage. On their arrival, they were received by the officers of the President's Secretariat. The President's Bodyguard (PBG) in their impressive white summer ceremonial attire lined the route from the South Court to the guest suites and rooms situated on the southern wing of Rashtrapati Bhavan. The grandchildren of President Dr Prasad also welcomed Vice President Johnson and Lady Bird by performing an *aarti* just as they had done when President Eisenhower had arrived at the Rashtrapati Bhavan 1959.

The Vice President and Lady Bird stayed in the Dwarka Suite. The Nalanda Suite was occupied by Stephen Smith and his wife, the brother-in-law and sister of the Vice President. Eleven members of the retinue were accommodated in Rashtrapati Bhavan, while the rest stayed at the Ashoka Hotel.

The President's Secretariat had made arrangements in advance for the Vice Presidential visit. It was not easy and they went into a tizzy trying to cope with the delegation's special requirements. Advisories were received indicating Vice President Johnson's special preferences and those of his entourage's. These were carefully noted and strenuous efforts were made to cater to the special requirements.

The US Embassy had informed the External Affairs Ministry that Vice President Johnson had certain preferences, which would have to be borne in mind while his food was prepared. As a butler reminisced, special care was taken by Rashtrapati Bhavan to serve food according to the dietary preferences contained in the advisories. He said that the Comptroller, President's Household (CPH) had specifically ensured that the cooks had practised making such fares.[8] Accordingly, "rich dessert" and "fried food" were avoided and "roasted and boiled food" was served.

Room Allocation Plan.

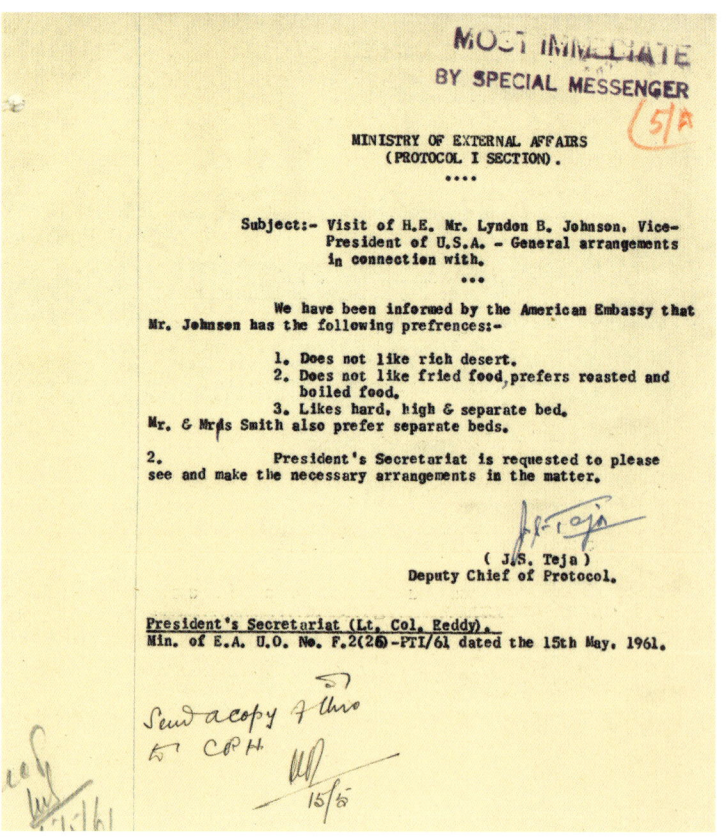

MEA advisory on "preferences" of Vice President Johnson.

Vice President Johnson (left) and Prime Minister Nehru at the latter's office in May 1961. Credit: PD

In addition to food preferences, the President's Secretariat also received, through the Ministry of External Affairs, a rather unusual request for a "hard, high and separate bed." It was no secret that such a bed would be difficult to buy 'off the shelf' for the nearly six-foot-four-inch Texan. The CPH and the Central Public Works Department (CPWD) of the President's Secretariat therefore swung into action to make a bed[9] for Vice President Johnson's use.

Security arrangements for the Vice President were a notch or two higher than those provided to most other Heads of State during their State Visits to India. They included a separate pilot vehicle and additional escort cars for all the Vice President's road journeys.

The first official engagement of the Vice President was a call on Prime Minister Jawaharlal Nehru at his office in the External Affairs Ministry. During the hour-long meeting, the two leaders mainly discussed issues relating to India's Third Five Year Plan and the United States' economic assistance to India.[10] During the meeting, Vice President Johnson also handed over a personal letter from John F Kennedy and communicated that President Kennedy would welcome any advice the Indian Prime Minister could provide on the subject of economic assistance that could be extended to countries in South-East Asia.[11] The situation prevailing in Indochina also came up for discussion.

The outcome of the first session between Prime Minister Nehru and Vice President Johnson was described by Professor John Galbraith, US Ambassador to India, as an "outstanding success." Summing up the proceedings, he said, "Both Nehru and Johnson spoke rather formally on education, which they favoured; poverty, which they opposed; freedom, which they endorsed; peace, which they wanted; and the third Five-Year Plan, which they praised."[12] Vice President Johnson was assisted during the talks by Professor Galbraith, Stephen Smith, Advisor to the Development Loan Fund and Carl Rowan, Deputy Assistant Secretary of State.[13] Prime Minister Nehru was assisted by RK Nehru, Secretary General of the External Affairs Ministry and J Desai, Foreign Secretary.[14]

Later that day at 5.30 pm, the US Vice President accompanied by Stephen Smith; Crockett, Assistant Secretary of State for Administration; Colonel Burris, Air Force Aide to the Vice President and Ambassador Galbraith and his wife, called on the President of India in his Study at Rashtrapati Bhavan. The meeting lasted for over 20 minutes. Afterwards, the Vice President and Lady Bird drove to *Rajghat* where they paid their respects to Mahatma Gandhi at his *samadhi*. Vice President Johnson placed Kashmiri roses at the monument and observed a moment's silence. The Vice President, known for his amiability, stopped and chatted with a few Indian college girls, and also posed for pictures with them at the memorial.

Next on the itinerary was a visit to the historic Red Fort. As the dignitaries were on their way, Vice President Johnson asked for the motorcade to make an unscheduled stop at Subhash Road (now *Netaji Subhash Marg*). To the despair of the security men, after the cavalcade came to a stop, the Vice President dashed straight into the crowd and made an impromptu speech of sorts. He spoke as if he were campaigning, something that he reportedly kept doing especially during his brief trip outside Delhi.[15] The similarity to campaigning was stark. It prompted Galbraith, who was accompanying Vice President Johnson, to exhort to a translator who was transcribing what the Vice President was speaking into Hindi, that "If Lyndon forgets and asks for votes, leave that out."[16]

When the Vice President addressed the crowd, he did not seem to require either a platform or a mike to be seen or heard. His height gave him a natural advantage over the physically shorter-built Indian audience. Amongst the things he told the crowd, was his impression that "India and America are friends, and they will ever so remain."[17] The sudden unscheduled stop was not, however, without any impact on the movement of the carefully planned motorcade. It threw the cavalcade out of gear, leading to confusion, chaos and jammed roads.

The evening was reserved for dinner with Pandit Nehru. However, before leaving for Teen Murti Bhavan, Vice President Johnson and Lady Bird had some unexpected visitors. President Dr Rajendra Prasad's grandchildren took special delight in visiting the Dwarka Suite.

The dinner in honour of the Vice President and his wife, at the Prime Minister's residence was a relaxed and informal affair. They walked around the sprawling gardens at the Prime Minister's residence and, Pandit Nehru showed off his pet tiger cubs, *Raja* and *Rani*, to the amused US Vice President and his wife.[18]

The next day at 7.50 am, Vice President Johnson left for Agra aboard a Pan American Airways (PAA) jet. In Agra, the Vice President obliged the press corps waiting at the airport, by answering a few questions. In a lighter vein and expressing delight at being in Agra, he said, "I am going to come back again, even if I was formally not invited... I will sit down and write the invitation myself like the school boy who did it when he was not invited to a dance party."[19]

From the airport, they proceeded straight to Bichpuri Community Development Block to see two villages. Here the

(L-R): Vice President Johnson and Lady Bird acknowledging greetings at Nagla village, Agra, in May 1961. Credit: PD

Vice President Johnson enjoying a bumpy ride in Agra in May 1961. Credit: US Embassy

Vice President Lyndon Johnson on a visit to Nagla village (Agra), perhaps giving credence to Prof. Galbraith's observation that the Vice President in this tour may forget that he is not campaigning and ask "for votes." (May 1961). Credit: US Embassy

visiting dignitaries freely interacted with the villagers at Nagla Patil Ram village.

Known for his fondness of children, the Vice President lifted a one-year-old toddler in his arms stating his desire for the girl to grow up, visit the United States and watch the proceedings of the Senate from the Vice President's Gallery. As if to establish his credibility, he signed an admission card to the US Senate Gallery and gave it to the child.[20]

The couple then visited the Taj Mahal. Enchanted by the 17th century mausoleum, Lady Bird remarked, "It is fabulous – breathtaking."[21] After having themselves photographed like virtually every other couple enthralled by the monument, which stands as a timeless embodiment of the love and adulation of a man for his wife, the Johnsons visited the Agra Fort. By lunch time, the Vice President and Lady Bird were back at Rashtrapati Bhavan.

Vice President Johnson had scheduled meetings with select Indian leaders after lunch, while Lady Bird went out for shopping and sightseeing. At 4.30 pm, the Indian Finance Minister, Morarji Desai called on the American Vice President. This was followed

Vice President Johnson with Lady Bird at Taj Mahal, Agra in May 1961. Credit: PD

by a call by Vice President Johnson on his Indian counterpart, Dr Radhakrishnan.

That evening, at 7.30, Professor Galbraith hosted a reception in honour of the American Vice President at 17, Ratendone Road (now *Amrita Shergil Marg*). After the reception, the Vice President attended a banquet hosted in his honour by his Indian counterpart at the Banquet Hall in Rashtrapati Bhavan.

Vice President Dr Radhakrishnan personally escorted his guests, Lyndon Johnson and Lady Bird, to the Ashok Hall after calling on them in the Sitting Room of the Dwarka Suite. Other invitees had, in the meantime, gathered in a horseshoe formation to be presented to the American Vice President by the Chief of Protocol, SK Banerjee. Over 100 guests including Indira Gandhi, Cabinet Ministers, the Ambassadors of USA, Thailand, Philippines and other senior officials were among those invited to this Banquet hosted in the Ashok Hall.

At the banquet, Lady Bird was seated to the right of the Indian Vice President, while Vice President Johnson sat next to Indira Gandhi. After dinner, Vice President Dr Radhakrishnan addressed the gathering. He welcomed the US Vice President and his wife and described the economic difficulties that India was facing. He also thanked the United States for taking an interest in India's development and growth.

Vice President Radhakrishnan underscored the critical importance of nations taking the right decisions. He said that the choices of a nation not only affect it but also humanity at large. All have to, he said, "rethink our past attitudes, to break with the past traditions of nationalism and militarism"[22] and "exercise some patience, self-restraint and criticism."[23] He referred to the concept of universalism embodied in philosophy, to emphasise the need for individual nations to subordinate their interest to their obligation to humanity. He exemplified his philosophical leaning by quoting Rabindranath Tagore thus:

> "My home is everywhere;
> I am in search of it;
> My country is in all countries,
> I will struggle to attain it."[24]

He also assured the Vice President Johnson of India's whole-hearted cooperation in the establishment of peace and friendship

Vice President Johnson (facing) delivering banquet speech at Rashtrapati Bhavan. Seated opposite is Vice President Dr Radhakrishnan. (May 1961). Credit: PD

among nations. Vice President Dr Radhakrishnan said that he did not claim that India was perfect but "Our attempt is to raise the material conditions of our country without breaking down the moral and spiritual values for which we have stood all these centuries, which have sustained us."[25] He concluded by proposing a toast to the health of the visiting Vice President.

In his reply, Vice President Johnson thanked India on behalf of his country and himself, for the warm welcome that was accorded to him, his wife and his entire delegation. He said that he was happily amazed by the hospitality, which he received in India calling it "most heart-warming." He concluded his banquet address by proposing a toast to "India's revered and honoured President, Dr Rajendra Prasad."[26]

With the banquet over, the official engagements of the "two-day goodwill mission to India"[27] of Vice President Lyndon Johnson came to an end.

The Ministry of External Affairs issued a press communiqué at the end of the visit on May 19, 1961, reflecting the content of the talks between Prime Minister Nehru and Vice President Johnson. The communiqué highlighted "President Kennedy's interest in the third Five Year Plan"[28] and suggested that America's aid to India would be "substantial in amount and effective in form." Both nations agreed that countries should strive to achieve the goal of "peace and freedom" for which the a priori requirement is freedom from "ignorance, poverty and disease."[29]

On the morning of May 20, 1961, at 9.00, the American Vice President and his team flew to Karachi, Pakistan, on the last leg of the seven-nation tour.

In Pandit Nehru's words, the visit of the US Vice President was characterised by a "frank and fair exchange of ideas."[30] The Indian Prime Minister's satisfaction at the meetings with Vice President Johnson was reflected in a comment in *The Times* (London) which quoted him as saying that they "hit it off well."[31]

The visit also resulted in some of the most interesting and free expressions of friendship by a US administration. President Kennedy in a letter thanked President Dr Prasad for the Indian carpet and an autographed photograph of himself, sent as gifts through Vice President Johnson. He thanked the President of India

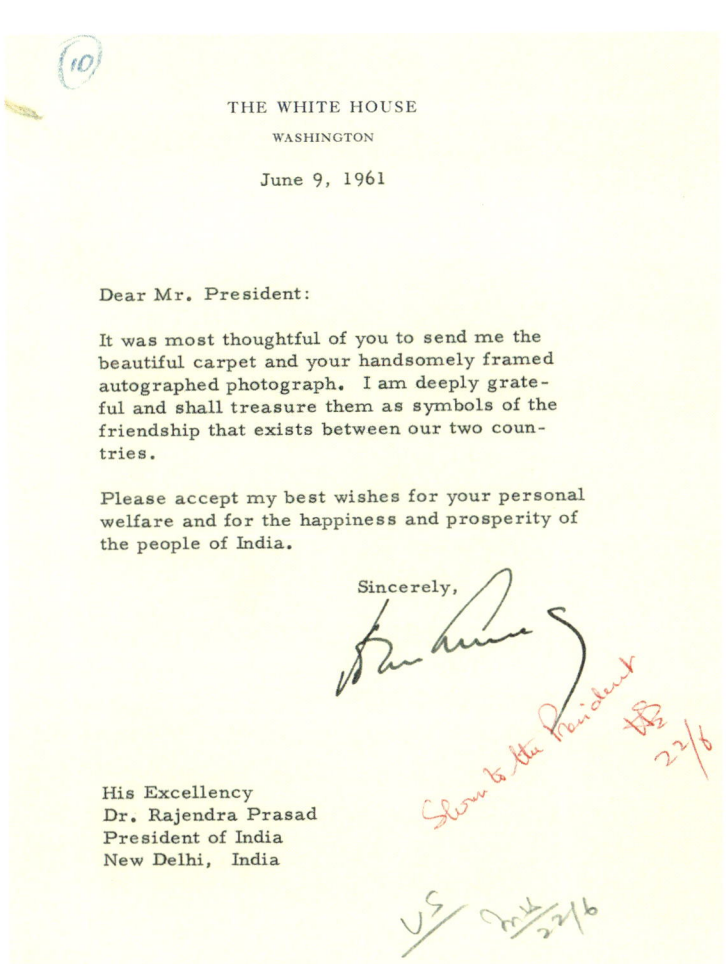

Letter of thanks from President John F Kennedy to President Dr Prasad.

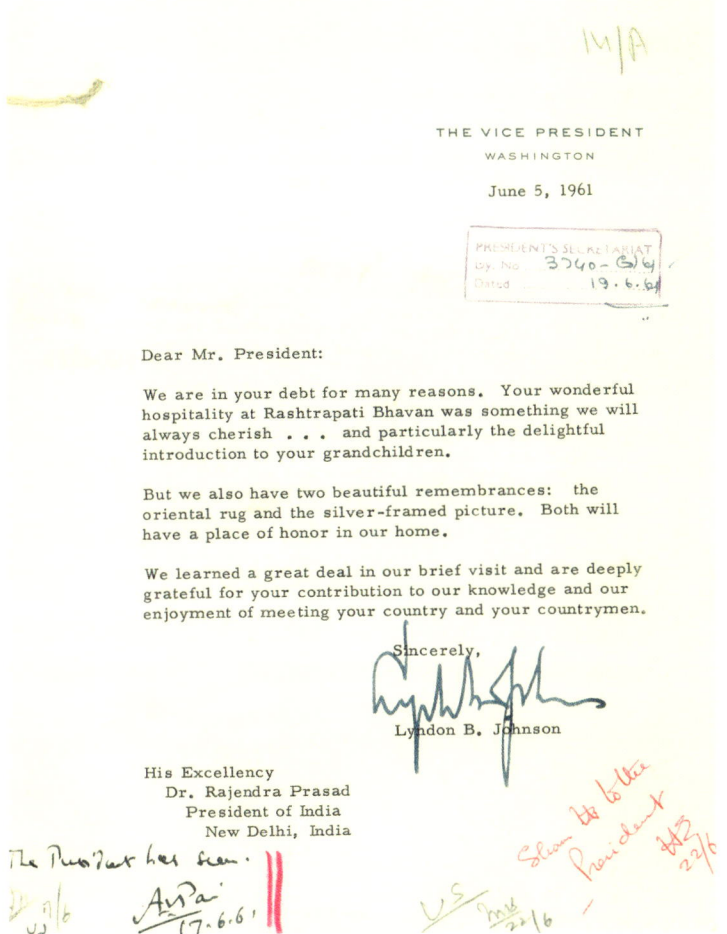

Letter of thanks from Vice President Johnson to President Dr Prasad.

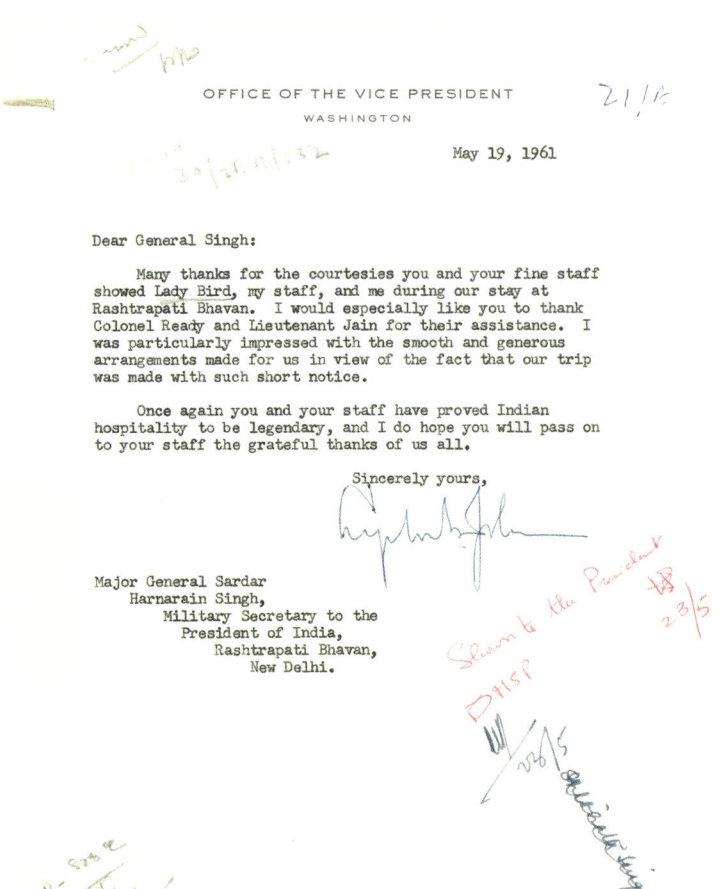

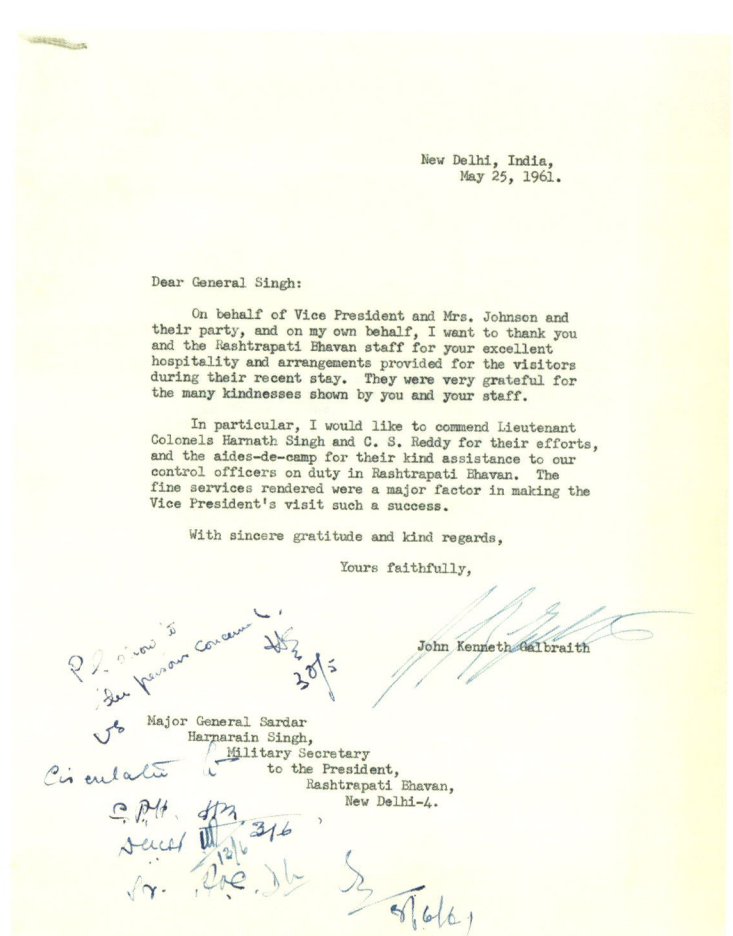

Letter of thanks from Vice President Johnson to
MSP, Major General Harnarain Singh.

Letter of thanks from US Ambassador John K Galbraith to
MSP Major General Harnarain Singh.

saying that it was "most thoughtful" of him to send the gifts, "the beautiful carpet" and President Dr Prasad's "handsomely framed autographed photograph." He added that he was, "deeply grateful and shall treasure them as symbols of the friendship that exists between the two countries."[32]

As presents, Lyndon Johnson received a carpet from President Dr Prasad and a Rajasthani punch bowl from the Government of India. Lady Bird Johnson received a fine *Benaras* brocade piece and a handbag.[33] Vice President Johnson personally acknowledged these gifts. He wrote a letter on June 5, 1961, to the President of India and thanked him. He referred to them as the "two beautiful remembrances" which he said, "will have a place of honor in our home." In the letter, Vice President Johnson further stated, "Your wonderful hospitality at Rashtrapati Bhavan was something we will always cherish...and particularly the delightful introduction to your grandchildren."[34]

In an appreciation of the warm hospitality that was extended to him, his wife and his entourage, Vice President Johnson, in a rather unusual gesture, sent a personal letter of thanks to the Military Secretary to the President (MSP), Major General Sardar Harnarain Singh. The Vice President expressed his warm sentiments for what

he said were "smooth and generous arrangements made for us in view of the fact that our trip was made with such short notice." Especially referring to their experience at Rashtrapati Bhavan, he wrote, "the courtesies you and your fine staff showed Lady Bird, my staff, and me during our stay at Rashtrapati Bhavan...have proved Indian hospitality to be legendary."[35]

A similar letter was also written by Ambassador Galbraith to the MSP on May 25, 1961, on behalf of the Vice President and Lady Bird thanking the Rashtrapati Bhavan staff, for what he said was the "excellent hospitality and arrangements provided for the visitors during their stay." He added that the guests were "very grateful for the many kindnesses shown by you and your staff." The Ambassador also specifically commended the services of Lieutenant Colonel Harnath Singh and CS Reddy for their efforts and the *aides-de-camp* (AsDC) for their assistance to the American officials. He added that the "fine services rendered were a major factor in making the Vice President's visit such a success." The letter was shown to the officers whose names were specifically mentioned and circulated to the CPH, Deputy MSP and senior AsDC.

After President Kennedy's assassination in 1963, Lyndon Johnson was sworn in as the 36th President of the United States.

He was sworn-in, in the US Presidential aircraft, making him the only President to take oath in air. He was elected President in 1964 with the widest popular margin in US history. Lyndon Johnson died on January 22, 1973. He was 64. Lady Bird died on July 11, 2007. She was 94.

Notes

(Endnotes)

[1] "Preserving Asia Against Communist Domination," *The Times of India* (New Delhi), May 15, 1961, p. 9.

[2] "LBJ: His Life and Times," LBJ Presidential Library, accessed June 5, 2015, http://www.lbjlibrary.org/lyndon-baines-johnson/timeline/

[3] "LBJ: Senate Campaign Trail, 1941" LBJ Presidential Library, accessed June 6, 2015, http://www.texasarchive.org/library/index.php?title=LBJ_Senate_Campaign_Trail,_1941

[4] "Kennedy Seeks Nehru's Advice," *The Times of India* (New Delhi), May 18, 1961, p. 7.

[5] "India's Economic Development," *The Hindu* (New Delhi), May 19, 1961, p. 1.

[6] Ibid.

[7] Ibid.

[8] Abdul Majid (2015), personal interview by Thomas Mathew, New Delhi, June 17, 2015.

[9] It could not, however, be ascertained if Johnson ultimately used the one procured by the President's Secretariat.

[10] "Kennedy seeks Nehru's advice," p. 1.

[11] K. Rangaswami, "Lyndon Johnson meets Nehru," *The Hindu* (New Delhi), May 19, 1961, p. 1.

[12] Rowald Evans and Robert Novak, *Lyndon B. Johnson: The Exercise of Power, A Political Biography* (London: George Allen and Unwin Ltd., 1967), p. 323.

[13] Rangaswami, "Lyndon Johnson," p. 1.

[14] "3rd Plan, Laos Discussed at Nehru-Johnson Meet," *The Hindustan Times* (New Delhi), May 19, 1961, p. 1.

[15] Robert Dallek, *The Flawed Giant: Lyndon Johnson and His Times 1961–1973* (New York: Oxford University Press, 1988), p.14

[16] Ibid., pp. 14–15.

[17] "Garlands For Johnson After Wayside Talk," *The Hindustan Times* (New Delhi), May 19, 1961, p. 1.

[18] "Johnson meets 'Raja' and 'Rani,'" *The Hindustan Times* (New Delhi), May 19, 1961, p. 4.

[19] "Invitation to Baby," *The Hindu* (New Delhi), May 21, 1961, p. 6.

[20] Ibid.

[21] Ibid.

[22] Ministry of External Affairs (1995), Foreign Affair Records 1960, Government of India, MEA Library, Foreign Affairs Records 1961, Volume VII, accessed May 28, 2015, http://mealib.nic.in/?pdf2549?000.

[23] Ibid.

[24] Ibid.

[25] Ibid.

[26] Ibid.

[27] K. Rangaswami, "Substantial U.S. Aid for India," *The Hindu*, May 20, 1961, p. 1.

[28] Ministry of External Affairs (1995), Foreign Affair Records 1960, Government of India, MEA Library, Foreign Affairs Records 1961, Volume VII, accessed May 28, 2015, http://mealib.nic.in/?pdf2549?000.

[29] Ibid.

[30] Ibid.

[31] "Substantial US aid for India," *The Times*, (London) May 20, 1961, p. 7.

[32] Records, President's Secretariat, Rashtrapati Bhavan, File No. 30/CER/132.

[33] "Prasad's Gift for Kennedy," *The Hindu*, May 21, 1961, p. 6.

[34] Records, President's Secretariat, Rashtrapati Bhavan, File No. 30/CER/132.

[35] Ibid.

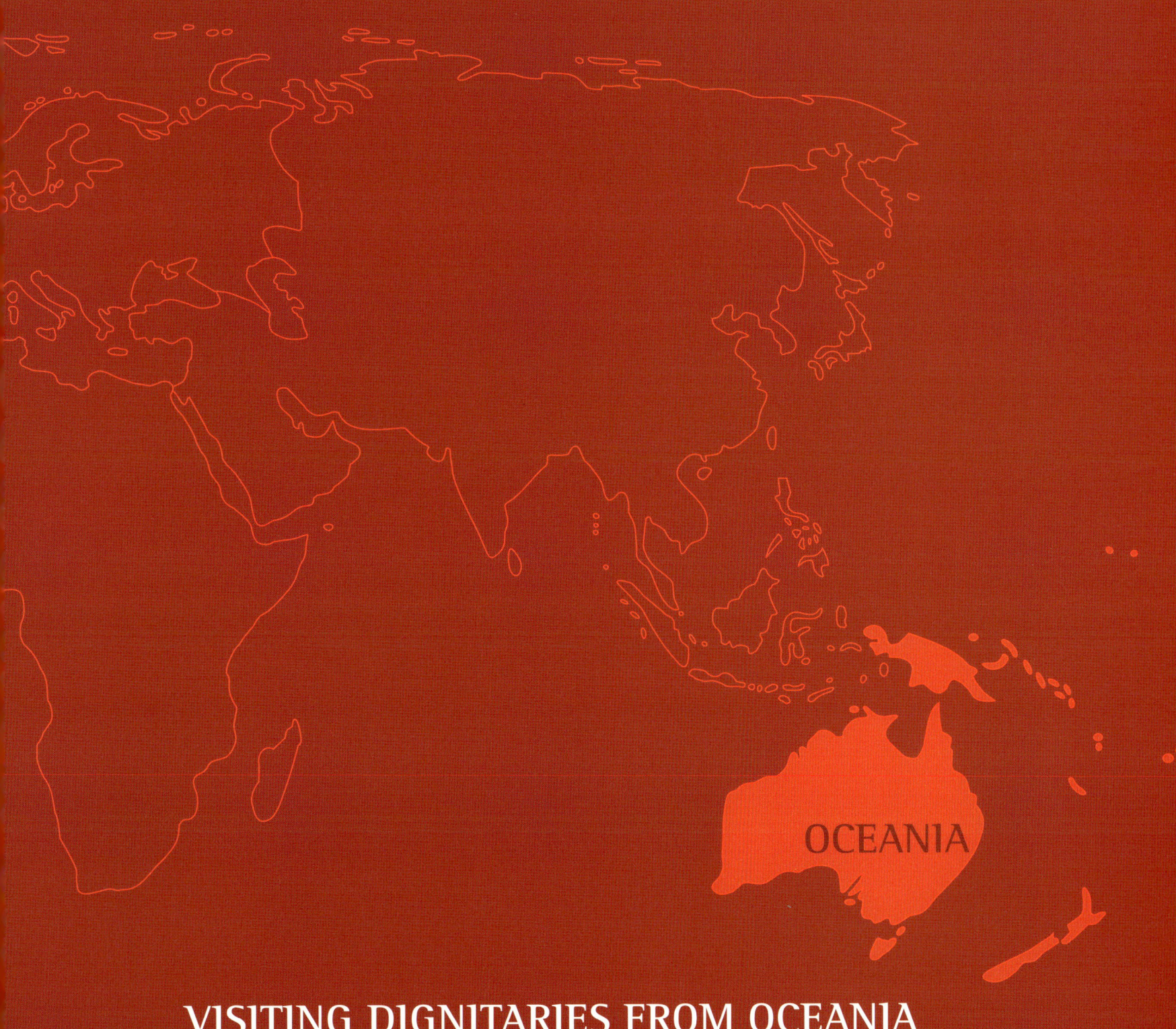

OCEANIA

VISITING DIGNITARIES FROM OCEANIA

NEW ZEALAND: Prime Minister Walter Nash

The Prime Minister of New Zealand, Walter Nash, paid a short three-day visit to India from March 17–21, 1958, as part of a longer Asian tour. It was his first visit to India and the first ever by a Head of Government of New Zealand.

Walter Nash's visit came just three months after he became Prime Minister. It began with a brief stop in Calcutta, late on the night of March 17. The Prime Minister had travelled to India from Hong Kong on board a BOAC (British Overseas Airway Corporation) flight, after he had attended the South East Asia Treaty Organisation (SEATO) meeting held in Manila, the Philippines. The Secretary of the Department of External Affairs, AD McIntosh and Private Secretary, Richard Taylor accompanied him. The Secretary to the New Zealand Trade Commissioner in Bombay, L Hamilton, joined the entourage in Calcutta. JB McGuire, the New Zealand Trade Commissioner in Bombay, was to join the delegation in Delhi.

Visit of

H.E. Mr Walter Nash

Prime Minister of New Zealand

The visit was undertaken purely as a gesture of goodwill with no declared agenda. It was, however, reported that Prime Minister Nash was interested in "strengthening his country's diplomatic representation in South-East Asian countries"[1] as they hardly had any representation in the region. New Zealand and India were both members of the Commonwealth of Nations and shared strong commercial ties. New Zealand was also a leading donor to India's development programmes and yet it had no diplomatic presence in India of the rank of High Commissioner except for a Trade Representative in Bombay. Wellington did not have any diplomatic presence in Pakistan and Ceylon either. It was in this context, to strengthen ties with the countries in the region that Prime Minister Nash undertook the visit.

Walter Nash, aged 76 at the time, was a well-known economist and an acknowledged internationalist. His foreign policy focussed on peace and the eradication of poverty, which had made him a popular figure in India.

Born on February 12, 1882, to a poor family in the town of Kidderminster, England, Walter Nash's early childhood was hard. His indigent family circumstances even compelled him to forego a scholarship to the prestigious King Charles I Grammar School, and take up work instead, for the money it would bring.

In 1909, Walter Nash moved to Wellington, New Zealand. He began his association with politics, when he assisted the Labour Party of New Zealand in the 1911 election campaign. Later, he helped establish a branch of the modern New Zealand Labour Party in 1918 when he moved to New Plymouth. By 1922, he was elected the Party's National Secretary.[2]

Quickly moving up the ladder, Walter Nash became Minister of Finance and Customs in the 1935 Labour Government and was made Deputy Prime Minister in 1940. He was

Facing page:
Prime Minister Walter Nash delivering banquet speech at Rashtrapati Bhavan. Seated opposite him is Prime Minister Nehru. (March 1958). Credit: PD

(R-L): Prime Minister Walter Nash with Lok Sabha Speaker Ayyangar at Parliament House in March 1958. Credit: PD

later elected Leader of the Party in 1950. In 1957, his party won a slim majority in the General Elections, but it was enough to make him the 27th Prime Minister of New Zealand. He was also the last Prime Minister of New Zealand to be born overseas and the oldest holder of the office.

The New Zealand Prime Minister and his entourage arrived at New Delhi's Palam Airport in a special Indian Air Force (IAF) Viscount aircraft Flight No. 402, that touched down in the capital 30-minutes past midnight on March 18, 1958. The Indian Defence Minister, VK Krishna Menon; the Deputy Minister of External Affairs, Lakshmi Menon and the Deputy Minister for Food, MV Krishnappa, warmly greeted him. Also present were the Chief of Protocol (COP), MRA Baig; the Australian High Commissioner, Peter Haydon and Councillors from the British and Canadian High Commissions. Prime Minister Jawaharlal Nehru, however, missed the reception due to a last minute change in the arrival time of the delegation, owing to the New Zealand Prime Minister's late departure for India.

After a rather quiet welcome, on account of the lateness of the hour, the visiting Prime Minister drove to Rashtrapati Bhavan in a Cadillac which was followed by a DeSoto and an Oldsmobile, all from the President's Garage. Unlike the usual ceremonial route that passes through Rajpath and Vijay Chowk, Prime Minister Nash was driven to Rashtrapati Bhavan via Kautilya Marg, Teen Murti

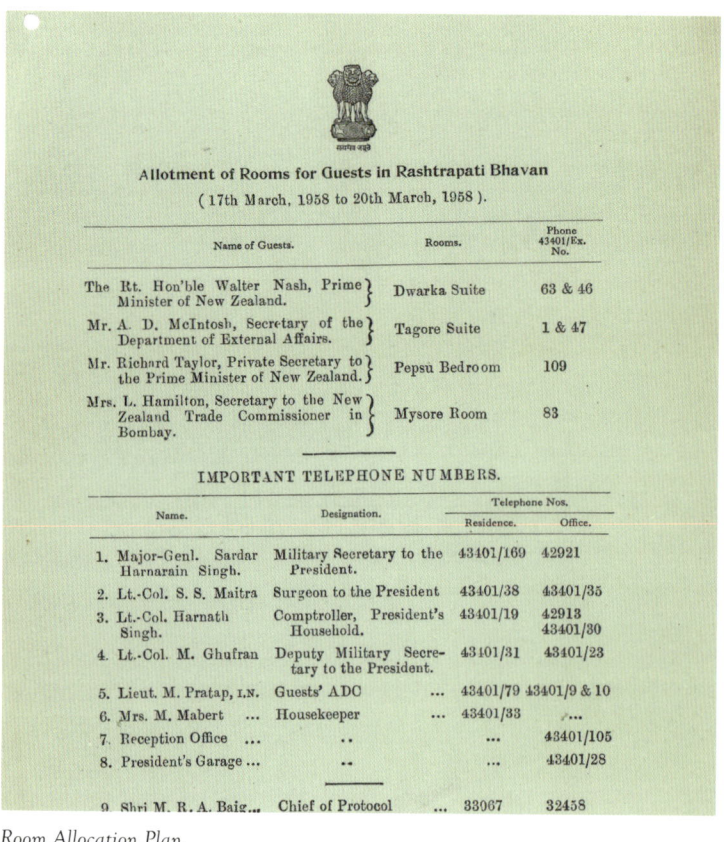

Room Allocation Plan.

Marg, South Avenue, Dalhousie Road, Freeman's Avenue and South Sunken Road.

On their arrival, the delegation was escorted to their respective rooms. Following protocol, Prime Minister Nash stayed at the regal Dwarka Suite. AD McIntosh and R Taylor stayed in the Tagore Suite and the Pepsu Bedroom respectively. L Hamilton stayed in the Mysore Room while JB McGuire decided to stay at the Ambassador Hotel.

At 9.30 the next morning, Prime Minister Nash visited *Rajghat* and placed a wreath at Mahatma Gandhi's *samadhi*. He later met Prime Minister Nehru and the two had an hour-long meeting.[3] The leaders were reported to have exchanged views on the international situation as well as the SEATO meeting in Manila.

The visiting Prime Minister subsequently met the Minister of Health, DP Karmarkar, at 11.30 am. The two held talks for nearly half-an-hour. The talks were dominated by a discussion on the progress of the construction of the All India Institute of Medical Sciences (AIIMS) for which New Zealand had sanctioned £ 1 million under the Colombo Plan that aimed at assisting poorer nations to help improve their living standards. New Zealand was one of the largest contributors to the Plan. More significantly, 40 per cent of its grant under the programme went to India.[4]

Minister of Food and Agriculture, AP Jain called on Prime Minister Nash thereafter, to discuss the progress of the Delhi milk schemes and other similar projects in the country. The milk schemes were also a component of the Colombo Plan and the Government of New Zealand had sanctioned £ 800,000 towards these.[5]

At 1.30 pm, Prime Minister Nash attended a lunch hosted by Health Minister Karmarkar in his honour. Fifty guests, including Prime Minister Nehru attended the lunch, which was held on the third floor of the Ashoka Hotel. Later that afternoon, at 3.00, Prime Minister Nash met Members of the Planning Commission at Udyog Bhavan. The Commission briefed the Prime Minister about the achievements made under India's First Five Year Plan and gave details about its next Five Year Plan which was under implementation. The Deputy Chairman of the Planning Commission, VT Krishnamachari; Chairman of the First Finance Commission of India, KC Neogy; Minister for Planning, Gulzari Lal Nanda and Defence Minister, Krishna Menon were among those who attended the meeting.

Thereafter, the Prime Minister visited the Lok Sabha to observe the proceedings of the House. After the session, the Speaker of the Lok Sabha, MA Ayyangar and the Chairman of the Rajya Sabha, Dr Radhakrishnan hosted tea for the visiting dignitary. He then returned to Rashtrapati Bhavan. At 6.30 pm, Prime Minister Nash and Prime Minister Nehru attended a Civic Reception held in his honour at the *Diwan–i–Khas* in the Red Fort.

The *Diwan–i–Khas* was exquisitely decorated for the reception. The venue was packed to capacity and it appeared that all 7000-8000 invitees were in attendance. The former President of the Municipal Corporation of Delhi, RN Agarwal welcomed Prime Minister Nash. He hailed the "fruitful co-operation" between the two countries and hoped that the visit would further strengthen the bilateral relationship between India and New Zealand.[6] In his reply, Prime Minister Nash lauded the close relations between New Zealand and India. Referring to the financial assistance to India, he said that it was not a "one-way" relationship. He said that his country had learnt a great deal from the Indians who "had come to New Zealand as had the New Zealanders who had come to India."[7] He referred to 60 Indian students receiving training in New Zealand, as "the picture of the quietness, humility, courtesy and dignity of life."[8]

Appreciating the life and work of Mahatma Gandhi, especially his steadfast adherence to *Ahimsa* and *Satyagraha*, Prime Minister Nash said that these were the "most priceless gifts to the world."[9] He was also gushing in his praise for Prime Minister Nehru. He said of him, "Not even in the warmest experiences, I have had in the last 76 years, has there been anything comparable to driving through the streets of Delhi and seeing its people with your Prime Minister this afternoon... I saw this afternoon how people worship him. He is worthy of all that you give him. The world owes him so much."[10]

Prime Minister Nehru, in his address, thanked his counterpart from New Zealand, for the aid and assistance that his country had been extending towards India. Praising New Zealand for its achievements, he called it India's "guiding star,"[11] "where there is neither a king nor a beggar."[12] At the reception, Prime Minister Nash was presented with a "silver plate and an engraved silver *surahi* (jug)," by RN Agarwal, as memorabilia.[13]

March 19, 1958 was a busy day for the Prime Minister of New Zealand. At 9.00 am, he visited the Delhi Milk Colony to get a first-hand experience of the projects that his country was supporting. This was followed by a visit to the Najafgarh Community Project, and then by a meeting with the Deputy Minister of Finance, BR Bhagat. At 1.30 pm, he attended a lunch hosted in his honour at the residence of the Australian High Commissioner.[14]

Prime Minister Nash visited AIIMS at 3.30 pm where he spent almost an hour. Three hours later, he was at Sapru House, where he addressed the Indian Council of World Affairs (ICWA), which was established as a think-tank in 1943 to study foreign affairs and international relations.[15]

Addressing the Council, Prime Minister Nash spoke about his country's defence policy and said that it was "'proud' of being a member of the Pact" of SEATO, and wished that India would also become a part of it.[16] However, he added, "I would not question Mr Nehru's judgment, of what is good for his country or his understanding of the peoples of Asia."[17] He elaborated that regional defence pacts like SEATO were necessary to avoid conflicts and promote peace. He voiced his support for collective security under the United Nations, and reaffirmed his conviction that disarmament had to "come about by agreement and not on the basis of fear."[18]

At 8.00 pm, Prime Minister Nehru hosted a grand State Banquet in honour of his counterpart at Rashtrapati Bhavan. Several Union Cabinet Ministers, Members of Parliament, members of the diplomatic corps and select senior Government officials attended it.

In his address after the meal, Prime Minister Nehru referred to the common problems of "peace and security," which made it imperative for both countries to work together and co-operate. Remarking on the irony of resorting to war to achieve peace, he said, "I have always thought that working for peace means adopting the methods of peace, because it seems to me rather odd that we should work for peace thinking of war, preparing for war, ever fearful of war, the two do not fit in."[19] He praised New Zealand for advancing the cause of peace and raised his glass in a toast to the "health of the Prime Minister of New Zealand."[20]

Prime Minister Nash was equally effusive in his reply. He praised the Indian leadership and the people, stating that "there was no country or continent or people that has made a greater contribution to the conditions that might make peace possible through the world."[21] He thanked Prime Minister Nehru for his appreciation of New

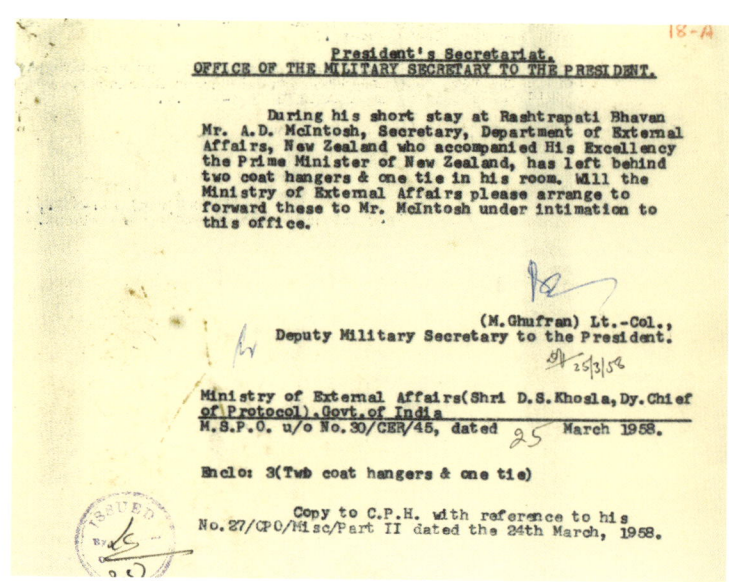

Communication from Office of the MSP to MEA regarding the return of AD McIntosh's belongings left in his suite at Rashtrapati Bhavan.

Zealand, and ended his address with the words, "I will take your goodwill and your good wishes back to my own country, and the 2¼ millions down there, and tell them 400 millions are thinking in the way you spoke tonight."[22] The evening concluded with a dance and music recital held in the Ashok Hall.

(Front row, L-R): Prime Minister Walter Nash (third) with Prime Minister Nehru at a cultural programme at Rashtrapati Bhavan in March 1958. Credit: PD

The next day at 8.00 am, Prime Minister Walter Nash left for Bombay from Palam Airport by IAC Flight No. 178. He was accorded a ceremonial departure and presented a Guard of Honour.

All the arrangements for the dignitaries' stay had been made by the President's Secretariat. Their meticulous attention to detail led them to discover that AD McIntosh had left two coat hangers and a tie behind in the Tagore Suite. The Deputy Military Secretary to the President (DMSP), Lieutenant Colonel Ghufran, requested the Ministry of External Affairs to ensure their safe return. The items were sent to the New Zealand Trade Commissioner's office in Bombay, from where they found their way to McIntosh.[23]

When Prime Minister Nash arrived in Bombay, the Chief Minister YB Chavan; Mayor, MV Dhonde and the Sheriff, JC Jain gave him an enthusiastic welcome at Santa Cruz Airport. The visiting Prime Minister then drove directly to the Aarey Milk Colony in Goregaon, accompanied by the Chief Minister. He was so pleased with the working of the Milk Colony that he indicated that his country would be willing to fund another such colony in Madras.[24]

Prime Minister Nash left for Colombo from Bombay on IAC Flight No. 171 on March 21, 1958, at 7.30 am after making a brief halt in Madras. He was given a warm send–off by YB Chavan, who presented him with an album of 30 photographs taken at the various functions held in the city in his honour.[25]

Speaking to correspondents during his brief halt in Madras, Prime Minister Nash emphasised the need for defence organisations like SEATO to check "any possible aggression by any power."[26] He praised Pandit Nehru saying that he was a person who "does not believe in fear. This makes for a better world than any other."[27] He reiterated his views on strengthening ties between the two countries, and said that his "country would very much like to see poverty banished from India as a prosperous India would be of great advantage to his country."[28]

On his return journey from Colombo, he made a night–halt in Bombay on March 23, 1958.[29]

Prime Minister Nash's visit played a vital role in the establishment of diplomatic relations between the two countries. This eventually led to the announcement of a High Commissioner's Office in New Delhi on October 16, 1958.

Walter Nash was Prime Minister of New Zealand until December 1960. He, however, continued to be a Member of Parliament. He died on June 4, 1968. He was 86.

Notes

[1] "New Zealand P.M.'s Talks in Delhi," *The Hindustan Times* (New Delhi), March 19, 1958, p. 1.

[2] Harris M. Lentz, *Heads of States and Governments: A Worldwide Encyclopaedia of Over 2,300 Leaders, 1945 through 1992* (London: Fitzroy Dearborn Publishers, 1995), p. 586.

[3] "Mr. Nash has Busy Day in Delhi," *The Times of India* (New Delhi), March 19, 1958, p. 1.

[4] "Nash Pays Tribute to Mahatma Gandhi," *The Hindustan Times* (New Delhi), March 19, 1958, p. 5.

[5] "Mr. Nash Praises Regional Pacts," *The Times* (London), March 20, 1958, p. 9.

[6] "Nash Pays Tribute to Mahatma Gandhi," p. 5.

[7] "Gandhian Ideals," *The Hindu* (New Delhi), March 20, 1958, p. 4.

[8] "Nash Pays Tribute to Mahatma Gandhi," p. 5.

[9] "Gandhian Ideals," p. 4.

[10] "Mr. Nash has Busy Day in Delhi," p. 1.

[11] Ibid.

[12] "Gandhian Ideals," p. 4.

[13] "Nash Pays Tribute to Mahatma Gandhi," p. 5.

[14] Records, President's Secretariat, Rashtrapati Bhavan, File No. 30/CER/45.

[15] Ibid.

[16] "SEATO Membership of New Zealand," *The Hindu* (New Delhi), March 22, 1958, p. 5.

[17] "Mr. Nash Praises Regional Pacts," p. 9.

[18] "Regional Pacts Promote Peace," *The Times of India* (New Delhi), March 20, 1958, p. 7.

[19] Ministry of External Affairs (1995), Government of India, MEA Library, Foreign Affairs Records 1958, Volume IV, accessed June 3, 2015, http://mealib.nic.in/?pdf2546?000

[20] Ibid.

[21] Ibid.

[22] Ibid.

[23] Records, President's Secretariat, File No. 30/CER/45.

[24] "Milk Project for Madras," *The Hindu* (New Delhi), March 22, 1958, p. 1.

[25] "New Zealand Premier," *The Hindu* (New Delhi), March 22, 1958, p. 1.

[26] "Milk Project for Madras," p. 1.

[27] Ibid.

[28] Ibid.

[29] "Departure for Karachi," *The Times of India* (New Delhi), March 25, 1958, p. 5.

Select Bibliography

PRIMARY SOURCES

GOVERNMENT SOURCES:

Academy of Sciences of the USSR. *Lenoid I. Brezhnev: Pages from his life*. New York: Simon and Schuster, 1979.

Department of State, U.S. Government, Office of the Historian, Foreign Relations of the United States, 1958–1960, Volume V, American Republics, Document 337, 1 December 1959, Washington. "Letter from President Eisenhower to Prime Minister Nehru." Accessed from http://history.state.gov/historicaldocuments/frus1958-60v15/d241.

Gerald R. Ford Presidential Library. *Leonid Brezhnev: The Man and His Style by Henry*. Accessed from www.fordlibrarymuseum.gov.

Gov.uk. "Past Prime Ministers–Clement Attlee." Accessed from: https://www.gov.uk/government/history/past-prime-ministers/clement-attlee.

LBJ Presidential Library. Accessed from http://www.lbjlibrary.org/.

Library and Archives Canada. "The Right Honourable John George Diefenbaker: Biography (1895–1979)." Accessed from https://www.collectionscanada.gc.ca/primeministers/h4-3331-e.html.

Ministry of External Affairs Library, Government of India, New Delhi, India. Accessed from http://www.mea.gov.in/.

National Archives of India, New Delhi.

Office of the Federal Register National Archives and Records Service, General Service Administration. *Public Papers of the Presidents of the United States: Richard Nixon, Containing the Public Messages, Speeches, and Statements of the President, 1969*. Washington: United States Government Printing Office, 1971.

Press Information Bureau, Government of India. http://pib.nic.in/.

Records, President's Secretariat, Rashtrapati Bhavan, India.

Regjeringen. Accessed from https://www.regjeringen.no/no/id4/.

The National Archives of the United States. Accessed from http://www.archives.gov.

NON-GOVERNMENTAL SOURCES:

Datta, C.L. *With Two Presidents*. New Delhi: Vikas Publishing House Pvt Ltd, 1970.

Eisenhower, Dwight D. *The White House Years, Waging Peace, 1956–1961*. London: William Heinemann Ltd., 1966.

Gooneratne, Yasmine. *Relative Merits: A Personal Memoir of the Bandaranaike Family of Sri Lanka*. London: C. Hurst & Company, 1986.

Jerry Hardman Brookshire. *Clement Attlee*. Manchester University Press, 1995.

Kapoor, Balwant R. *My Days at Rashtrapati Bhavan: The Memoirs of an Air Force ADC to President Dr. Rajendra Prasad*. New Delhi: Jnanda Prakashan (P&D), 2013.

Kissinger, Henry. *White House Years*. London: Simon & Schuster, 2011.

Menon, K.P.S. *Memories and Musings*. New Delhi: Allied Publishers Private Ltd., 1979.

Nixon, Richard. *Leaders:Profiles and Reminiscences of Man who have shaped the Modern World, Leaders*. New York: Warner Book, 1982.

Nixon, Richard. *The Memoirs of Richard Nixon: Volume I*. New York: Warner Books, 1978.

Noon, Feroz Khan. *From Memory*. Lahore: Ferozsons, 1966.

Sihanouk, Norodom and Wilfred Burchett. *My war with the CIA: The memoirs of Prince Norodom Sihanouk as related to Wilfred Burchett*. Harmondsworth: Penguin Books, 1974.

Choudhary, Valmiki., ed. *Dr. Rajendra Prasad: Correspondence and Select Documents*, Volume 21 (January 1960 – February 1963). New Delhi: Allied Publishers Limited, 1992.

S.W.R.D. Bandaranaike, Speeches and Writings. Colombo: Information Division of the Department of Broadcasting and Information, 1963.

Selected Works of Jawaharlal Nehru, 1 February–31 May 1955 –Series 2, Volume 28. New Delhi: Jawaharlal Nehru Memorial Fund, 2001.

Selected Works of Jawaharlal Nehru,1 November – 31 December 1957–Series 2, Volume 40. New Delhi: Jawaharlal Nehru Memorial Fund, 2009.

Society for the Study of State Governments, Journal, Volume 3–4, Pennsylvania State University, 1970.

The Citizen King: Biography of Mahendra Bir Bikram Shah Deva The Ruler of Nepal. New Delhi: Nepal Trading Corporation, 1959.

SECONDARY SOURCES:

BOOKS:

Ahmad, Ziauddin. *Shaheed–e–Millat, Liaquat Ali Khan, Builder of Pakistan*. Karachi: Royal Book Company, 1990.

Aitken, Jonathan. *Nixon: A Life*. London: Weidenfeld& Nicolson, 1993.

Bacon, Edwin. "Reconsidering Brezhnev." In Edwin Bacon and Mark Sandle, ed., *Brezhnev Reconsidered*,. 1–21. New York: Palgrave Macmillan, 2002.

Bradford, Sarah. *Queen Elizabeth II: Her Life in Our Time*. London: Viking, 2012.

Butler, Arthur S.G., *The Architecture of Sir Edwin Lutyens: Volume II*. London: Country Life Limited, 1950.

Dallek, Robert. *Lyndon B. Johnson: Portrait of a President*. New York: Oxford University Press, 2004.

Dallek, Robert. *The Flawed Giant: Lyndon Johnson and His Times 1961–1973*. New York: Oxford University Press, 1998.

Darlymple,William. *City of Djinns: A Year in Delhi*. Gurgaon: Penguin Books India, 2004.

Dean, Vera Micheles. *New Patterns of Democracy in India*. Cambridge: Harvard University Press, 1959.

Evans, Rowald and Robert Novak. *Lyndon B. Johnson: The Exercise of Power, A Political Biography*. London: George Allen and Unwin Ltd., 1967.

Figueira, Daurius. Tubal Uriah Butler of Trinidad and Tobago *Kwame Nkrumah of Ghana: The Road to Independence*. Lincoln: iUniverse, 2007.

Franklin, Daniel P. *Pitiful Giants: Presidents in Their Final Terms*. London: Palgrave Macmillan, 2014.

Home, Alistair. *Kissinger 1973, The Crucial Year*. New York: Simon & Schuster, 2009.

Kazimi, Mohammed Reza. *Liaquat Ali Khan: His Life and Work*. Karachi: Oxford University Press, 2003.

Krishnamurti, Y.G. *His Majesty King Mahendra Bir Bikram Shah Dev: An Analytical Biography*. Bombay: The Nityanand Society, 1963.

Kux, Dennis. *India and the United States: Estranged Democracies, 1941–1991*. Washington DC: National Defence University Press, 1993.

Kwame Nkrumah–Panaf Great Lives. London: Panaf Books, 1974.

Lacouture, Jean. *Nasser: A Biography*. London: Secker & Warburg, 1973.

Lentz, Harris M. *Heads of States and Governments: A Worldwide Encyclopedia of Over 2,300 Leaders, 1945 through 1992*. London: Fitzroy Dearborn Publishers, 1995.

Maung, Maung. *Burma and General Ne Win*. Bombay: Asia Publishing House, 1969.

McMahon, Robert J. *The Cold War on the Periphery: The United States, India, and Pakistan*. New York: Columbia University Press, 1994.

Morrah, Dermot., ed. *The Queen's visit: Elizabeth II in India and Pakistan*. London: Asia Publishing House, 1961.

Muni, S.D., *Foreign Policy of Nepal* (Delhi: National Publishing House, 1973.

Rizvi, Hasan Askari. "Party Politics in Nepal." In Verinder Grover, ed. *Nepal: Government and Politics*. New Delhi: Deep and Deep Publications, 2000.

Shaha, Rishikesh. *Three Decades and Two Kings (1960-1990): Eclipse of Nepal's Partyless Monarchic Rule*. New Delhi: Sterling Publishers, 1990.

Shlaim, Avi. *Lion of Jordan: The Life of King Hussein in War and Peace*. London: Penguin, 2008.

Slade, Arthur. *John Diefenbaker: An Appointment with Destiny*. Quebec: XYZ Publishing, 2001.

Smith, Sally Bedell. *Elizabeth the Queen: The Woman Behind the Throne*. London: Penguin, 2012.

Touhey, Ryan M., *Conflicting Visions: Canada and India in the Cold War World, 1946-76*. Vancouver: University of British Columbia Press, 2015.

Wahab, Shaista and Barry Youngerman. *A Brief History of Afghanistan*. New York: Infobase Publishing, 2007.

Witte, Sam. *Gamal Abdel Nasser*. New York: Rosen Publishing Group, 2004.

JOURNAL ARTICLES:

Addo-Fening, Robert. "Gandhi and Nkrumah: A Study of Non-Violence and Non-Co-operation Campaigns in India and Ghana as an Anti-Colonial Strategy." *Transactions of the Historical Society of Ghana*, 13, no.1 (June 1972): 82.

Campbell, John C., "Tito: The Achievement and the Legacy." *Foreign Affairs*, 58, no.5, (Summer 1980):1055.

Cook, C.P., "Burma: The Era of Ne Win," *The World Today*, 26, no.6, (June 1, 1970): 261.

Djilas, Aleksa. "Tito's Last Secret: How Did He Keep the Yugoslavs Together?" *Foreign Affairs*, 74, no.4, (July 1, 1995): 116.

Halivni, Tzipora Hager. "The Birkenau Revolt: Poles Prevent a Timely Insurrection," *Jewish Social Studies*, 41, no. 2 (Spring 1979): 125.

Maclean, Fitzroy., "Tito: A Study." *Foreign Affairs*, 28, no.2, (January 1950): 232.

Pharo, Helge. "Altruism, Security and the Impact of Oil: Norway's Foreign Economic Assistance Policy, 1958-1971." *Contemporary European History* ,12, no. 4 (2003): 530.

NEWSPAPERS:

Asian Tribune (Bangkok)

Cairns Post

Chicago Tribune

Hindusthan Standard (New Delhi)

The Cornell Daily Sun

The Economic Times (New Delhi)

The Florence Times

The Guardian (London)

The Hindu (New Delhi)

The Hindustan Times (New Delhi)

The New Indian Express (Chennai)

The New York Times

The News (Karachi)

The Phnom Penh Post

The Statesman (New Delhi)

The Telegraph (London)

The Times (London)

The Times of India (New Delhi)

JOURNALS/MAGAZINES:

Foreign Affairs (Council on Foreign Relation, New York City, New York)

Life (Time Inc., New York, NY)

Newsweek (Newsweek Inc., New York, NY)

The Economist (The Economist Newspaper Ltd., London)

Time (Time Inc., New York, NY)

WEBSITES:

Encyclopedia Britannica. www.britannica.com.

Pakistan Herald. www.pakistanherald.com.

Gallup. "Presidential Approval Ratings -- Gallup Historical Statistics and Trends." http://www.gallup.com.

Norwegian Encyclopaedia. "Einar Gerhardsen." https://snl.no/Einar_Gerhardsen.

Russiapedia. "Prominent Russians: Anastas Mikoyan." http://russiapedia.rt.com/prominent-russians/politics-and-society/anastas-mikoyan/.

BBC News. "The Legacy of Yugoslavia's Marshal Tito." http://news.bbc.co.uk/2/hi/europe/8636034.stm.

Nauka w Polsce. "100th Anniversary of the Birth of Joseph Cyrankiewicz–"eternal premiere" of" PRL." http://naukawpolsce.pap.pl/aktualnosci/news,381531,100-rocznica-urodzin-jozefa-cyrankiewicza---wiecznego-premiera-prl-u.html.

Acknowledgements

The President, Shri Pranab Mukherjee, was the reason for this book. His irrepressible penchant for recording history, translated into his encouragement to write a book on the visits of Heads of States/Heads of Governments and leaders to India who stayed at the Rashtrapati Bhavan or the Government House as it was called. The objective was to record their experience in the country, their meetings with the Indian leaders and how Rashtrapati Bhavan was the home away from home for these leaders. Without his constant reminder and monitoring, it would have been difficult to summon the extra energy, stamina and commitment to complete this arduous work.

The Secretary to the President, Smt. Omita Paul's unrelenting pressure to complete the work before July 25, 2015— a no mean challenge, matched the President's encouragement. She was persuasive, insistent and demanding. It left no wiggle room. If it were not for her unrelenting coaxing and support, this book would not have seen the light of day.

If it were not for the extra hours of work and unflinching commitment of Sadhana Rout, ADG, Publications Division and her team, including Harini Srinivasan, who burned the midnight oil executing ably her editorial task, it would not have been possible to complete the book in this short time. They accomplished what publishers seldom do.

I am grateful to MV Bhanumathi, my friend and colleague, for painstakingly going through the manuscript and for her suggestions on improving the work. I cannot of course fail to thank George Thomas who was great on his computers, verified dates, data, facts and made suggestions that not only improved the quality of this work, but also saved it from typos. I also owe him an apology for taking away from him the last two months of freedom after which he has to attend his Civil Services training programme.

The assistance of Major Adarsh Sharma of the President's Bodyguard was invaluable. An officer with a keen eye, he painstakingly combed the drafts pointing out unwitting discrepancies that had crept in. He was ably assisted by the computer whiz kid, Deepika Sharma, who worked tirelessly and meticulously, selecting the images for this book, working on them and advising on their positioning in the book as also pointing out issues that required further clarification.

I cannot but acknowledge the commitment of my research team consisting of Damini Kukreja, Chetna Gupta and Remya Thomas. Without their invaluable assistance, it would not have been possible to sift through thousands of clippings of newspapers from 1947, in search of relevant information for the work.

I owe my gratitude to Anubhav Das of ZinkID Media and his team for their valuable assistance in the design of the introduction, the selection of the photos in it and their layout, in a punishingly short time.

I am thankful to my personal staff, Arun Gupta and Varun Ranjan for virtually burning the midnight oil for months in office, helping me with the correction of drafts without even taking a day's break. The former was available to me any time of the day or night to help me with the work. JK Sharma, my PPS coordinated the administrative aspect of the work. I also have to thank my other supporting staff, Arvind Prasad, K. Sahu and Subash Kumar for taking care of the team by seeing that they lacked nothing while we worked.

– Dr Thomas Mathew

About the Author and Photographer

THOMAS MATHEW is a career civil servant, a Ph.D. in international relations and the Additional Secretary to the President. He has worked in Kerala, his home cadre and in several ministries and departments in the centre. His published works include the book, *India–US Relations under the Obama Administration* (ed.) with its lead chapter and several articles in leading journals. He was also the Chair of the Report on the *Development of Nuclear Energy Sector in India*. He writes regularly for leading Indian and foreign dailies and journals on Defence and Finance. He has dozens of publications to his credit. He is a keen photographer and an avid birdwatcher. His last published book was on the birds of Rashtrapati Bhavan, titled, "Winged Wonders of Rashtrapati Bhavan" (2014). It was released by Hon'ble Prime Minister Narendra Modi.